AF207893

Cuba

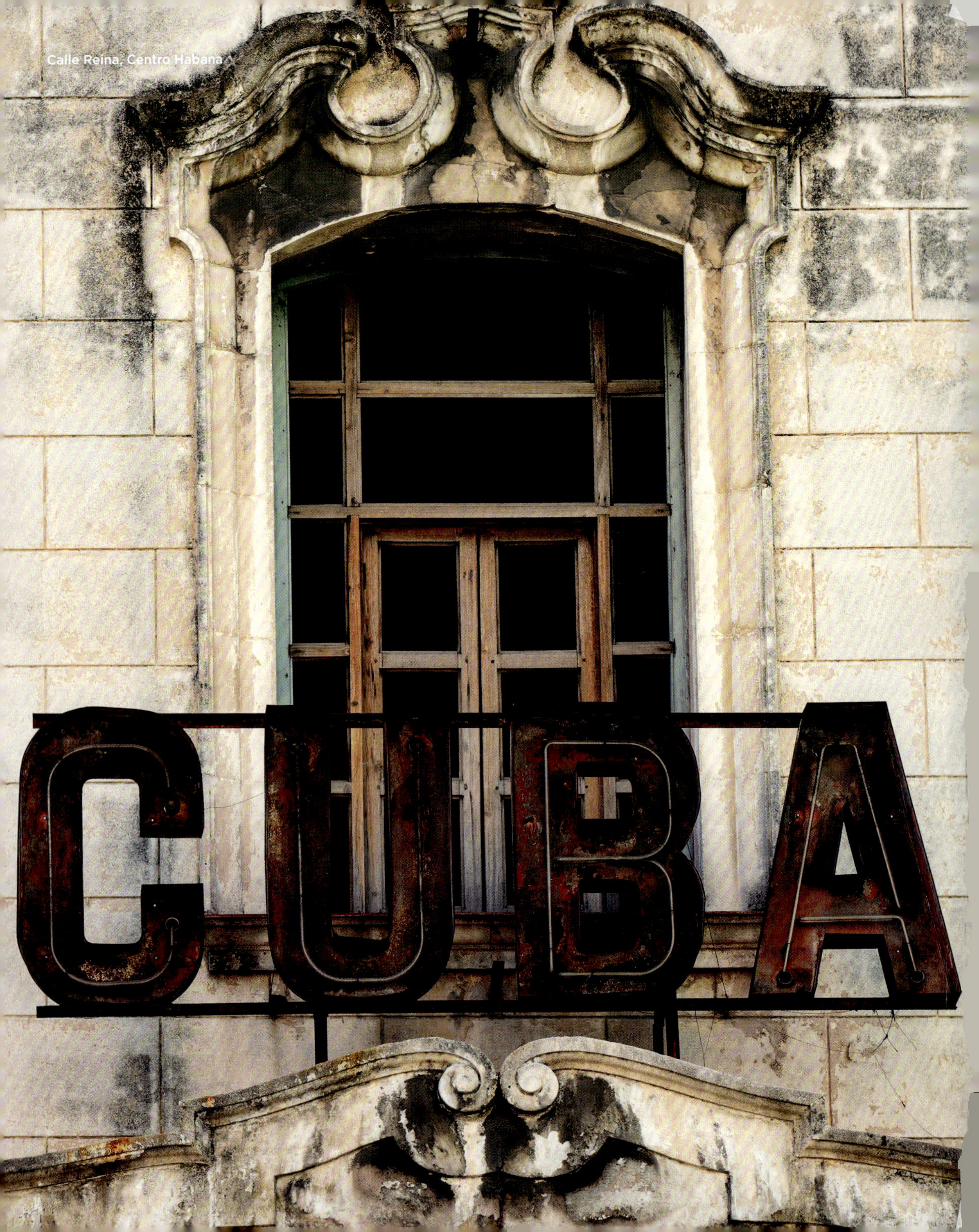
Calle Reina, Centro Habana
CUBA

Cuba

Karl-Heinz Raach

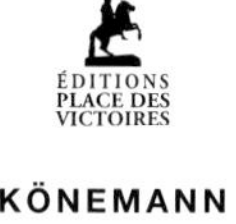

ÉDITIONS
PLACE DES
VICTOIRES

KÖNEMANN

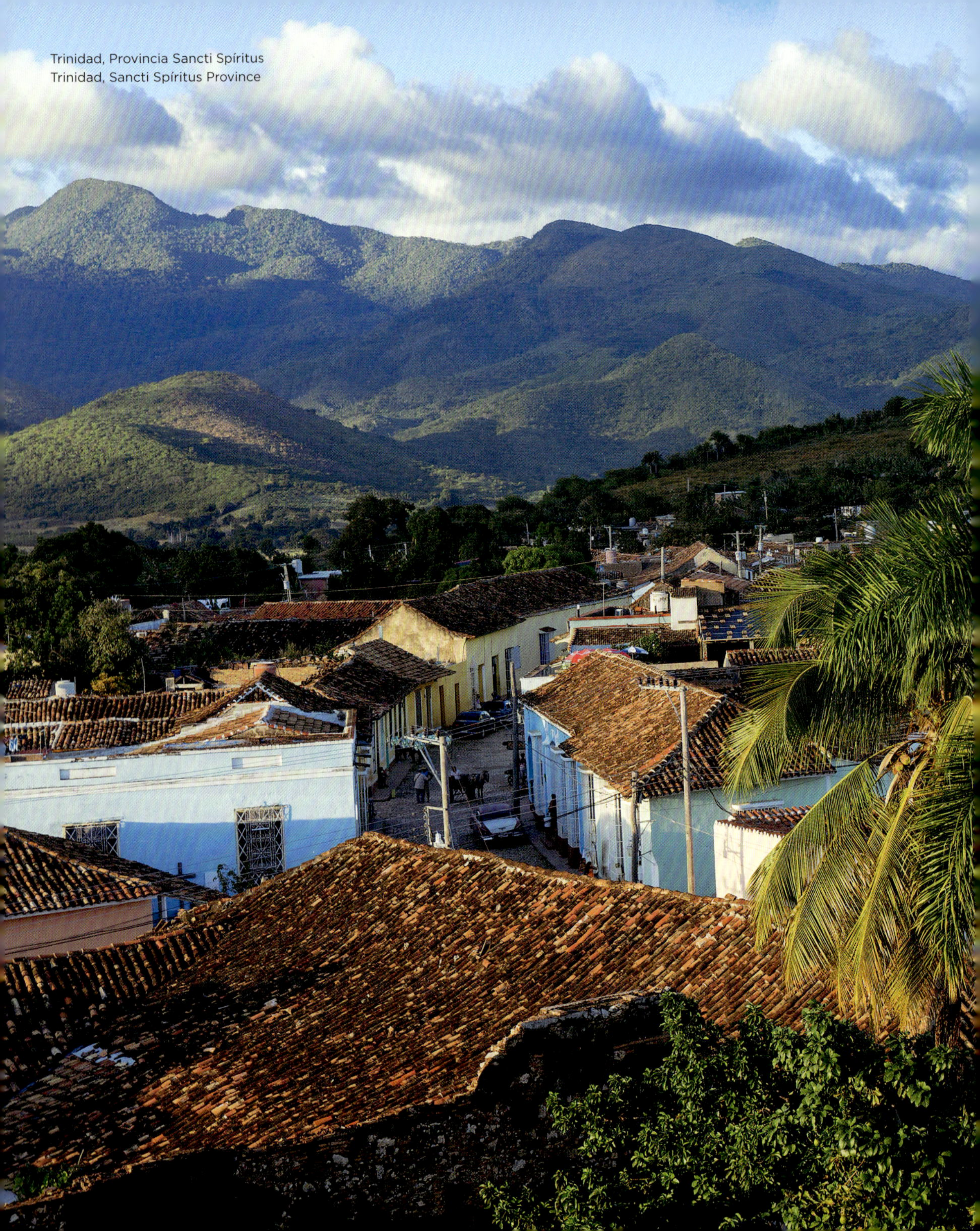
Trinidad, Provincia Sancti Spíritus
Trinidad, Sancti Spíritus Province

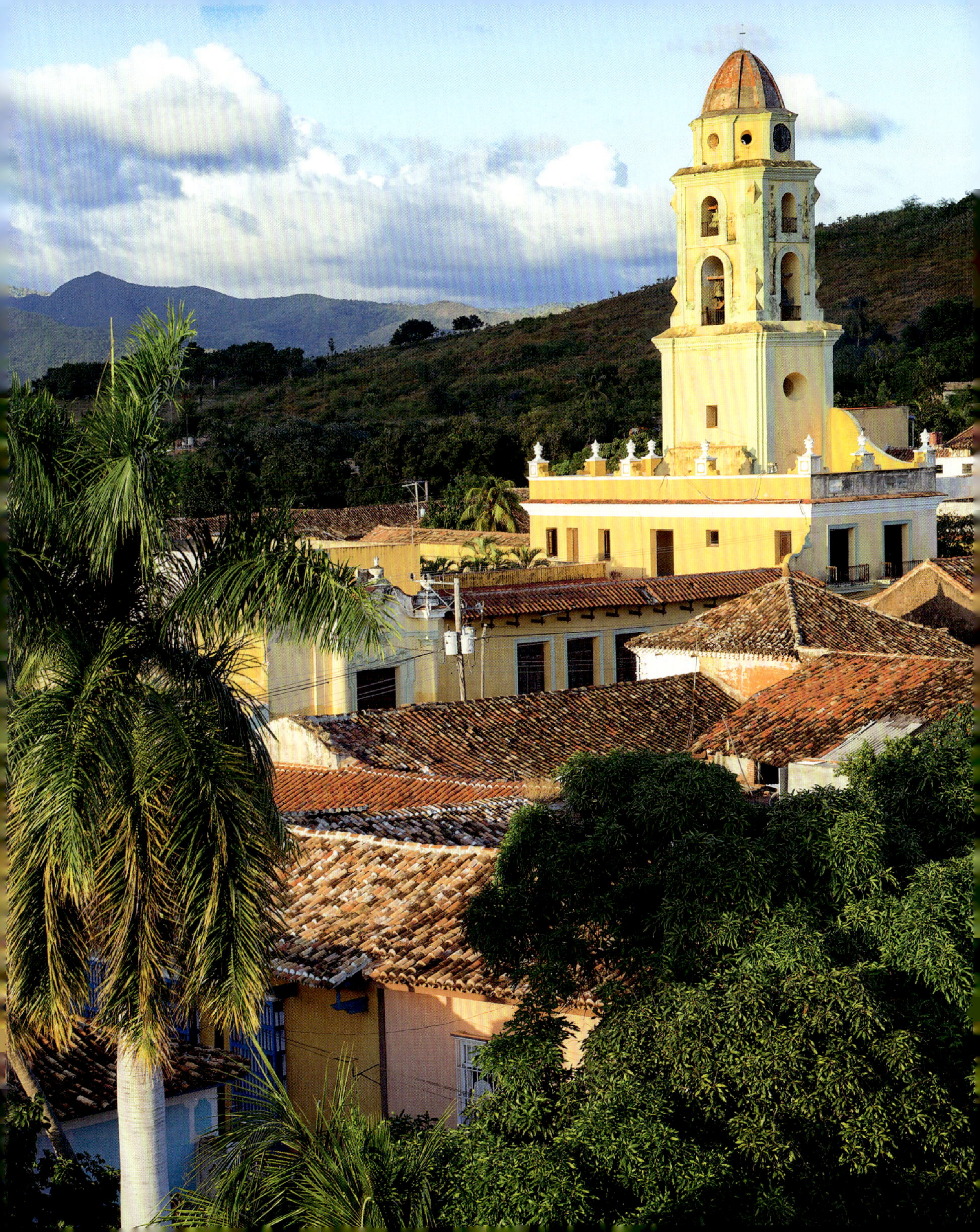

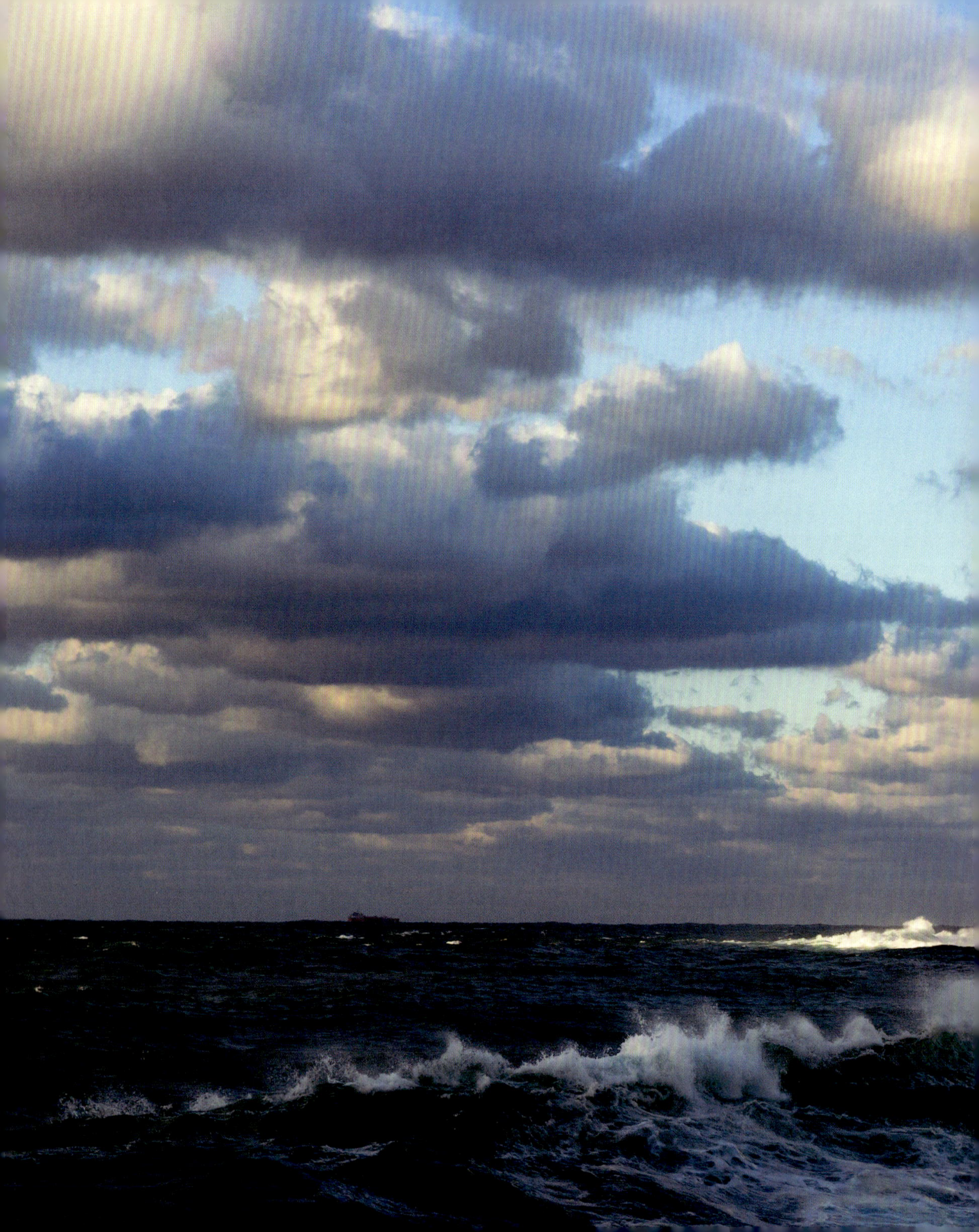

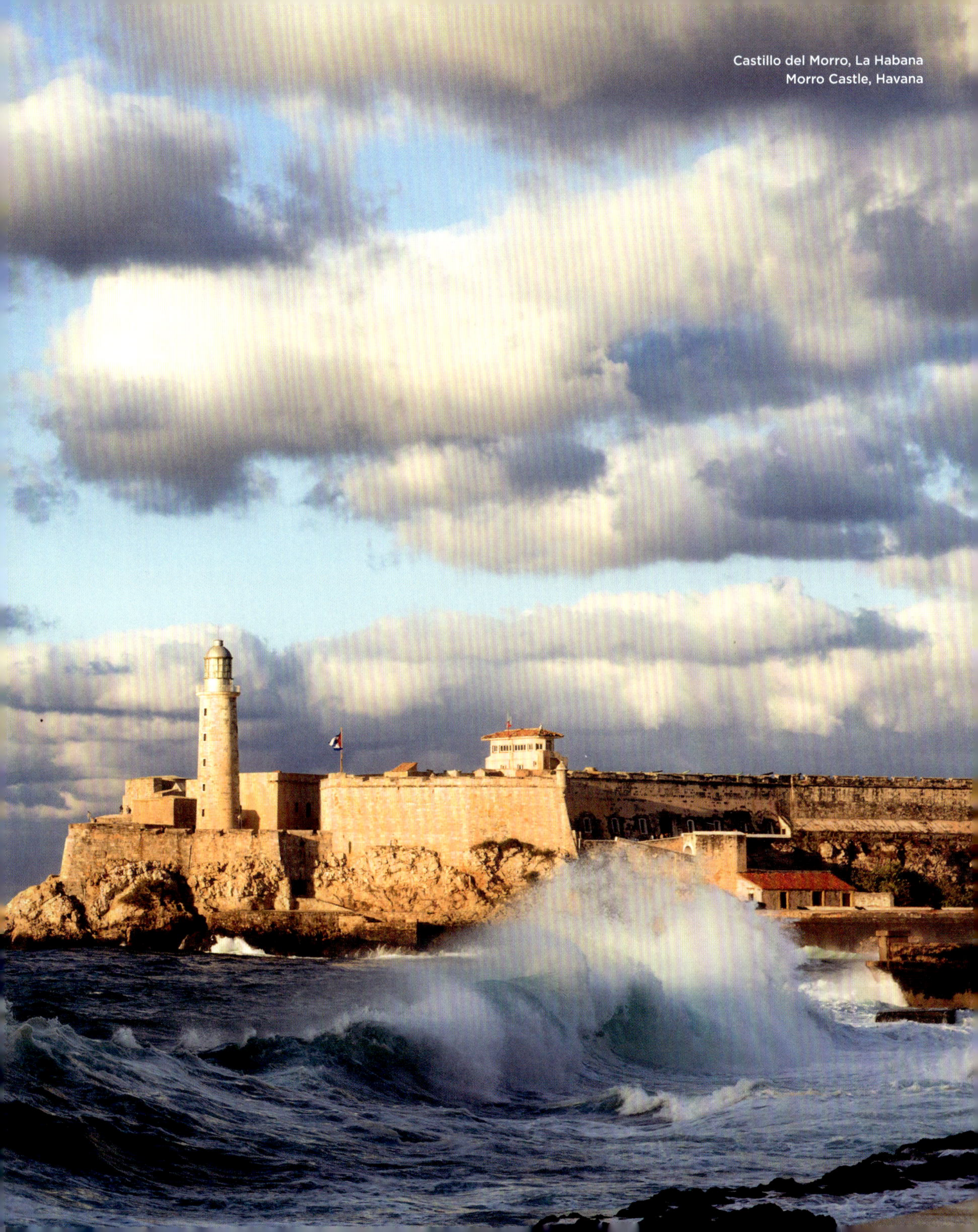
Castillo del Morro, La Habana
Morro Castle, Havana

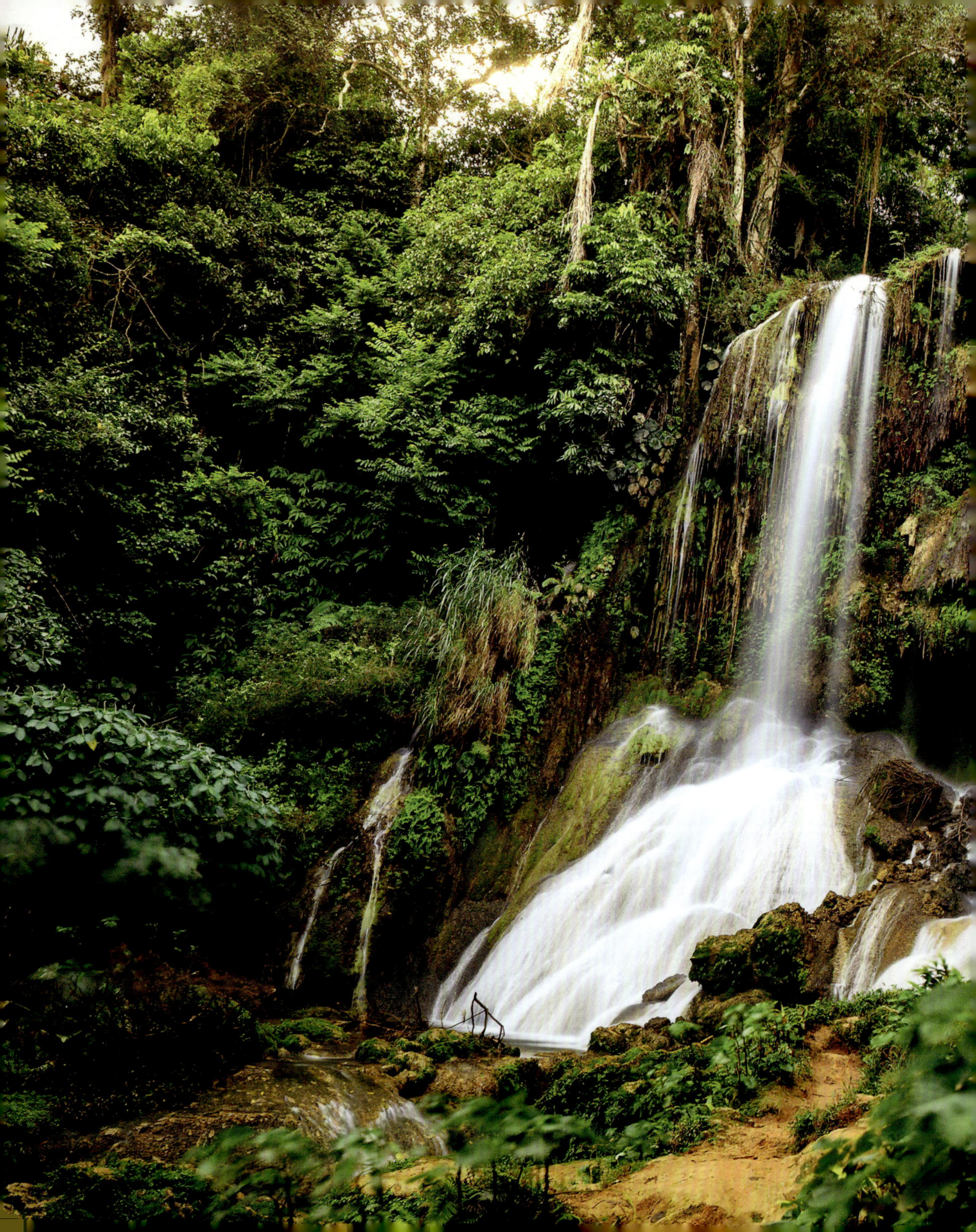

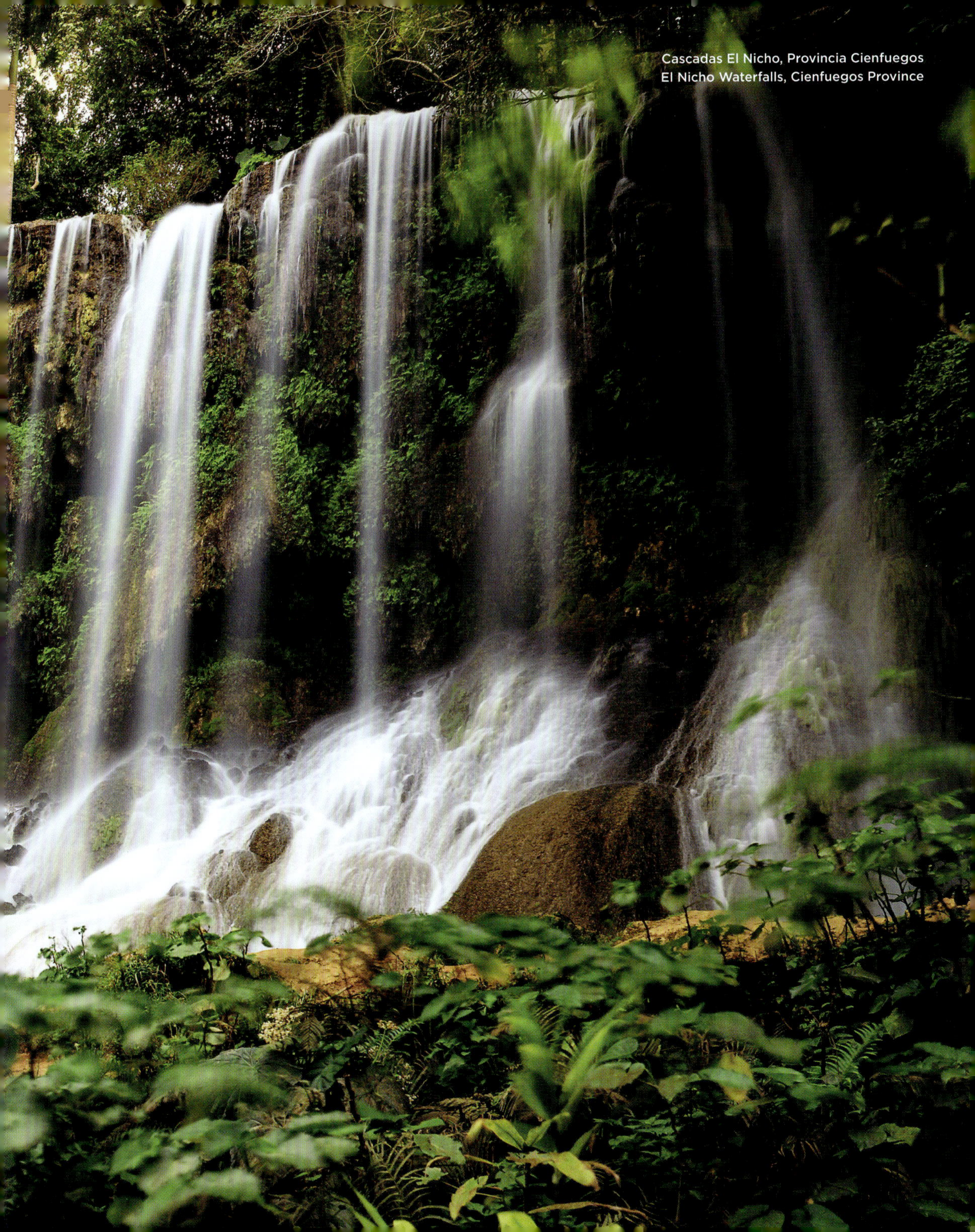
Cascadas El Nicho, Provincia Cienfuegos
El Nicho Waterfalls, Cienfuegos Province

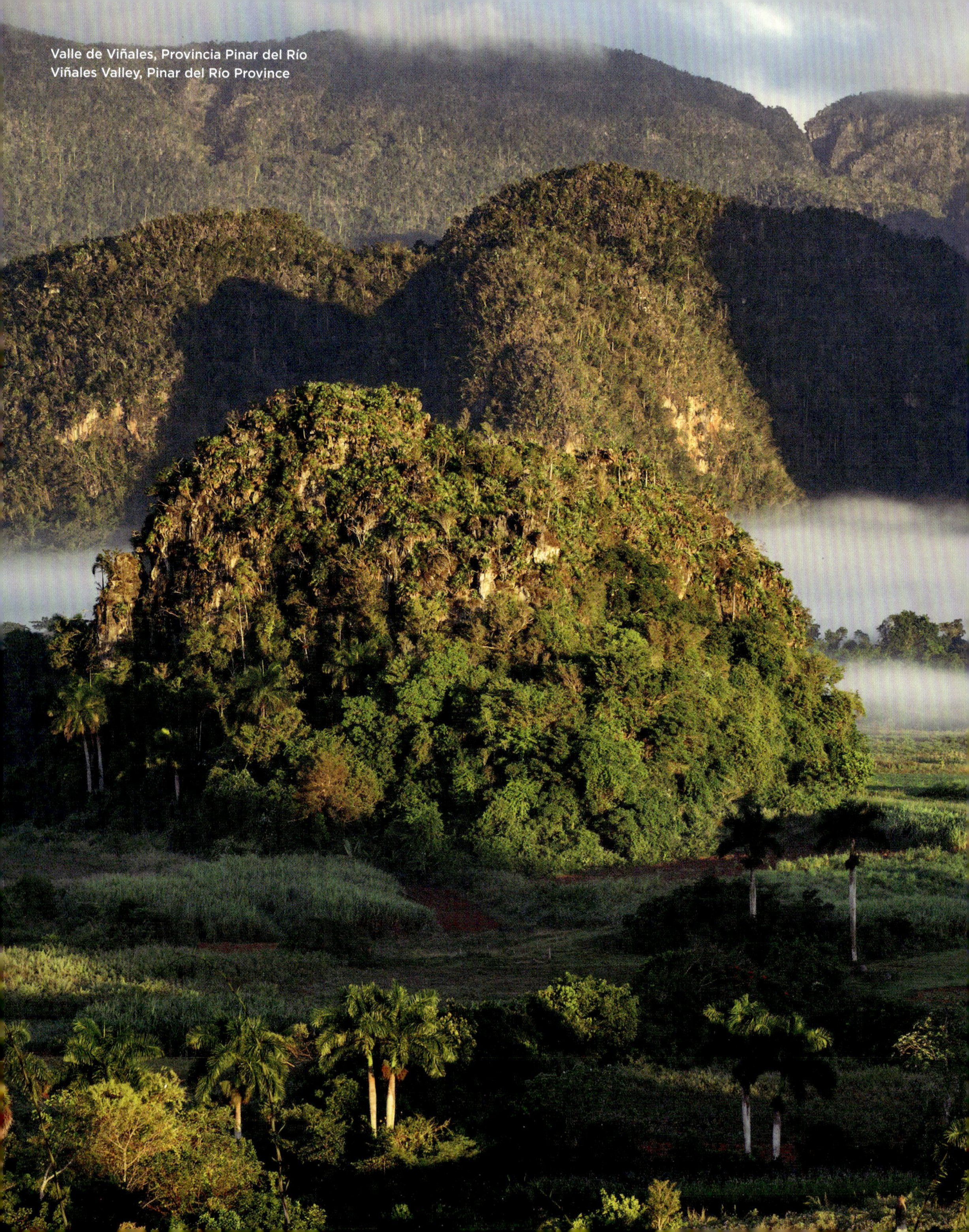
Valle de Viñales, Provincia Pinar del Río
Viñales Valley, Pinar del Río Province

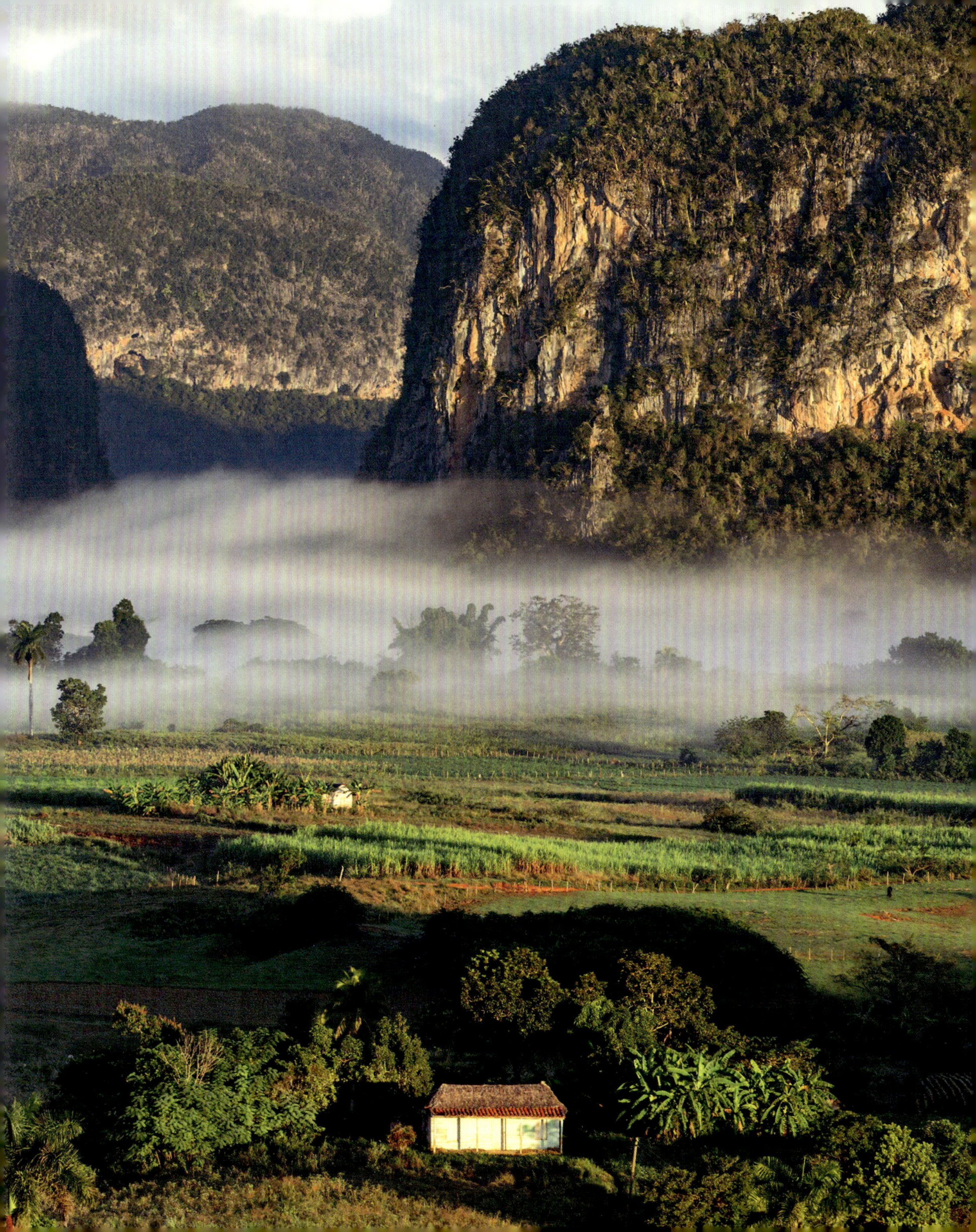

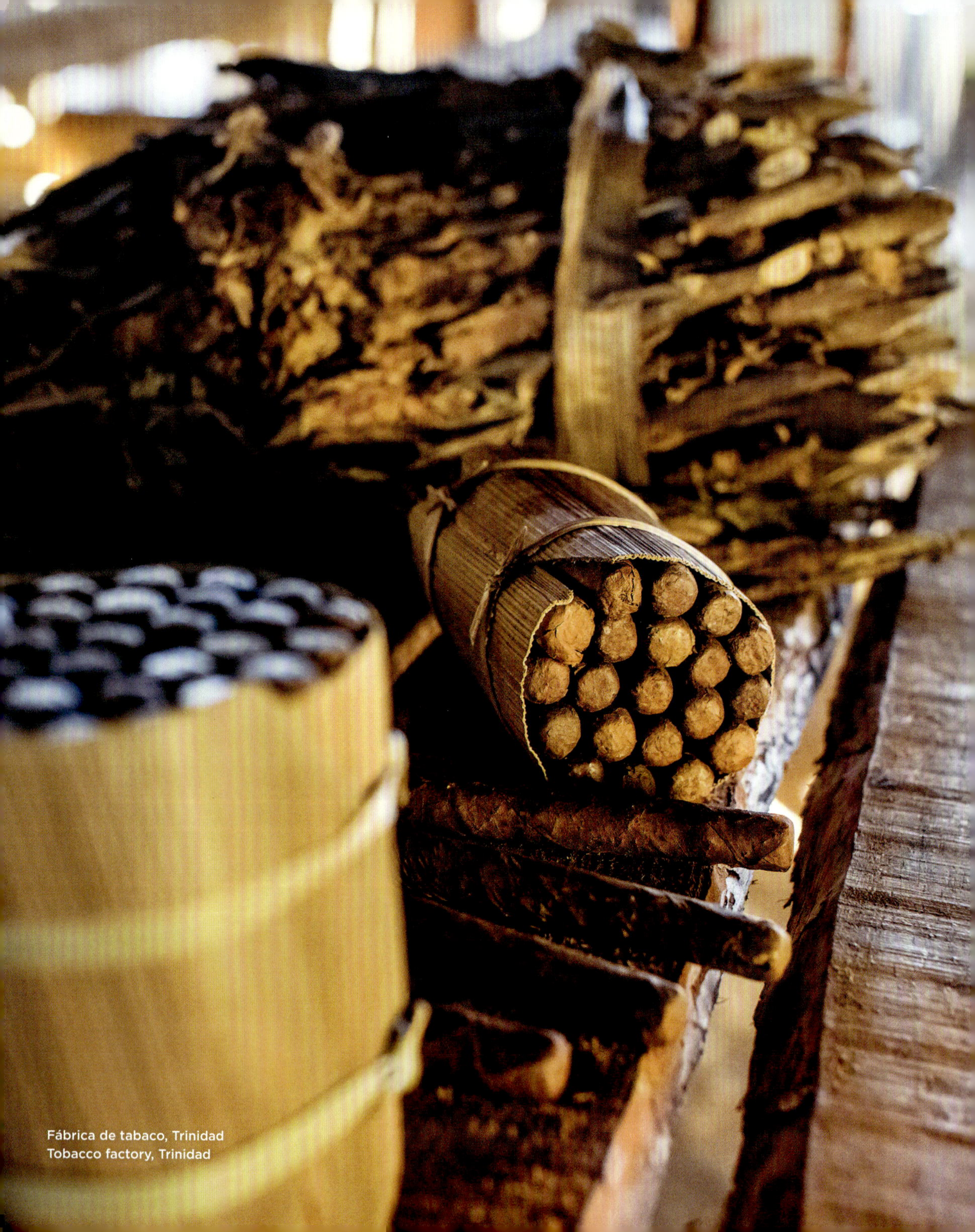

Fábrica de tabaco, Trinidad
Tobacco factory, Trinidad

Contents · Sommaire · Inhalt · Índice · Inhoud

Cuba

Cuba is synonymous with sugar and cigars, rum and revolution, classic cars and socialism, dream beaches and music. But it is also a country that has protected one-fifth of its surface area, including tropical rainforests, extensive swamps and mangrove forests. The flora and fauna of Cuba make up the Caribbean's greatest biodiversity. With an area of 11,860 km² (4579 sq. mi.) distributed over the main island, the secondary island of Isla de la Juventud and several archipelagos with over 4000 small and tiny islands, Cuba is the largest Antilles island but is still a relatively small country. Nevertheless, Cuba has often been the focus of world attention—through the revolution of 1959, the rocket crisis of 1962, the invasion at the Bay of Pigs, and the US base at Guantánamo. Musically, the island is almost a Great Power. No other country of this size has influenced popular music as much as Cuba. The colonial heritage, including slavery and sugar monoculture, has shaped the island as much as the massive US dominance of the 20th century. The megacity Havana, once a mafia playground, glitters today with its colonial old town, but other jewels of colonial architecture like Trinidad and the 'secret capital' Santiago also attract a lot of tourism, which is the main source of income for the state and for very many Cubans. The fact that a large portion of the population receives their salary in pesos but needs foreign currency to survive is one of the many absurdities of Cuban everyday life that can be found all over the country.

Cuba

Cuba est réputée pour son sucre et ses cigares, son rhum et sa révolution, ses vieilles voitures et son socialisme, ses plages paradisiaques et sa musique. Pourtant, ce n'est pas tout, un cinquième du pays a été déclaré zone naturelle protégée. Ses forêts pluvieuses tropicales, ses marécages étendus et ses forêts de mangrove abritent une flore et une faune présentant la plus riche biodiversité des Caraïbes. Avec une superficie de 11860 km², répartis entre l'île de Cuba, l'île de la Jeunesse voisine et plusieurs archipels comptant plus de 4 000 petits et moyens îlots, Cuba est un pays relativement petit, même s'il englobe la plus grande île des Caraïbes. Elle se retrouve pourtant régulièrement au centre de l'attention mondiale, qu'il s'agisse de la révolution de 1959, la crise des missiles de 1962, le débarquement de la baie des Cochons ou la base militaire de Guantánamo. En matière de musique, Cuba relève d'une « grande puissance ». Aucun autre pays de cette taille n'a autant influencé la musique populaire mondiale. L'héritage colonial, associé à l'esclavage et à la monoculture de la canne à sucre, a énormément imprégné l'île, tout comme la domination despotique des États-Unis au xxᵉ siècle. La Havane, ancien terrain d'action de la mafia, compte aujourd'hui un million d'habitants et rayonne avec sa vieille ville coloniale. Divers autres joyaux architecturaux de cette époque, dont Trinidad et la « capitale clandestine » Santiago, génèrent également un important tourisme, principale source de revenus du pays et de nombreux Cubains. Une grande partie de la population perçoit en effet un salaire en pesos, mais ne peut survivre sans devises étrangères ; telle est l'une des nombreuses aberrations du pays.

Kuba

Kuba steht für Zucker und Zigarren, Rum und Revolution, Oldtimer und Sozialismus, Traumstrände und Musik. Aber es ist auch ein Land, das ein Fünftel seiner Fläche unter Naturschutz gestellt hat, darunter tropische Regenwälder, ausgedehnte Sumpfgebiete und Mangrovenwälder, deren Flora und Fauna den größten Artenreichtum der Karibik bilden. Mit einer Fläche von 11860 km², die sich auf die Hauptinsel, die Nebeninsel Isla de la Juventud und mehrere Archipele mit über 4000 kleinen und winzigen Inseln verteilt, ist Kuba zwar die größte Antilleninsel, aber doch ein relativ kleines Land. Trotzdem stand Kuba immer wieder im Blickpunkt der Weltöffentlichkeit – durch die Revolution von 1959, die Raketenkrise 1962, die Invasion in die Schweinebucht, den US-Stützpunkt Guantánamo. Musikalisch ist die Insel geradezu eine Großmacht. Kein anderes Land dieser Größe hat weltweit die populäre Musik so beeinflusst wie Kuba. Das koloniale Erbe, darunter Sklaverei und Zucker-Monokultur, hat die Insel ebenso geprägt wie die gewaltige US-amerikanische Dominanz im 20. Jahrhundert. Die Millionenstadt Havanna, einst ein Mafia-Spielplatz, glänzt heute mit ihrer kolonialen Altstadt, aber auch andere Juwelen der Kolonialarchitektur wie Trinidad und die ‚heimliche Hauptstadt' Santiago ziehen viel Tourismus an, die Haupteinnahmequelle des Staates und sehr vieler Kubaner. Dass ein Großteil der Bevölkerung das Gehalt in Pesos bezieht, zum Überleben aber Devisen braucht, ist eine der vielen Absurditäten des kubanischen Alltags, denen man überall im Land begegnet.

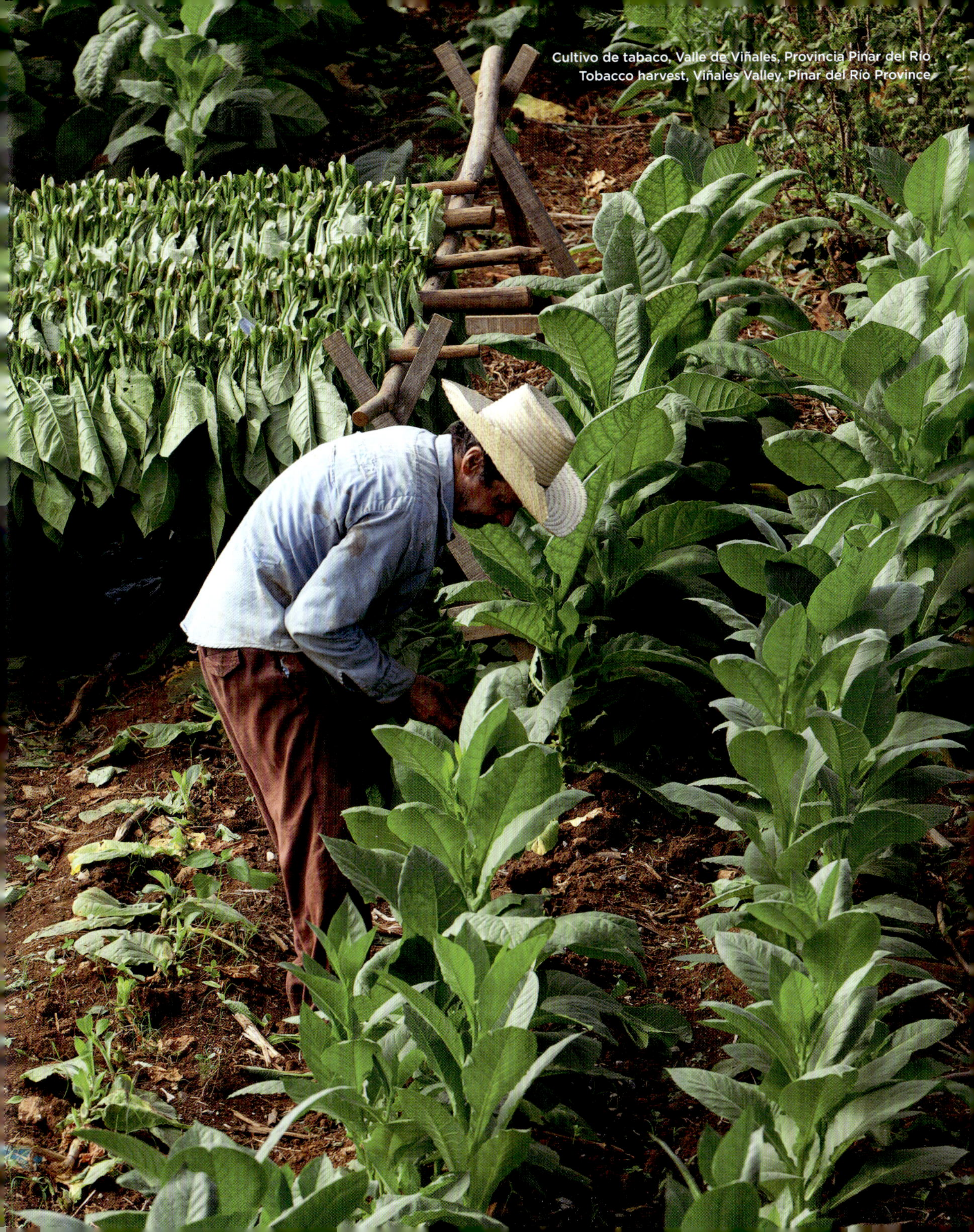

Cultivo de tabaco, Valle de Viñales, Provincia Pinar del Río
Tobacco harvest, Viñales Valley, Pinar del Río Province

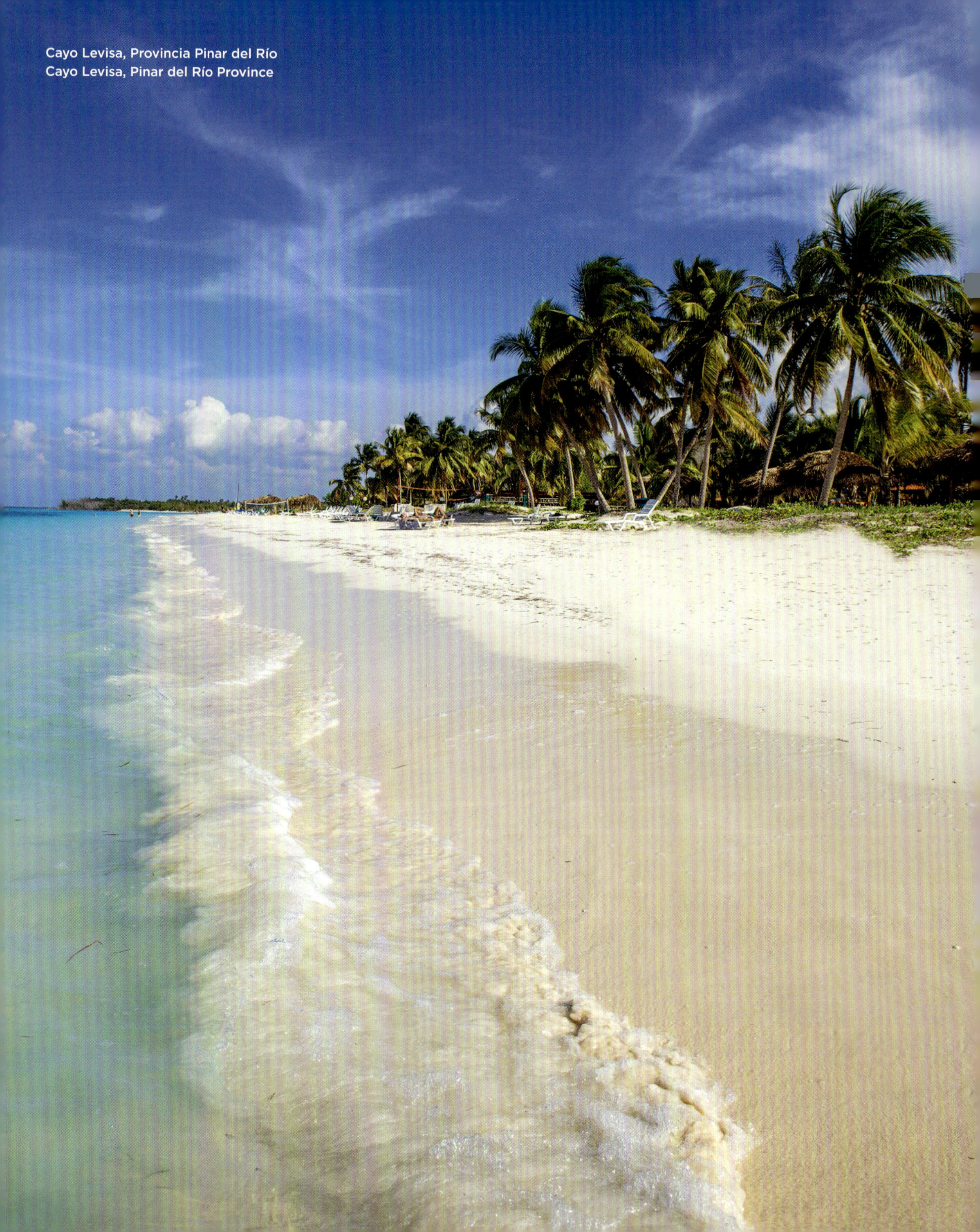
Cayo Levisa, Provincia Pinar del Río
Cayo Levisa, Pinar del Río Province

Cuba

Lo más representativo de Cuba son el azúcar y los cigarros, el ron y la revolución, los vehículos clásicos y el socialismo, las playas de ensueño y la música. Pero también es un país con una quinta parte de su superficie protegida, incluidas selvas tropicales, extensos pantanos y manglares, cuya flora y fauna constituyen la mayor biodiversidad del Caribe. Con una superficie de 11860 km² repartidos en la isla principal, la isla secundaria Isla de la Juventud y varios archipiélagos con más de 4000 pequeñas y diminutas islas, Cuba es la isla más grande de las Antillas, pero sigue siendo un país relativamente pequeño. Sin embargo, el país se convierte una y otra vez en el centro de atención de la atención mundial (a través de la revolución de 1959, la crisis de los cohetes de 1962, la invasión de Bahía de Cochinos, la base estadounidense de Guantánamo). Musicalmente, la isla es casi una gran potencia. Ningún otro país de este tamaño ha influido tanto en la música popular como Cuba. La herencia colonial, incluyendo la esclavitud y el monocultivo de azúcar, ha dado forma a la isla tanto como el dominio masivo de Estados Unidos en el siglo XX. La megaciudad de La Habana, que en su día fue un patio de recreo de la mafia, brilla hoy en día con su casco antiguo colonial, pero también otras joyas de la arquitectura colonial como Trinidad y la "capital secreta" de Santiago atraen mucho turismo, que constituye la principal fuente de ingresos del estado y de muchos cubanos. El hecho de que una gran parte de la población reciba su salario en pesos pero necesite divisas para sobrevivir es uno de los muchos disparates de la vida cotidiana cubana que se pueden encontrar en todo el país.

Cuba

Cuba significa açúcar e charutos, rum e revolução, carros clássicos e socialismo, praias de sonho e música. Mas é também um país que protegeu um quinto da sua superfície, incluindo florestas tropicais, extensos pântanos e florestas de mangue, cuja flora e fauna constituem a maior biodiversidade do Caribe. Com uma área de 11860 km² dividida entre a ilha principal, a ilha secundária "Isla de la Juventud" e os vários arquipélagos com mais de 4000 ilhas pequenas e minúsculas, Cuba é a maior ilha das Antilhas, mas ainda é um país relativamente pequeno. No entanto, Cuba sempre esteve no foco da opinião pública mundial – passando pela revolução de 1959, pela crise dos foguetes de 1962, pela invasão da Baía dos Porcos, chegando até a base norte-americana de Guantánamo. Musicalmente, a ilha é quase uma grande potência. Nenhum outro país deste tamanho influenciou tanto a música popular como Cuba. A herança colonial, incluindo a escravatura e a monocultura do açúcar, influenciou a ilha tanto quanto o domínio massivo dos EUA no século XX. A megacidade de Havana, outrora já foi o palco da máfia, brilha hoje com sua cidade velha colonial, mas também outras jóias da arquitetura colonial como Trinidad e a 'capital secreta' Santiago atraem muito turismo, a principal fonte de renda do Estado e muitos cubanos. O fato de uma grande parte da população receber seu salário em pesos, mas precisar de moeda estrangeira para sobreviver, é um dos muitos absurdos da vida cotidiana cubana que são encontrados em todo o país.

Cuba

Cuba staat bekend om suiker en sigaren, rum en revolutie, oldtimers en socialisme, droomstranden en muziek. Maar het is ook een land dat een vijfde van zijn oppervlakte heeft beschermd, waaronder tropische regenwouden, uitgestrekte moerassen en mangrovebossen, waarvan de flora en fauna de grootste biodiversiteit van het Caribisch gebied vormen. Met een oppervlakte van 11860 km² wat over het hoofdeiland, het omliggende eiland Isla de la Juventud en verschillende archipels met meer dan 4000 kleine eilanden is verdeeld, maakt Cuba weliswaar het grootste eiland van de Antillen, maar nog steeds een relatief klein land. Desondanks stond Cuba herhaaldelijk in het middelpunt van de belangstelling van de wereldopinie – door de revolutie van 1959, de raketcrisis van 1962, de invasie van de Varkensbaai, de Amerikaanse basis Guantánamo. Muzikaal gezien is het eiland bijna een heerschappij. Geen enkel ander land van deze omvang heeft zoveel invloed gehad op de populaire muziek als Cuba. Het koloniale erfgoed, waaronder de slavernij en de suikermonocultuur, heeft het eiland evenzeer gevormd als de massale Amerikaanse dominantie in de 20e eeuw. De miljoenenstad Havana, ooit een maffia speeltuin, straalt vandaag de dag met zijn koloniale historische stad, maar ook andere koloniale architectuur zoals Trinidad en de 'geheime hoofdstad' Santiago trekken veel toerisme aan en is de belangrijkste bron van inkomsten van de staat en heel veel Cubanen. Het feit dat een groot deel van de bevolking hun salaris in peso's ontvangt, maar vreemde valuta nodig heeft om te overleven, is een van de vele absurditeiten van het Cubaanse dagelijks leven die in het hele land te vinden zijn.

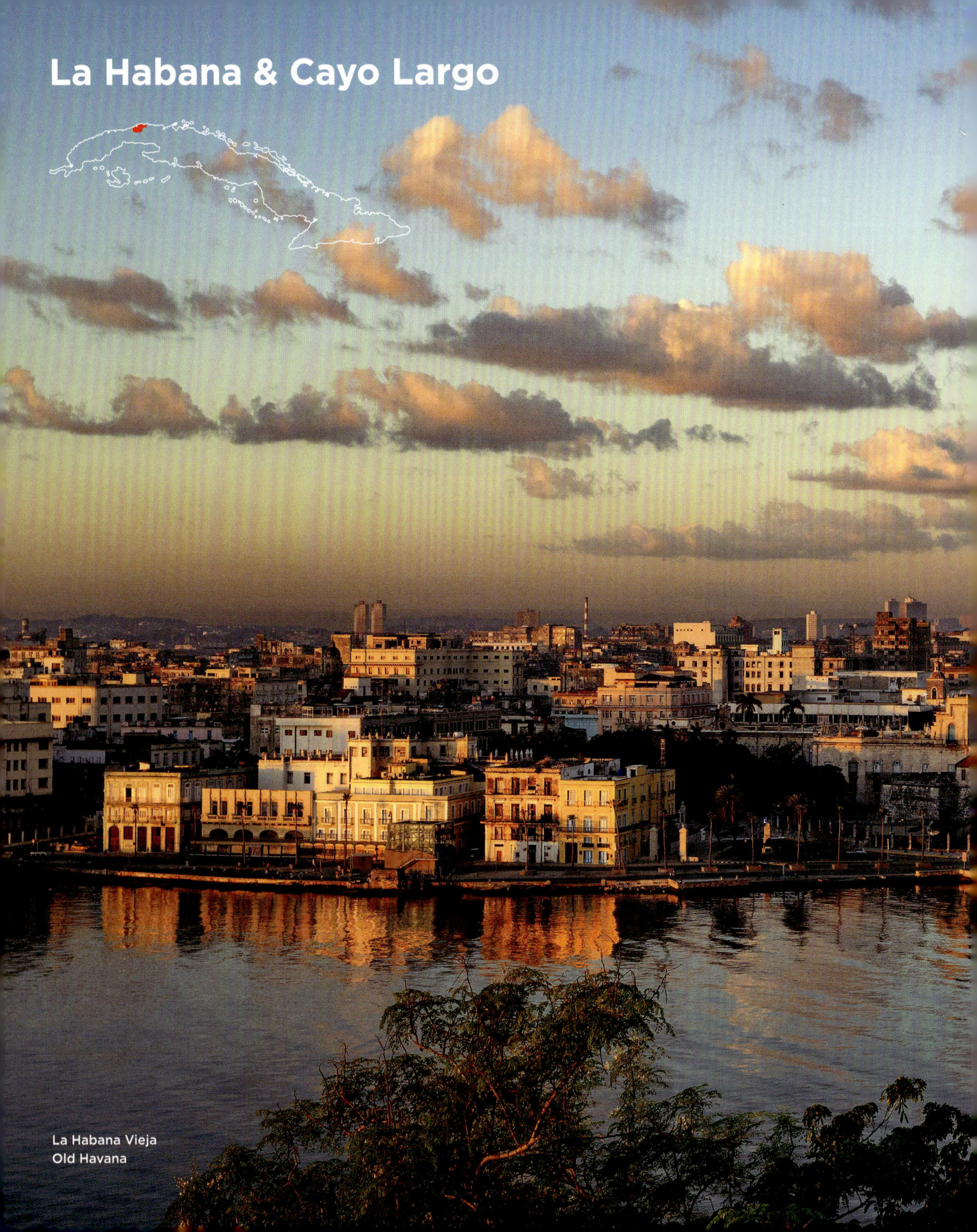

La Habana Vieja
Old Havana

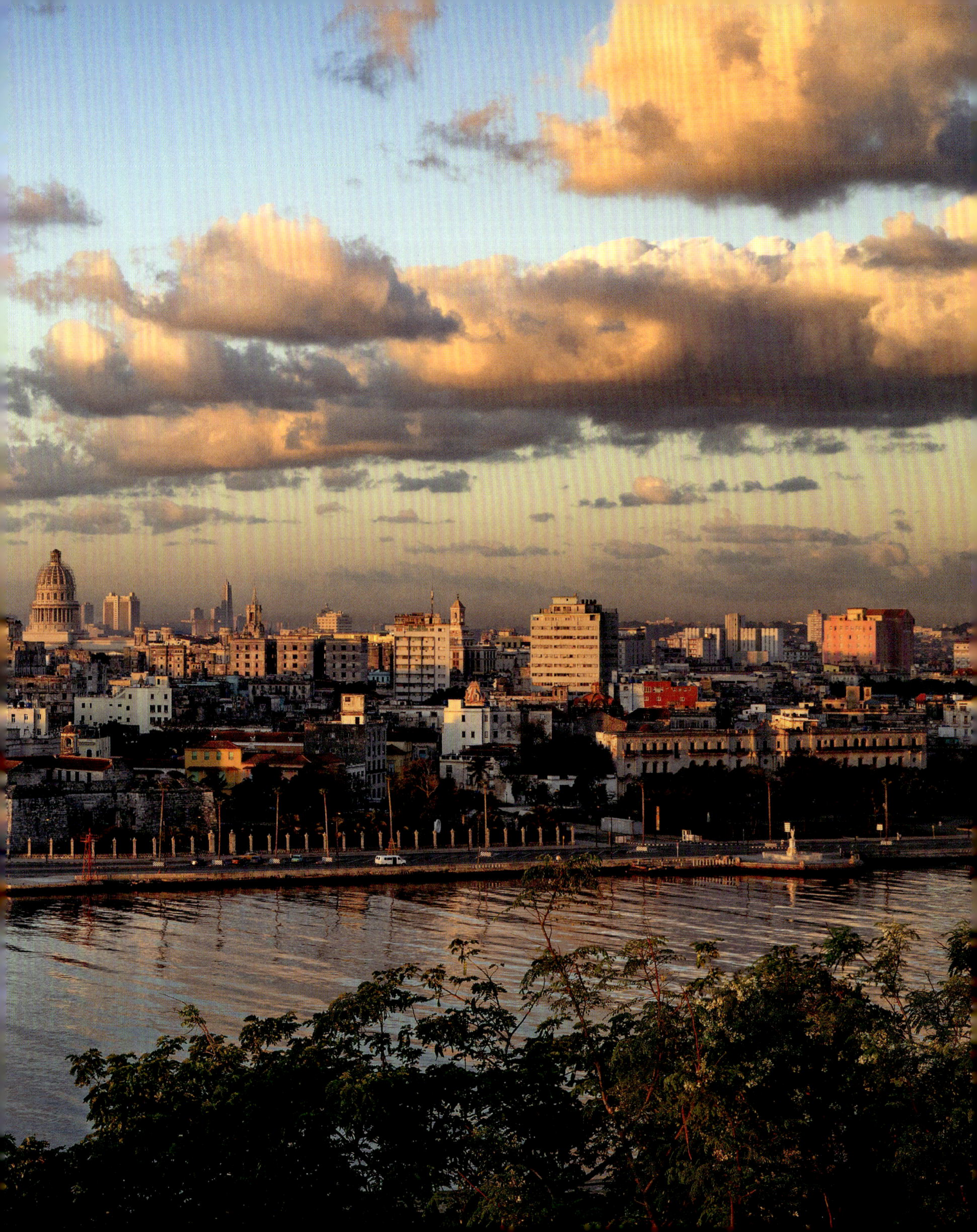

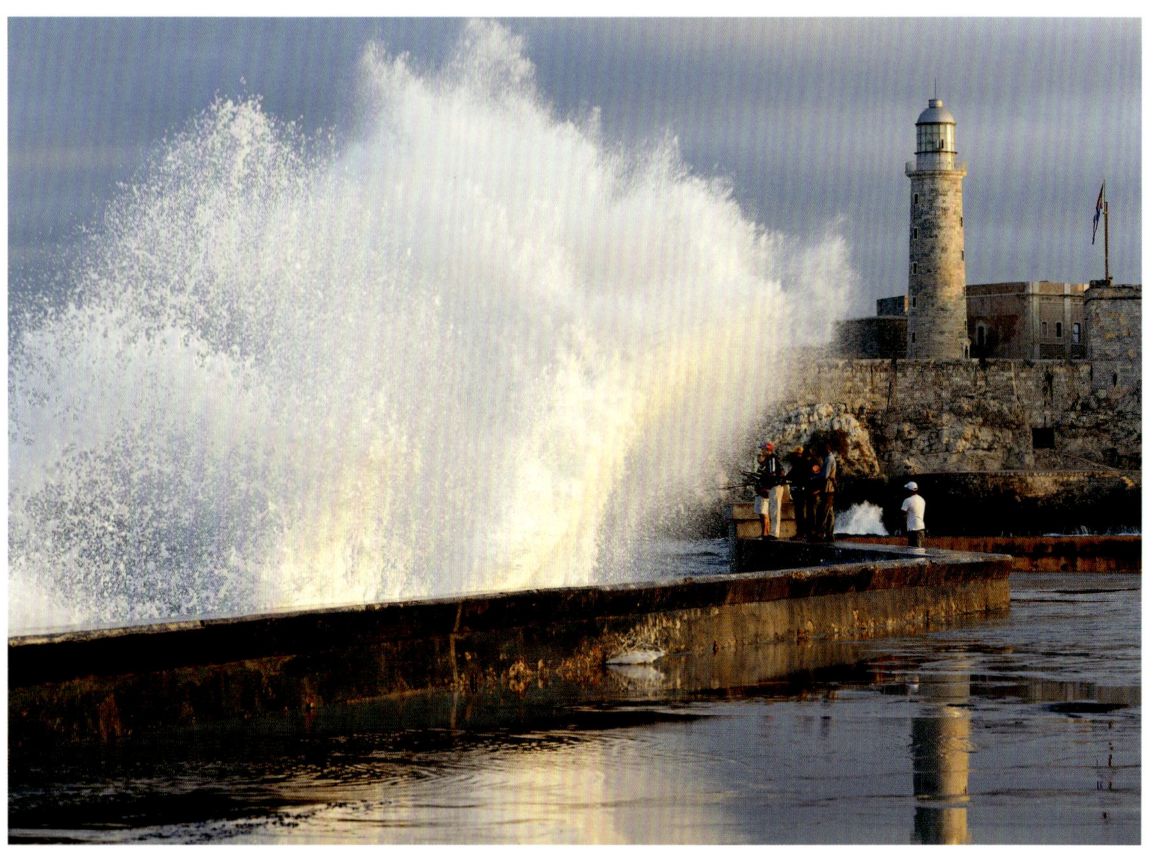

Castillo del Morro, La Habana
Morro Castle, Havana

Havana

The metropolis of Havana has a very special flair. Musicians and poets have compared Havana to a bubbling stew, to a gigantic melting pot whose "ingredients" are the extremely different cultures and people—Native Americans, Spanish colonial rulers and settlers, pirates, African slaves, European adventurers, British occupiers, Chinese immigrants, Americans (marines, industrialists, tourists), mafias and fortune-hunters, sugar barons and rebels. All have left their mark here over the past five centuries. Havana, the "ugly beauty", is a city of contradictions and contrasts.

La Havane

La métropole de La Havane possède un charme particulier. Musiciens et poètes l'ont comparée à un creuset bouillonnant, un gigantesque melting-pot, brassant les cultures et les individus aux origines les plus diverses : autochtones indiens, colons espagnols, pirates, esclaves africains, aventuriers européens, occupants britanniques, immigrés chinois, Américains (marines, industriels et touristes), patrons de la mafia, baroudeurs, barons du sucre et rebelles. Tous ont exercé leur influence sur la ville au cours des cinq siècles derniers. La Havane, la « belle vilaine », est une ville de contrastes et de contradictions.

Havanna

Die Metropole Havanna hat ein ganz besonderes Flair. Musiker und Dichter haben Havanna mit einem brodelnden Eintopf verglichen, mit einem gigantischen Melting-Pot, dessen „Zutaten" äußerst unterschiedliche Kulturen und Menschen sind – indianische Ureinwohner, spanische Kolonialherren und Siedler, Piraten, afrikanische Sklaven, europäische Abenteurer, britische Besatzer, chinesische Einwanderer, US-Amerikaner (Marines, Industrielle, Touristen), Mafiabosse und Glücksritter, Zuckerbarone und Rebellen. Alle haben hier in den vergangenen fünf Jahrhunderten ihre Spuren hinterlassen. Havanna, die „hässliche Schöne", ist eine Stadt der Widersprüche und Gegensätze.

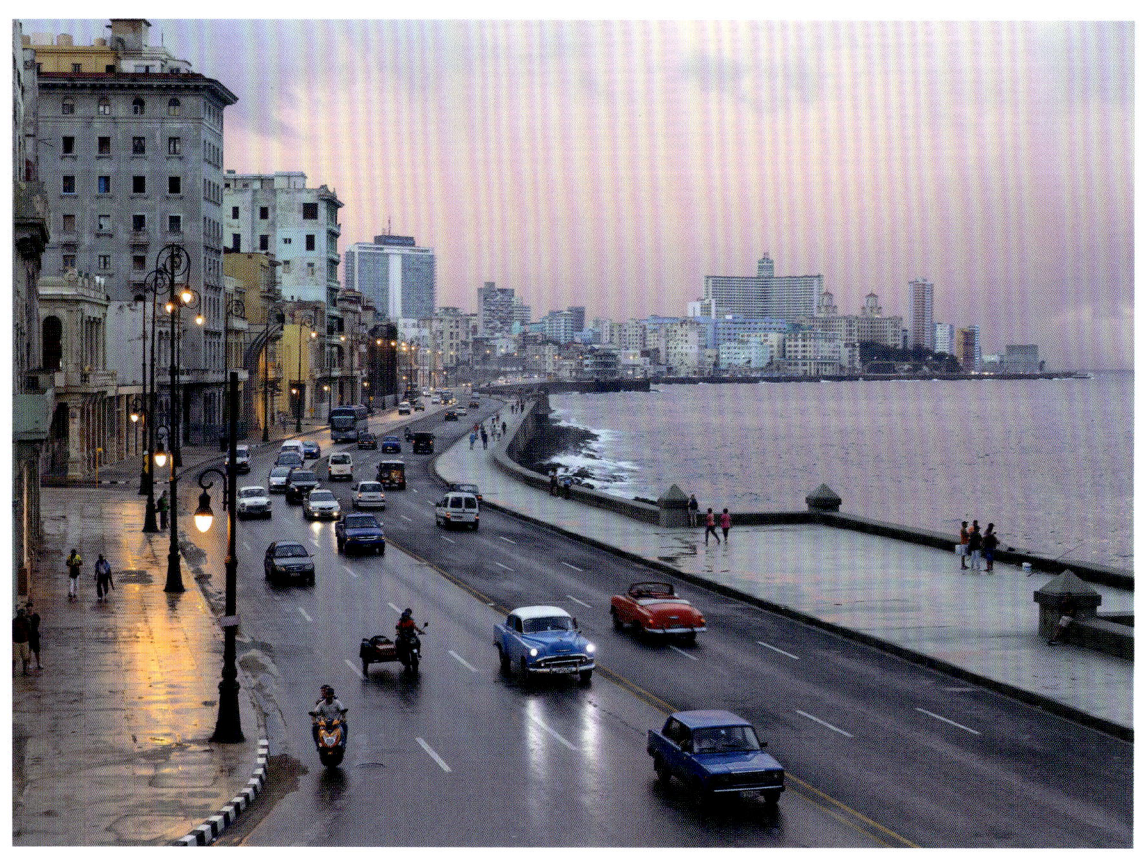

Malecón

La Habana

La metrópoli de La Habana tiene un toque muy especial. Músicos y poetas han comparado La Habana con una olla hirviendo, con un gigantesco crisol cuyos "ingredientes" son culturas y pueblos extremadamente diferentes: indios americanos, gobernantes y colonos coloniales españoles, piratas, esclavos africanos, aventureros europeos, ocupantes británicos, inmigrantes chinos, estadounidenses (marineros, industriales, turistas), mafiosos y cazafortunas, barones del azúcar y rebeldes. Todos ellos han dejado su huella aquí en los últimos cinco siglos. La Habana, la "fea belleza", es una ciudad de contradicciones y contrastes.

Havana

A metrópole de Havana tem um toque muito especial. Músicos e poetas compararam Havana a um guisado borbulhante, a um gigantesco caldeirão cujos "ingredientes" são culturas e pessoas extremamente diferentes – nativos americanos, governantes e colonizadores coloniais espanhóis, piratas, escravos africanos, aventureiros europeus, ocupantes britânicos, imigrantes chineses, americanos (fuzileiros navais, industriais, turistas), máfias e caçadores de fortunas, barões do açúcar e rebeldes. Todos deixaram a sua marca aqui nos últimos cinco séculos. Havana, a "beleza feia", é uma cidade de contradições e contrastes.

Havana

De metropool Havana heeft een heel bijzondere flair. Muzikanten en dichters hebben Havana vergeleken met een borrelende stoofpot, met een gigantische smeltkroes waarvan de 'ingrediënten' extreem verschillende culturen en mensen zijn – inheemse Amerikanen, Spaanse koloniale heersers en kolonisten, piraten, Afrikaanse slaven, Europese avonturiers, Britse bezetters, Chinese immigranten, Amerikanen (mariniers, industriëlen, toeristen), maffiabazen, gelukszoekers, suikerbaronnen en rebellen. Allen hebben hier in de afgelopen vijf eeuwen hun sporen achtergelaten. Havana, de 'lelijke schoonheid', is een stad van tegenstellingen en contrasten.

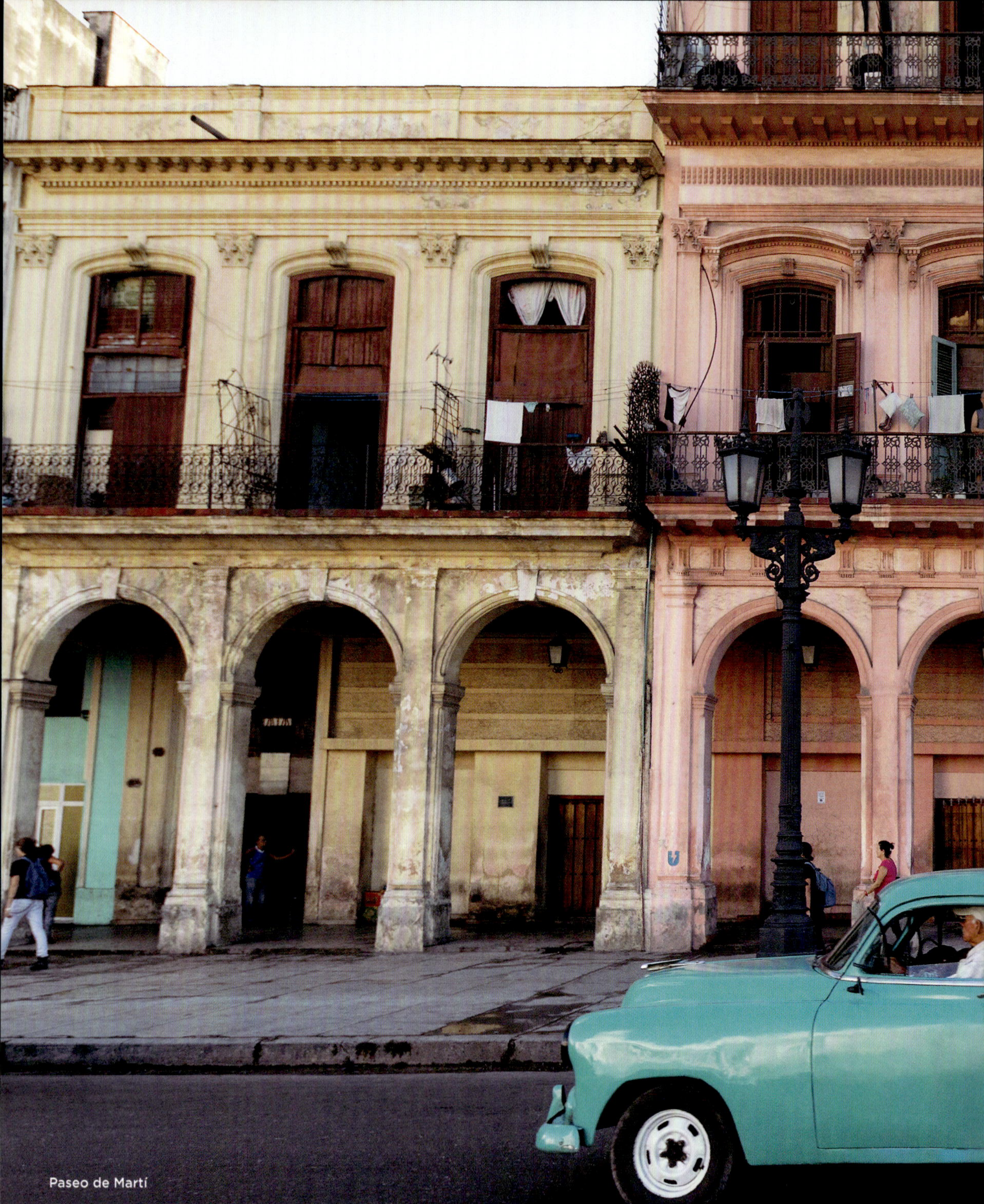
Paseo de Martí

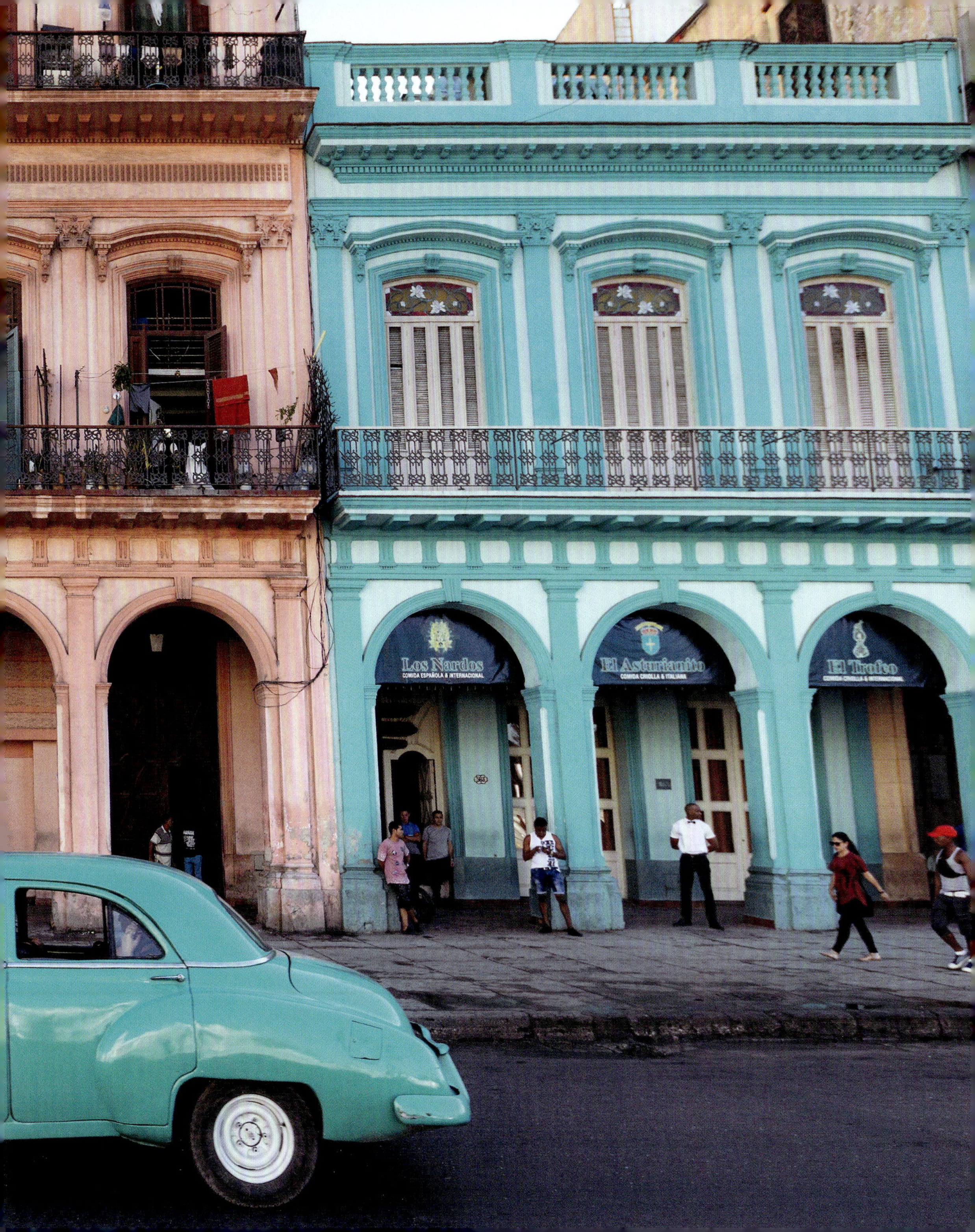

Los Nardos
COMIDA ESPAÑOLA & INTERNACIONAL
El Asturianito
COMIDA CRIOLLA & ITALIANA
El Trofeo
COMIDA CRIOLLA & INTERNACIONAL

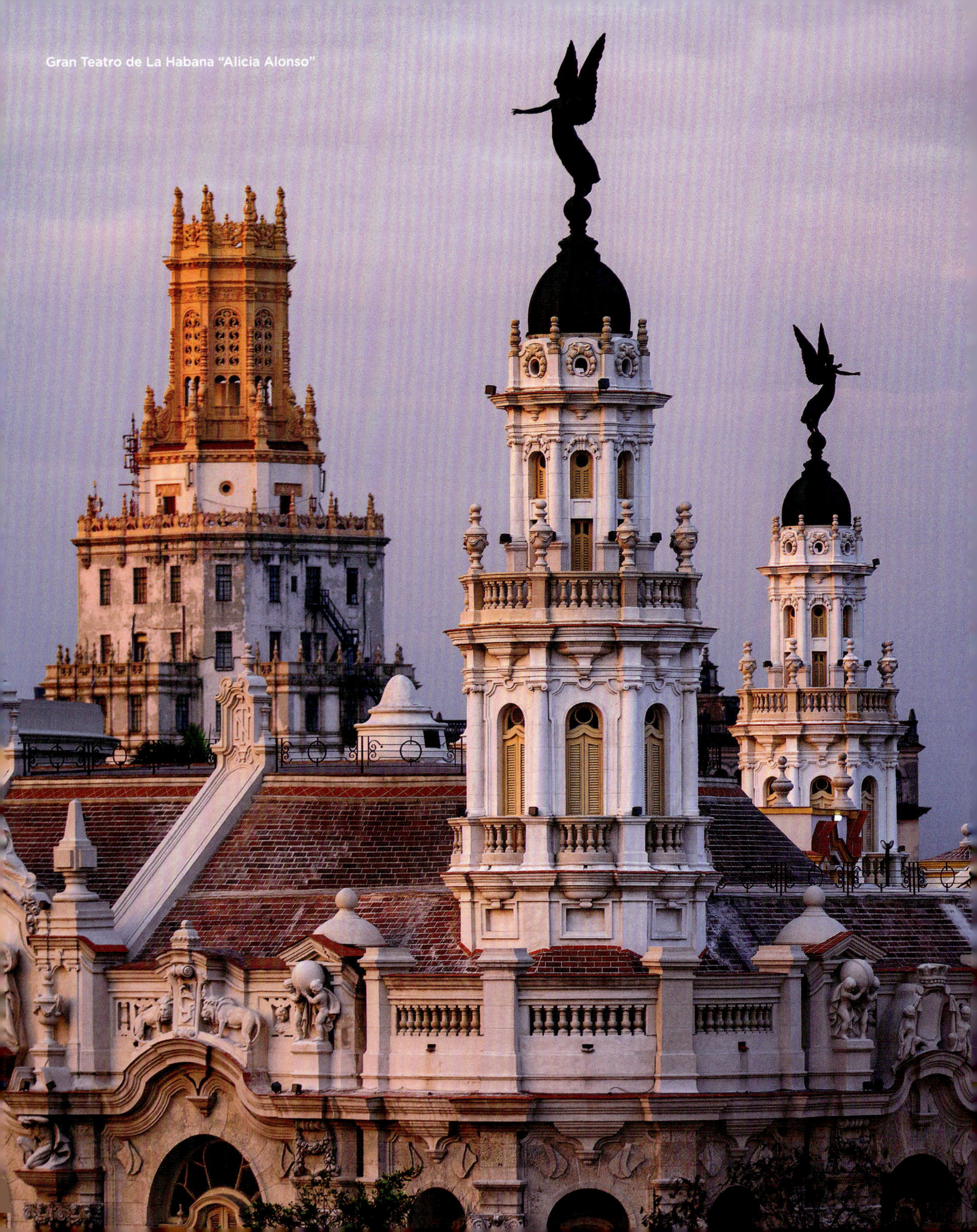

Gran Teatro de La Habana "Alicia Alonso"

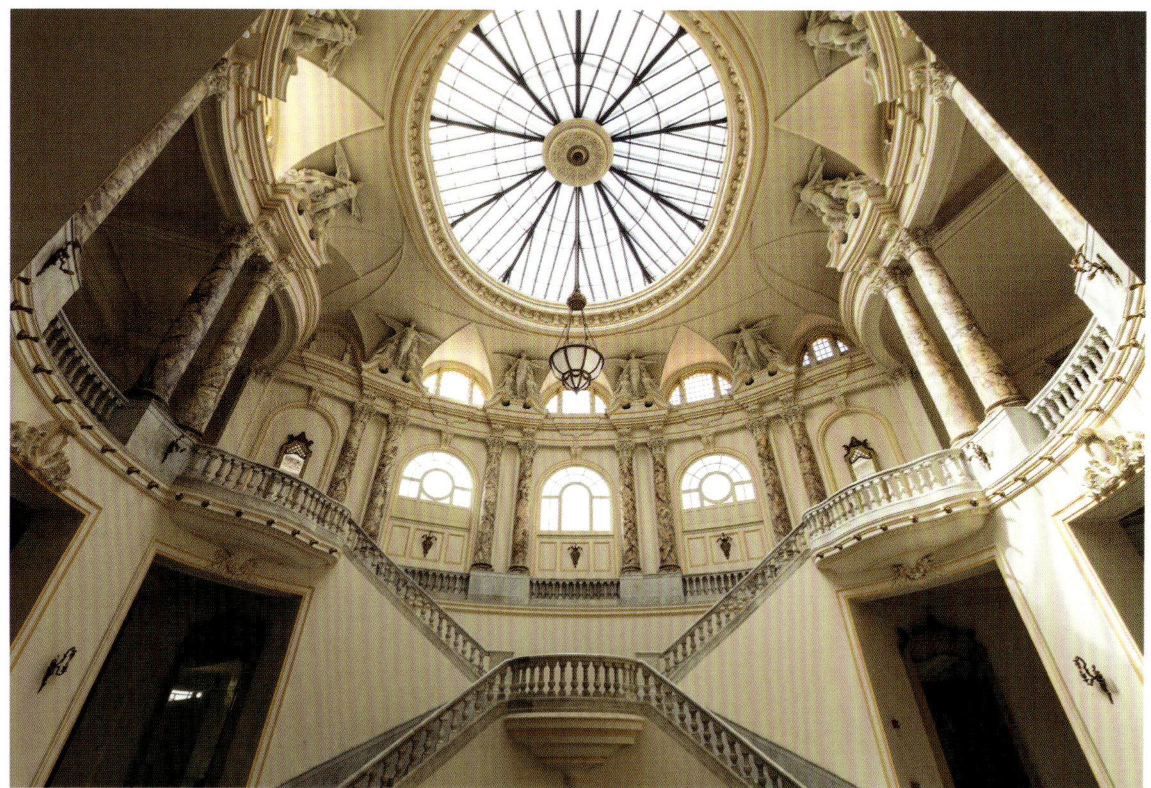

Gran Teatro de La Habana "Alicia Alonso"

Gran Teatro de La Habana "Alicia Alonso"

This neo-baroque magnificent building, named after the Cuban dance legend Alicia Alonso, is the seat of the National Ballet and the State Opera, and with its 2000 seats is one of the largest theatres in Latin America. Enrico Caruso and Sarah Bernhardt have previously performed here, and Barack Obama gave his historic speech to the Cuban people in the Great Hall in 2016.

Gran Teatro de La Habana "Alicia Alonso"

El magnífico edificio neobarroco, que lleva el nombre de la leyenda de la danza cubana Alicia Alonso, es la sede del Ballet Nacional y de la Ópera del Estado y, con su espacio para 2000 personas, uno de los mayores teatros de América Latina. Enrico Caruso y Sarah Bernhardt ya han actuado aquí, y Barack Obama dio su histórico discurso al pueblo cubano en el Gran Salón en 2016.

Grand Théâtre de La Havane Alicia Alonso

Le somptueux bâtiment néobaroque, baptisé du nom de la légendaire ballerine Alicia Alonso, est le siège du Ballet National, l'Opéra national du pays, et avec une jauge de 2000 places, l'une des plus grandes salles de spectacle d'Amérique latine. Il a accueilli sur ses planches Enrico Caruso et Sarah Bernhardt, et Barack Obama y tint, en 2016, son discours historique adressé au peuple de Cuba.

Gran Teatro de La Habana "Alicia Alonso"

O magnífico edifício neobarroco, nomeado em homenagem à lenda da dança cubana Alicia Alonso, é a sede do Ballet Nacional e da Ópera Estadual e, com 2000 lugares, é um dos maiores teatros da América Latina. Enrico Caruso e Sarah Bernhardt já se apresentaram aqui, e Barack Obama fez seu discurso histórico ao povo cubano no Grande Salão em 2016.

Gran Teatro de La Habana "Alicia Alonso"

Das neobarocke Prachtgebäude, benannt nach der kubanischen Tanzlegende Alicia Alonso, ist Sitz des Nationalballetts und der Staatsoper und mit 2000 Plätzen eines der größten Schauspielhäuser Lateinamerikas. Hier standen schon Enrico Caruso und Sarah Bernhardt auf der Bühne, und im Großen Saal hielt Barack Obama 2016 seine historische Rede an das kubanische Volk.

Gran Teatro de La Habana 'Alicia Alonso'

Het prachtige barokke gebouw, genoemd naar de Cubaanse danslegende Alicia Alonso, is de zetel van het Nationale Ballet en de Staatsopera en is met 2000 zitplaatsen een van de grootste theaters in Latijns-Amerika. Enrico Caruso en Sarah Bernhardt hebben hier al opgetreden en Barack Obama gaf in het jaar 2016 in de grote zaal zijn historische toespraak voor de Cubaanse bevolking.

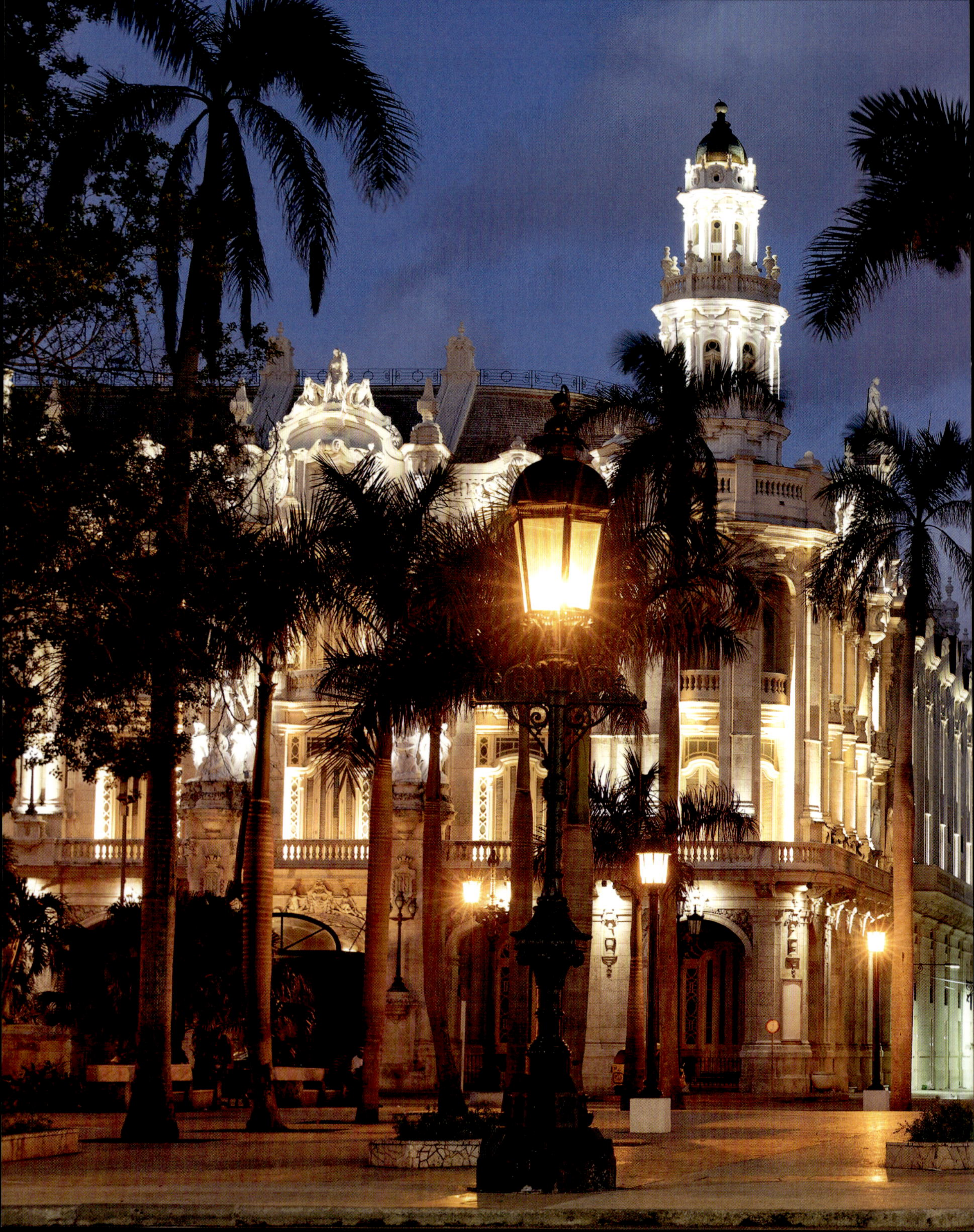

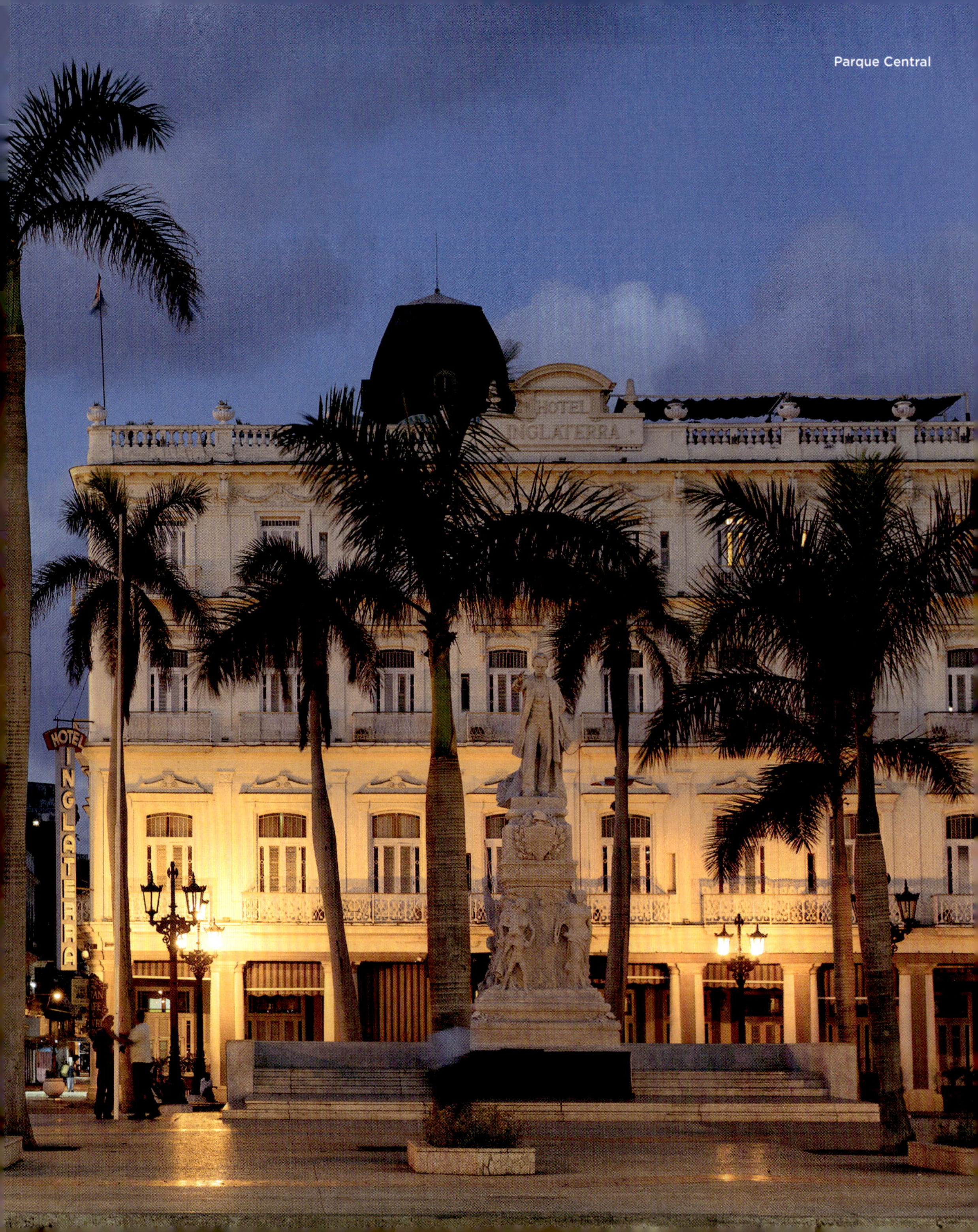
HOTEL
INGLATERRA
HOTEL
INGLATERRA

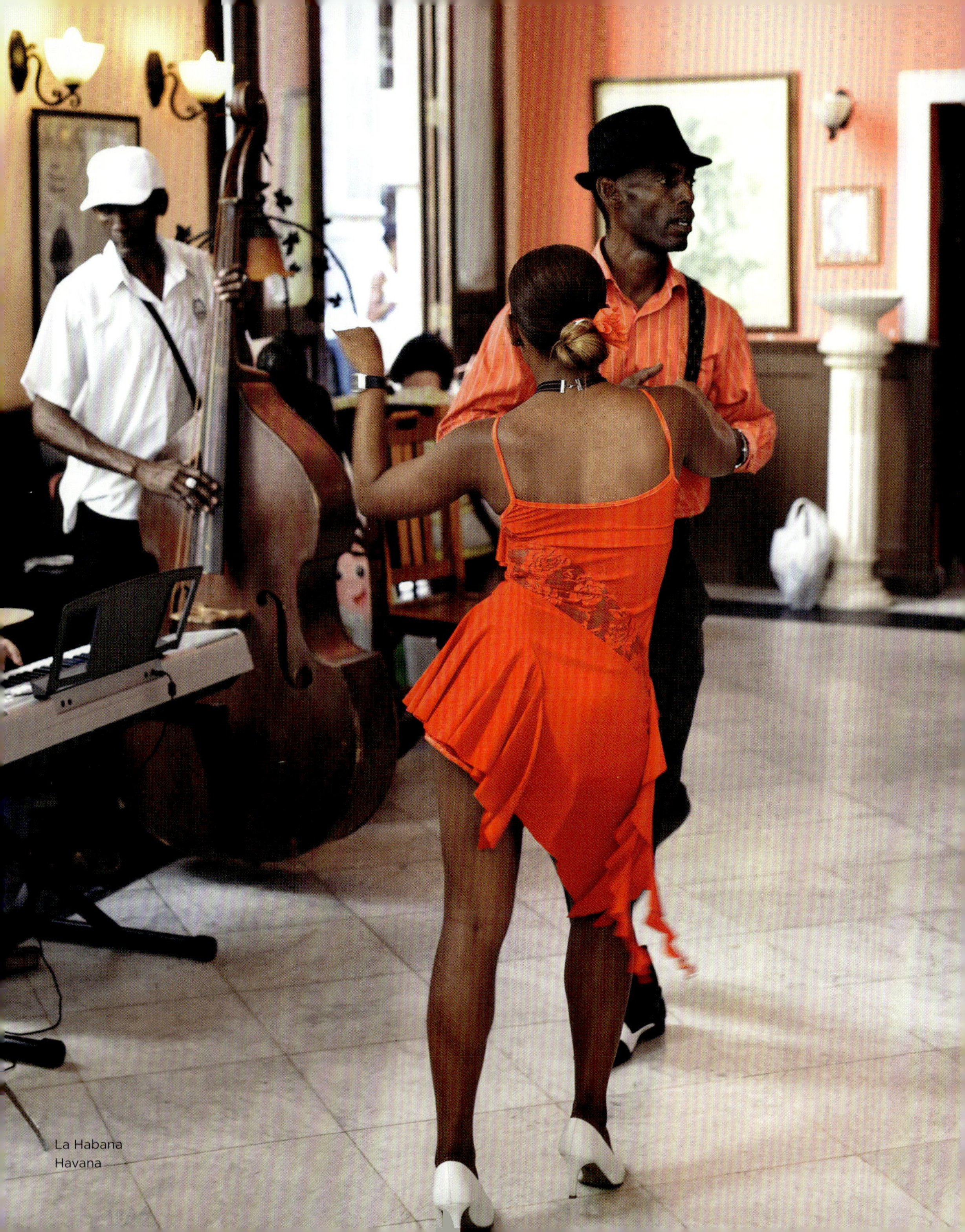

La Habana
Havana

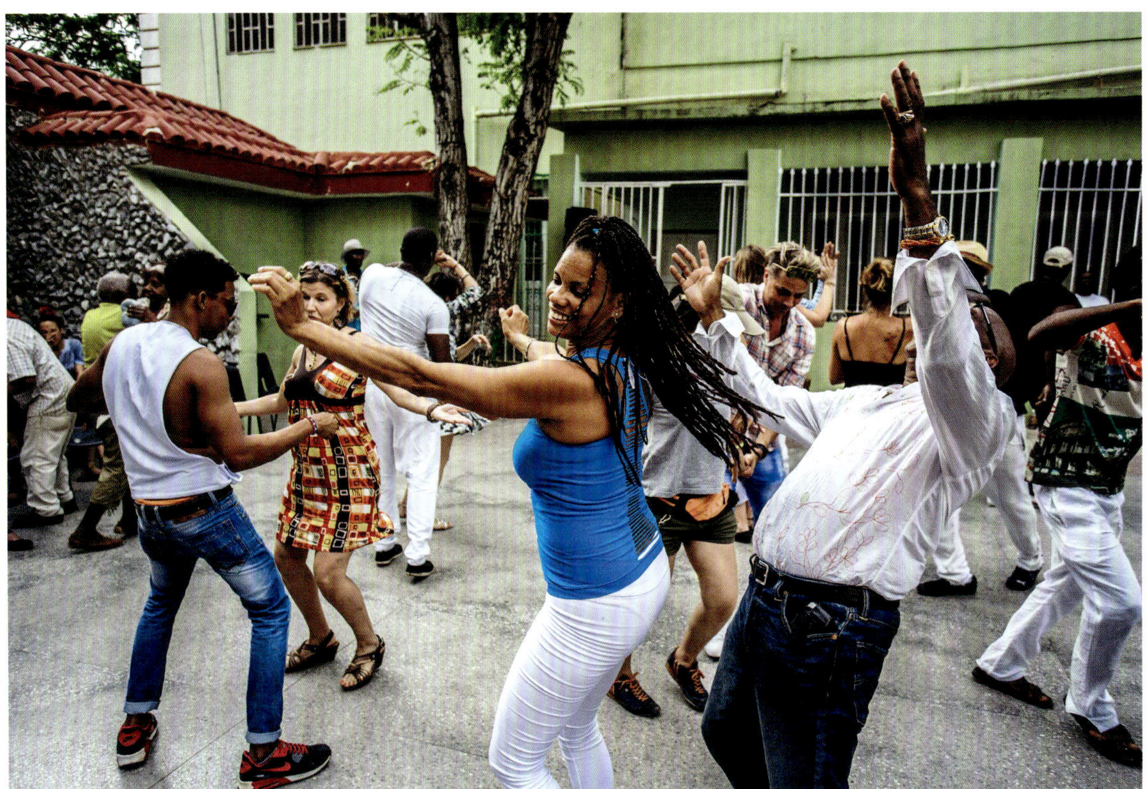

La Habana
Havana

The Island of Sound

Ever since the worldwide success of the *Buena Vista Social Club,* it has become clear that Cuba is an "island of sound", where music and dance are food. Whether it's the syncopated national rhythm Son, the rumba that migrated from the slave barracks to the salons, or the mambos and chachachás of the 1950s—Cuba has been exporting music and dance all over the world for decades.

La isla sonora

A más tardar desde el éxito mundial del *Buena Vista Social Club* está claro: Cuba es una "isla sonora" que se alimenta de la música y la danza. Ya sea el ritmo nacional sincopado son, la rumba que emigró de las barracas de esclavos a los salones o los mambos y chachachás de los años 50, Cuba lleva décadas exportando música y bailes por todo el mundo.

L'île de la musique

Si certains en doutaient encore, le succès mondial du *Buena Vista Social Club* l'a définitivement prouvé : à Cuba, la musique et la danse sont des denrées vitales. Qu'il s'agisse du *son,* rythme national syncopé né dans les baraques des esclaves et aujourd'hui joué dans les salons, de la rumba immigrée ou du mambo et du cha-cha-cha des années 1950, Cuba exporte, depuis des décennies, ses musiques et ses danses dans le monde entier.

A Ilha dos Sons

O mais tardar, desde o sucesso mundial do *Buena Vista Social Club,* ficou claro: Cuba é uma "ilha sonora" onde a música e a dança são alimentos. Seja o ritmo nacional sincopado Son, a rumba que migrou das cabanas dos escravos para os salões ou os mambos e chachachachás dos anos 50 – Cuba exporta música e dança para todo o mundo há décadas.

Die klingende Insel

Spätestens seit dem Welterfolg des *Buena Vista Social Club* ist klar: Kuba ist eine „klingende Insel", auf der Musik und Tanz Lebensmittel sind. Ob der synkopierte Nationalrhythmus Son, die aus den Sklavenbaracken in die Salons gewanderte Rumba oder die Mambos und Chachachás der 1950er-Jahre – Kuba exportiert seit Jahrzehnten Musik und Tänze in die ganze Welt.

Het Klankeiland

Sinds het wereldwijde succes van de *Buena Vista Social Club* is het duidelijk: Cuba is een 'Klankeiland' waar muziek en dans eten zijn. Of het nu gaat om het gesyncopeerde nationale ritme Son, de rumba die van de slavenkazerne naar de salons migreerde of de mambo's en Cha-Cha-Chas van de jaren vijftig – Cuba exporteert al decennia lang muziek en dansen over de hele wereld.

Music

Nothing in Cuba is purely white or black. This applies to the kitchen as well as to art, but above all it applies to the phenomenon of Cuban music, which is incredibly rich in variations, mixing all the sounds that come to the island in order to self-confidently create its very own sound—a polyphonic acoustic cloud that rises above the streets of Havana.

Musique

À Cuba, rien n'est déterminé ni figé, ce principe vaut en cuisine comme en art. Il est au cœur du phénomène de la musique cubaine, aux innombrables variantes. Elle a assimilé toutes les sonorités débarquées sur l'île pour façonner un style absolument unique, conscient de ses origines, telle une nuée acoustique polyphonique planant au-dessus des rues de La Havane.

Musik

Nichts in Kuba ist nur weiß oder nur schwarz, das gilt für die Küche wie die Kunst. Doch vor allem gilt es für das Phänomen der ungemein variantenreichen kubanischen Musik, die alles miteinander vermengte, was an Klängen auf die Insel kam, um daraus selbstbewusst einen ganz eigenen Sound zu kreieren – eine vielstimmige akustische Wolke, die über den Straßen Havannas liegt.

Música

Nada en Cuba es solo blanco o negro, y esto se aplica tanto a la cocina como al arte. Pero sobre todo se aplica al fenómeno de la música cubana, que es increíblemente rica en variaciones, ya que mezcló todos los sonidos que llegaron a la isla para crear con confianza su propio sonido, una nube acústica polifónica que se extiende sobre las calles de La Habana.

Música

Nada em Cuba é só branco ou só preto, isso se aplica tanto à cozinha como à arte. Mas, acima de tudo, aplica-se ao fenómeno da música cubana, que é incrivelmente rica em variedade, misturando todos os sons, que chegaram à ilha, para criar com confiança o seu próprio som único – uma nuvem acústica polifónica que pode ser encontrado nas ruas de Havana.

Muziek

Niets in Cuba is alleen maar wit of alleen zwart, dit geldt voor zowel de keuken als voor de kunst. Het geldt vooral voor het fenomeen van de Cubaanse muziek, wat ongelofelijk variatierijk is, waarbij alle geluiden die naar het eiland zijn gekomen zo een eigen geluid creëren – een polyfone akoestische wolk die boven de straten van Havana ligt.

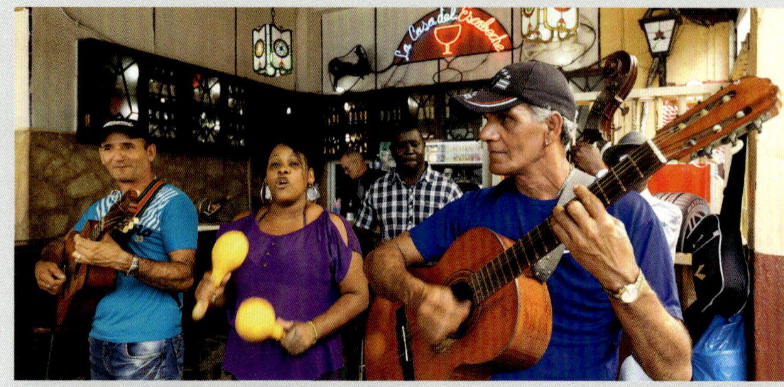
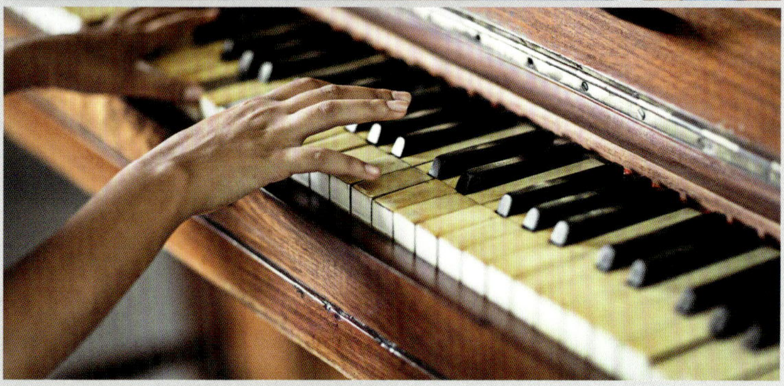
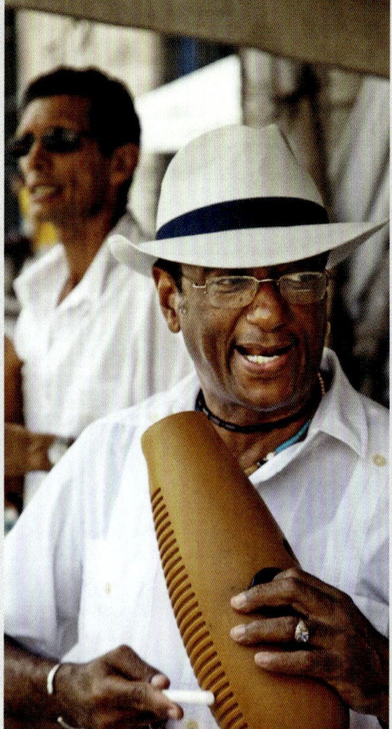
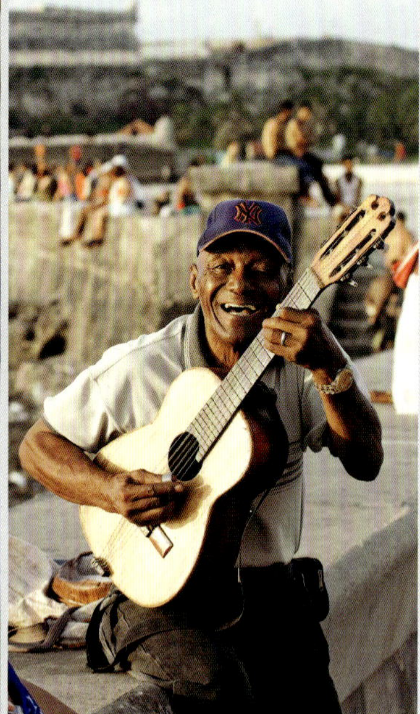

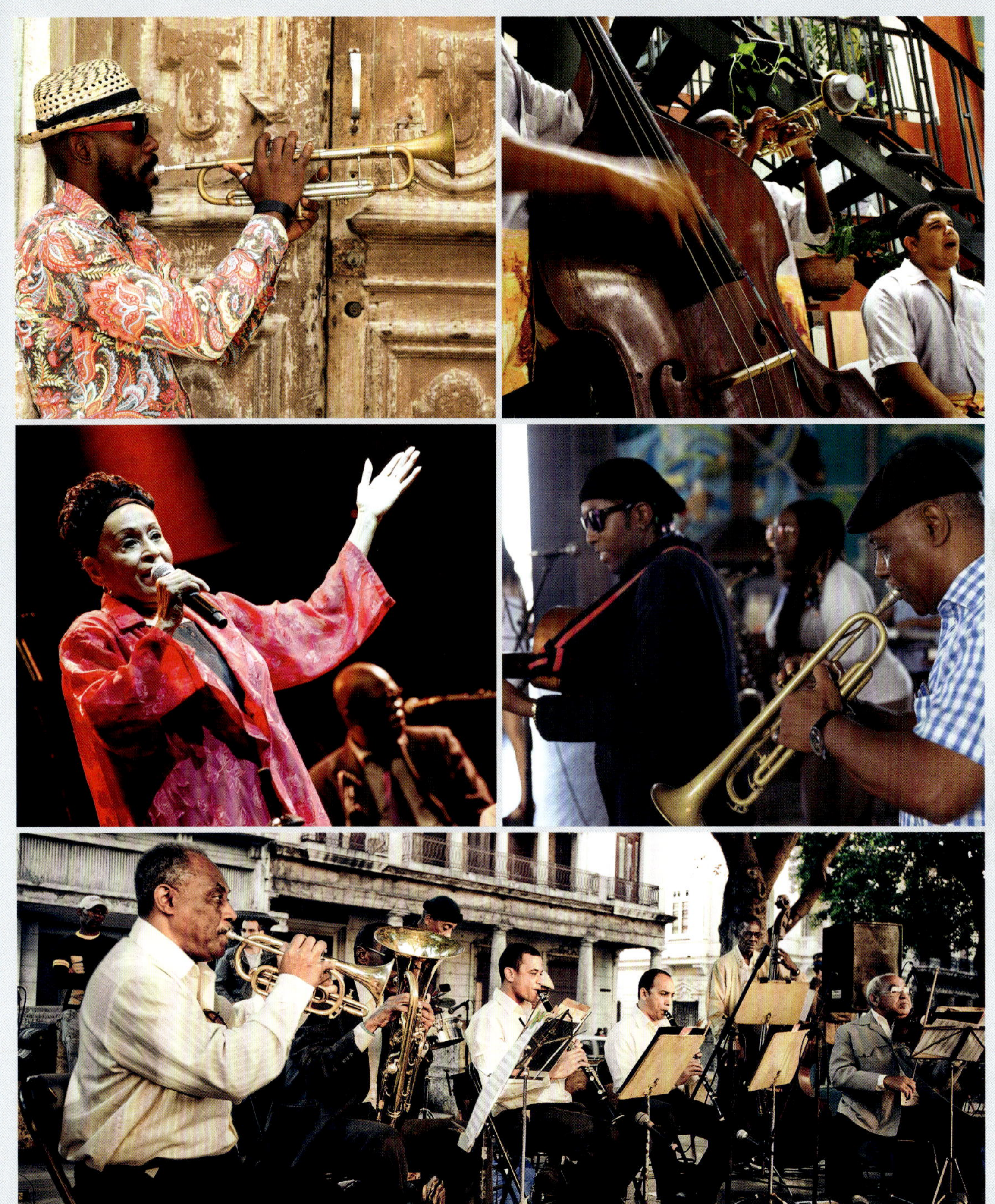

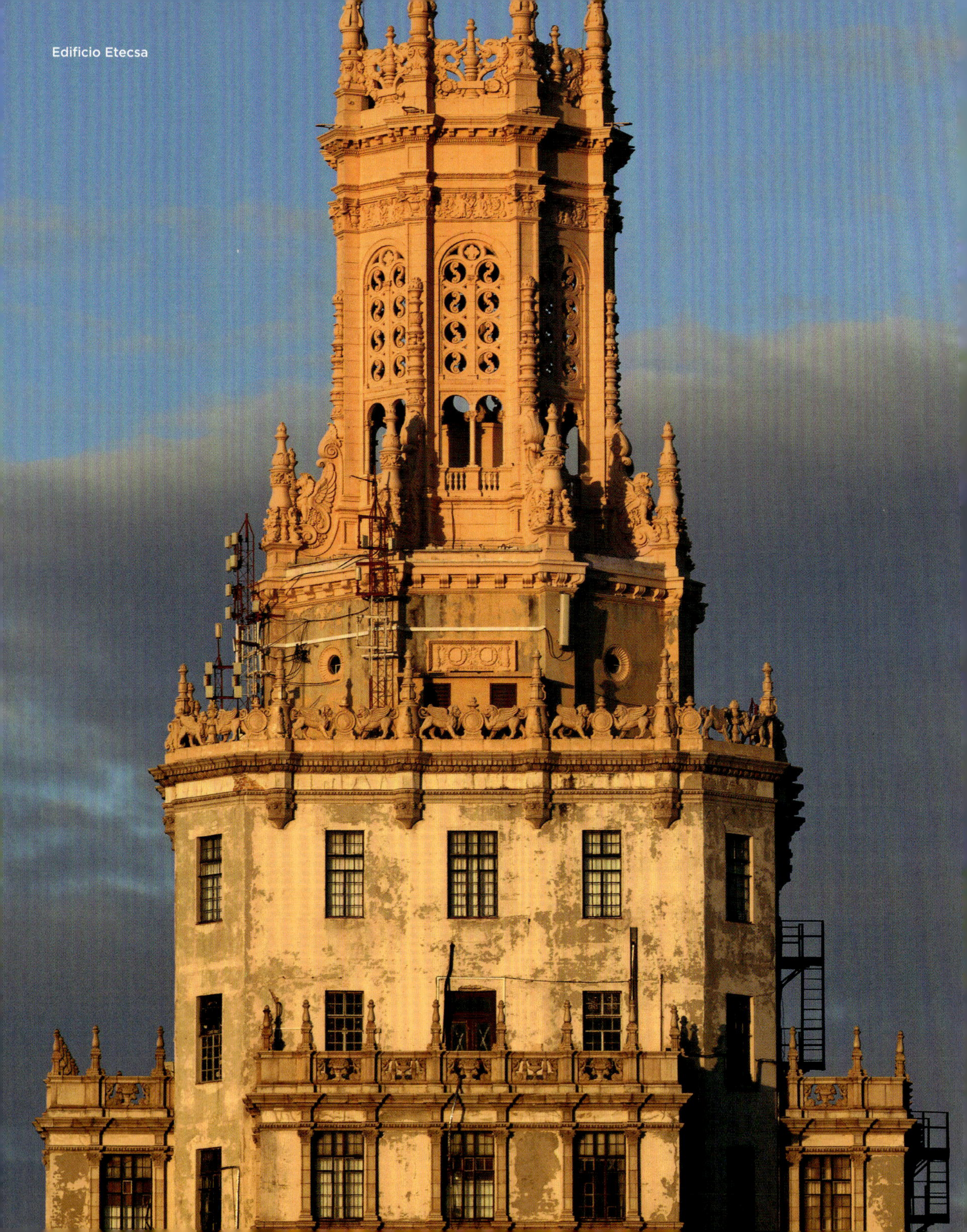
Edificio Etecsa

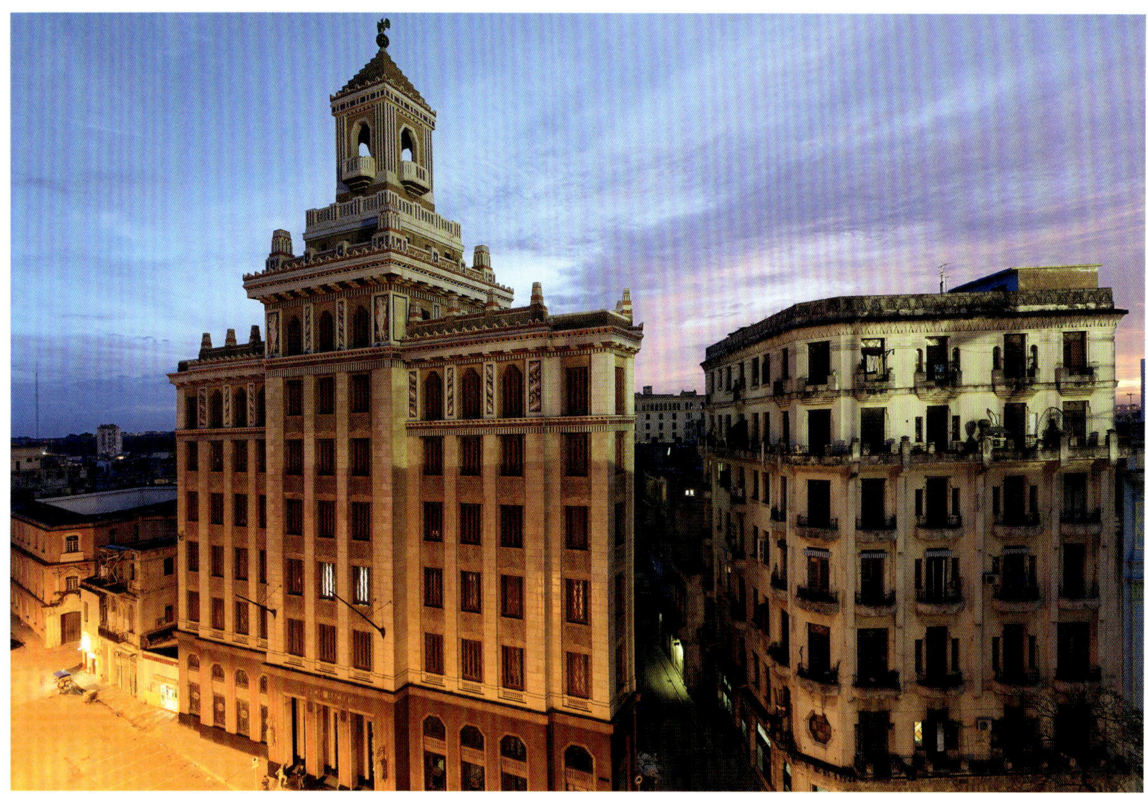

Edificio Bacardi

Edificio Etecsa and Edificio Bacardí

When the skyscraper of the Cuban telephone company Etecsa was built in 1927, it dominated the panorama of Havana with its unique tower at a height of 62 m (203 ft). The Edificio Bacardí, former seat of the legendary Rum brand and a prime example of Art Deco architecture, dates from the same period (1930). After the revolution in 1959, the family emigrated to the USA.

Edificio Etecsa y Edificio Bacardí

Cuando se construyó el rascacielos de la compañía telefónica cubana Etecsa en 1927, dominaba el panorama de La Habana con su corona idiosincrásica a 62 m de altura. El Edificio Bacardí, antigua sede de la legendaria marca de ron y ejemplo de arquitectura Art Déco, data de la misma época (1930). Después de la revolución de 1959, la familia se fue a Estados Unidos.

Edificio Etecsa et Edificio Bacardí

Lorsque l'immeuble de la société téléphonique cubaine Etecsa fut érigé en 1927, sa couronne originale dominait à 62 m la ligne des toits de La Havane. L'Edificio Bacardí, ancien siège de la légendaire marque de rhum et exemple éclatant d'architecture Art déco, date également de cette époque (1930). Au lendemain de la révolution de 1959, la famille émigra aux États-Unis.

Edificio Etecsa e Edificio Bacardí

Quando o arranha-céus da companhia telefônica cubana Etecsa foi construído em 1927, dominava o panorama de Havana com sua coroa idiossincrática a 62 m de altura. O Edificio Bacardí, antiga sede da lendária marca de Rum, e exemplar da arquitetura Art Deco, data do mesmo período (1930). Depois da revolução de 1959, a família foi para os EUA.

Edificio Etecsa und Edificio Bacardí

Als das Hochhaus der kubanischen Telefongesellschaft Etecsa 1927 erbaut wurde, dominierte es mit seiner eigenwilligen Krone in 62 m Höhe das Panorama Havannas. Aus derselben Zeit (1930) stammt das Edificio Bacardí, früher Sitz der legendären Rum-Marke und Paradebeispiel der Architektur des Art déco. Nach der Revolution 1959 ging die Familie in die USA.

Edificio Etecsa en Edificio Bacardí

Toen de wolkenkrabber van de Cubaanse telefoonmaatschappij Etecsa in 1927 werd gebouwd, domineerde hij het panorama van Havana met zijn eigenzinnige kroon op 62 m hoogte. Het Edificio Bacardí, de voormalige zetel van het legendarische merk Rum en het belangrijkste voorbeeld van Art Deco architectuur, dateert uit dezelfde periode (1930). Na de revolutie in 1959 ging de familie naar de VS.

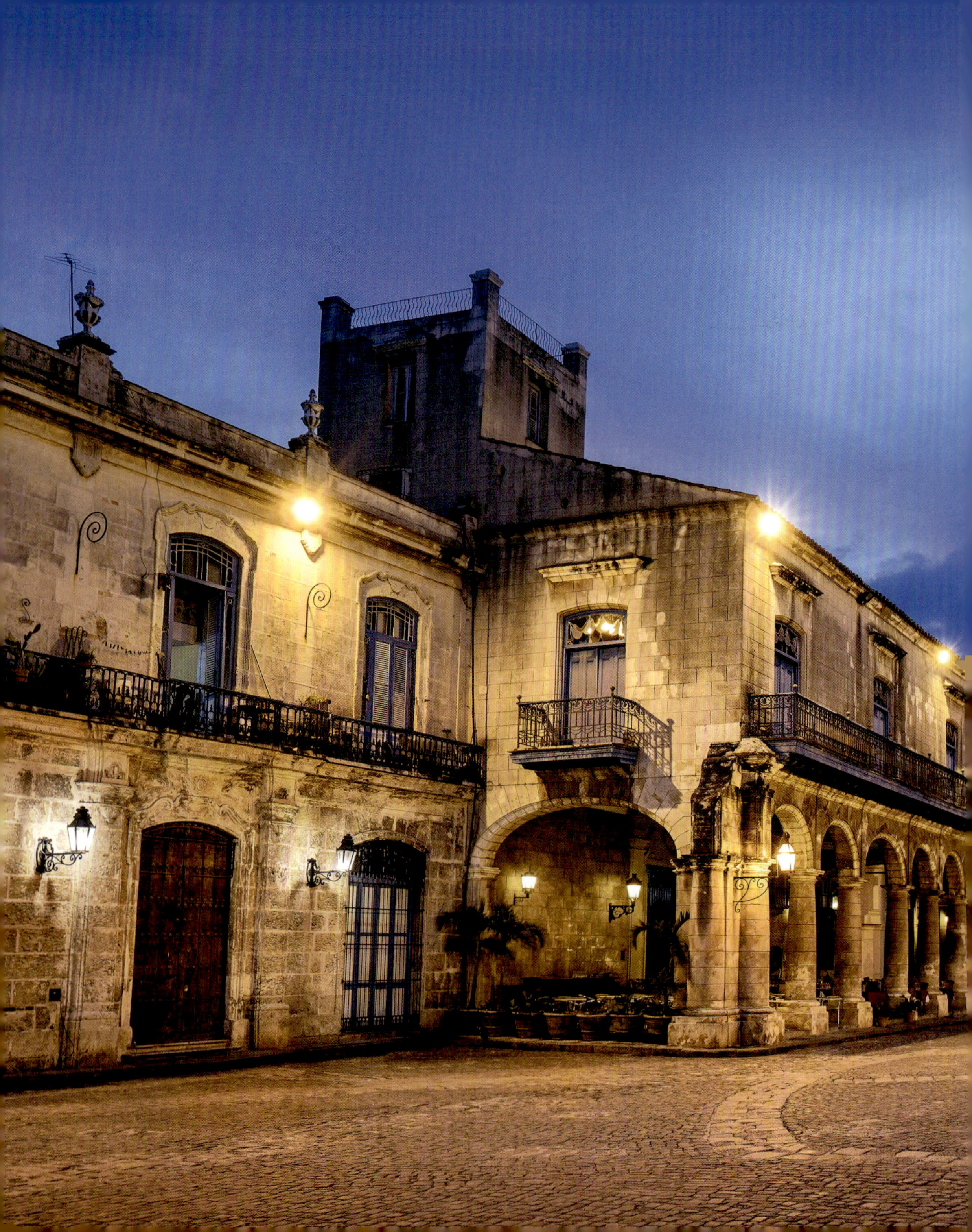

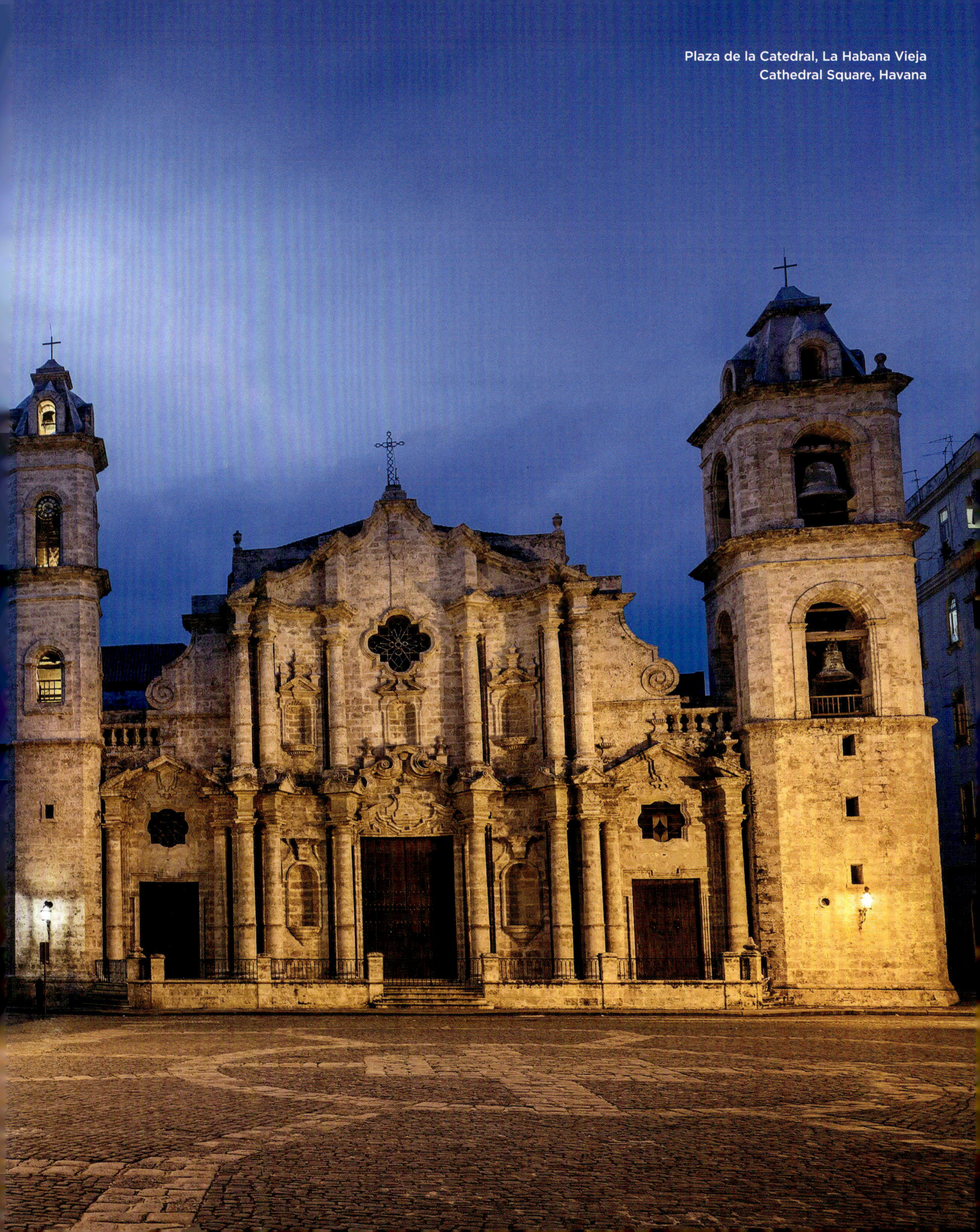

Plaza de la Catedral, La Habana Vieja
Cathedral Square, Havana

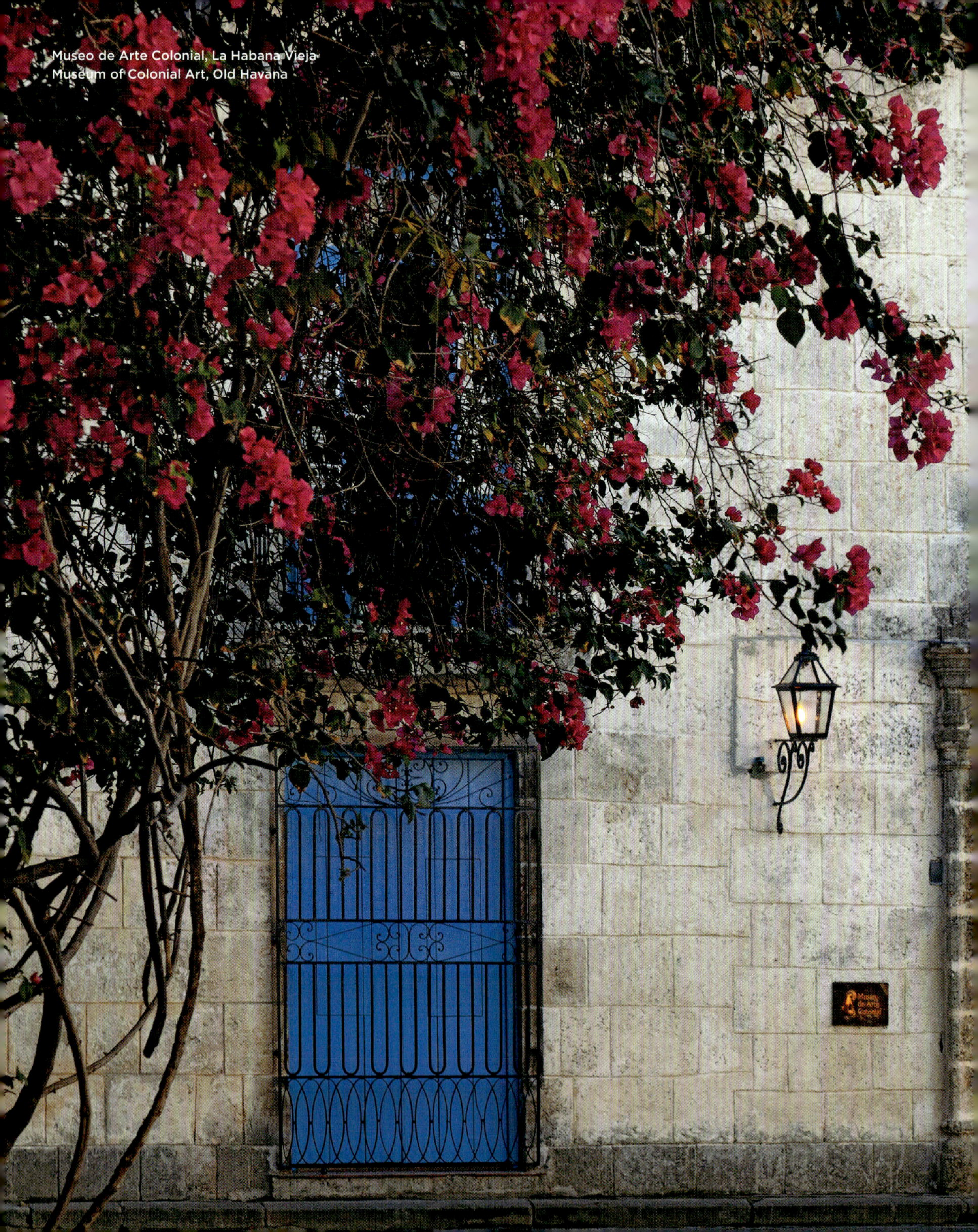

Museo de Arte Colonial, La Habana Vieja
Museum of Colonial Art, Old Havana

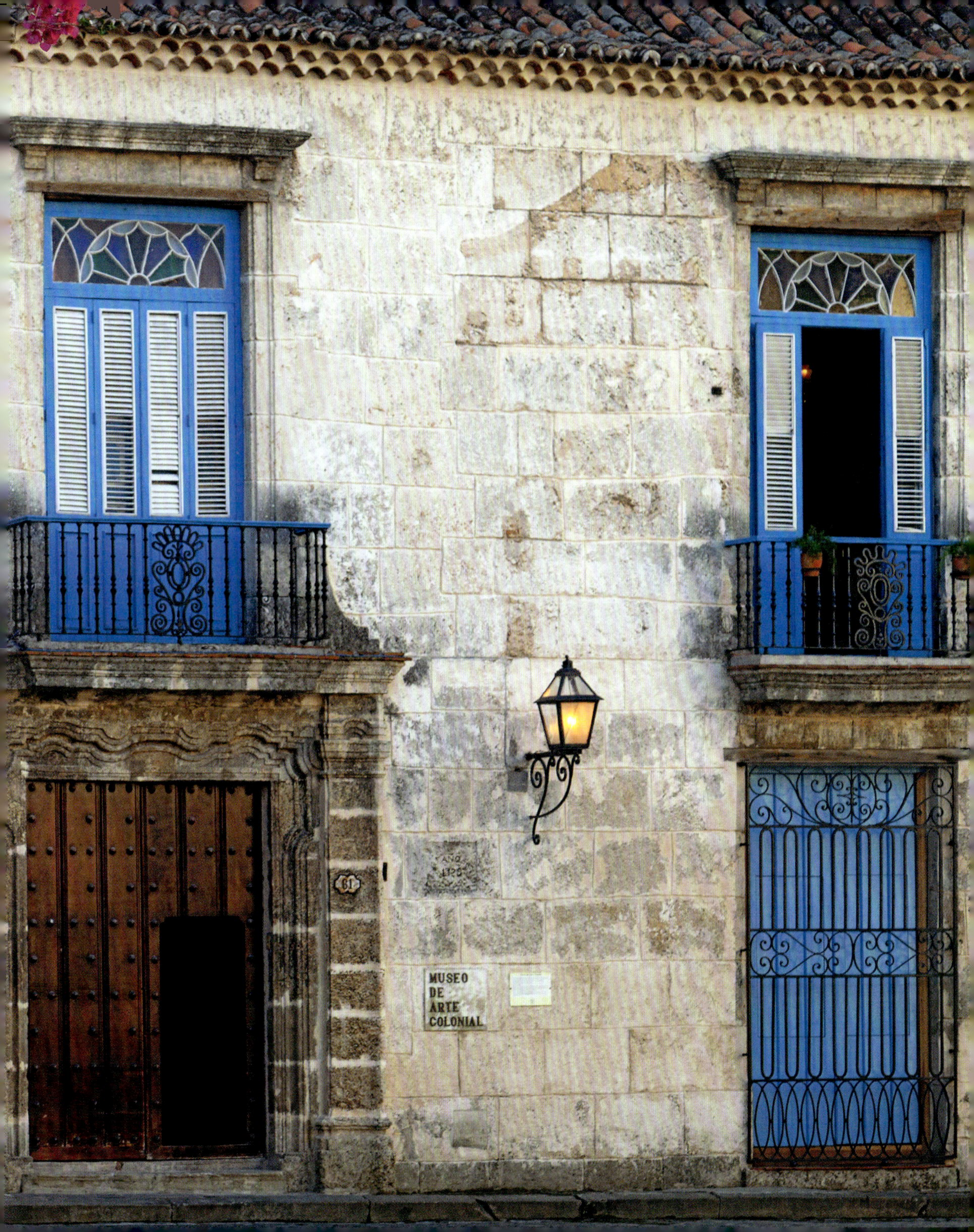
MUSEO
DE
ARTE
COLONIAL

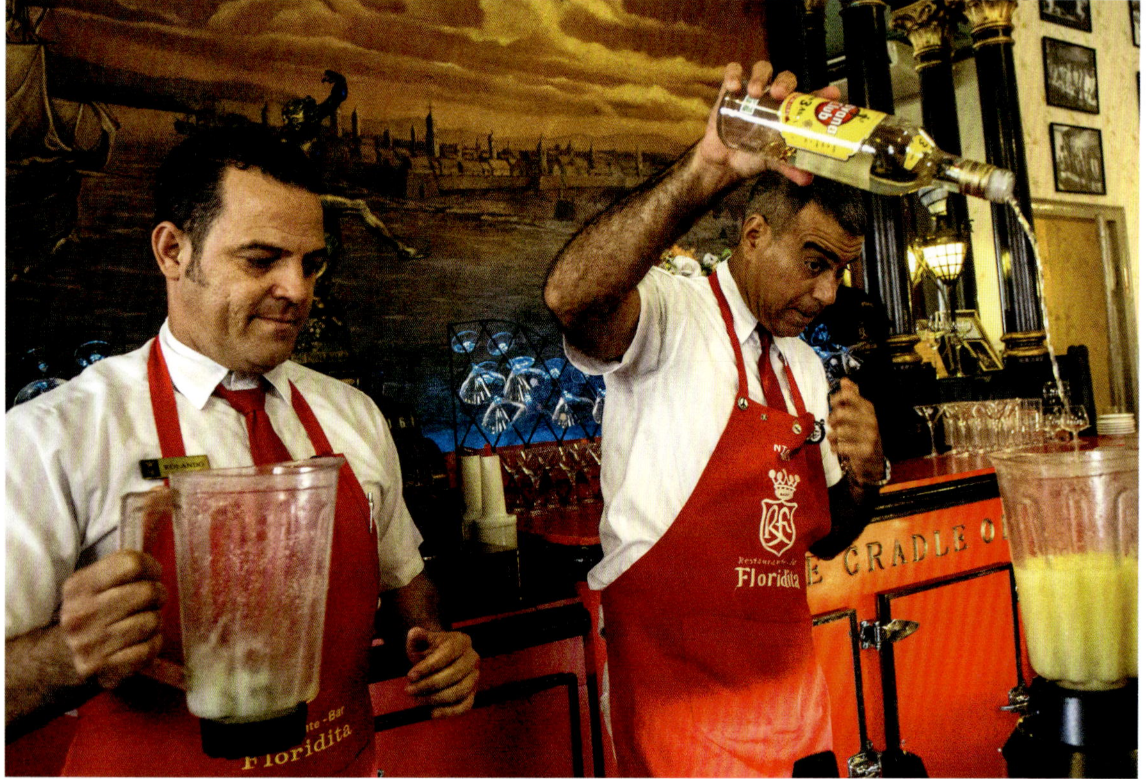

El Floridita, La Habana Vieja
El Floridita, Old Havana

El Floridita

Ernest Hemingway made the traditional bar El Floridita world-famous in the 1950s. Here, he drank his favorite daiquiri cocktail, consisting of rum, sugar syrup, lime juice and crushed ice. Even today "Papa Hemingway" sits as a bronze figure at the bar and has his special daiquirí (no sugar, double rum) served daily.

El Floridita

Ernest Hemingway hizo famoso en los años 50 el tradicional bar El Floridita, ya que aquí se bebió su cóctel favorito, el Daiquirí, que consiste en ron, jarabe de azúcar, jugo de limón y hielo picado. Incluso hoy en día, la figura de bronce de "Papa Hemingway" está sentada en la barra y recibe su daiquirí especial (sin azúcar, doble ron) servido diariamente.

El Floridita

Dans les années 1950, Ernest Hemingway apporta au bar traditionnel El Floridita la célébrité mondiale. Il y dégustait son cocktail préféré, le daïquiri, composé de rhum, de sirop de canne, de jus de limette et de glace pilée. Aujourd'hui encore, un buste de «Papa Hemingway» trône sur le comptoir en bronze et se voit servir chaque jour un daïquiri spécial (sans sucre, mais avec double dose de rhum).

El Floridita

Ernest Hemingway tornou o tradicional bar El Floridita mundialmente famoso nos anos 50, onde bebeu o seu cocktail favorito, o Daiquirí, composto por rum, xarope de açúcar, sumo de lima e gelo picado. Ainda hoje "Papa Hemingway" senta-se como uma figura de bronze no bar e recebe seu daiquirí especial (sem açúcar, rum duplo) servido diariamente.

El Floridita

Ernest Hemingway machte die traditionsreiche Bar El Floridita in den 1950er Jahren weltberühmt, denn hier trank er seinen Lieblingscocktail Daiquirí, bestehend aus Rum, Zuckersirup, Limettensaft und gestoßenem Eis. Noch heute sitzt „Papa Hemingway" als Bronzefigur an der Theke und bekommt täglich seinen Spezial-Daiquirí (kein Zucker, doppelt Rum) serviert.

El Floridita

Ernest Hemingway maakte in de jaren vijftig de traditionele bar El Floridita wereldberoemd, hier dronk hij zijn favoriete cocktail Daiquiri, bestaande uit rum, suikerstroop, limoensap en gemalen ijs. Papa Hemingway' zit vandaag de dag nog steeds als bronzen figuur aan de bar en krijgt dagelijks zijn speciale daiquiri (geen suiker, dubbele rum) geserveerd.

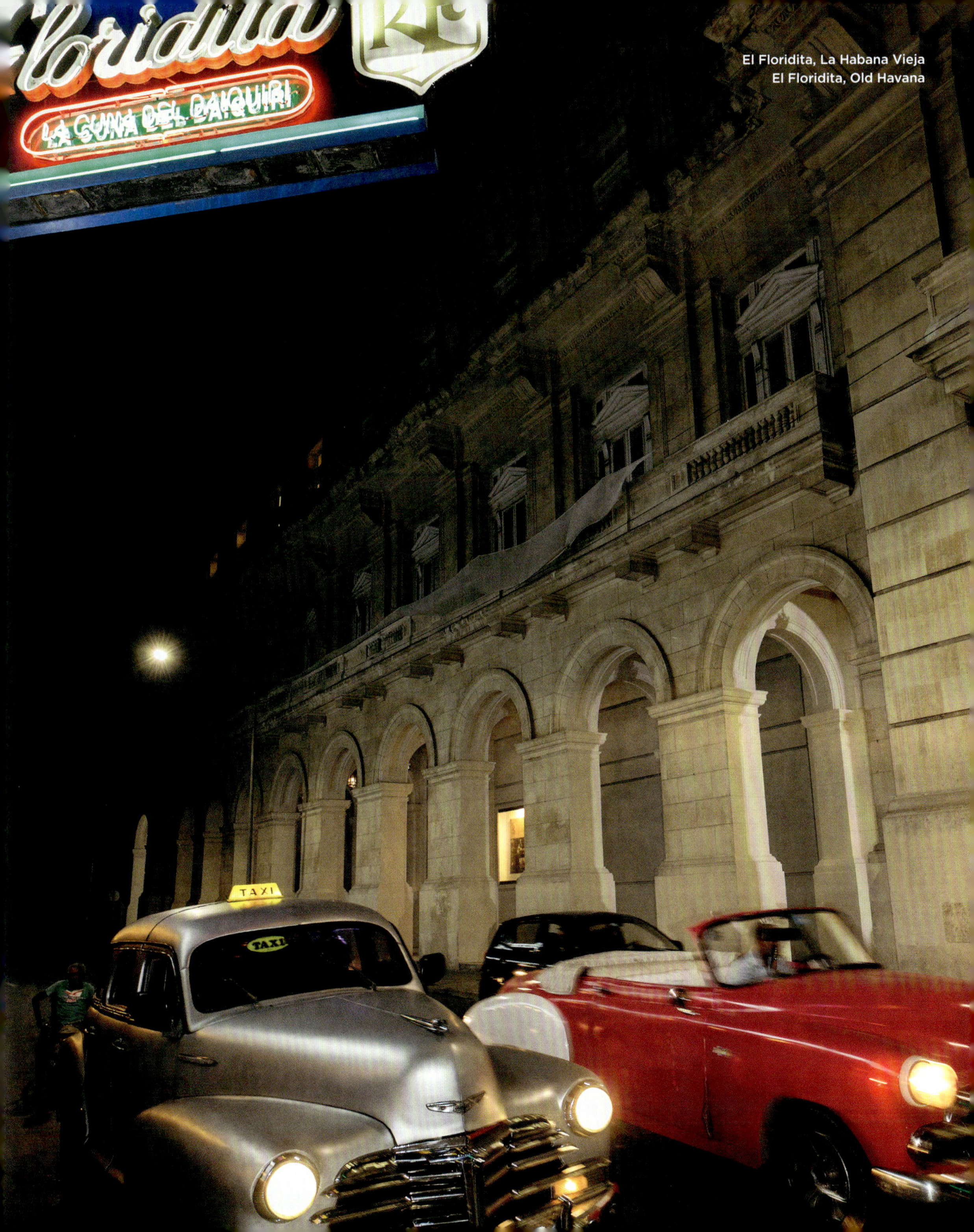

El Floridita, La Habana Vieja
El Floridita, Old Havana

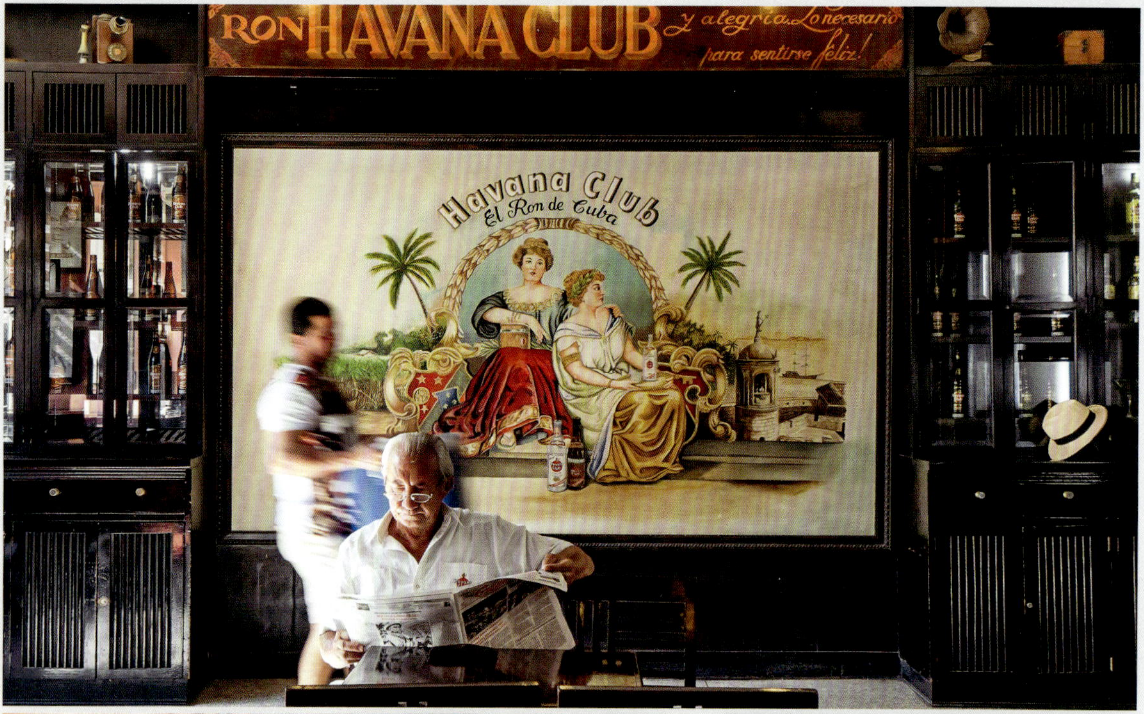

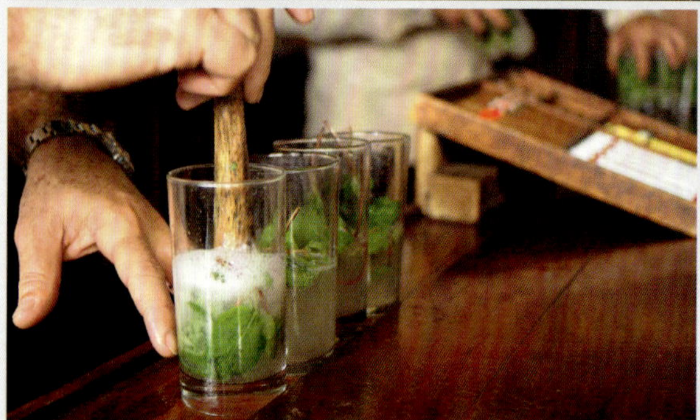

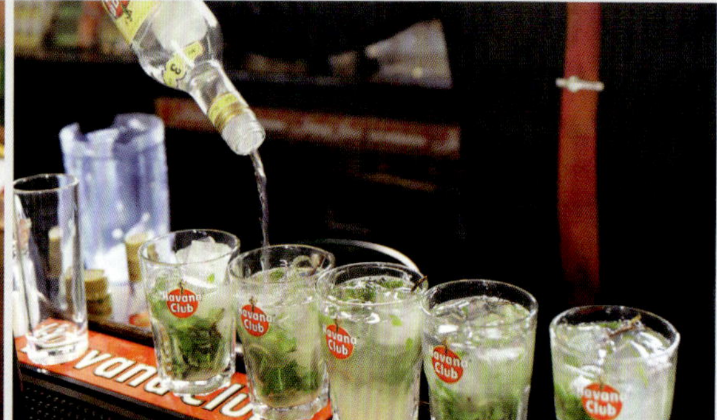

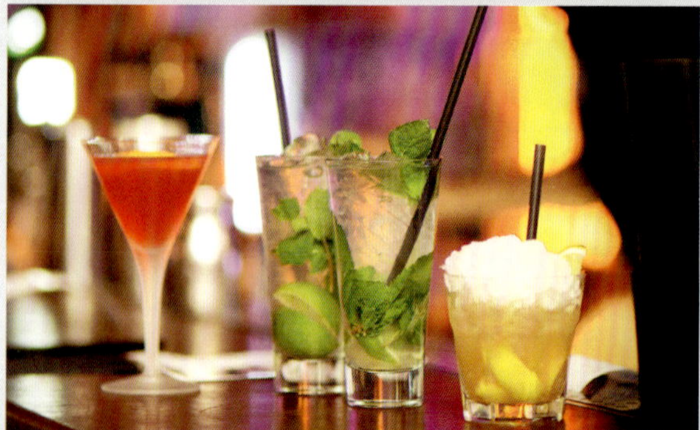

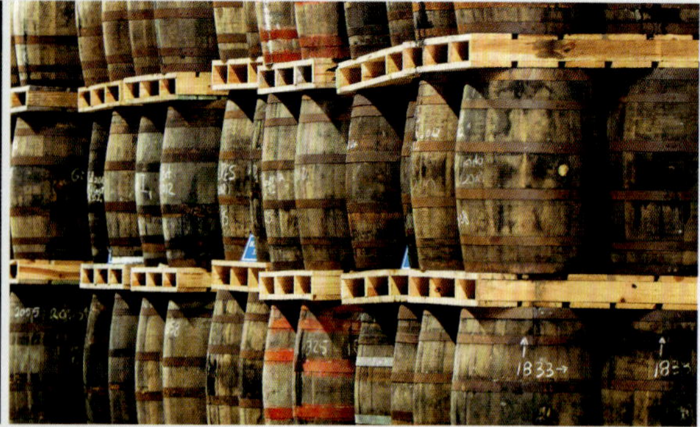

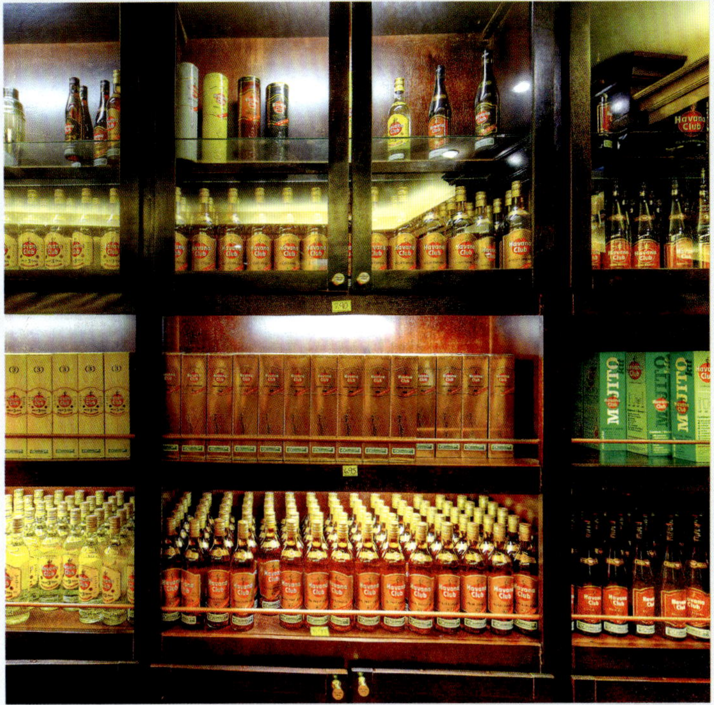

Rum

Rum, the Cuban national drink, is distilled from molasses, a by-product of sugar cane processing. For famous cocktails such as mojito, Ron Collins, daiquirí and Cuba libre, light rum is used, which is matured in oak barrels for a maximum of three years *(Añejo 3 años)*. On the other hand, the amber-colored seven-year-old rum is drunk pure.

Rhum

Le rhum, boisson nationale cubaine, est obtenu à partir de la mélasse, sous-produit de l'industrie de la canne à sucre. Pour les célèbres cocktails, tels que le mojito, le Ron Collins, le daïquiri et le Cuba libre, on utilise un rhum blanc, dont les plus vieux ont maturé jusqu'à 3 ans en fût de chêne *(añejo 3 años)*. Le rhum ambré, vieilli pendant sept ans, se déguste plutôt pur.

Rum

Aus Melasse, einem Nebenprodukt der Zuckerrohr-Verarbeitung, wird das kubanische Nationalgetränk Rum gebrannt. Für die berühmten Cocktails wie Mojito, Ron Collins, Daiquirí und Cuba libre wird heller Rum verwendet, der höchstens bis zu drei Jahren in Eichenfässern gereift ist *(Añejo 3 años)*. Den bernsteinfarbenen siebenjährigen Rum trinkt man dagegen pur.

Ron

El ron, la bebida nacional cubana, se destila de la melaza, un subproducto del procesamiento de la caña de azúcar. Para los famosos cócteles como el Mojito, Ron Collins, Daiquirí y Cuba libre, se utiliza ron ligero, que se madura en barricas de roble durante un máximo de tres años (Añejo 3 años). Por otro lado, el ron de siete años de color ámbar se bebe puro.

Rum

A bebida nacional cubana Rum é destilada a partir do melaço, um subproduto do processamento da cana-de-açúcar. Para os famosos cocktails como Mojito, Ron Collins, Daiquirí e Cuba libre, utiliza-se rum claro, que é amadurecido em barris de carvalho durante um período máximo de três anos *(Añejo 3 años)*. O rum de sete anos de cor âmbar, por outro lado, é bebido puro.

Rum

De Cubaanse nationale drank Rum wordt bereid uit de bijproducten van suikerriet, vooral melasse. Voor de beroemde cocktails zoals Mojito, Ron Collins, Daiquiri en Cuba libre wordt lichte rum gebruikt, die maximaal drie jaar in eikenhouten vaten gerijpt wordt *(Añejo 3 años)*. De amberkleurige zeven jaar oude rum wordt daarentegen zuiver gedronken.

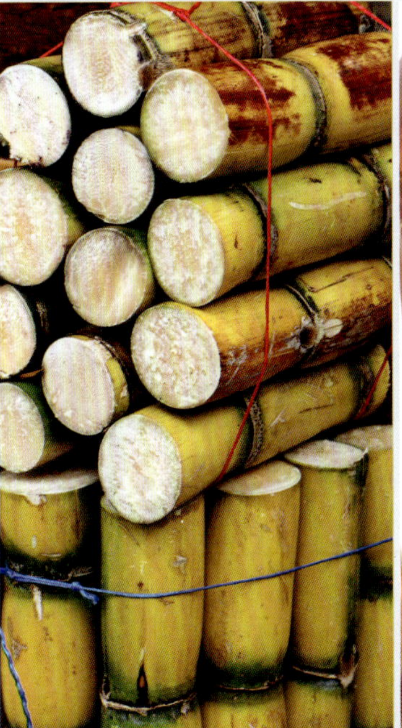

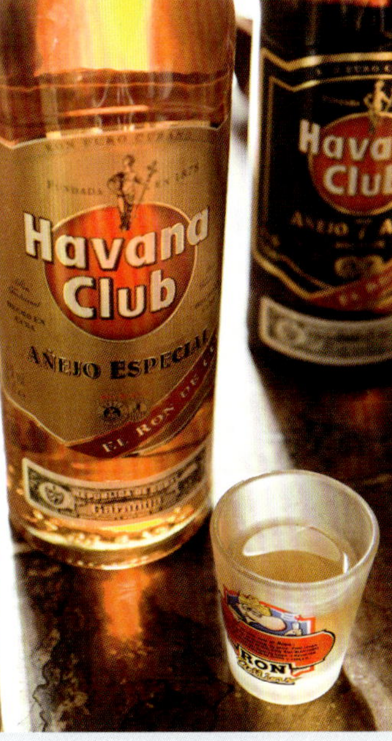

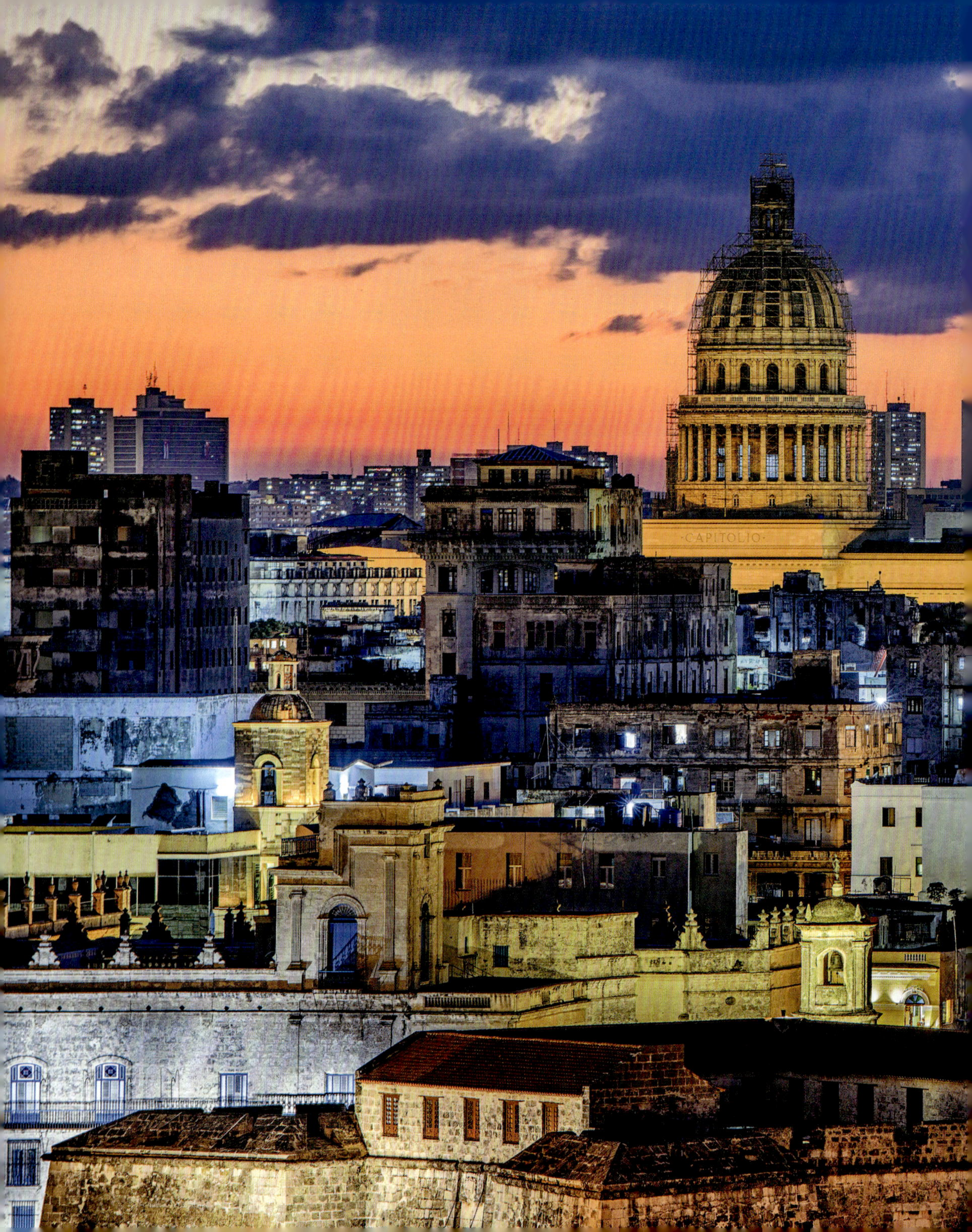

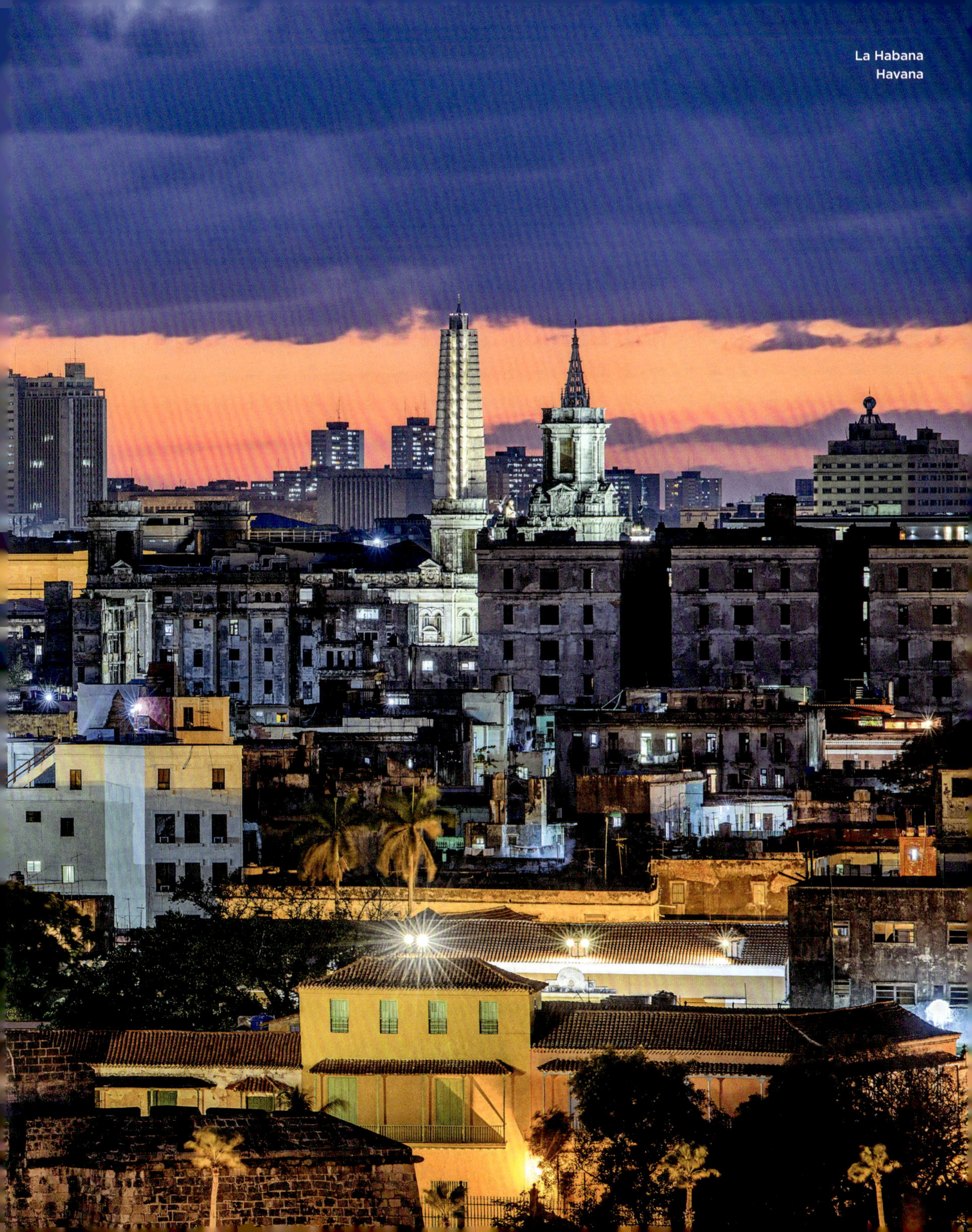
La Habana
Havana

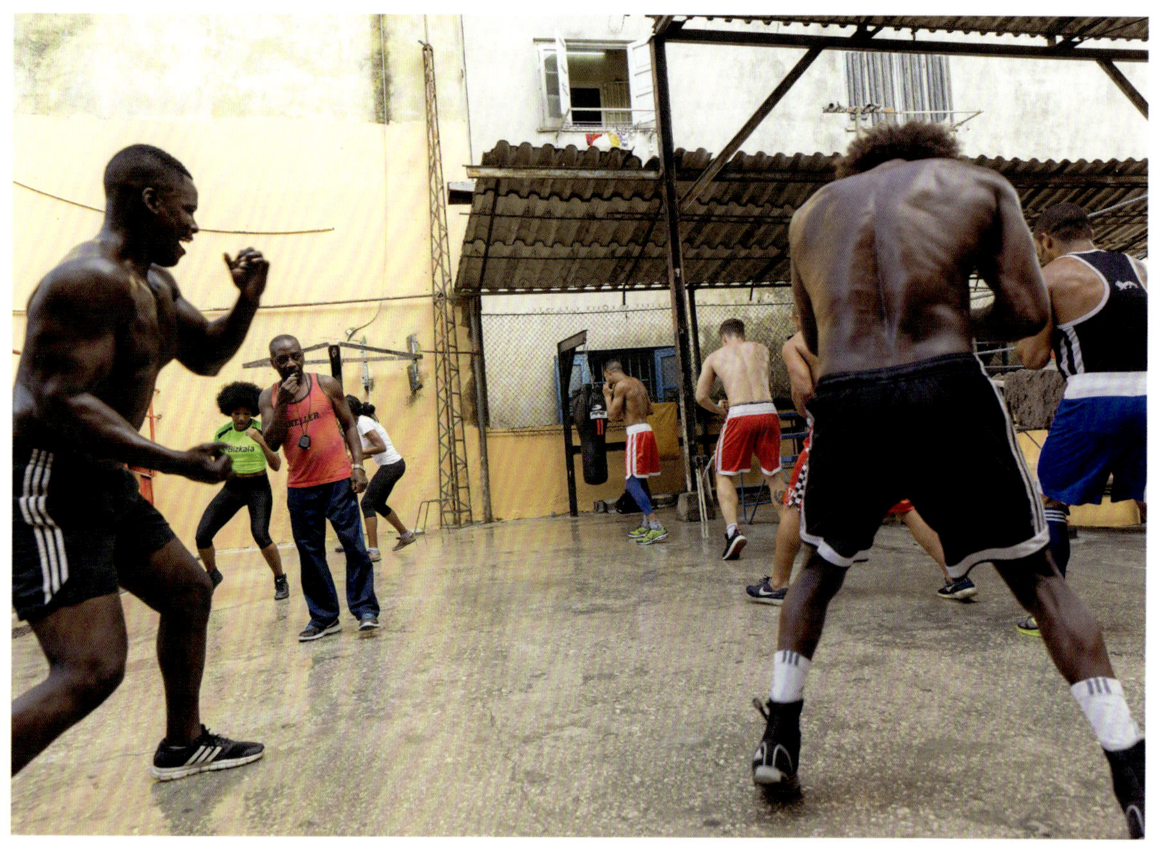

Gimnasio de Boxeo Rafael Trejo, La Habana Vieja
Rafael Trejo Boxing Gym, Old Havana

Boxing

Boxing in Cuba is a both male national sport and at the same time a subculture. Professional boxing has only been allowed again since 2013, but in recent decades Cuban amateur and Olympic boxers have won countless medals worldwide. There is a high level of training in the backyards of Havana, because those with boxing talent have excellent opportunities for social advancement. The Gimnasio de Boxeo Rafael Trejo in Havana is regarded as a talent factory that has produced many top athletes. Cuban boxers have developed their very own boxing style, which combines the hardness of boxing with a feeling for dance and rhythm.

Boxe

À Cuba, la boxe est le sport national masculin mais également une sous-culture. La pratique professionnelle n'est à nouveau autorisée que depuis 2013 mais, dans un cadre amateur et au niveau olympique, les boxeurs cubains ont remporté d'innombrables médailles au cours des dernières décennies. Dans les arrière-cours de La Havane, les jeunes s'entraînent assidûment car les meilleurs bénéficieront des plus grandes chances d'ascension sociale. Le Gimnasio de Boxeo Rafael Trejo est le creuset des jeunes talents qui a façonné de nombreux sportifs de haut niveau. Les boxeurs cubains ont développé un style très particulier, associant la rudesse de la boxe à la sensibilité de la danse et du rythme.

Boxen

Boxen ist in Kuba männlicher Nationalsport und Subkultur zugleich. Das Profiboxen ist zwar erst seit 2013 wieder erlaubt, aber im Amateursport und beim olympischen Boxen holten kubanische Boxer in den letzten Jahrzehnten weltweit unzählige Medaillen. In den Hinterhöfen Havannas wird fleißig trainiert, denn Boxtalente haben beste Chancen auf sozialen Aufstieg. Das Gimnasio de Boxeo Rafael Trejo in Havanna gilt als Talentschmiede, die viele Spitzensportler hervorgebracht hat. Die kubanischen Boxer haben einen ganz eigenen Box-Stil entwickelt, der die Härte des Boxens mit dem Gefühl für Tanz und Rhythmus verbindet.

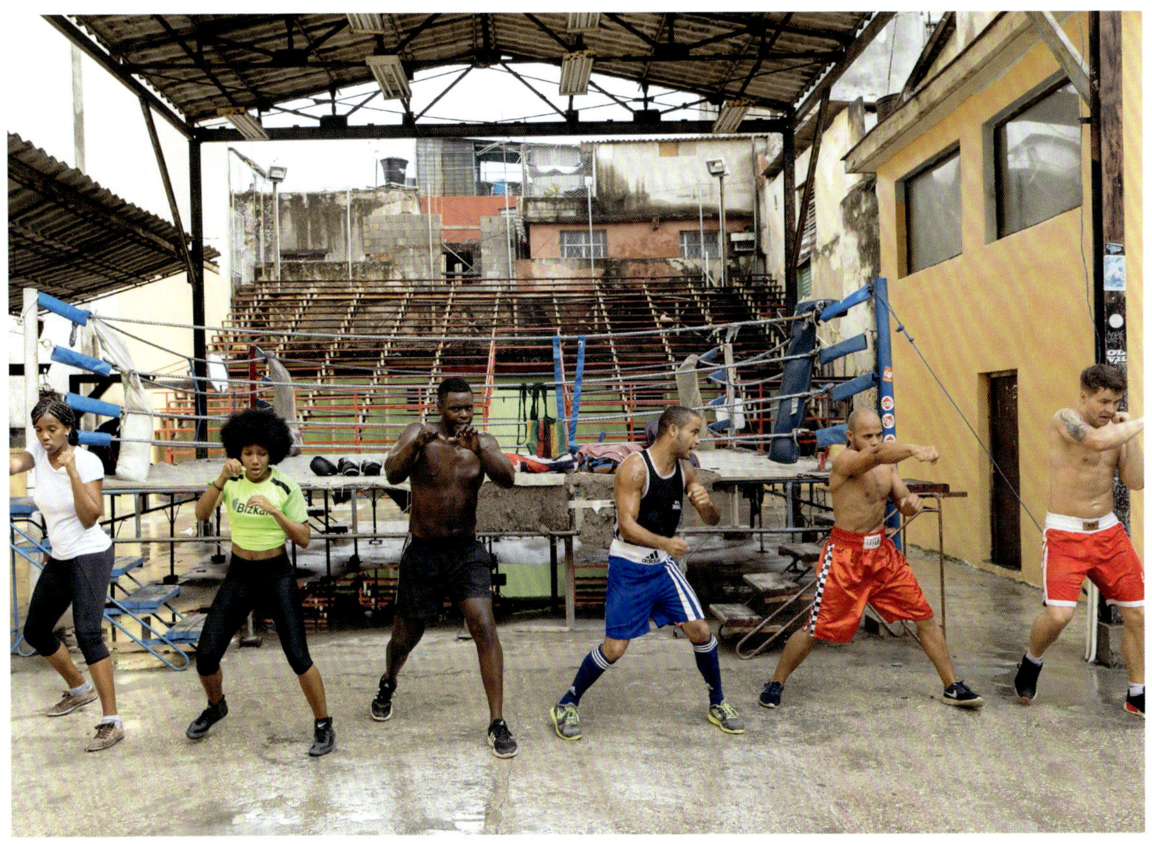

Gimnasio de Boxeo Rafael Trejo, La Habana Vieja
Rafael Trejo Boxing Gym, Old Havana

Boxeo

El boxeo en Cuba es un deporte nacional
masculino y subcultura al mismo tiempo.
El boxeo profesional solo se permite desde
2013, pero en el deporte amateur y el
boxeo olímpico los boxeadores cubanos
han ganado innumerables medallas en
todo el mundo en las últimas décadas. Hay
mucha capacitación en los patios traseros
de La Habana, porque los talentos del
boxeo tienen las mejores oportunidades
de progreso social. El Gimnasio de
Boxeo Rafael Trejo en La Habana se
considera una fábrica de talento que ha
producido muchos atletas de alto nivel.
Los boxeadores cubanos han desarrollado
su propio estilo de boxeo, que combina
la dureza del boxeo con una sensación de
baile y ritmo.

Boxe

O boxe em Cuba é ao mesmo tempo
um esporte nacional masculino e uma
subcultura. Apesar do boxe profissional só
ter sido permitido novamente desde 2013,
no esporte amador e no boxe olímpico
os boxeadores cubanos conquistaram
inúmeras medalhas em todo o mundo nas
últimas décadas. Nos quintais de Havana
encontra-se muito treino, porque os
talentos do boxe têm as melhores chances
para o avanço social. O Ginásio de Boxeio
Rafael Trejo em Havana é considerado uma
fábrica de talentos que já produziu muitos
atletas de topo. Os boxeadores cubanos
desenvolveram o seu próprio estilo de
boxe, que combina a dureza do boxe com
uma sensação de dança e ritmo.

Boksen

Boksen in Cuba is een mannelijke
nationale sport en subcultuur tegelijkertijd.
Professioneel boksen is pas sinds 2013
weer toegestaan, maar in de amateursport
en het Olympisch boksen hebben
Cubaanse boksers de afgelopen decennia
wereldwijd talloze medailles gewonnen.
Er wordt veel getraind in de achtertuinen
van Havana, omdat bokstalenten de beste
kansen hebben op sociale vooruitgang.
De Rafael Trejo Boxing Gym in Havana
wordt beschouwd als een talentenfabriek
die veel topsporters heeft voortgebracht.
De Cubaanse boksers hebben hun eigen
boksstijl ontwikkeld, die de hardheid van
het boksen combineert met een gevoel
voor dans en ritme.

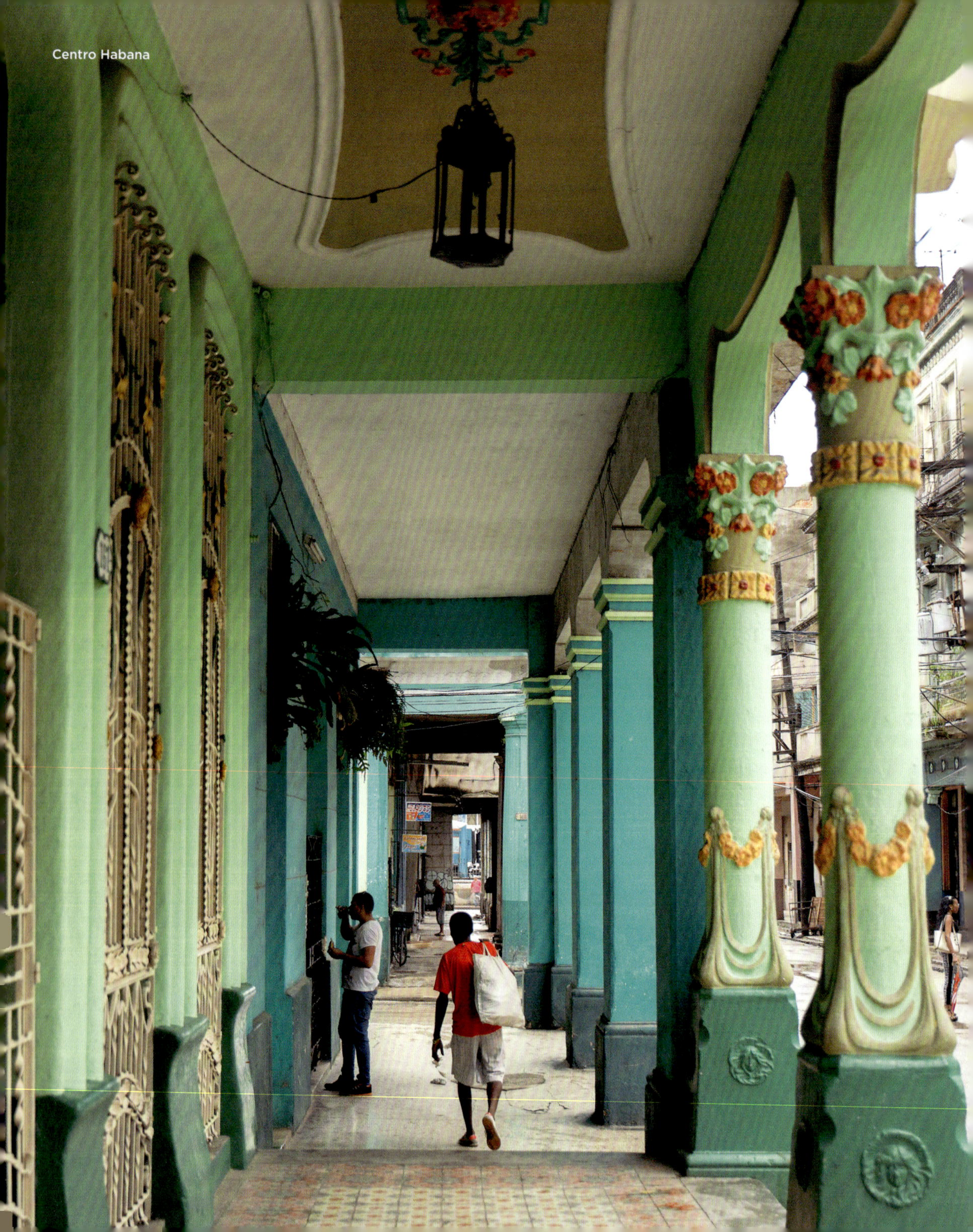

Centro Habana

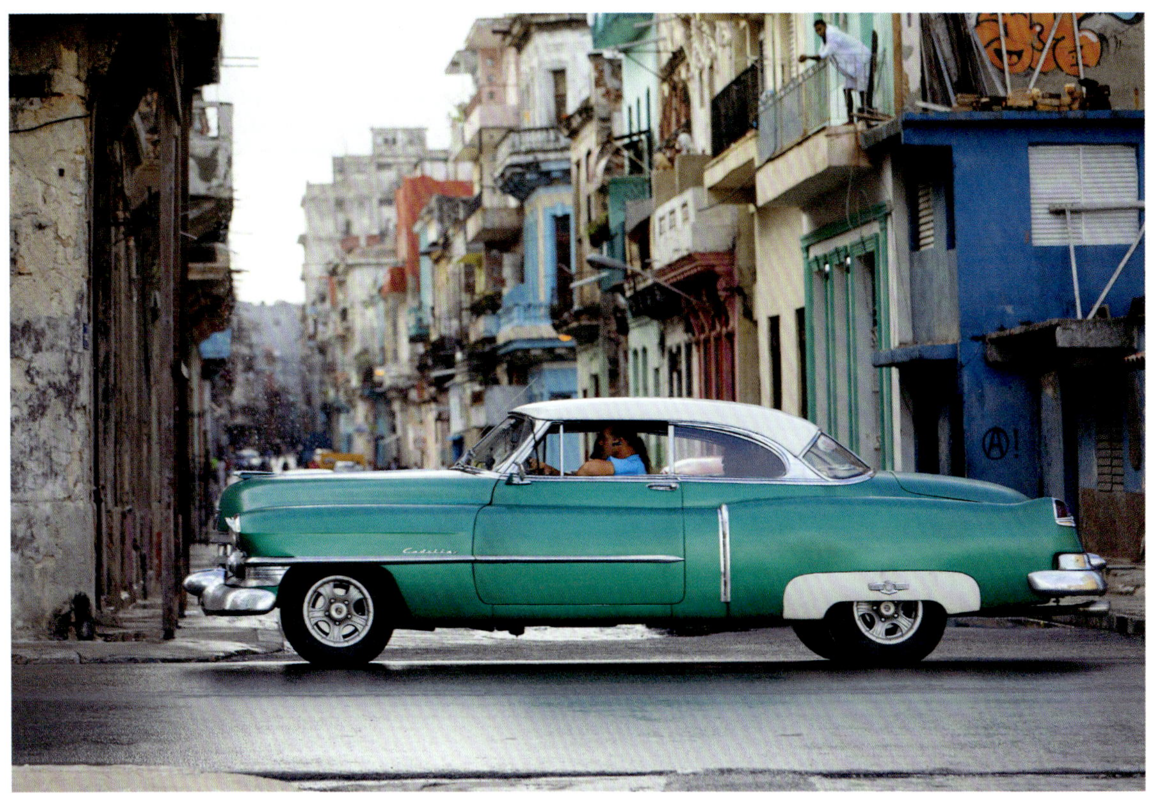

Calle San Lázaro, Centro Habana

The City of Columns

Shade is a precious commodity in Cuba, and this is why Havana has become the "City of Columns", a "stacking place of columns", a "primeval forest of columns", wrote the Cuban writer Alejo Carpentier. Countless colonnades were created in order to allow people to cross the city from the harbor fortress to the outskirts, protected from the dazzling sun.

La ciudad de las columnas

La sombra es un bien muy valioso en Cuba. Por eso La Habana se ha convertido en la "ciudad de las columnas", un "emporio de columnas", una "selva de columnas", escribió el escritor cubano Alejo Carpentier. Se crearon innumerables colonias para cruzar la ciudad desde la fortaleza del puerto hasta las afueras, protegidas del sol resplandeciente.

La cité des colonnes

À Cuba, l'ombre est un bien précieux. C'est pour cette raison que La Havane est devenue la « cité des colonnes », « un empire de colonnes, une jungle de colonnes », écrivait l'auteur cubain Alejo Carpentier. D'innombrables colonnades ont été bâties pour pouvoir traverser la ville à l'abri du soleil accablant, depuis la forteresse du port jusqu'aux quartiers périphériques.

A cidade das colunas

A sombra é um bem precioso em Cuba. É por isso que Havana se tornou a "Cidade das Colunas", um "armazém de colunas", uma "floresta primitiva de colunas", escreveu o escritor cubano Alejo Carpentier. Inúmeras colunatas foram criadas para atravessar a cidade da fortaleza do porto para os arredores, protegidos do sol resplandecente.

Die Stadt der Säulen

Schatten ist in Kuba ein kostbares Gut. Deshalb sei Havanna zur „Stadt der Säulen" geworden, zu einem „Säulenstapelplatz", einem „Säulenurwald", schrieb der kubanische Schriftsteller Alejo Carpentier. Zahllose Kolonaden wurden geschaffen, um, geschützt vor der gleißenden Sonne, die Stadt von der Hafenfestung bis in die Außenbezirke durchqueren zu können.

De stad van de kolommen

Schaduw is een kostbaar goed in Cuba. Dit is de reden waarom volgens de Cubaanse schrijver Alejo Carpentier Havana de 'Stad van de Kolommen', een 'stapelplaats van zuilen', een 'oerwoud van zuilen' is geworden. Talloze zuilenrijen werden opgericht om de stad vanaf de havenburcht tot aan de rand van de stad tegen de felle zon te beschermen.

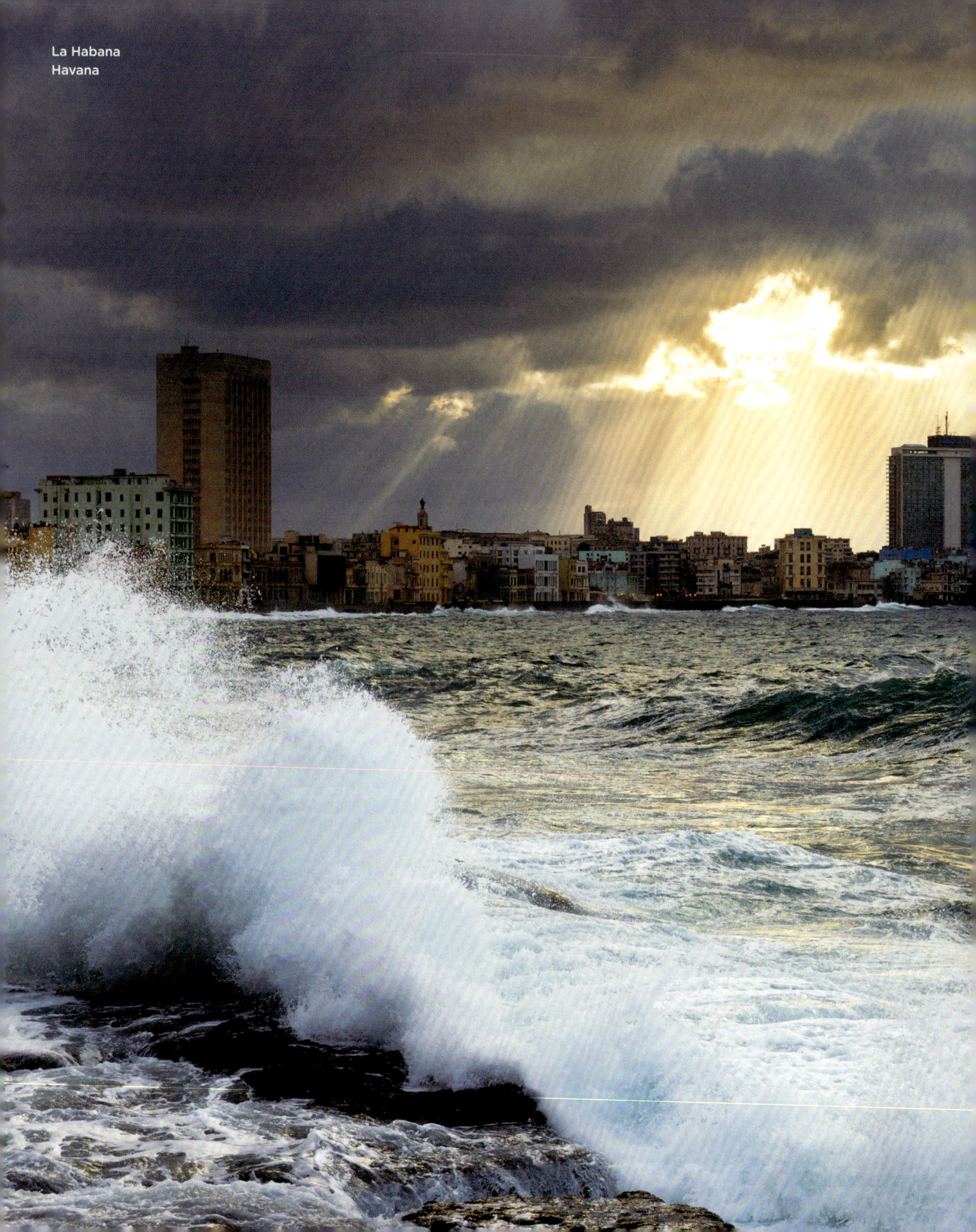
La Habana
Havana

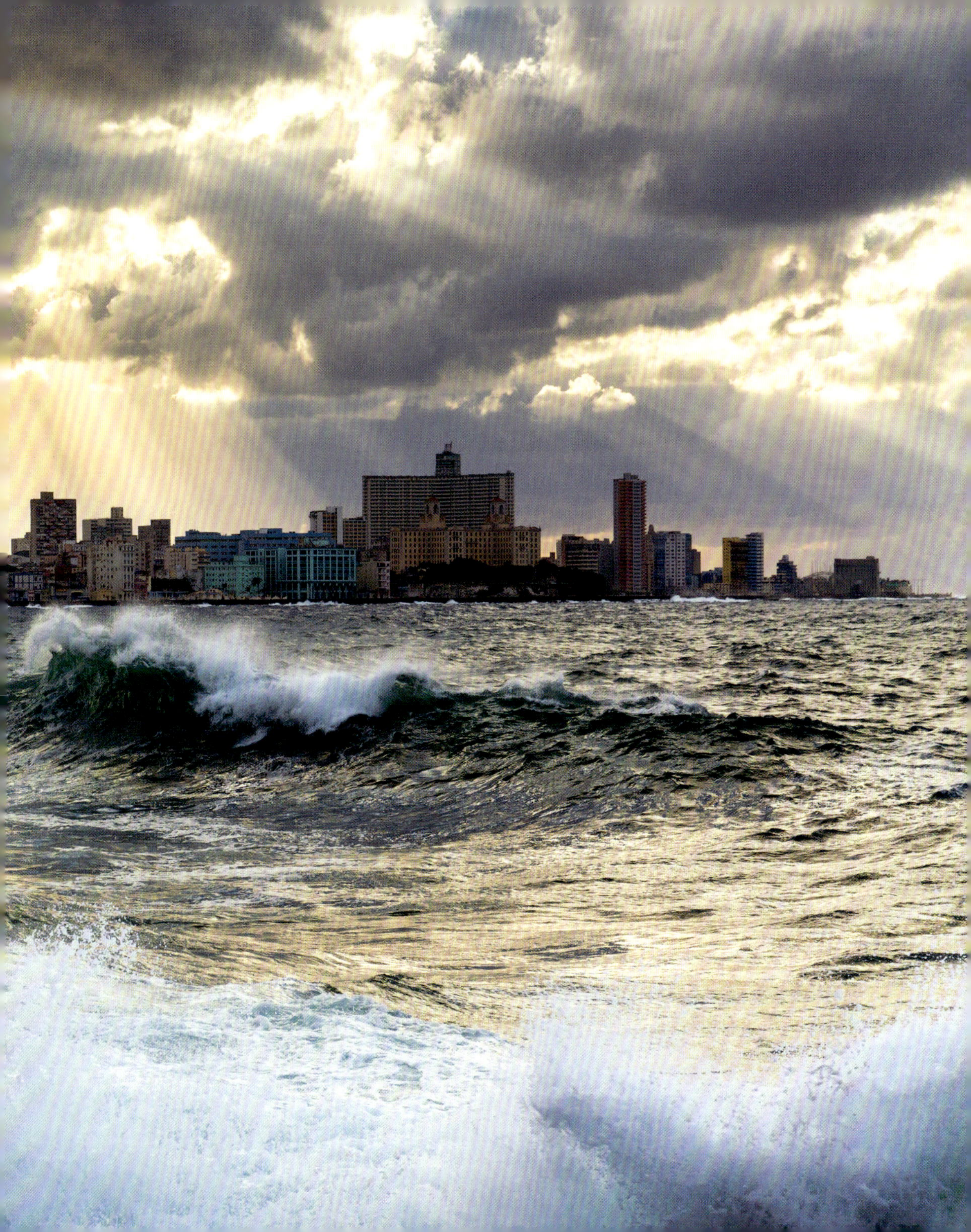

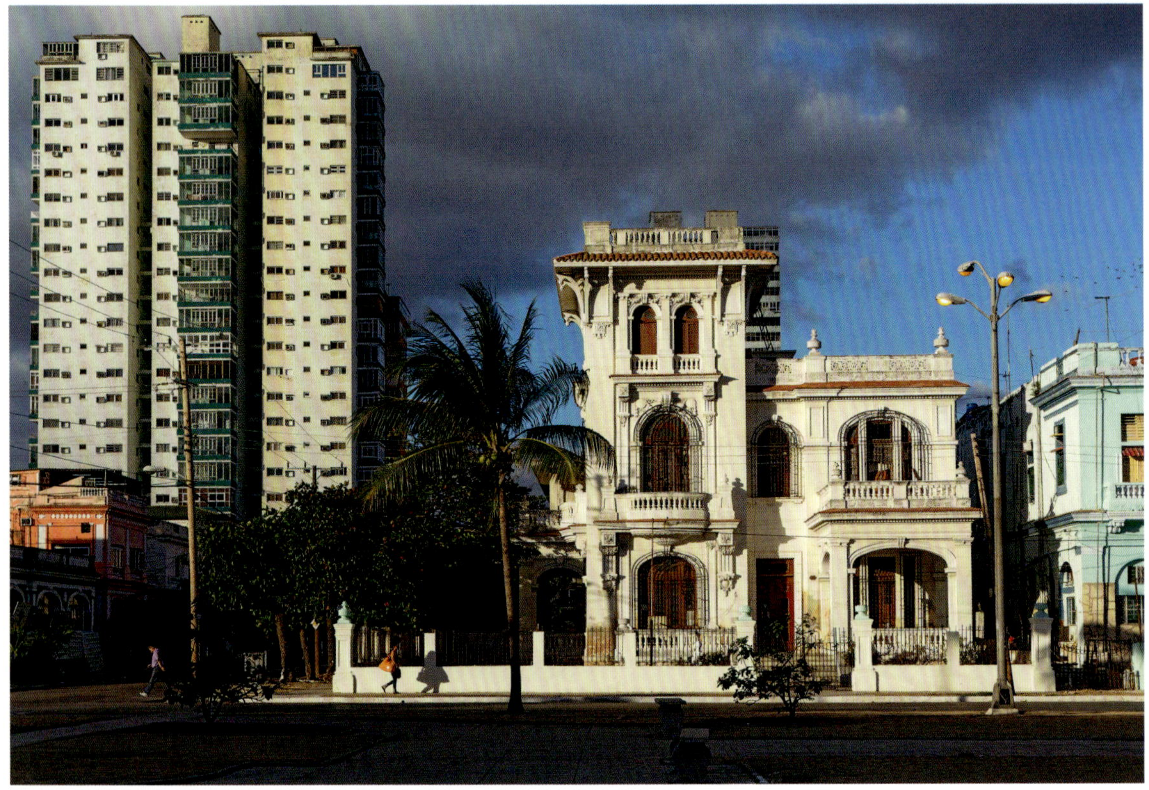

Avenida de los Presidentes, Vedado

Mixture of Styles in Vedado

The city centre of Vedado was created at the beginning of the 20th century, and is a district of architectural contradictions. Elegant villas and townhouses in neoclassical, neo-Gothic, Art Deco and Art Nouveau styles stand next to skyscrapers from the 1950s. Some of them are hotels and were built by the Mafia, for example the Capri and the Riviera.

Estilo mixto en Vedado

El centro de la ciudad de Vedado se creó a principios del siglo XX y es un barrio de contradicciones arquitectónicas. Elegantes villas y casas adosadas de estilo neoclásico, neogótico, Art Déco y Art Nouveau se encuentran junto a rascacielos de los años 50. Algunos de ellos son hoteles y, como el Capri y la Riviera, fueron construidos por la mafia.

Mélange des styles à Vedado

Le centre-ville de Vedado, bâti au début du xxᵉ siècle, est un quartier riche de contrastes architecturaux. Les villas et maisons de ville de style néoclassique, néogothique, Art déco et Art nouveau y côtoient des immeubles des années 1950. Certains, tel le Capri et la Riviera, abritent des hôtels et ont été érigés par la mafia.

Mistura de estilos em Vedado

O centro da cidade de Vedado foi criado no início do século XX e é um bairro de contradições arquitetónicas. Vilas e moradias elegantes em estilo neoclássico, neogótico, Art Deco e Art Nouveau estão ao lado de arranha-céus dos anos 50. Alguns deles são hotéis e foram, como o Capri e o Riviera, construídos pela máfia.

Stilmix in Vedado

Das Stadtzentrum Vedado entstand Anfang des 20. Jahrhunderts und ist ein Viertel der architektonischen Widersprüche. Elegante Villen und Stadthäuser im Stil des Neoklassizismus, der Neogotik, des Art déco und Jugendstils stehen neben Hochhäusern aus den 1950er-Jahren. Einige davon sind Hotels und wurden, wie das Capri und das Riviera, von der Mafia gebaut.

Stijlvolle mix in Vedado

Het stadscentrum van Vedado werd in het begin van de 20e eeuw gecreëerd en is een kwart van de architectonische tegenstrijdigheden. Elegante villa's en herenhuizen in neoklassieke, neogotische, art deco en art nouveau stijl staan naast wolkenkrabbers uit de jaren vijftig. Sommige van hen zijn hotels en werden zoals de Capri en de Riviera door de maffia gebouwd.

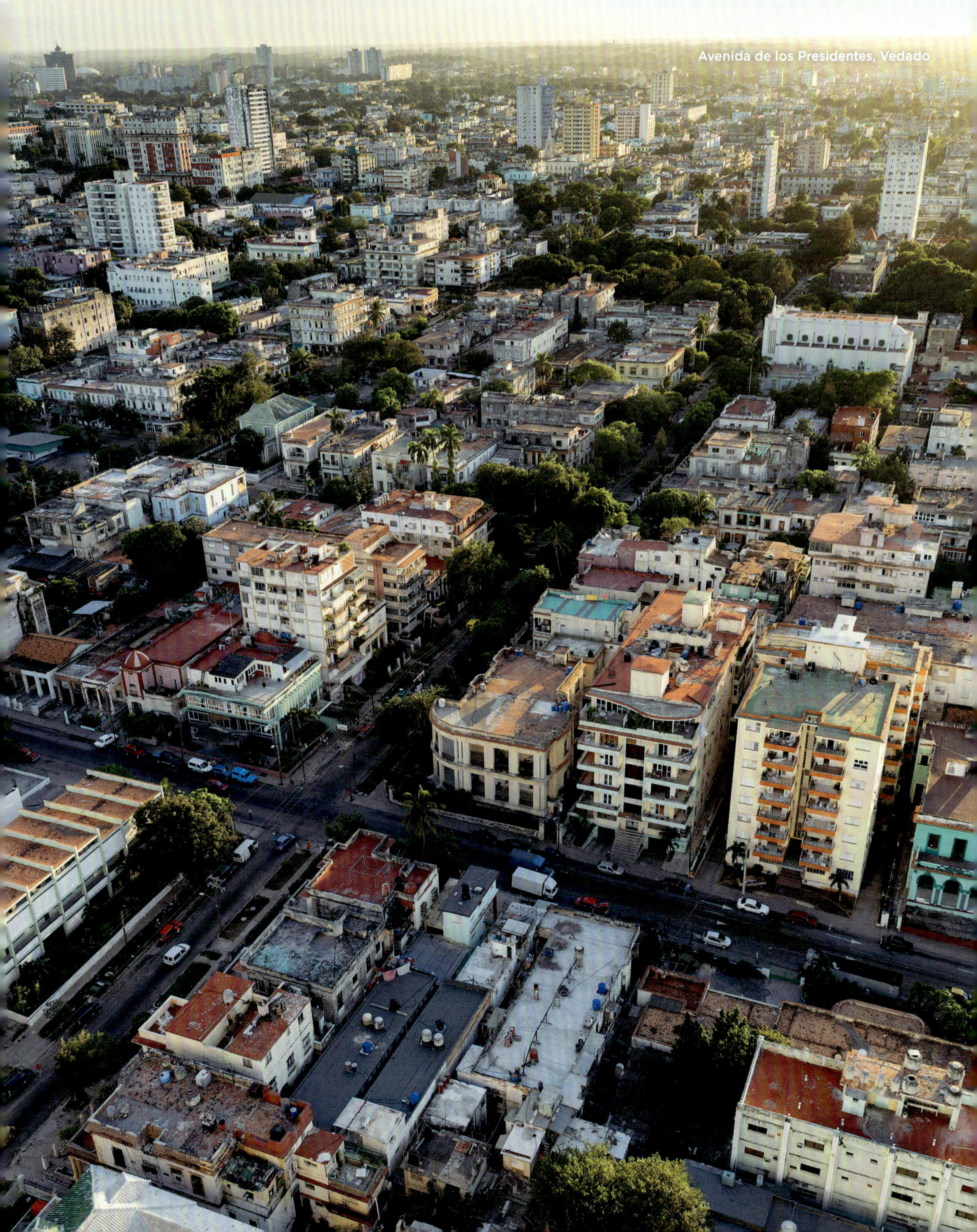

Avenida de los Presidentes, Vedado

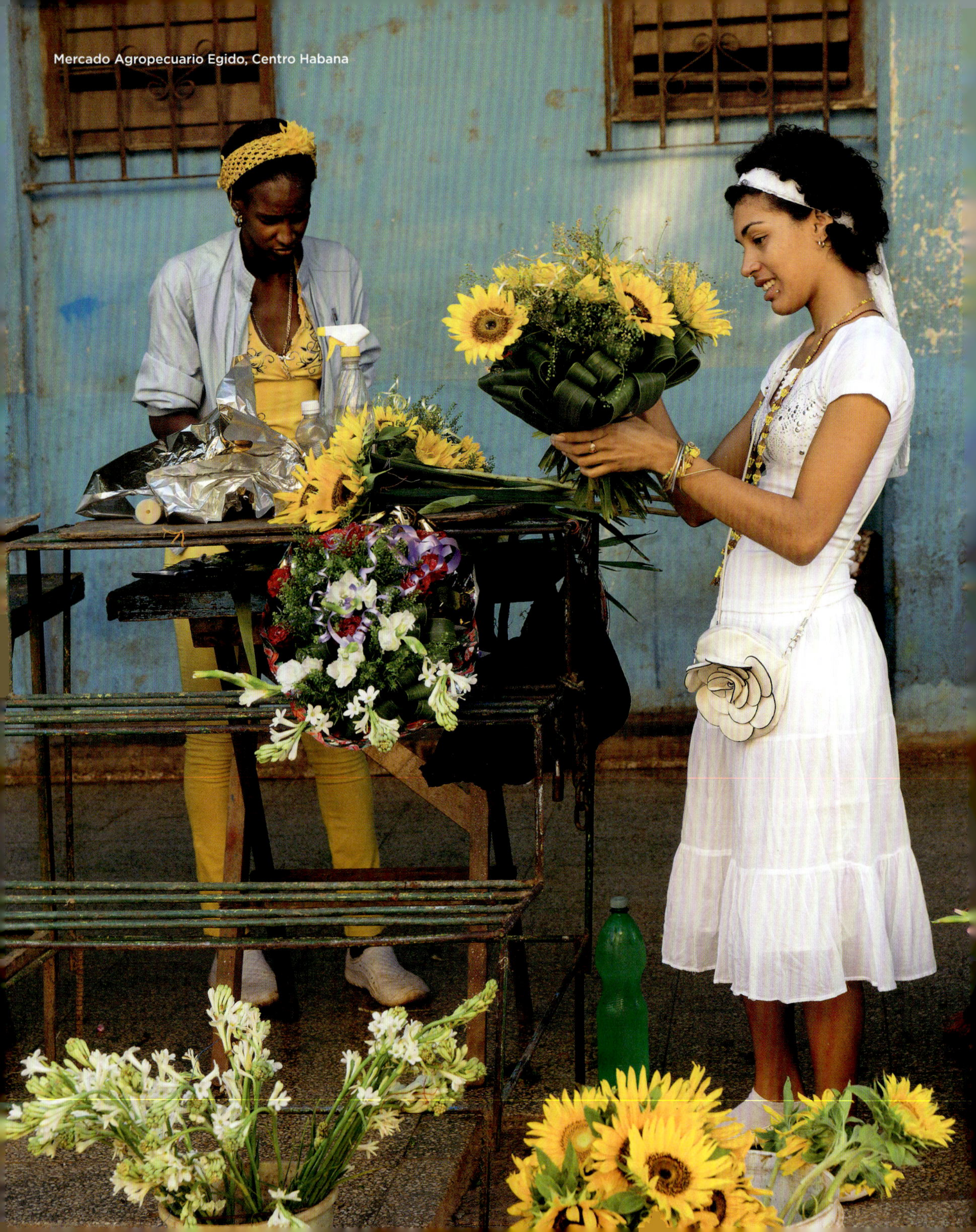
Mercado Agropecuario Egido, Centro Habana

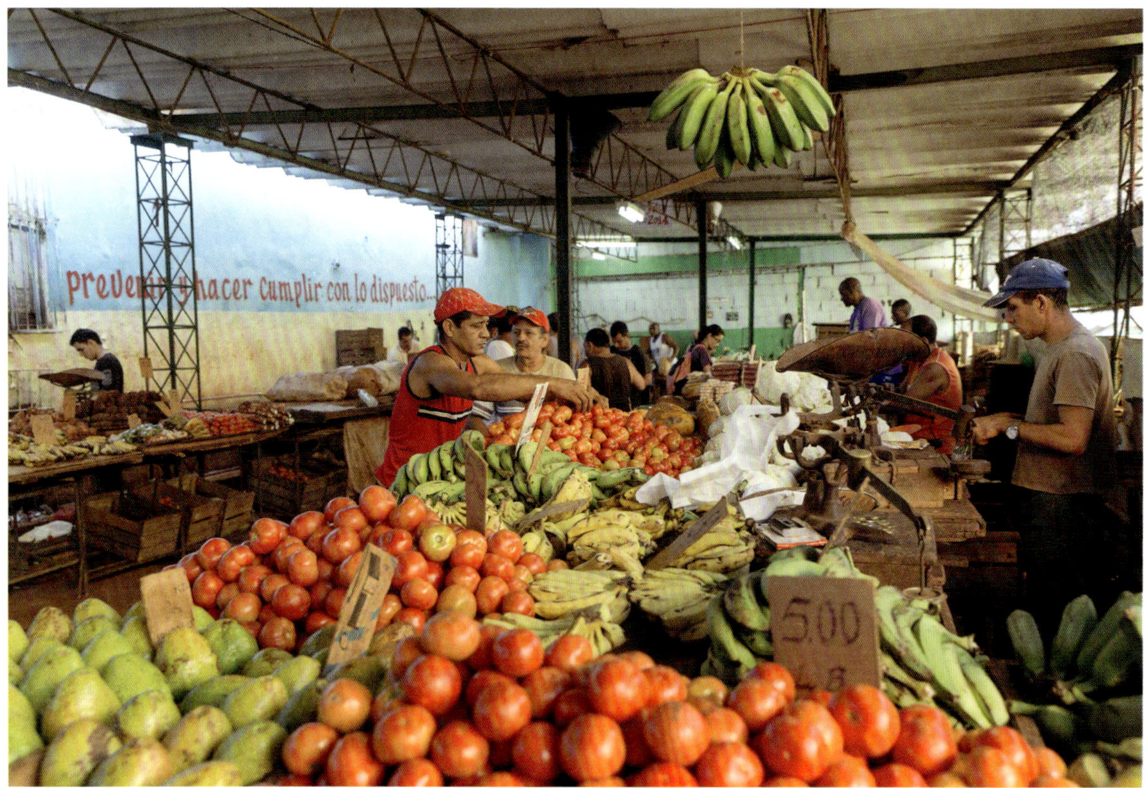

Mercado Agropecuario Egido, Centro Habana

Independent Farmers' Markets

Everyday life and the supply of goods have improved somewhat since the severe economic crisis of the 1990s, at least in Havana. At independent farmers' markets such as the Mercado Agropecuario Egido in the Centro district of Havana, Cuban pesos (CUP) are also used to buy fruit and vegetables, albeit at elevated prices relative to the average income.

Marchés paysans en plein air

La vie quotidienne et l'offre de marchandises se sont un peu améliorées, tout au moins à La Havane, depuis la terrible crise économique des années 1990. Sur les marchés paysans en plein air, tels que le Mercado Agropecuario Egido du quartier Centro, il est possible de se ravitailler, y compris avec des pesos cubains (CUP), en fruits et légumes, certes à des prix très élevés par rapport au salaire moyen.

Freie Bauernmärkte

Das Alltagsleben und das Warenangebot haben sich seit der schweren Wirtschaftskrise der 1990er-Jahre zumindest in Havanna immerhin ein wenig verbessert. Auf freien Bauernmärkten wie dem Mercado Agropecuario Egido im Stadtteil Centro bekommt man auch für kubanische Pesos (CUP) Obst und Gemüse, allerdings zu gesalzenen Preisen, gemessen am üblichen Einkommen.

Mercados libres de agricultores

La vida cotidiana y la oferta de bienes han mejorado un poco desde la grave crisis económica de los años noventa, al menos en La Habana. En mercados de agricultores independientes como el Mercado Agropecuario Egido en el distrito Centro de La Habana, también se pueden comprar frutas y verduras con pesos cubanos (CUP), aunque a precios desorbitados en comparación con los ingresos habituales.

Mercados livres de agricultores

A vida cotidiana e a oferta de bens melhoraram um pouco desde a grave crise econômica da década de 1990, pelo menos em Havana. Em mercados de agricultores independentes, como o Mercado Agropecuário Egido, no distrito de Havana, no bairro do Centro, pode-se comprar frutas e verduras em pesos Cubanos (CUP), embora a preços salgados em comparação com a renda média.

Vrije boerenmarkten

Het dagelijks leven en het warenaanbod zijn sinds de ernstige economische crisis van de jaren negentig, althans in Havana, enigszins verbeterd. Op onafhankelijke boerenmarkten zoals de Mercado Agropecuario Egido in de staddeel Centro krijgt men ook groenten en fruit wanneer met de Cubaanse peso's (CUP) wordt betaald, echter tegen gezouten prijzen in vergelijking met het gebruikelijke inkomen.

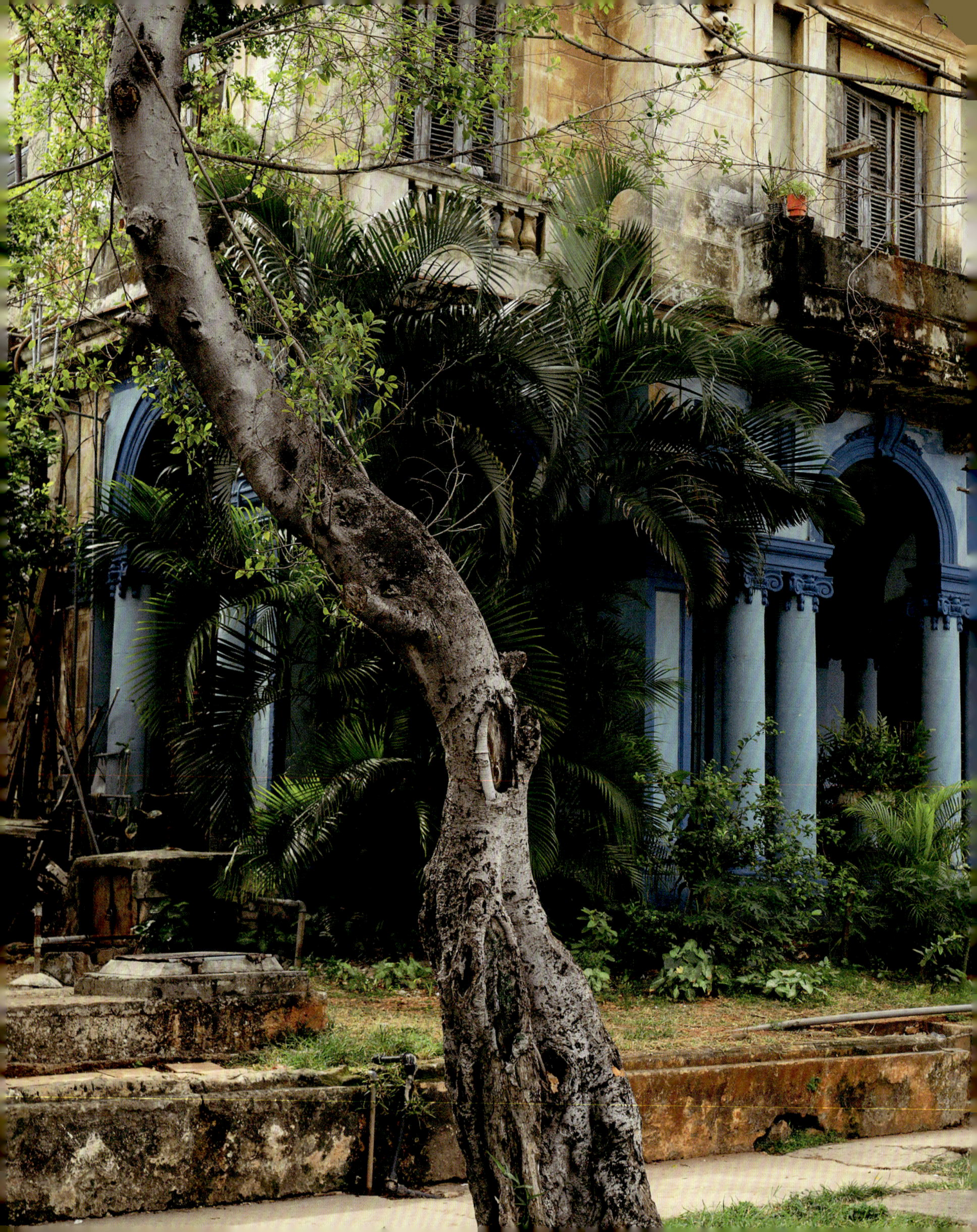

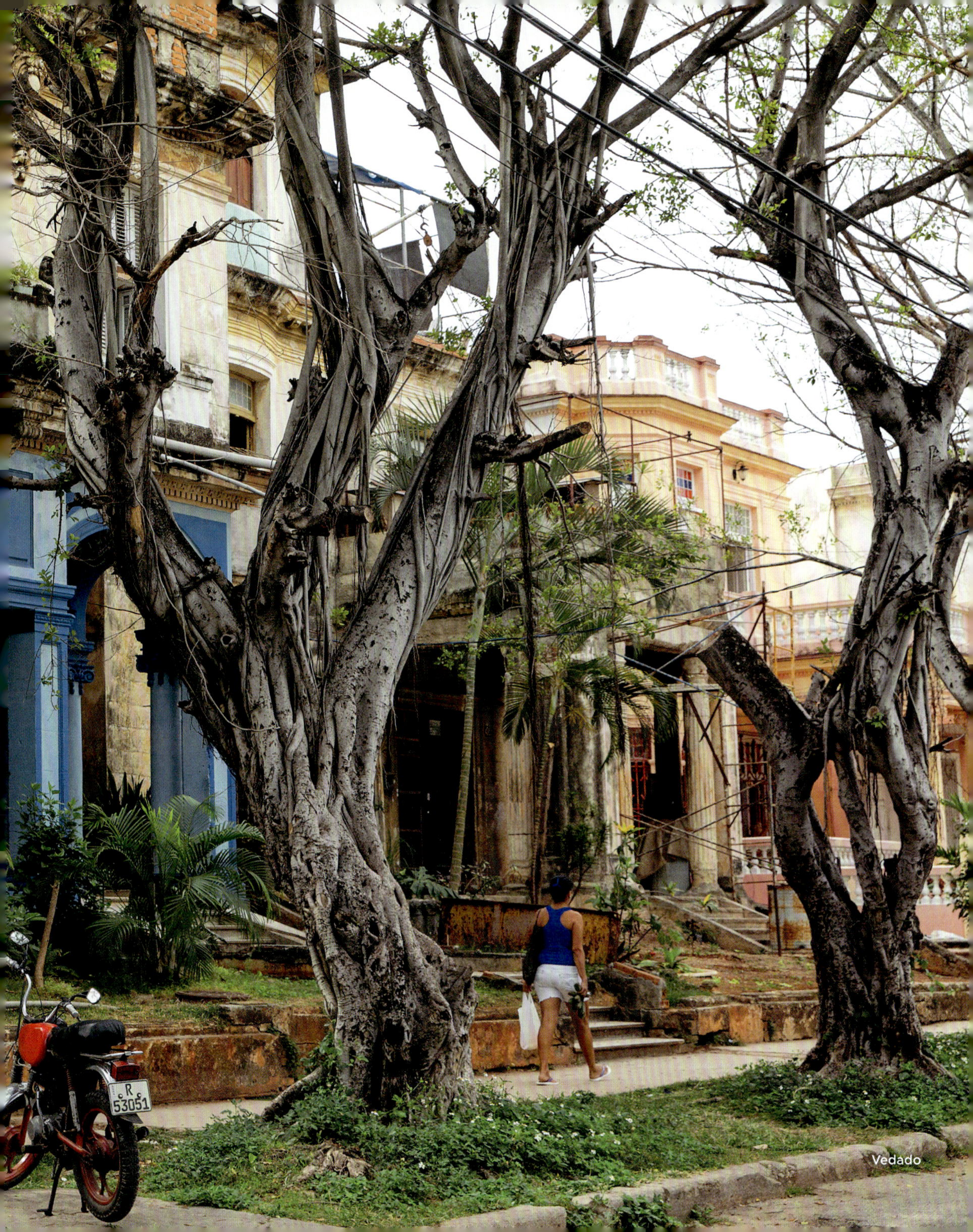

Vedado

Villas in Havana

Most of Havana's villas and townhouses were nationalized after the revolution, and very few are still privately owned today. The former splendid ambience has suffered a lot in recent decades, and it has by no means a romantic patina. It is difficult and almost impossible to obtain building materials for the necessary renovations and maintenance, particularly for private individuals.

Les villas de La Havane

La majorité des villas et maisons de ville de La Havane ont été nationalisées après la révolution et aujourd'hui, très peu sont encore des propriétés privées. La splendeur d'autrefois s'est énormément décrépie au cours des dernières décennies et s'est parée d'une patine qui n'a rien de romantique. Pour les particuliers surtout, il est difficile, voire impossible, d'obtenir les matériaux de construction nécessaires à la rénovation et à l'entretien de ces demeures.

Villen in Havanna

Die meisten Villen und Stadthäuser Havannas wurden nach der Revolution verstaatlicht, nur sehr wenige sind heute noch in Privatbesitz. Das ehemals prachtvolle Ambiente hat in den letzten Jahrzehnten sehr gelitten und eine keineswegs romantische Patina angesetzt. Vor allem für Privatleute ist es schwierig bis unmöglich, an Baumaterial für notwendige Renovierungen und die Instandhaltung zu kommen.

Villas en La Habana

La mayoría de las villas y casas adosadas de La Habana fueron nacionalizadas después de la revolución, y solo unas pocas son aún de propiedad privada. El antiguo espléndido ambiente ha sufrido mucho en las últimas décadas y tiene una pátina no romántica. Especialmente para los particulares es difícil o imposible conseguir materiales de construcción para realizar las reformas y el mantenimiento necesarios.

Vilas em Havana

A maioria das vilas e moradias de Havana foram nacionalizadas após a revolução, apenas muito poucas são ainda hoje propriedade privada. O ambiente anteriormente magnífico sofreu muito nas últimas décadas e criou-se uma pátina nada romântica. Especialmente para pessoas privadas é difícil conseguir materiais de construção para renovações e manutenção necessárias.

Villa's in Havana

De meeste villa's en herenhuizen in Havana werden na de revolutie genationaliseerd, maar tegenwoordig zijn nog maar weinig in particulier bezit. De voormalige prachtige sfeer heeft de laatste decennia veel te lijden gehad en heeft de romantische glans verloren. Vooral voor particulieren is het moeilijk om aan bouwmaterialen te komen voor noodzakelijke renovaties en onderhoud.

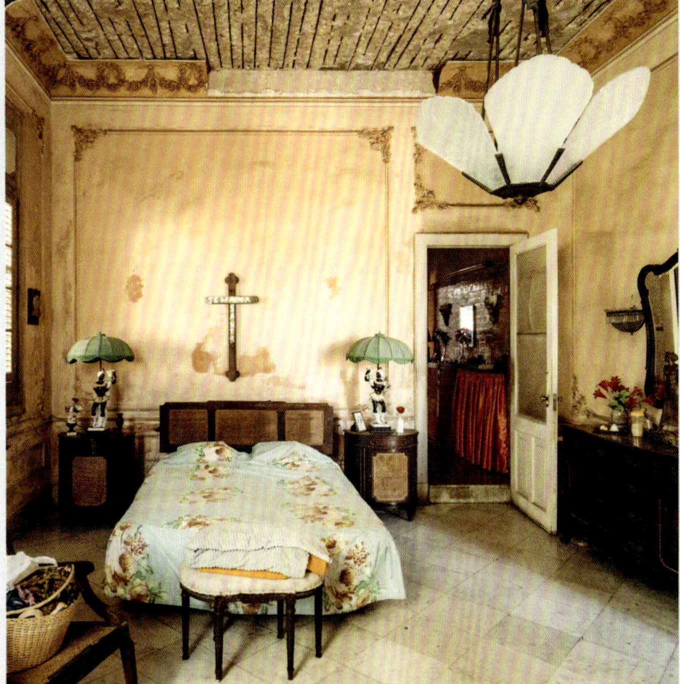

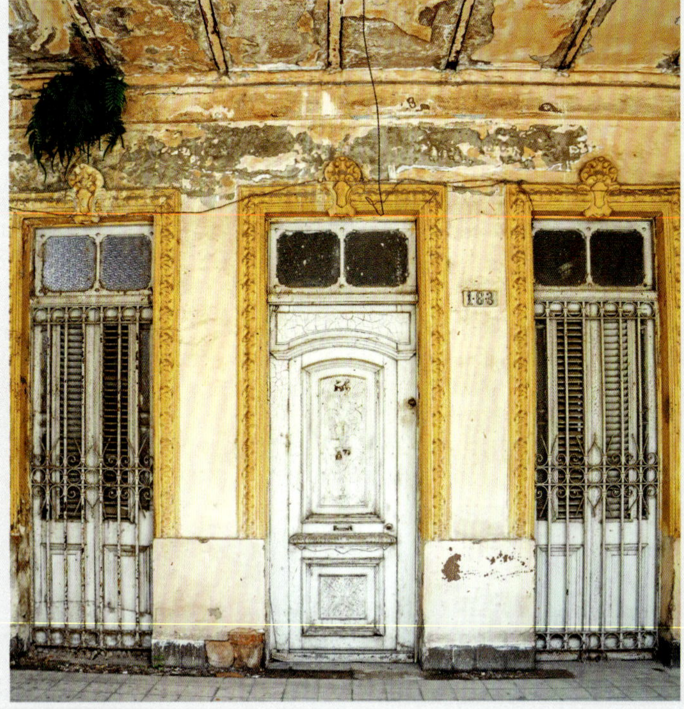

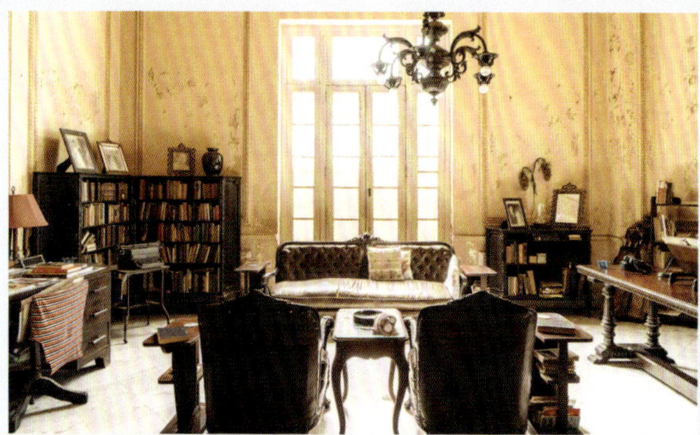
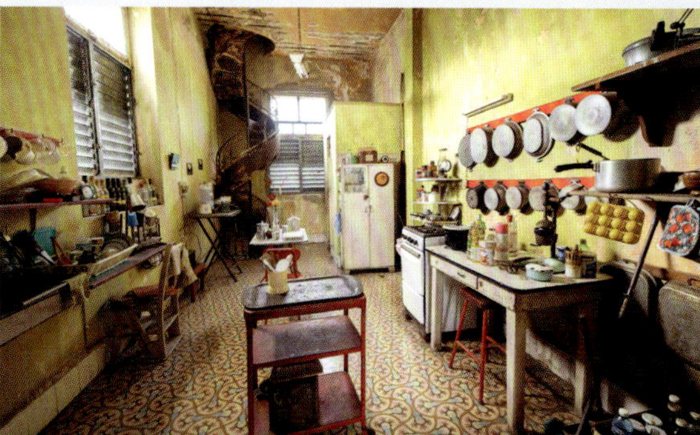
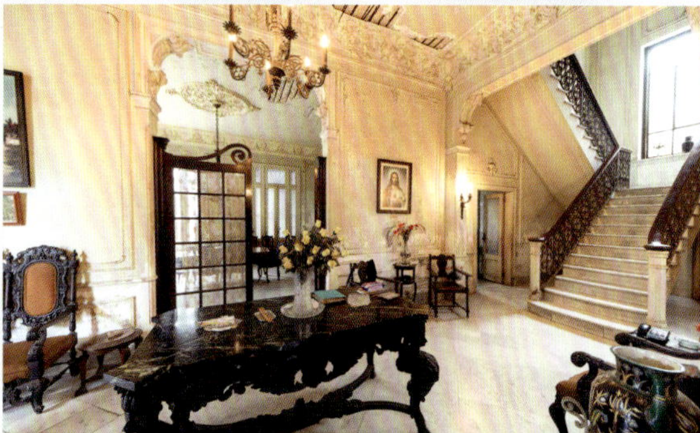
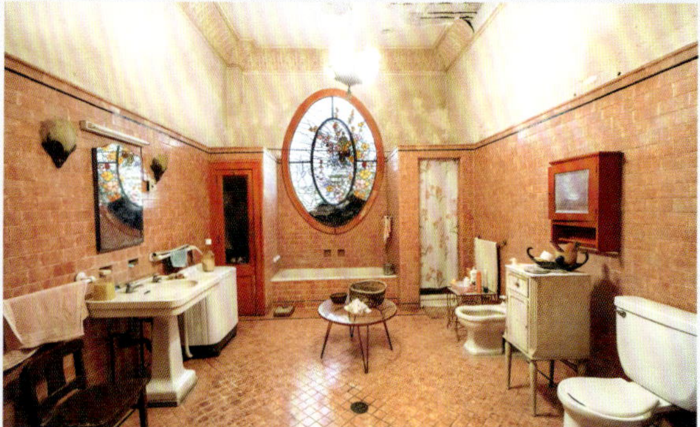

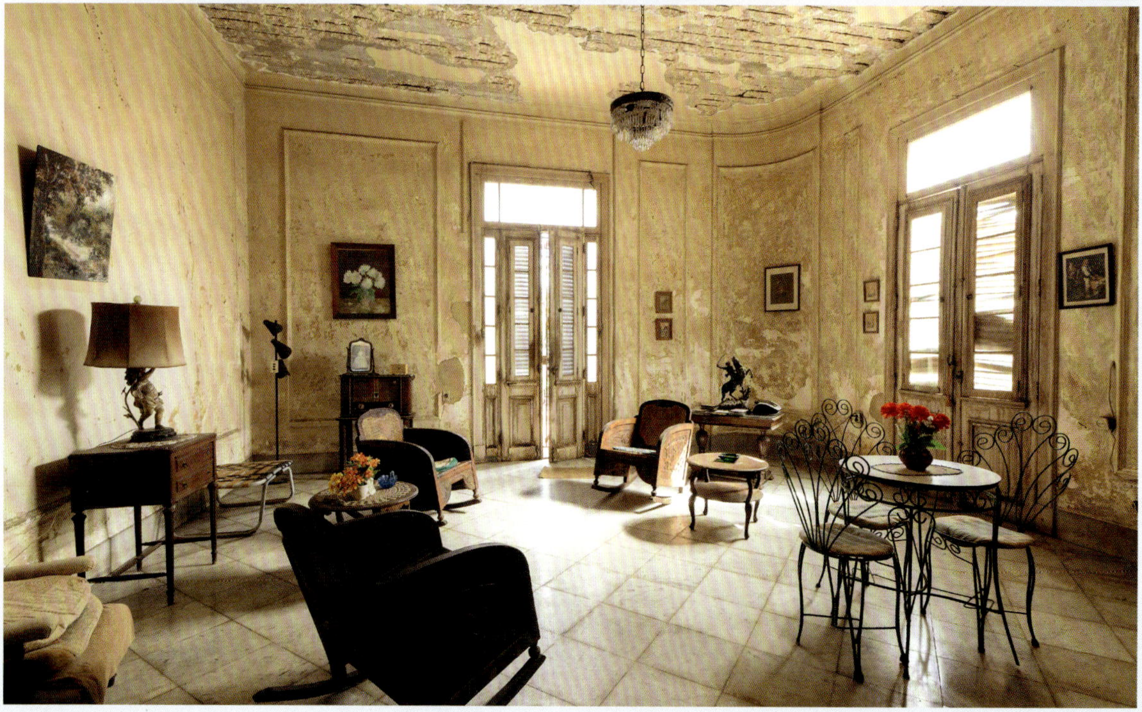

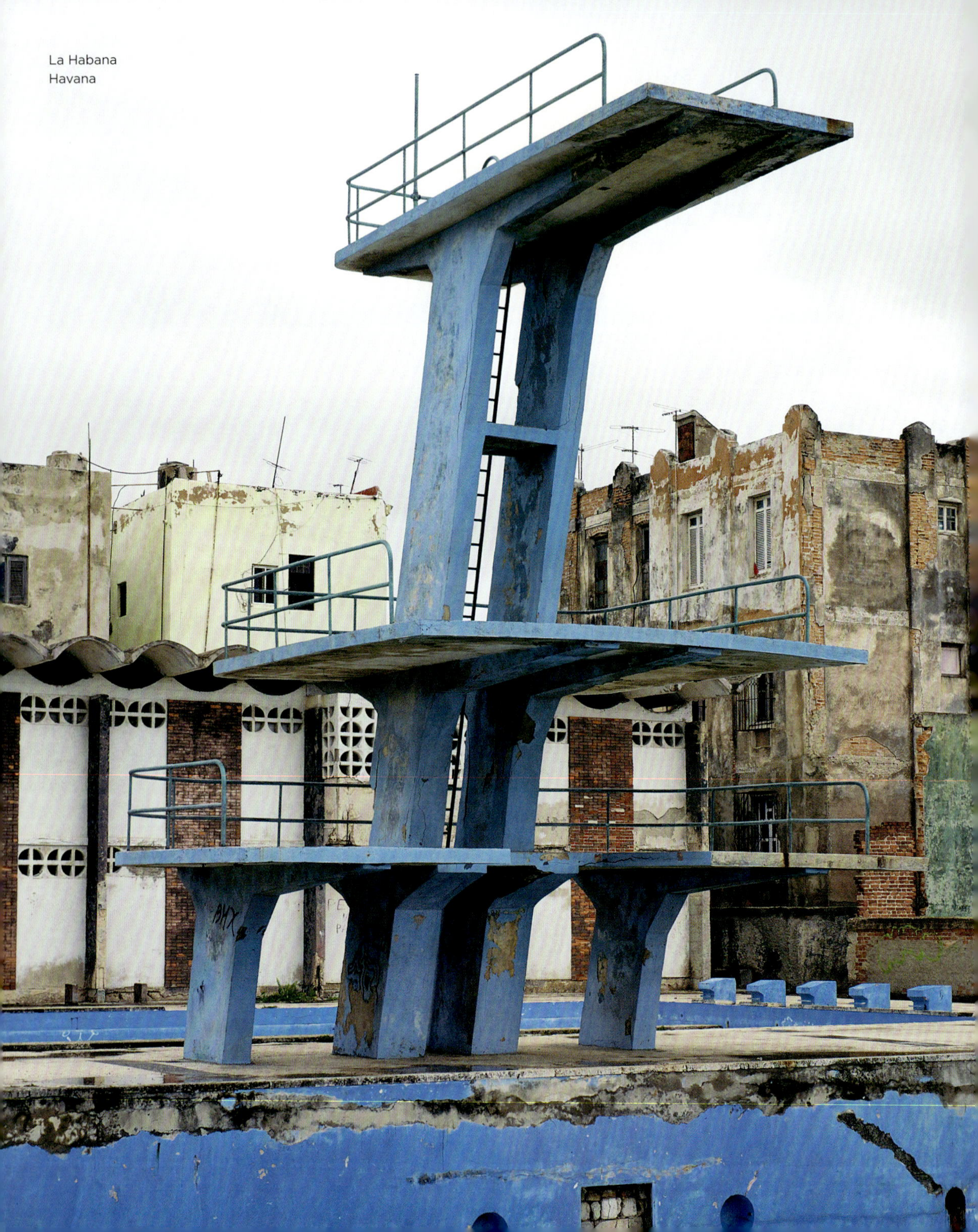

La Habana
Havana

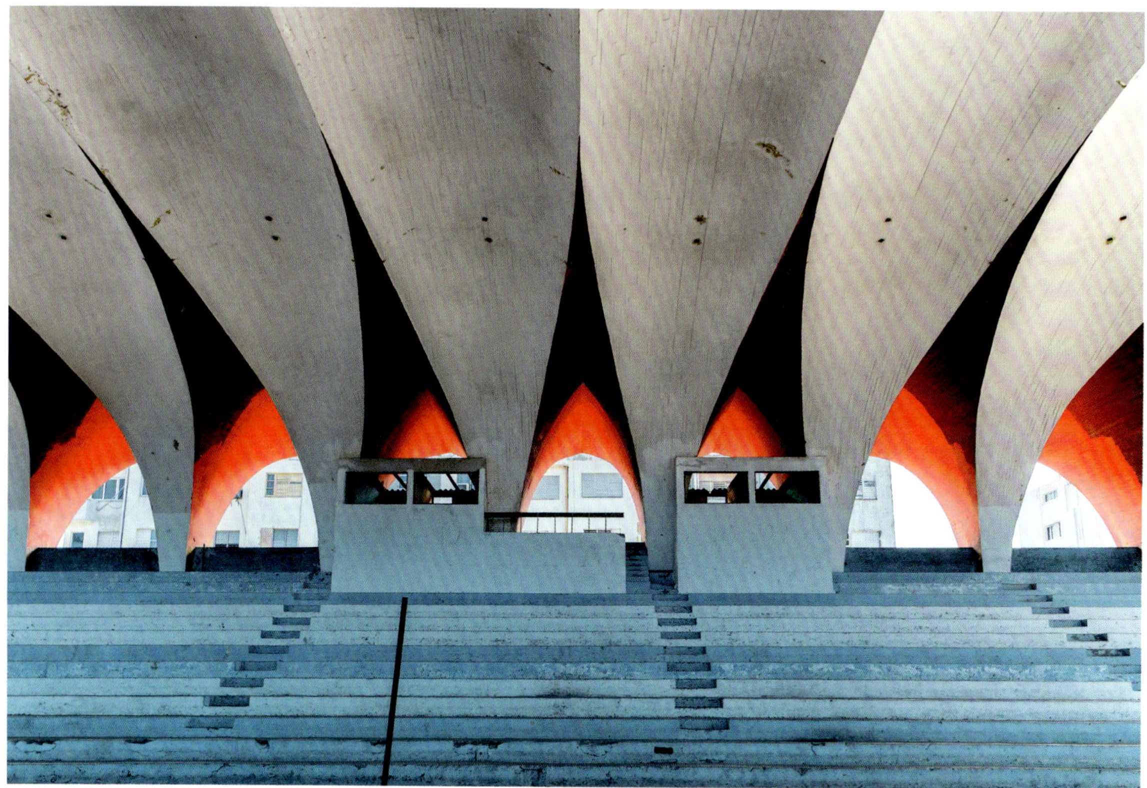

El estadio, Vedado

National Sport *Béisbol*

Baseball (Cuban: *béisbol*) is the legacy of American dominance in Cuba, and is a national passion. The professional league was abolished after 1959, but *béisbol* still has a high status and Cuban players collect many medals in Olympic competitions. The stadium with its striking roof is located directly on the Malecón.

Deporte nacional béisbol

El béisbol es el legado de la dominación norteamericana en Cuba y una pasión nacional. Después de 1959, se abolió la liga profesional, pero el béisbol todavía tiene un estatus alto y los jugadores cubanos recogen muchas medallas en las competiciones olímpicas. El estadio con su llamativo techo está situado directamente en el Malecón.

Le *béisbol*, sport national

Le base-ball (en espagnol de Cuba : *béisbol*), hérité de la présence américaine, est aujourd'hui une passion nationale. La ligue professionnelle a été supprimée après 1959, mais le *béisbol* a conservé son importance jusqu'à aujourd'hui et les joueurs cubains ont remporté de nombreuses médailles lors des rencontres olympiques. Le stade, au toit remarquable, est situé à proximité du Malecón.

Desporto nacional beisebol

O beisebol (cubano: *béisbol*) é o legado do domínio americano em Cuba e uma paixão nacional. Depois de 1959, a liga profissional foi abolida, mas o beisebol ainda tem até hoje um alto status e os jogadores cubanos conquistam muitas medalhas em competições olímpicas. O estádio com o telhado marcante está localizado diretamente sobre o Malecón.

Nationalsport *béisbol*

Baseball (kubanisch: *béisbol*) ist das Erbe der US-amerikanischen Dominanz in Kuba und eine nationale Leidenschaft. Nach 1959 wurde die Profiliga abgeschafft, aber *béisbol* hat bis heute einen hohen Stellenwert und die kubanischen Spieler sammeln bei olympischen Wettkämpfen viele Medaillen ein. Das Stadion mit der markanten Überdachung liegt direkt am Malecón.

Nationale sport *béisbol*

Honkbal (Cubaans: *béisbol*) is de erfenis van de Amerikaanse dominantie in Cuba en een nationale passie. Na 1959 werd de professionele competitie afgeschaft, maar *béisbol* heeft nog steeds een hoge status en de Cubaanse spelers verzamelen veel medailles in Olympische competities. Het stadion met het opvallende dak ligt direct aan de Malecón.

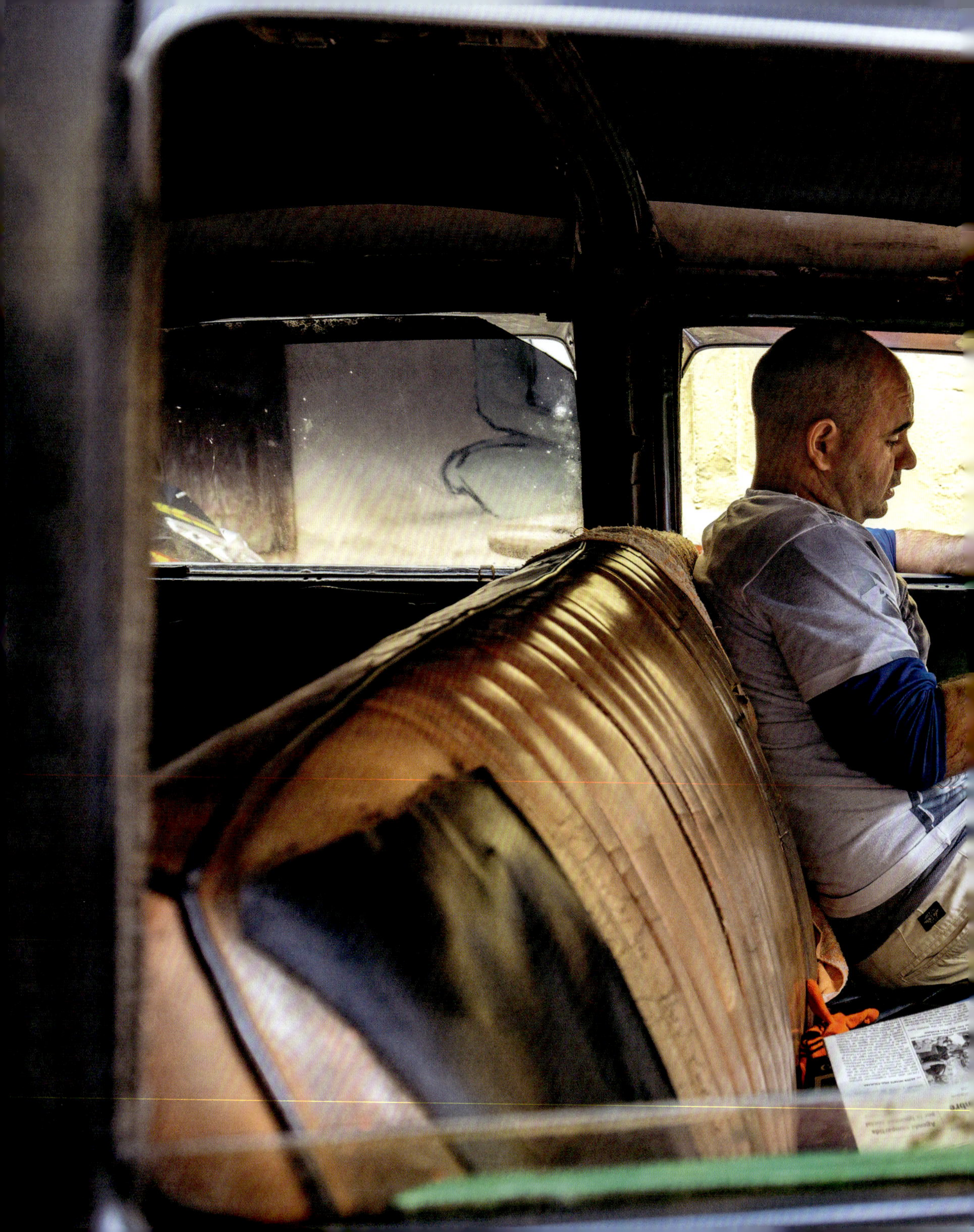

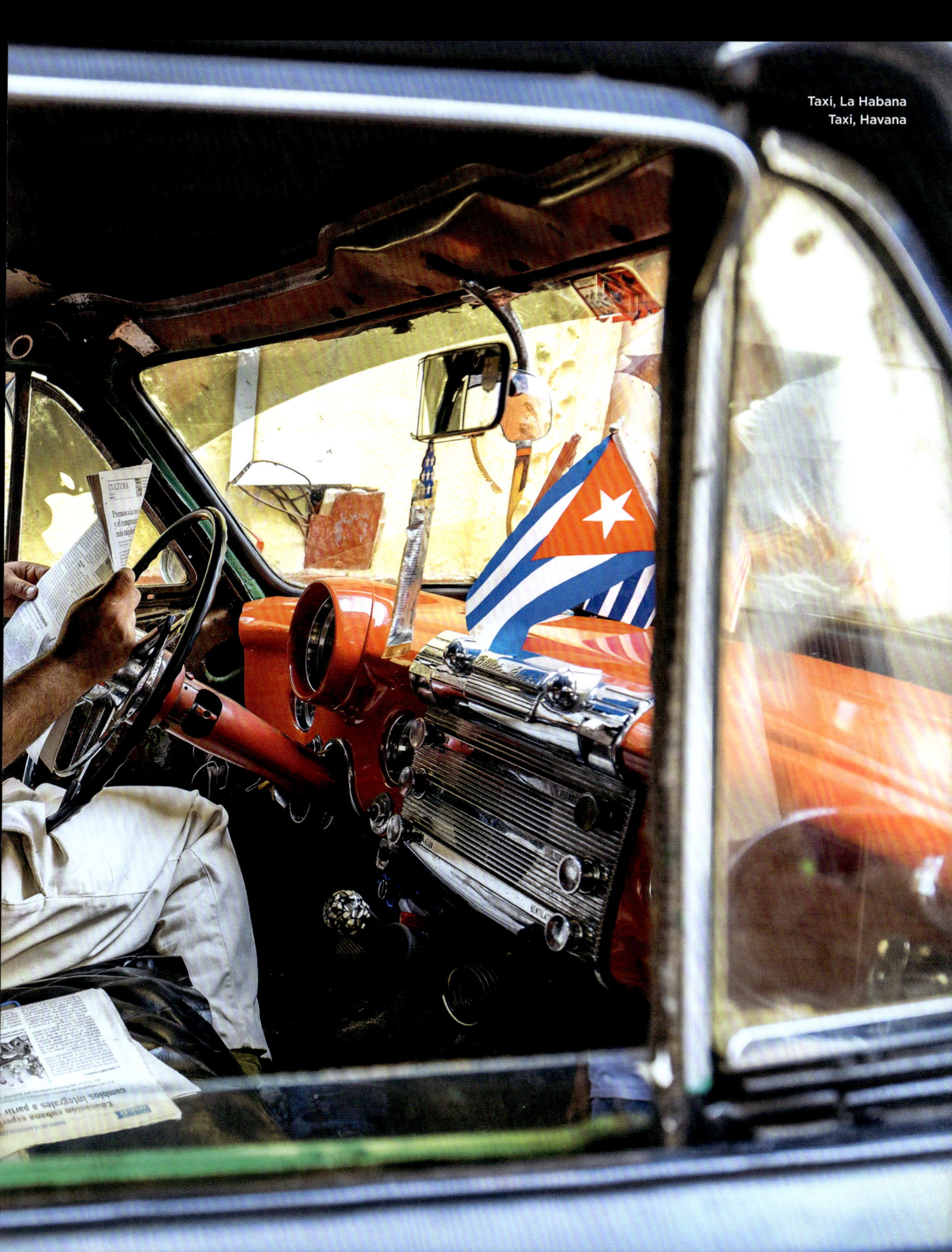

Taxi, La Habana
Taxi, Havana

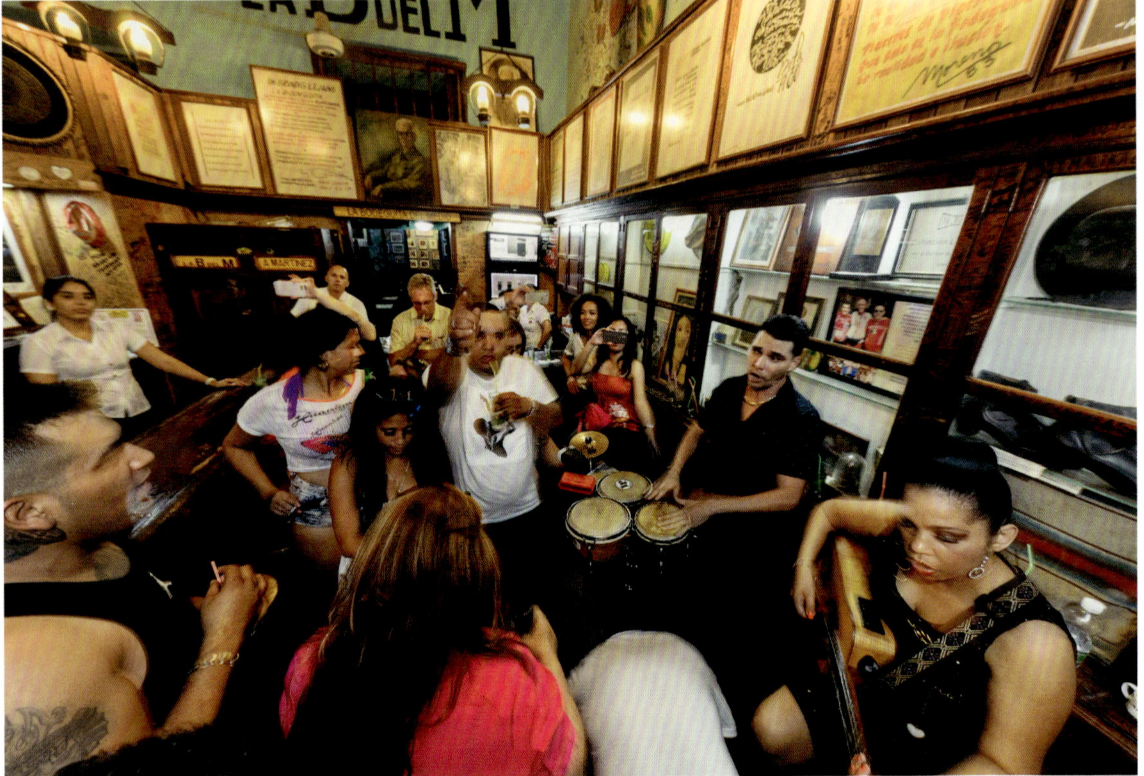

La Bodeguita del Medio, La Habana Vieja
Bodeguita del Medio, Old Havana

Bodeguita del Medio

The Bodeguita del Medio, the most famous bar in Cuba, is located in Calle Empedrado in the heart of the old town. In the past, workers from the surrounding printing houses ate here, then journalists, artists and intellectuals joined in. Hemingway drank his Mojito in the Bodegita, the landmark bar that is now a place of pilgrimage for tourists.

Bodeguita del Medio

Au cœur de la vieille ville, dans la calle Empedrado, est installé le bar le plus célèbre de Cuba, la Bodeguita del Medio. Autrefois, les ouvriers des imprimeries environnantes venaient y déjeuner, puis ce furent les journalistes, les artistes et les intellectuels. Hemingway y dégustait des mojitos, spécialité de ce minuscule bar devenu un lieu de pèlerinage pour touristes.

Bodeguita del Medio

Im Herzen der Altstadt in der Calle Empedrado liegt die Bodeguita del Medio, die berühmteste Bar Kubas. Früher aßen hier die Arbeiter aus den umliegenden Druckereien, dann kamen Journalisten, Künstler und Intellektuelle hinzu. Hemingway trank in der Bodegita seinen Mojito, das Markenzeichen der winzigen Bar, die heute ein Wallfahrtsort für Touristen ist.

Bodeguita del Medio

La Bodeguita del Medio, el bar más famoso de Cuba, se encuentra en el corazón del casco antiguo de la ciudad, en la calle Empedrado. En el pasado, los trabajadores de las imprentas de los alrededores comían aquí. Luego se unieron periodistas, artistas e intelectuales. Hemingway bebió su mojito en la Bodegita, la marca registrada del pequeño bar que ahora es un lugar de peregrinación para los turistas.

Bodeguita del Medio

O Bodeguita del Medio, o bar mais famoso de Cuba, está localizado no coração da cidade velha de Calle Empedrado. No passado, os trabalhadores das tipografias dos arredores vinham comer aqui, depois vinheram os jornalistas, os artistas e os intelectuais. Hemingway bebia seu Mojito aqui na Bodegita, a marca registrada do pequeno bar que agora é um lugar de peregrinação para turistas.

Bodeguita del Medio

De Bodeguita del Medio, de bekendste bar van Cuba, ligt in het hart van de oude stad in Calle Empedrado. Vroeger aten de arbeiders van de omliggende drukkerijen hier, waarna journalisten, kunstenaars en intellectuelen zich er bij aansloten. Hemingway dronk zijn Mojito in de Bodegita, het handelsmerk van het kleine café dat nu een bedevaartsoord voor toeristen is.

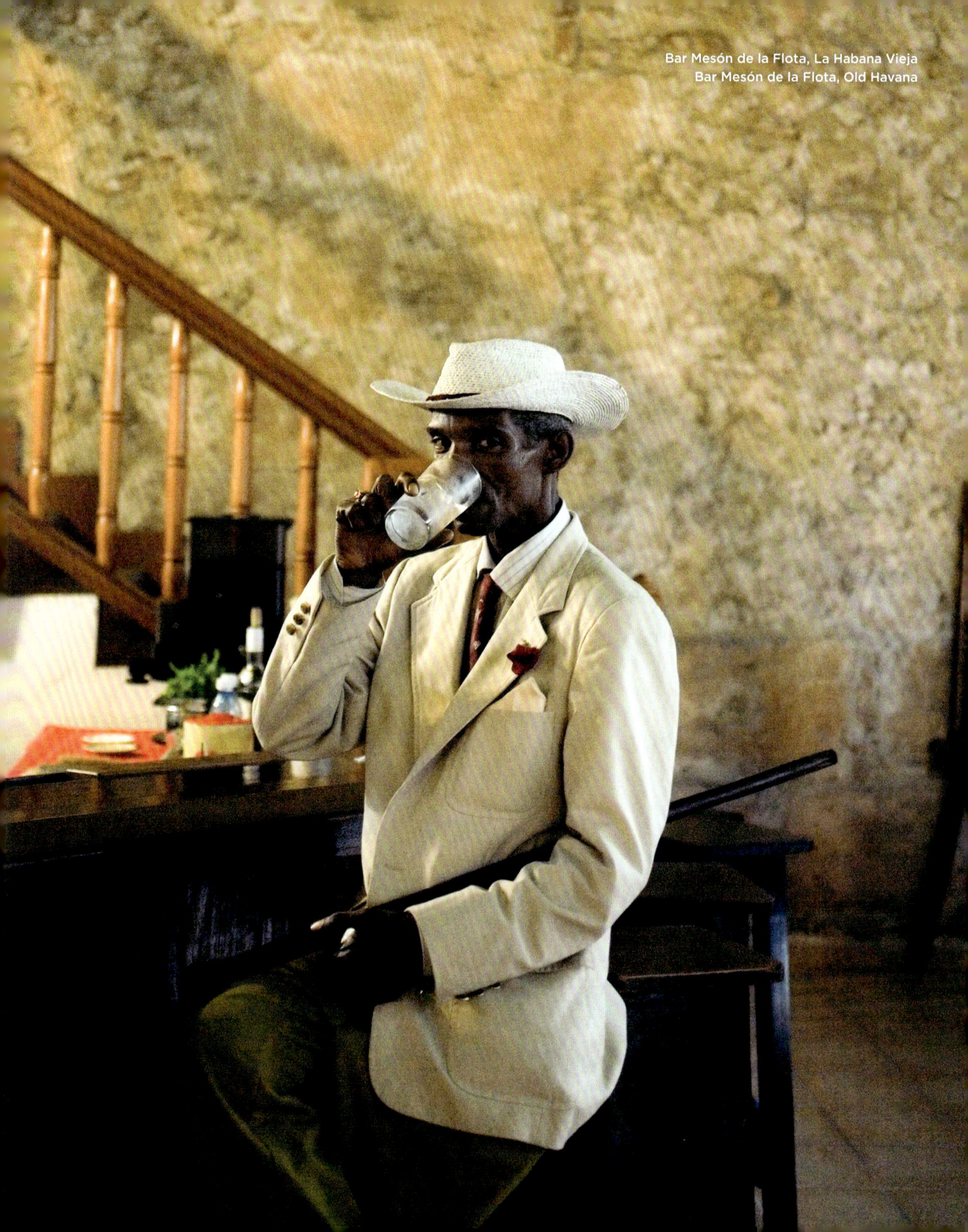

Bar Mesón de la Flota, La Habana Vieja
Bar Mesón de la Flota, Old Havana

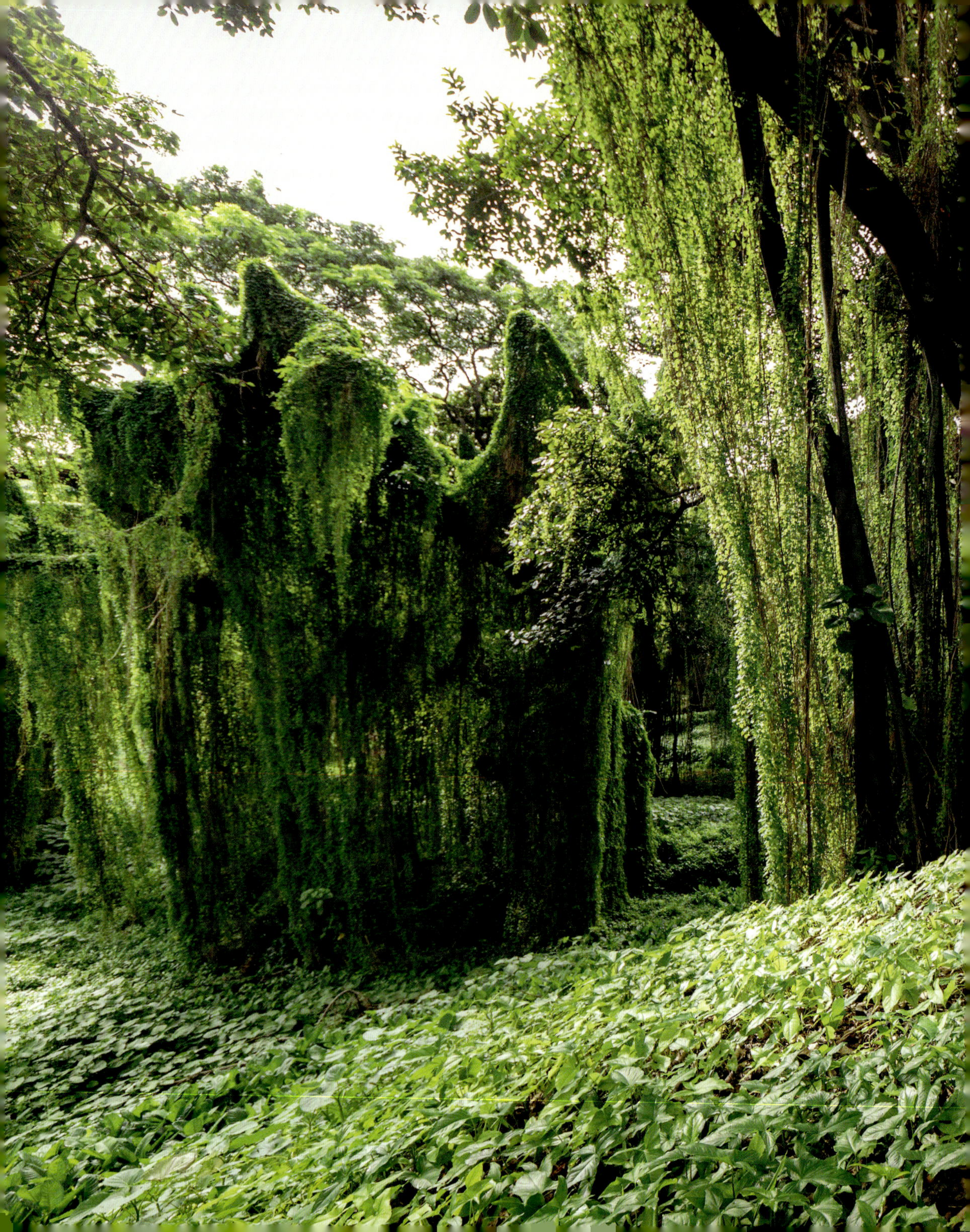

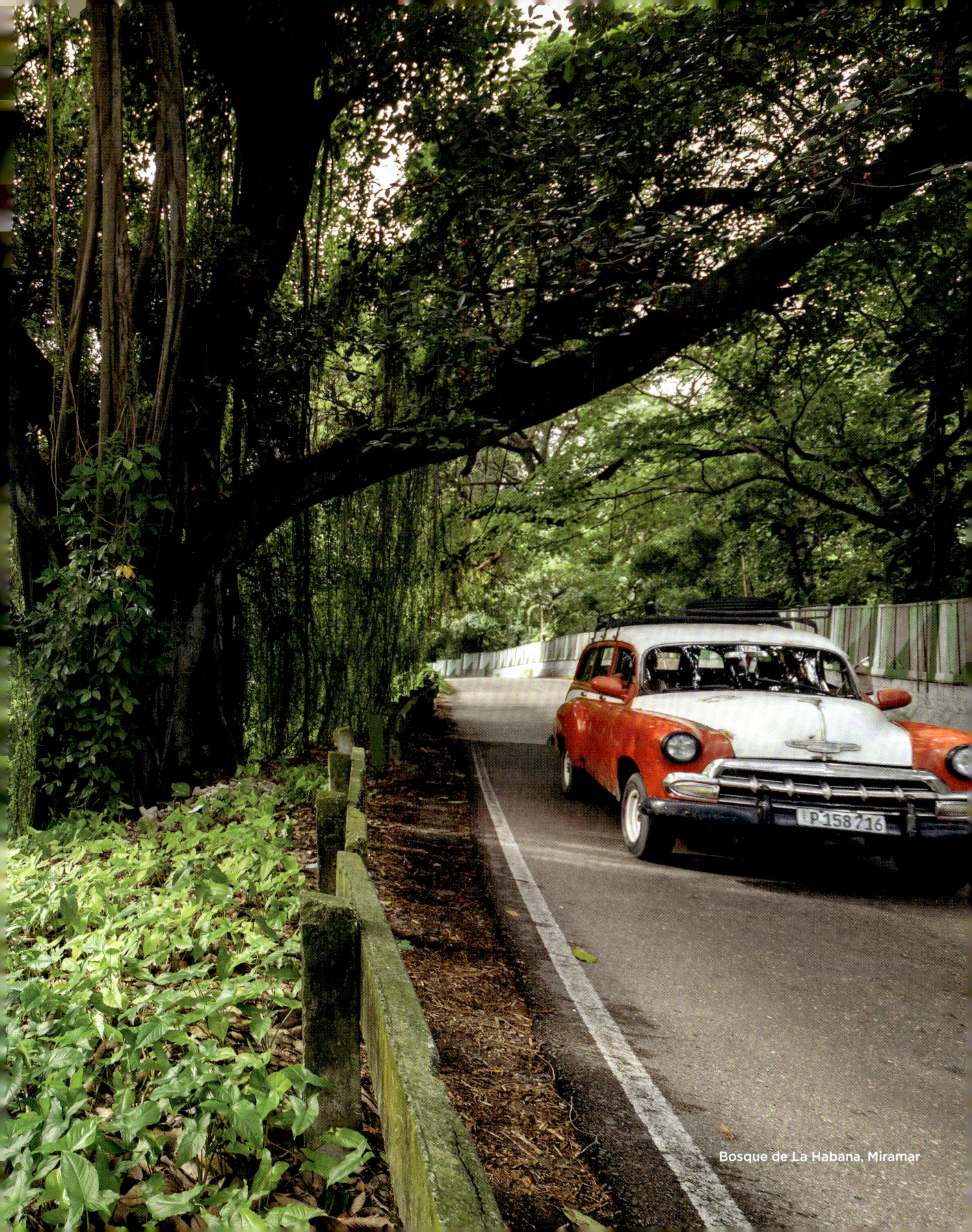

Bosque de La Habana, Miramar

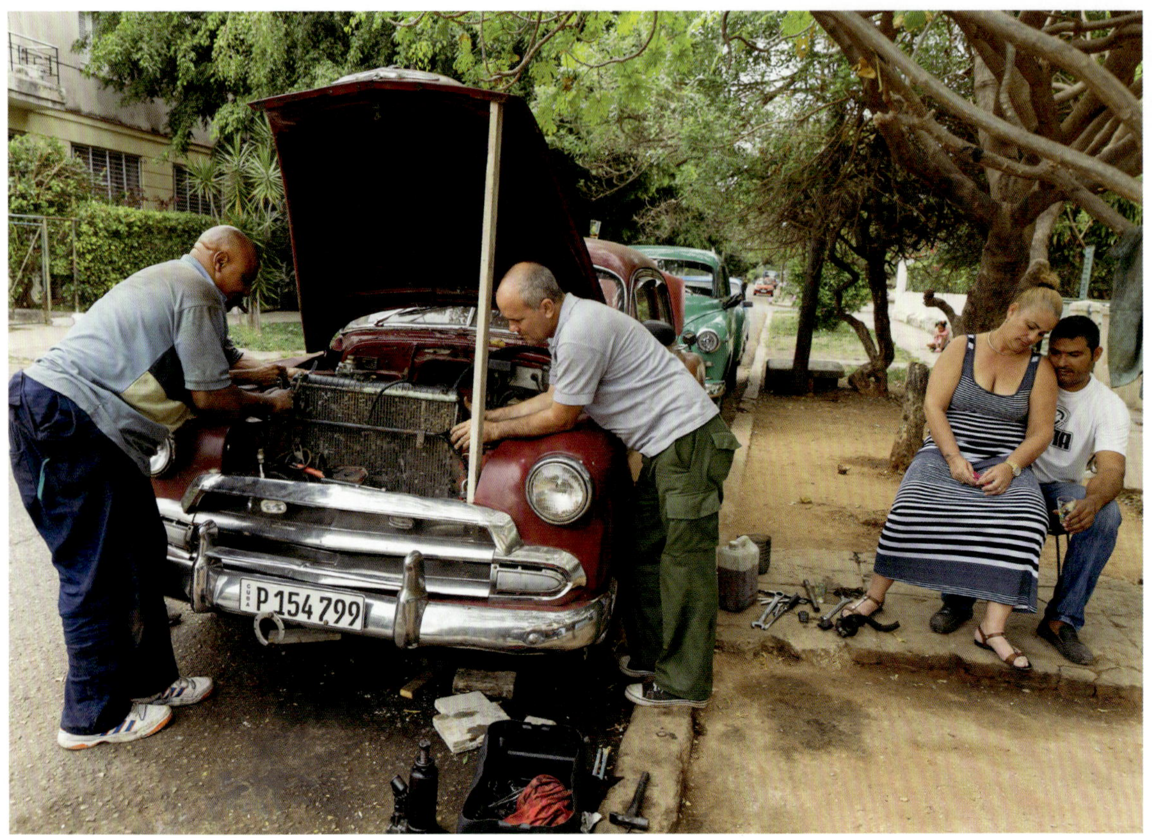

Vedado

Classic Cars

Scenes like this are often seen on the streets of Havana. These decrepit vehicles are extremely prone to breakdowns of all kinds, and countless potholes threaten aging axles and fragile tires. If you are on the road in a vintage collective taxi (colectivo), you have to expect forced stops. The taxi drivers are small entrepreneurs (cuentapropistas) and have to pay high taxes, depending on the condition of their classic cars. Factory-new mid-range cars, also available in Cuba for some years now, are unfortunately not a cheaper alternative because of their exorbitant prices (up to €150,000/$165,500 US); the average monthly wage in Cuba is €20 ($23 US).

Vieux tacots

Les scènes de ce type ne sont pas rares dans les rues de La Havane. Les véhicules délabrés sont victimes de pannes de toutes sortes et d'innombrables nids-de-poule mettent à mal leurs essieux anciens et leurs pneus épuisés. Quiconque décide d'emprunter un taxi collectif (colectivo) doit compter avec ce type d'imprévu. Les chauffeurs sont de petits entrepreneurs (cuentapropistas) soumis, en fonction de l'état de leur outil de travail, à de très lourds impôts. La commercialisation de voitures neuves de classe moyenne est autorisée depuis quelques années, mais elles ne constituent en aucun cas une alternative, car leur prix est exorbitant (jusqu'à 150 000 €) au regard du salaire moyen (avoisinant 20 €)

Oldtimer

Szenen wie dieser begegnet man auf den Straßen Havannas häufig. Die altersschwachen Gefährte sind äußerst anfällig für Pannen jeder Art, und unzählige Schlaglöcher bedrohen betagte Achsen und mürbe Reifen. Wer mit einem Oldtimer-Sammeltaxi (colectivo) unterwegs ist, muss mit Zwangspausen rechnen. Die Taxifahrer sind Kleinunternehmer (cuentapropistas) und müssen, je nach Zustand ihres Oldtimers, hohe Steuern zahlen. Fabrikneue Mittelklassewagen, seit einigen Jahren auch auf Kuba käuflich, sind wegen ihrer exorbitanten Preise (bis zu 150 000 €) leider keine Alternative, denn der monatliche Durchschnittslohn liegt in Kuba bei 20 €.

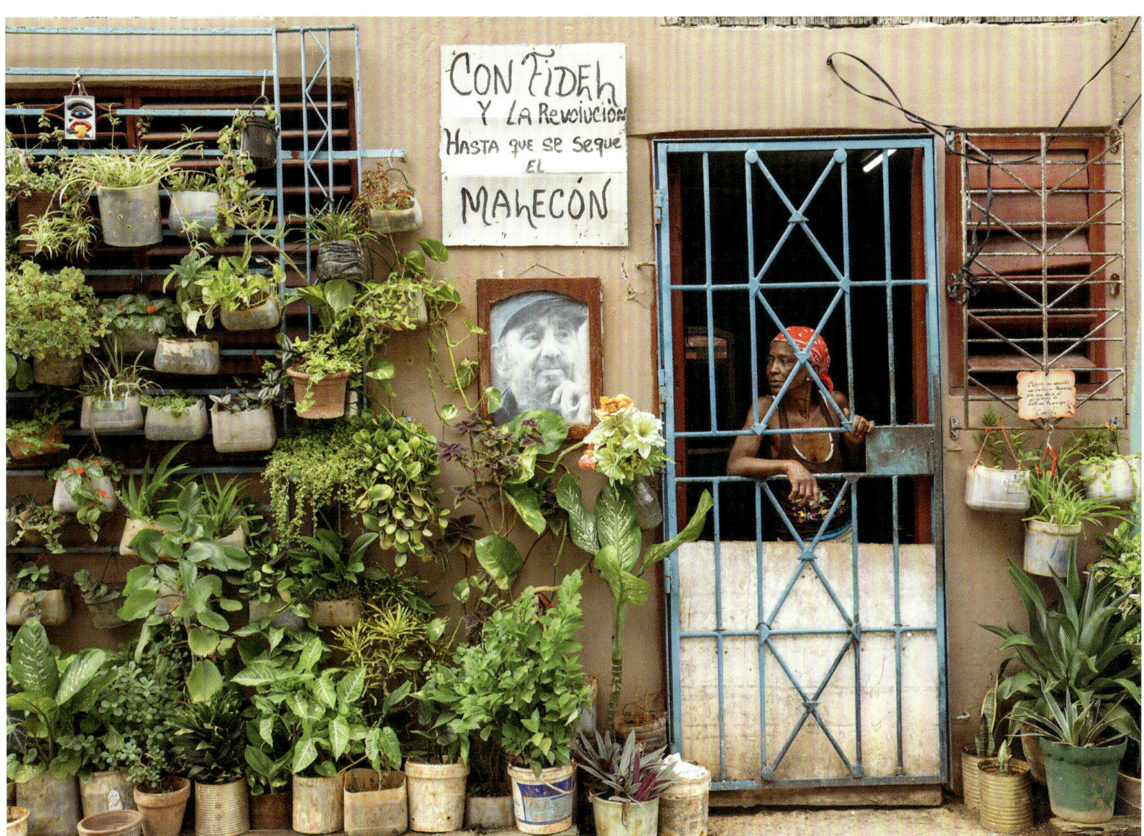

Centro Habana

Oldtimer

Escenas como esta se ven a menudo en las calles de La Habana. Estos viejos compañeros son extremadamente propensos a sufrir averías de todo tipo, y los innumerables baches son una amenaza para los ejes antiguos y los frágiles neumáticos. Aquellos que van por la carretera en un taxi colectivo de época tienen que contar con los descansos forzados. Los taxistas son pequeños empresarios *(cuentapropistas)* y tienen que pagar altos impuestos, dependiendo de la condición de sus coches clásicos. Desgraciadamente, los coches nuevos de clase media de fábrica, que desde hace algunos años también están disponibles en Cuba, no son una alternativa debido a sus precios desorbitados (hasta 150 000 €), y que el salario medio mensual en Cuba es de 20 €.

Carros Clássicos

Cenas como estas são frequentemente vistas nas ruas de Havana. Os velhos companheiros são extremamente propensos a avarias de todos os tipos, e os incontáveis buracos ameaçam eixos velhos e pneus quebradiços. Quem viaja com um táxi de carro clássico coletivo *(colectivo)*, deve contar com pausas forçadas. Os taxistas são pequenos empresários *(cuentapropistas)* e têm que pagar impostos altos, dependendo da condição de seus carros clássicos. Os carros novos de classe média, há alguns anos também disponíveis em Cuba, infelizmente não podem ser vistos como uma alternativa devido aos seus preços exorbitantes (até 150 000 €), porque o salário médio mensal em Cuba é de 20 €.

Oldtimer

Dit soort scènes zijn vaak te zien in de straten van Havana. De oude metgezellen zijn zeer gevoelig voor allerlei storingen en talloze kuilen bedreigen oude assen en broze banden. Als je onderweg bent in een vintage collectieve taxi *(colectivo)*, moet je rekening houden met gedwongen pauzes. De taxichauffeurs zijn kleine ondernemers *(cuentapropistas)* en moeten hoge belastingen betalen, afhankelijk van de staat van hun klassieke auto. Nieuwe middenklasse auto's, die sinds enkele jaren ook in Cuba verkrijgbaar zijn, zijn helaas geen alternatief vanwege hun extreem hoge prijzen (tot € 150 000), het gemiddelde maandloon in Cuba bedraagt € 20.

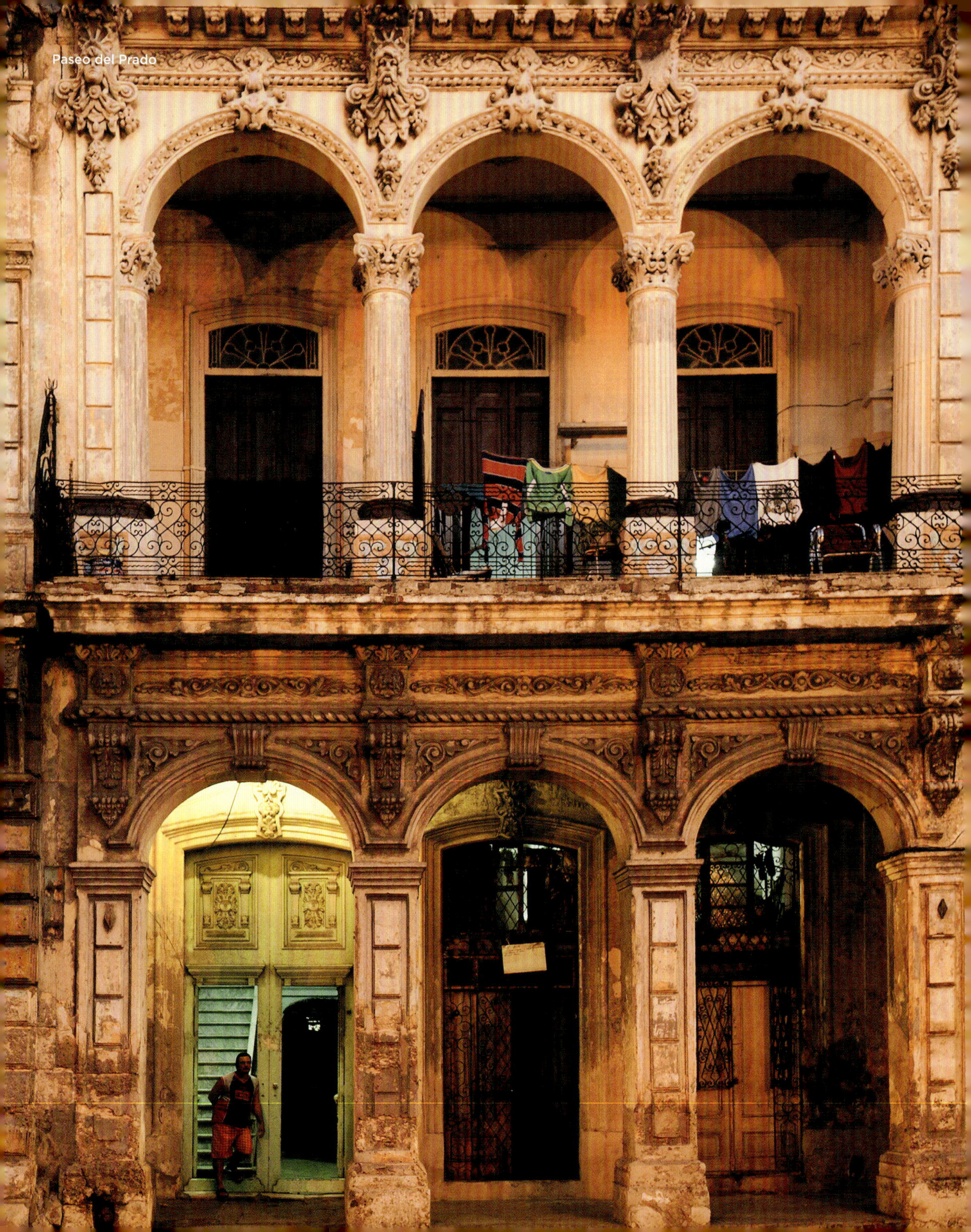
Paseo del Prado

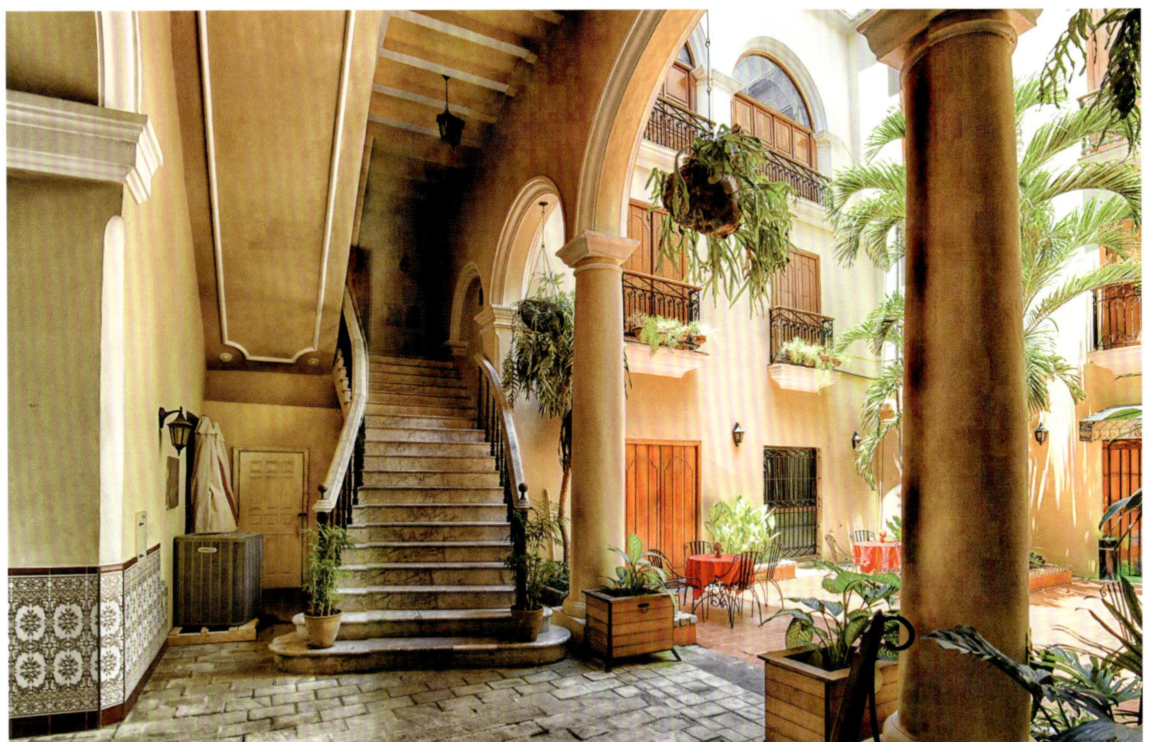

La Habana Vieja
Old Havana

Housing Shortage in Havana

The everyday life of most Habaneros does not take place in restored colonial houses with idyllic patios. Many people live in formerly splendid townhouses which today are in need of renovation or are in danger of collapsing. The apartments were divided into many small and often windowless units with false ceilings, and are hopelessly overcrowded.

Déficit habitacional en La Habana

La vida cotidiana de la mayoría de los habaneros no tiene lugar en casas coloniales restauradas con patios idílicos. Muchas personas viven en casas adosadas que en su día fueron espléndias, pero que ahora necesitan urgentemente una reforma o están en peligro de derrumbarse. Los apartamentos se dividieron en muchas unidades pequeñas y a menudo sin ventanas con techos falsos y están superpoblados.

Crise du logement à La Havane

Le quotidien de la majorité des Habaneros se déroule loin des belles demeures coloniales agrémentées d'un patio idyllique. Beaucoup occupent des maisons de ville autrefois somptueuses, mais qui nécessiteraient aujourd'hui d'être rénovées ou menacent franchement de s'effondrer. Elles ont été compartimentées à l'aide de mezzanines en de nombreuses petites unités, parfois dépourvues de fenêtre, et désespérément surpeuplées.

Excassez de moradia em Havana

A vida quotidiana da maioria dos Habaneros não acontece em casas coloniais restauradas com pátios idílicos. Muitas pessoas vivem em moradias anteriormente esplêndidas, que hoje precisam de renovação ou correm o risco de desmoronar. Os apartamentos foram divididos em muitas unidades pequenas e muitas vezes sem janelas com tetos falsos e são irremediavelmente superlotados.

Wohnungsnot in Havanna

Der Alltag der meisten Habaneros findet nicht in restaurierten Kolonialhäusern mit idyllischen Patios statt. Viele Menschen leben in ehemals prächtigen Stadthäusern, die heute renovierungsbedürftig oder einsturzgefährdet sind. Die Wohnungen wurden mit Zwischendecken in viele kleine und oft fensterlose Einheiten unterteilt und sind hoffnungslos überbelegt.

Huisvestingsproblemen in Havana

Het dagelijkse leven van de meeste Habaneros vindt niet in gerestaureerde koloniale huizen met idyllische terrassen plaats. Veel mensen wonen in voormalige prachtige herenhuizen, die vandaag de dag aan renovatie toe zijn of zelfs dreigen in te storten. De appartementen werden verdeeld in vele kleine en vaak raamloze eenheden met verlaagde plafonds en zijn overvol.

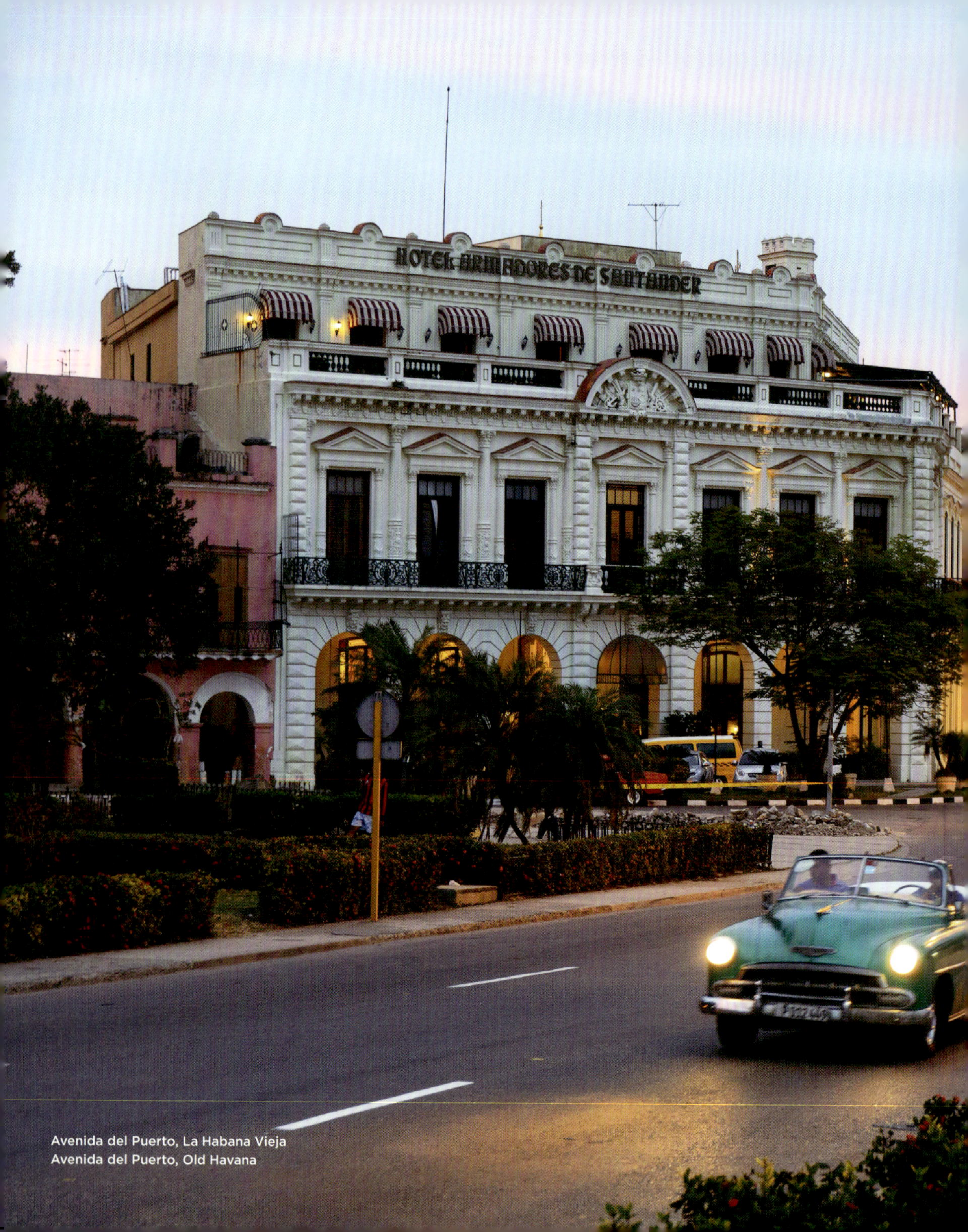

Avenida del Puerto, La Habana Vieja
Avenida del Puerto, Old Havana

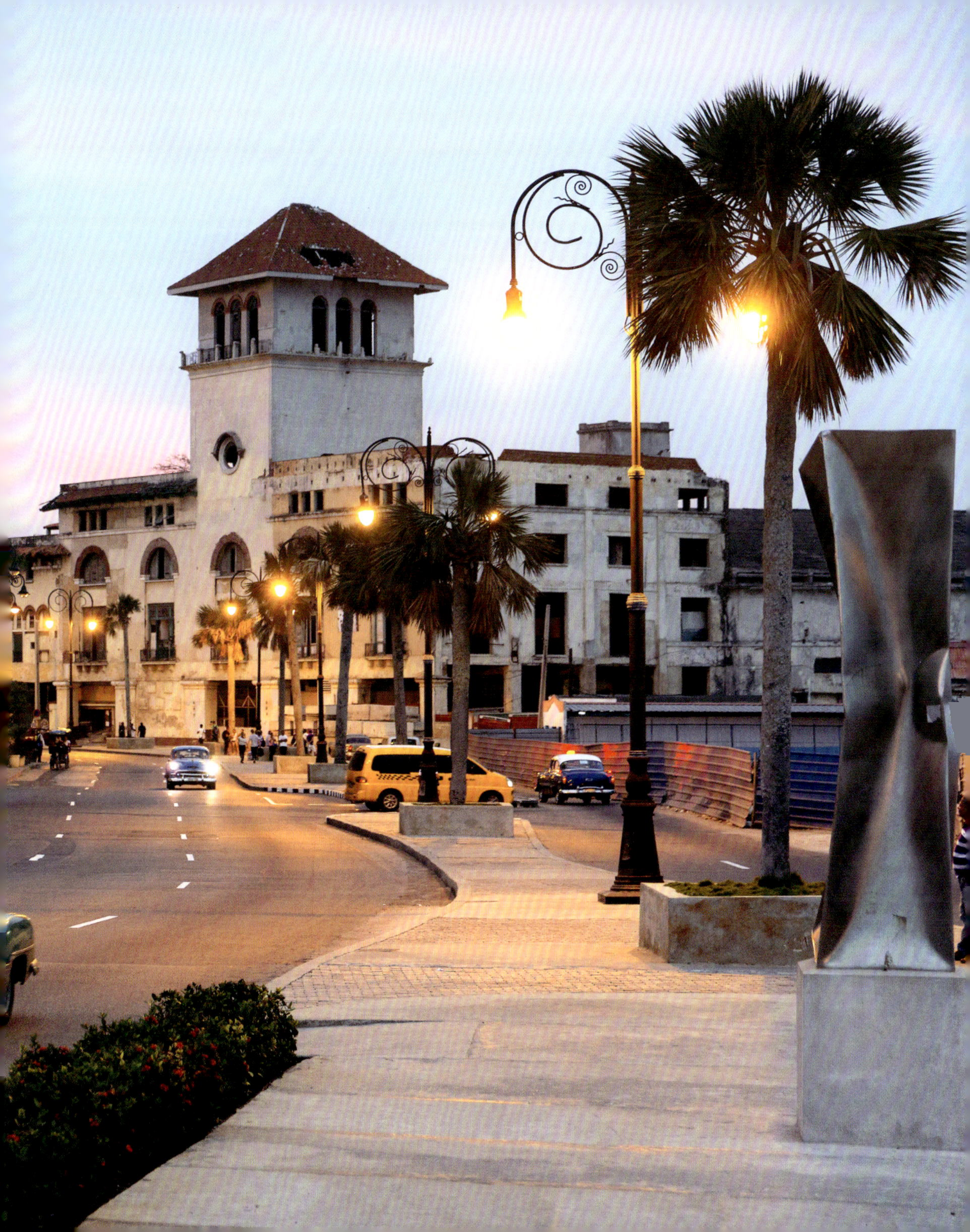

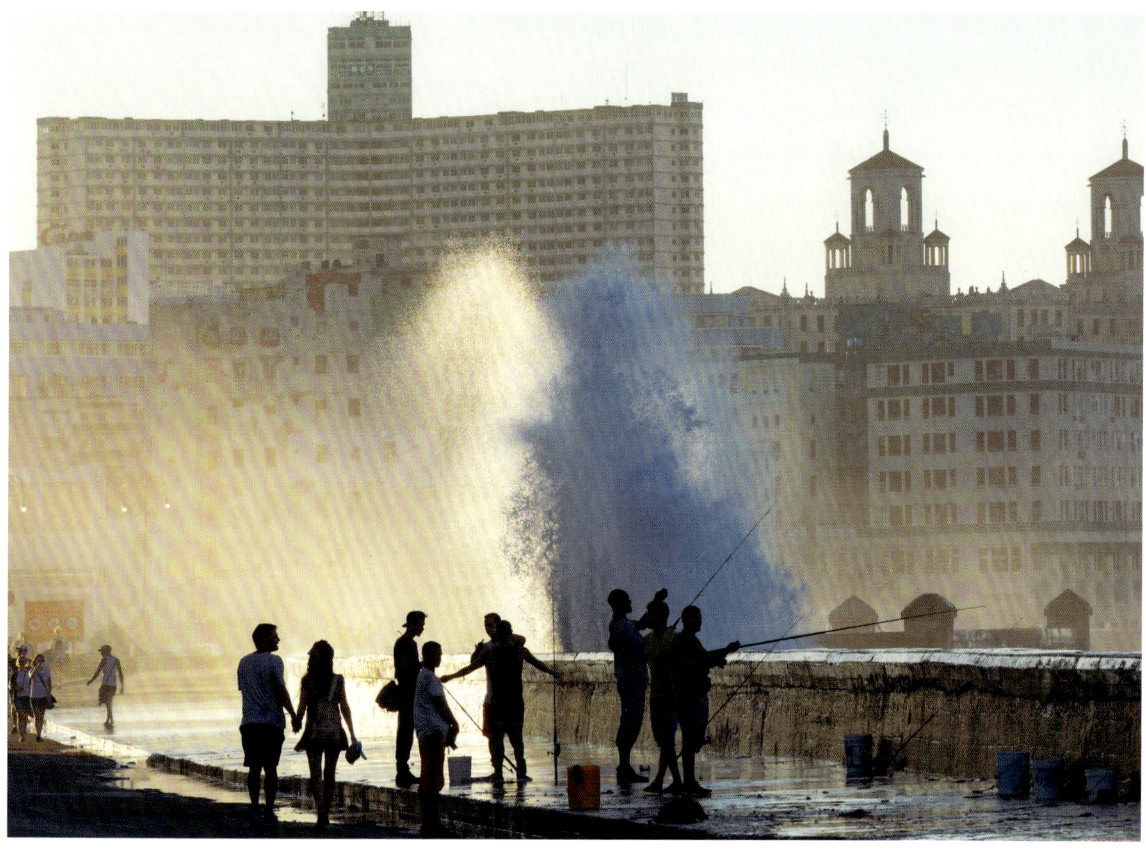

Malecón

Malecón

Havana lives with its face to the sea. The Malecón, the 8 km (5 mi.) long, legendary waterfront promenade between the old town and the Miramar villa district is the lifeline, promenade and public living room of the city. As the sun gradually sets, young and old are drawn to the "Boulevard of Longing" to cool off, enjoy the sea breeze, chat, arrange business, make music. On the low wall sit lovers, lonely people, merchants, whole families and countless anglers who hope for a good catch for dinner. They are only permitted to fish from the shore, boats are forbidden.

Malecón

La Havane est tournée vers le large. Le Malecón est une promenade en front de mer de 8 km de long qui relie la vieille ville et le quartier résidentiel de Miramar. C'est une ligne de vie, un lieu pour flâner et le salon officiel de la ville. Alors que le soleil décline, jeunes et moins jeunes se dirigent vers le « boulevard de la nostalgie » pour se rafraîchir, profiter de la brise marine, bavarder, conclure des affaires ou jouer de la musique. Sur la digue sont assis les amoureux, les esseulés, les marchands, les familles et d'innombrables pêcheurs espérant la bonne prise qui améliorera le dîner. Ils ne peuvent pêcher en mer, car les bateaux sont interdits.

Malecón

Havanna lebt mit dem Gesicht zum Meer. Der Malecón, die 8 km lange, legendäre Uferpromenade zwischen der Altstadt und dem Villenviertel Miramar, ist Lebenslinie, Flaniermeile und öffentliches Wohnzimmer der Stadt. Wenn die Sonne allmählich untergeht, zieht es Jung und Alt zum „Boulevard der Sehnsucht", um abzukühlen, die Meeresbrise zu genießen, zu plaudern, Geschäfte zu verabreden, Musik zu machen. Auf dem Mäuerchen sitzen Verliebte, Einsame, Händler, ganze Familien und zahllose Angler, die auf einen guten Fang für das Abendessen hoffen. Angeln dürfen sie nur von Land aus, Boote sind verboten.

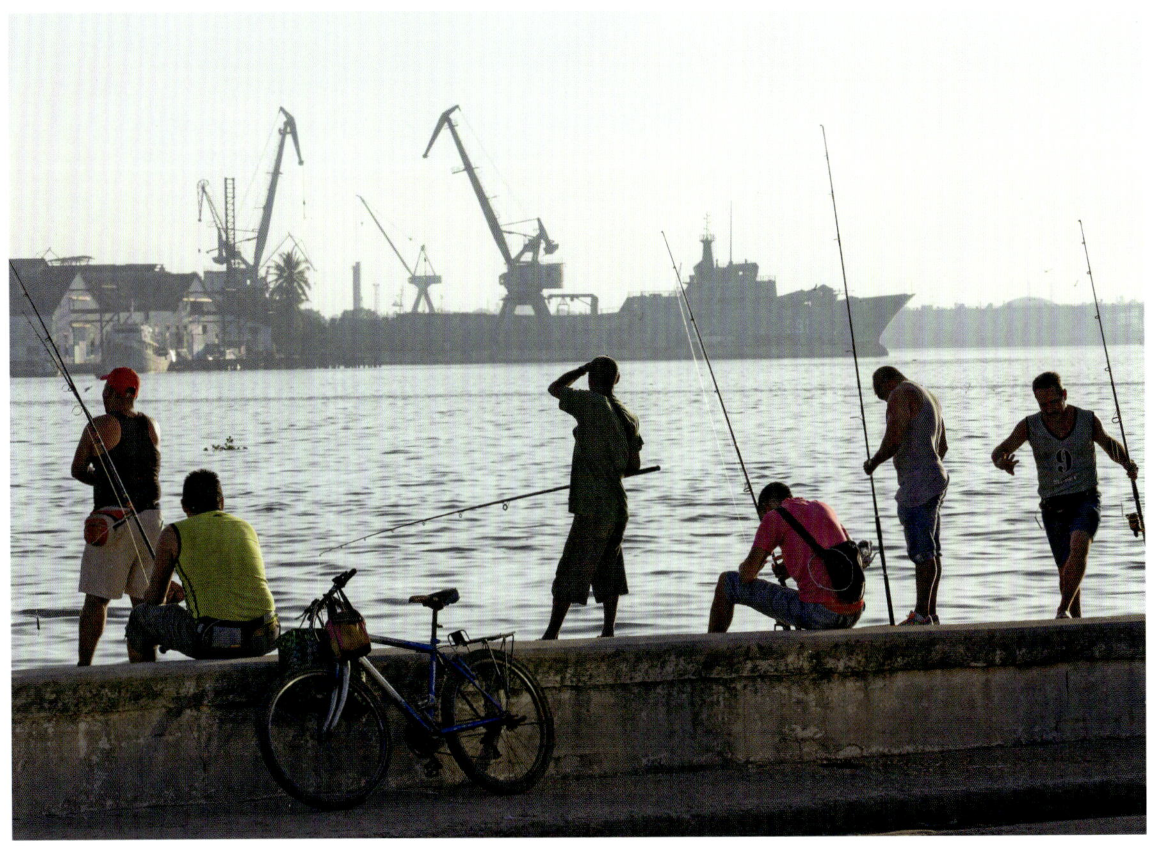

Malecón

Malecón

La Habana vive con su cara al mar. El Malecón, el legendario paseo marítimo de 8 km de largo entre el casco antiguo y el barrio de las villas de Miramar, es la línea de vida, el paseo marítimo y el salón público de la ciudad. Cuando el sol se va poniendo, jóvenes y mayores se sienten atraídos por el "Boulevard de la nostalgia" para refrescarse, disfrutar de la brisa del mar, charlar, hacer negocios o tocar música. En la pequeña pared se sientan amantes, gente solitaria, comerciantes, familias enteras e innumerables pescadores que esperan una buena pesca para la cena. Solo se les permite pescar desde tierra; los barcos están prohibidos.

Malecón

Havana vive com a sua face voltada para o mar. O Malecón, o lendário passeio de 8 km de extensão à beira-mar entre a cidade velha e o distrito de Miramar, é a linha de vida, o passeio e a sala de estar pública da cidade. Quando o sol se põe gradualmente, jovens e velhos são atraídos para a "Avenida da Saudade" para se refrescar, desfrutar da brisa do mar, conversar, organizar negócios e fazer música. Na pequena parede sentam-se amantes, pessoas solitárias, comerciantes, famílias inteiras e inúmeros pescadores, que esperam por uma boa captura para o jantar. Só lhes é permitido pescar em terra, os barcos são proibidos.

Malecón

Havana kijkt uit op de zee. De Malecón, de 8 km lange, legendarische promenade aan het water tussen de oude stad en de villawijk van Miramar, is de levenslijn, de boulevard en de openbare woonkamer van de stad. Wanneer de zon geleidelijk aan ondergaat, worden jong en oud aangetrokken tot de 'Boulevard van verlangen' om af te koelen, te genieten van de zeewind, te kletsen, zaken te regelen, muziek te maken. Op de kleine muur zitten geliefden, eenzame mensen, kooplieden, hele families en talloze vissers die hopen op een goede vangst voor het avondeten. Ze mogen alleen vanaf het land vissen, boten zijn verboden.

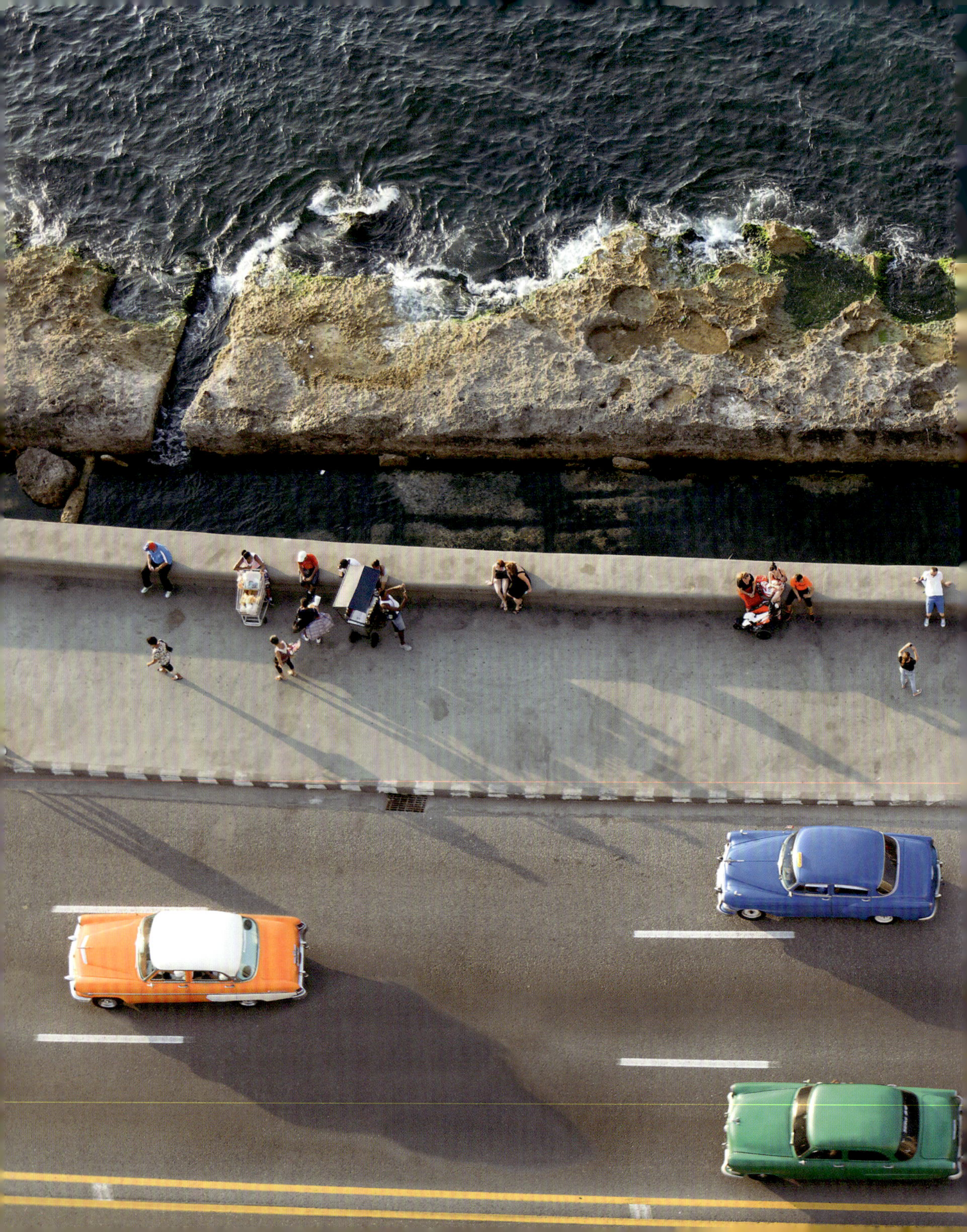

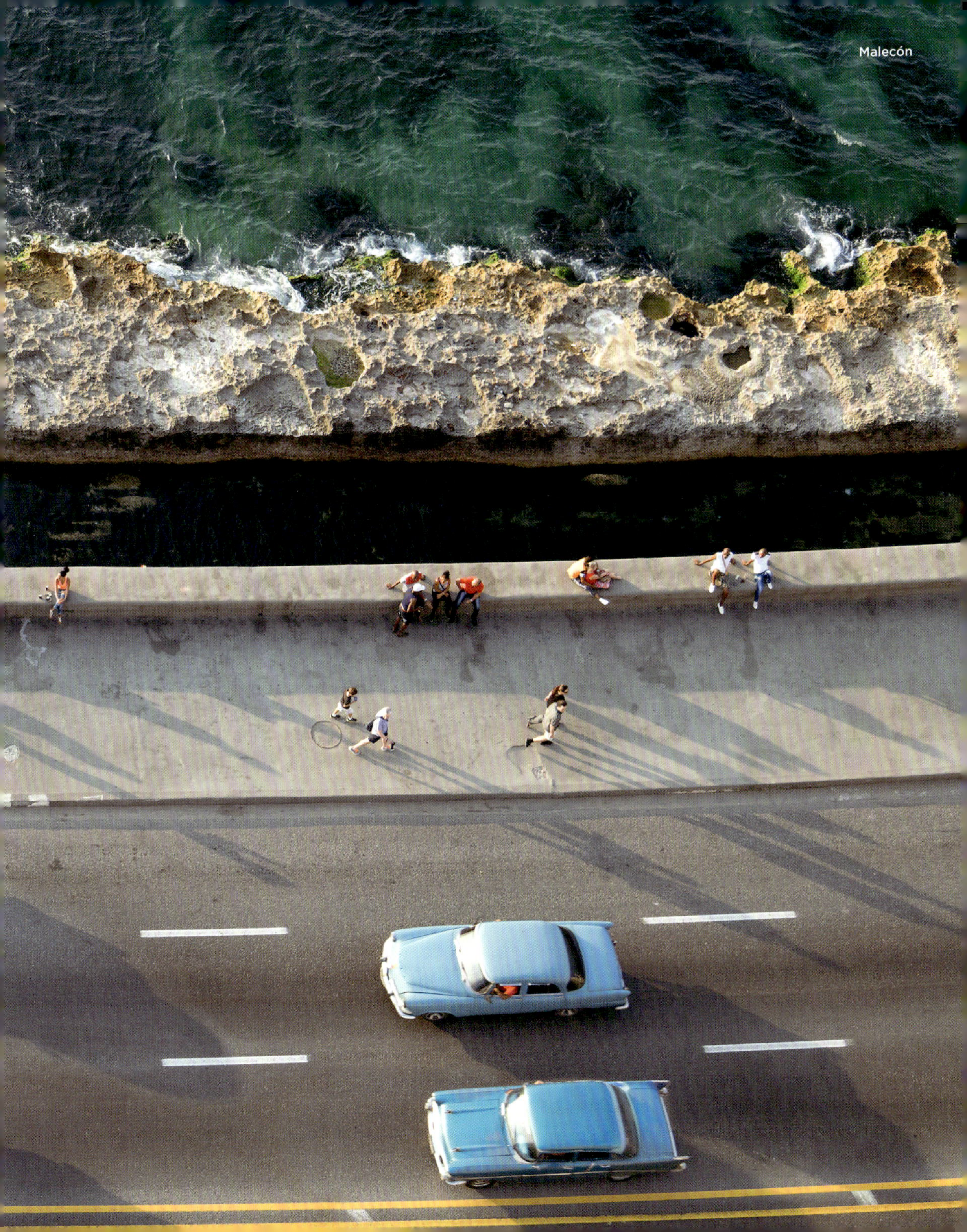
Malecón

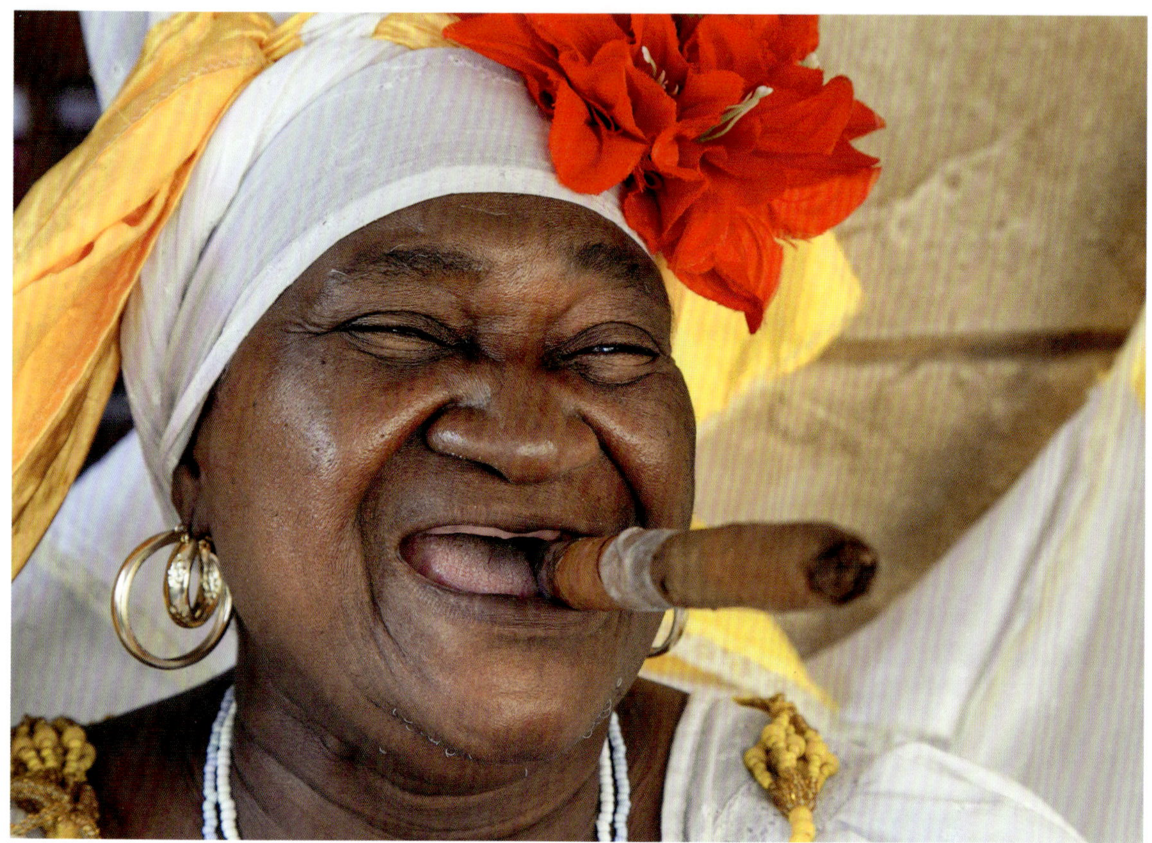

Mujer cubana
Cuban woman

Santería

On the streets of Havana, you can see everywhere white dressed believers from the Afro-Cuban mixed religion Santería. The Santeros believe that every human being is assigned to one of over twenty deities (oríchas), which in colonial times had to be equated with Catholic saints, since the gods of slaves were officially forbidden in Catholic Cuba. The sea goddess Yemayá, known as Virgen de Regla, is Havana's patron saint, and Ochún, goddess of love and mistress of fresh water, is Cuba's patron saint as Virgen del Cobre. Those who are "assigned" to Ochún have yellow attributes, and white chains stand for Obatalá, the god of peace.

Santería

Dans les rues de La Havane, on croise nombre d'adeptes de la religion syncrétique afro-cubaine Santería, vêtus de blanc. Pour les *Santeros,* tout individu est rattaché à l'une des divinités *(oríchas)* d'un panthéon qui en compte plus de vingt. Au cours de la période coloniale, elles ont dû être associées à des saints catholiques, car les dieux des esclaves étaient officiellement interdits. Ainsi, la déesse de la mer, Yemayá, est, en tant que Virgen de Regla, la sainte patronne de La Havane et Ochún, déesse de l'amour et maîtresse des eaux douces, est la Virgen del Cobre, sainte patronne de Cuba. L'adepte « attaché » à Ochún porte des attributs jaunes, celui d'Obatalá, dieu de la paix, des cordons blancs.

Santería

Auf den Straßen Havannas sieht man überall weiß gekleidete Gläubige der afrokubanischen Mischreligion Santería. Die Santeros glauben, dass jeder Mensch einer der über zwanzig Gottheiten *(oríchas)* zugeordnet ist, die in der Kolonialzeit mit katholischen Heiligen gleichgesetzt werden mussten, da die Götter der Sklaven im katholischen Kuba offiziell verboten war. Ihre Meeresgöttin Yemayá ist als Virgen de Regla Schutzherrin Havannas, und Ochún, Liebesgöttin und Herrin des Süßwassers, ist als Virgen del Cobre Patronin Kubas. Wer Ochún „zugeordnet" ist, trägt gelbe Attribute, weiße Ketten stehen für Obatalá, den Friedensgott.

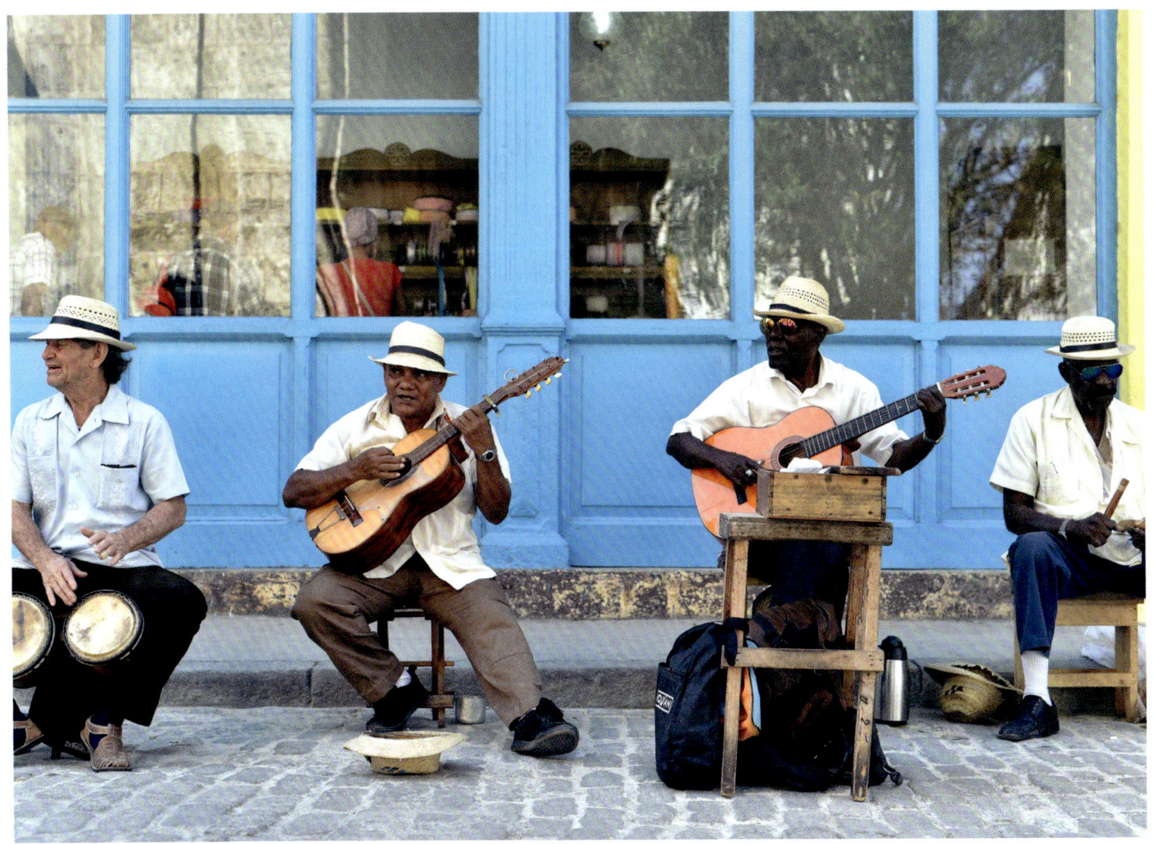

Músicos, La Habana Vieja
Musicians, Old Havana

Santería

En las calles de La Habana se ven por
todas partes creyentes de la Santería de
religión mixta afrocubana vestidos de
blanco. Los santeros creen que todo ser
humano está asignado a una de las más de
veinte deidades *(oríchas)*, que en tiempos
coloniales tenían que ser equiparadas con
santos católicos, ya que los dioses de los
esclavos estaban oficialmente prohibidos
en la Cuba católica. Su diosa marina
Yemayá es la patrona de La Habana como
la Virgen de Regla, y Ochún, diosa del
amor y dueña del agua dulce, es la patrona
de Cuba como la Virgen del Cobre. Los que
están "asignados" a Ochún tienen atributos
amarillos, las cadenas blancas representan
a Obatalá, el dios de la paz.

Santería

Nas ruas de Havana, se vê por toda parte
crentes vestidos de branco da religião
mista afro-cubana Santería. Os Santeros
acreditam que todo ser humano está
influenciado por a uma das mais de vinte
divindades *(oríchas)*, que na era colonial
tiveram que ser equiparadas aos santos
católicos, já que os deuses dos escravos na
Cuba católica eram oficialmente proibidos.
Sua deusa do mar Iemanjá (Yemayá em
Cuba) é a santa padroeira de Havana
como "Virgen de Regla", e Oxum, deusa
do amor e senhora da água doce, é a
santa padroeira de Cuba como "Virgen del
Cobre". Aqueles que são "influenciados"
por Oxum usam atributos amarelos,
correntes brancas representam Obatalá, o
deus da paz.

Santería

In de straten van Havana, ziet men overal
witte geklede gelovigen van de Afro-
Cubaanse gemengde Santería religie.
De Santeros geloven dat ieder mens is
toegewezen aan een van de meer dan
twintig godheden *(oríchas)*, die in de
koloniale tijd gelijkgesteld moesten worden
met katholieke heiligen, omdat de goden
van de slaven officieel verboden waren
in het katholieke Cuba. Haar zeegodin
Yemayá is Havana's beschermheilige als
Virgen de Regla, en Ochún, godin van de
liefde en minnares van zoet water, is Cuba's
beschermheilige als Virgen del Cobre.
Degenen die 'toegewezen' zijn aan Ochún
hebben gele attributen, witte kettingen
staan voor Obatalá, de god van de vrede.

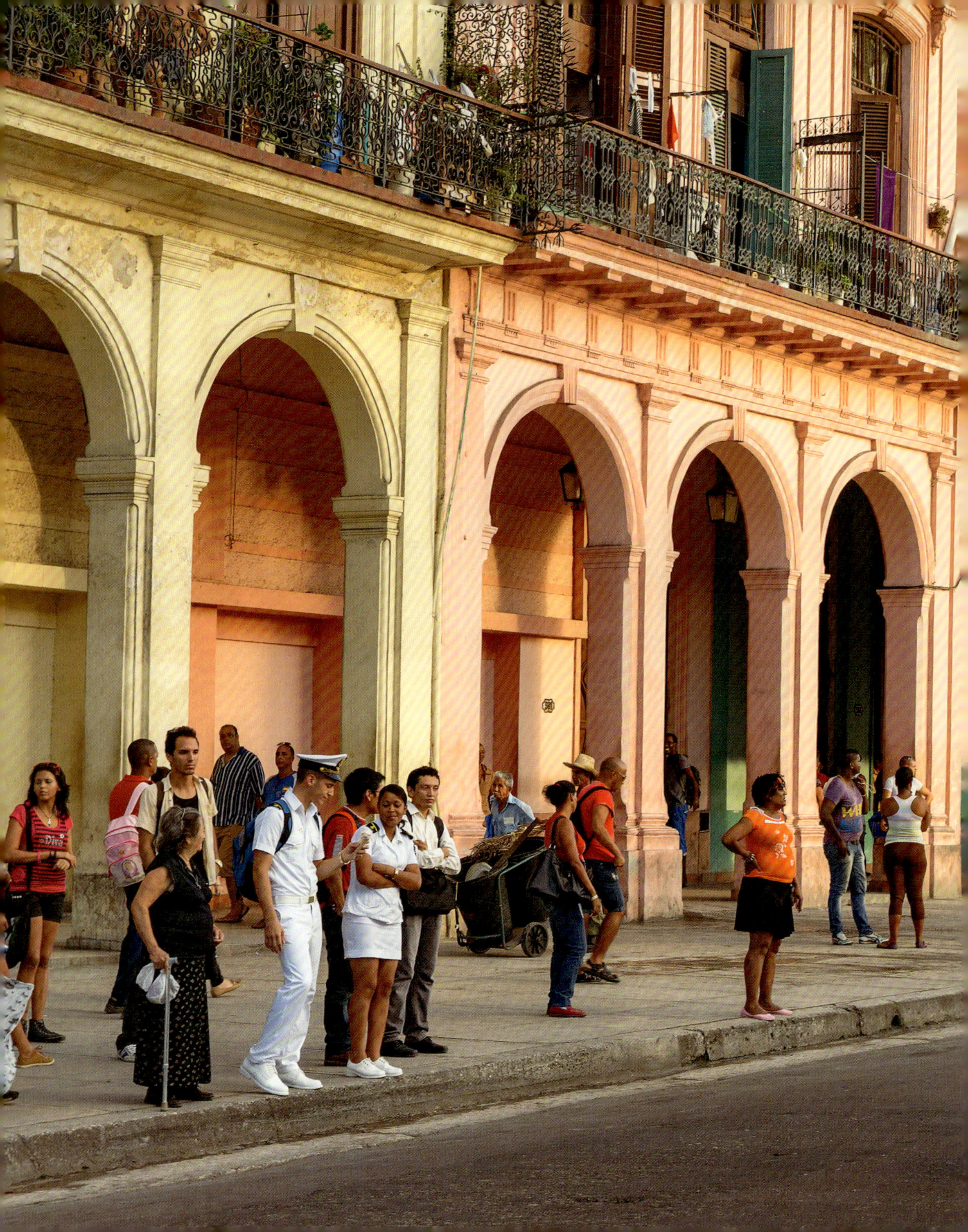

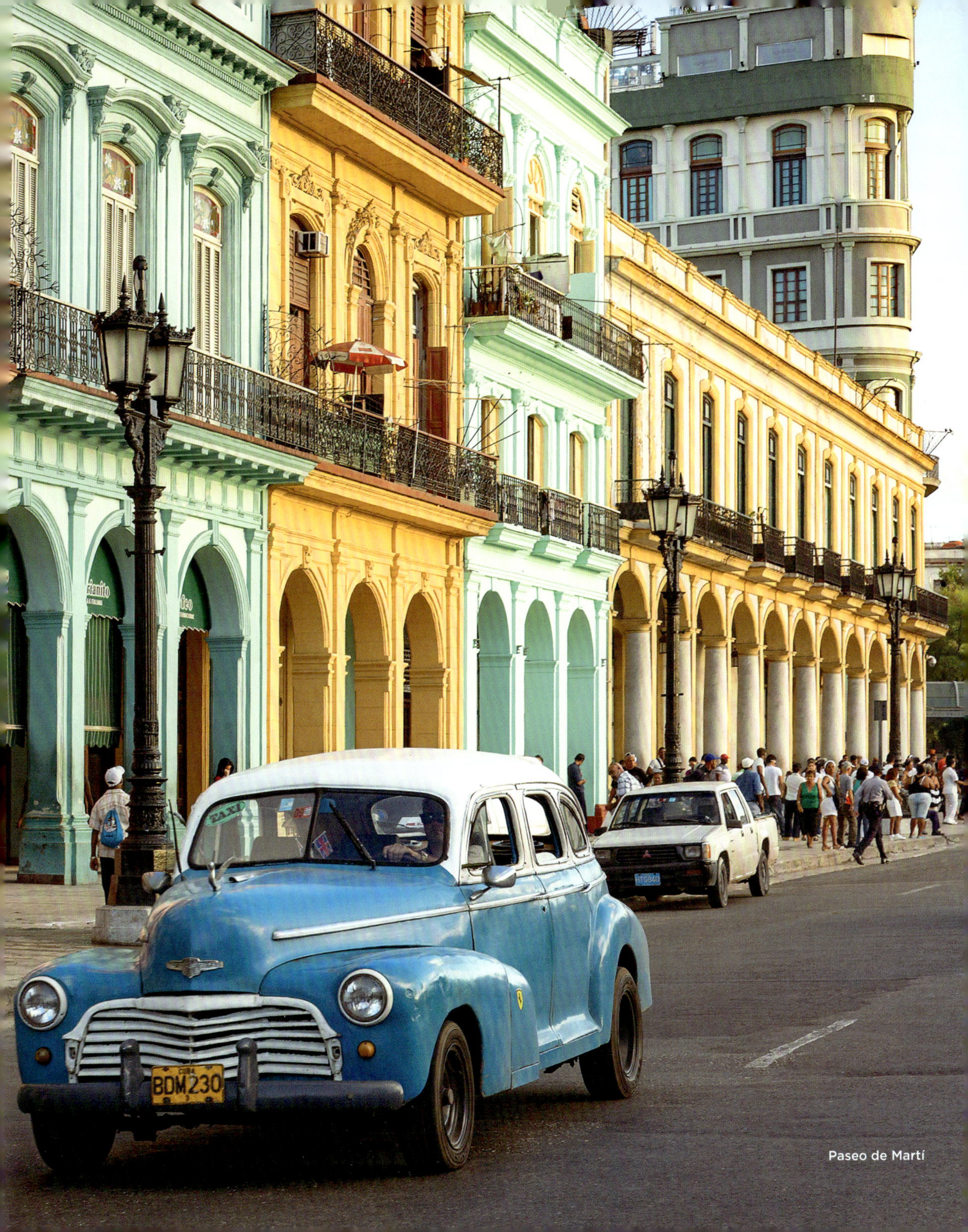

Paseo de Martí

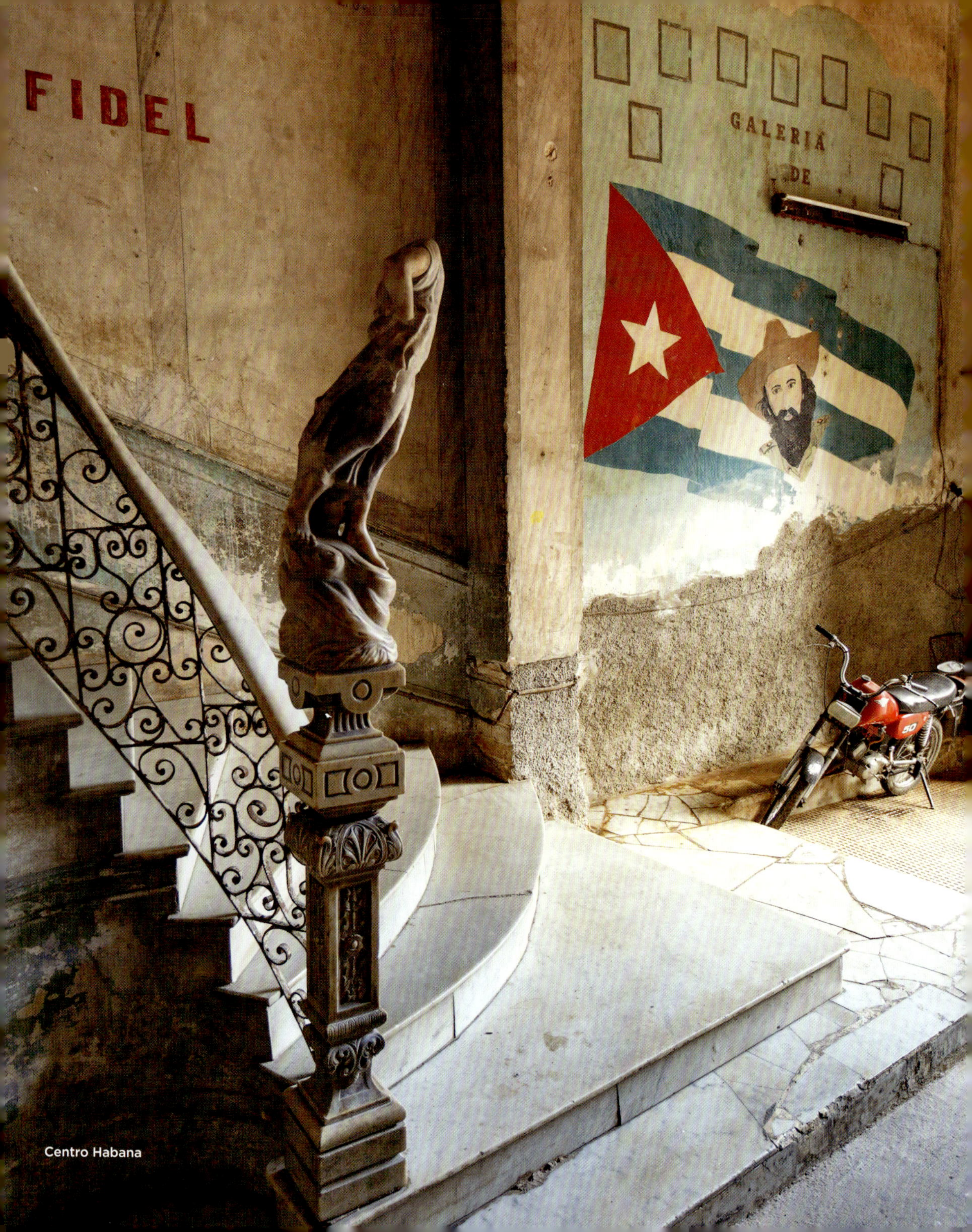

Centro Habana

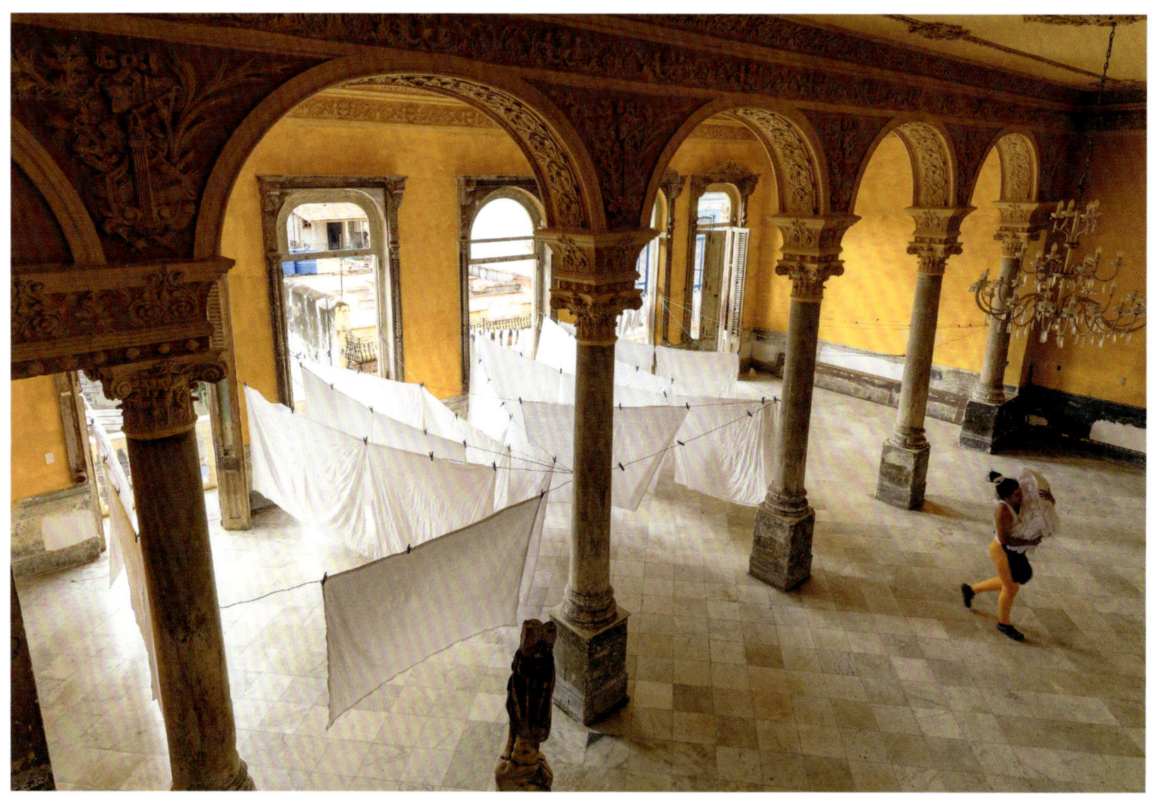

Centro Habana

La Guarida in Centro Habana

Cuba's most famous private restaurant
is popular with artists, royalty and
international jet setters. It is located on
the top floor of a once luxurious manor
house that has become a residential
building, which explains the laundry in
the marble entrance hall. Tomás Gutiérrez
Alea shot his film classic *Strawberry and
Chocolate* here.

La Guarida à Centro Habana

Le restaurant privé le plus célèbre de
Cuba est apprécié des artistes, des têtes
couronnées et de la jet-set du monde
entier. Il occupe le dernier étage d'une
maison de maître autrefois somptueuse,
qui fut transformée en immeuble
d'habitation, ce qui explique la présence
de linge séchant dans le hall d'entrée en
marbre. C'est ici que Tomás Gutiérrez Alea
tourna *Fraise et Chocolat,* film devenu
un classique.

La Guarida in Centro Habana

Das berühmteste Privatrestaurant Kubas ist
beliebt bei Künstlern, gekrönten Häuptern
und beim internationalen Jetset. Es liegt in
der oberen Etage eines ehemals luxuriösen
Herrenhauses, aus dem ein Wohnhaus
wurde, was die Wäsche in der marmornen
Eingangshalle erklärt. Hier drehte Tomás
Gutiérrez Alea seinen Filmklassiker *Erdbeer
und Schokolade.*

La Guarida en el Centro Habana

El restaurante privado más famoso de
Cuba es popular entre los artistas, la
Realeza y la jet set internacional. Está
situado en el último piso de una antigua
casa señorial de lujo, que se ha convertido
en un edificio residencial, lo que explica la
lavandería en el vestíbulo de entrada de
mármol. Aquí Tomás Gutiérrez Alea rodó la
clásica película *Fresa y chocolate.*

La Guarida no Centro Habana

O restaurante privado mais famoso de
Cuba é popular entre os artistas, a realeza
e o jet set internacional. Ele está localizado
no último andar de uma casa senhorial
outrora luxuosa, que se tornou um
edifício residencial, o que explica a roupa
estendida no hall de entrada de mármore.
Aqui Tomás Gutiérrez Alea filmou seu
clássico *Morango e chocolate.*

La Guarida in Centro Habana

Cuba's beroemdste privé-restaurant is
populair bij kunstenaars, vorsten en de
internationale jetset. Het is gelegen op de
bovenste verdieping van een ooit luxueuze
herenhuis, dat is uitgegroeid tot een
residentieel gebouw, wat ook de wasserij
in de marmeren foyer verklaart. Hier heeft
Tomás Gutiérrez Alea zijn filmklassieker
Fresa y chocolate opgenomen.

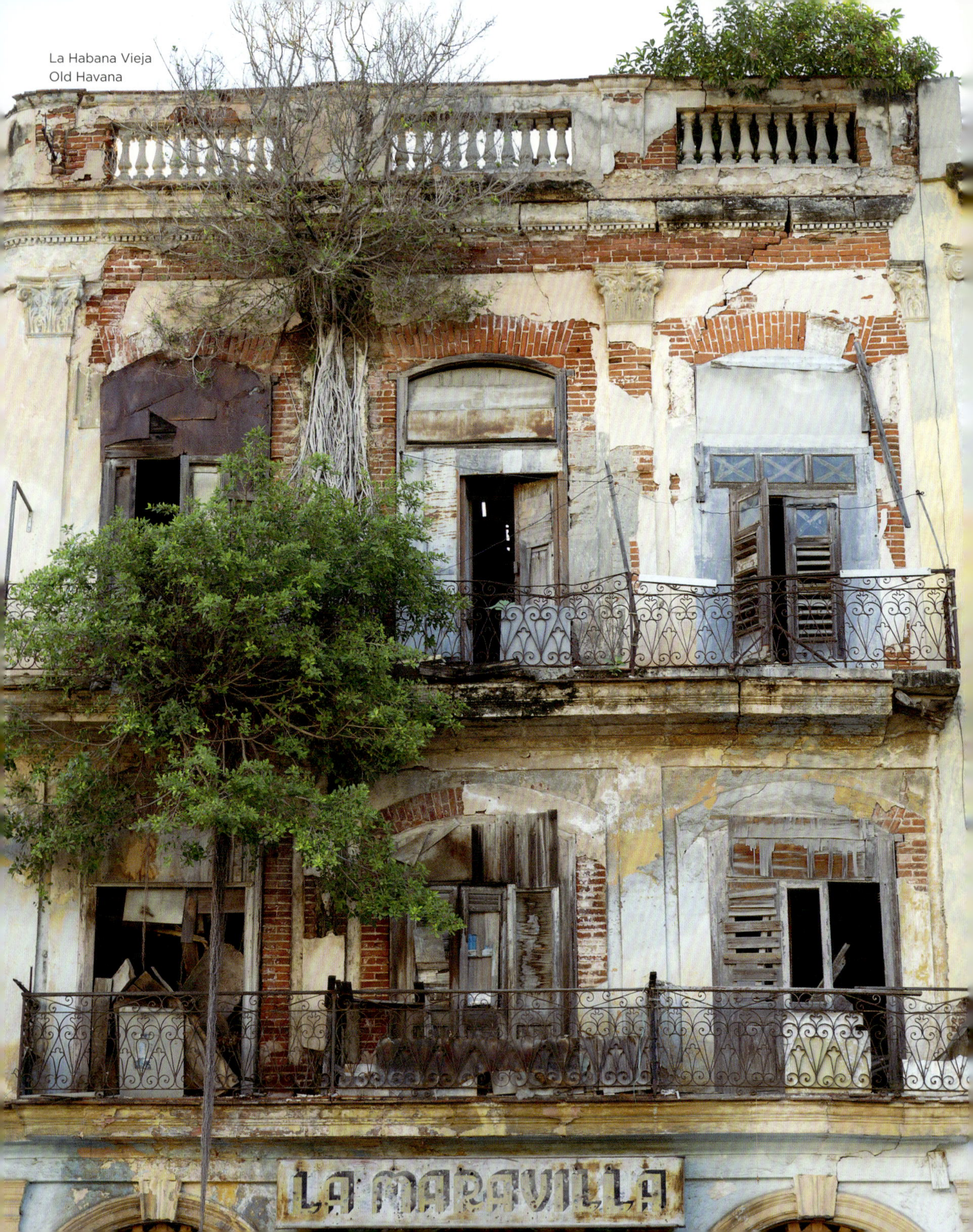
La Habana Vieja
Old Havana
LA MARAVILLA

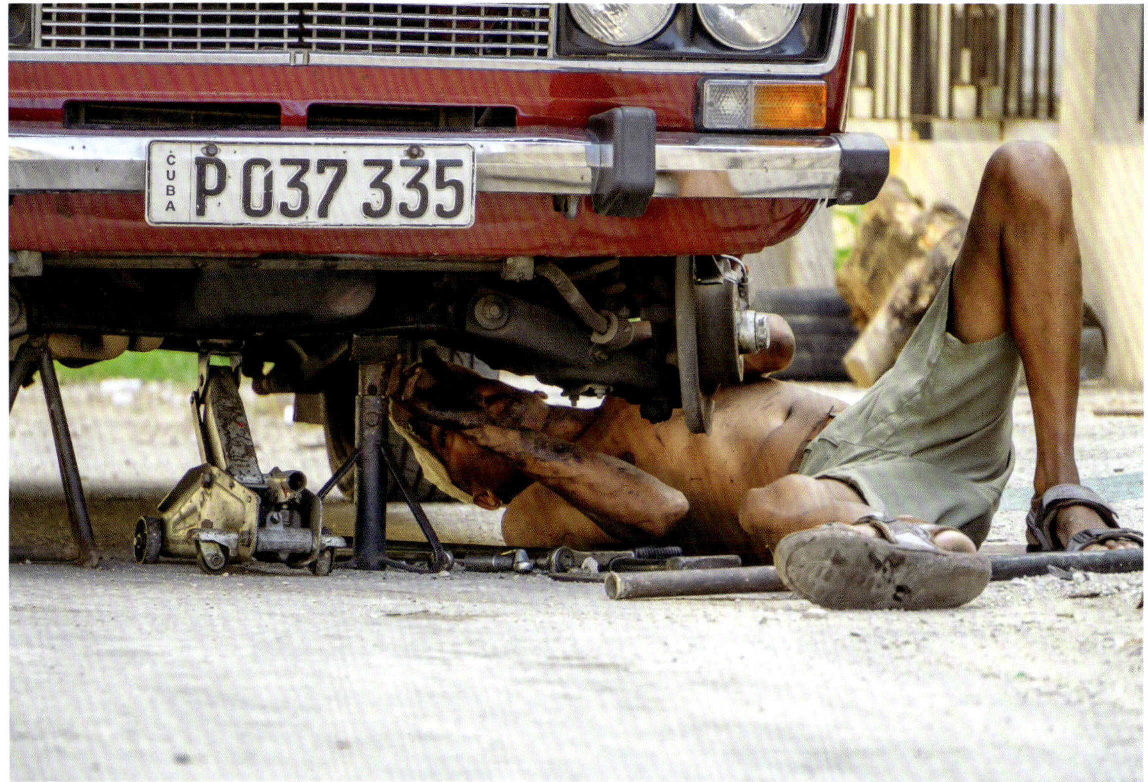

La Habana Vieja
Old Havana

The Battle Against Decay

Havana has been struggling against decay, often in vain. Whole streets in Centro Habana are threatened by collapse, as are many houses in the districts *(barrios)* such as Luyanó or Santos Suárez that are less frequented by tourists. As poetic as they may seem at first sight, the many ruins are not very enchanting for their inhabitants.

Lucha contra el deterioro

La Habana lucha con esfuerzo y a menudo en vano contra el deterioro. Calles enteras en Centro Habana están amenazadas por el colapso, al igual que muchas casas en los barrios menos frecuentados como Luyanó o Santos Suárez. Las numerosas ruinas, por muy poéticas que parezcan a simple vista, no son muy encantadoras para sus habitantes.

Lutter contre la décrépitude

La Havane lutte laborieusement et souvent en vain contre la décrépitude. Des rues entières de Centro Habana sont menacées d'effondrement, tout comme de nombreuses maisons des quartiers *(barrios)* peu fréquentés par les touristes, tels que Luyanó ou Santos Suárez. Les nombreuses ruines, si elles peuvent paraître formidablement poétiques à première vue, n'ont pas grand-chose d'enchanteur pour leurs habitants.

Luta contra a decadência

Havana luta laboriosamente, e muitas vezes em vão, contra a decadência. Ruas inteiras no Centro de Habana estão ameaçadas de colapso, assim como muitas casas nos bairros menos frequentados pelos turistas, como Luyanó ou Santos Suárez. As muitas ruínas, por mais poéticas que possam parecer à primeira vista, não são muito encantadoras para os seus habitantes.

Kampf gegen den Verfall

Havanna kämpft mühsam und oft vergeblich gegen den Verfall. Ganze Straßenzüge in Centro Habana sind vom Einsturz bedroht, ebenso viele Häuser in den wenig von Touristen frequentierten Vierteln *(barrios)* wie Luyanó oder Santos Suárez. Die vielen Ruinen, so poetisch sie auch auf den ersten Blick wirken mögen, sind für ihre Bewohner wenig zauberhaft.

Gevecht tegen verval

Havana worstelt moeizaam en vaak tevergeefs tegen verval. Hele straten in Centro Habana dreigen in te storten, net als veel huizen in de minder bezochte wijken *(barrios)* zoals Luyanó of Santos Suárez. De vele ruïnes, hoe poëtisch ze op het eerste gezicht ook lijken, zijn niet erg betoverend voor hun inwoners.

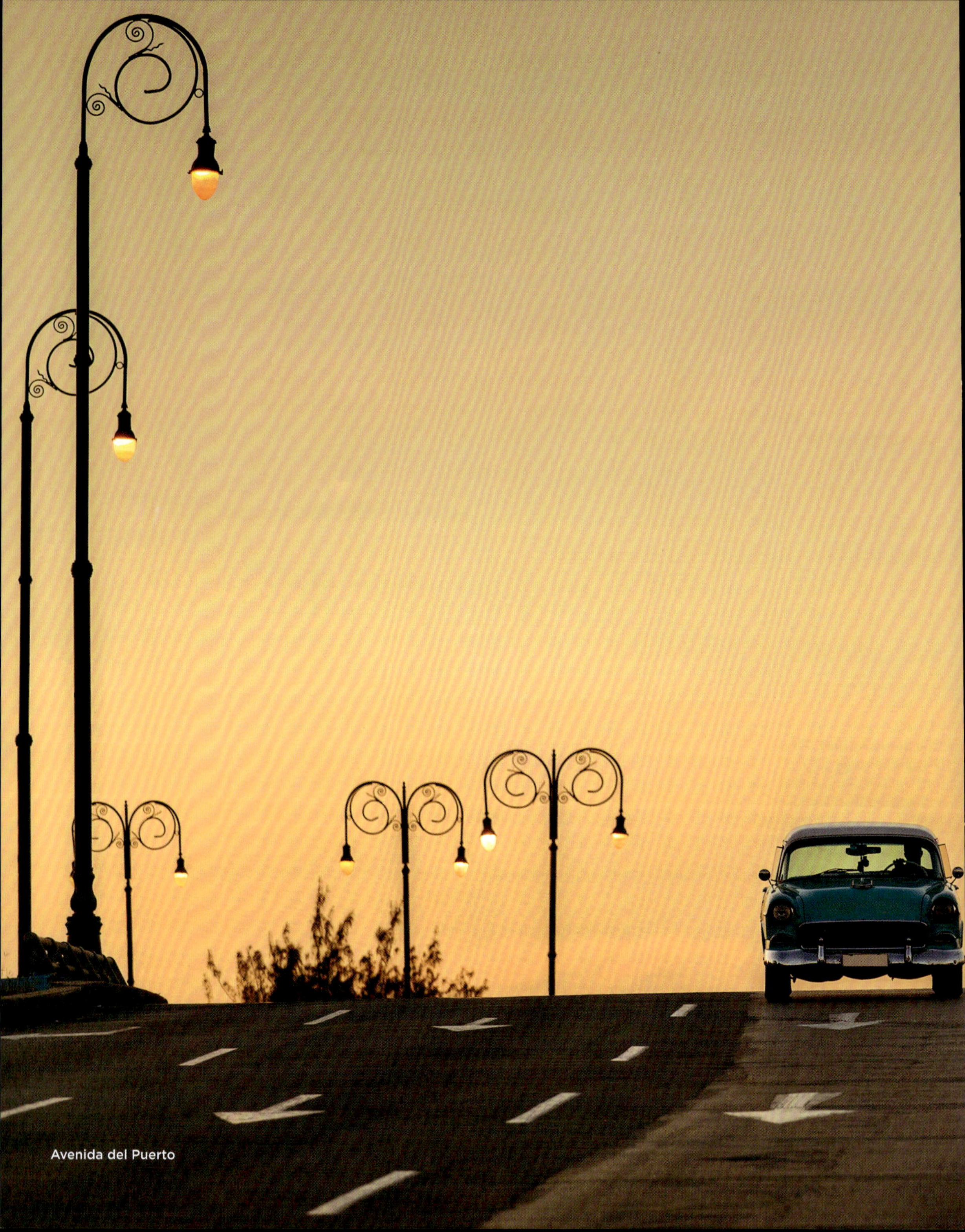
Avenida del Puerto

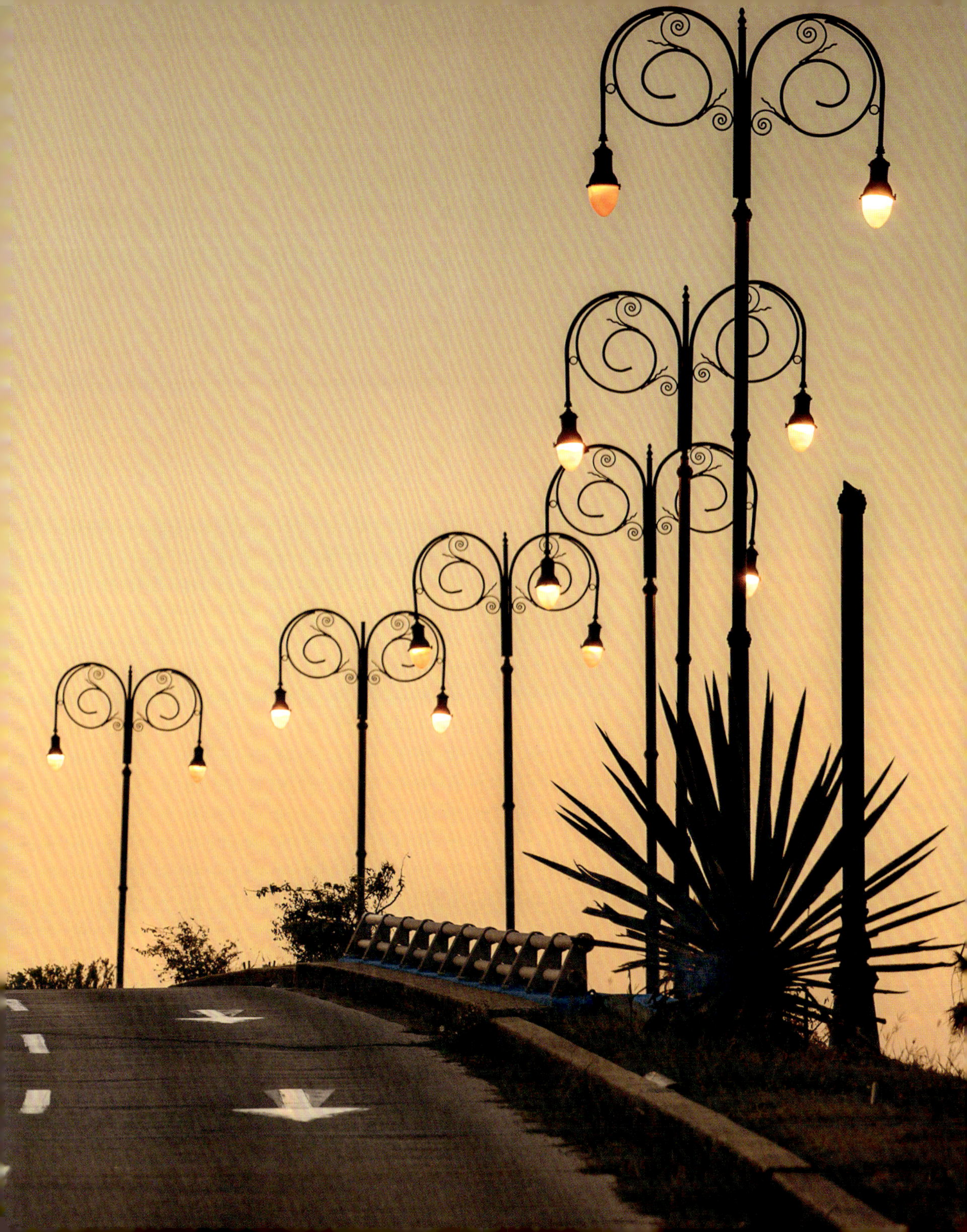

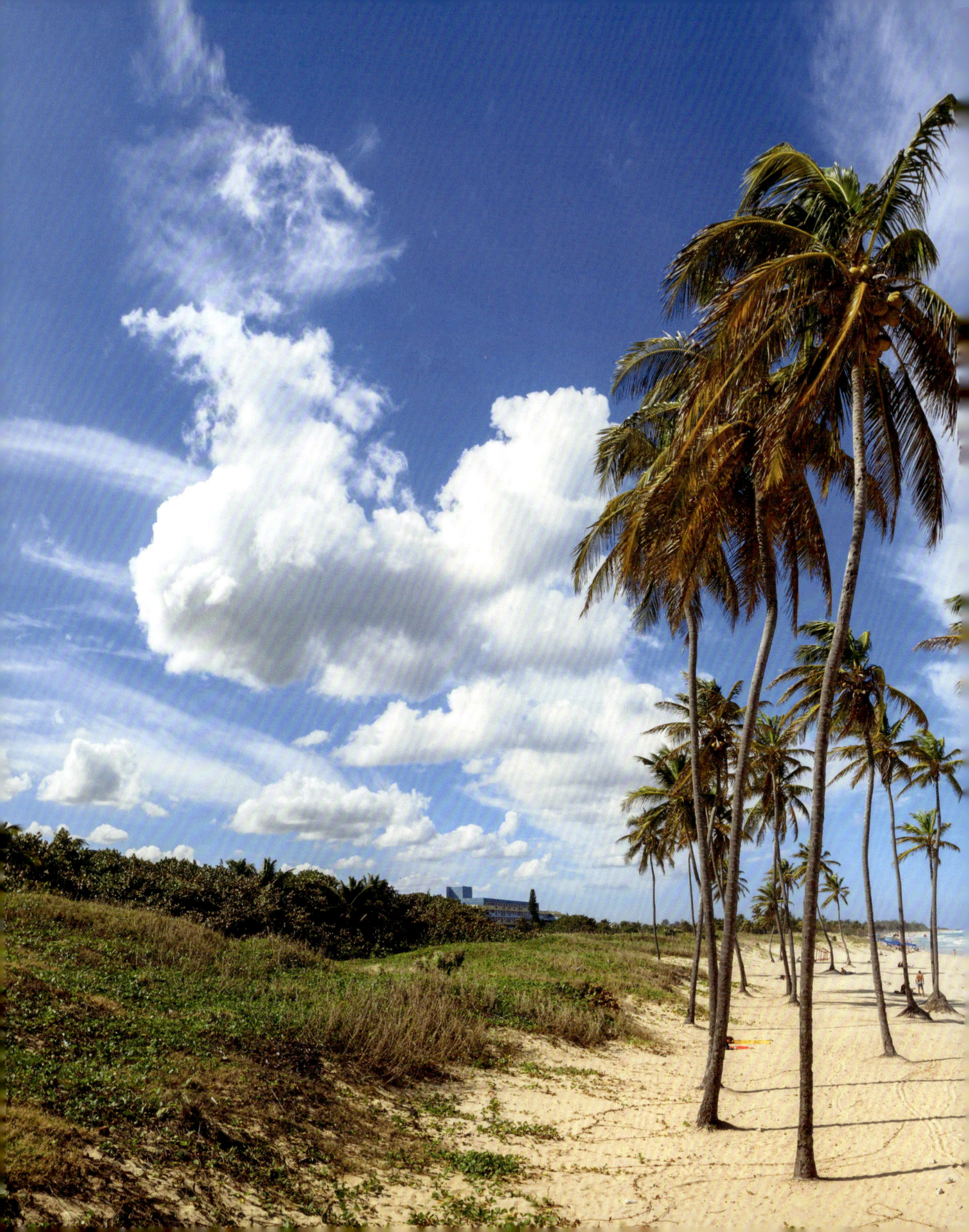

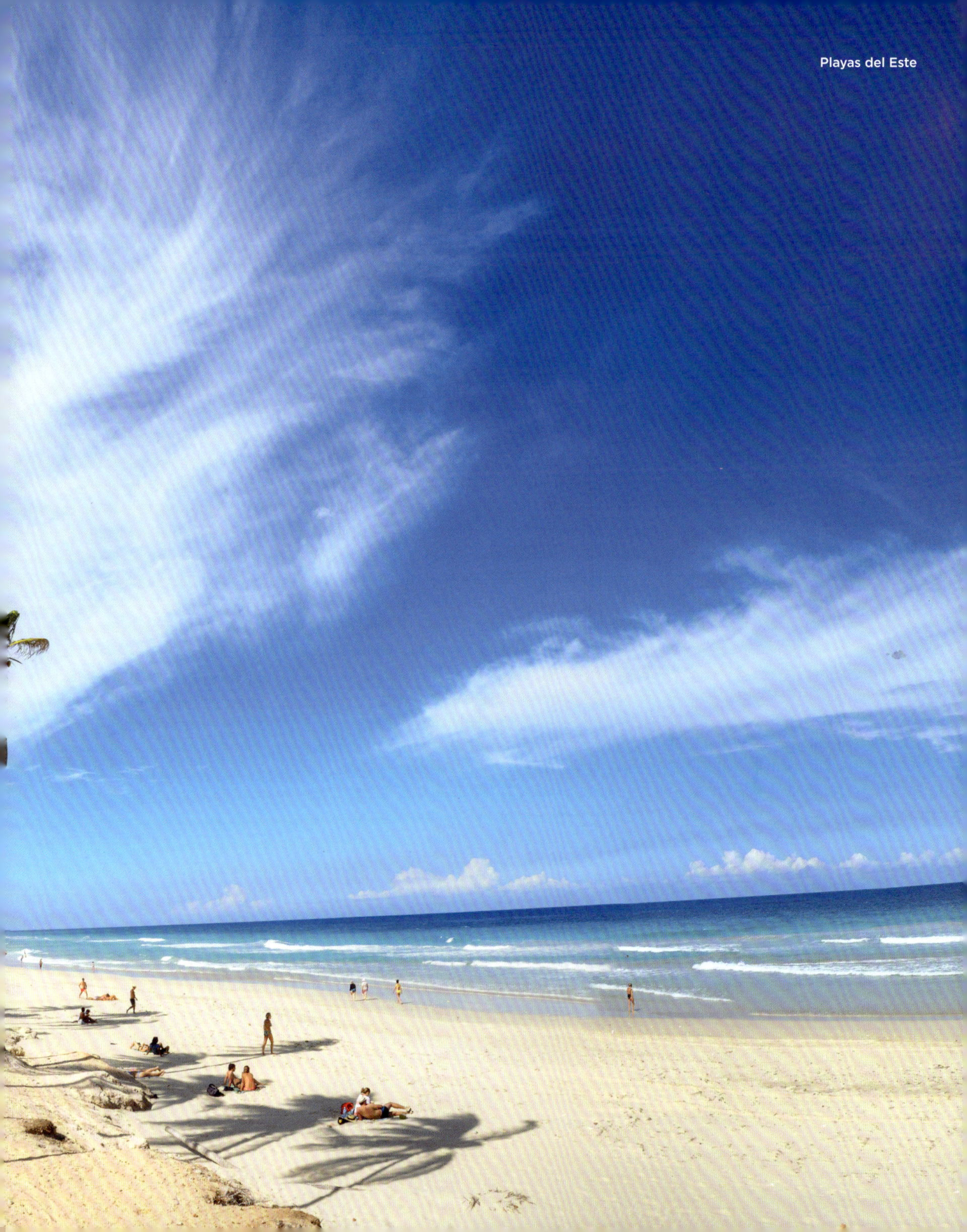
Playas del Este

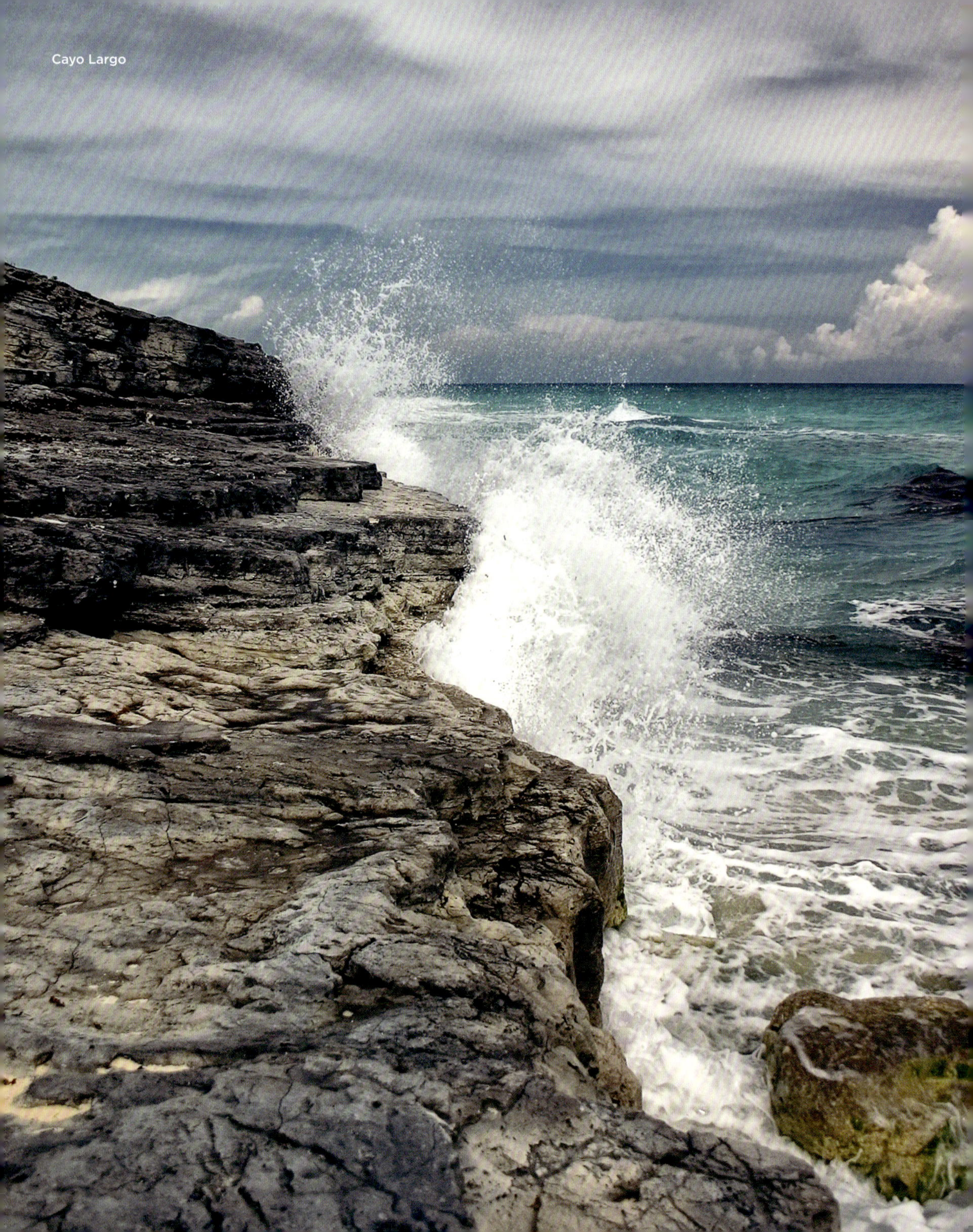
Cayo Largo

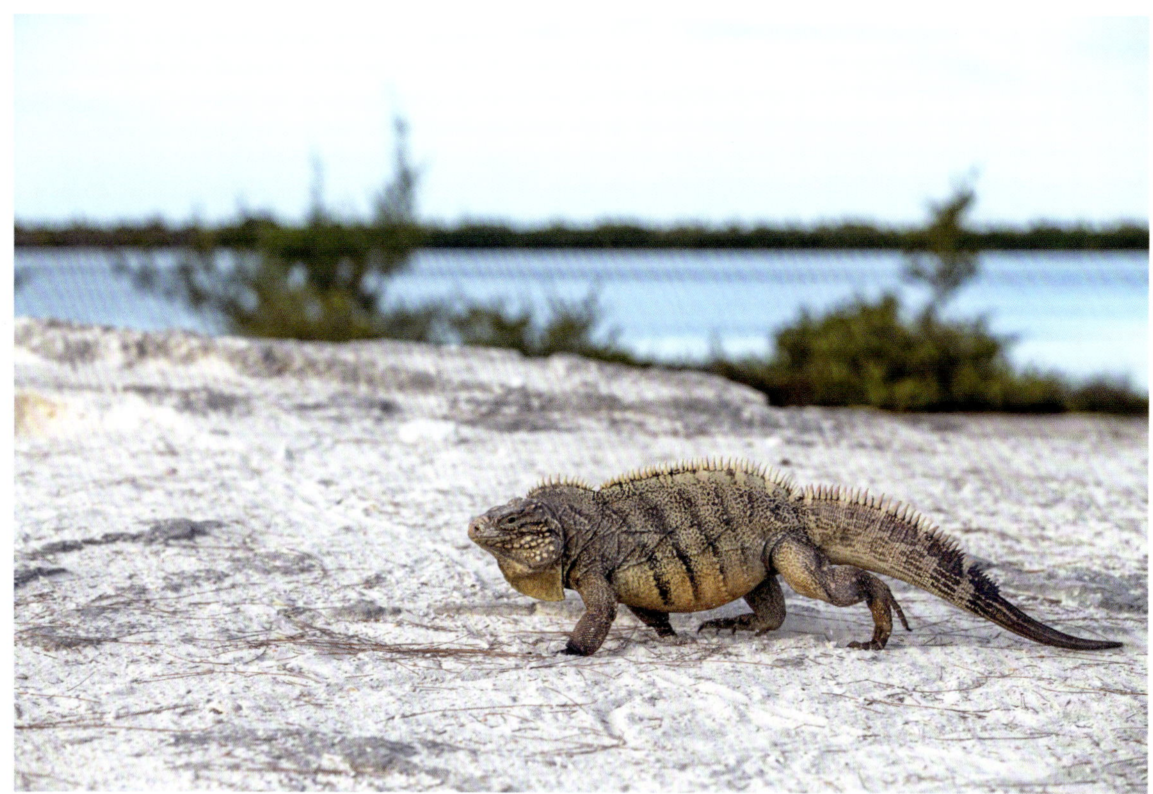

Iguana, Cayo Largo

Cayo Largo

Cayo Largo belongs to the archipelago Los Canarreos, which lies to the south of the main island and consists essentially of a 25 km (15 mi.) long and 3 km (1.8 mi.) wide icing sugar white sandy beach—a natural paradise. Between April and December, various species of turtles lay their eggs on Playa Tortuga, and hundreds of iguanas live on the tiny neighboring island of Cayo Iguana.

Cayo Largo

Cayo Largo pertenece al archipiélago de Los Canarreos, al sur de la isla principal, y consiste principalmente en una playa de arena blanca como el azúcar de 25 km de largo y 3 km de ancho: un paraíso natural. En Playa Tortuga, entre abril y diciembre, varias especies de tortugas ponen sus huevos, y cientos de iguanas viven en la pequeña isla vecina de Cayo Iguana.

Cayo Largo

Cayo Largo est un îlot de l'archipel Los Canarreos, situé au sud de son île principale. Il est essentiellement constitué d'une plage de sable fin blanc de 25 km de long et 3 km de large. Dans ce paradis naturel, entre avril et décembre, diverses espèces de tortues viennent pondre sur la Playa Tortuga, alors que le minuscule îlot voisin, Cayo Iguana, abrite des centaines de reptiles.

Cayo Largo

Cayo Largo pertence ao arquipélago de Los Canarreos, ao sul da ilha principal e consiste essencialmente de uma praia de areia branca como açúcar em pó de 25 km de comprimento e 3 km de largura – um paraíso natural. Na Playa Tortuga, entre abril e dezembro, várias espécies de tartarugas desovam e centenas de iguanas vivem na pequena ilha vizinha de Cayo Iguana.

Cayo Largo

Cayo Largo gehört zum Archipel Los Canarreos südlich der Hauptinsel und besteht im Wesentlichen aus einem 25 km langen und 3 km breiten puderzuckerweißen Sandstrand – ein Naturparadies. An der Playa Tortuga legen zwischen April und Dezember verschiedene Schildkrötenarten ihre Eier ab, und auf der winzigen Nachbarinsel Cayo Iguana leben hunderte Leguane.

Cayo Largo

Cayo Largo behoort tot de archipel Los Canarreos ten zuiden van het hoofdeiland en bestaat voornamelijk uit een 25 km lang en 3 km breed zandstrand zo wit als talkpoeder – een natuurlijk paradijs. Op Playa Tortuga leggen tussen april en december verschillende soorten schildpadden hun eieren, en op het kleine eilandje Cayo Iguana leven honderden leguanen.

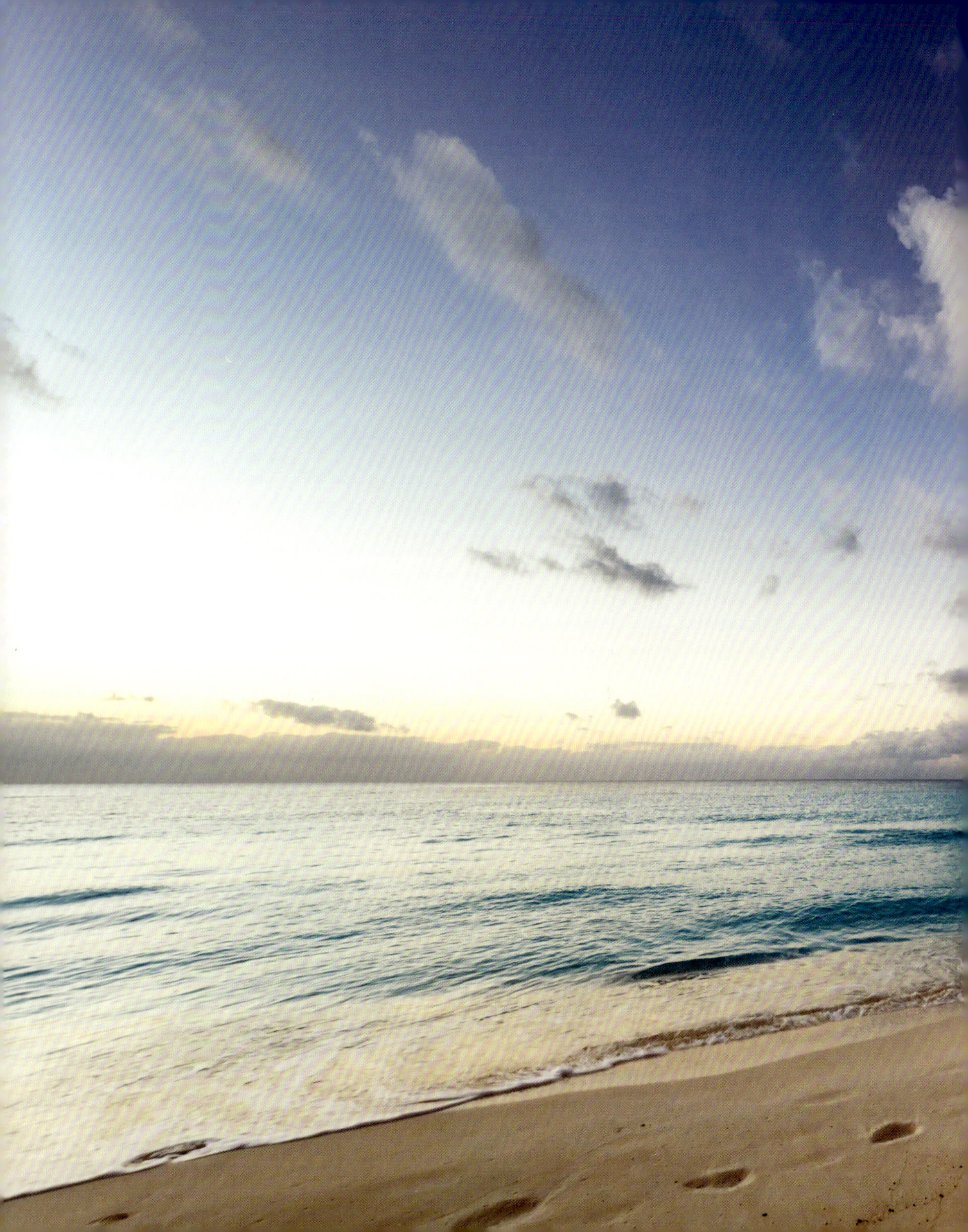

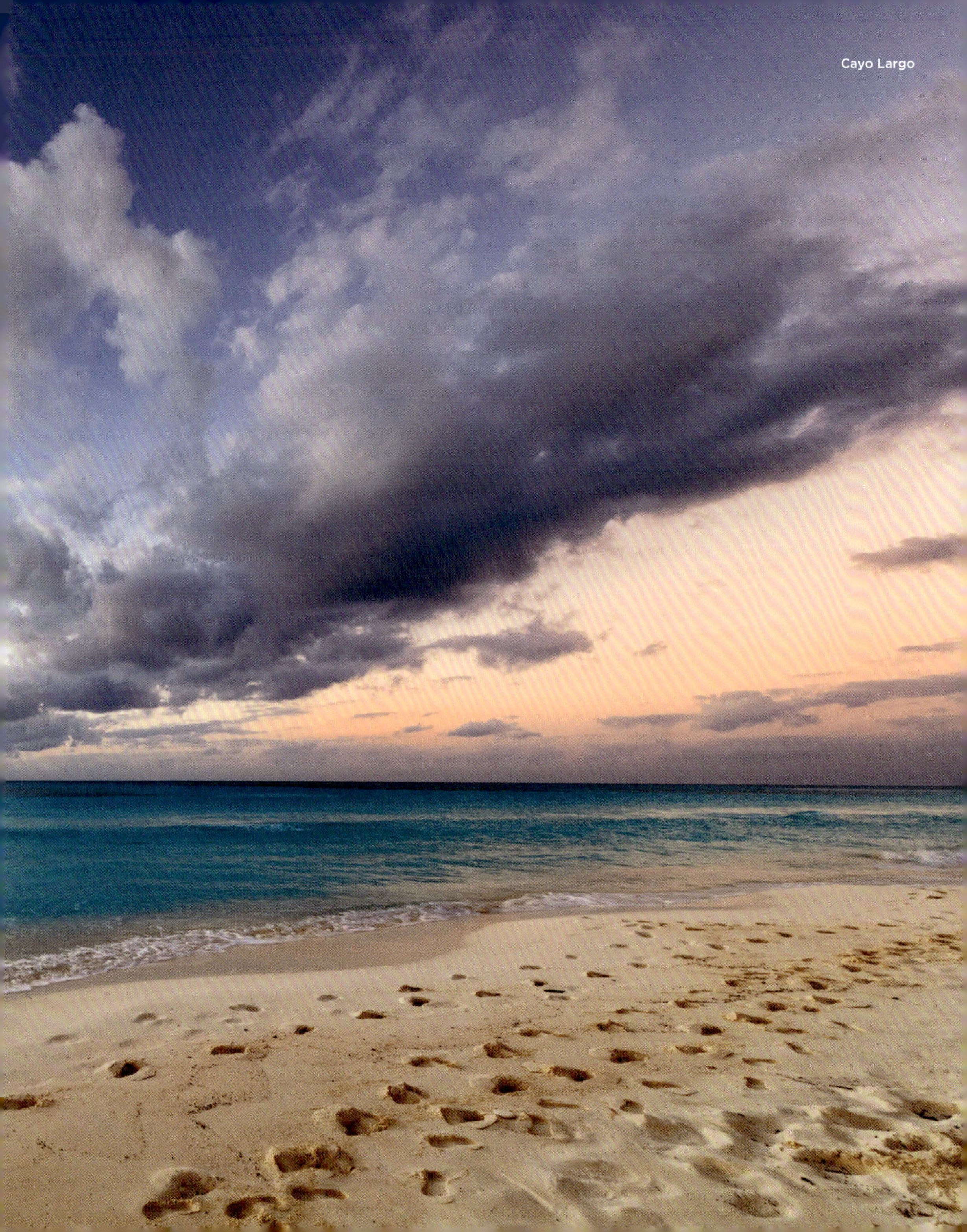
Cayo Largo

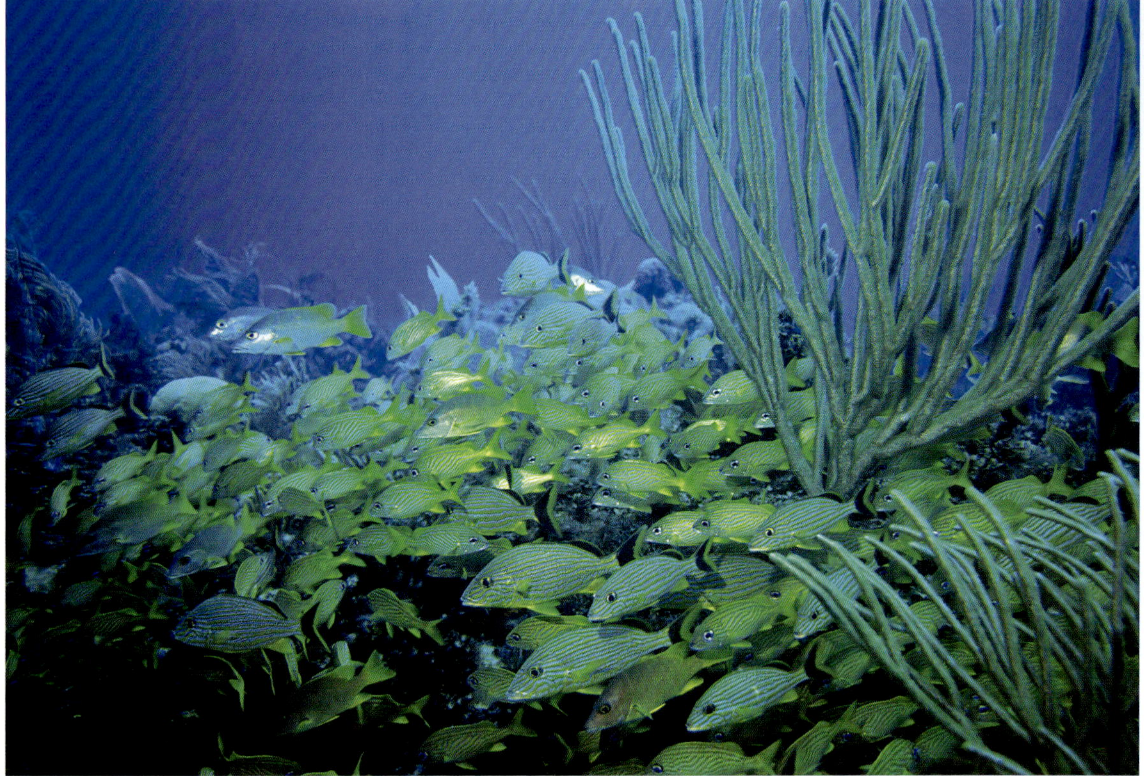

Haemulon sciurus, Cayo Largo
Blue striped grunt, Cayo Largo

Underwater World off Cayo Largo

The coral reefs and wreckage of sunken ships off Cayo Largo are a hotspot for divers, and the underwater world rich in sea life by Playa Sirena is one of the best preserved in the world. However, one problem is the bizarre, poisonous lionfish that originate from the Red Sea and the Indian Ocean, and are displacing the native fish species.

Le monde sous-marin de Cayo Largo

Les récifs coralliens et les épaves des navires ayant sombré au large de Cayo Largo en font un haut lieu de la plongée, alors que le monde sous-marin et la riche faune de la Playa Sirena comptent parmi les mieux préservés du monde. Toutefois, l'arrivée de rascasses volantes venimeuses, originaires de la mer Rouge et de l'océan Indien, menace aujourd'hui les espèces locales.

Unterwasserwelt vor Cayo Largo

Die Korallenriffe und Wrackteile gesunkener Schiffe vor Cayo Largo sind ein Hotspot für Taucher, und die fischreiche Unterwasserwelt vor Playa Sirena gehört zu den am besten erhaltenen weltweit. Ein Problem sind allerdings die bizarren, giftigen Rotfeuerfische, die aus dem Roten Meer und dem Indischen Ozean kommen und die heimischen Fischarten verdrängen.

Mundo submarino frente a Cayo Largo

Los arrecifes de coral y los restos de naufragios de barcos hundidos en Cayo Largo son un punto importante para los buceadores, y el rico mundo submarino de peces en Playa Sirena es uno de los mejor conservados del mundo. Un problema, sin embargo, es el extraño y venenoso pez león colorado que viene del Mar Rojo y del Océano Índico y echa a las especies de peces nativas.

Mundo submarino em frente a Cayo Largo

Os recifes de corais e partes naufragadas de navios afundados em Cayo Largo são um hotspot para mergulhadores, e o mundo subaquático rico em peixes da Playa Sirena é um dos mais bem preservados do mundo. Um problema, no entanto, é o bizarro e venenoso peixe-leão que vem do Mar Vermelho e do Oceano Índico e expulsa as espécies nativas de peixes.

Onderwaterwereld Cayo Largo

De koraalriffen en wrakstukken van gezonken schepen voor de kust van Cayo Largo zijn een hotspot voor duikers, en de visrijke onderwaterwereld voor de kust van Playa Sirena is een van de best bewaarde ter wereld. Een probleem is echter de bizarre, giftige koraalduivels die uit de Rode Zee en de Indische Oceaan afkomstig zijn en de inheemse vissoorten verdringen.

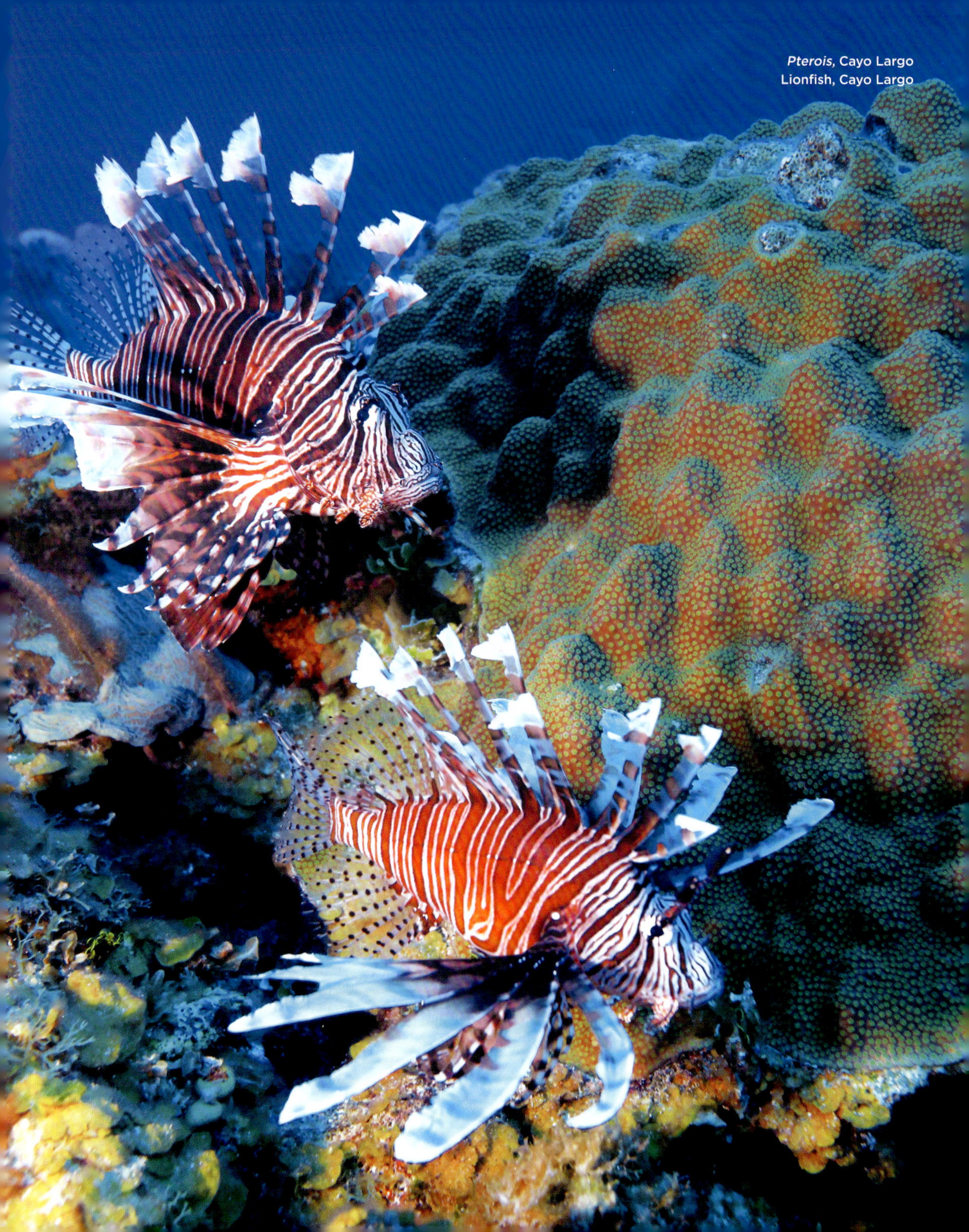

Pterois, Cayo Largo
Lionfish, Cayo Largo

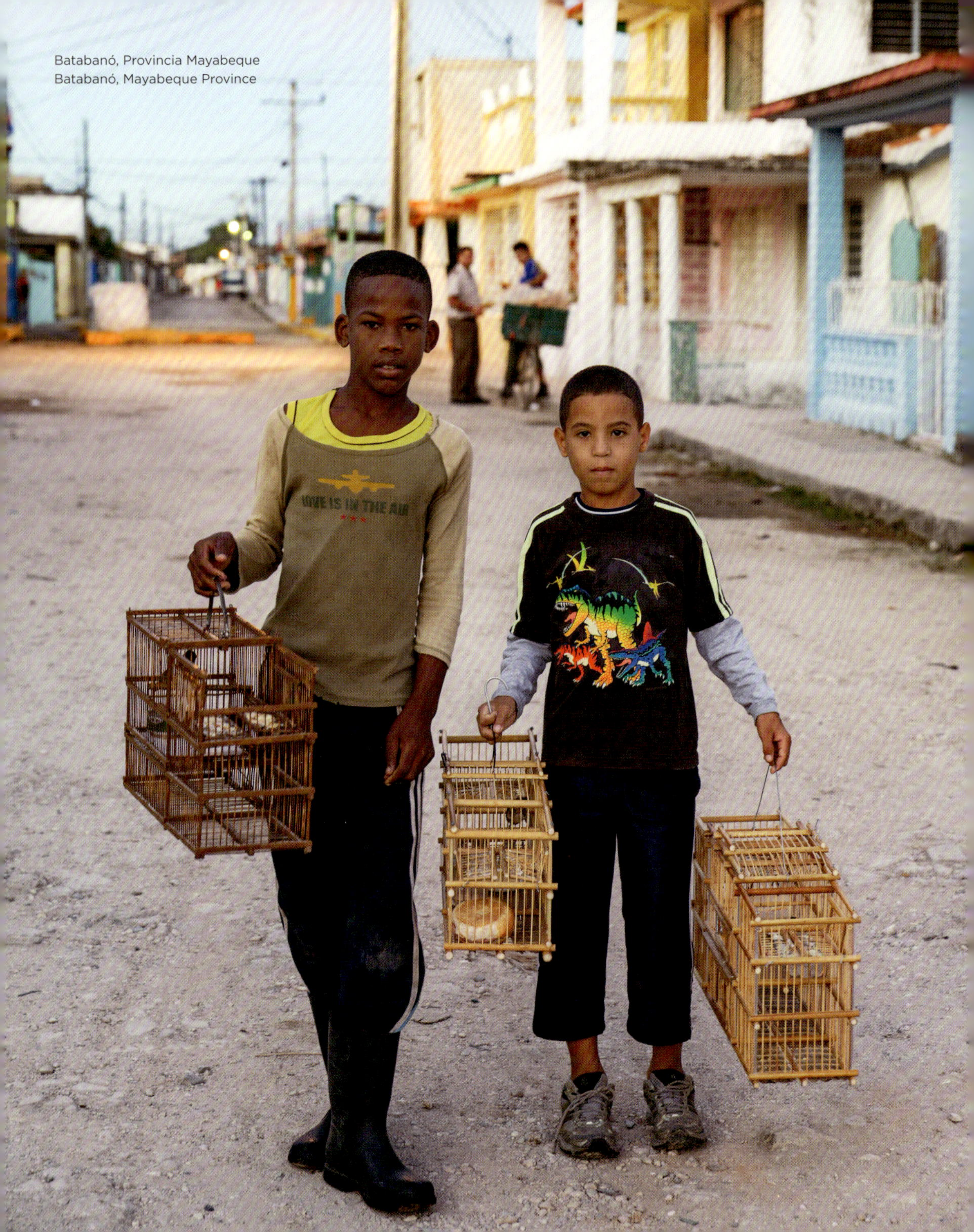

Batabanó, Provincia Mayabeque
Batabanó, Mayabeque Province

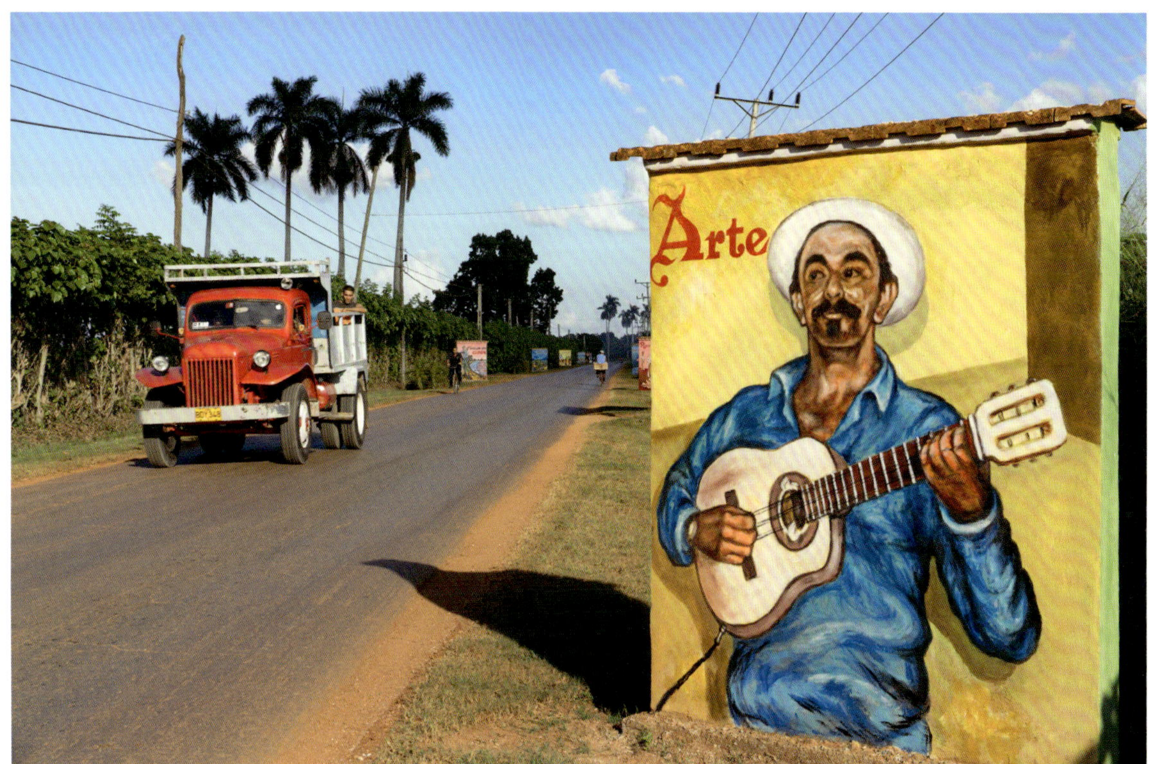

San Antonio de los Baños, Provincia Artemisa
San Antonio de los Baños, Artemisa Province

Caged Birds
Although it is a tradition particularly in Trinidad to walk through the streets with bird cages, this custom is also popular in rural regions of Cuba. It is possible that the keeping of songbirds has been passed down from the indigenous people. Song birds are also popular in Cuba as an item of exchange, they also used for singing competitions.

Cages à oiseaux
Si la tradition est surtout présente à Trinidad, il est également d'usage et souvent fort apprécié dans les régions centrales de Cuba de se promener dans la rue avec des cages à oiseaux. L'élevage d'oiseaux chanteurs pourrait avoir été hérité des pratiques des peuples autochtones indiens. Les oiseaux sont aussi employés à Cuba en tant que monnaie d'échange ; on les laisse chanter sans retenue.

Vogelkäfige
Zwar ist es vor allem in Trinidad Tradition, mit Vogelkäfigen durch die Straßen zu spazieren, doch der Brauch ist in ländlichen Regionen Kubas ebenfalls beliebt. Möglicherweise ist die Haltung von Singvögeln von den indianischen Ureinwohnern überliefert. Auch als Tauschobjekt sind Singvögel sind in Kuba beliebt, man lässt sie gern um die Wette singen.

Jaulas de pájaros
Aunque es una tradición, especialmente en Trinidad, caminar por las calles con jaulas de pájaros, la costumbre también es popular en las regiones rurales de Cuba. Es posible que la cría de aves cantoras haya sido transmitida por los pueblos indígenas. Las aves cantoras también son populares en Cuba como objeto de intercambio, y a los cubanos les gusta apostar con ellas.

Gaiolas para pássaros
Embora seja uma tradição, especialmente em Trinidad, caminhar pelas ruas com gaiolas de pássaros, o costume também é popular nas regiões rurais de Cuba. É possível que a criação de pássaros canoros tenha sido transmitida pelos povos indígenas. Os pássaros canoros também são populares em Cuba como um objeto de troca, eles gostam de deixá-los cantar para fazer apostas.

Vogelkooien
Hoewel het vooral in Trinidad een traditie is om met vogelkooien door de straten te lopen, is het gebruik ook populair in de landelijke gebieden van Cuba. Het is mogelijk dat het houden van zangvogels is doorgegeven door de inheemse volkeren. Zangvogels zijn ook in Cuba populair als ruilobject, men laat ze graag als weddenschap tegen elkaar zingen.

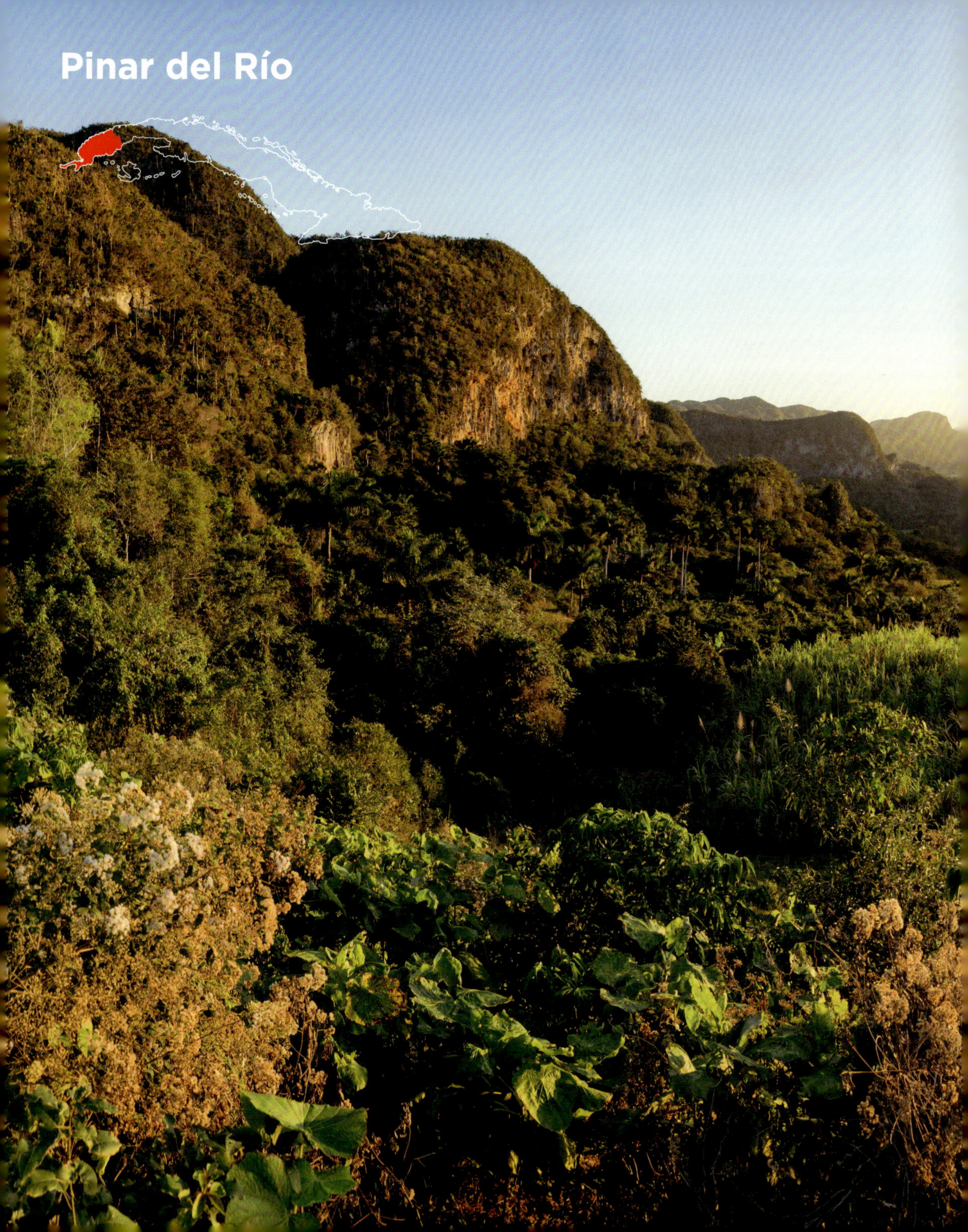
Pinar del Río

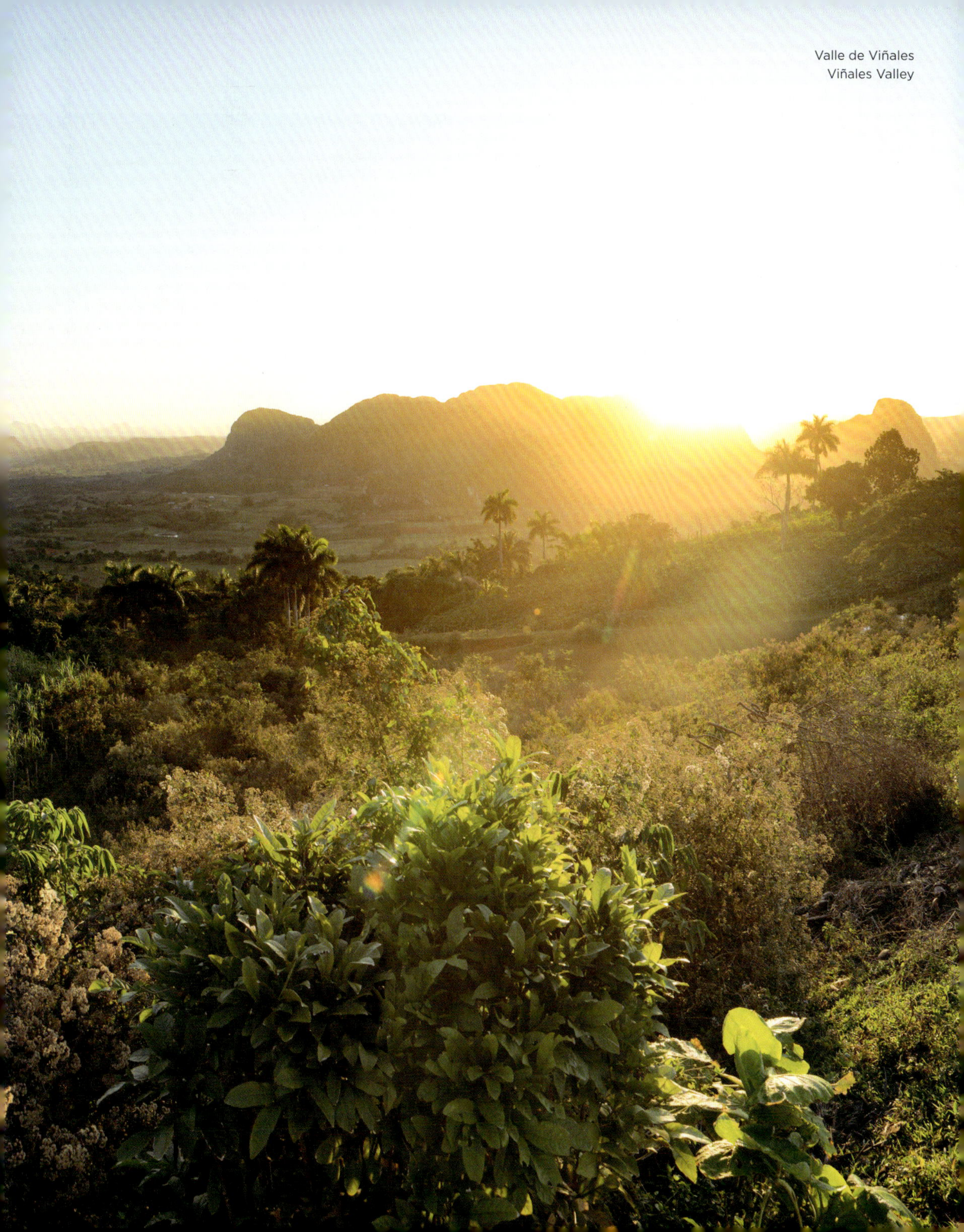

Valle de Viñales
Viñales Valley

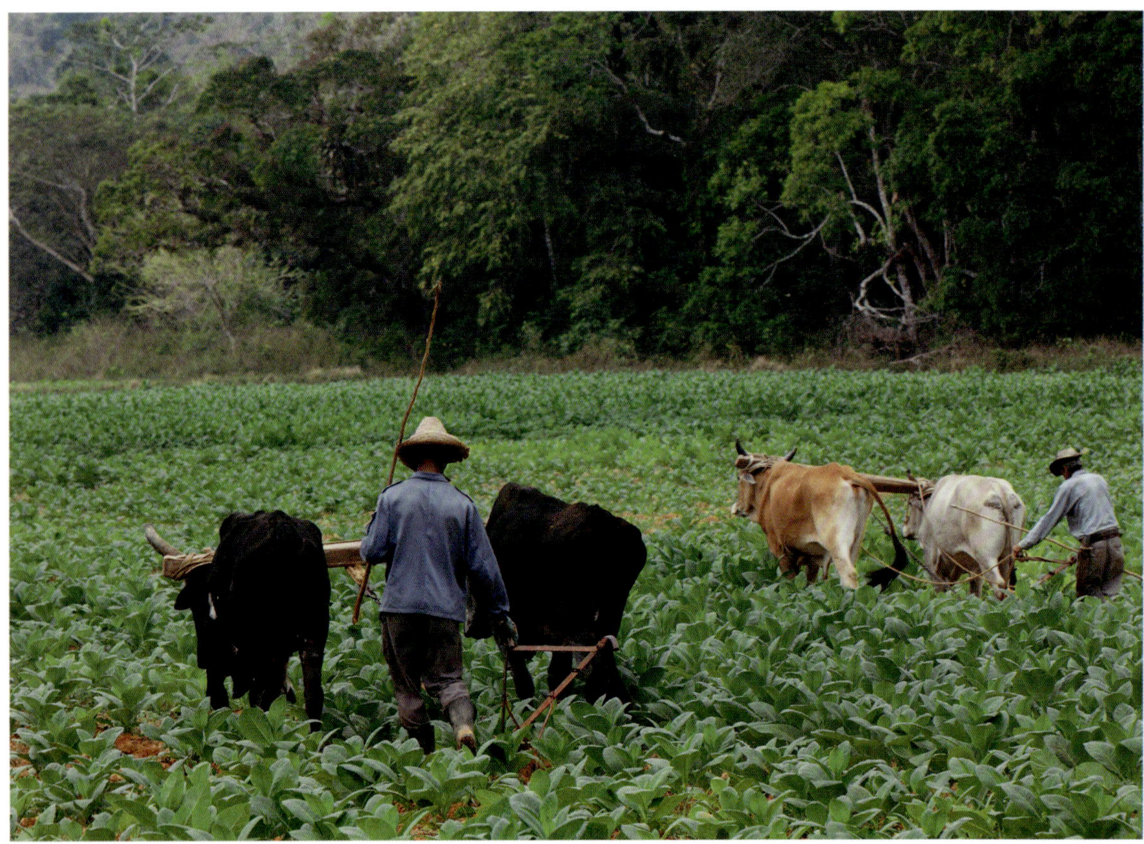

Plantación de tabaco, Valle de Viñales
Tobacco field, Viñales Valley

Pinar del Río

Cave fans, nature lovers, divers and
passionate cigar smokers must make their
way to the west, to the province of Pinar
del Río. Here, in the midst of a bizarre
landscape the best tobacco varieties in the
world grow around the legendary "tobacco
village" of Viñales. Like misshapen
cigars, green overgrown sandstone
cones (mogotes) rise out of the flat land.
Under the ground the scene is similarly
spectacular. Underground rivers and
streams have created a widely branched
cave system in which the indigenous
Indians lived before the Spanish times.

Pinar del Río

Amateurs de grottes, amoureux de la
nature, plongeurs et fumeurs de cigares
passionnés se doivent de visiter la province
de Pinar del Río, à l'extrême ouest de l'île.
C'est ici que sont cultivées les meilleures
variétés de tabac du monde autour du
légendaire «village du tabac», Viñales.
L'étrangeté du paysage local tient à la
présence de mogotes, monticules oblongs
calcaires couverts de végétation, qui
parsèment la plaine tels des cigares mal
façonnés. Sous terre, la structure est
tout aussi étrange. Fleuves et ruisseaux
ont creusé un vaste réseau de grottes
qu'habitaient les Indiens autochtones avant
la période hispanique.

Pinar del Río

Höhlenfans, Naturliebhaber, Taucher und
passionierte Zigarrenraucher müssen sich
obligatorisch auf den Weg nach Westen
machen, in die Provinz Pinar del Río. Hier
wachsen die besten Tabaksorten der
Welt rund um das legendäre „Tabakdorf"
Viñales, inmitten einer bizarren Landschaft:
Wie aus der Form geratene Zigarren
ragen grün überwucherte Kalksandstein-
Kegel (Mogotes) aus dem tischflachen
Boden. Unter der Erde geht es ähnlich
spektakulär zu. Unterirdische Flüsse und
Bäche haben hier ein weit verzweigtes
Höhlensystem geschaffen, in dem vor
den spanischen Zeiten die indianischen
Ureinwohner lebten.

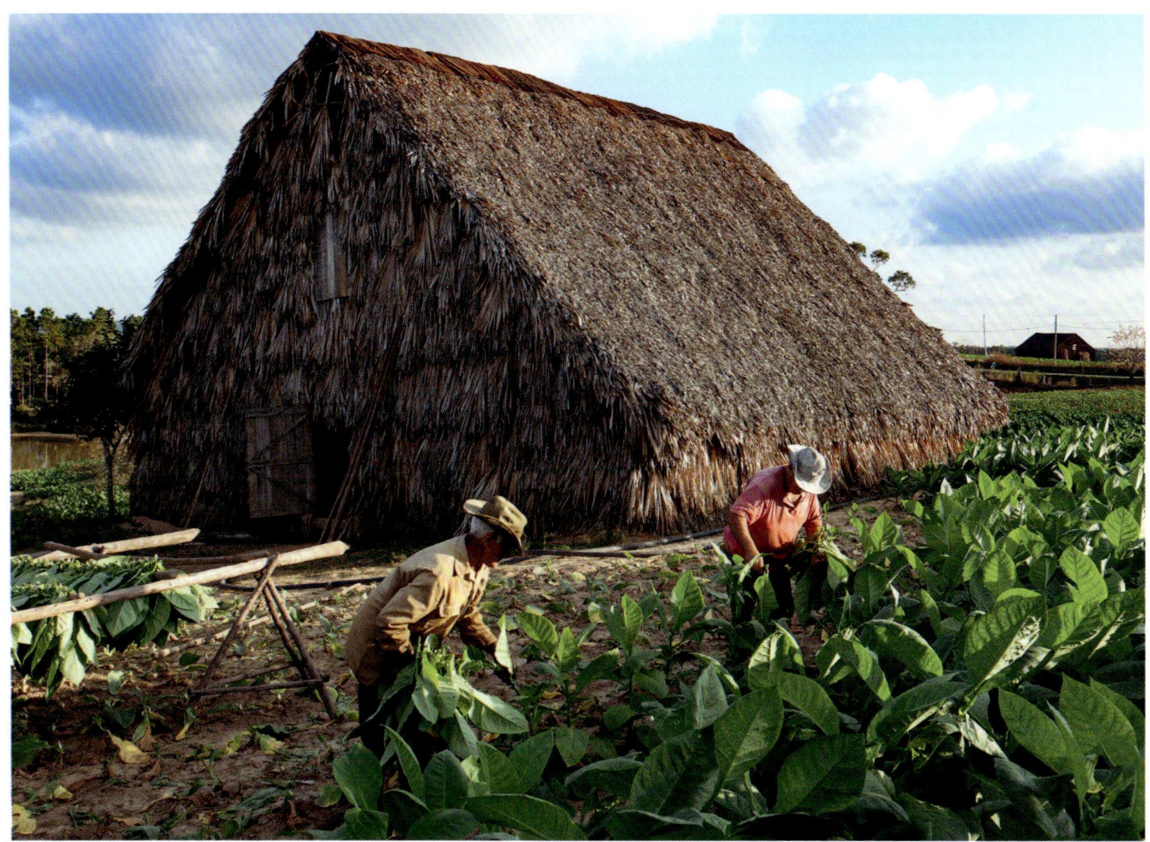

Cosecha de tabaco, Valle de Viñales
Tobacco harvest, Viñales Valley

Pinar del Río

Aficionados a las cavernas, amantes
de la naturaleza, buzos y apasionados
fumadores de puros deben dirigirse
hacia el oeste, hacia la provincia de Pinar
del Río. Aquí, las mejores variedades de
tabaco del mundo crecen alrededor del
legendario "pueblo del tabaco" de Viñales,
en medio de un paisaje extraño: como
los puros que han perdido su forma, los
conos de lima arenosa (mogotes) verdes
y cubiertos de vegetación se levantan del
suelo llano. Debajo del suelo hay cosas
igual de espectaculares. Los ríos y arroyos
subterráneos han creado un sistema de
cuevas ampliamente ramificado, en el que
los indígenas vivían antes de los tiempos
de los españoles.

Pinar del Río

Fãs das cavernas, amantes da natureza,
mergulhadores e fumantes apaixonados
por charutos devem seguir para o oeste,
para a província de Pinar del Río. Aqui, as
melhores variedades de tabaco do mundo
crescem em torno da lendária "aldeia do
tabaco" Viñales, no meio de uma paisagem
bizarra: como os charutos que ficaram
fora de forma, os cones de pedra calcária
verdes (mogotes) emergem do solo plano.
O subsolo é igualmente espetacular. Os
rios e córregos subterrâneos criaram aqui
um sistema de cavernas amplamente
ramificado, no qual os índios americanos
nativos viviam antes da época espanhola.

Pinar del Río

Grottenliefhebbers, natuurliefhebbers,
duikers en gepassioneerde sigarenrokers
moeten naar het westen reizen, naar
de provincie Pinar del Río. Rondom het
legendarische 'tabaksdorp' Viñales groeien
de beste tabakssoorten ter wereld, en
dit midden in een apart landschap: zoals
uit vorm geraakte sigaren steken groene,
begroeide kegels uit kalkzandsteen
(mogotes) uit de tafelvormige bodem.
Ook onder de grond is het spectaculair.
Ondergrondse rivieren en beekjes hebben
hier een wijd vertakt grottensysteem
gecreëerd, waarin de inheemse indianen
voor de Spaanse tijd leefden.

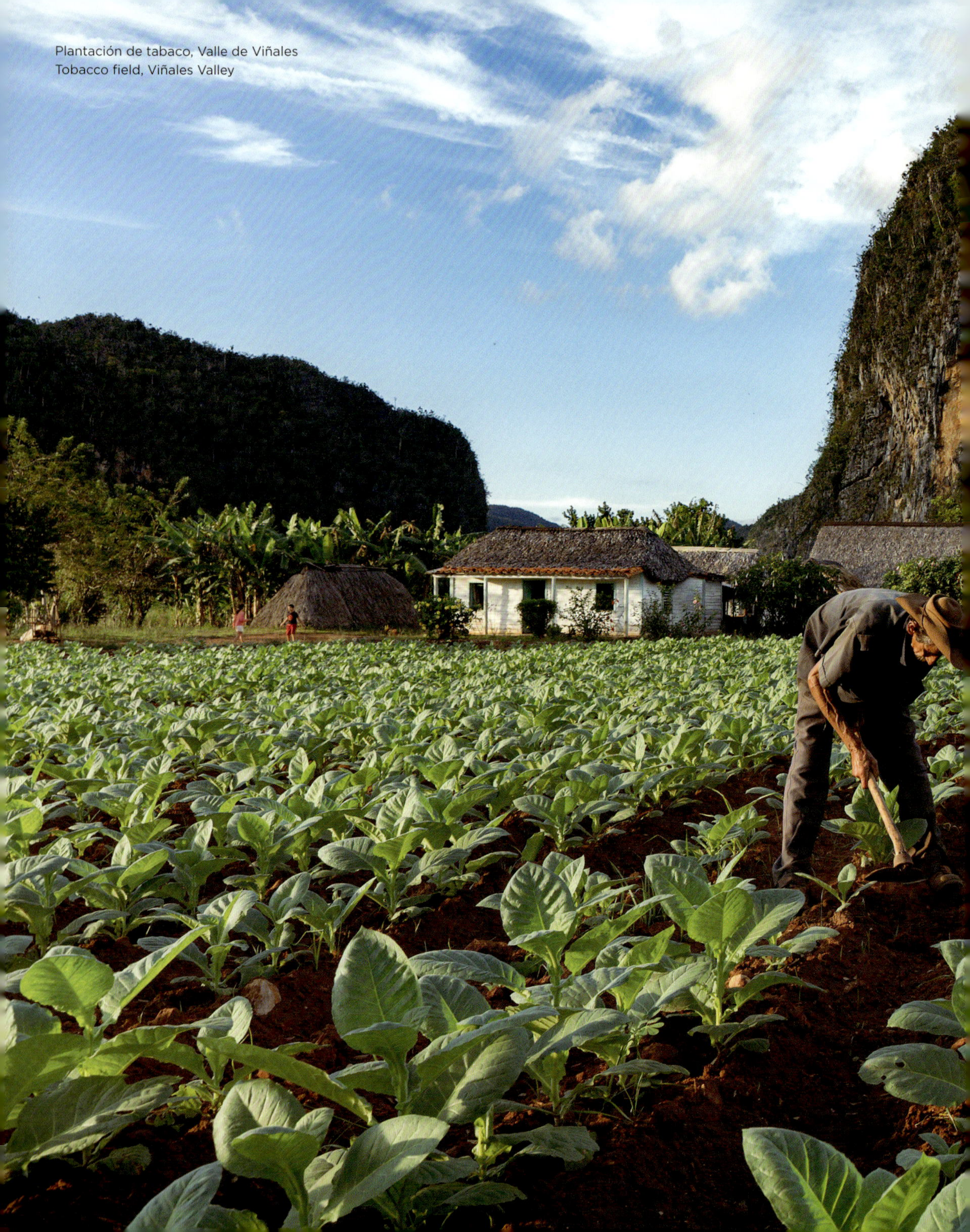

Plantación de tabaco, Valle de Viñales
Tobacco field, Viñales Valley

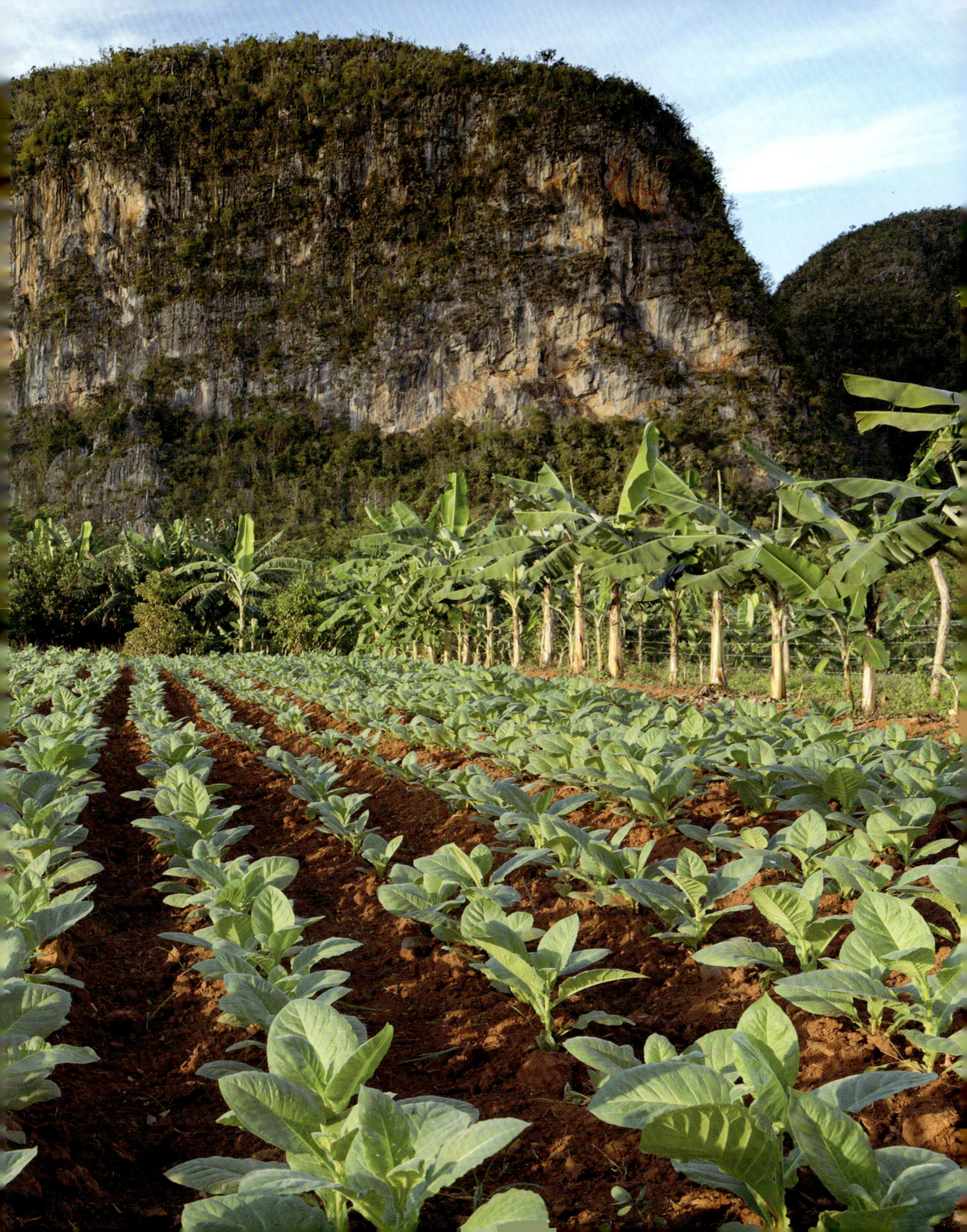

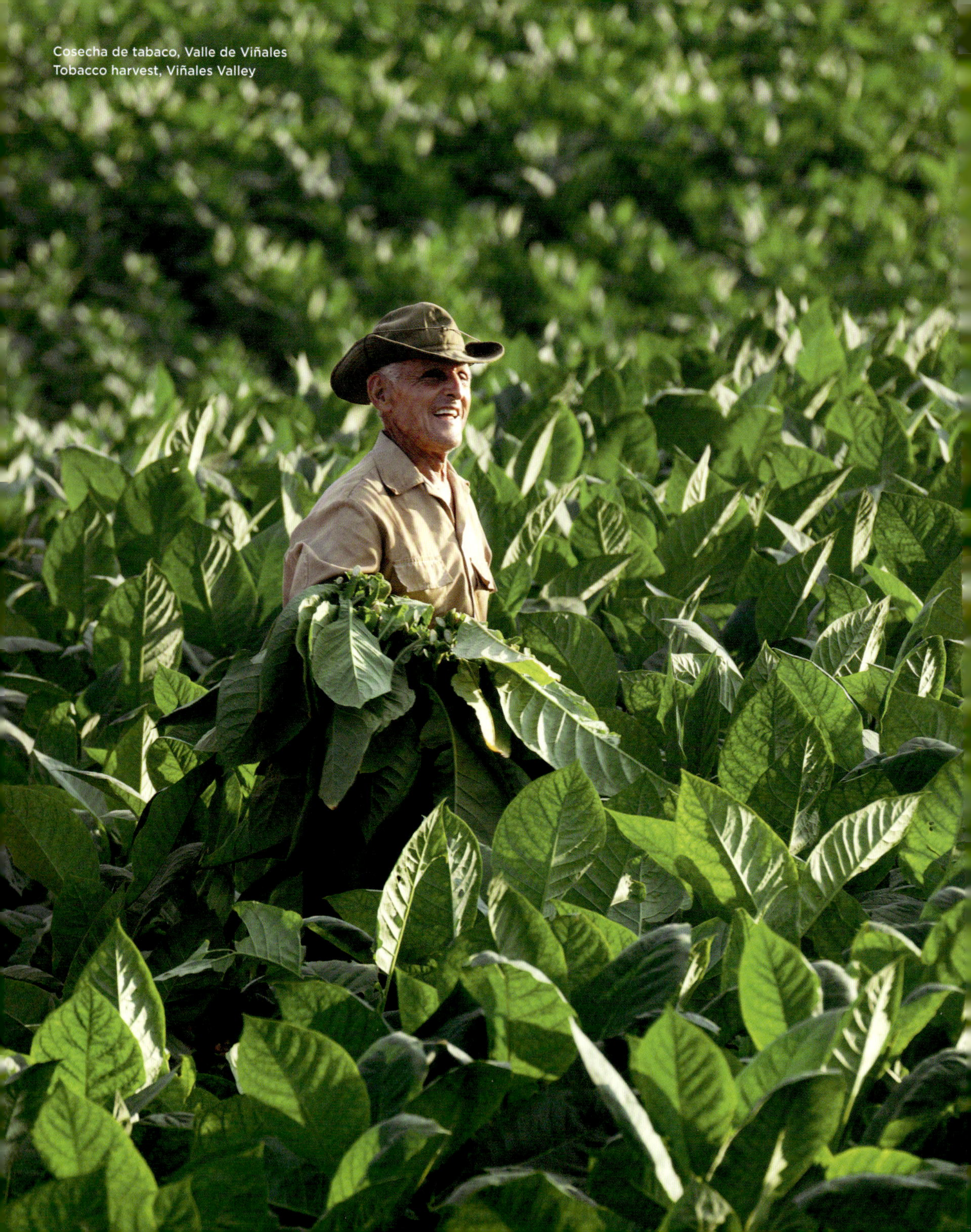

Cosecha de tabaco, Valle de Viñales
Tobacco harvest, Viñales Valley

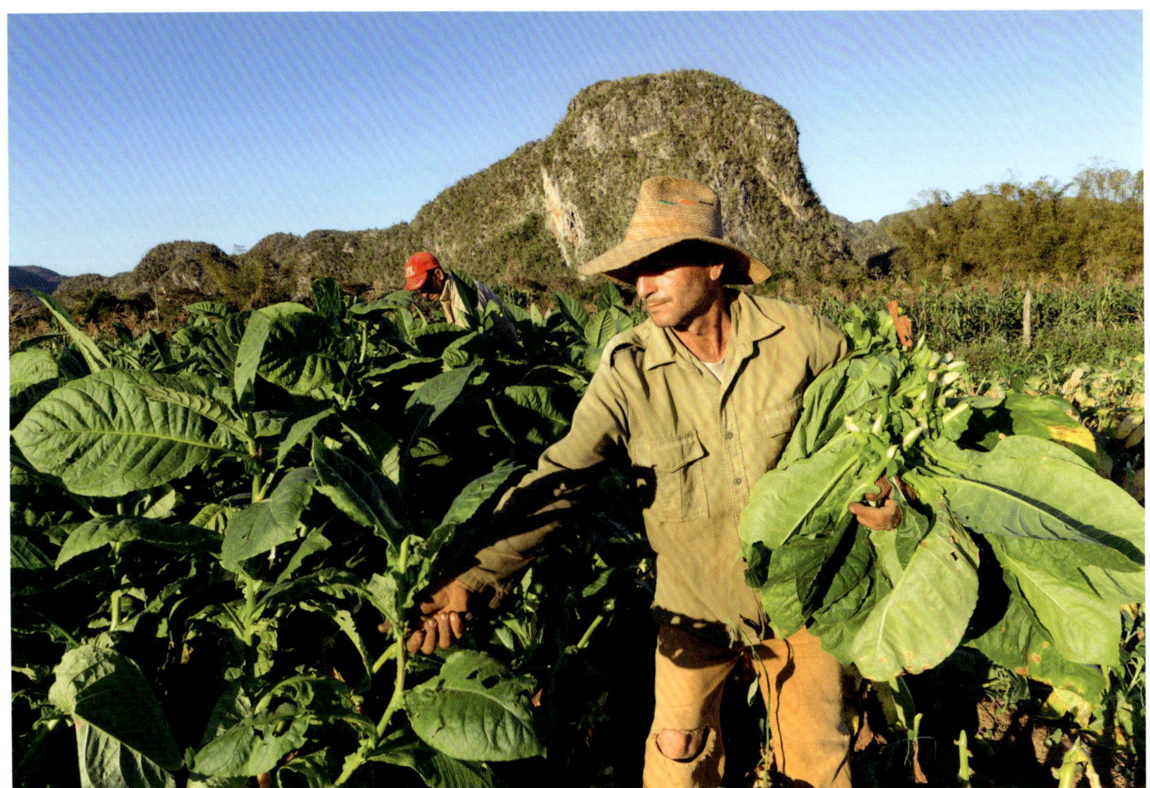

Cosecha de tabaco, Valle de Viñales
Tobacco harvest, Viñales Valley

Tobacco crop

Tobacco is a fussy plant: it requires light, but not direct sun; moisture, but not too much; warmth, but not too warm; cool nights, but no sudden drops in temperature. It must be continually cleared of flowers, weeds and pests. Sowing begins after the rainy season at the end of October, and harvesting takes place from January to April.

Cosecha de tabaco

El tabaco es una planta muy delicada: necesita luz, pero no sol directo; humedad, pero no demasiado; calidez, pero no calor; noches frescas, pero bajadas de temperatura. Una y otra vez debe ser liberada de flores, malezas y bichos. La siembra comienza después de la temporada de lluvias a finales de octubre, y la cosecha se realiza de enero a abril.

Récolte du tabac

Le tabac est une plante capricieuse : il a besoin de lumière mais craint les rayons directs du soleil, d'humidité mais pas trop, de tiédeur mais pas de chaleur, de nuits fraîches mais sans variations de température. Il doit en permanence être débarrassé des fleurs, des mauvaises herbes et de la vermine. Les semailles se font après la saison des pluies, fin octobre, et la récolte, entre janvier et avril.

Colheita de tabaco

O tabaco é uma planta com um carácter muito especial: ela precisa de luz, mas sem sol direto, umidade, mas não muito, aquecimento, mas sem calor, noites frias, mas sem queda na temperatura. Constantemente deve ser libertada de flores, ervas daninhas e vermes. A semeadura começa depois da estação das chuvas, no final de outubro, e a colheita acontece de janeiro a abril.

Tabakernte

Tabak ist eine kapriziöse Pflanze: Sie braucht Licht, aber keine direkte Sonne, Feuchtigkeit, allerdings nicht zu viel, Wärme, jedoch keine Hitze, kühle Nächte, aber keinen Temperatursturz. Immer wieder muss sie von Blüten, Unkraut und Ungeziefer befreit werden. Die Aussaat beginnt nach der Regenzeit Ende Oktober, geerntet wird von Januar bis April.

Tabaksoogst

Tabak is een humeurige plant: het heeft licht nodig, maar geen directe zonlicht, vocht, maar niet te veel, warmte, maar geen hitte, koele nachten, maar geen temperatuurdaling. Het moet steeds weer worden bevrijd van bloemen, onkruid en ongedierte. Het zaaien begint eind oktober na het regenseizoen, de oogst vindt plaats van januari tot april.

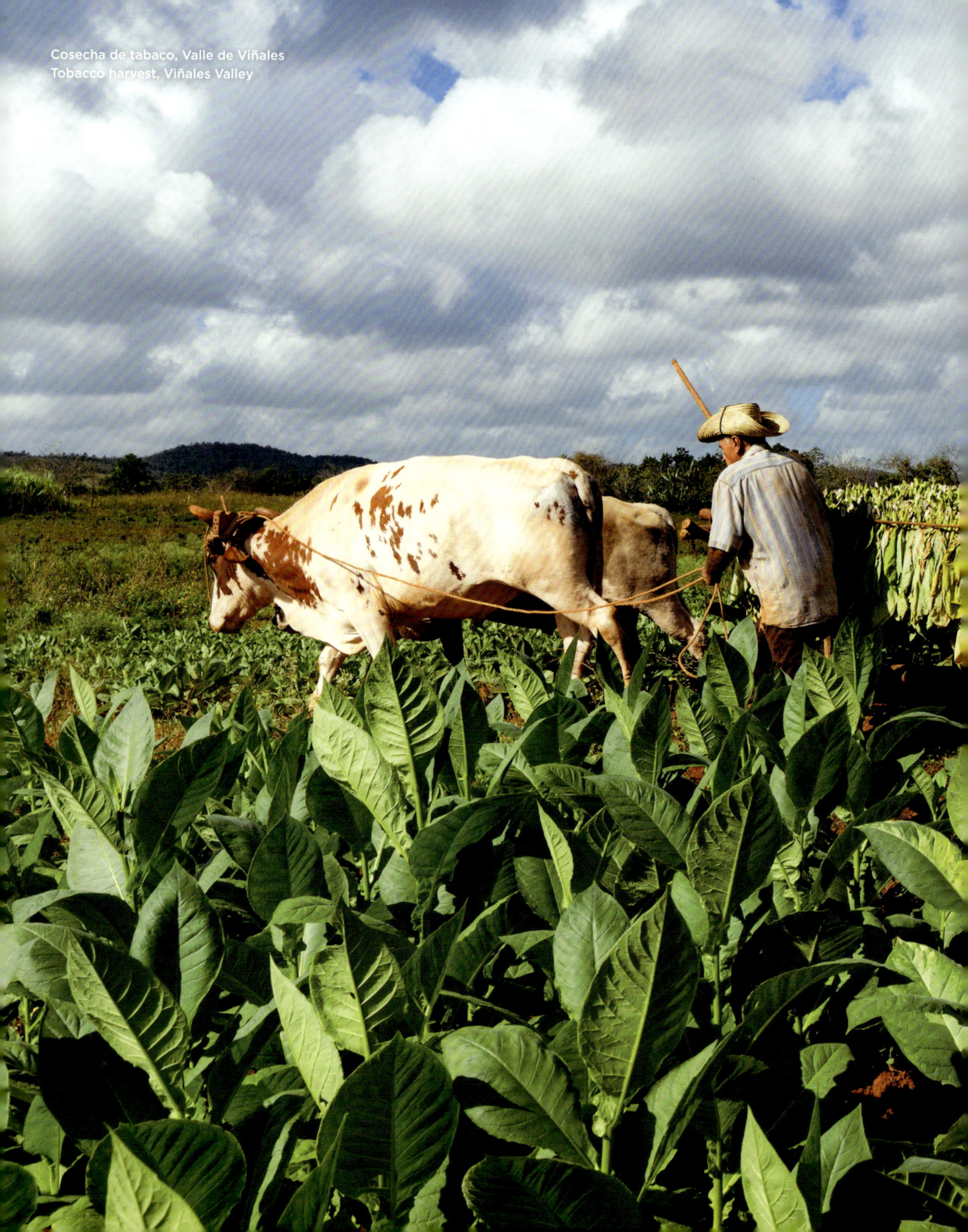

Cosecha de tabaco, Valle de Viñales
Tobacco harvest, Viñales Valley

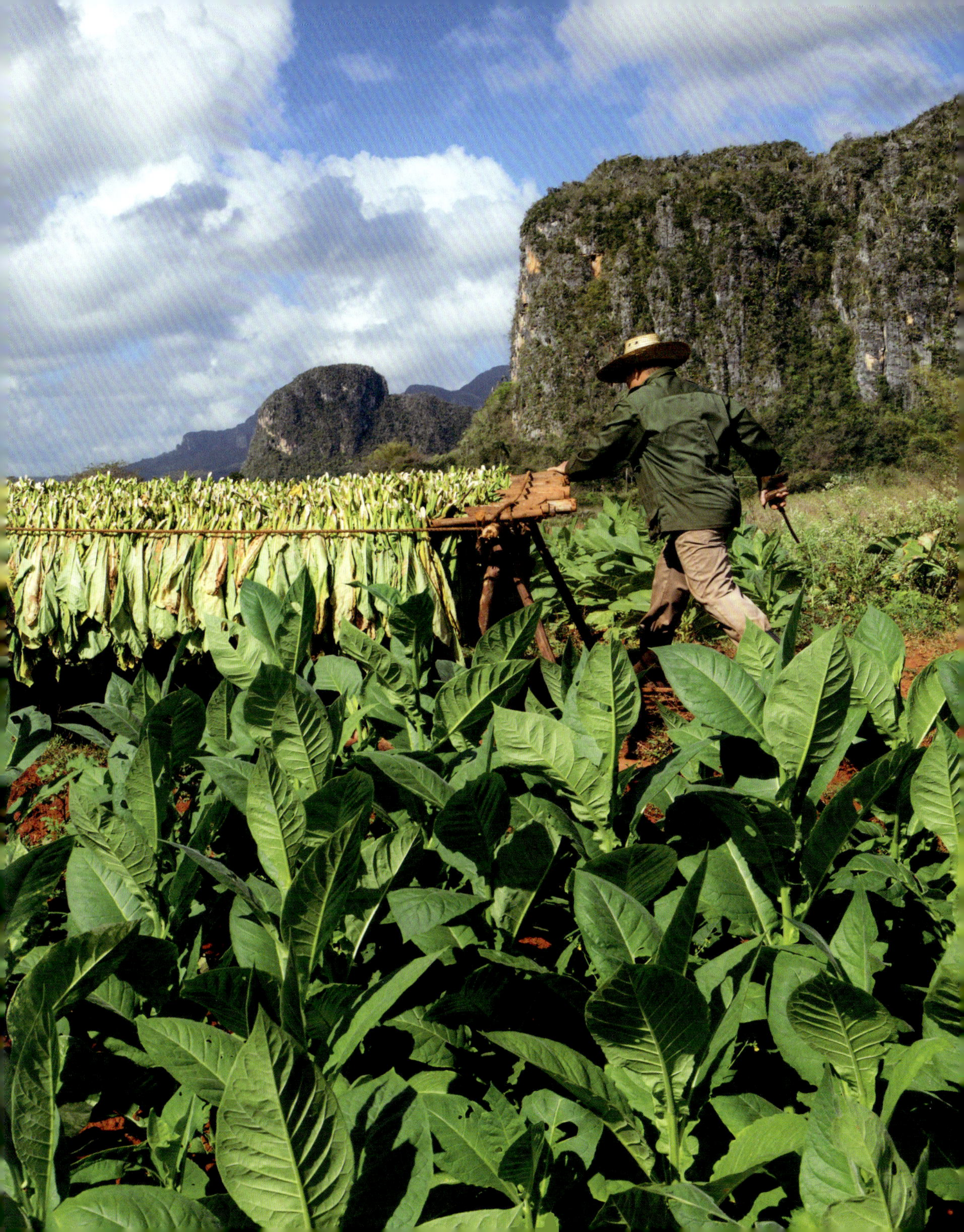

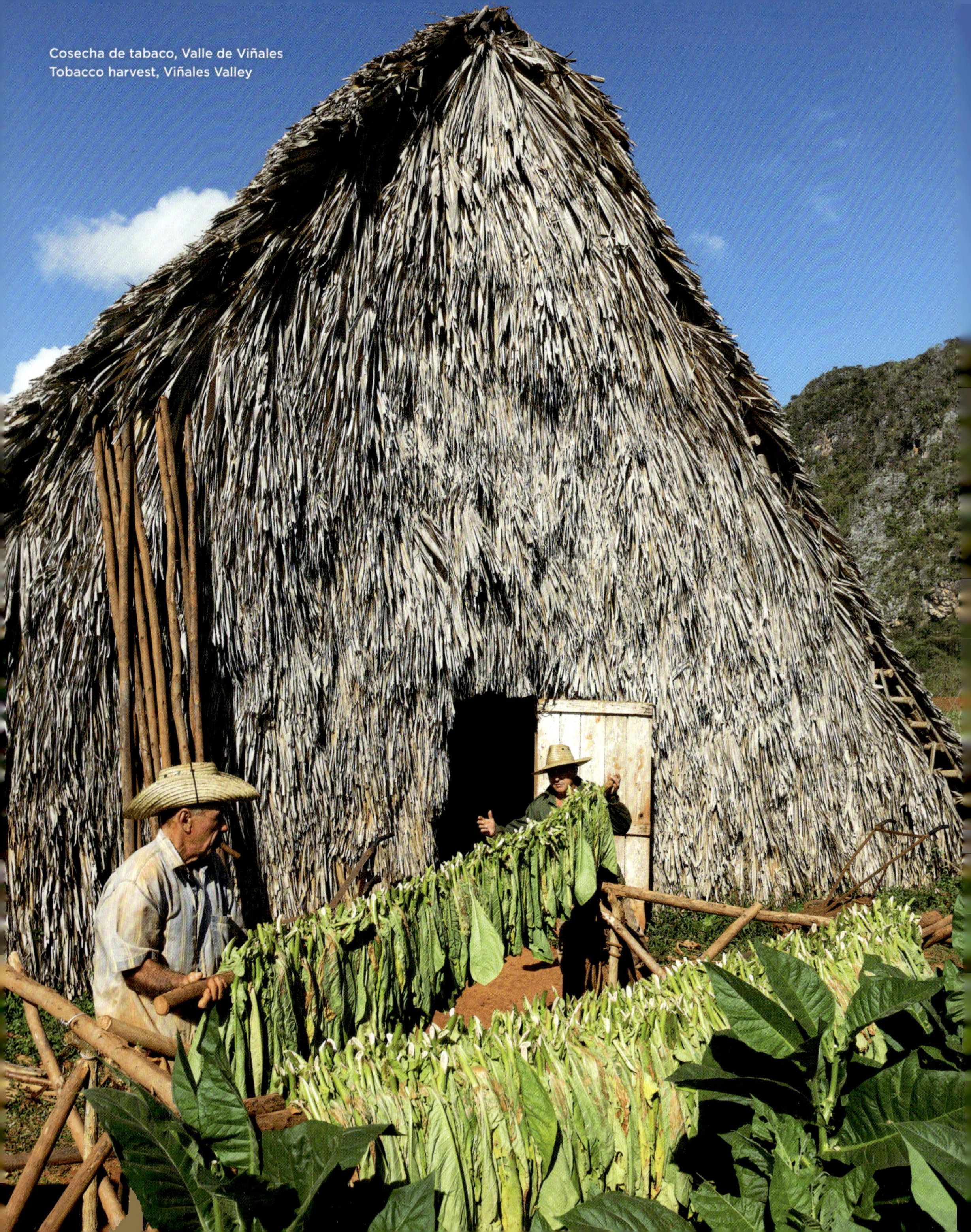

Cosecha de tabaco, Valle de Viñales
Tobacco harvest, Viñales Valley

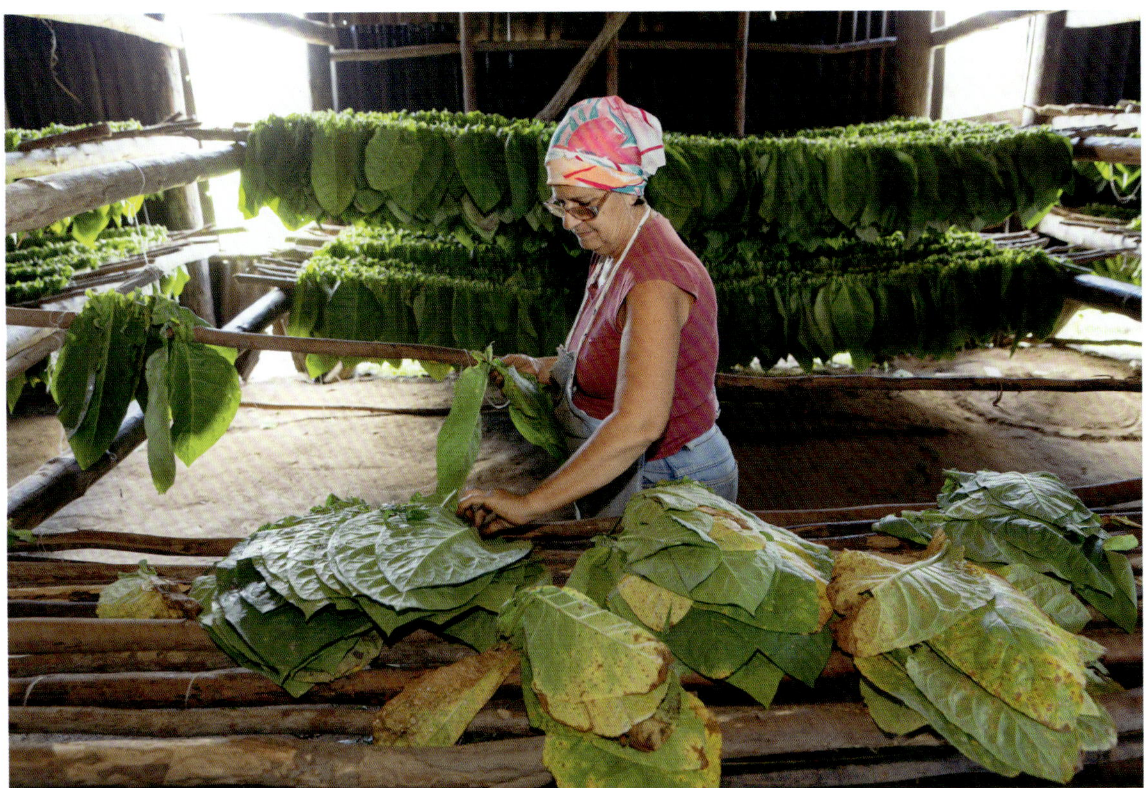

Procesado del tabaco, Valle de Viñales
Tobacco processing, Viñales Valley

Casa de Tabaco

The tobacco leaves are dried and fermented in these windowless sheds, where they sweat out their moisture and steam in their own vapor. The drier they become, the higher they must be hung under the roof. Later, the leaves are moistened and fermented for up to three times in order to achieve uniform quality and color.

Casa de tabaco

Les feuilles de tabac sont mises à sécher et à fermenter dans des remises aveugles. Elles macèrent dans la chaleur qu'elles exhalent et éliminent ainsi leur humidité. À mesure qu'elles sèchent, les ouvriers les rapprochent du toit. Les feuilles sont ensuite réhumidifiées et passent par un processus de fermentation pouvant comporter jusqu'à 3 cycles, afin de parvenir à une qualité et une couleur homogènes.

Casa de Tabaco

In den fensterlosen Schuppen werden die Blätter getrocknet und fermentiert. Sie kochen in ihrem eigenen Hitzedunst und schwitzen ihre Feuchtigkeit aus. Je trockener sie werden, desto höher müssen sie unter das Dach gehängt werden. Später werden die Blätter befeuchtet und bis zu drei Mal fermentiert, um eine gleichmäßige Qualität und Färbung zu erzielen.

Casa de Tabaco

Las hojas se secan y fermentan en cobertizos sin ventanas. Hierven en su propio vapor de calor y sudan su humedad. Cuanto más secos se ponen, más alto tienen que colgarse bajo el techo. Posteriormente, las hojas se humedecen y fermentan hasta tres veces para conseguir una calidad y un color uniformes.

Casa de Tabaco

As folhas são secas e fermentadas no galpão sem janelas. Elas cozinham no seu próprio vapor de calor e "suam" a sua humidade. Quanto mais secas ficam, mais alto têm de ser penduradas debaixo do telhado. Posteriormente, as folhas são humedecidas e fermentadas até três vezes para obter uma qualidade e cor uniformes.

Casa de Tabaco

De bladeren worden in een schuur zonder ramen gedroogd en gefermenteerd. Ze koken in hun eigen hittedamp en zweten hun vocht uit. Hoe droger ze worden, des te hoger ze onder het dak moeten worden opgehangen. Later worden de bladeren tot drie keer bevochtigd en gefermenteerd om zo een uniforme kwaliteit en kleur te verkrijgen.

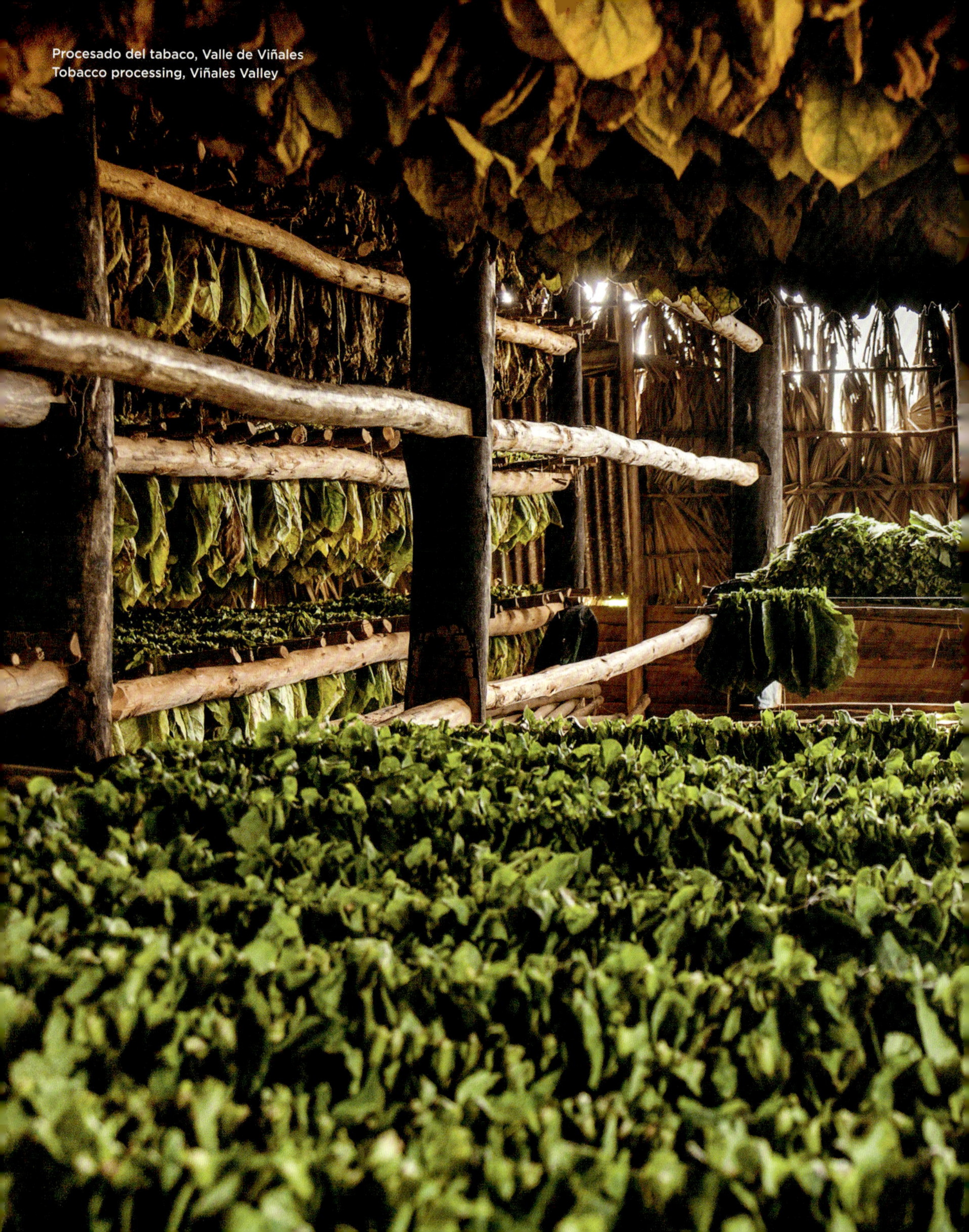
Procesado del tabaco, Valle de Viñales
Tobacco processing, Viñales Valley

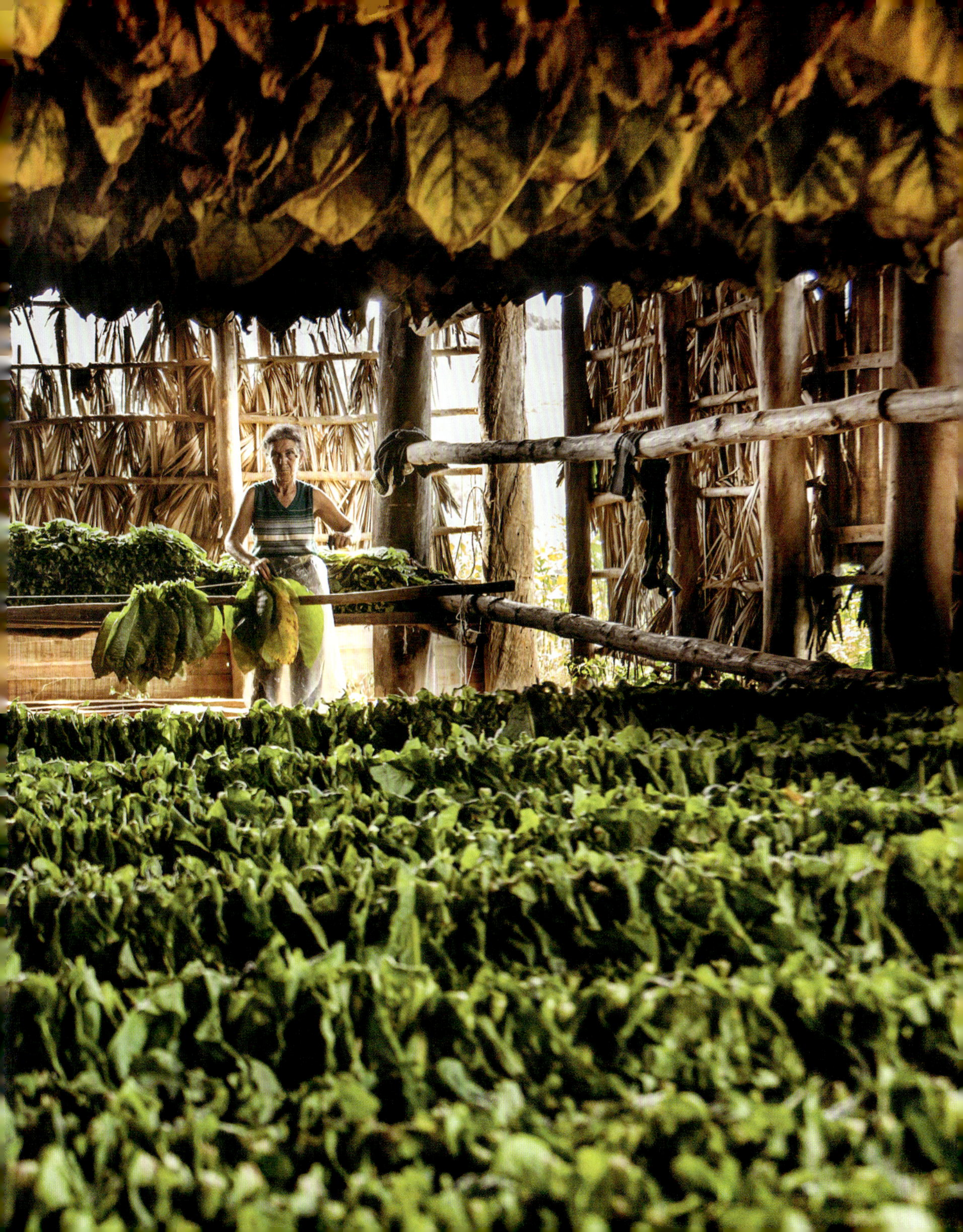

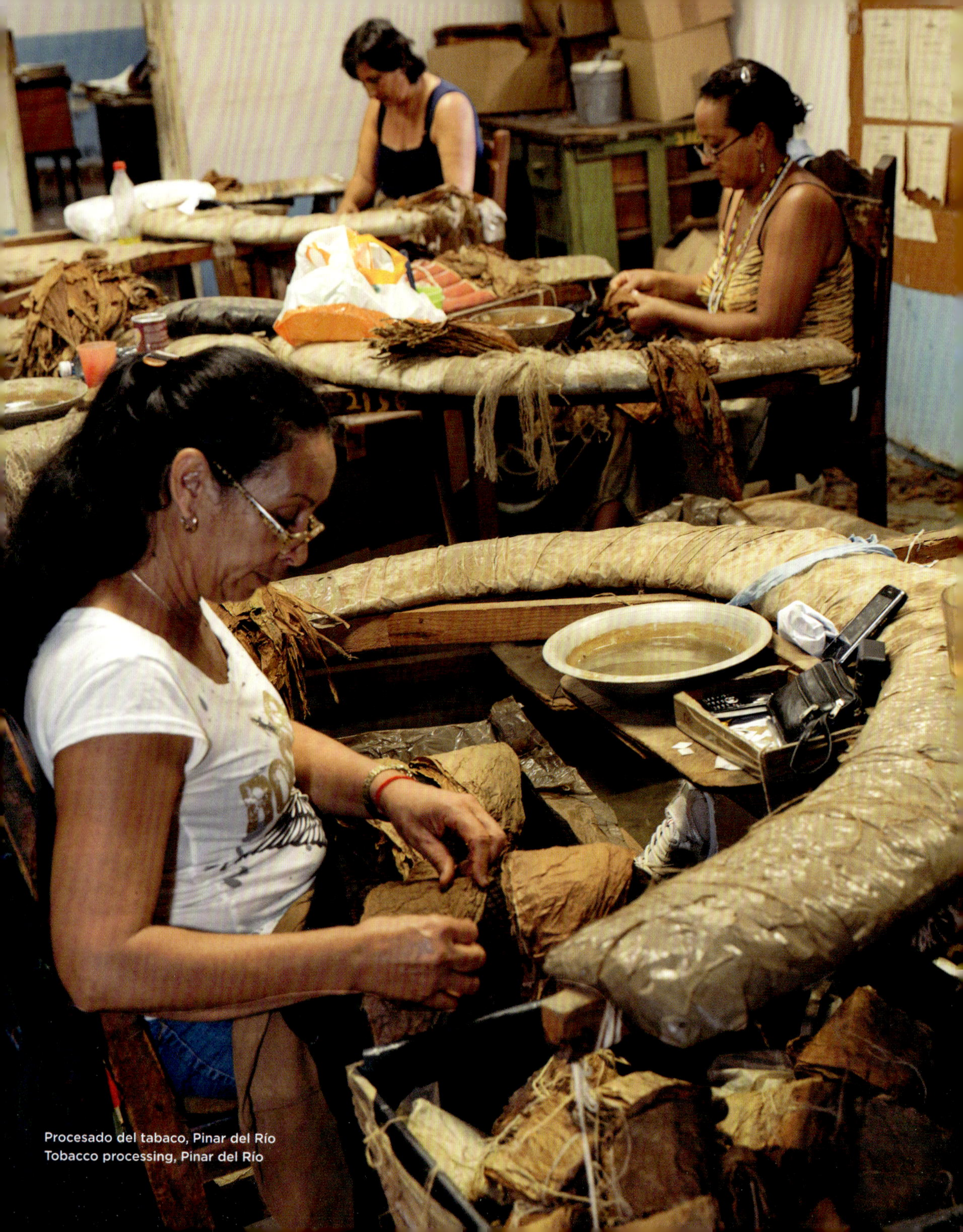

Procesado del tabaco, Pinar del Río
Tobacco processing, Pinar del Río

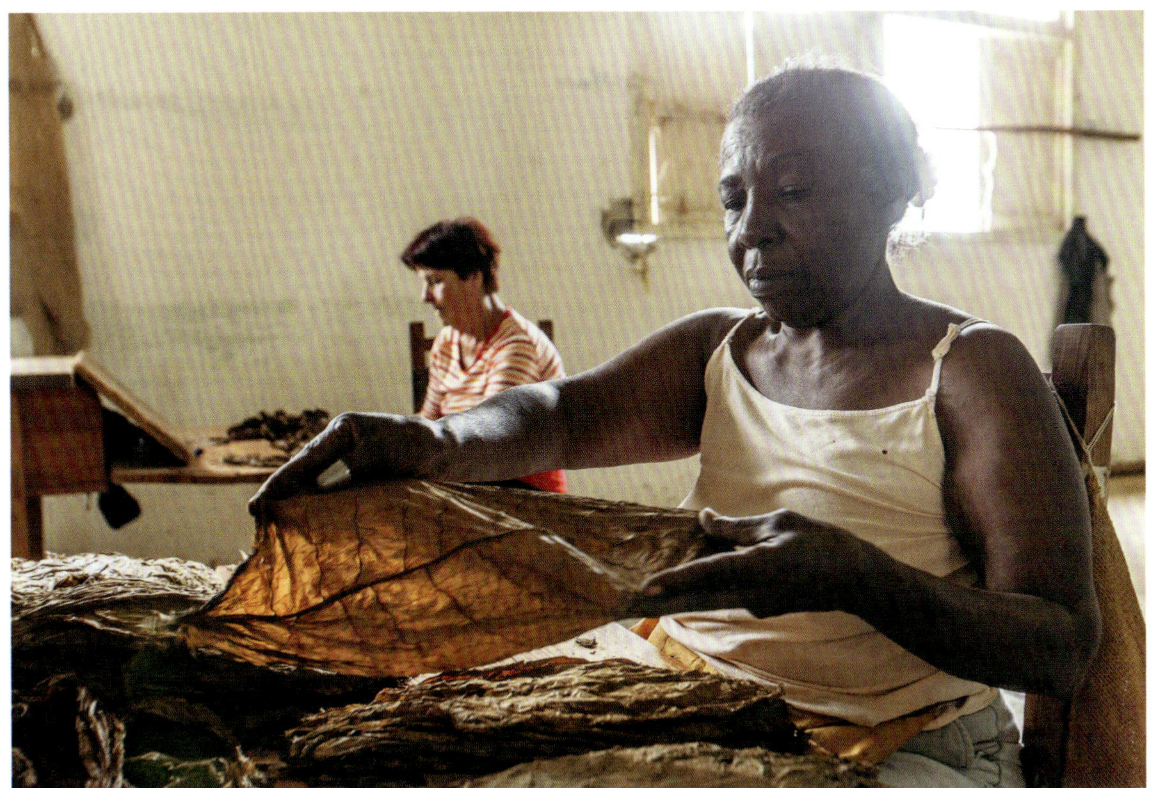

Procesado del tabaco, Pinar del Río
Tobacco processing, Pinar del Río

Tobacco is Handmade

"You can't just plant the tobacco, you have to marry it", states a Cuban proverb. The path to making a cigar is long, laborious and painstaking. In the tobacco factory the workers (mostly women) moisten the dried tobacco leaves and smooth them, and then the central rib of each leaf is cut out.

El tabaco es un trabajo manual

"No se puede plantar el tabaco, hay que casarse con él", dice un proverbio cubano. El proceso hasta obtener un cigarro es largo, laborioso y complicado. En la fábrica de tabaco, los trabajadores (en su mayoría, mujeres) humedecen las hojas de tabaco seco y las alisan. Luego se corta la línea central de cada hoja.

Le tabac, un travail manuel

« Le tabac ne se cultive pas, il s'épouse », dit-on à Cuba. Et en effet, la transformation de la plante en cigare nécessite un travail long, exigeant et pénible. Dans les ateliers, les ouvriers (presque uniquement des femmes) humidifient les feuilles de tabac séchées et les étalent à plat. Ils retirent ensuite la nervure centrale de chaque feuille.

O tabaco é feito à mão

"Você não pode simplesmente plantar tabaco, você tem que se casar com ele", diz um provérbio cubano. O caminho para um charuto é um trabalho manual longo, trabalhoso e cansativo. Na fábrica de tabaco, os trabalhadores (principalmente mulheres trabalham aqui) humedecem as folhas secas do tabaco e as alisam. Em seguida, a nervura central de cada folha é cortada.

Tabak ist Handarbeit

„Den Tabak kann man nicht einfach pflanzen, man muss ihn heiraten", sagt ein kubanisches Sprichwort. Der Weg zur Zigarre ist lang, aufwändig und mühsame Handarbeit. In der Tabakfabrik feuchten die Arbeiterinnen (meist arbeiten hier Frauen) die getrockneten Tabakblätter an und streichen sie glatt. Danach wird die Zentralrippe jedes Blattes herausgetrennt.

Tabak is handenarbeid

Een Cubaans spreekwoord luidt: 'Je kunt de tabak niet zomaar planten, je moet er mee trouwen.' De weg naar een sigaar is lang, omslachtig en moeizaam. In de tabaksfabriek bevochtigen de arbeiders (meestal vrouwen) de gedroogde tabaksbladeren en maken ze glad. Vervolgens wordt de centrale rib van elk blad uitgesneden.

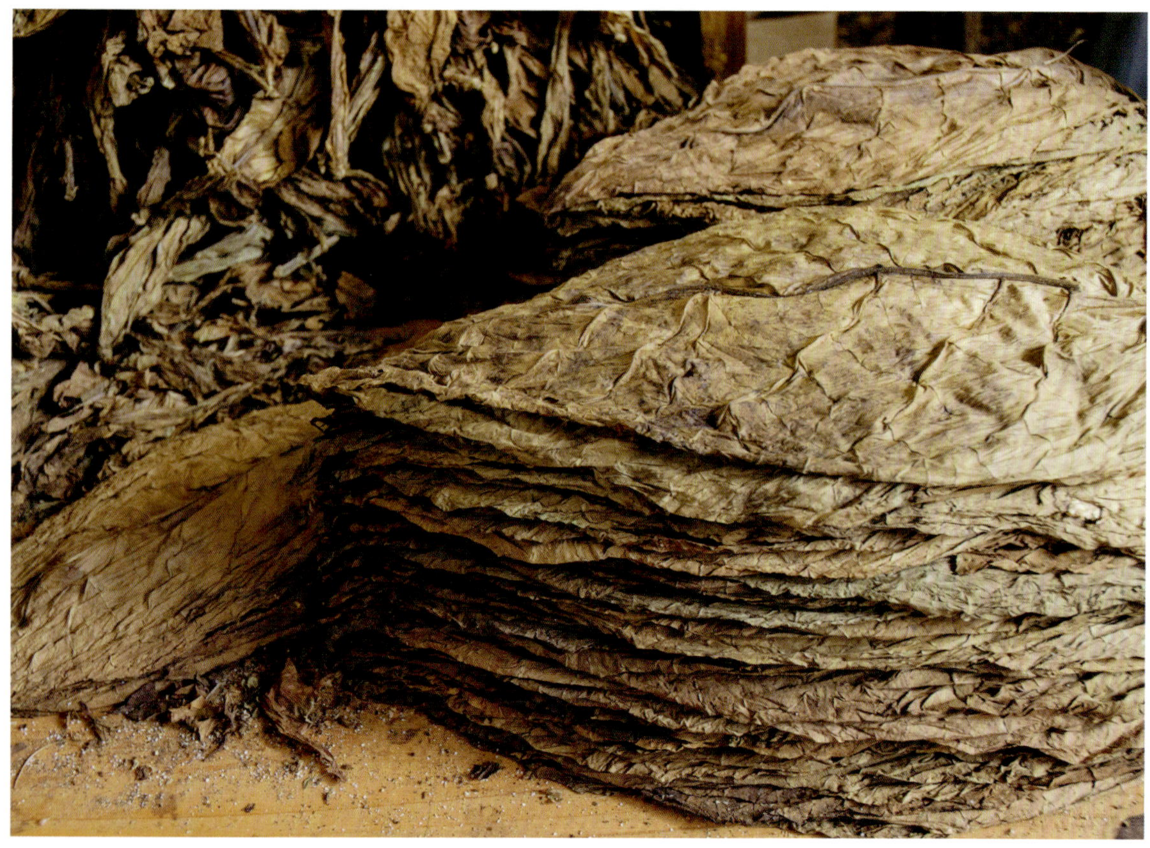

Procesado del tabaco, Pinar del Río
Tobacco processing, Pinar del Río

Valuable Leaves

It took some time before the Spanish crown recognized the value of the strange plants which the Indians "smoked", but the custom of "fog drinking" finally spread to Europe, and soon the tobacco leaves became "brown gold" for Spain. In fact, not all tobacco leaves are the same: Corojo plants are used exclusively as cigar wrappers, while the Criollo plants are used to inside the cigar because they provide the aroma. The lower *(volado)*, middle *(seco)* and upper *(ligero)* leaves each have their own flavor and are separated at harvest.

Précieuses feuilles

Il fallut un certain temps avant que la couronne d'Espagne ne prête attention à cette étrange plante avec laquelle les Indiens « s'enfumaient ». La pratique des « buveurs de nuages » se répandit alors dans toute l'Europe et les feuilles de tabac se changèrent rapidement pour l'Espagne en « or brun ». Mais, attention, toutes les feuilles de tabac ne se valent pas : celles de la variété Corojo sont exclusivement utilisées pour la cape des cigares et celles de la plante Criollo pour la tripe et la sous-cape, car elles offrent un arôme plus puissant. Les feuilles inférieures *(volado)*, centrales *(seco)* et supérieures *(ligero)* présentent un parfum différent et sont séparées lors de la récolte.

Wertvolle Blätter

Es dauerte, bis die spanische Krone den Wert der merkwürdigen Pflanzen erkannte, mit denen sich die Indios „einräucherten". Doch die Sitte des „Nebeltrinkens" breitete sich schließlich auch in Europa aus, und bald avancierten die Tabakblätter für Spanien zum „braunen Gold". Tatsächlich sind nicht alle Tabakblätter gleich: Die Corojo-Pflanzen werden ausschließlich als Deckblätter der Zigarren verwendet, die Criollo-Pflanzen dagegen für Einlage und Umblatt der Zigarre, denn sie liefern das Aroma. Die unteren *(volado)*, mittleren *(seco)* und oberen Blätter *(ligero)* haben jeweils eine eigene Geschmacksnote und werden bei der Ernte getrennt.

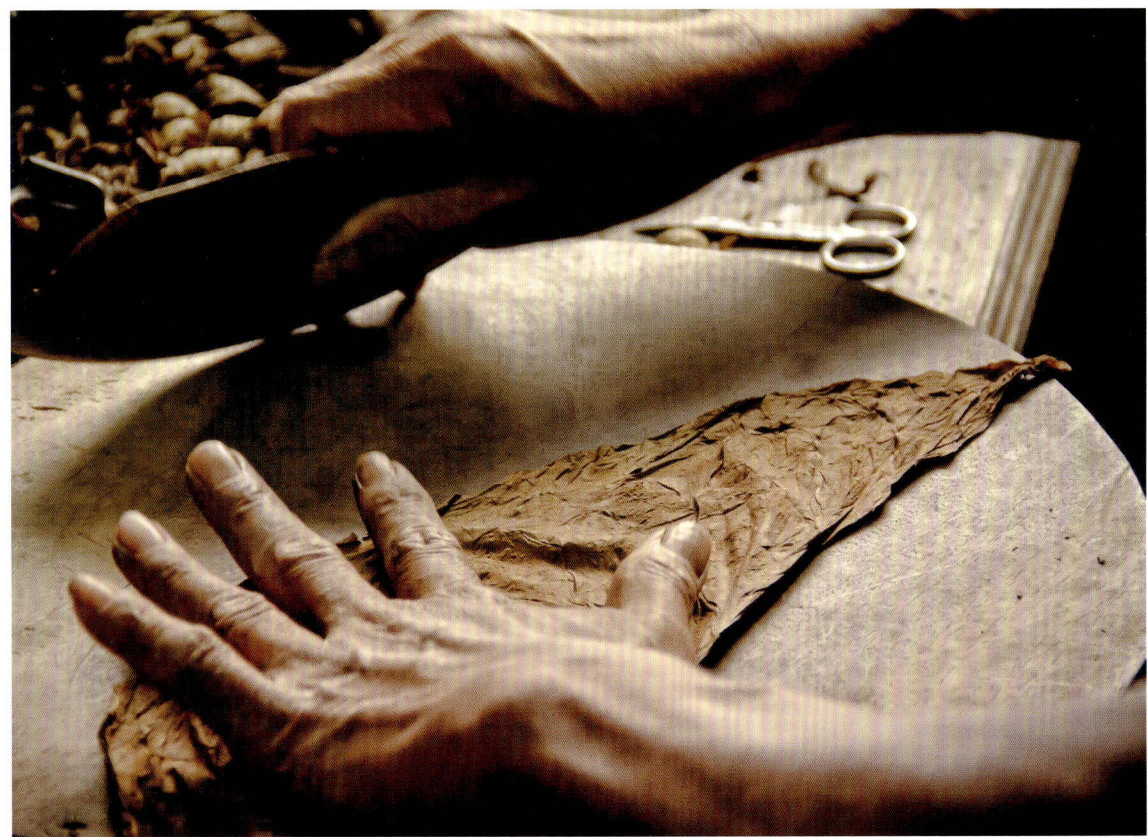

Procesado del tabaco, Pinar del Río
Tobacco processing, Pinar del Río

Hojas valiosas

La Corona española tardó en reconocer el valor de las extrañas plantas con las que los indios "ahumaban". Pero la costumbre de "beber la niebla" finalmente se extendió a Europa, y pronto las hojas de tabaco se convirtieron en "oro marrón" para España. De hecho, no todas las hojas de tabaco son iguales: las plantas de corojo se utilizan exclusivamente como envoltorios de puros, mientras que las plantas de criollo se utilizan para insertar y envolver el puro, porque proporcionan el aroma. Las hojas inferiores *(volado)*, medias *(seco)* y superiores *(ligero)* tienen cada una su propio sabor y se separan al momento de la cosecha.

Folhas valiosas

Demorou um pouco até que a coroa espanhola reconhecesse o valor das plantas estranhas que os índios costumavam "fumar". Mas o costume de "beber névoa" finalmente se espalhou pela Europa, e logo as folhas de tabaco se tornaram "ouro marrom" para a Espanha. De fato, nem todas as folhas de tabaco são iguais: as plantas de Corojo são usadas exclusivamente como cobertura para os charutos, enquanto as de Criollo são usadas para inserir e embalar o charuto, pois fornecem o aroma. As folhas inferiores *(volado)*, as médias *(seco)* e as superiores *(ligero)* têm cada uma o seu sabor próprio e são separadas no momento da colheita.

Waardevolle bladeren

Het duurde tot de Spaanse regering de waarde van de vreemde planten die de indianen als geneesachtig kruid en een stimulerend middel gebruikten erkende. Maar het verspreidde zich uiteindelijk ook naar Europa, en al snel werden de tabaksbladeren 'bruin goud' voor Spanje. In feite zijn niet alle tabaksbladeren hetzelfde: de Corojo-planten worden uitsluitend gebruikt als sigarenverpakking, terwijl de Criollo-planten worden gebruikt om de sigaar te vullen en te binden, en zo de aroma levert. De onderste *(volado)*, middelste *(seco)* en bovenste *(ligero)* bladeren hebben elk hun eigen smaak en worden bij de oogst gescheiden.

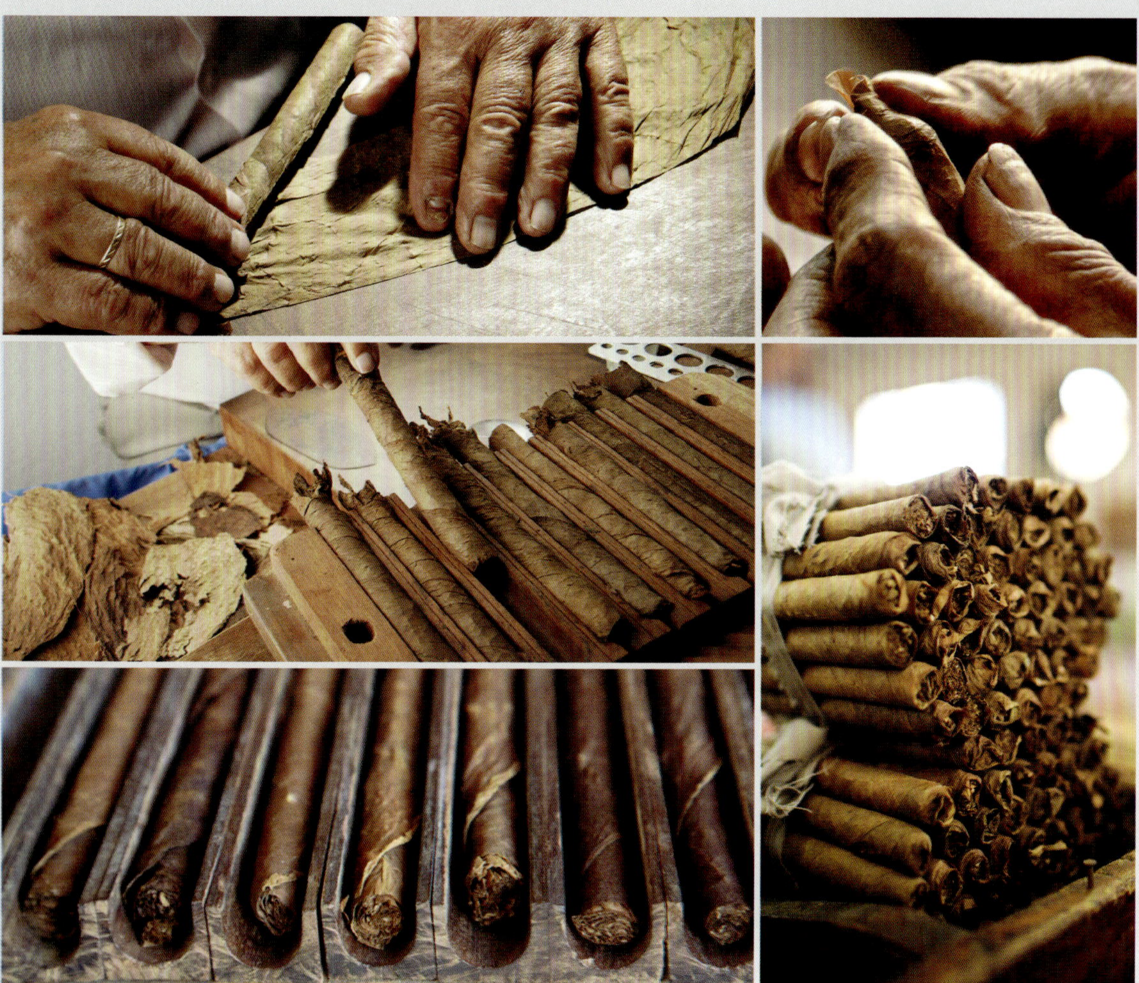

The Path to a Havana Cigar

The tobacco filler is shaped in a grooved box before the cigars are wrapped in the casing, for which the most flawless tobacco leaves are used. The hand-rolled cigars are bundled and sorted by the quality inspectors according to length and diameter. The cigars are placed in the cigar boxes in a specific color sequence: the darkest cigar on the left, the lightest on the right. Any other sequence indicates a counterfeit. Whichever exclusive names the cigars bear, whether Cohiba, Montecristo, H. Upmann, Partagás or Romeo y Julieta—the precious works of art are destined to go up in smoke.

La naissance du cigare de La Havane

Le tabac servant à la tripe est mis en forme sur des plaques rainurées, avant d'être enveloppé d'une cape pour laquelle on sélectionne les feuilles les plus impeccables possible. Les cigares roulés à la main sont mis en fagots et vérifiés par des contrôleuses de qualité qui les trient par diamètre et longueur. Dans les caisses, les cigares sont rangés dans un ordre précis en fonction de leur couleur : à gauche les plus foncés, à droite les plus clairs. Un rangement différent indiquerait qu'il s'agit d'une contrefaçon. Et pourtant, quel que soit le nom exclusif qu'elles portent (Cohiba, Montecristo, H. Upmann, Partagás ou Romeo y Julieta), ces pièces artisanales coûteuses partent toutes en fumée.

Der Weg zur Havanna-Zigarre

In einem Rillenkasten wird der Einlage-Tabak in Form gebracht, bevor man die Zigarren mit dem Mantel umwickelt, für den man die makellosesten Tabakblätter nimmt. Die handgerollten Zigarren werden gebündelt und von den Qualitätsprüferinnen nach Länge und Durchmesser sortiert. In den Zigarrenkisten liegen die Zigarren in einer bestimmten Farbreihenfolge: links die dunkelste, rechts die hellste Zigarre. Eine andere Reihenfolge weist auf eine Fälschung hin. Doch welche exklusiven Namen die Zigarren auch tragen, ob Cohiba, Montecristo, H. Upmann, Partagás oder Romeo y Julieta – die kostbaren Kunstwerke sind dazu bestimmt, in Rauch aufzugehen.

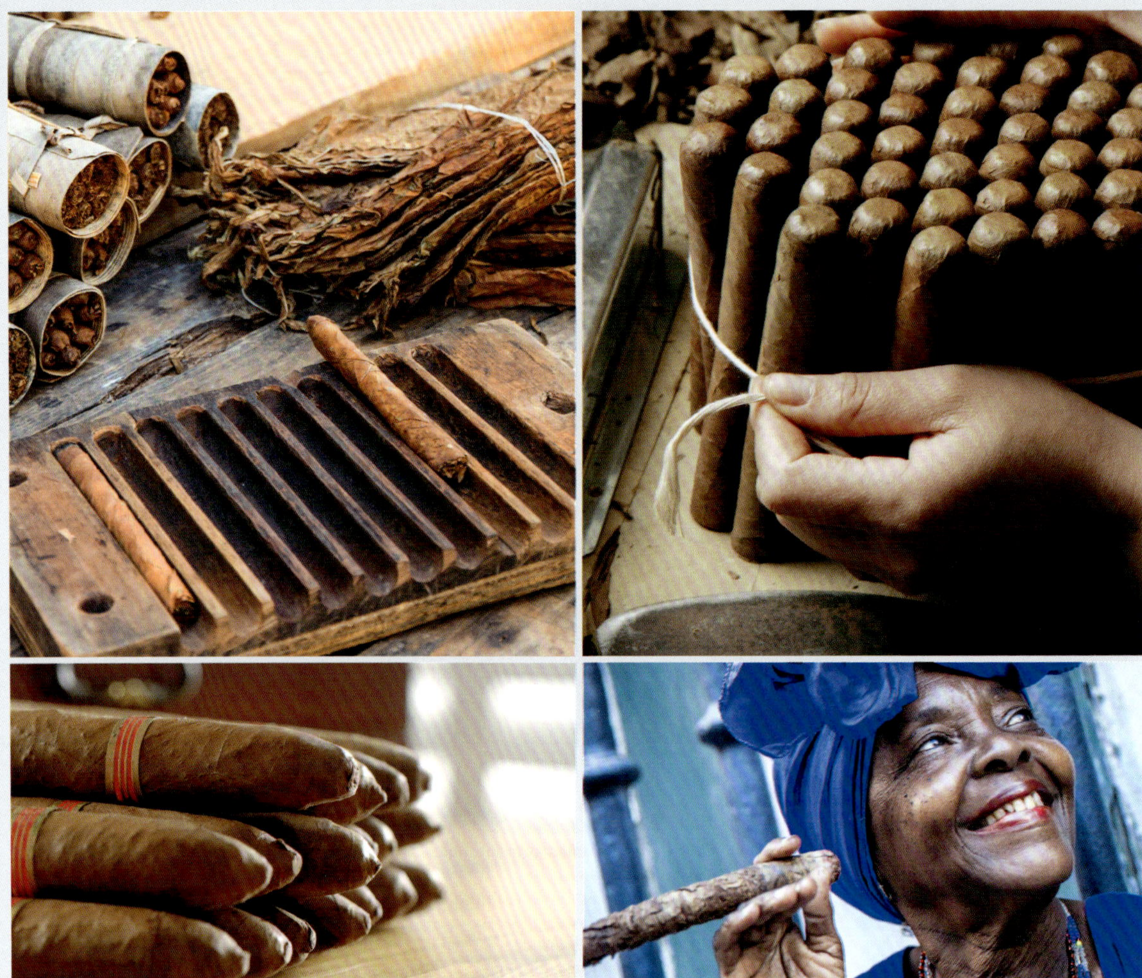

El camino al cigarro habano

En una caja estriada, el tabaco de relleno se forma antes de envolver los puros con el manto, para lo cual se utilizan las hojas de tabaco más perfectas. Los cigarros enrollados a mano son agrupados y clasificados por los inspectores de calidad en función de su longitud y diámetro. En las cajas de puros, los puros se encuentran en una determinada secuencia de colores: el puro más oscuro a la izquierda, el más claro a la derecha. Si la secuencia es distinta, es porque el producto está falsificado. Pero cualquiera que sea el nombre exclusivo que lleven los cigarros, ya sea Cohiba, Montecristo, H. Upmann, Partagás o Romeo y Julieta, las preciosas obras de arte están destinadas a esfumarse.

O caminho para o charuto de Havana

Em uma caixa ranhurada, o tabaco do enchimento é modelado antes de envolver os charutos no revestimento, para o qual as folhas de tabaco mais perfeitas são usadas. Os charutos enrolados à mão são agrupados e classificados pelos inspetores de qualidade de acordo com o comprimento e o diâmetro. Nas caixas de charutos, os charutos encontram-se numa determinada sequência de cores: o charuto mais escuro à esquerda, o mais claro à direita. Outra sequência indica uma falsificação. Mas quaisquer que sejam os nomes exclusivos dos charutos, sejam eles Cohiba, Montecristo, H. Upmann, Partagás ou Romeo y Julieta – as preciosas obras de arte estão destinadas a virar fumaça.

De weg van Havana sigaren

In een gegroefde doos wordt de vullingstabak gevormd voordat de sigaren in de vacht worden gewikkeld, hiervoor worden de meest onberispelijke tabaksbladeren gebruikt. De met de hand gerolde sigaren worden gebundeld en door de kwaliteitsinspecteurs gesorteerd op lengte en diameter. In de sigarendoosjes liggen de sigaren in een bepaalde kleurvolgorde: de donkerste sigaar links, de lichtste sigaar rechts. Een andere reeks wijst op een vervalsing. Maar welke exclusieve namen de sigaren ook dragen, of het nu gaat om Cohiba, Montecristo, H. Upmann, Partagás of Romeo y Julieta – de kostbare kunstwerken zijn bestemd om in rook op te gaan.

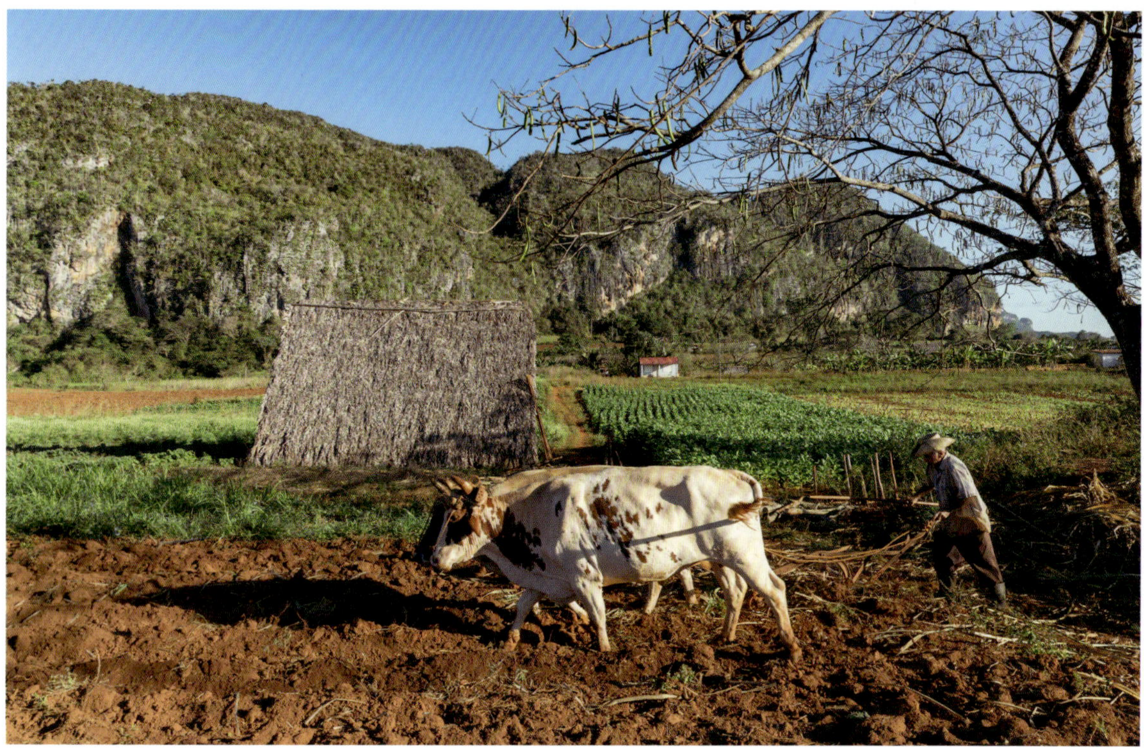

Valle de Viñales
Viñales Valley

Traces of the Natives

There are only few traces remaining of the original inhabitants natives of Cuba, the Siboneyes, Taínos and Guanahatabeyes. These include the palm straw-covered huts *(bohíos)* that can be seen all over the country. The naming and cultivation of maize, jukka, boniato, potatoes and tobacco can also be traced back to them, as can the name of the island itself: Cubanacán became Cuba.

Huellas de los nativos

De los extintos nativos de Cuba, los Siboneyes, Taínos y Guanahatabeyes, solo quedan unos pocos vestigios. Estos incluyen los bohíos cubiertos de paja de palma que se pueden ver en todo el país. El cultivo y la denominación del maíz, la jukka, el boniato, la papa y el tabaco también se remontan a ellos, al igual que el nombre de la isla en sí: Cubanacán se convirtió en Cuba.

Les vestiges des peuples autochtones

Des peuples aborigènes de Cuba aujourd'hui éteints, Siboneyes, Taïnos et Guanajatabeys, il ne reste que peu de vestiges. On trouve encore des huttes recouvertes de chaume de palmier *(bohíos)* dans tout le pays. La culture et les appellations espagnoles de plantes telles que le maïs, le yucca, la patate douce, la pomme de terre et le tabac sont également héritées de ces populations, tout comme le nom de l'île, dérivé de « Cubanacán ».

Vestígios dos nativos

Dos povos indígenas extintos de Cuba, os Siboneyes, Taínos e Guanahatabeyes, restam poucos vestígios. Isto inclui as cabanas cobertas de palha de palmeira *(bohíos)* que podem ser vistas em todo o país. Também o cultivo e a designação de milho, jukka, boniato, batata e tabaco, devem-se a eles, assim como o nome da própria ilha: Cubanacán tornou-se Cuba.

Spuren der Ureinwohner

Von den ausgelöschten Ureinwohnern Kubas, den Siboneyes, Taínos und Guanahatabeyes, gibt es nur noch wenige Spuren. Dazu gehören die palmstrohgedeckten Hütten *(bohíos)*, die man überall auf dem Land sieht. Auch Anbau und Bezeichnung von Mais, Jukka, Boniato, Kartoffeln, Tabak geht auf sie zurück, ebenso wie der Name der Insel selbst: aus Cubanacán wurde Cuba.

Sporen van de inboorlingen

Van de uitgestorven Cubaanse inboorlingen, de Siboneyes, Taíno's en Guanahatabeyes, zijn nog maar weinig sporen over. Zo zijn er onder andere de met palmstro bedekte hutten *(bohíos)* die overal in het land te vinden zijn. Ook de teelt en benaming van maïs, jukka, boniato, aardappelen en tabak zijn hier ook van terug te herleiden, zoals ook de naam van het eiland zelf: uit Cubanacán is Cuba geworden.

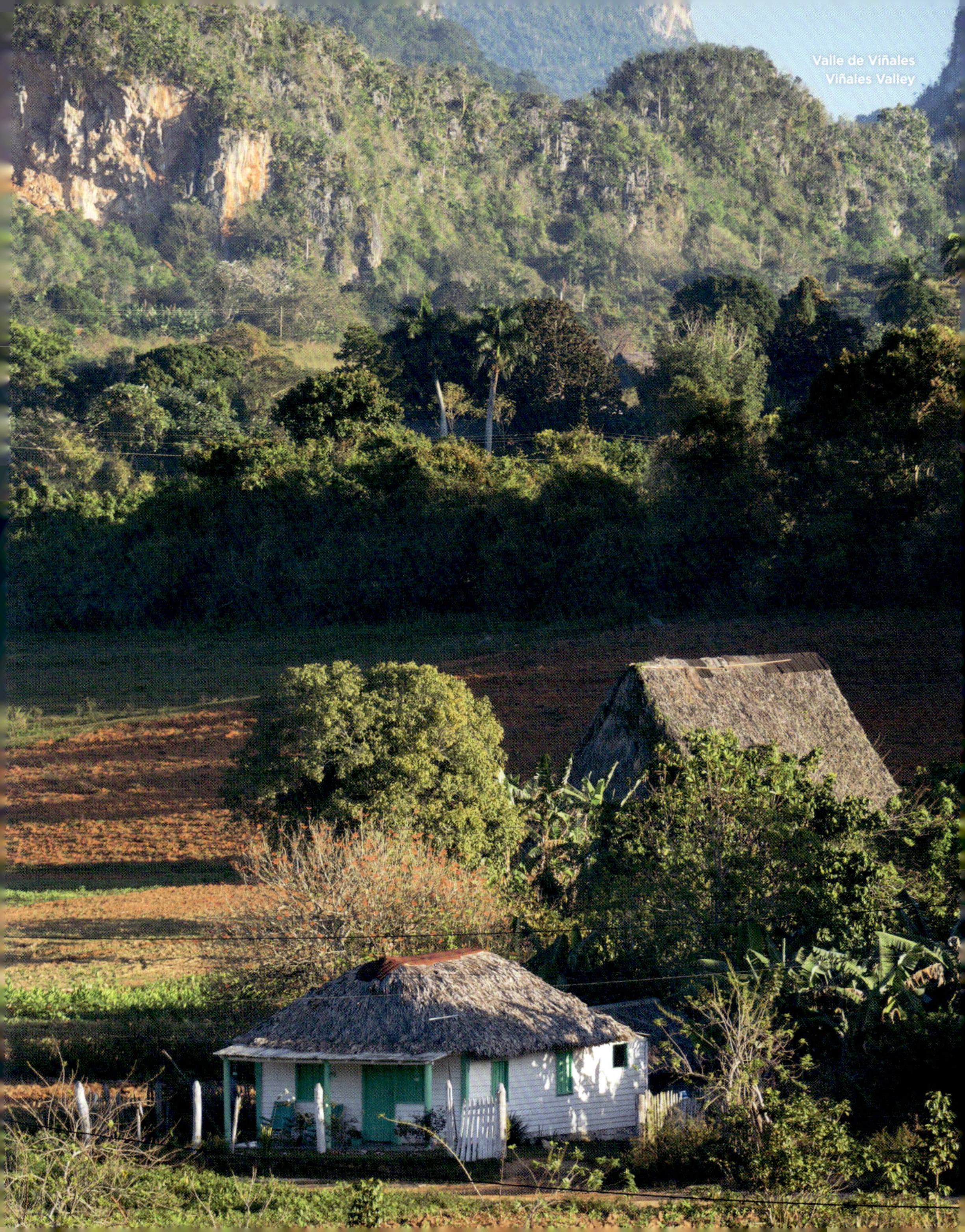

Valle de Viñales
Viñales Valley

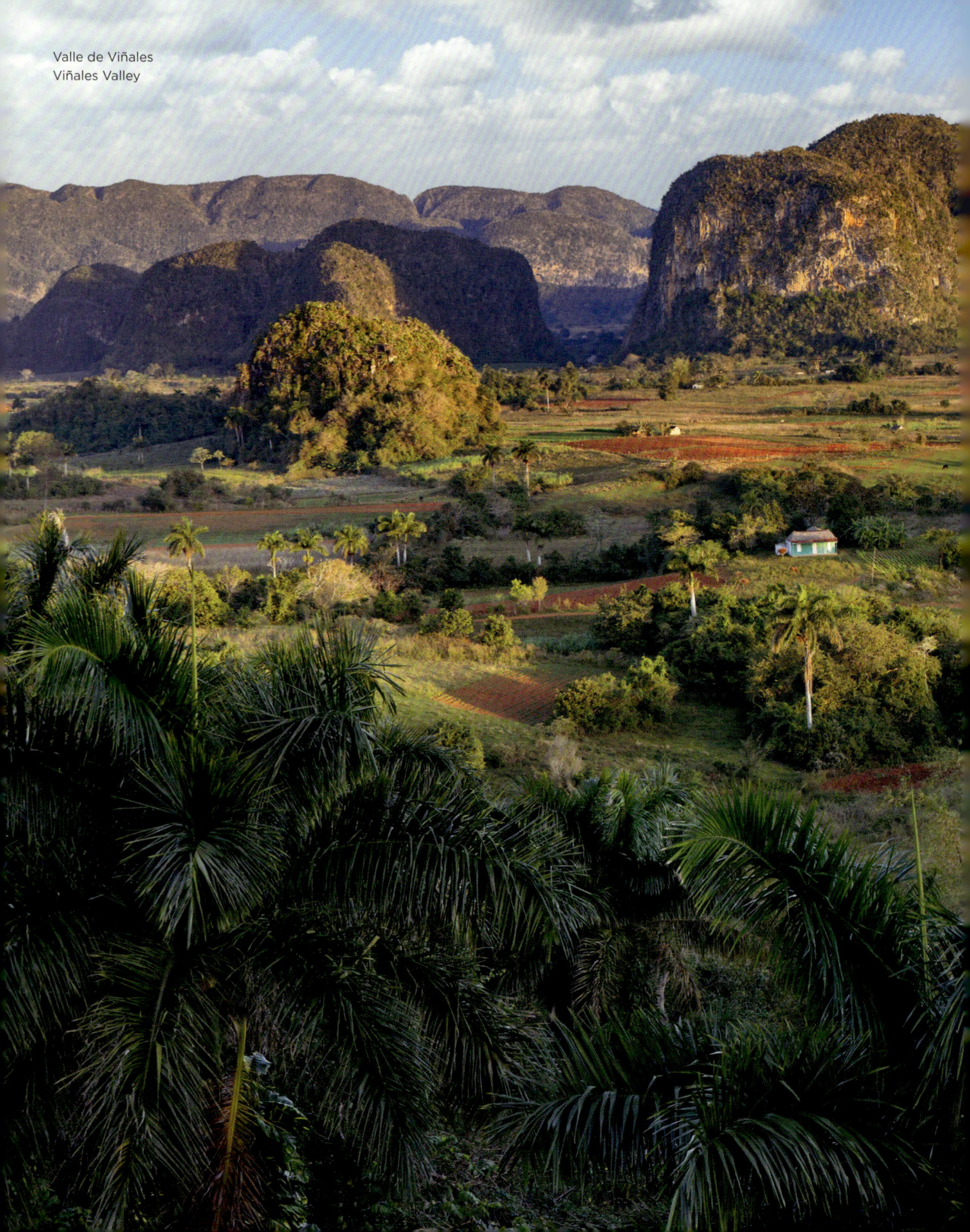

Valle de Viñales
Viñales Valley

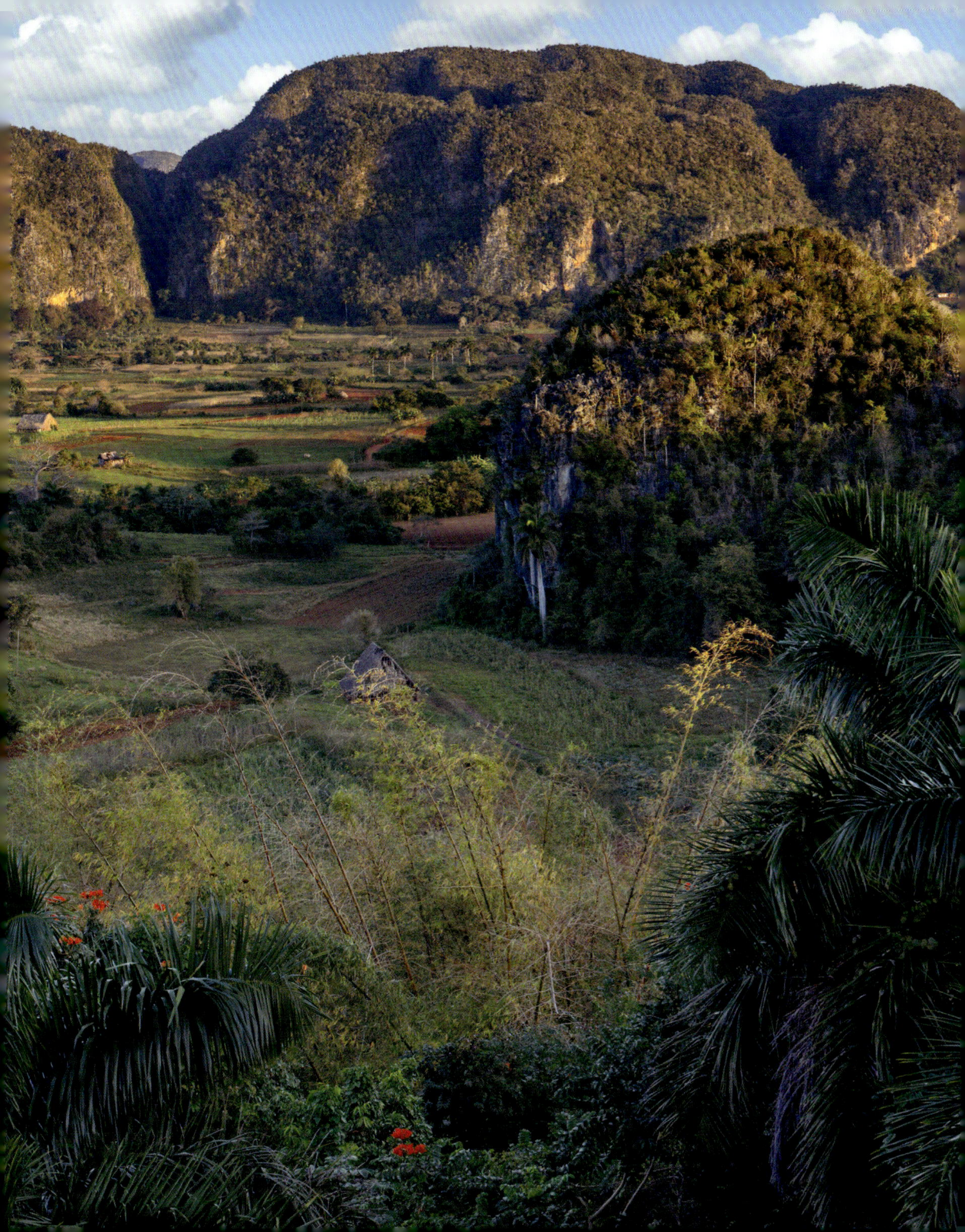

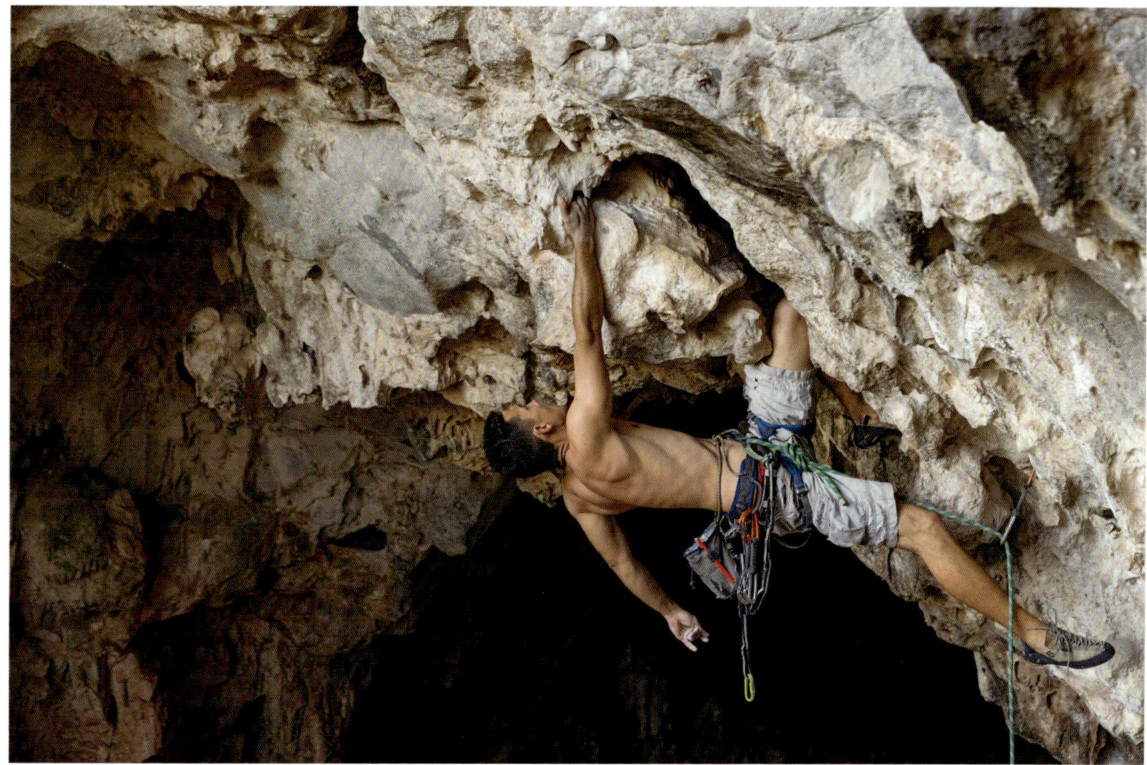

Valle de Viñales
Viñales Valley

The Caves of Santo Tomás

Before the arrival of the Spanish, the Guanahatabeyes, a hunter gatherer tribe, lived in the pine forests on the banks of the Guamá River. They used the countless caves dug into the rock by the branches of the river as shelters. The Santo Tomás Caves are the largest cave system in Cuba, with seven levels and extending over 46 km (28 mi.).

Las cuevas de Santo Tomás

Antes de la llegada de los españoles, los guanahatabeyes, un pueblo de cazadores y recolectores, vivían en los bosques de pinos a orillas del río Guamá. Utilizaron las innumerables cuevas excavadas en la roca por los brazos del río como refugios. El sistema de cuevas más grande de Cuba son las Cuevas de Santo Tomás, que tienen siete pisos y se extienden a lo largo de 46 km.

Les hauteurs de Santo Tomás

Avant l'arrivée des Espagnols, le peuple de chasseurs-cueilleurs Guanajatabey vivait dans les pinèdes bordant les rives du Río Guamá. Ils installaient leur refuge dans les innombrables grottes creusées dans la roche par les bras de la rivière. Le plus vaste réseau de grottes de Cuba se situe à Santo Tomás; il présente à certains endroits une hauteur équivalant à 7 étages et s'étend sur 46 km de long.

As Cavernas de Santo Tomás

Antes da chegada dos espanhóis, os Guanahatabeyes, um povo de caçadores e coletores, viviam nas florestas de pinheiros às margens do rio Guamá. Eles usavam como abrigos as inúmeras cavernas escavadas na rocha pelos braços do rio. O maior sistema de cavernas de Cuba é o das Cavernas de Santo Tomás, com sete andares e mais de 46 km de extensão.

Die Höhlen von Santo Tomás

In den Pinienwäldern an den Ufern des Río Guamá lebten vor Ankunft der Spanier die Guanahatabeyes, ein Volk von Jägern und Sammlern. Sie benutzten die unzähligen Höhlen, die die Flussarme in das Felsgestein gegraben hatten, als Zufluchtsorte. Das größte Höhlensystem Kubas sind die Höhlen von Santo Tomás, sie haben sieben Etagen und ziehen sich über 46 km.

Cueva de Santo Tomas

De Guanahatabeyes, een volk van jagers en verzamelaars leefden voor de komst van de Spanjaarden in de dennenbossen aan de oever van de Guamá rivier. Ze gebruikten de talloze grotten die door de rivierarm in de rotsen waren uitgegraven als schuilplaatsen. Het grootste grottensysteem in Cuba is de Santo Tomás Grotten 'Cueva de Santo Tomas', die zeven verdiepingen hebben en zich over 46 km uitstrekken.

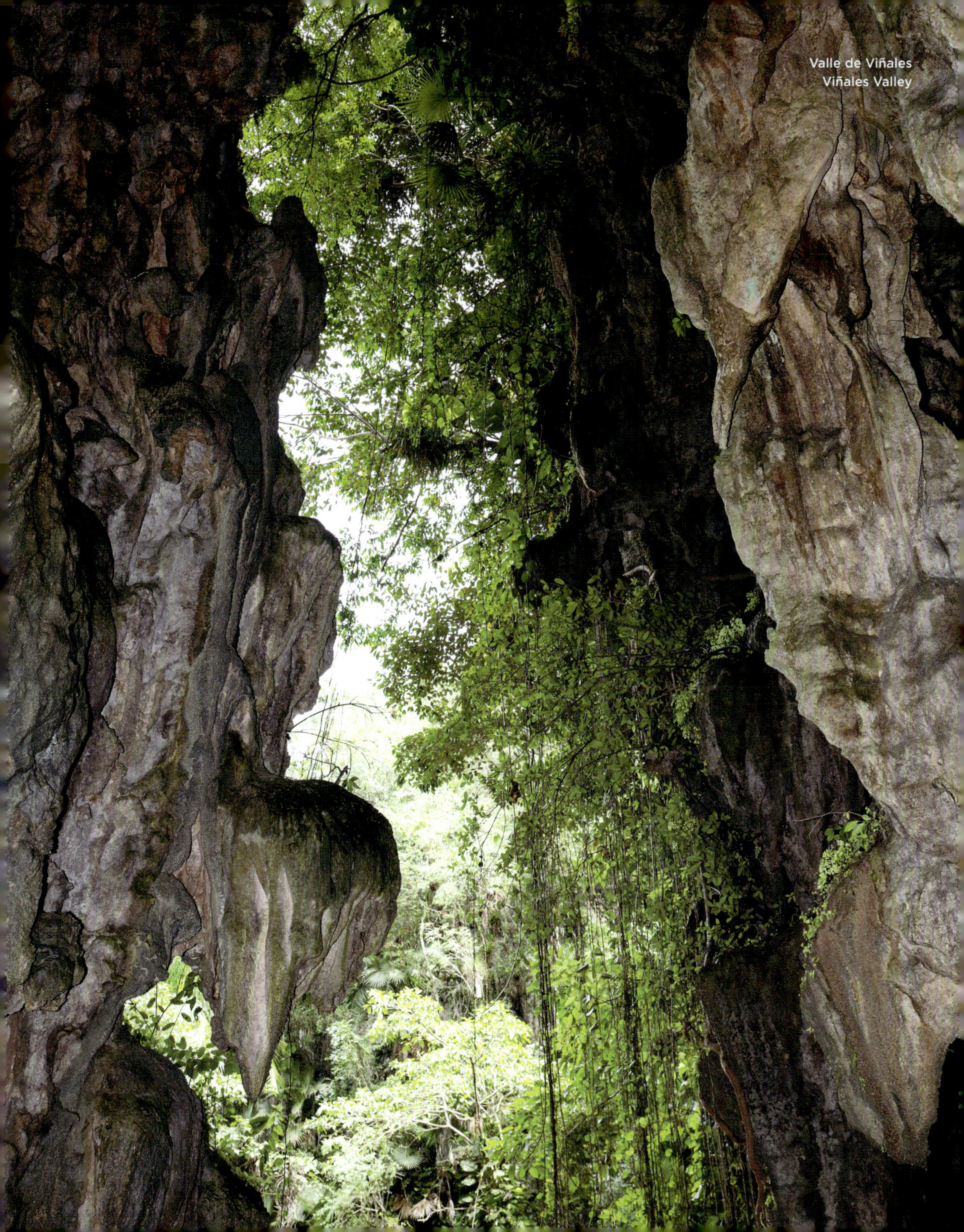
Valle de Viñales
Viñales Valley

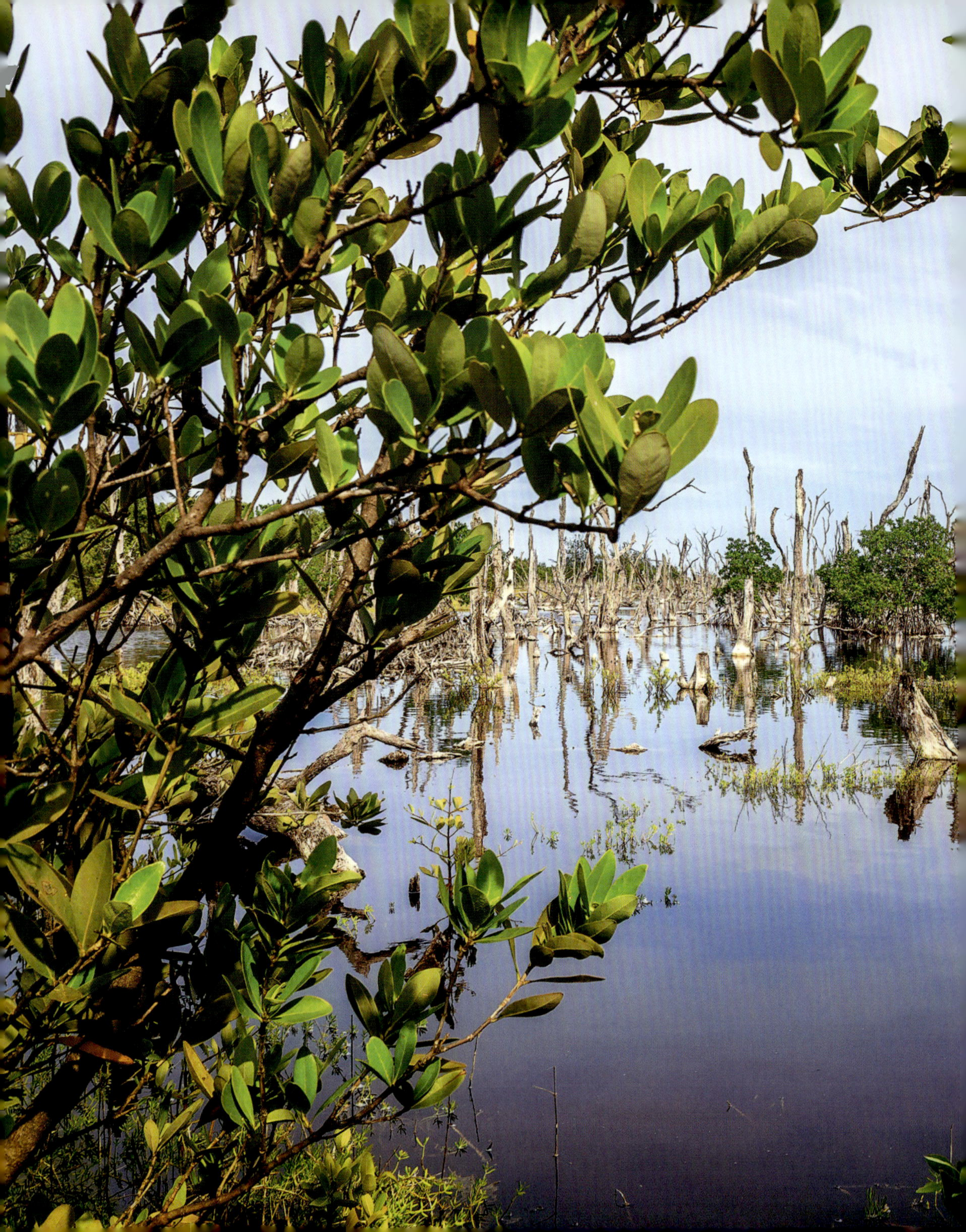

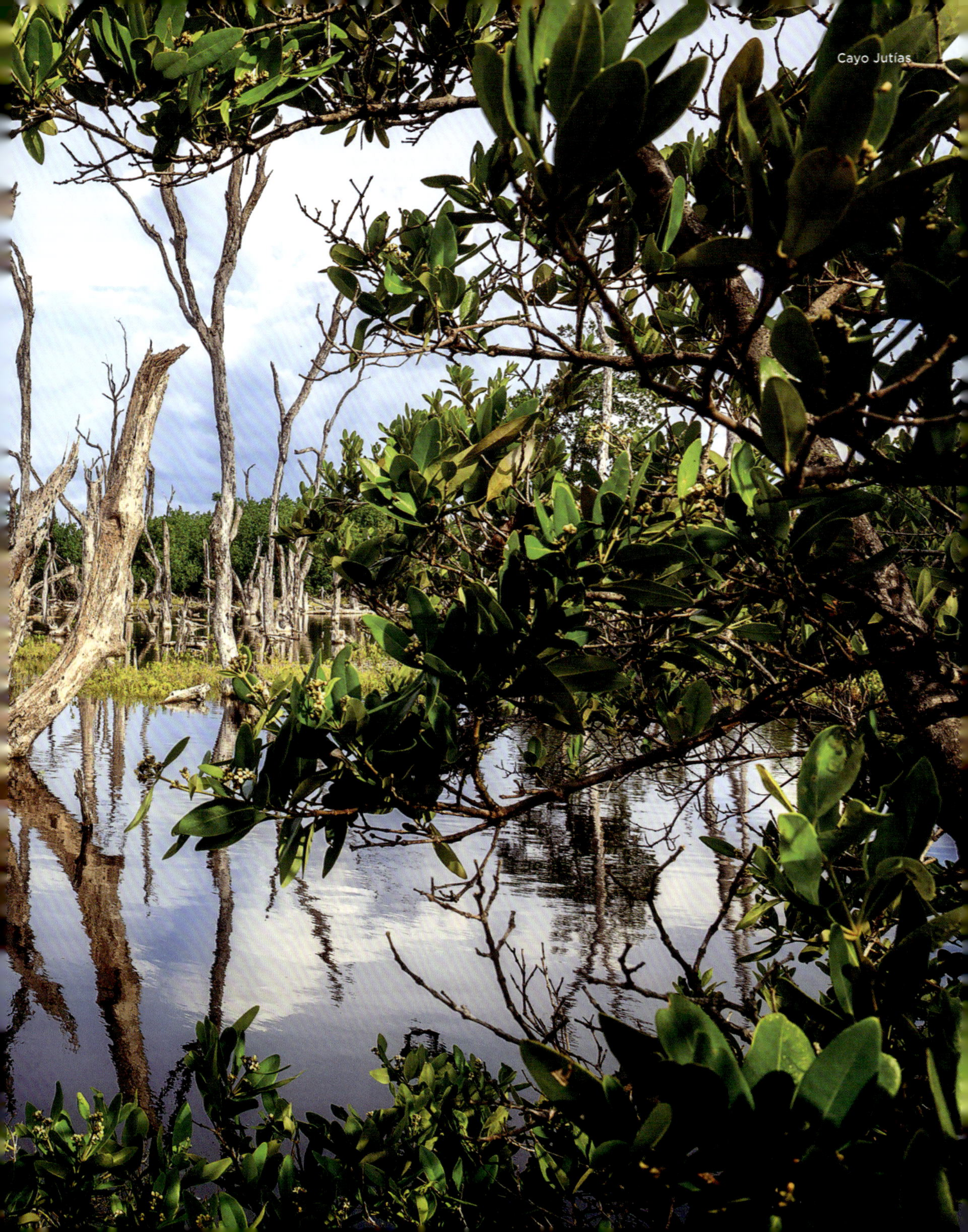
Cayo Jutías

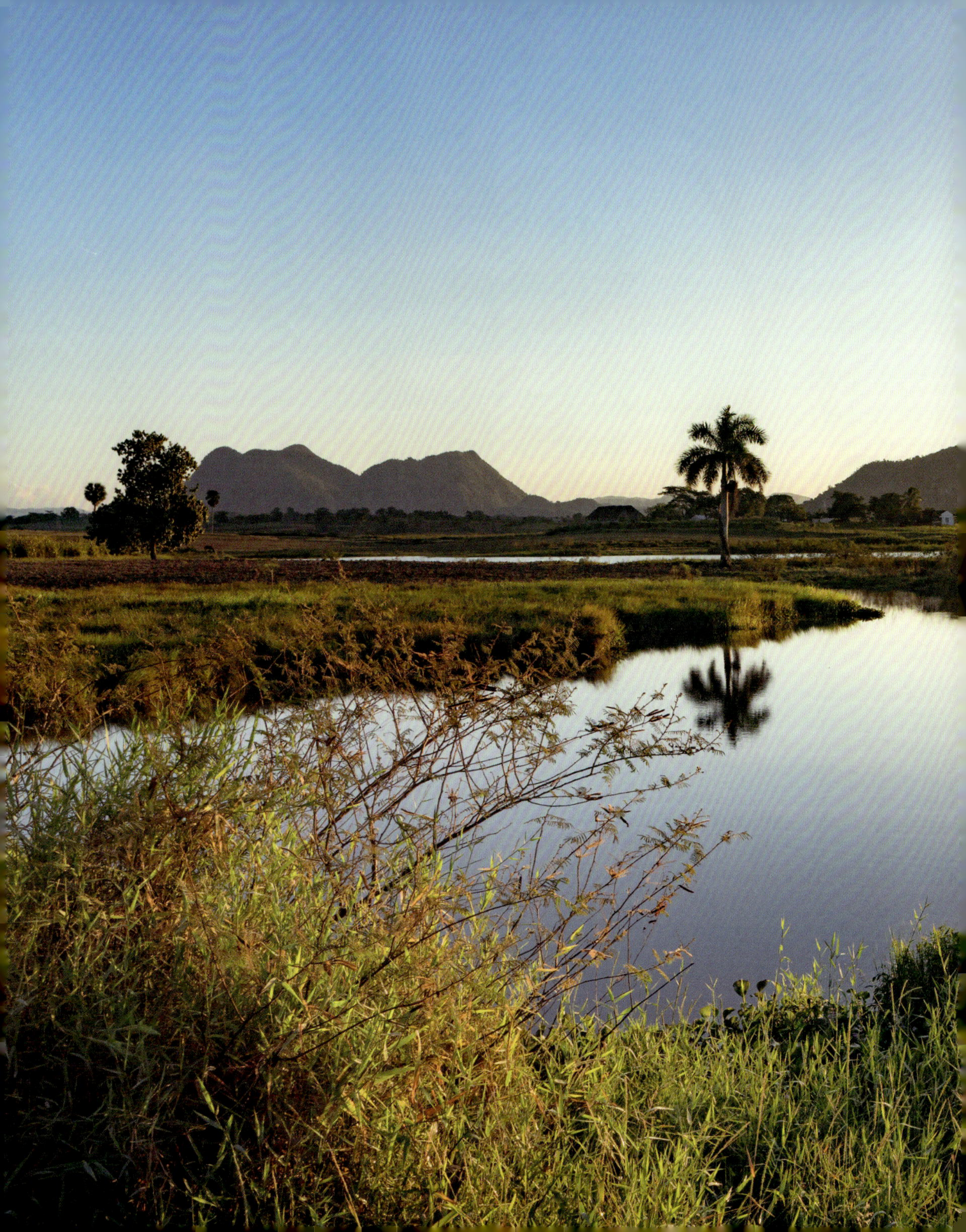

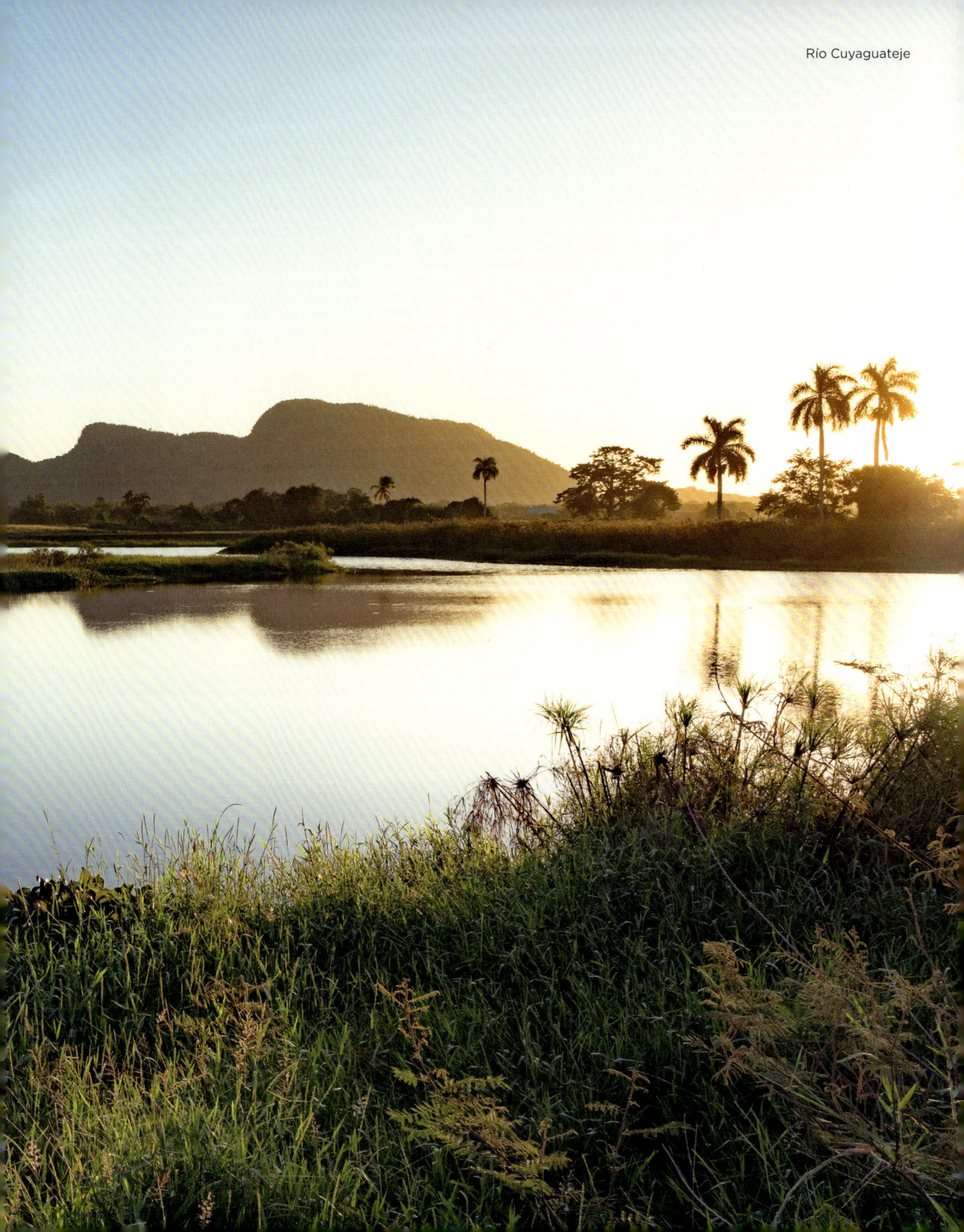

Río Cuyaguateje

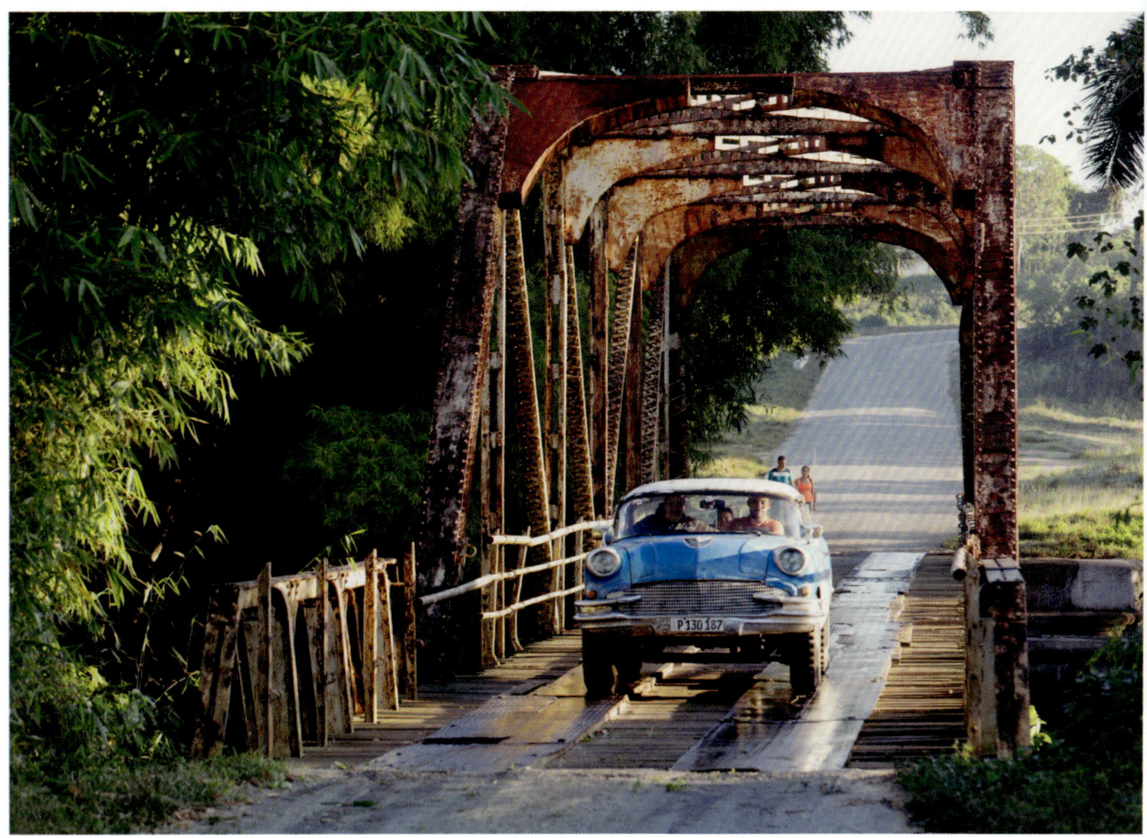

Guane

Che Guevara

The revolutionary icon Ernesto "Che" Guevara (1928–1967) is everywhere in Cuba. "El Che", as he is known, smiles from the walls of houses even in the remotest villages; his world-famous portrait can be found in schools, public buildings and on kitsch postcards. This charismatic comandante from Argentina fought with the rebel army in the Sierra Maestra, was Minister of Industry and headed the National Bank. However, he ordered the execution of 216 people as "counterrevolutionaries" in the fortress La Cabaña in Havana, and noted in his diary that the killings were "a necessity for the Cuban people".

L'icône Che Guevara

À Cuba, l'icône révolutionnaire Ernesto Che Guevara (1928–1967) est omniprésente. Le « Che » orne les murs des maisons dans les moindres villages, et son portrait mondialement célèbre est affiché dans les écoles, les bâtiments officiels et sur des cartes postales d'un kitch exceptionnel. Le charismatique *comandante* d'origine argentine combattit avec l'armée rebelle dans la sierra Maestra, puis devint ministre de l'Industrie et directeur de la Banque nationale. Il fit également exécuter, dans la forteresse La Cabaña de La Havane, au moins 216 personnes « contre-révolutionnaires », justifiant dans son journal ces fusillades comme « une nécessité pour le peuple cubain ».

Ikone Che Guevara

In Kuba ist die Revolutions-Ikone Ernesto „Che" Guevara (1928–1967) allgegenwärtig. „El Che", wie er in Kuba heißt, lächelt noch im entlegensten Dorf von einer Hauswand, sein weltberühmtes Konterfei findet man an Schulen, öffentlichen Gebäuden und schrillen Kitschpostkarten. Der charismatische Comandante aus Argentinien kämpfte mit der Rebellenarmee in der Sierra Maestra, war Industrieminister und leitete die Nationalbank. Allerdings ließ er in der Festung La Cabaña in Havanna mindestens 216 Menschen als „Konterrevolutionäre" hinrichten und notierte in seinem Tagebuch, Erschießungen seien „eine Notwendigkeit für das kubanische Volk".

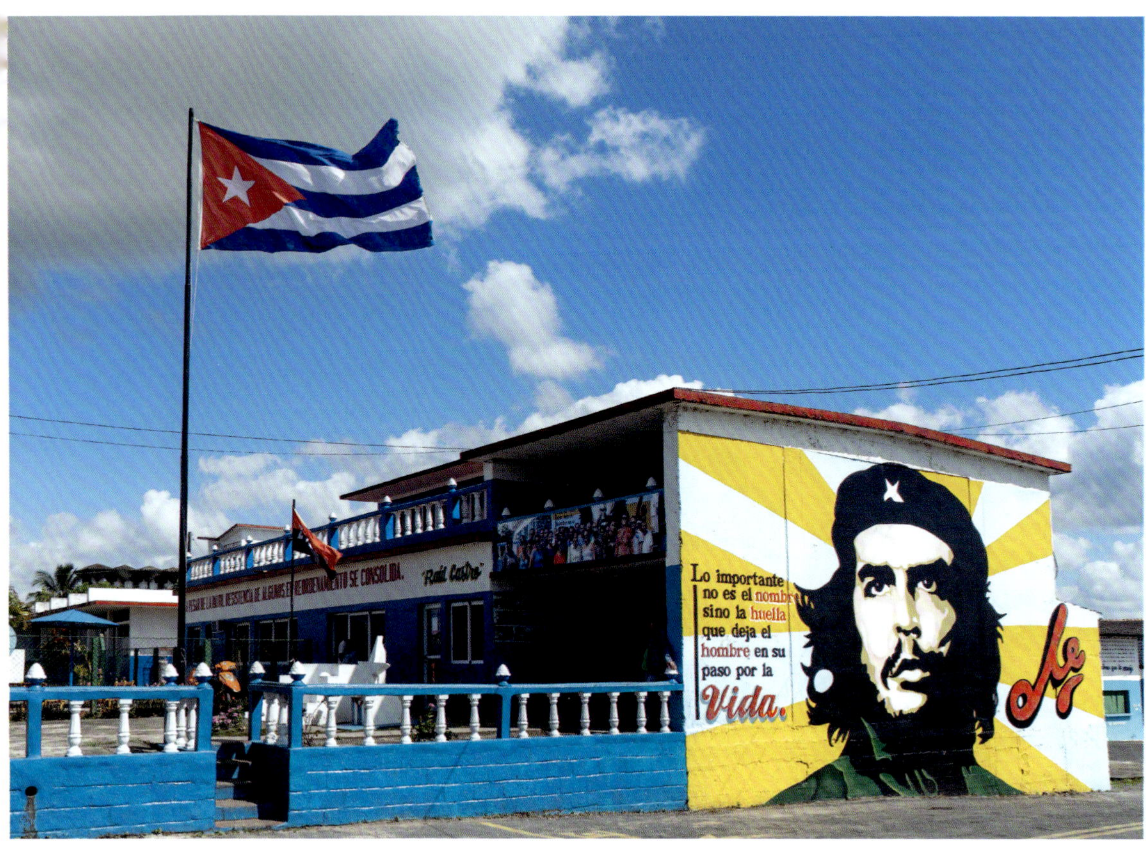

Guane

Icono Che Guevara

El icono revolucionario Ernesto "Che" Guevara (1928–1967) es omnipresente en Cuba. "El Che", como se le llama en Cuba, sonríe desde la pared de una casa incluso en el pueblo más remoto; su famoso retrato se puede encontrar en escuelas, edificios públicos y postales chillonas. El carismático comandante argentino luchó con el ejército rebelde en la Sierra Maestra, fue ministro de Industria y dirigió el Banco Nacional. Sin embargo, al menos 216 personas fueron ejecutadas como "contrarrevolucionarios" en la fortaleza de La Cabaña en La Habana y señaló en su diario que los tiroteos eran "una necesidad para el pueblo cubano".

Ícone Che Guevara

O ícone revolucionário Ernesto "Che" Guevara (1928–1967) é onipresente em Cuba. O "El Che", como é chamado em Cuba, ainda sorri em um muro de uma casa mesmo na aldeia mais remota; seu retrato mundialmente famoso pode ser encontrado em escolas, edifícios públicos e cartões postais kitsch. O carismático comandante argentino lutou com o exército rebelde na Serra Maestra, foi Ministro da Indústria e chefiou o Banco Nacional. No entanto, executou pelo menos 216 pessoas na fortaleza La Cabaña em Havana como "contra-revolucionárias" e em seu diário anotou que os tiroteios eram "uma necessidade para o povo cubano".

Che Guevara

In Cuba is de revolutionaire icoon Ernesto 'Che' Guevara (1928–1967) alomvertegenwoordigd. Hij wordt in Cuba ook wel 'El Che' genoemd. Je vindt zijn portret zelfs op muren van de huizen van de verste dorpen; daarnaast vindt je zijn wereldberoemde portret ook in scholen, openbare gebouwen en op schrille kitscherige ansichtkaarten terug. De charismatische commandant uit Argentinië vocht met het rebellenleger in de Sierra Maestra, hij was minister van Industrie en leidde de Nationale Bank. Hij liet echter minstens 216 mensen als 'contrarevolutionairen' executeren in het fort La Cabaña in Havana en merkte in zijn dagboek op dat schietpartijen 'een noodzaak waren voor het Cubaanse volk'.

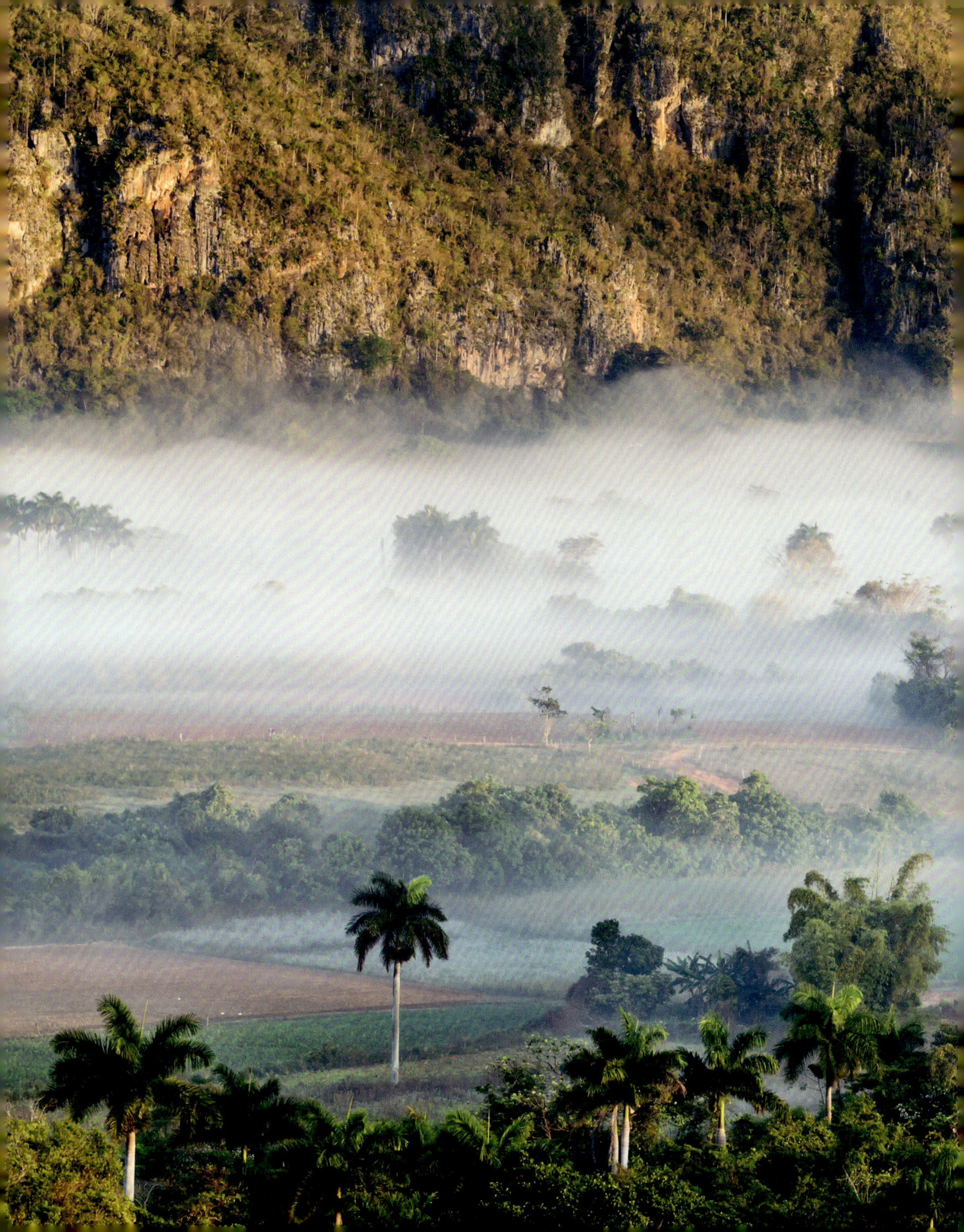

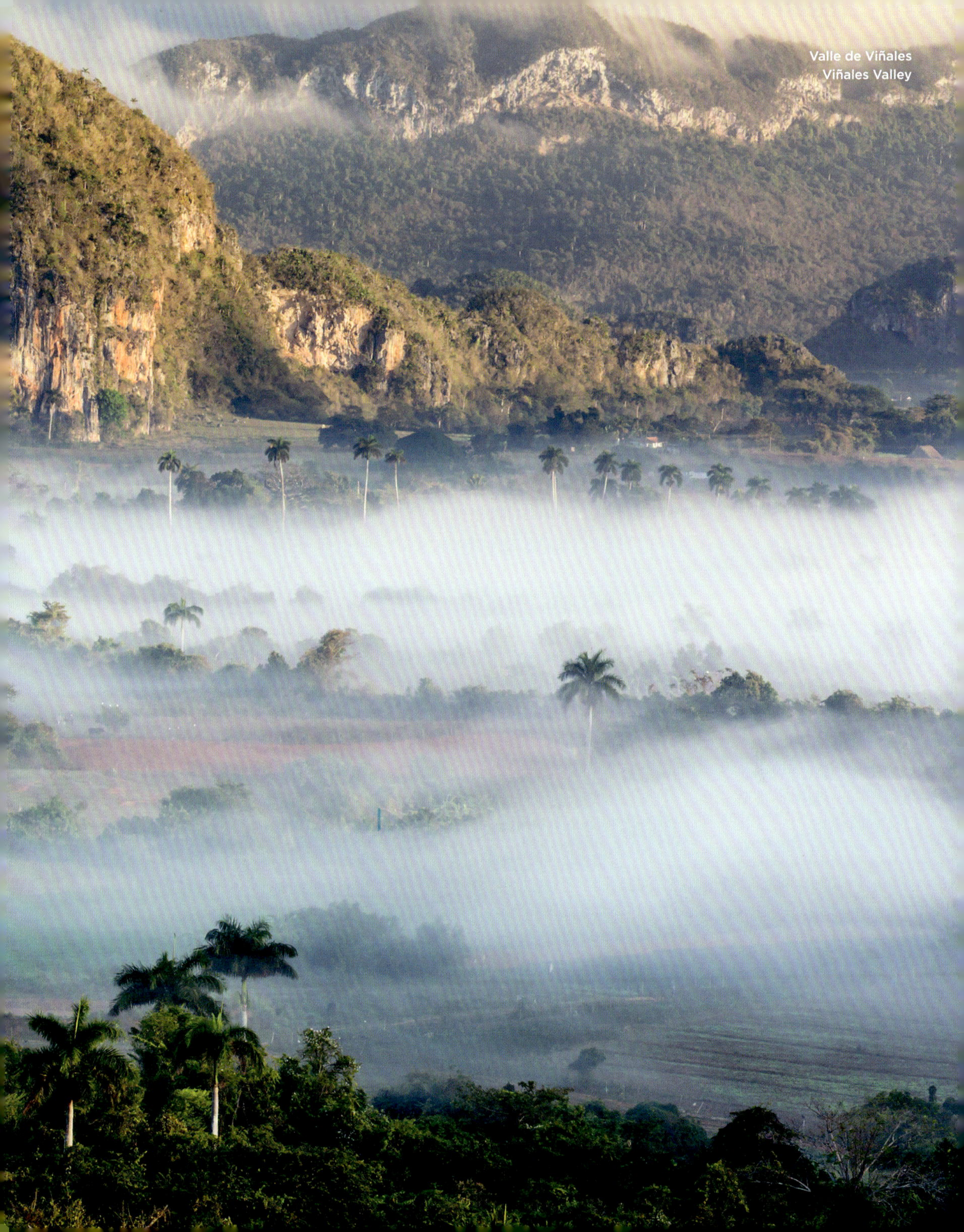
Valle de Viñales
Viñales Valley

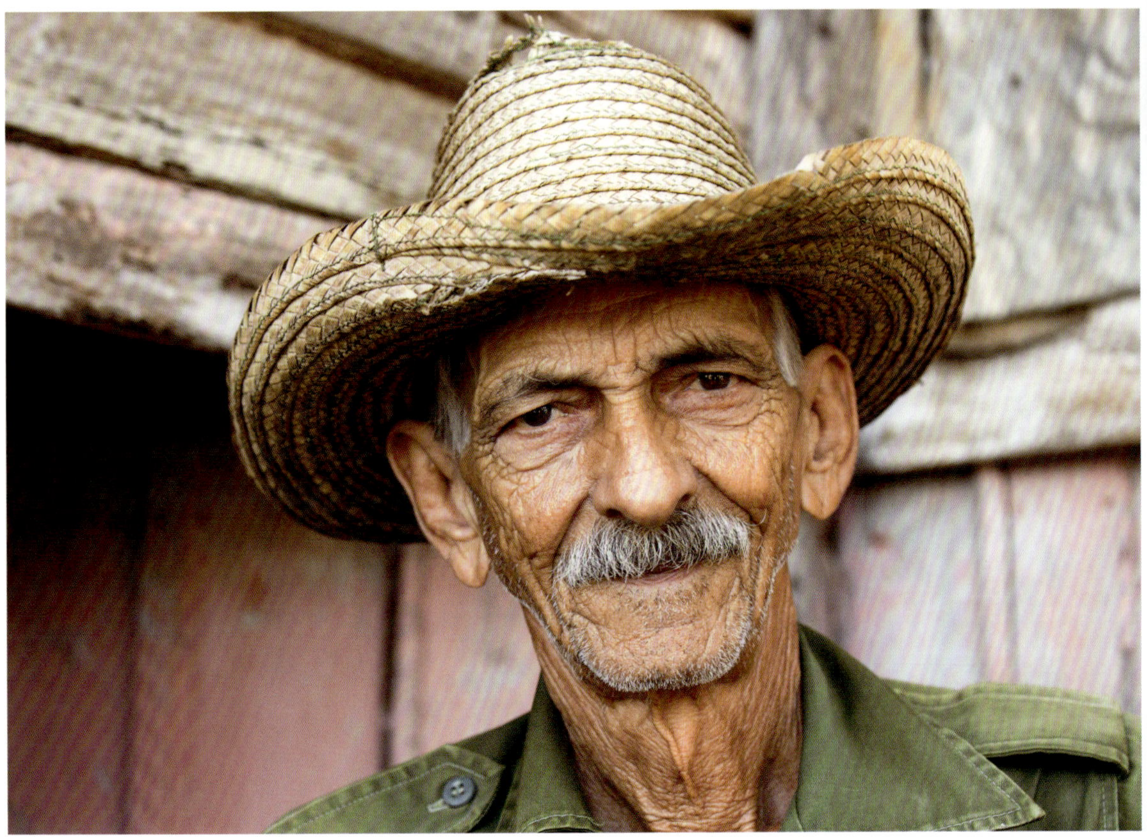

Valle de Viñales
Viñales Valley

The Vegueros

The proud tobacco farmers of Pinar del Río call themselves *vegueros,* from Spanish *vega* (floodplain). They are mostly of Spanish origin (mainly from the Canary Islands), which can also be noticed in the music of Pinar del Río. In the 18th century the vegueros rebelled against the draconian Spanish trade monopoly on tobacco and tax increases, and in 1720 they were bloodily defeated. Today the vegueros must sell 90 percent of their harvest to the state at fixed prices. "Vegueros" is also the name of a special type of cigar with an aroma and taste that is tailored for Cuban cigar smokers and which has only been exported since the 1990s.

Les Vegueros

Les fiers cultivateurs de tabac de Pinar del Río se surnomment eux-mêmes *vegueros,* de l'espagnol *vega* (prairie). La plupart sont d'origine espagnole (notamment des îles Canaries), ce qui transparaît également dans la musique de la région. Au XVIIIe siècle, les Vegueros se rebellèrent contre le strict monopole commercial de l'Espagne sur le tabac et les impôts, mais furent réprimés dans le sang en 1720. Aujourd'hui, ils doivent vendre 90 % de leur récolte à prix fixe à l'État. « Vegueros » est également une variété de cigares spécifique, dont l'arôme et le goût sont très appréciés des fumeurs cubains et exportés depuis les années 1990.

Die Vegueros

Die stolzen Tabakbauern in Pinar del Río nennen sich selbst *vegueros,* von spanisch *vega* (Aue). Sie sind größtenteils spanischer Herkunft (v. a. von den Kanarischen Inseln), was auch in der Musik Pinar del Ríos hörbar ist. Im 18. Jahrhundert rebellierten die Vegueros gegen das drakonische spanische Handelsmonopol auf Tabak und Steuererhöhungen, 1720 wurden sie blutig niedergeschlagen. Heute müssen die Vegueros 90 Prozent der Ernte zu Fixpreisen an den Staat verkaufen. „Vegueros" heißt auch eine besondere Zigarrensorte, deren Aroma und Geschmack auf die kubanischen Zigarrenraucher abgestimmt ist und die erst seit den 1990er Jahren auch exportiert wird.

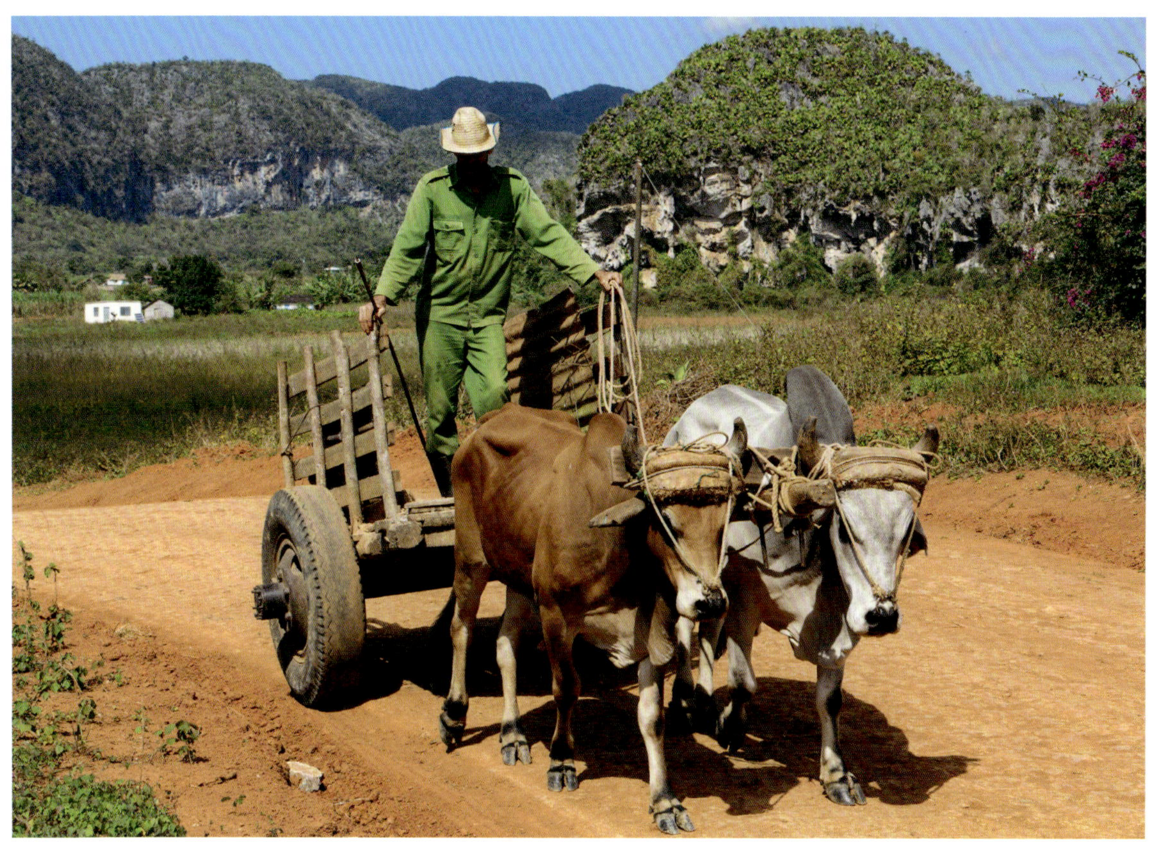

Valle de Viñales
Viñales Valley

Los Vegueros

Los orgullosos cultivadores de tabaco de Pinar del Río se llaman a sí mismos "vegueros", de la vega española. Son en su mayoría de origen español (principalmente canario), lo cual también se puede reconocer al escuchar la música de Pinar del Río. En el siglo XVIII, los vegueros se rebelaron contra el dramático monopolio comercial español por el tabaco y los aumentos de impuestos, y en 1720 fueron derrotados de forma muy sangrienta. Actualmente, los vegueros tienen que vender el 90 por ciento de la cosecha al estado a precios fijos. "Vegueros" es también el nombre de un tipo especial de puro cuyo aroma y sabor están adaptados a los fumadores cubanos y que solo se exporta desde los años noventa.

Os Vegueros

Os orgulhosos produtores de tabaco de Pinar del Río se autodenominam *vegueros* do espanhol *vega* (planície de inundação). Eles são principalmente de origem espanhola (principalmente das Ilhas Canárias), que também podem ser ouvidos na música de Pinar del Río. No século XVIII, os vegueros rebelaram-se contra o draconiano monopólio comercial espanhol do tabaco e o aumento dos impostos e, em 1720, foram derrotados de forma sangrenta. Hoje os vegueros têm que vender 90 por cento da colheita para o Estado a preços fixos. "Vegueros" é também o nome de um tipo especial de charuto, cujo aroma e sabor são adaptados aos fumadores cubanos e que só começou a ser exportado a partir dos anos 90.

De Vegueros

De trotse tabakstelers in Pinar del Río noemen zichzelf *vegueros*, afkomstig uit de Spaanse *vega*. Ze zijn grotendeels van Spaanse afkomst (voornamelijk afkomstig van de Canarische Eilanden), wat ook te horen is in de muziek van Pinar del Río. In de 18e eeuw kwamen de Vegueros in opstand tegen het draconische Spaanse handelsmonopolie op tabak en belastingverhogingen, en in 1720 werden ze bloedig verslagen. Tegenwoordig moeten de Vegueros 90 procent van de oogst tegen vaste prijzen aan de staat verkopen. Vegueros is ook de naam van een speciaal type sigaar waarvan het aroma en de smaak zijn aangepast aan de Cubaanse sigarenrokers en die pas sinds de jaren negentig wordt geëxporteerd.

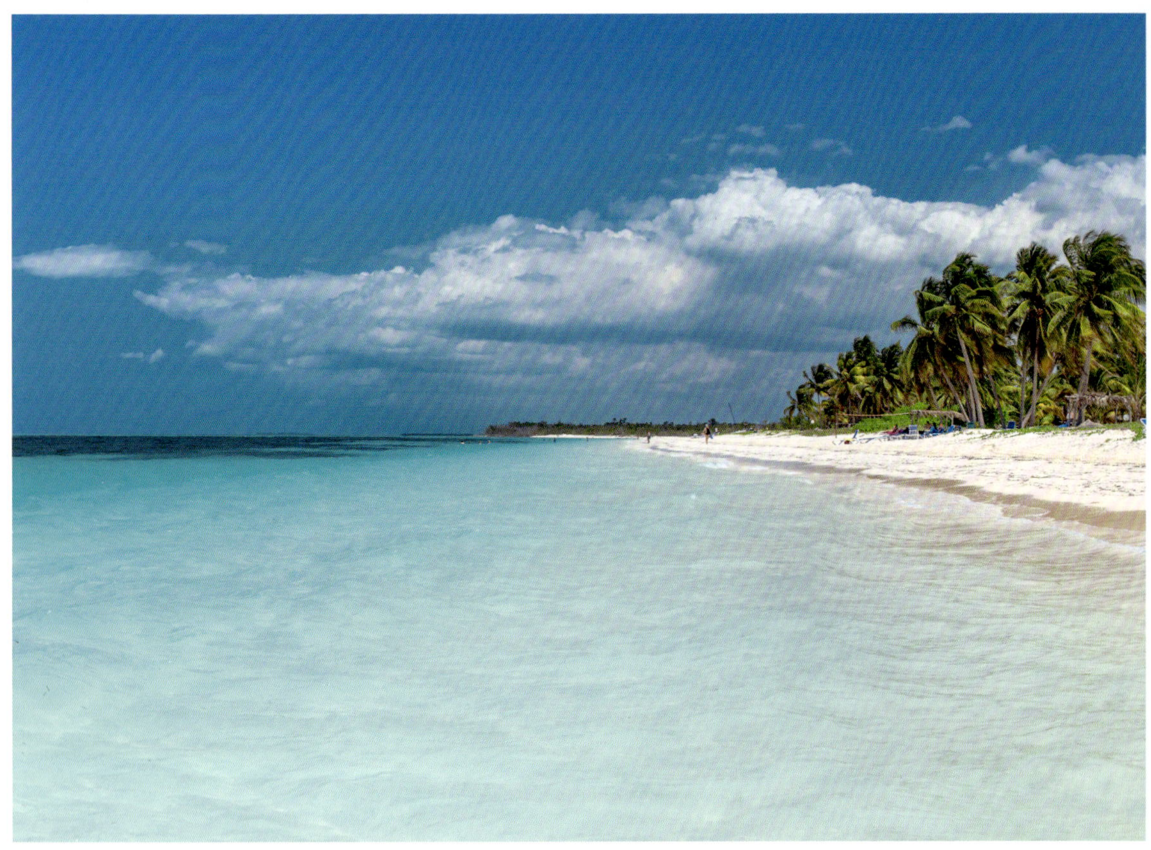

Cayo Levisa

Cayo Jutías

The two islands of Cayo Levisa and Cayo Jutías, which belong to the archipelago Los Colorados, are located off the north coast of Pinar del Ríos. Cayo Levisa can be reached by ferry, and Cayo Jutías can reached by crossing a 4 km (2.5 mi.) long dam. The south side of the Cayo is covered with dense mangrove forests, and fine sandy white beaches lie on the north side. Because many specimens of the tree rats *(jutías)* that are related to porcupines lived on the Cayo, the islet carries this name. There is no tourist infrastructure or hotels on Cayo Jutías, just a simple restaurant and a lot of untouched nature.

Cayo Jutías

Les deux îlots Cayo Levisa et Cayo Jutías, intégrés à l'archipel Los Colorados, sont situés au large de la côte nord de Pinar del Ríos. Un ferry permet d'atteindre Cayo Levisa et une digue de 4 km rejoint Cayo Jutías. Les régions sud des cayos sont couvertes de forêts de mangrove denses, alors que les plages de sable fin occupent les côtes nord. Cayo Jutías doit son nom à l'importante population de hutias, rats arboricoles cousins du porc-épic, présente sur l'îlot. Exempt d'infrastructure touristique et d'hôtels, ce cayo offre un unique restaurant et une magnifique nature vierge.

Cayo Jutías

Vor der Nordküste Pinar del Ríos liegen die beiden Inselchen Cayo Levisa und Cayo Jutías, die zum Archipel Los Colorados gehören. Cayo Levisa ist mit der Fähre zu erreichen, nach Cayo Jutías führt ein 4 km langer Damm. Die Südseite des Cayos ist mit dichten Mangrovenwäldern bewachsen, die feinsandigen weißen Strände liegen an der Nordseite. Weil auf dem Cayo viele Exemplare der mit den Stachelschweinen verwandten Baumratten *(jutías)* lebten, trägt das Inselchen diesen Namen. Eine touristische Infrastruktur und Hotels gibt es nicht auf Cayo Jutías, nur ein einfaches Restaurant und viel unberührte Natur.

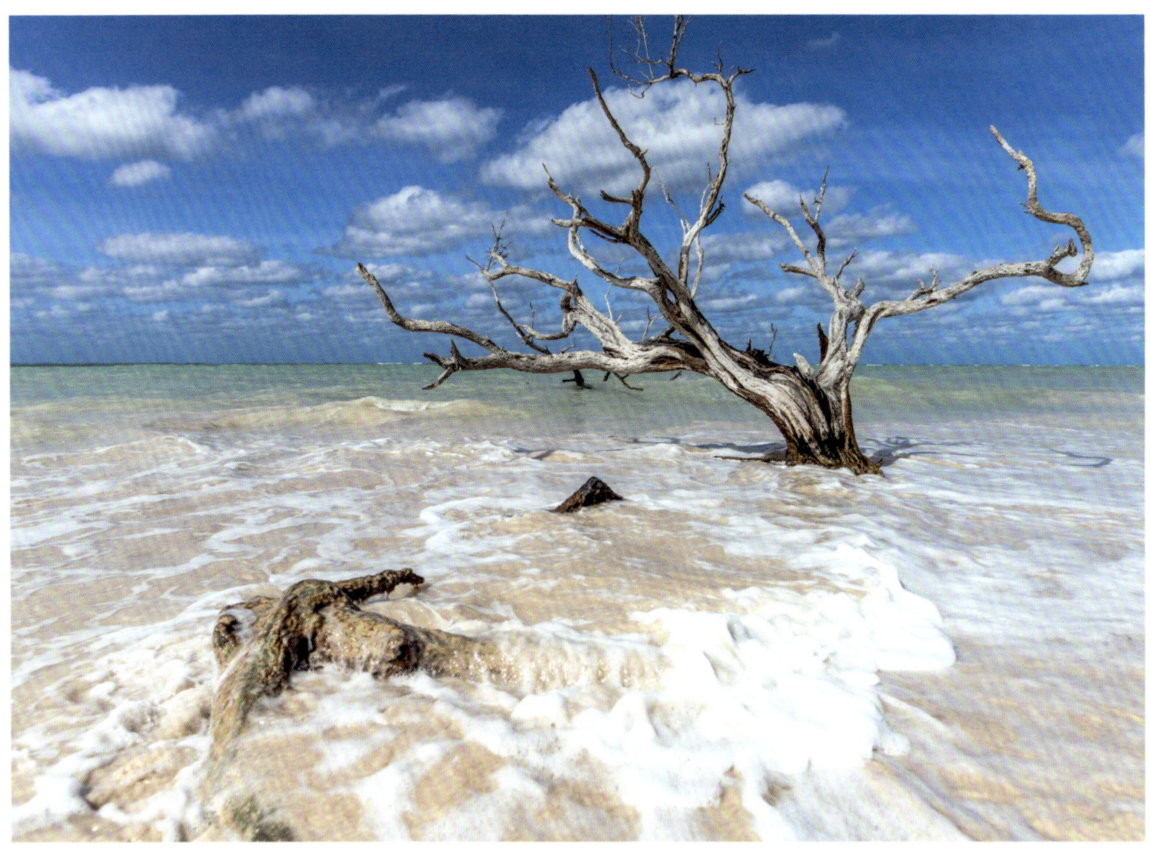

Cayo Jutías

Cayo Jutías

Las dos islas Cayo Levisa y Cayo Jutías, que pertenecen al archipiélago "Los Colorados", están situadas en la costa norte de Pinar del Ríos. Se puede llegar a Cayo Levisa en ferry, y a Cayo Jutías se llega a través de una presa de 4 km de longitud. El lado sur del Cayo está cubierto de densos bosques de manglares; las playas de arena fina y blanca se encuentran en el lado norte. Debido a que muchos especímenes de las ratas arbóreas (*jutías*) relacionadas con los puercoespines vivían en el Cayo, el islote lleva este nombre. No hay infraestructura turística ni hoteles en Cayo Jutías, sino solo un simple restaurante y mucha naturaleza virgen.

Cayo Jutías

As duas pequenas ilhas Cayo Levisa e Cayo Jutías, que pertencem ao arquipélago Los Colorados, estão localizadas na costa norte de Pinar del Río. Cayo Levisa pode ser alcançado por balsa, Cayo Jutías é alcançado por uma barragem de 4 km de comprimento. O lado sul do Cayo é coberto por densas florestas de mangue, as praias de areia branca e fina ficam no lado norte. Como em Cayo existia uma grande quantidade dos roedores rutías (*jutías*) relacionadas com os porcos-espinhos , o ilhéu tem este nome. Não há infraestrutura turística e hotéis em Cayo Jutías, apenas um simples restaurante e muita natureza intocada.

Cayo Jutías

Voor de noordkust van Pinar del Ríos liggen de twee eilanden Cayo Levisa en Cayo Jutías, die tot de archipel Los Colorados behoren. Cayo Levisa kan met de veerboot worden bereikt, Cayo Jutías kan door een 4 km lange dam worden bereikt. De zuidkant van de Cayo is bedekt met dichte mangrovebossen, de fijne witte zandstranden liggen aan de noordkant. Omdat op de Cayo veel exemplaren van de boomratten (*jutías,* verwant aan stekelvarkens) leefden, draagt het eilandje deze naam. Er is geen toeristische infrastructuur en hotels op Cayo Jutías, alleen een eenvoudig restaurant en veel ongerepte natuur.

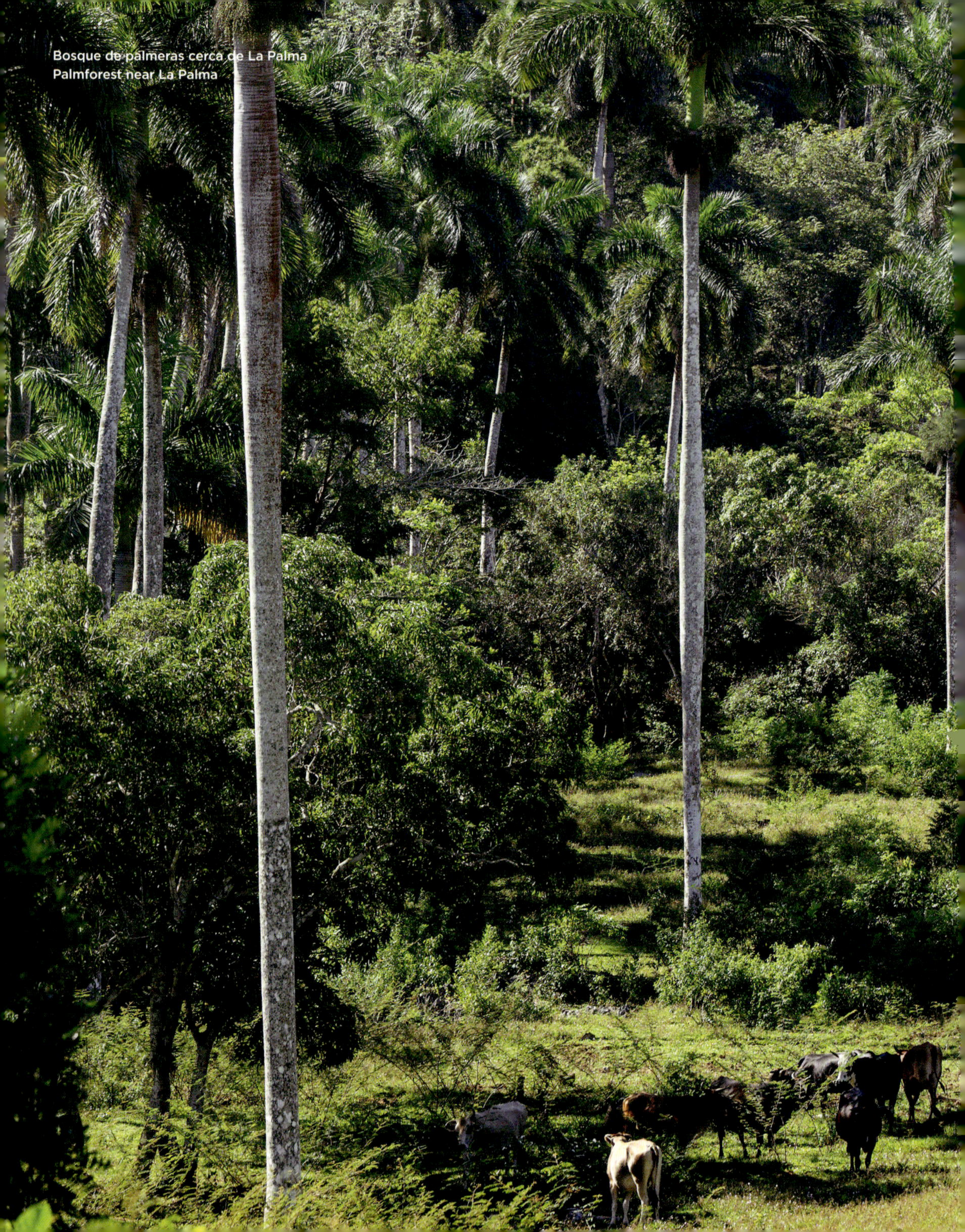
Bosque de palmeras cerca de La Palma
Palmforest near La Palma

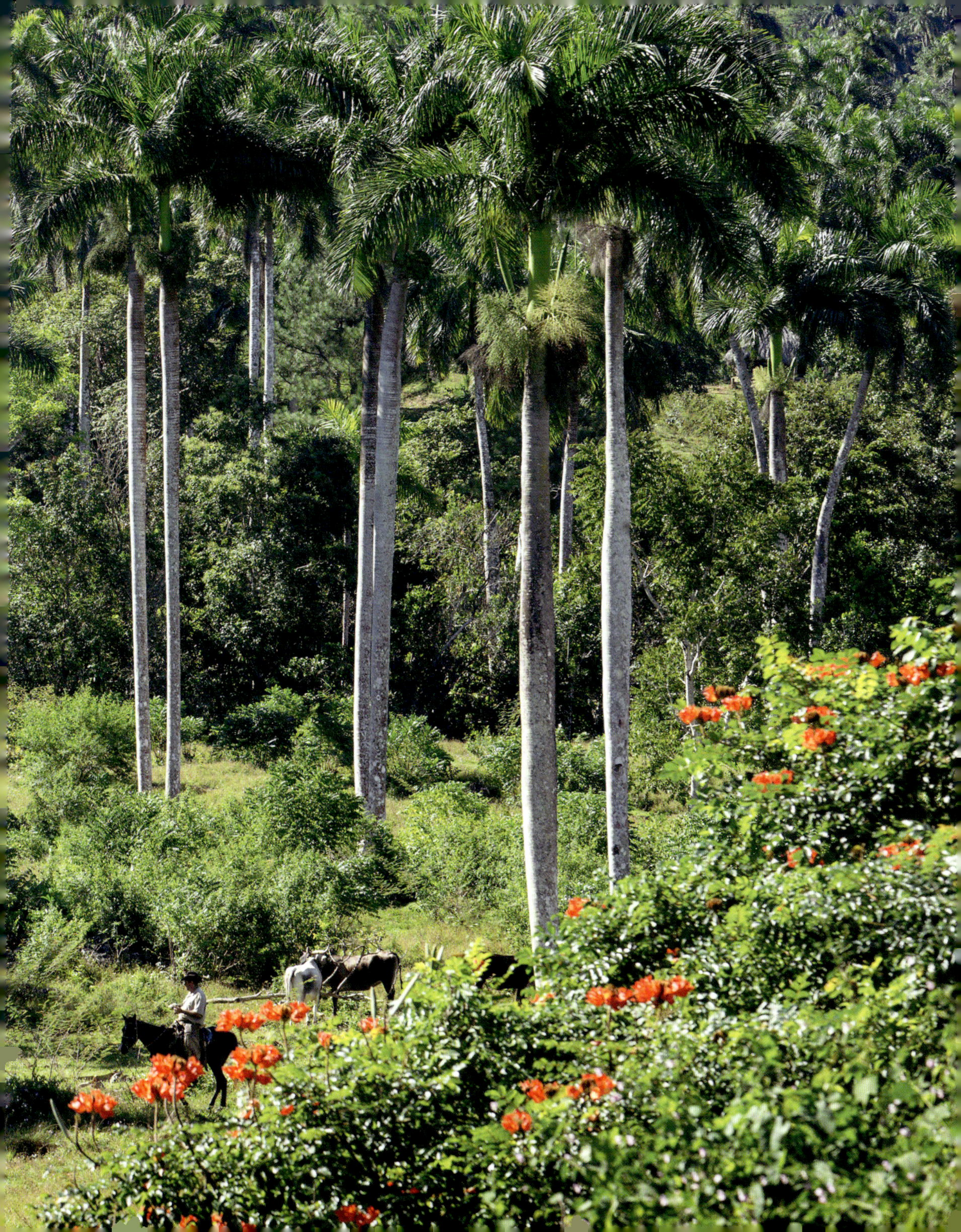

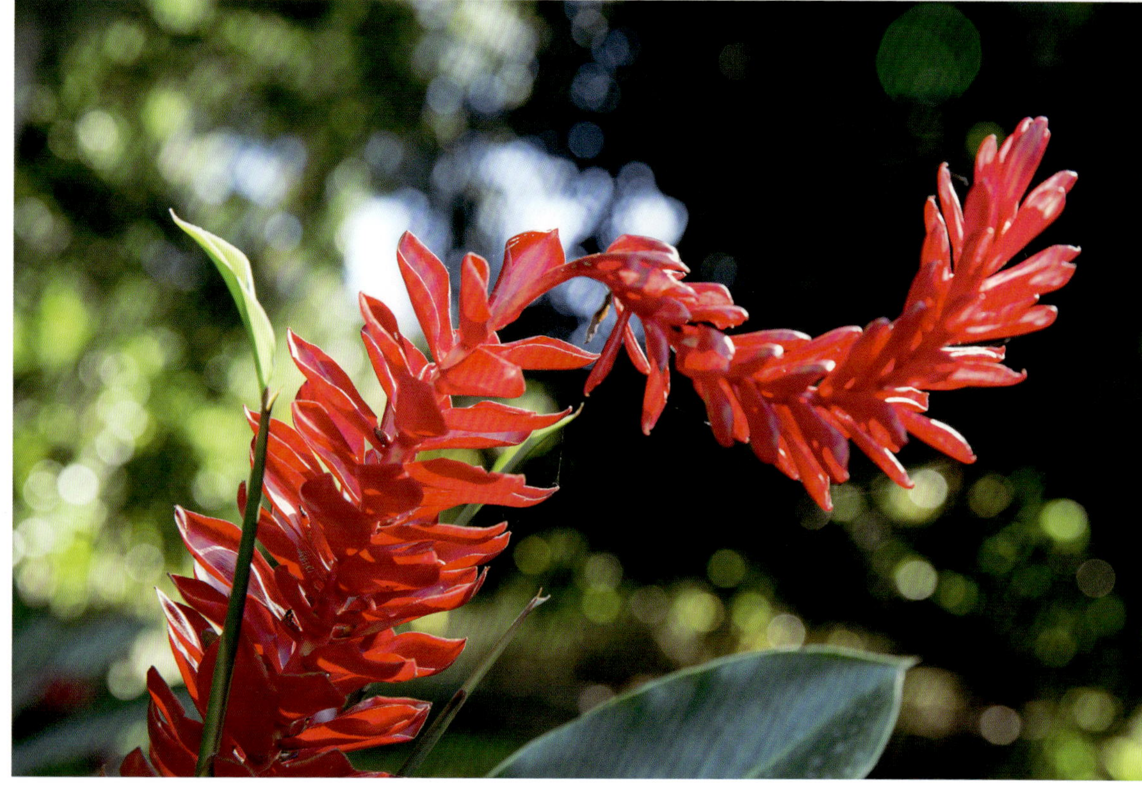

Jardín Botánico Soroa
Botanical Garden Soroa

Soroa

The 30 m (100 ft) waterfall of Soroa (El Salto) magically produces a permanent rainbow, so it is also called "rainbow cascade". The main attractions of the Botanical Garden near Soroa are the more than 700 orchid species that have been cultivated here since 1943. They bloom from December to March, and almost a third of them are endemic to Cuba.

Soroa

La cascada de 30 m de profundidad de Soroa (El Salto) evoca un arco iris permanente, por lo que también se le llama "cascada del arco iris". El principal atractivo del Jardín Botánico cerca de Soroa son las más de 700 especies de orquídeas que se han cultivado aquí desde 1943. Florecen de diciembre a marzo, y casi un tercio de ellas son endémicas de Cuba.

Soroa

La chute d'eau de 30 m de Soroa, El Salto, fait apparaître un arc-en-ciel permanent. C'est pourquoi elle est également surnommée « cascade arc-en-ciel ». Le jardin botanique de Soroa est particulièrement célèbre pour ses 700 variétés d'orchidées, cultivées depuis 1943. Elles fleurissent de décembre à mars ; un tiers environ sont endémiques de Cuba.

Soroa

A cachoeira em Soroa (El Salto) de 30 m de profundidade evoca um arco-íris permanente, por isso também é chamada de "cascata do arco-íris". A principal atração do Jardim Botânico perto de Soroa são as mais de 700 espécies de orquídeas que foram cultivadas aqui desde 1943. Elas florescem de dezembro a março, quase um terço das quais é endémico em Cuba.

Soroa

Der 30 m tiefe Wasserfall von Soroa (El Salto) zaubert einen Dauer-Regenbogen, deshalb nennt man ihn auch „Regenbogen-Kaskade". Hauptattraktion des Botanischen Gartens bei Soroa sind die über 700 Orchideenarten, die hier seit 1943 gezüchtet werden. Sie blühen von Dezember bis März, knapp ein Drittel davon ist in Kuba endemisch.

Soroa

De 30 m diepe waterval van Soroa (El Salto) tovert een permanente regenboog en wordt daarom ook wel 'regenboogcascade' genoemd. De belangrijkste attractie van de Botanische Tuin bij Soroa zijn de meer dan 700 orchideeënsoorten die hier sinds 1943 zijn verbouwd. Ze bloeien van december tot maart, bijna een derde daarvan is endemisch voor Cuba.

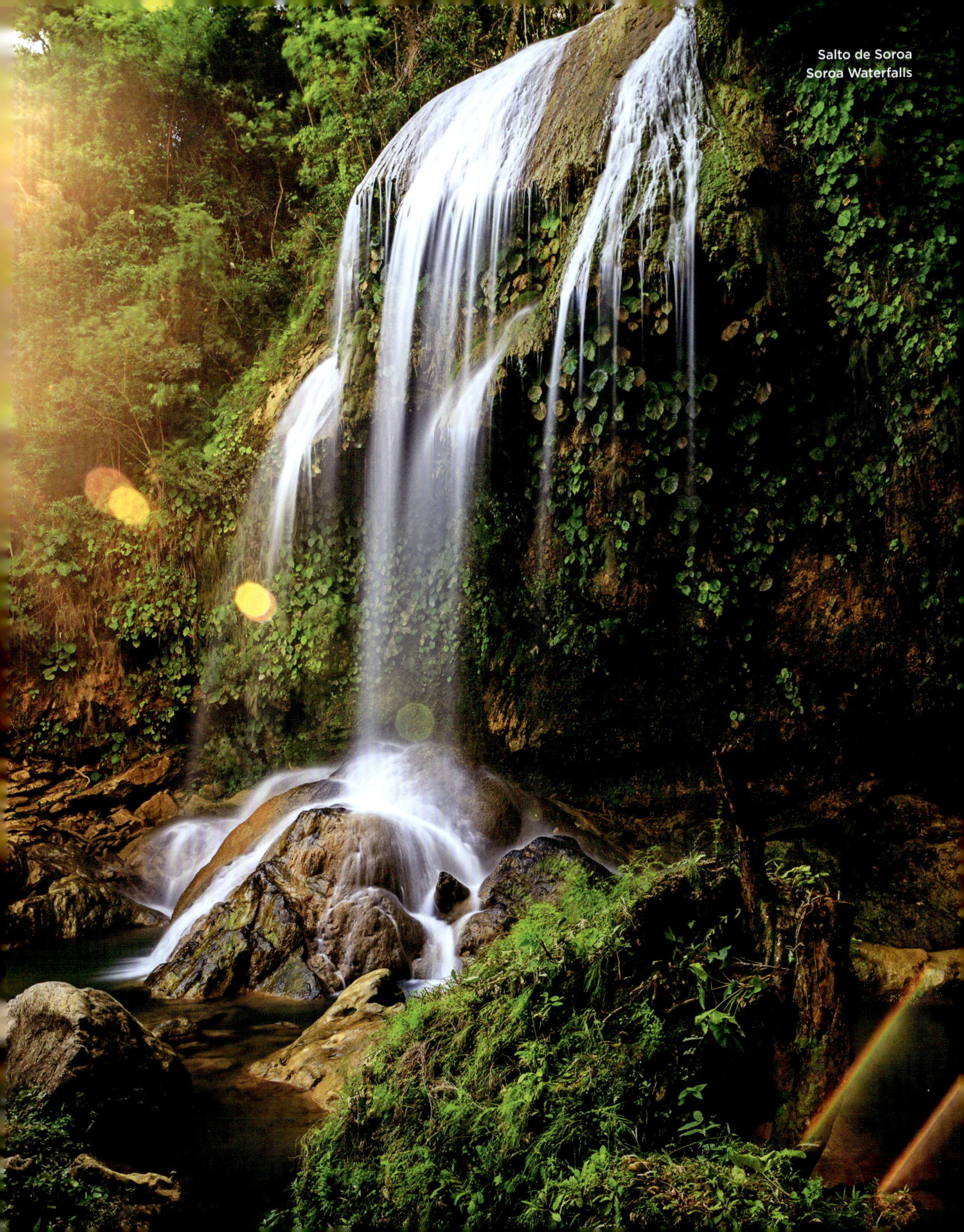
Salto de Soroa
Soroa Waterfalls

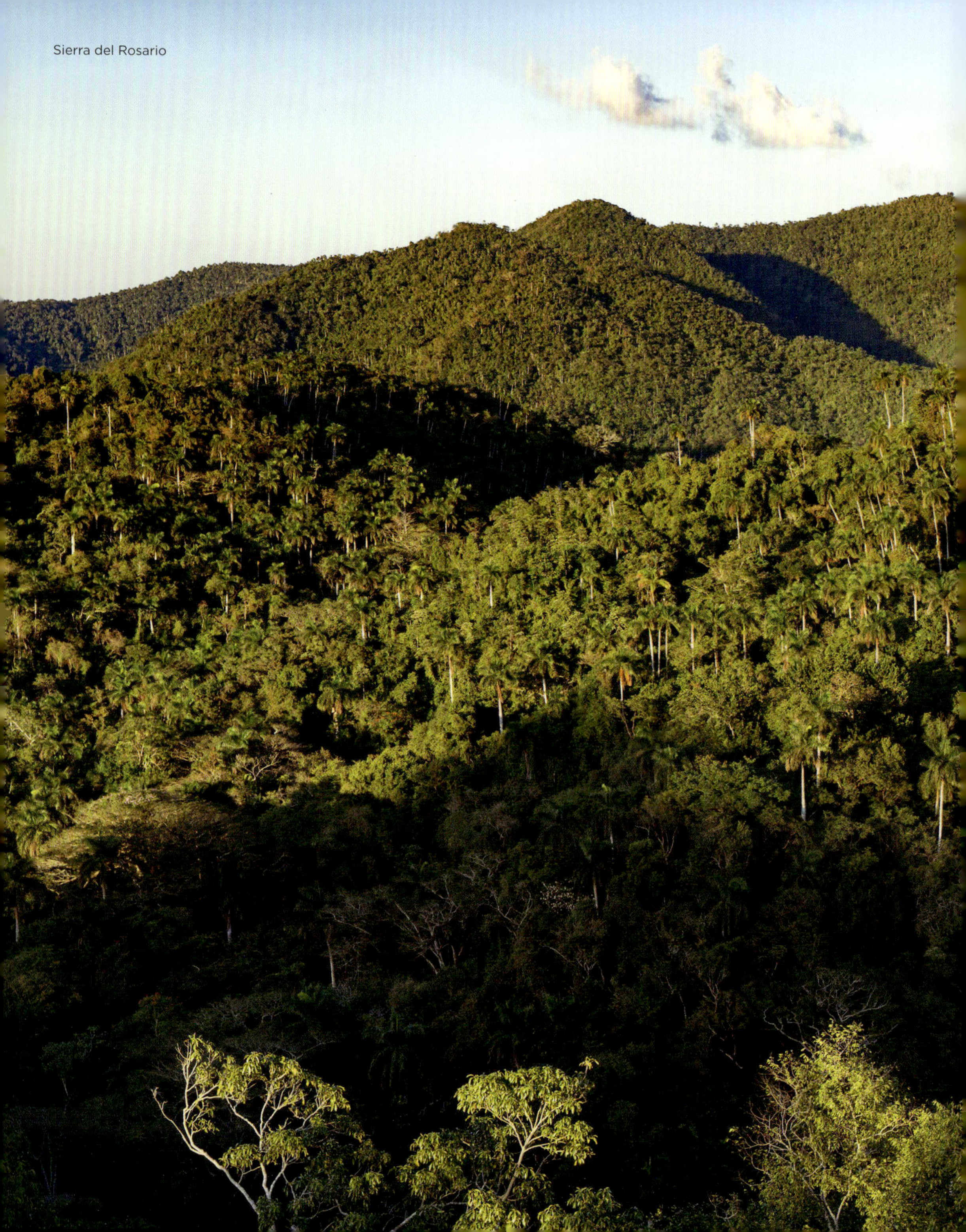
Sierra del Rosario

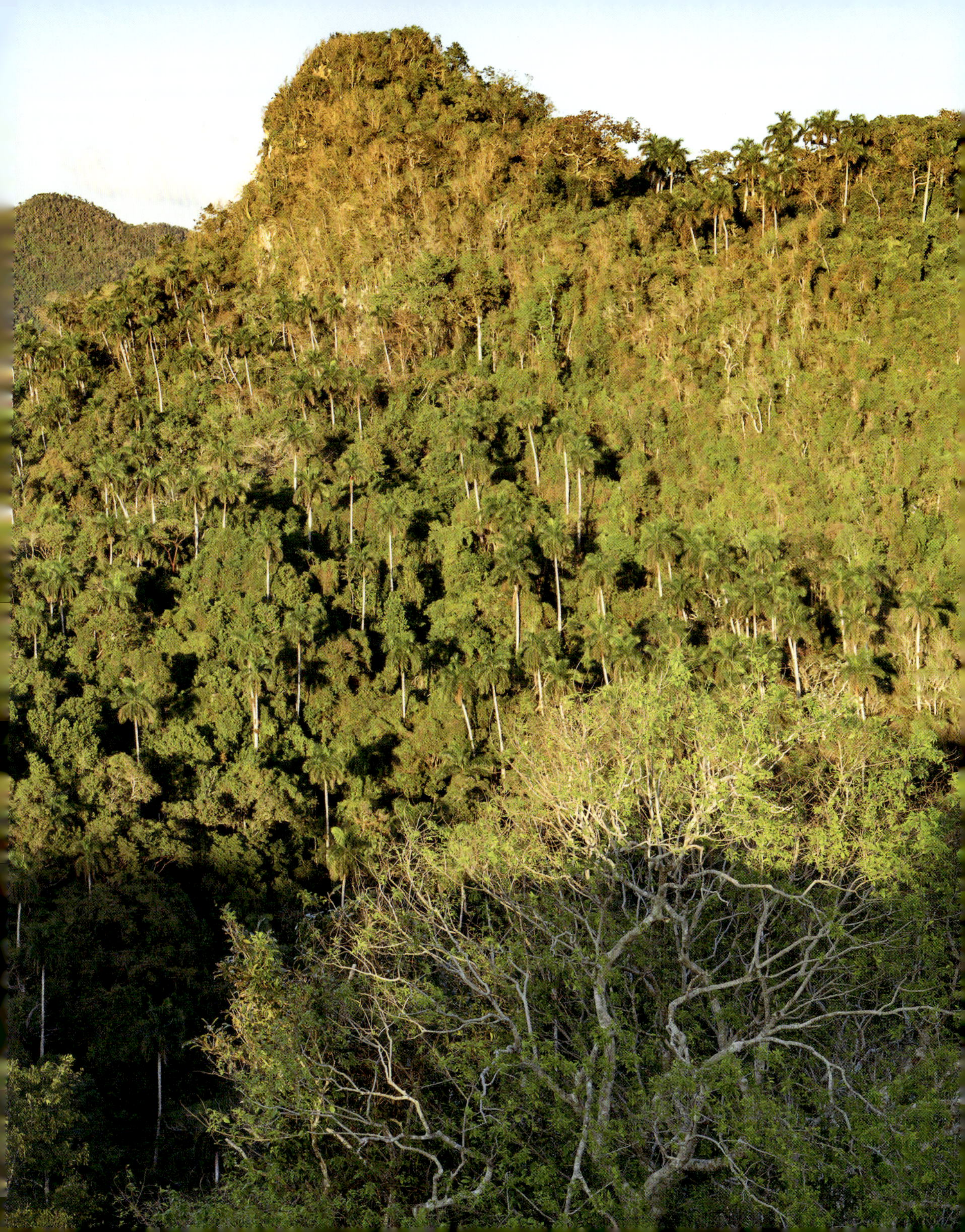

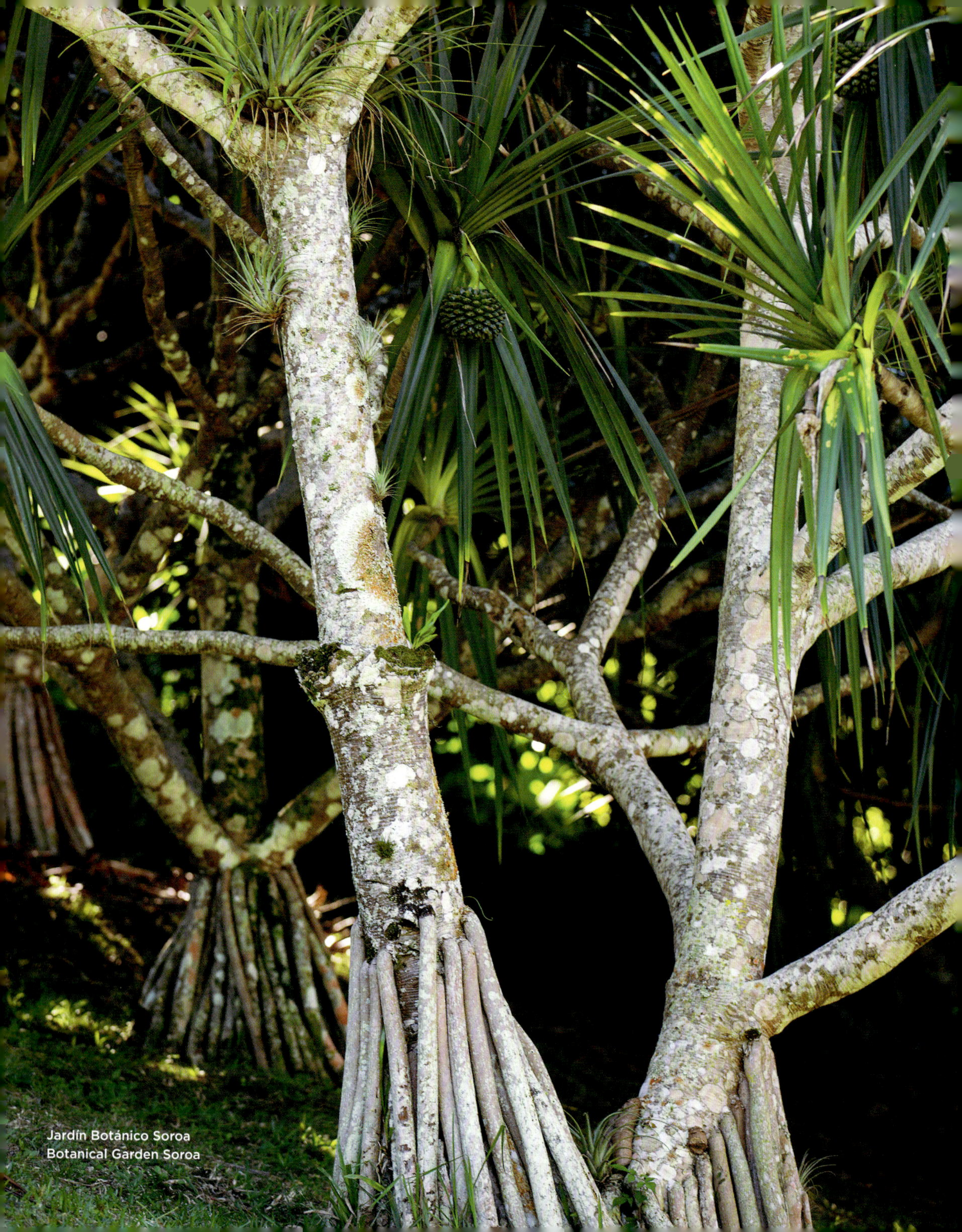

Jardín Botánico Soroa
Botanical Garden Soroa

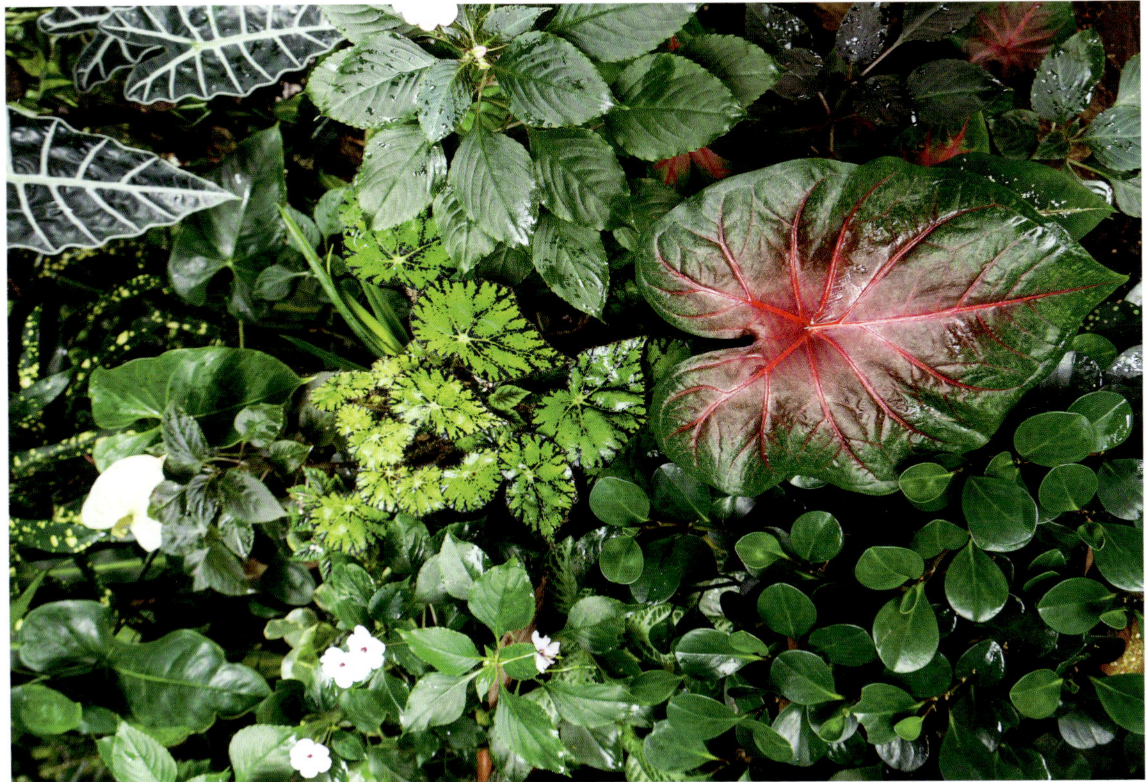

Jardín Botánico Soroa
Botanical Garden Soroa

Botanical Garden of Soroa

This Botanical Garden is located in the Sierra del Rosario, a biosphere reserve with a cooler microclimate due to its height and dense vegetation. The orchid garden is one of the largest in the world at 3.5 hectares (8 acres). In addition, about a thousand other plant species grow here, partly from Cuba but also from other tropical regions.

Jardín Botánico de Soroa

El Jardín Botánico está ubicado en la Sierra del Rosario, una reserva de la biosfera con un microclima más fresco debido a su altura y densa vegetación. Con sus 3,5 hectáreas, el jardín de orquídeas es uno de los más grandes del mundo. Además, aquí crecen unas mil especies de plantas, en parte de Cuba, pero también de otras regiones tropicales.

Le jardin botanique de Soroa

Le jardin botanique est situé dans la sierra del Rosario, réserve de biosphère dans laquelle règne un microclimat légèrement plus frais, conséquence de l'altitude et de la densité de la végétation. Le jardin des orchidées de 3,5 ha est le plus vaste du monde. Il compte en outre environ un millier d'autres espèces de plantes, originaires de Cuba et d'autres régions tropicales.

Jardim Botânico de Soroa

O Jardim Botânico está localizado na Sierra del Rosario, uma reserva da biosfera com um microclima ligeiramente mais fresco devido à sua altura e vegetação densa. O jardim de orquídeas é um dos maiores do mundo, com 3,5 ha. Além disso, cerca de mil outras espécies de plantas crescem aqui, algumas de Cuba, mas também de outras regiões tropicais.

Botanischer Garten von Soroa

Der Botanische Garten liegt in der Sierra del Rosario, einem Biosphärenreservat, in dem aufgrund der Höhe und der dichten Vegetation ein etwas kühleres Mikroklima herrscht. Der Orchideengarten ist mit 3,5 ha einer der größten der Welt. Außerdem wachsen hier noch rund tausend weitere Pflanzenarten, teilweise aus Kuba, aber auch aus anderen Tropenregionen.

Botanische tuin van Soroa

De Botanische Tuin ligt in de Sierra del Rosario, een biosfeerreservaat met een koeler microklimaat door de hoogte en de dichte vegetatie. De orchideeëntuin is met 3,5 hectare een van de grootste ter wereld. Daarnaast groeien hier nog ongeveer duizend andere plantensoorten, deels uit Cuba, maar ook uit andere tropische gebieden.

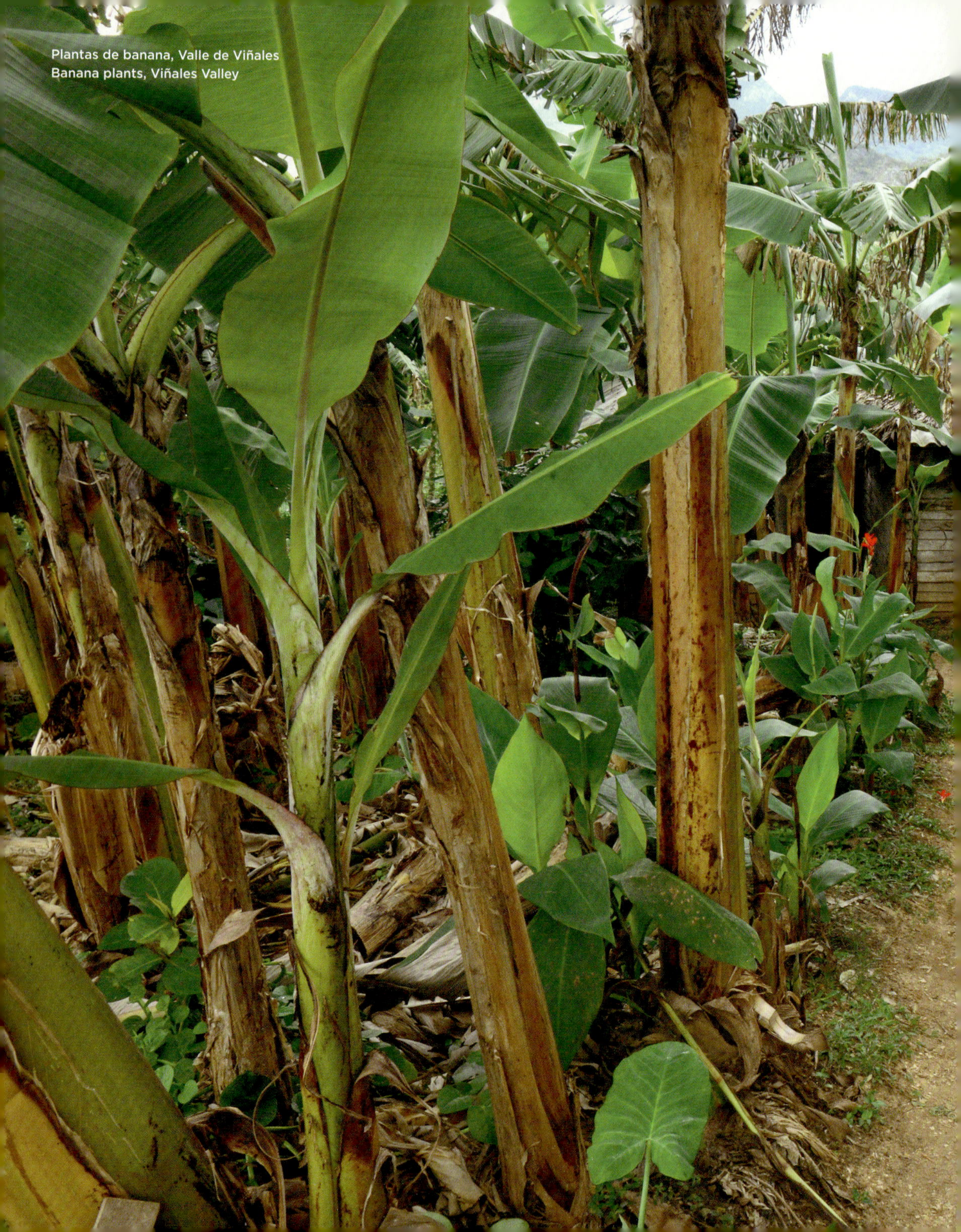
Plantas de banana, Valle de Viñales
Banana plants, Viñales Valley

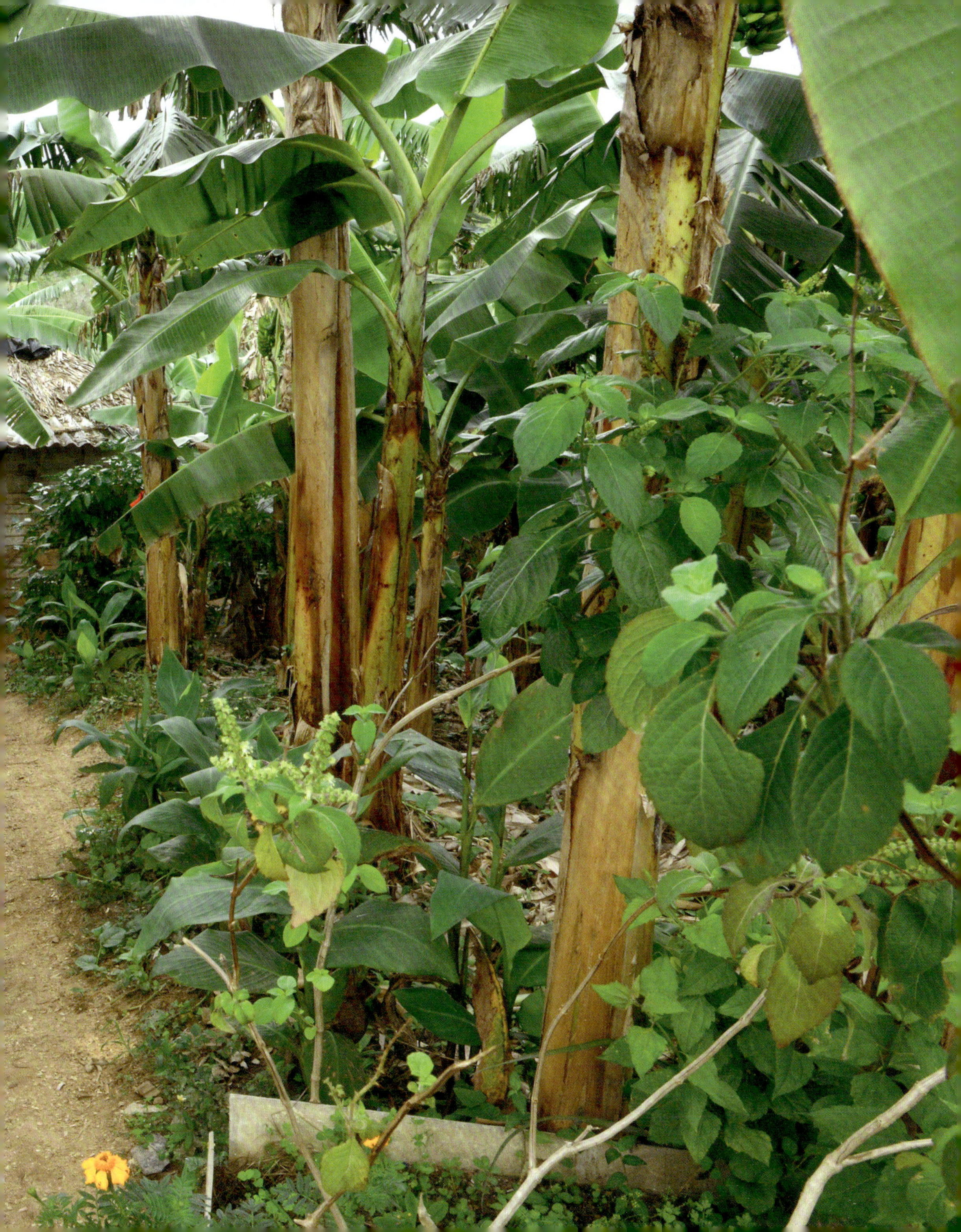

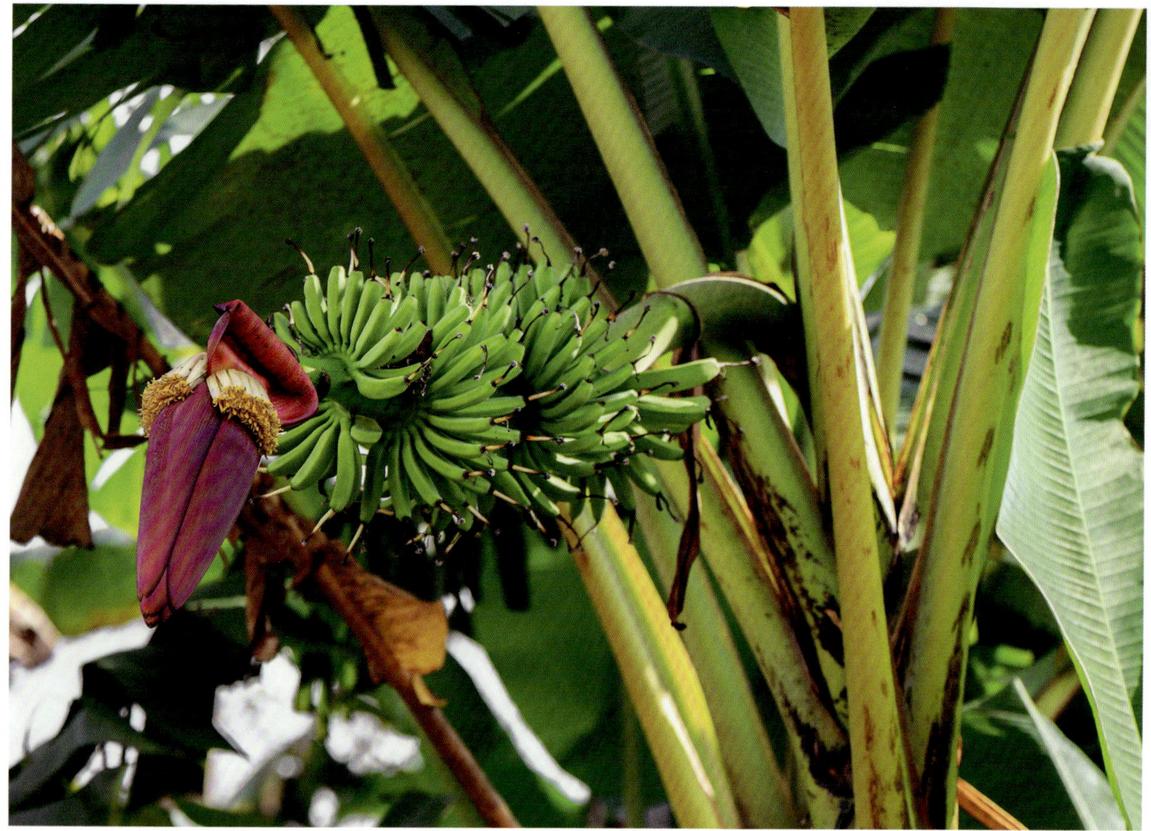

Plantas de banana, Valle de Viñales
Banana plants, Viñales Valley

Plantains

A jungle of banana trees surrounding a cottage is a common sight in the countryside. Many (tobacco) farmers are at least partially self-sufficient. Agriculture is a hot topic in Cuba because the there is a lack of food for the population. It is an advantage if at least some basic foods such as plantains are available. Cut into slices and fried twice *(tostones)*, these should not be missing from any meal. Cuban cuisine is traditionally very starchy, and you can also find tubers such as manioc *(yuca)* and malanga (also known in Europe as tannia) on the menu.

Banane plantain

Dans tout le pays, on retrouve ce paysage de petites maisons enfouies au cœur d'une jungle de bananiers. De nombreux cultivateurs de tabac produisent, au moins en partie, leur propre nourriture. L'agriculture à Cuba est un sujet ardent, car l'approvisionnement de la population en denrées est déficient. Ainsi, il est très avantageux de disposer, à portée de main, de certains aliments de base tels que les bananes plantains. Découpées en rondelles et frites deux fois *(tostones)*, elles complètent tous les repas. La cuisine cubaine est traditionnellement très riche en féculents, notamment en tubercules, tels que le manioc (ou yuca) et le malanga (ou tania).

Kochbananen

Ein Dschungel aus Bananenstauden rund um das Wohnhäuschen ist ein verbreitetes Bild auf dem Land. Viele (Tabak-)Bauern sind zumindest teilweise Selbstversorger. Das Thema Landwirtschaft ist in Kuba ein heißes Eisen, denn die Versorgung der Bevölkerung mit Lebensmitteln ist sehr mangelhaft. Da ist es von Vorteil, wenn zumindest einige Grundnahrungsmittel wie Kochbananen greifbar sind, die, in Scheiben geschnitten und doppelt frittiert *(tostones)*, bei keinem Essen fehlen dürfen. Die kubanische Küche ist traditionell sehr stärkehaltig, auf dem Teller finden sich auch Knollenfrüchte wie Maniok *(yuca)* und Malanga, in Europa bekannt als Tannia.

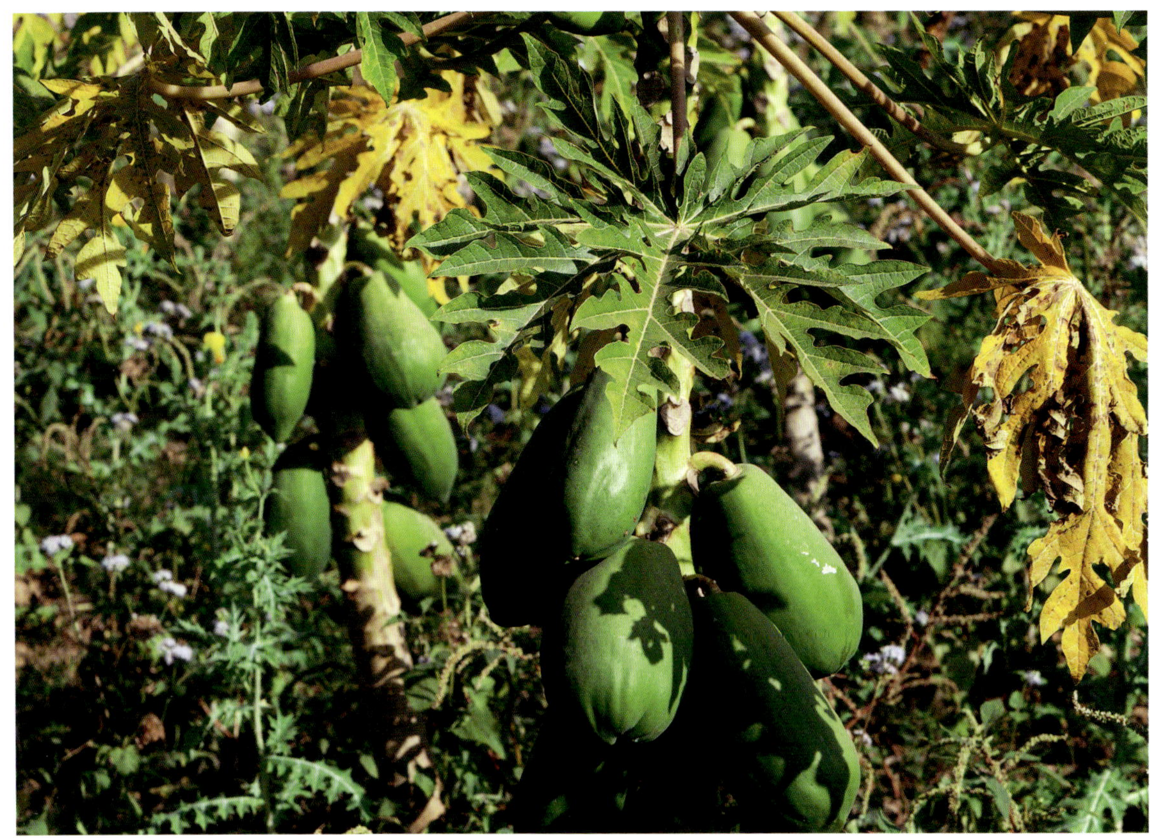

Carica papaya, Valle de Viñales
Papaya, Viñales Valley

Plátanos

Una jungla de arbustos de plátanos
alrededor de la cabaña es una vista
común en el campo. Muchos agricultores
(de tabaco) son al menos parcialmente
autosuficientes. La agricultura es un tema
candente en Cuba, porque el suministro
de alimentos a la población es muy
deficiente. Es una ventaja si se dispone de
al menos algunos alimentos básicos como
los plátanos, que, cortados en rodajas y
fritos dos veces (tostones), no deberían
faltar en ninguna comida. La cocina cubana
es tradicionalmente muy almidonada, y
en el plato también se pueden encontrar
tubérculos como el manihot (yuca) y el
malanga, conocido en Europa como tannia.

Banana-da-terra

Uma selva de bananeiras em torno da casa
de moradia é uma visão comum no campo.
Muitos agricultores (de tabaco) são pelo
menos parcialmente autossuficientes. A
agricultura é um tema delicado em Cuba,
porque o abastecimento da população
com alimentos é muito deficiente.
Portanto, é uma vantagem se pelo menos
alguns alimentos básicos, tais como
bananas-da-terra, estiverem disponíveis,
as quais, cortadas em fatias e fritas duas
vezes (tostones), não devem faltar em
nenhuma refeição. A cozinha cubana é
tradicionalmente muito rica em amido,
no prato você também pode encontrar
tubérculos como mandioca (yuca) e taioba,
conhecido na Europa como Tannia.

Bakbananen

Een jungle van bananenstruiken rond het
woonhuis is een veel voorkomend gezicht
op het platteland. Veel (tabaks)boeren zijn
op zijn minst gedeeltelijk zelfvoorzienend.
Landbouw is een hot topic in Cuba,
omdat de voedselvoorziening van de
bevolking zeer gebrekkig is. Daarom is
het een voordeel als er minstens enkele
basisvoedingsmiddelen zoals bakbananen
beschikbaar zijn. Deze bakbananen worden
in plakken gesneden en daarna twee keer
gebakken (tostones) en die bij geen enkele
maaltijd mag ontbreken. De Cubaanse
keuken is van oudsher erg zetmeelrijk, op
het bord vind je ook knollen zoals Maniok
(yuca) en Malanga, in Europa bekend
als Tannia.

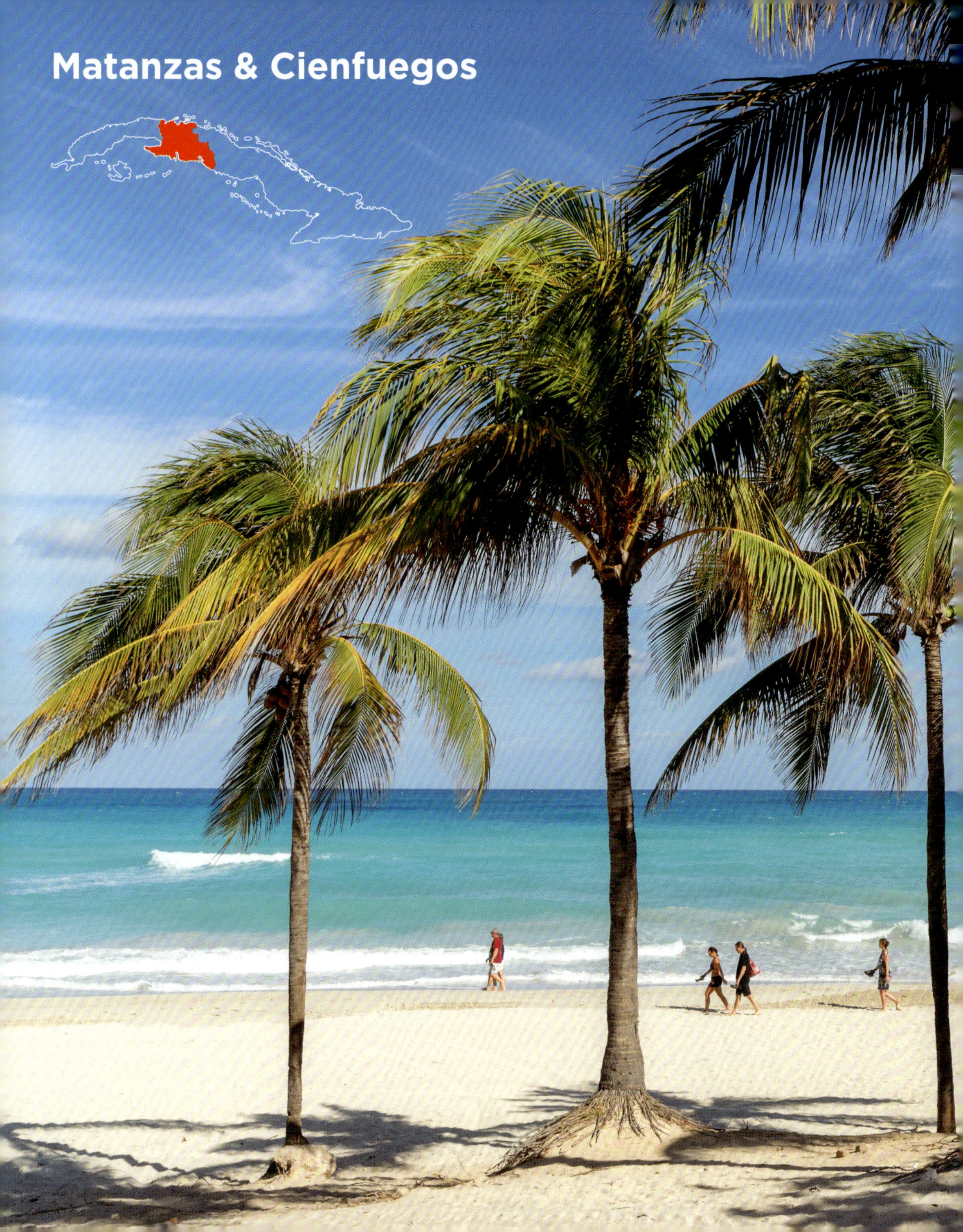
Matanzas & Cienfuegos

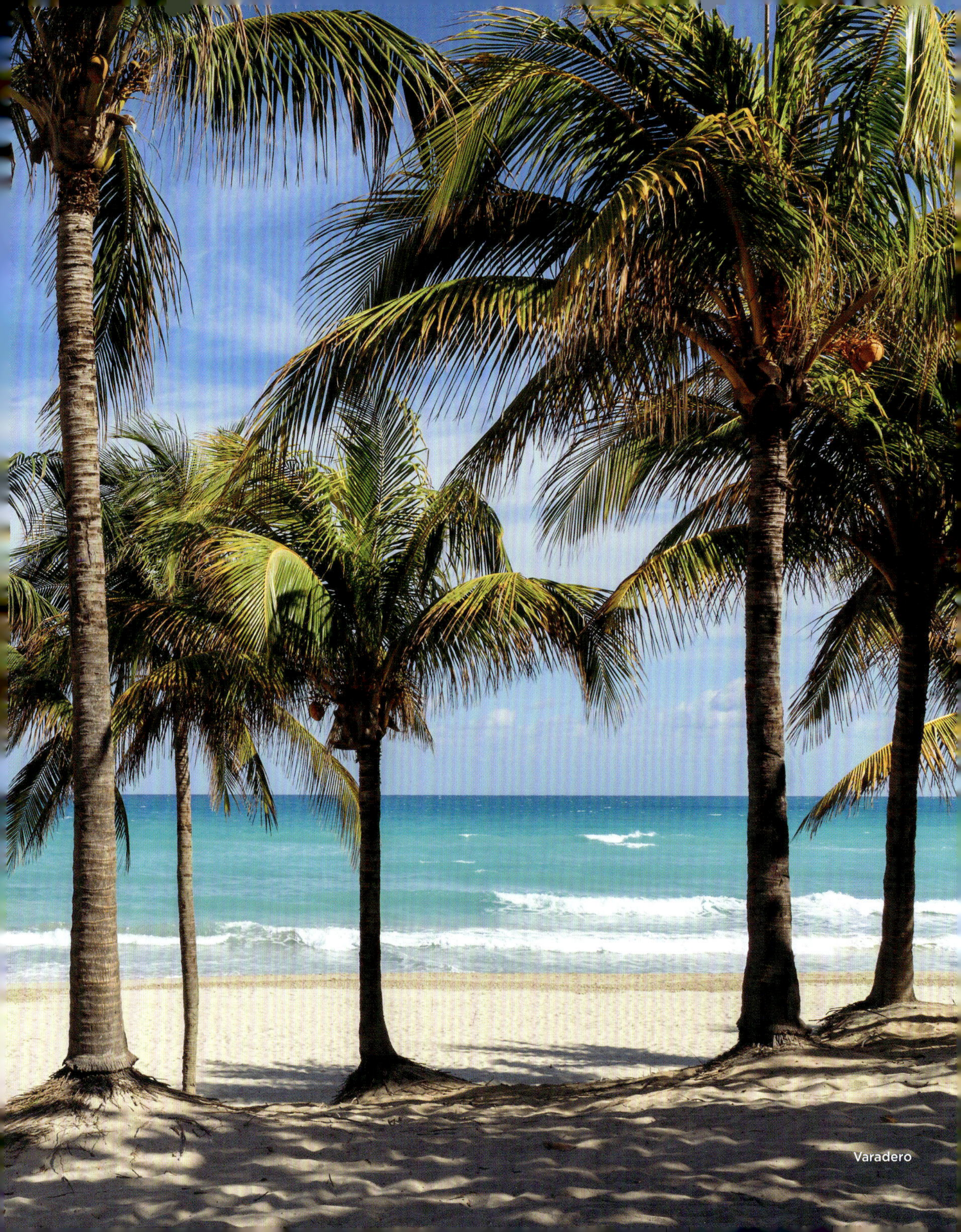

Varadero

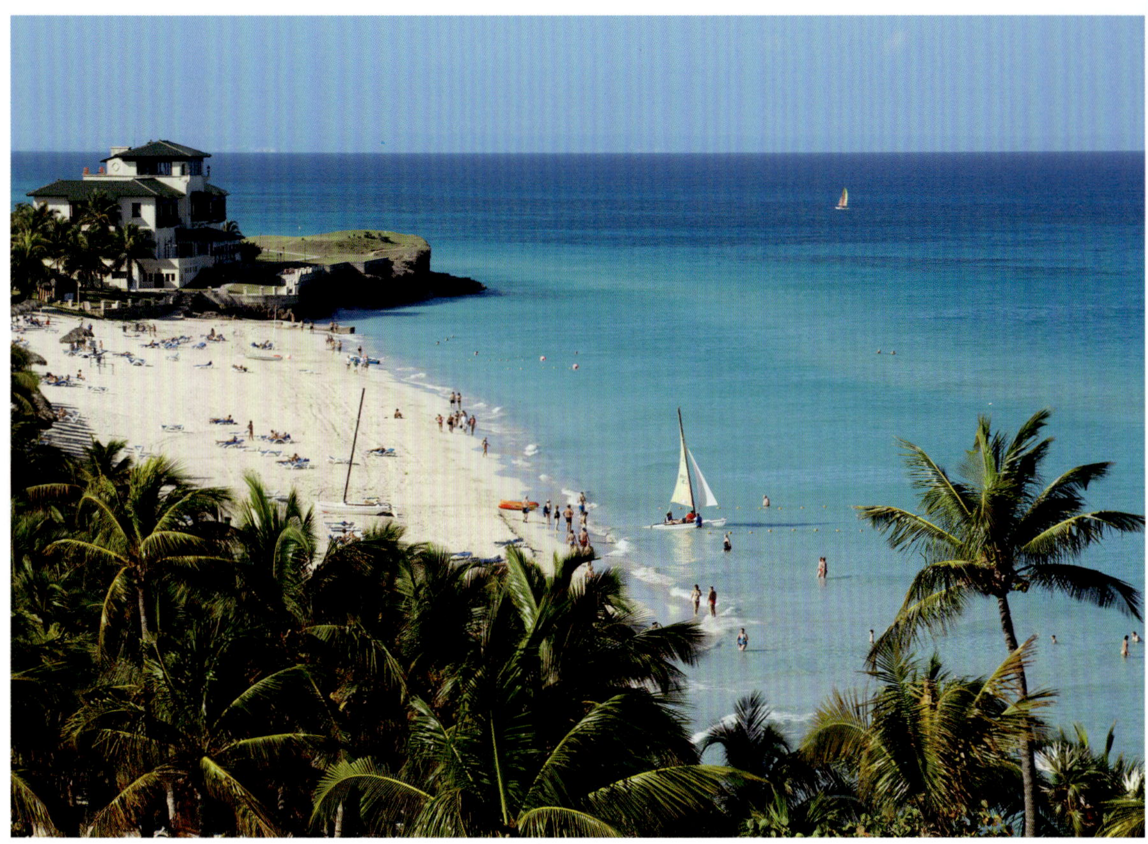

Varadero

Matanzas and Cienfuegos

To the east of the province of Havana begins the land of "green gold", as the Spanish called sugar cane. They cultivated it in endless plantations as a monoculture, and then had it harvested by slaves. On the north coast, dream beaches such as the 20 km (12 mi.) white sandy beach of Varadero on the Hicacos peninsula are tempting. On the south coast, the charming town of Cienfuegos offers French flair. A contrast is the Montemar Nature Park on the Zapata Peninsula, with its huge marshlands. Right next to it lies the Bay of Pigs, at the southern end of which the failed invasion by the CIA and exiled Cubans took place in Playa Girón in 1961.

Matanzas et Cienfuegos

À l'est de la province de La Habana débute le pays de « l'or vert », surnom donné à la canne à sucre par les Espagnols, qui la cultivaient en monoculture dans d'infinies plantations où travaillaient leurs esclaves. La côte nord est occupée par des plages paradisiaques, dont celle de Varadero, qui déploie ses 20 km de sable blanc sur la presqu'île Hicacos. Sur la côte sud, la charmante petite ville de Cienfuegos exhale un charme français. Le parc naturel de Montemar, sur la presqu'île de Zapata, compose un paysage fort contrasté d'immenses marécages. Il jouxte la baie des Cochons, à la pointe sud de laquelle, sur la Playa Girón, échoua le débarquement de la CIA et d'exilés cubains en 1961.

Matanzas und Cienfuegos

Östlich der Provinz Havanna beginnt das „Land des grünen Goldes", wie die Spanier das Zuckerrohr nannten, das sie auf endlosen Plantagen in Monokultur anbauen und von Sklaven schneiden ließen. An der Nordküste locken Traumstrände wie der 20 km lange, weiße Sandstrand von Varadero auf der Halbinsel Hicacos. An der Südküste wartet das charmante Städtchen Cienfuegos mit französischem Flair auf. Ein Kontrastprogramm ist der Naturpark Montemar auf der Zapata-Halbinsel mit riesigen Sumpfgebieten. Gleich daneben liegt die Schweinebucht, an deren südlichem Ende 1961 in Playa Girón die gescheiterte Invasion von CIA und Exilkubanern stattfand.

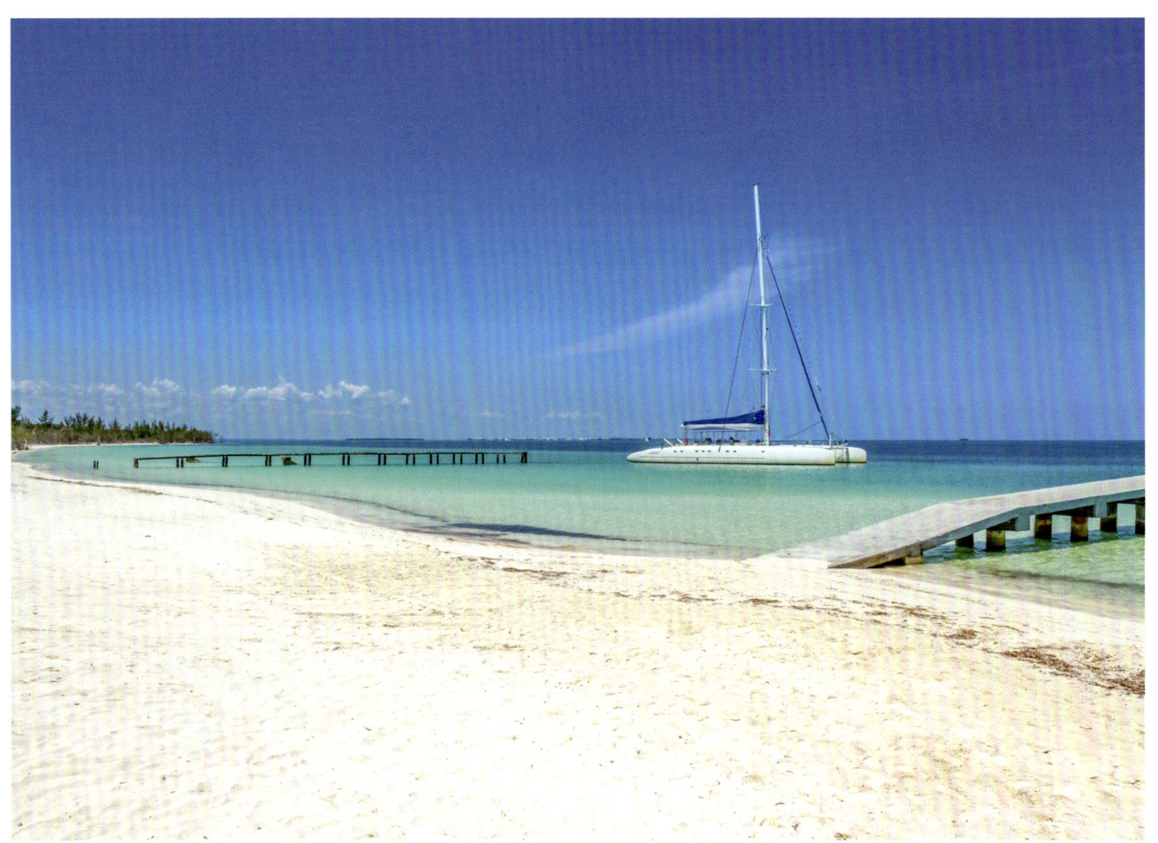

Varadero

Matanzas y Cienfuegos

Al este de la provincia de La Habana comienza la "tierra de oro verde", como los españoles llamaban a la caña de azúcar, que cultivaban en interminables plantaciones en monocultivo y que habían sido cortadas por esclavos. En la costa norte, playas de ensueño como la de Varadero, en la península de Hicacos, de 20 km de largo y arena blanca, son tentadoras. En la costa sur, la encantadora ciudad de Cienfuegos ofrece un ambiente francés. Un contraste es el Parque Natural de Montemar en la Península de Zapata con sus enormes pantanos. Justo al lado se encuentra Bahía de Cochinos, en cuyo extremo sur tuvo lugar la fallida invasión de CIA y el exilio cubano en Playa Girón en 1961.

Matanzas e Cienfuegos

Ao leste da província de Havana começa a "terra do ouro verde", como os espanhóis chamavam a cana-de-açúcar, que cultivaram em plantações sem fim em monocultura e que eram cortadas por escravos. Na costa norte, praias de sonho como a praia de areia branca de Varadero, de 20 km de extensão, na península de Hicacos, são tentadoras. Na costa sul, a encantadora cidade de Cienfuegos oferece um toque francês. Um programa de contraste é o Parque Natural de Montemar, na Península de Zapata, com os seus enormes pântanos. Mesmo ao seu lado está a Baía dos Porcos, no extremo sul da qual a fracassada invasão da CIA e dos cubanos no exílio ocorreu em Playa Girón, em 1961.

Matanzas en Cienfuegos

Ten oosten van de provincie Havana begint het 'land van groen goud', zoals de Spanjaarden het suikerriet noemen. Dit werd op eindeloze plantages in de monocultuur verbouwd en door slaven gesneden. Aan de noordkust zijn droomstranden zoals het 20 km lange witte zandstrand van Varadero op het schiereiland Hicacos. Aan de zuidkust biedt het charmante stadje Cienfuegos Franse flair. Een contrast is het Montemar Natuurpark op het schiereiland Zapata met zijn enorme moeraslanden. Vlak ernaast ligt de Varkensbaai, aan het zuidelijke uiteinde waar de mislukte invasie van de CIA en de Cubanen in ballingschap in Playa Girón in 1961 plaatsvond.

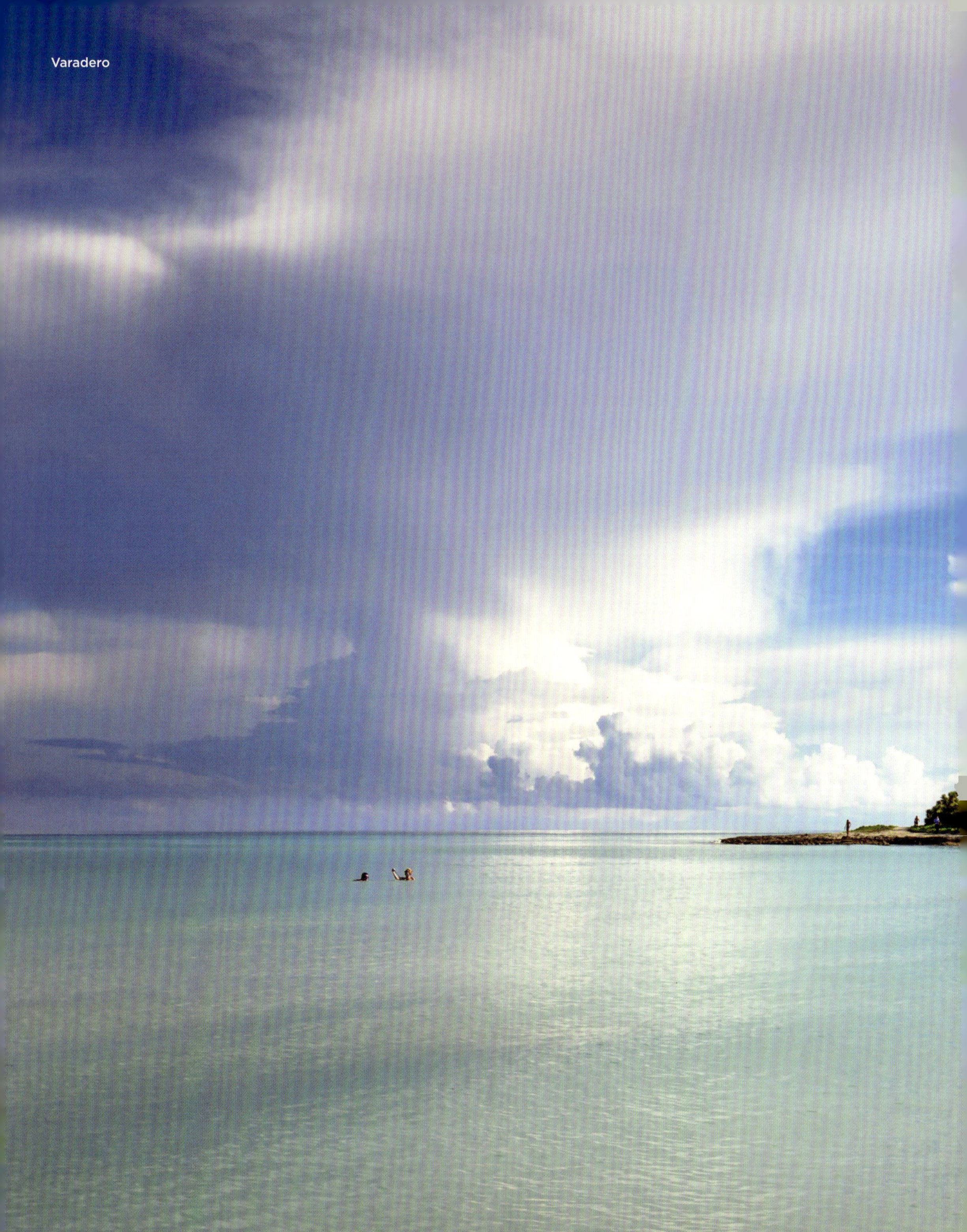
Varadero

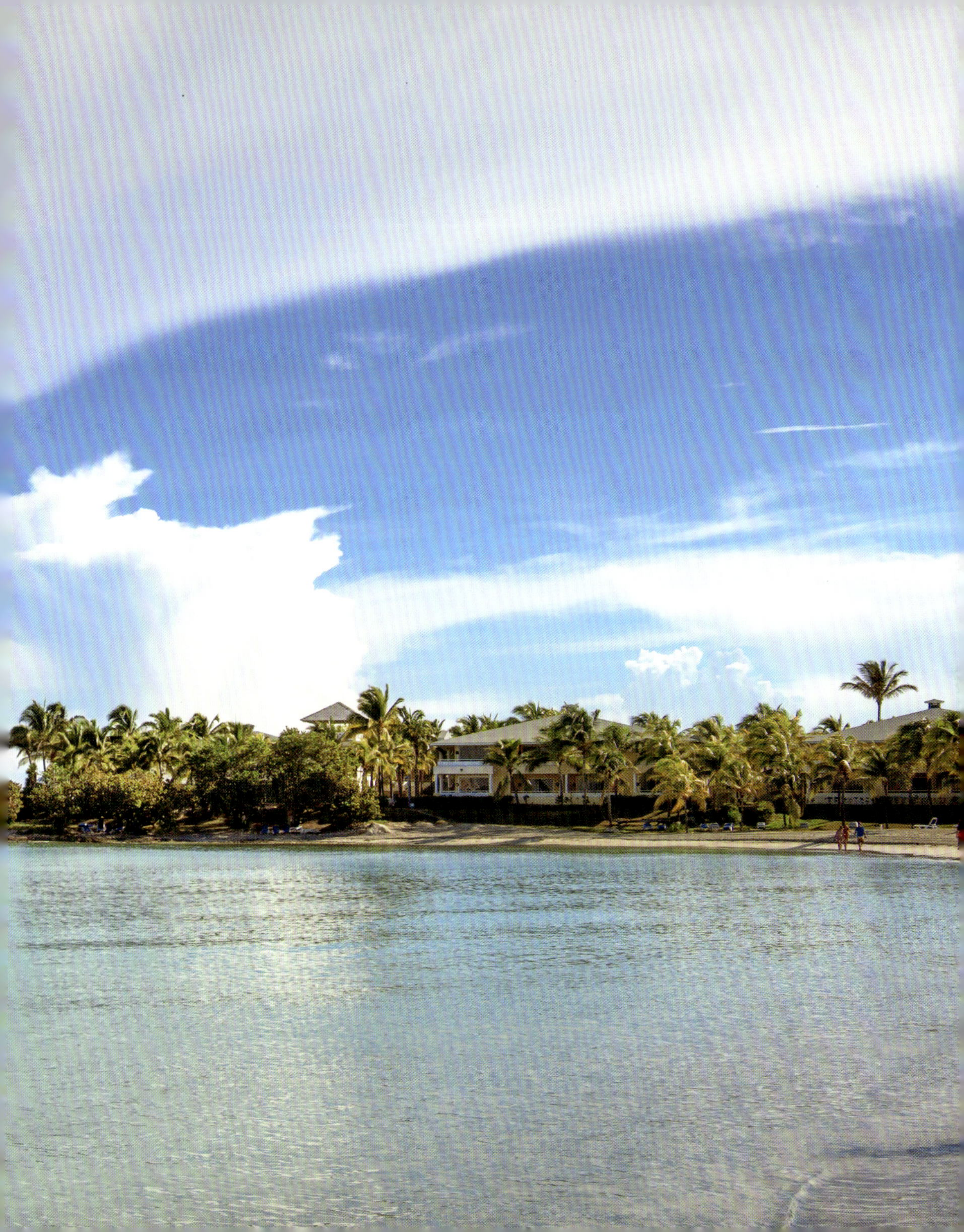

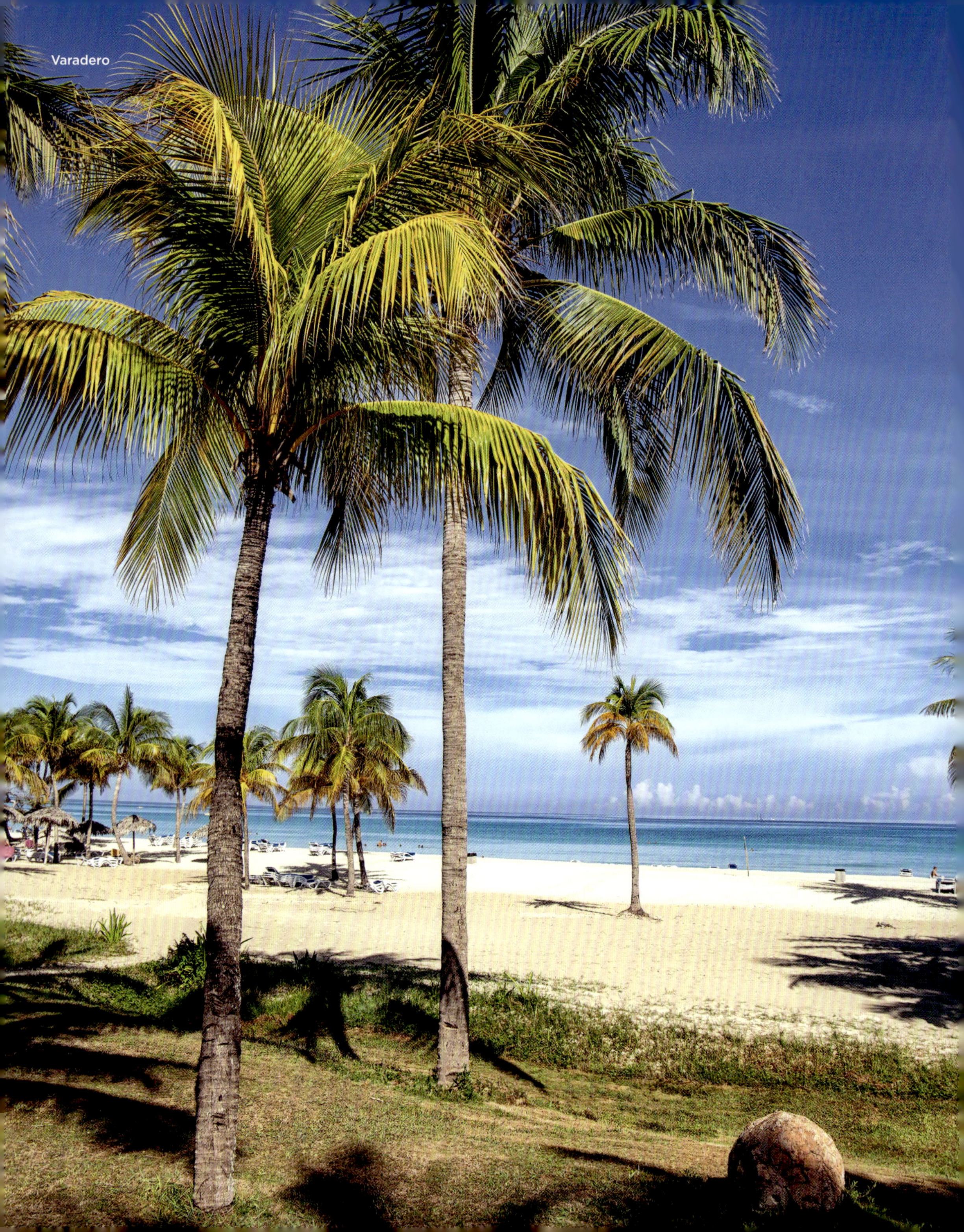
Varadero

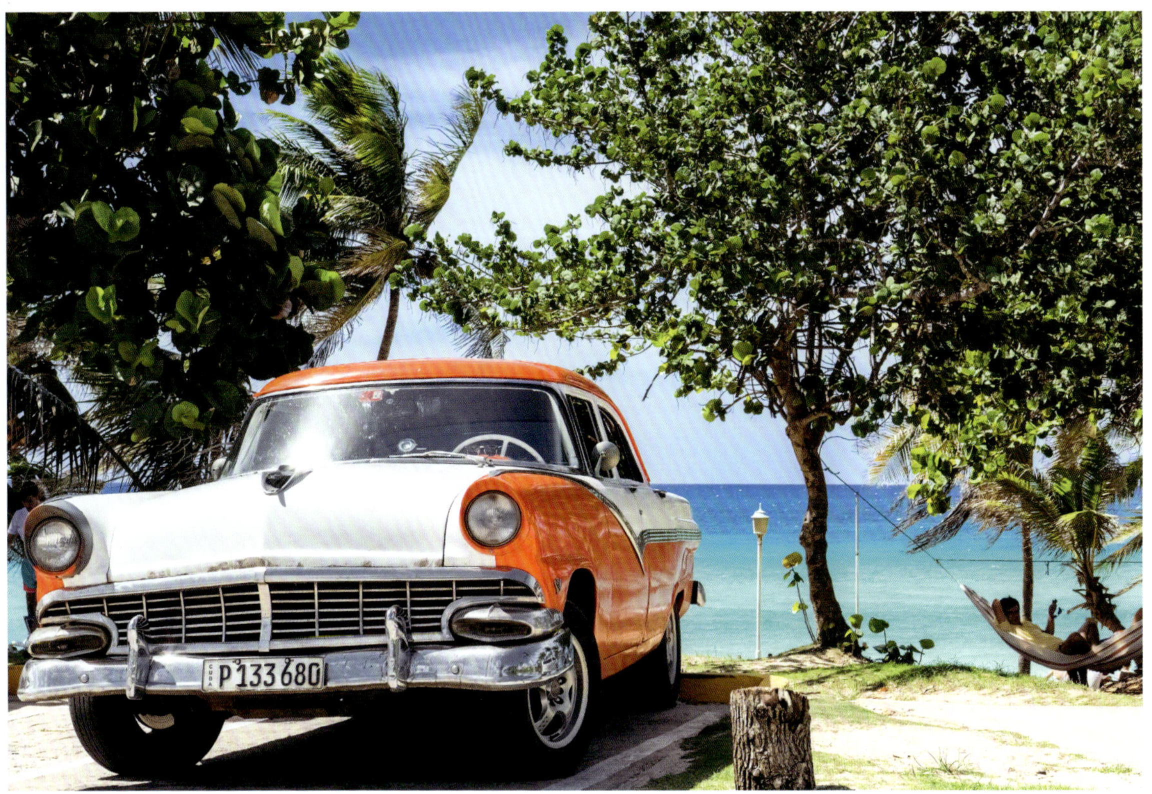

Varadero

Varadero

Sugar magnates from Matanzas built their villas in Varadero. In the 1920s, rich Americans joined them, for example the chemical and arms manufacturer DuPont, as well as Mafia boss Al Capone and his friend, dictator Batista. Before the Spaniards arrived, Hicacos Indians lived in the caves of the peninsula, for example in the Cueva de Bellamar and in the Cueva de Ambrosio.

Varadero

Los magnates del azúcar de Matanzas construyeron sus villas en Varadero. En la década de 1920, se añadieron los americanos ricos, como el fabricante de productos químicos y armas DuPont, así como el jefe de la mafia Al Capone y su amigo, el dictador Batista. Antes de la llegada de los españoles, los indios Hicacos vivían en las cuevas de la península, por ejemplo, en la Cueva de Bellamar y en la Cueva de Ambrosio.

Varadero

Les magnats du sucre de Matanzas firent construire leurs villas à Varadero. Dans les années 1920, les riches Américains les y rejoignirent, et parmi eux, l'industriel de la chimie et fabricant d'armes DuPont, le mafioso Al Capone et son ami le dictateur Batista. Avant l'arrivée des Espagnols, les grottes de la presqu'île étaient habitées par les Indiens Hicaco, notamment les Cuevas de Bellamar et la Cueva de Ambrosio.

Varadero

Os magnatas do açúcar de Matanzas construíram as suas moradias em Varadero. Na década de 1920, chegaram os americanos ricos, como o fabricante de produtos químicos e de armas DuPont, bem como o chefe da máfia Al Capone e seu amigo, o ditador Batista. Antes da chegada dos espanhóis, os índios Hicacos viviam nas cavernas da península, por exemplo, na Cueva de Bellamar e na Cueva de Ambrosio.

Varadero

Zuckermagnaten aus Matanzas bauten sich in Varadero ihre Villen. In den 1920er-Jahren kamen reiche US-Amerikaner hinzu wie der Chemie- und Waffenfabrikant DuPont sowie Mafiaboss Al Capone und sein Freund Diktator Batista. Vor Ankunft der Spanier lebten in den Höhlen der Halbinsel Hicacos-Indianer, z.B. in der Cueva de Bellamar und in der Cueva de Ambrosio.

Varadero

Suikermagnaten uit Matanzas bouwden in Varadero hun villa's. In de jaren twintig kwamen daar rijke Amerikanen bij, zoals de chemische en wapenproducent DuPont, maar ook maffiabaas Al Capone en zijn vriend, dictator Batista. Voor de komst van de Spanjaarden woonden de Hicacos indianen in de grotten van het schiereiland, bijvoorbeeld in de Cueva de Bellamar en in de Cueva de Ambrosio.

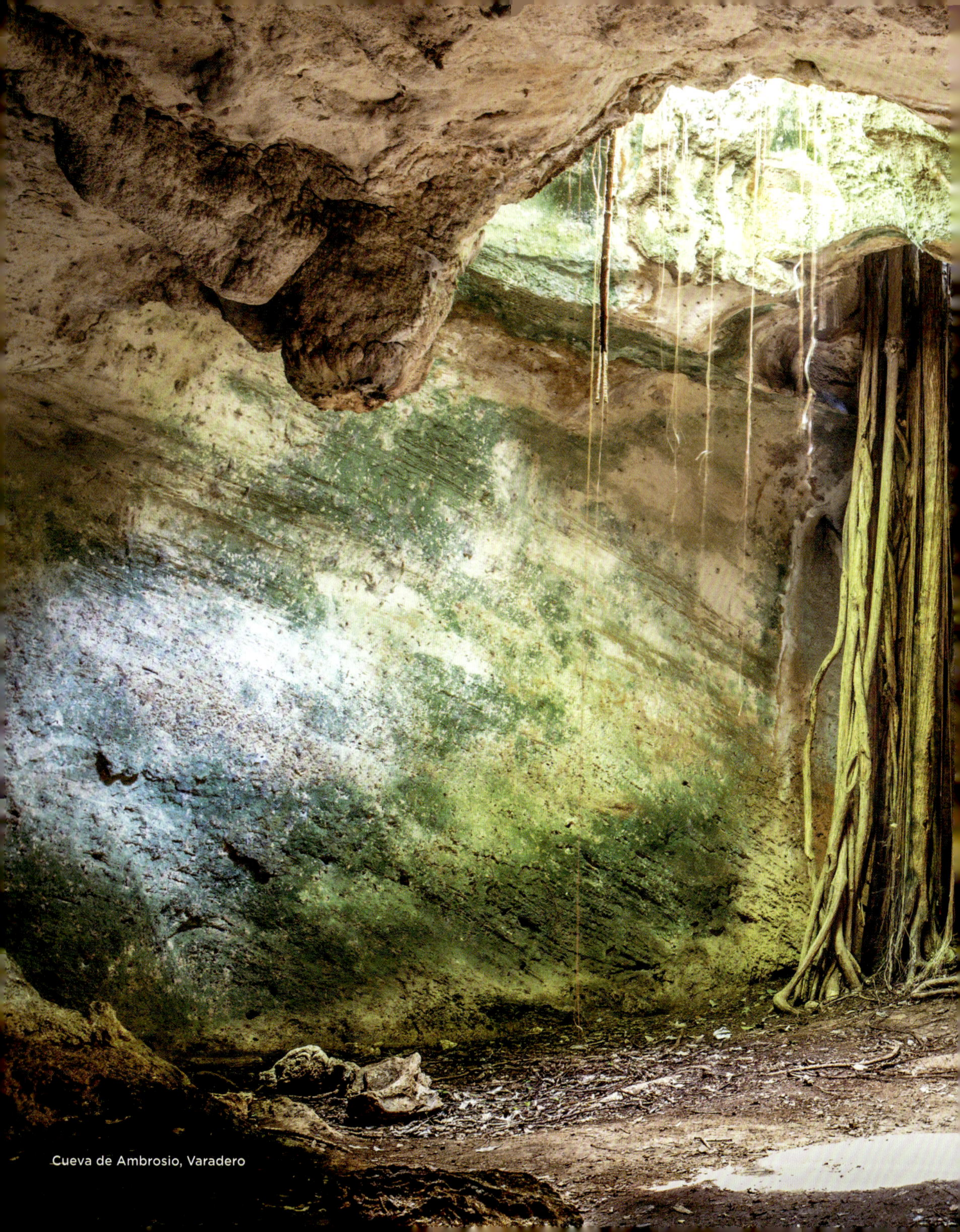

Cueva de Ambrosio, Varadero

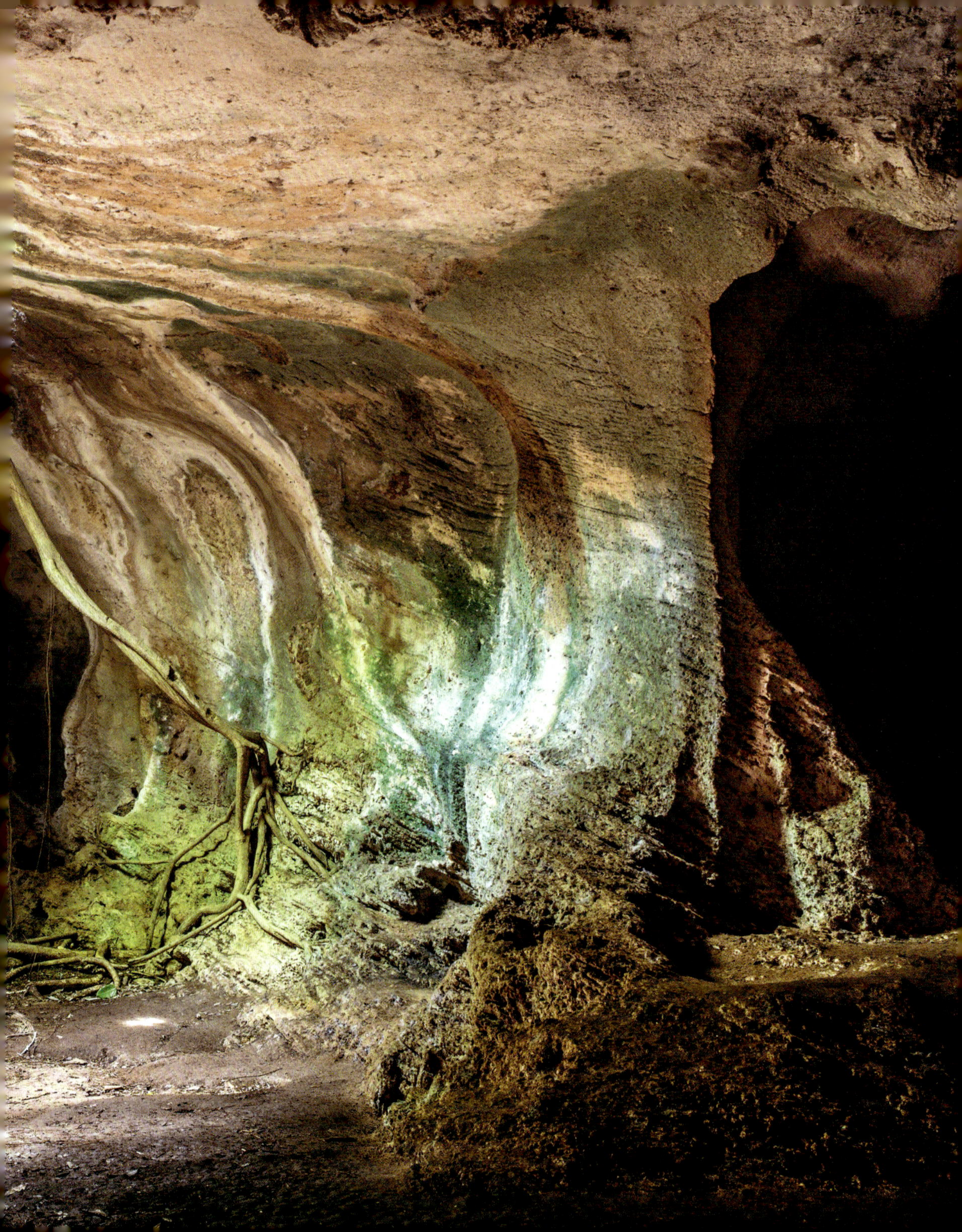

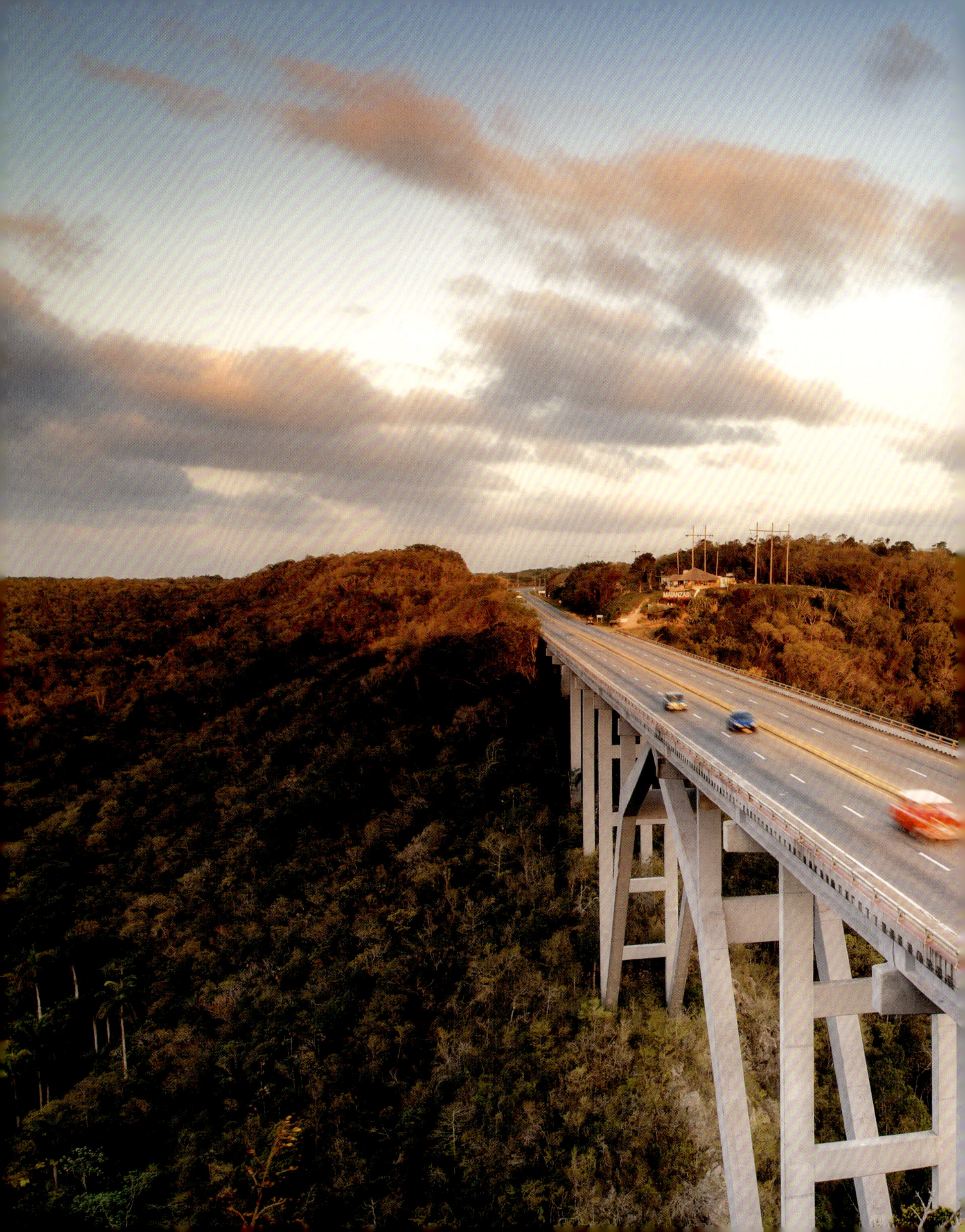

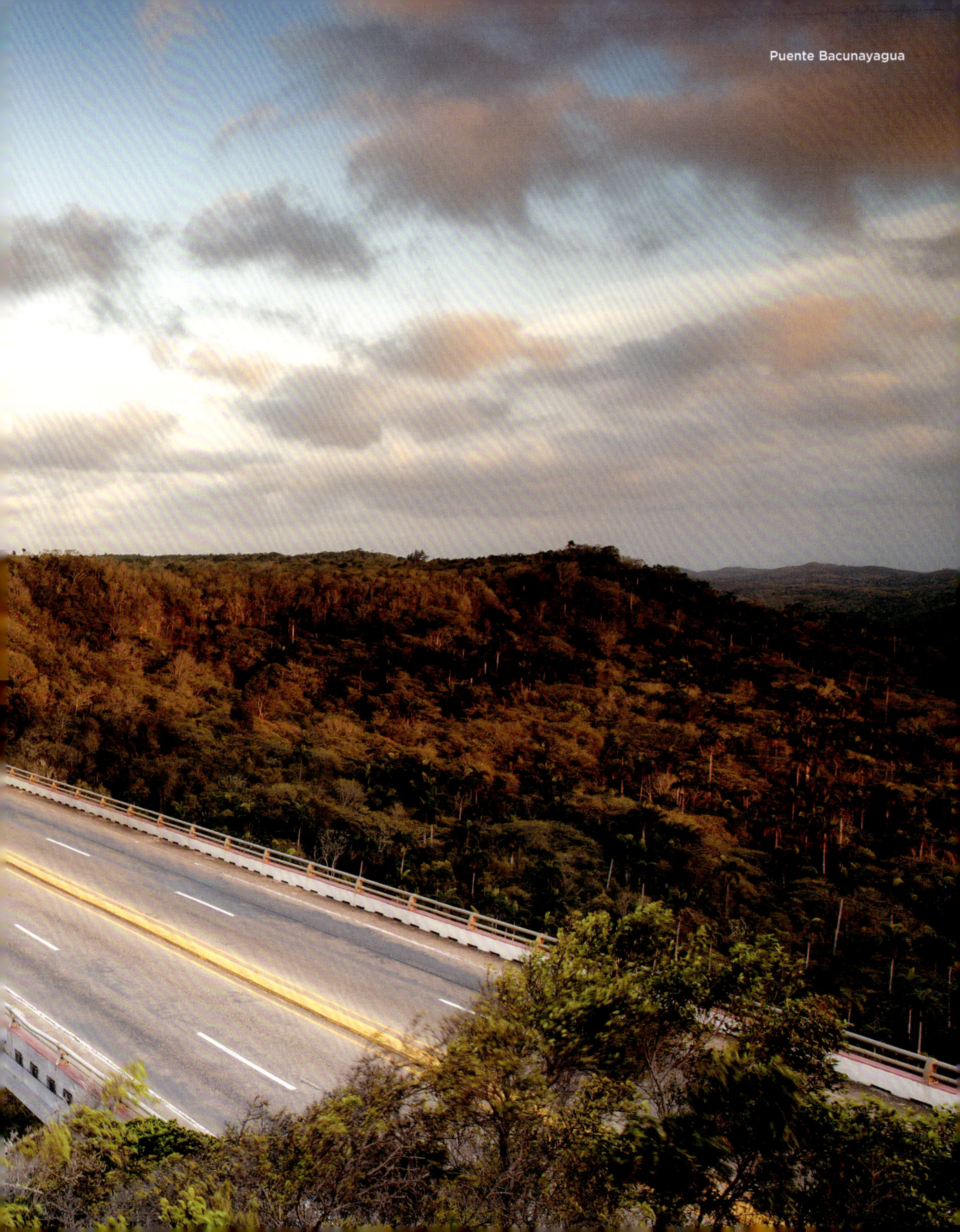
Puente Bacunayagua

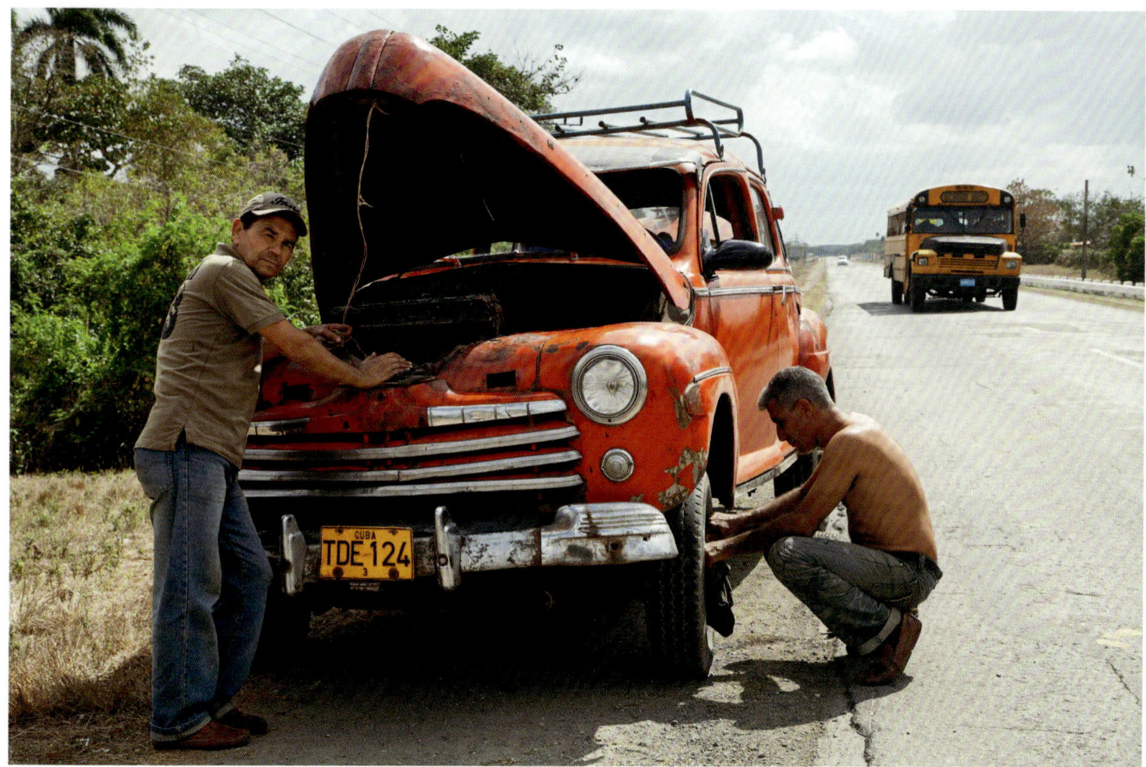

Carretera Central

On the Carretera Central

Breakdowns are part of everyday life on the Carretera Central and the country roads because many of these creaking museum pieces have hundreds of thousands, if not more than a million kilometers under their belt. The very existence of these old US cars mocks the laws of the market, car mechanics and the environment, wrote Cuba's best-known crime writer Leonardo Padura.

En la Carretera Central

Las averías forman parte de la vida cotidiana en la Carretera Central y en las carreteras rurales, porque muchas de las piezas de museo que gimen tienen cientos de miles, si no más de un millón de kilómetros a sus espaldas. La existencia misma de los viejos automóviles estadounidenses se burla de las leyes del mercado, de la mecánica automotriz y del medio ambiente, escribió Leonardo Padura, el escritor criminalista más conocido de Cuba.

Sur la Carretera Central

Les pannes font partie du quotidien sur la Carretera Central et sur les grandes routes : les pièces de musée grinçantes comptent en effet des centaines de milliers de kilomètres au compteur, voire un million pour certaines. « Ces vieilles voitures américaines bafouent les lois du marché, de la mécanique automobile et de l'environnement », écrivait l'auteur de polars le plus célèbre de Cuba, Leonardo Padura.

Na Carretera Central

As avarias fazem parte da vida quotidiana na Carretera Central e nas estradas rurais, porque muitas das peças de museu guinchantes têm centenas de milhares, se não mais de um milhão de quilómetros nas costas. A própria existência dos velhos carros americanos despreza as leis do mercado, da mecânica dos carros e do meio ambiente, escreveu o mais conhecido escritor cubano de crimes, Leonardo Padura.

Auf der Carretera Central

Pannen gehören zum Alltag auf der Carretera Central und den Landstraßen, denn viele der ächzenden Museumsstücke haben Hunderttausende, wenn nicht über eine Million Kilometer auf dem Buckel. Allein die Existenz der alten US-Autos verhöhne die Gesetze des Marktes, der Automechanik und der Umwelt, schrieb Kubas bekanntester Krimiautor Leonardo Padura.

Op de Carretera Central

Motorpech is een onderdeel van het dagelijks leven op de Carretera Central en de landwegen, dit omdat veel van deze museumstukken honderdduizenden, zo niet meer dan een miljoen kilometer op de teller hebben. Alleen het bestaan van de oude Amerikaanse auto's zelf is een bespotting van de wetten van de markt, automonteurs en het milieu, schreef Cuba's bekendste misdaadschrijver Leonardo Padura.

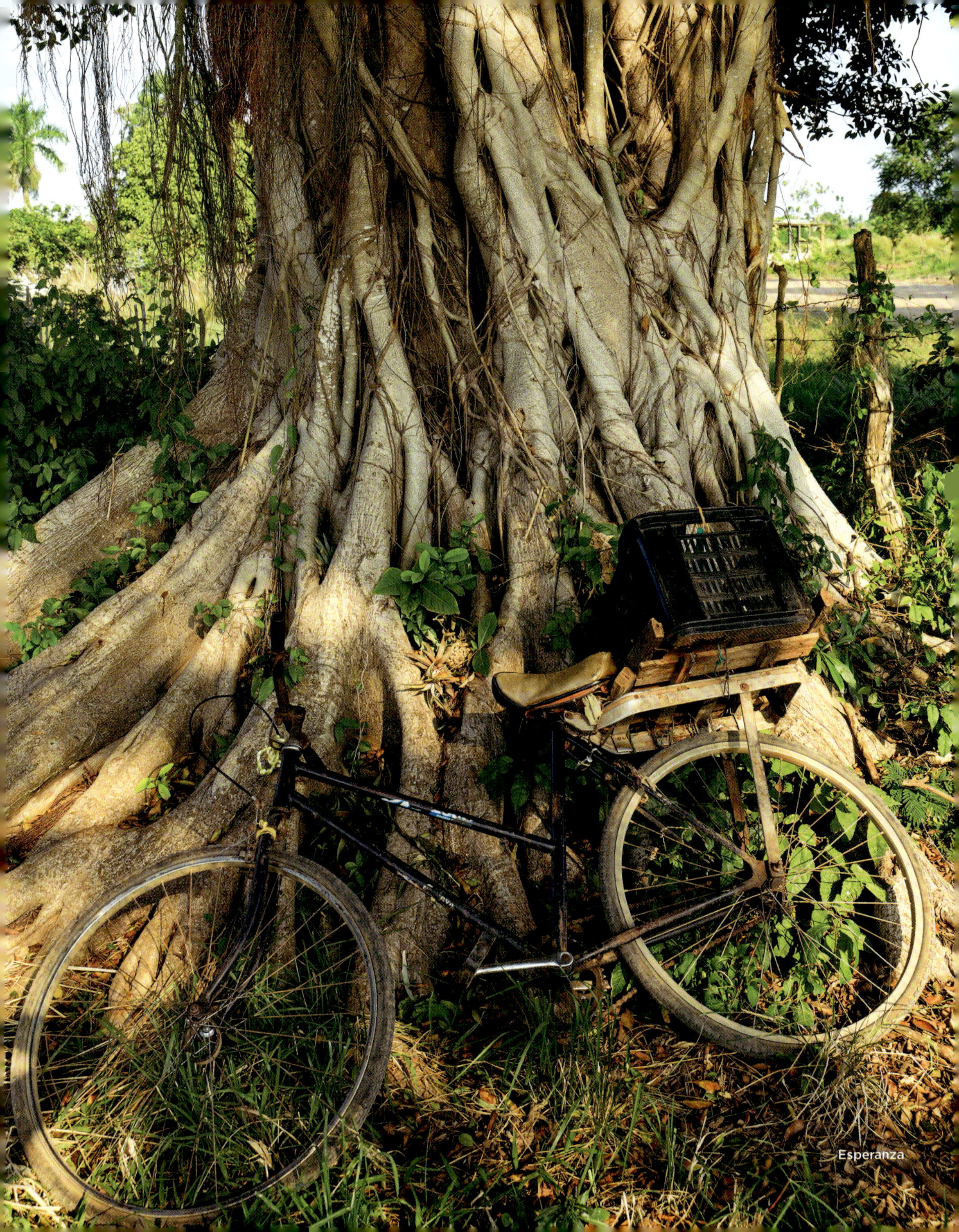
Esperanza

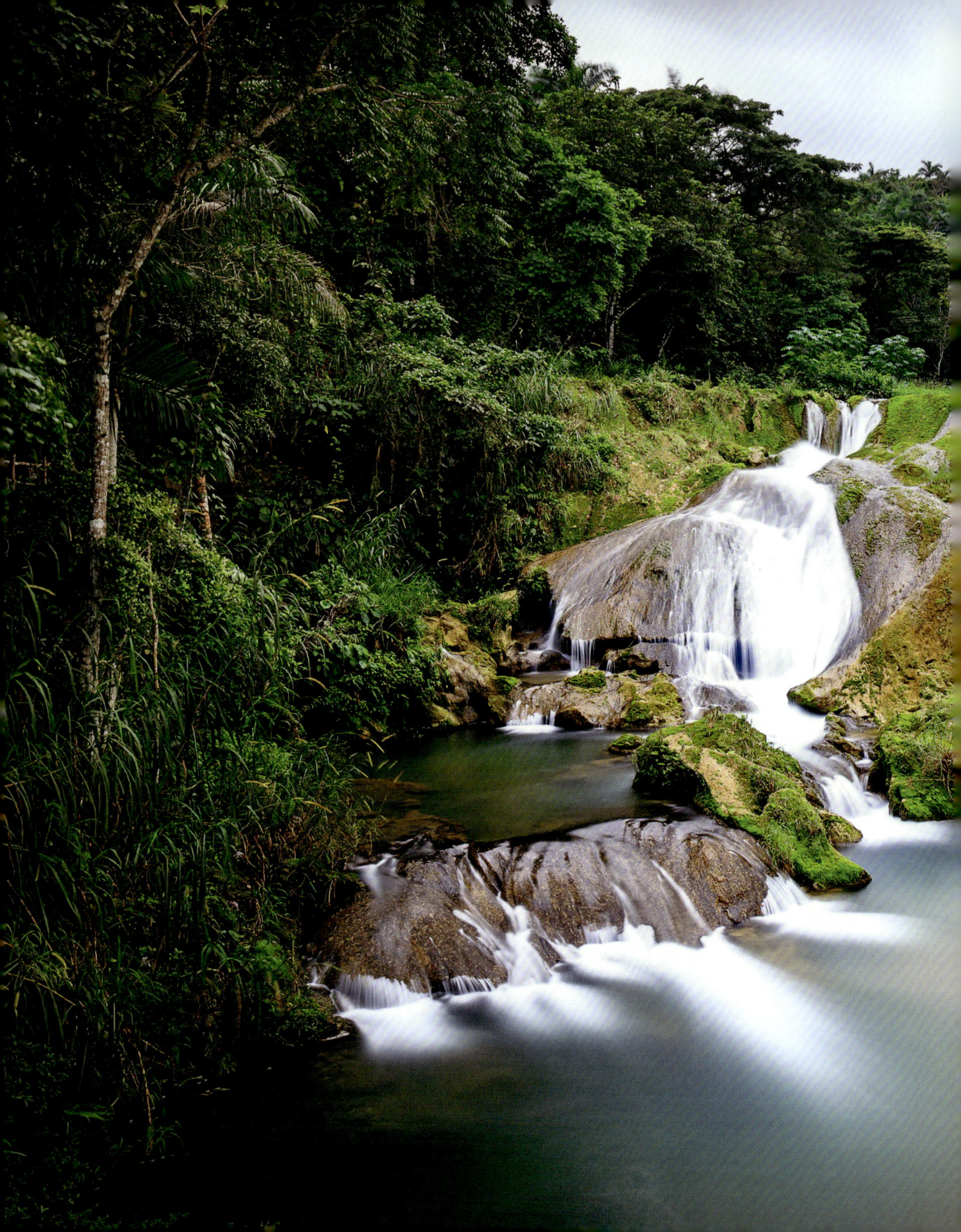

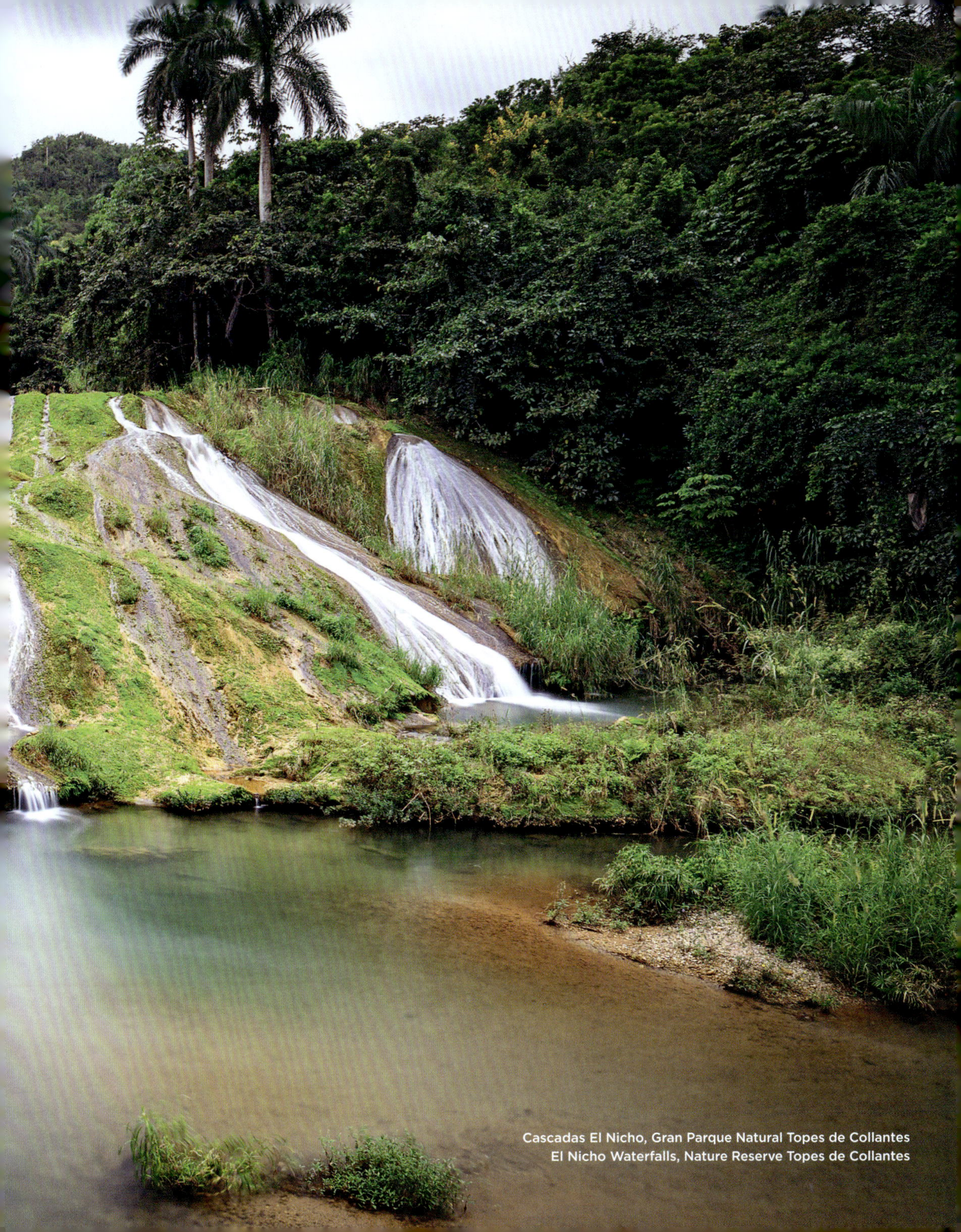

Cascadas El Nicho, Gran Parque Natural Topes de Collantes
El Nicho Waterfalls, Nature Reserve Topes de Collantes

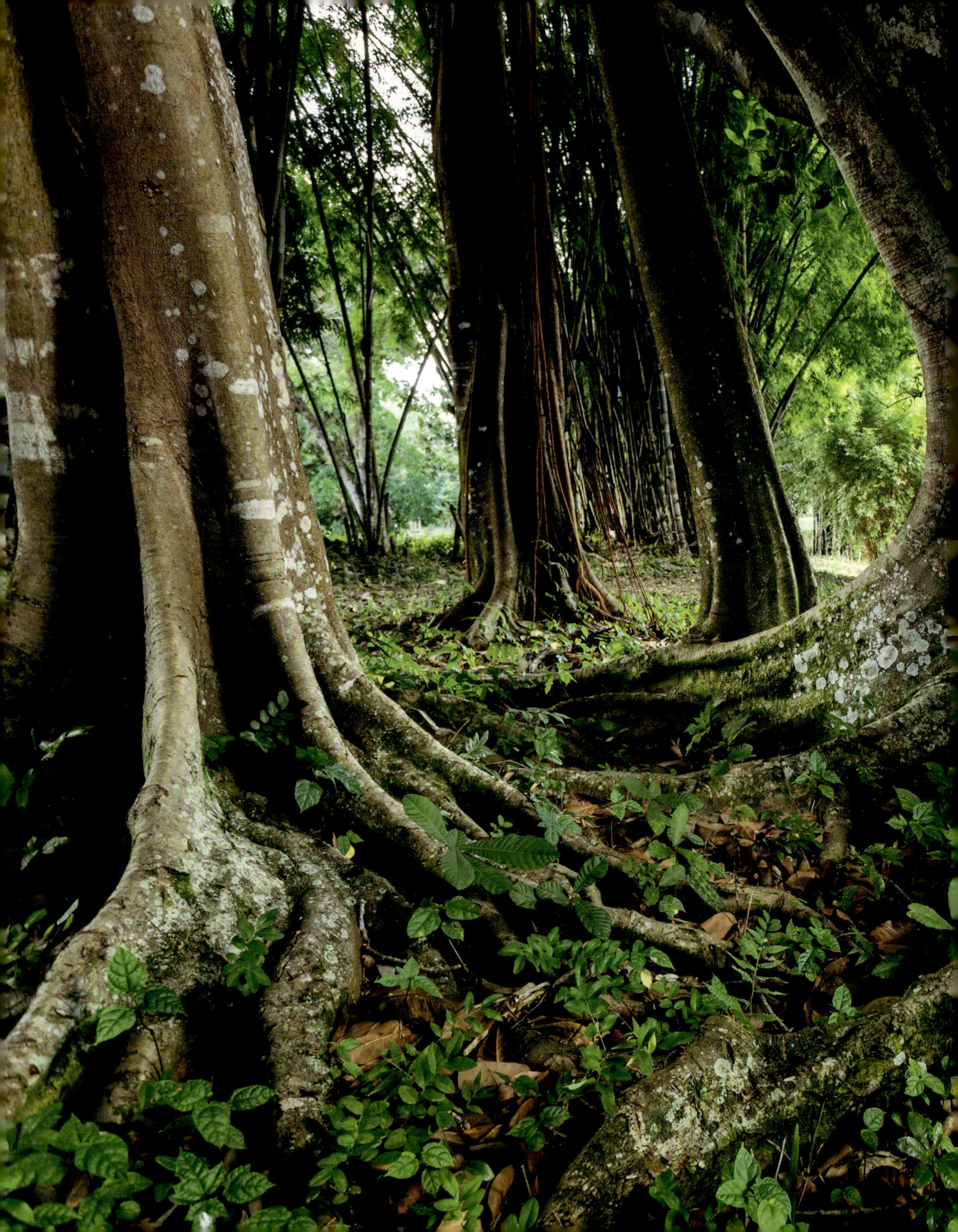

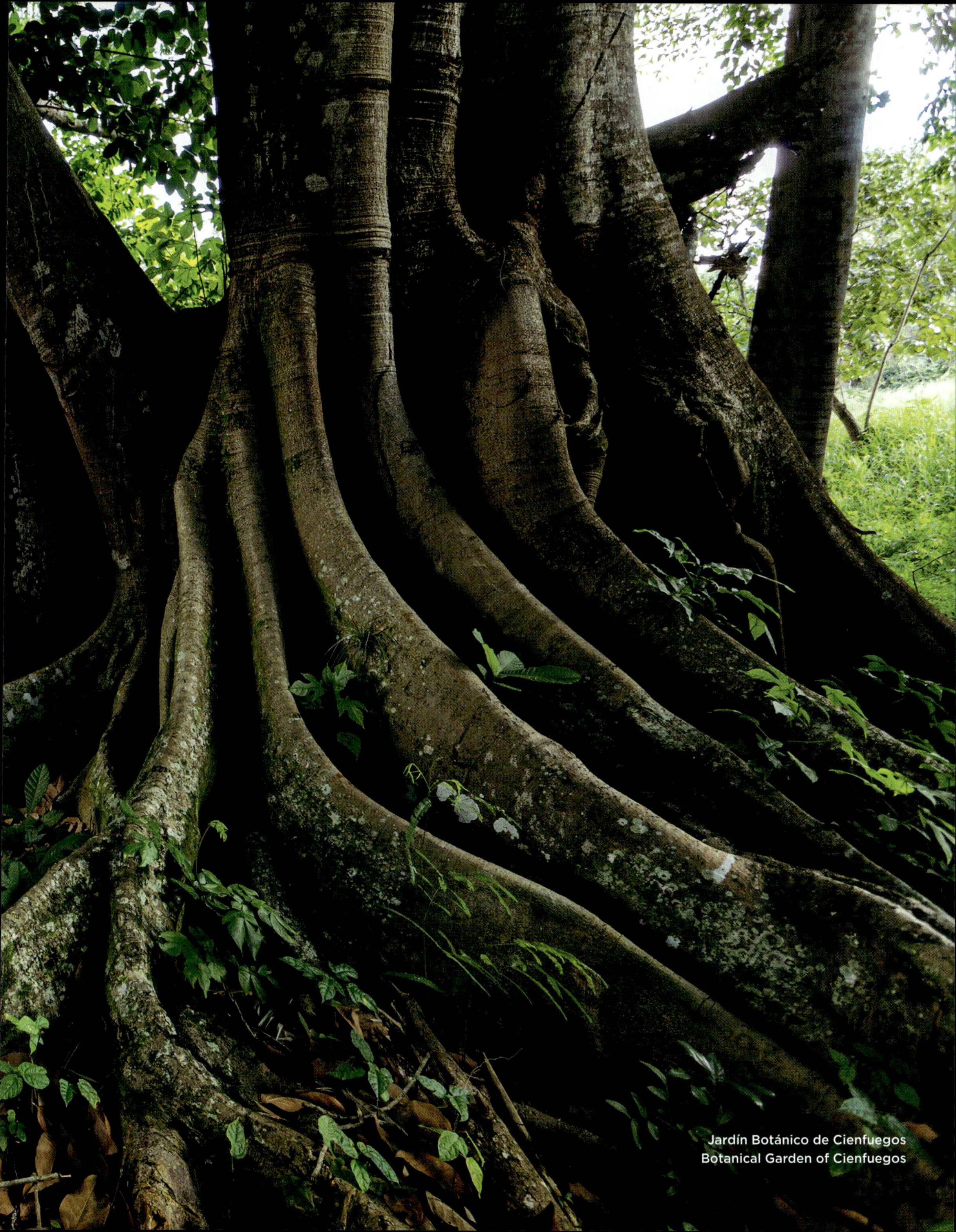
Jardín Botánico de Cienfuegos
Botanical Garden of Cienfuegos

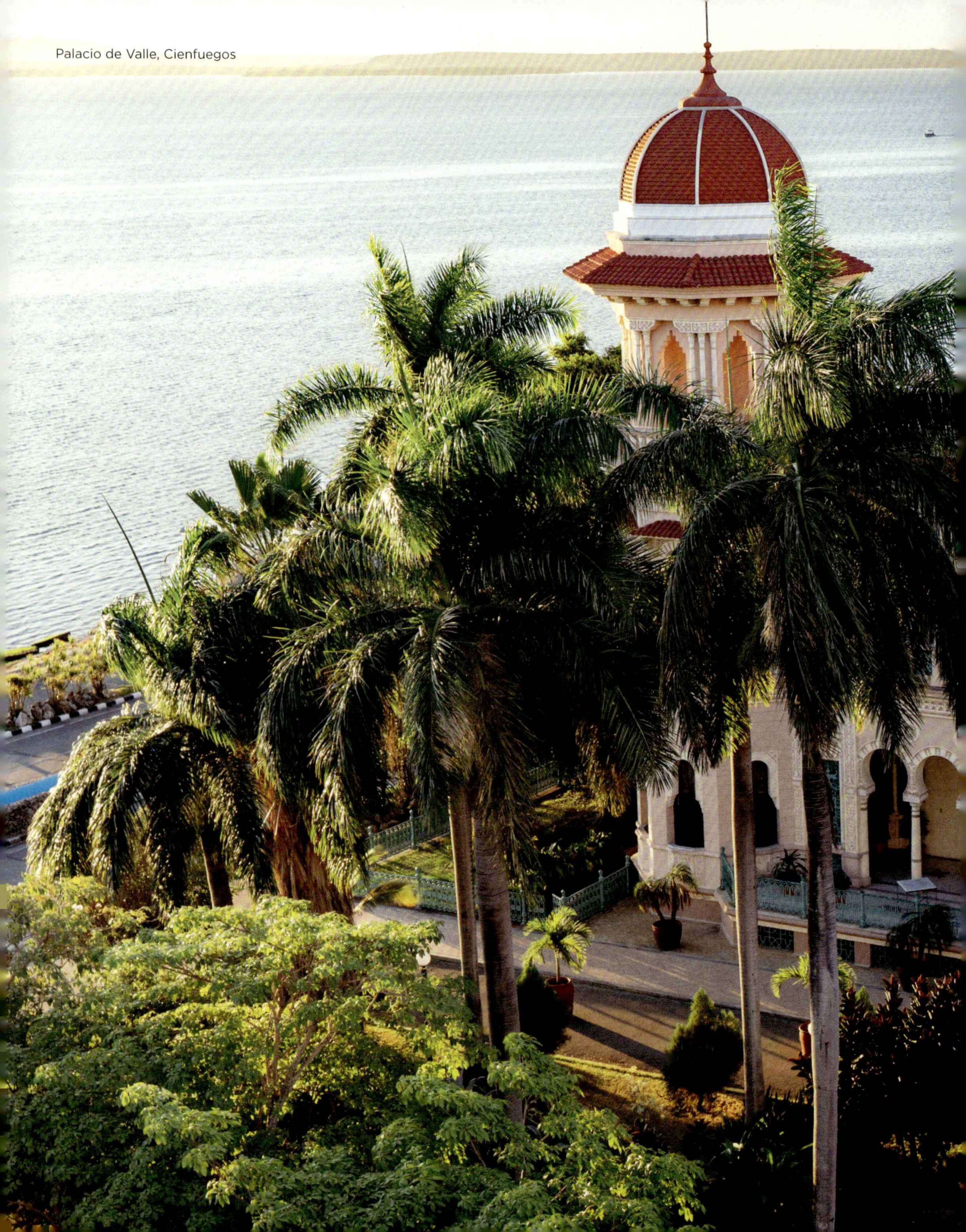

Palacio de Valle, Cienfuegos

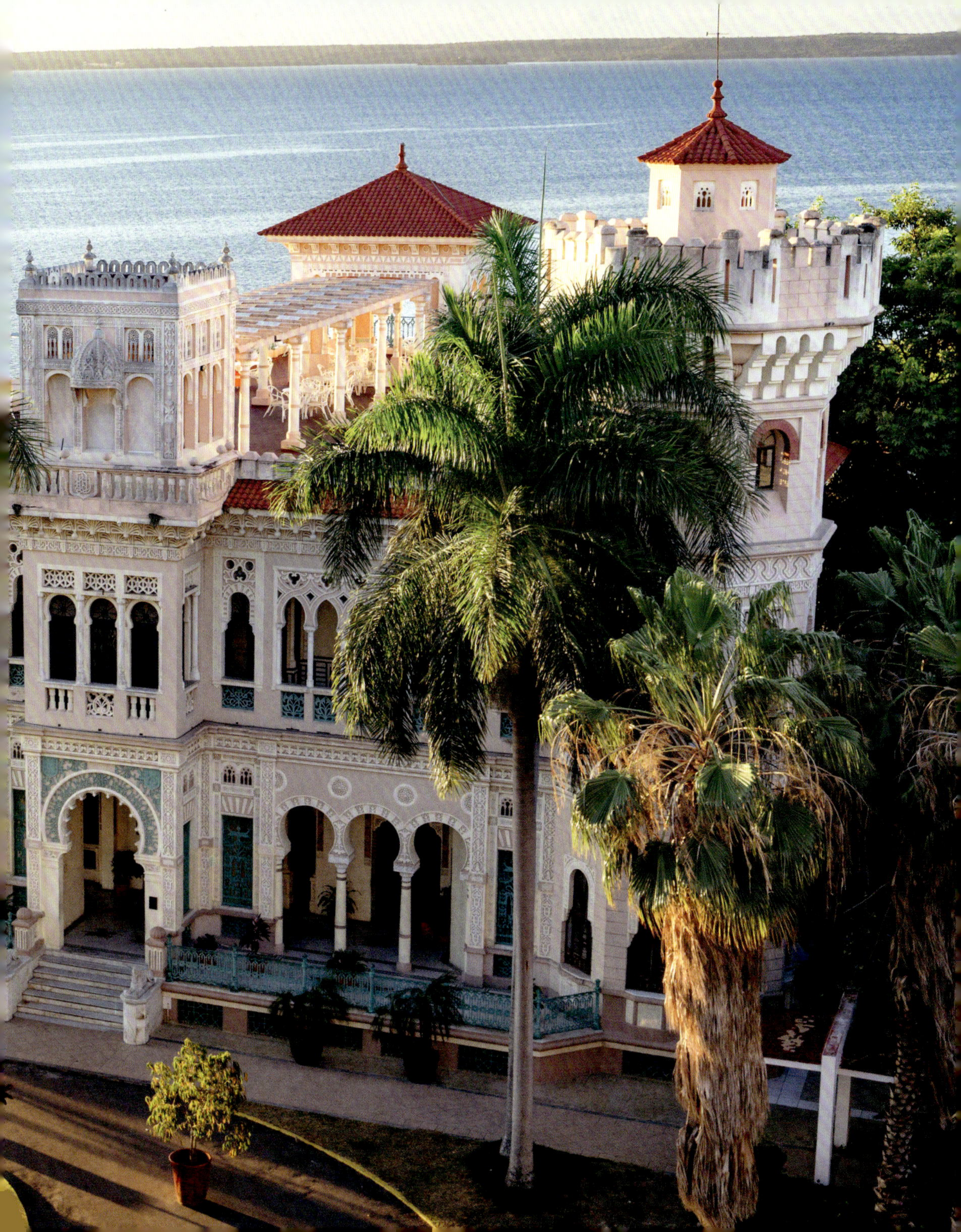

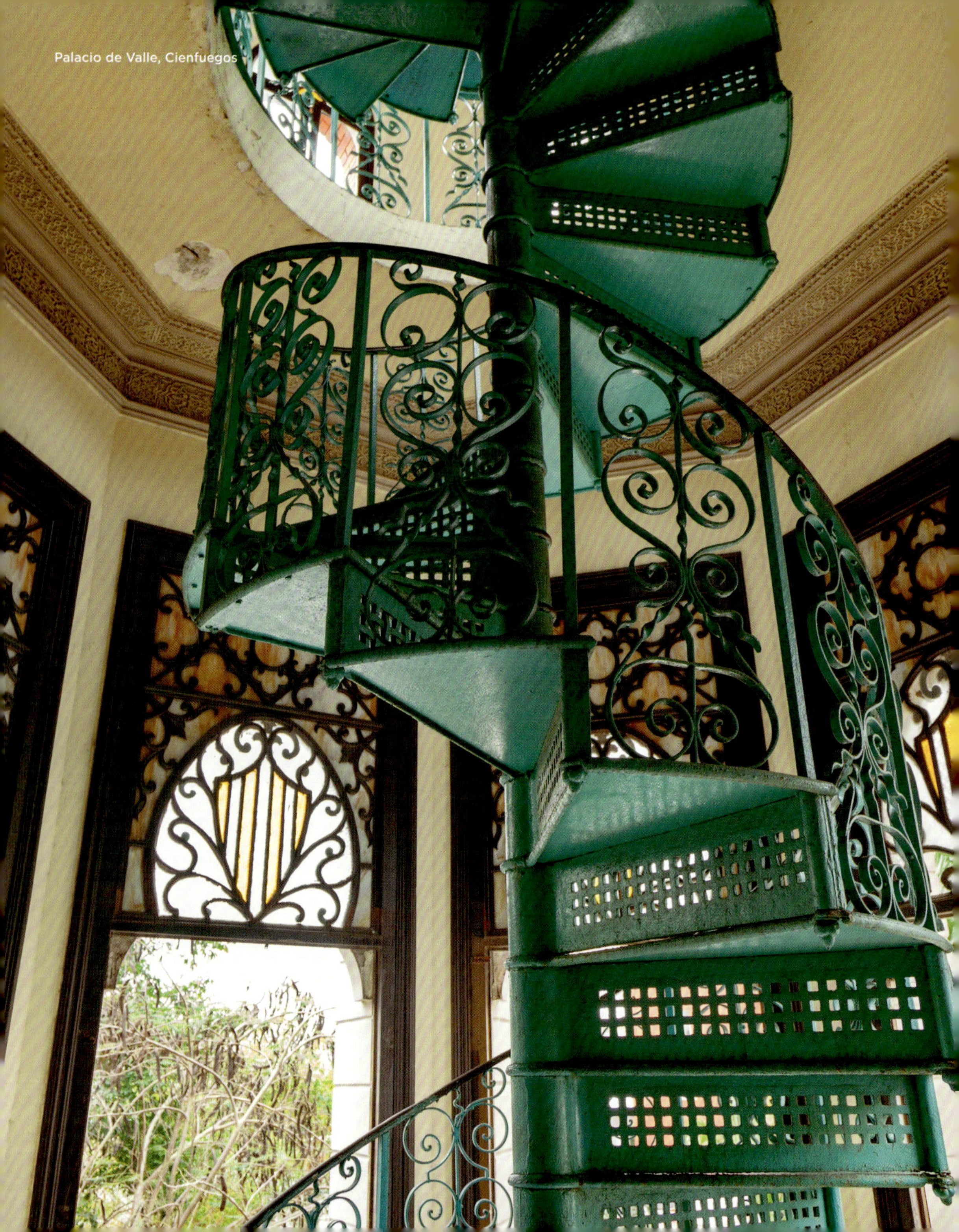
Palacio de Valle, Cienfuegos

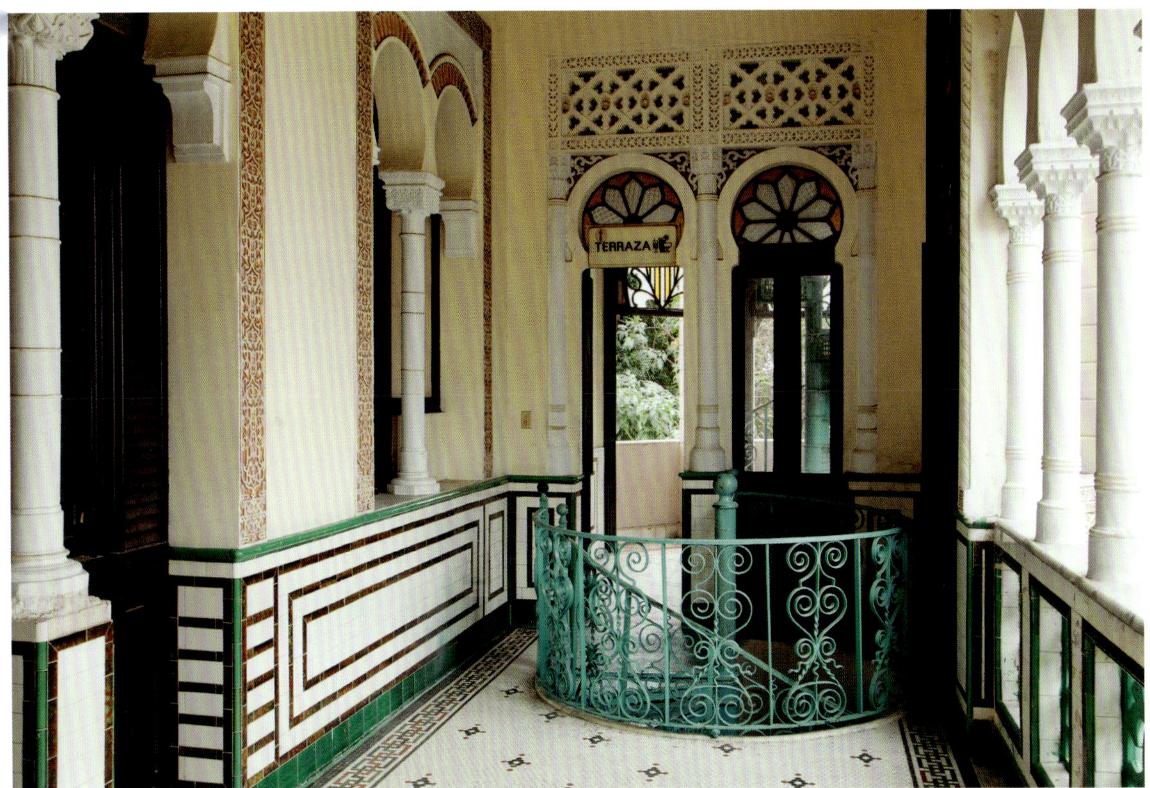

Palacio de Valle, Cienfuegos

Palacio del Valle, Cienfuegos
The Palacio del Valle was built between 1913 and 1917 by the Spanish sugar millionaire Don Ciscle del Valle y Blanco in memory of the Moorish splendor of the Alhambra. The interior of the palace with its exquisite woodcarvings is also reminiscent of the famous model. With its small towers and cornices, the Palacio del Valle looks like an oversized wedding cake.

Palacio del Valle, Cienfuegos
El Palacio del Valle fue construido por el millonario azucarero español Don Ciscle del Valle y Blanco entre 1913 y 1917 en memoria del esplendor morisco de la Alhambra. También el interior del palacio recuerda al famoso modelo con tallas en madera preciosa. Con sus pequeñas torres y cornisas, el Palacio del Valle parece un enorme pastel de boda.

Palacio de Valle, Cienfuegos
Le Palacio de Valle fut érigé entre 1913 et 1917 à la demande de Don Ciscle del Valle y Blanco, marchand de sucre prospère, en hommage au somptueux palais mauresque, l'Alhambra. Son décor intérieur évoque également les précieux reliefs en bois de son modèle. Truffé de tourelles et de corniches, le Palacio de Valle ressemble à une pièce montée géante.

Palácio del Valle, Cienfuegos
O Palácio del Valle foi construído pelo milionário espanhol Don Ciscle del Valle y Blanco entre 1913 e 1917, em memória do esplendor mourisco da Alhambra. Também o interior do palácio lembra o famoso modelo com esculturas em madeira preciosa. Com suas pequenas torres e cornijas, o Palacio del Valle parece um bolo de casamento superdimensionado.

Palacio del Valle, Cienfuegos
Den Palacio del Valle ließ der spanische Zuckermillionär Don Ciscle del Valle y Blanco 1913 bis 1917 bauen, in Erinnerung an die maurische Pracht der Alhambra. Auch das Innere des Palastes erinnert mit kostbaren Holzschnitzereien an das berühmte Vorbild. Mit seinen Türmchen und Simsen wirkt der Palacio del Valle wie eine überdimensionierte Hochzeitstorte.

Palacio del Valle, Cienfuegos, Cienfuegos
Het Palacio del Valle werd tussen 1913 en 1917 door de Spaanse suikermiljonair Don Ciscle del Valle y Blanco gebouwd, dit ter nagedachtenis aan de Moorse pracht en praal van het Alhambra. Ook het interieur van het paleis doet met kostbaar houtsnijwerk denken aan het beroemde model. Het Palacio del Valle ziet er met zijn kleine torens en kroonlijsten uit als een oversized bruidstaart.

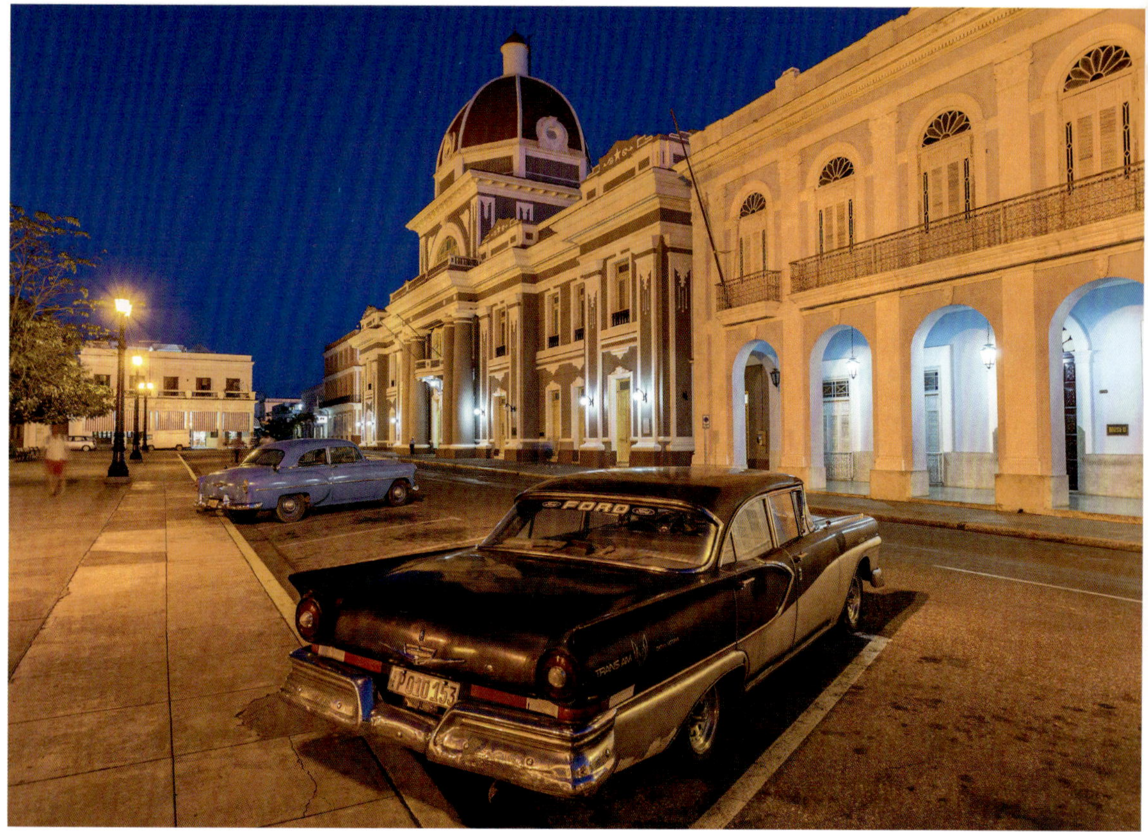

Teatro Tomás Terry, Cienfuegos

Cienfuegos

Cienfuegos, the "Pearl of the South", is a charming little town on the south coast, with many candy-colored colonial buildings, a boulevard modeled on the Champs-Élysées, a very pretty riverside promenade and a marina. In the evening you can stroll around the magnificent music pavilion at Parque Martí, the central square flanked by well-kept colonial buildings. One of the attractions is the neoclassical Teatro Terry, which sugar baron Tomás Terry built in 1889 and inaugurated in 1890 with a magnificent *Aida* performance. The elegant interior with its sumptuous Cuban precious woods and ceiling frescoes is well worth seeing.

Cienfuegos

Cienfuegos, la « perle du Sud », est une charmante petite ville de la côte sud exhibant moult constructions coloniales acidulées, une voie somptueuse inspirée des Champs-Élysées, un front de mer ravissant et un port de plaisance. Le soir, on y flâne aux abords du splendide pavillon de musique du Parque José Martí, place centrale flanquée de bâtiments coloniaux soignés. L'une des principales attractions, le Teatro Terry néoclassique, fut commandée par le baron du sucre Tomás Terry en 1889 et son inauguration en 1890 donna lieu à une pompeuse représentation d'*Aïda*. L'aménagement intérieur mérite une visite : il fait la part belle aux bois précieux cubains et aux plafonds illuminés de fresques.

Cienfuegos

Cienfuegos, die „Perle des Südens", ist ein charmantes Städtchen an der Südküste, mit vielen bonbonfarbenen Kolonialbauten, einer den Champs-Élysées nachempfundenem Prachtstraße, einer sehr hübschen Uferpromenade und einem Yachthafen. Abends flaniert man rund um den prächtigen Musikpavillon am Parque Martí, dem von gepflegten Kolonialbauten flankierten zentralen Platz. Eine der Attraktionen ist das neoklassizistische Teatro Terry, das der Zuckerbaron Tomás Terry 1889 erbauen und 1890 mit einer prunkvollen *Aida*-Aufführung einweihen ließ. Die elegante Innenausstattung mit kostbaren kubanischen Edelhölzern und Deckenfresken ist sehenswert.

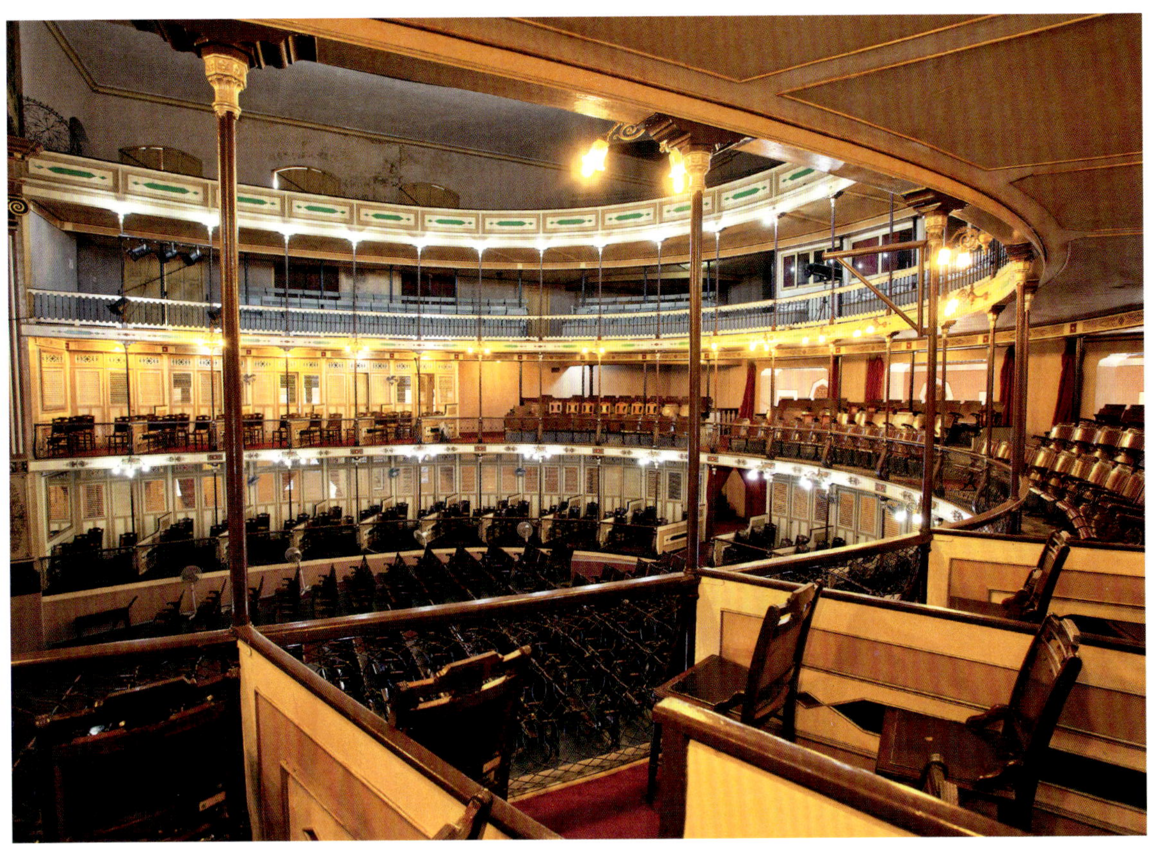

Teatro Tomás Terry, Cienfuegos

Cienfuegos

Cienfuegos, la "perla del sur", es una pequeña y encantadora ciudad en la costa sur, con muchos edificios coloniales de colores dulces, un boulevard que imita los Campos Elíseos, un precioso paseo a orillas del río y un puerto deportivo. Por la noche se puede pasear por el magnífico pabellón de música del Parque Martí, la plaza central flanqueada por edificios coloniales en buen estado. Uno de los atractivos es el neoclásico Teatro Terry, que el magnate del azúcar Tomás Terry construyó en 1889 e inauguró en 1890 con una magnífica actuación de *Aida*. El elegante interior con preciosas maderas preciosas cubanas y frescos en el techo es digno de ver.

Cienfuegos

Cienfuegos, a "Pérola do Sul", é uma encantadora pequena cidade na costa sul, com muitos edifícios coloniais em cores doces, uma avenida inspirada nos Champs-Élysées, um bonito passeio ribeirinho e uma marina. À noite, você passeia pelo magnífico pavilhão de música do Parque Martí, a praça central rodeada por edifícios coloniais bem conservados. Uma das atrações é o neoclássico Teatro Terry, que o barão do açúcar Tomás Terry construiu em 1889 e inaugurou em 1890 com uma magnífica apresentação de *Aida*. Vale a pena ver o elegante interior com valiosas madeiras nobres cubanas e afrescos no teto.

Cienfuegos

Cienfuegos, de 'Parel van het Zuiden', is een charmant stadje aan de zuidkust, met veel snoepkleurige koloniale gebouwen, een boulevard naar het voorbeeld van de Champs-Élysées, een zeer mooie promenade langs de rivier en een jachthaven. 's Avonds wandel je rond in het prachtige muziekpaviljoen van het Parque Martí, het centrale plein geflankeerd door goed onderhouden koloniale gebouwen. Een van de attracties is het neoklassieke Teatro Terry, dat in 1889 door suikerbaron Tomás Terry werd gebouwd en in 1890 werd ingehuldigd met een prachtige *Aida* voorstelling. Het elegante interieur met kostbaar Cubaans hout en plafondfresco's is zeker een bezoek waard.

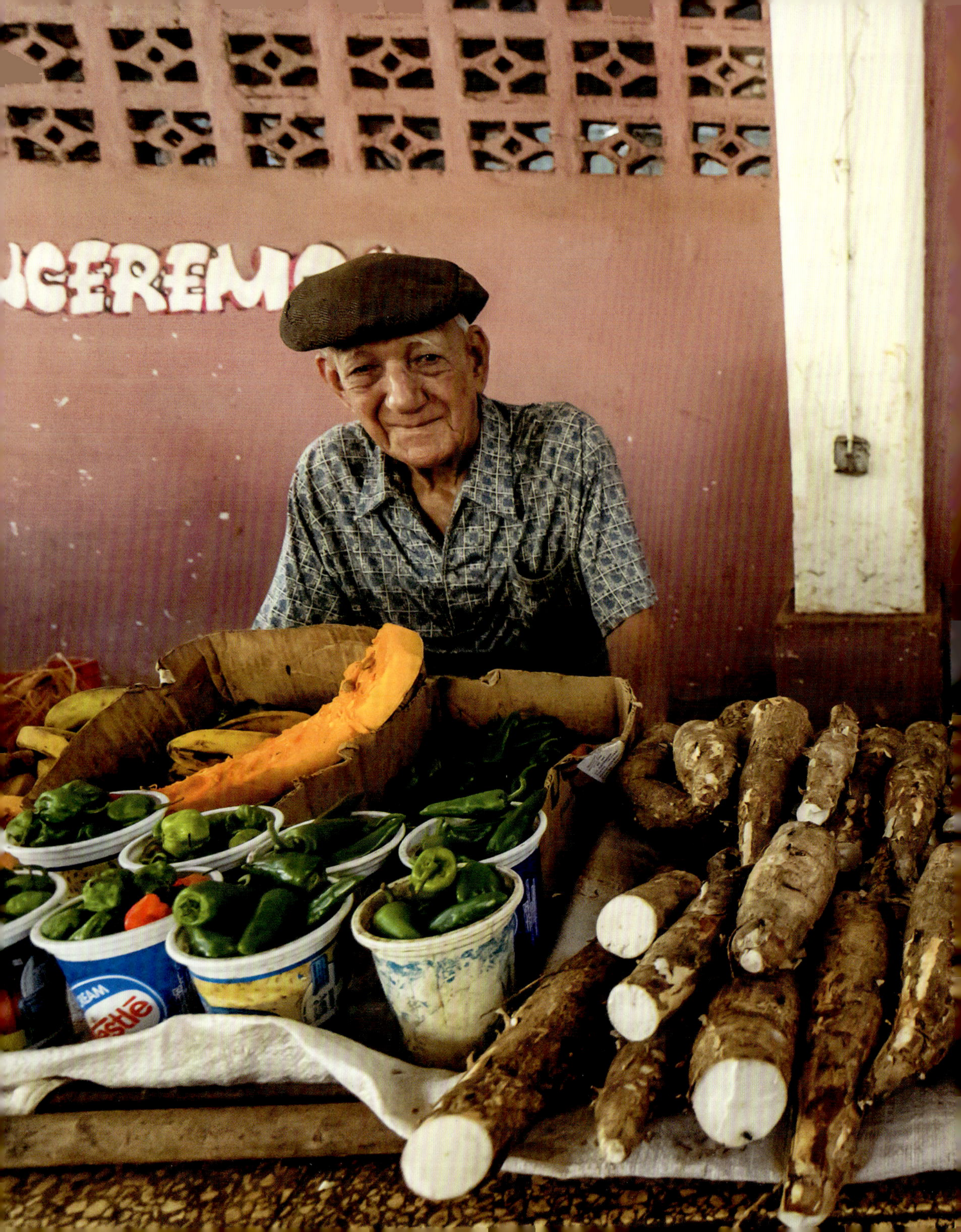
NGEREMO

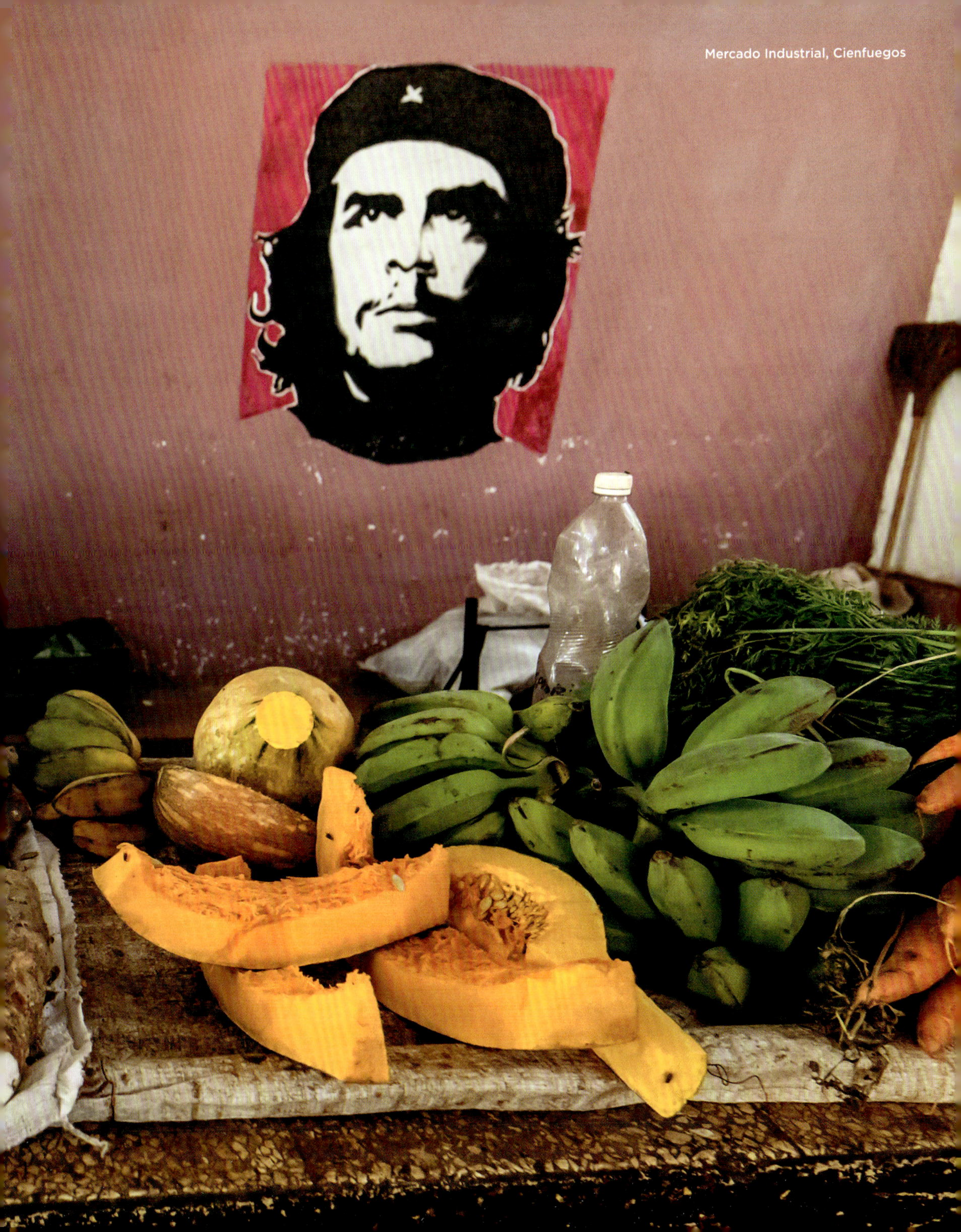

Mercado Industrial, Cienfuegos

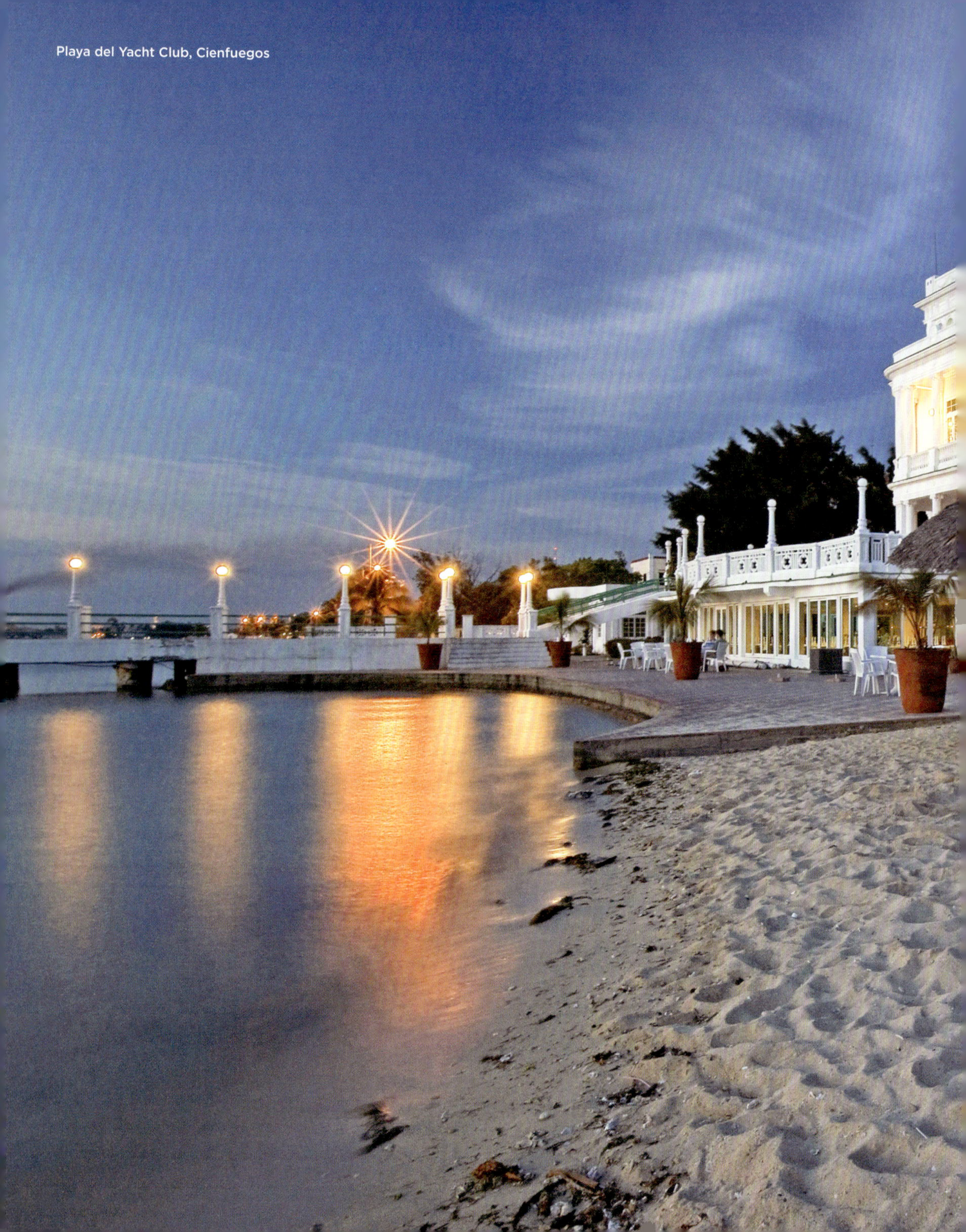
Playa del Yacht Club, Cienfuegos

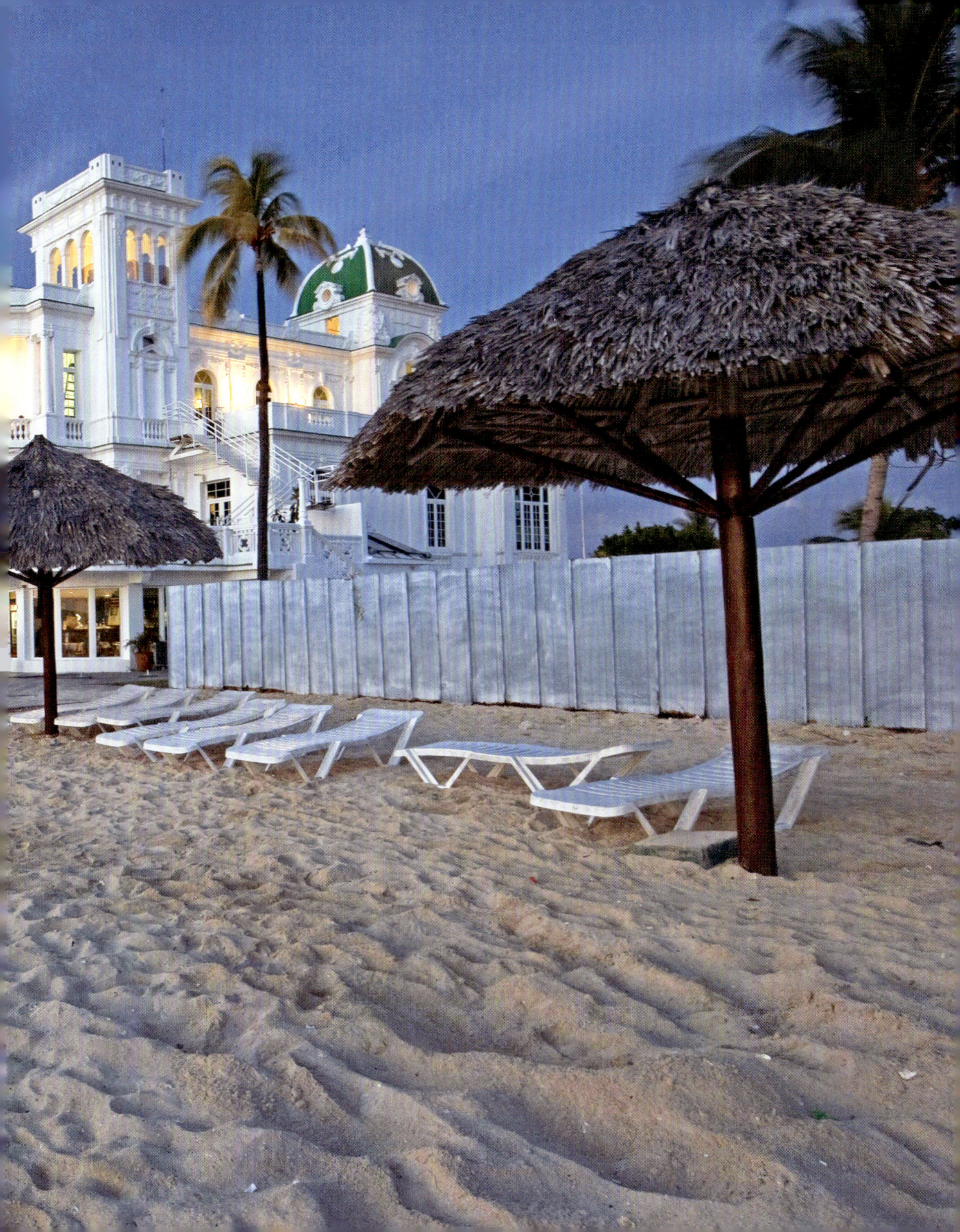

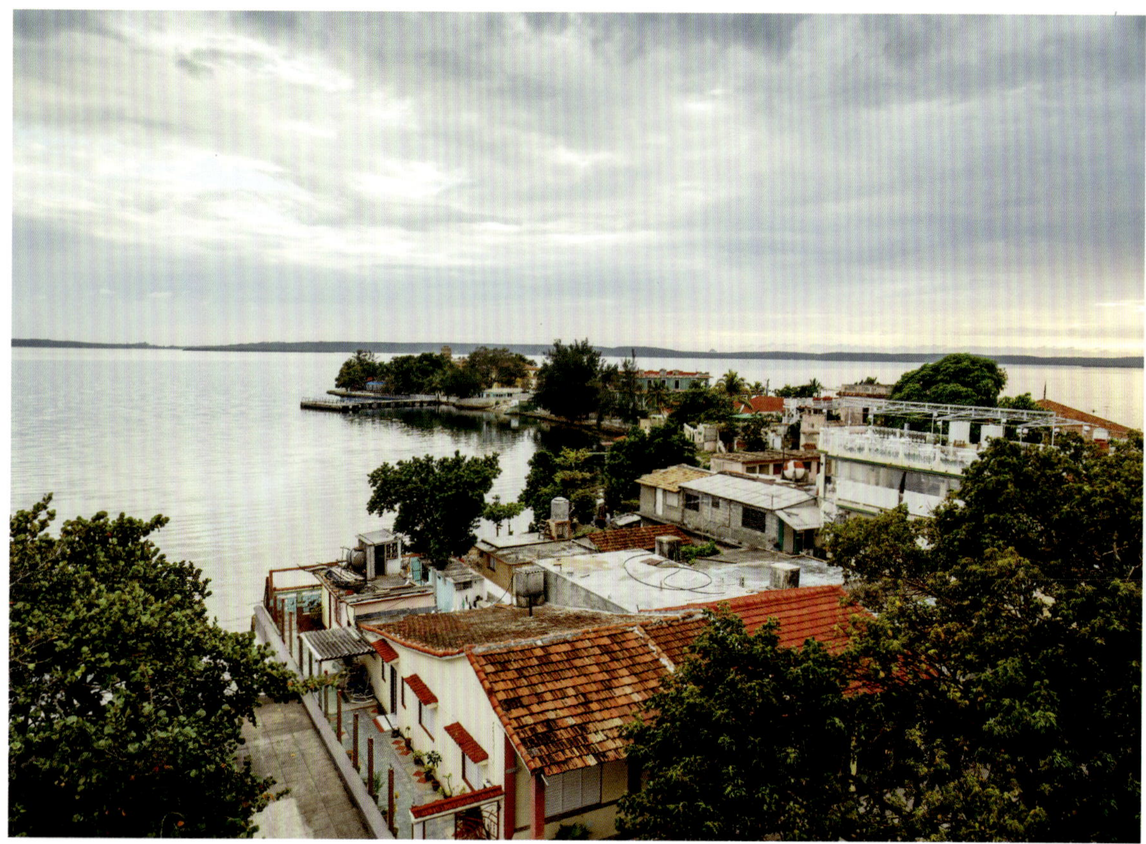

La Punta, Cienfuegos

Jagua Bay

Cienfuegos is located at the northern end
of a 21 km (13 mi.) long bay which forms a
deep natural harbor into which three rivers
flow. Around 1650, even before the city
was founded, Spanish settlers and Indians
lived peacefully together on the banks of
the three rivers. This was mainly due to the
Spanish Father Bartolomé de las Casas,
who protected the Indios from the Spanish
soldiers. The bay is named after Jagua,
the Indian goddess of agriculture, fishing
and fertility, granddaughter of the sun and
moon. The peninsula Punta Gorda with
its faded wooden villas extends far into
the bay.

La baie Jagua

Cienfuegos est située au nord d'une baie
de 21 km de long, port naturel profond
dans lequel se jettent trois fleuves.
Vers 1650, avant la fondation du pays,
colons espagnols et Indiens cohabitaient
paisiblement sur les rives des trois fleuves.
Cette bonne entente était essentiellement
l'œuvre du père espagnol Bartolomé de
Las Casas, qui protégeait les Indiens des
agressions espagnoles. La baie porte le
nom de la déesse indienne de la culture, de
la pêche et de la fertilité, Jagua, petite-fille
du Soleil et de la Lune. La presqu'île Punta
Gorda, avec ses villas en bois délavées,
s'avance loin dans la baie.

Die Jagua-Bucht

Cienfuegos liegt am nördlichen Ende
einer 21 km langen Bucht, die einen
tiefen natürlichen Hafen bildet, in den
drei Flüsse münden. Um 1650, noch vor
der Stadtgründung, lebten spanische
Siedler und Indios friedlich an den Ufern
der drei Flüsse zusammen. Dies war vor
allem dem spanischen Pater Bartolomé
de las Casas zu verdanken, der die
Indios vor Übergriffen der spanischen
Soldaten schützte. Benannt ist die Bucht
nach Jagua, der indianischen Göttin
des Ackerbaus, des Fischfangs und der
Fruchtbarkeit, Enkelin der Sonne und des
Mondes. Die Halbinsel Punta Gorda mit
ihren verwaschenen Holzvillen ragt weit in
die Bucht.

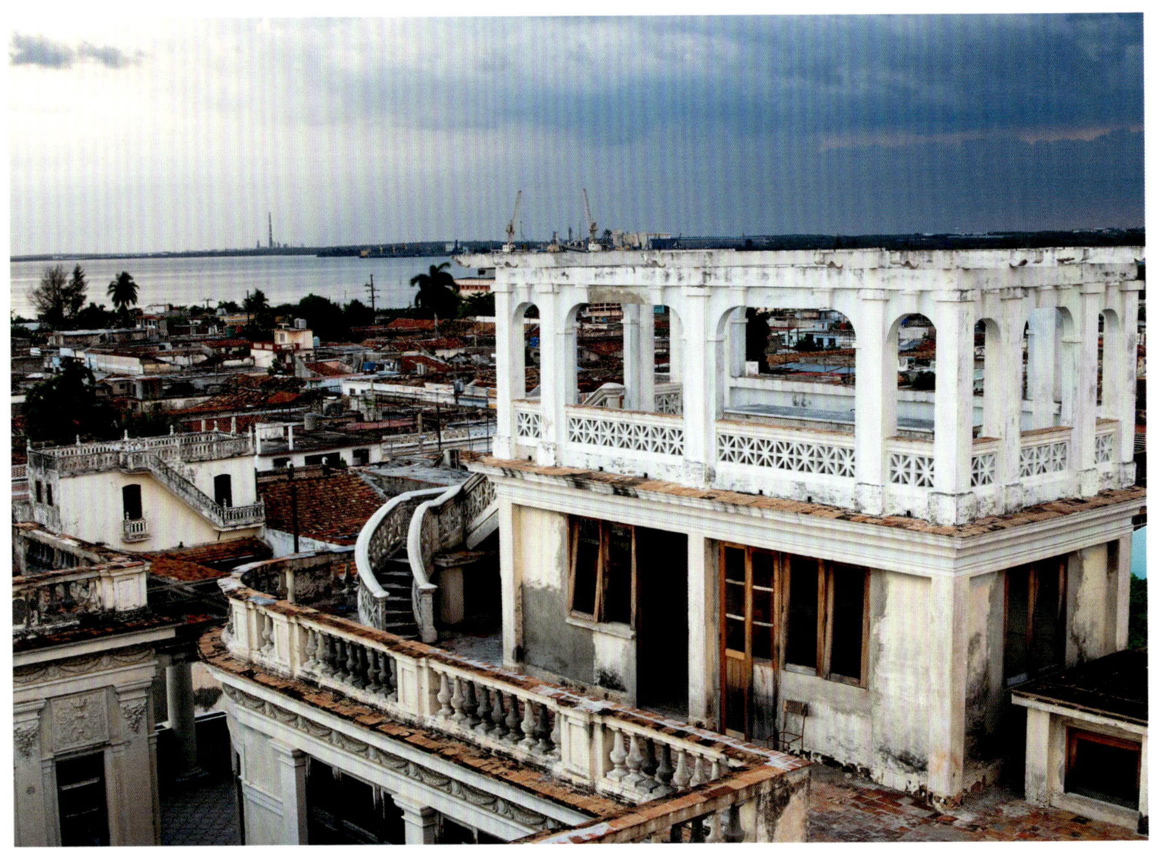

Cienfuegos

Bahía de Jagua

Cienfuegos se encuentra en el extremo norte de una bahía de 21 km de longitud que forma un profundo puerto natural en el que desembocan tres ríos. Alrededor de 1650, incluso antes de la fundación de la ciudad, los colonos españoles y los indios vivían pacíficamente juntos en las orillas de los tres ríos. Esto se debió principalmente al padre Bartolomé de las Casas, que protegió a los indios de los soldados españoles. La bahía lleva el nombre de Jagua, la diosa india de la agricultura, la pesca y la fertilidad, nieta del sol y la luna. La península de Punta Gorda con sus villas de madera destartaladas se eleva muy adentro en la bahía.

A Baía de Jagua

Cienfuegos está localizada no extremo norte de uma baía de 21 km de comprimento, que forma um profundo porto natural, para o qual fluem três rios. Por volta de 1650, mesmo antes da fundação da cidade, colonos e índios espanhóis viviam juntos pacificamente nas margens dos três rios. Isso se deve principalmente ao padre espanhol Bartolomé de las Casas, que protegeu os índios dos ataques dos soldados espanhóis. A baía tem o nome de Jagua, a deusa indígena da agricultura, pesca e fertilidade, neta do sol e da lua. A península de Punta Gorda, com suas vilas de madeira desbotadas, se ergue na baía.

Jagua Baai

Cienfuegos ligt aan het noordelijke uiteinde van een 21 km lange baai, die een diepe natuurlijke haven vormt en waar drie rivieren in uitmonden. Rond 1650, nog voordat de stad werd gesticht, leefden de Spaanse kolonisten en indianen vreedzaam samen aan de oevers van de drie rivieren. Dit was vooral te danken aan de Spaanse pater Bartolomé de las Casas, die de Indianen beschermde tegen de Spaanse soldaten. De baai is vernoemd naar Jagua, de Indiase godin van de landbouw, visserij en vruchtbaarheid, kleindochter van de zon en de maan. Het schiereiland Punta Gorda met zijn uitgespoelde houten villa's steekt ver in de baai uit.

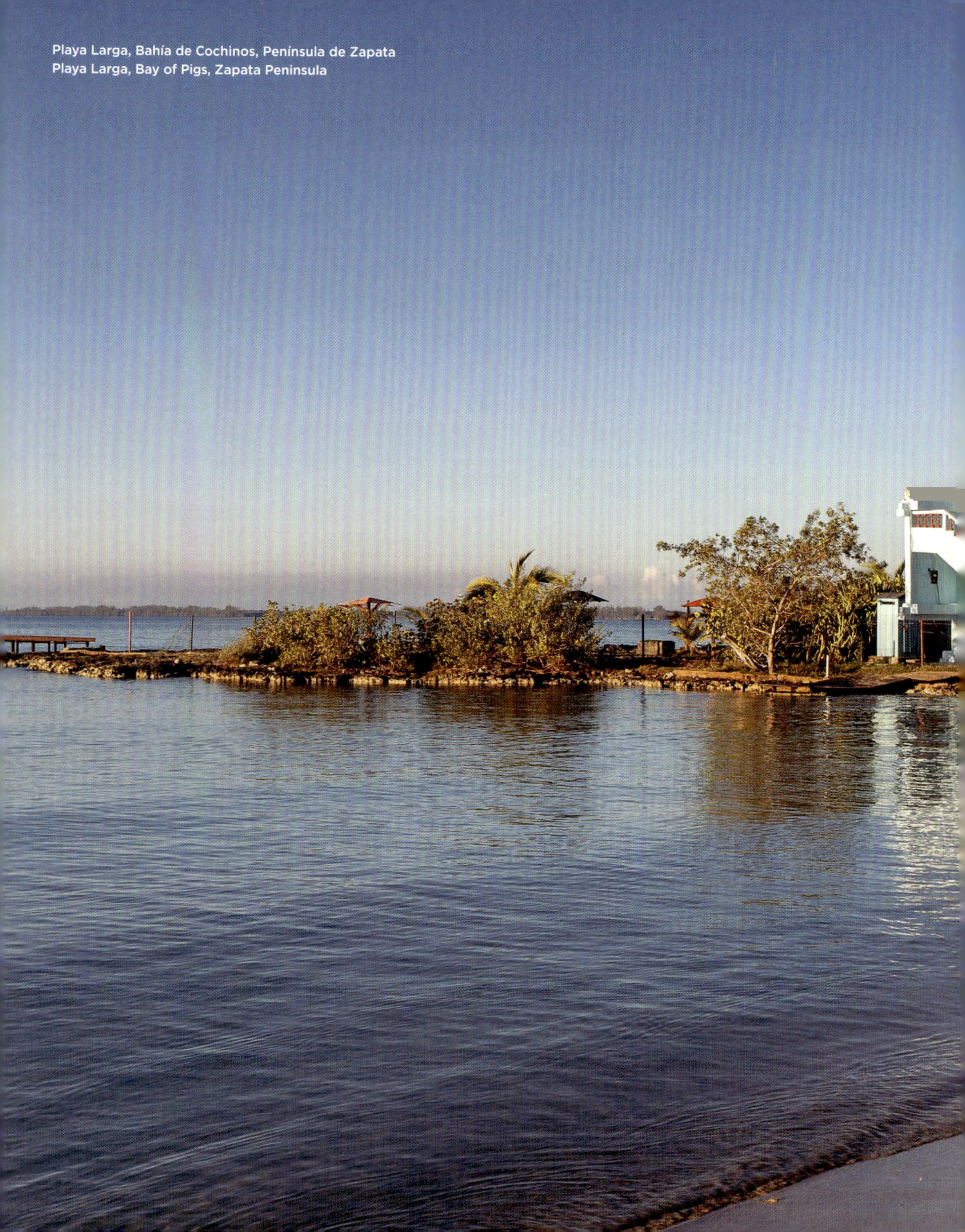

Playa Larga, Bahía de Cochinos, Península de Zapata
Playa Larga, Bay of Pigs, Zapata Peninsula

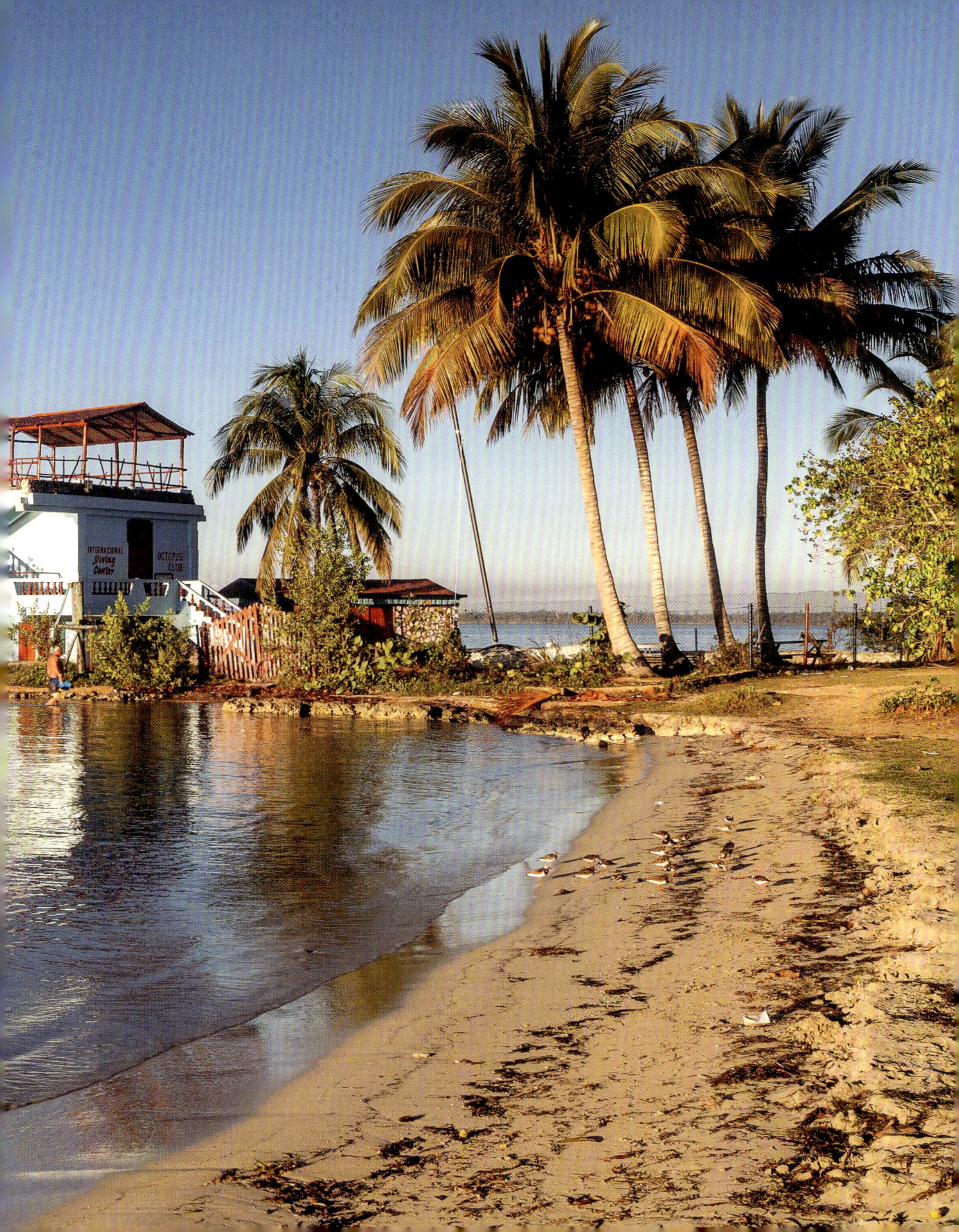

INTERNACIONAL
Diving Center
OCTOPUS
CLUB

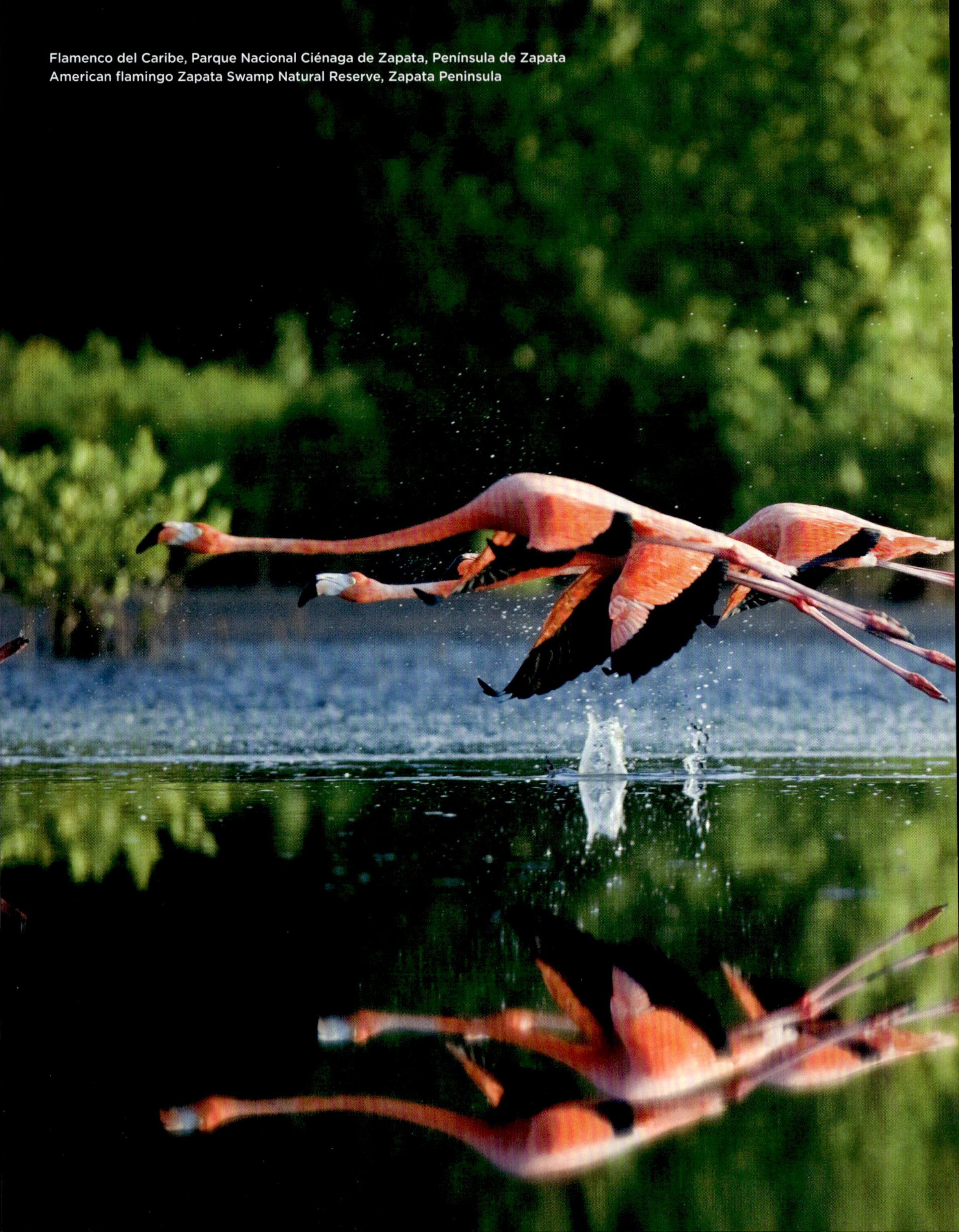

Flamenco del Caribe, Parque Nacional Ciénaga de Zapata, Península de Zapata
American flamingo Zapata Swamp Natural Reserve, Zapata Peninsula

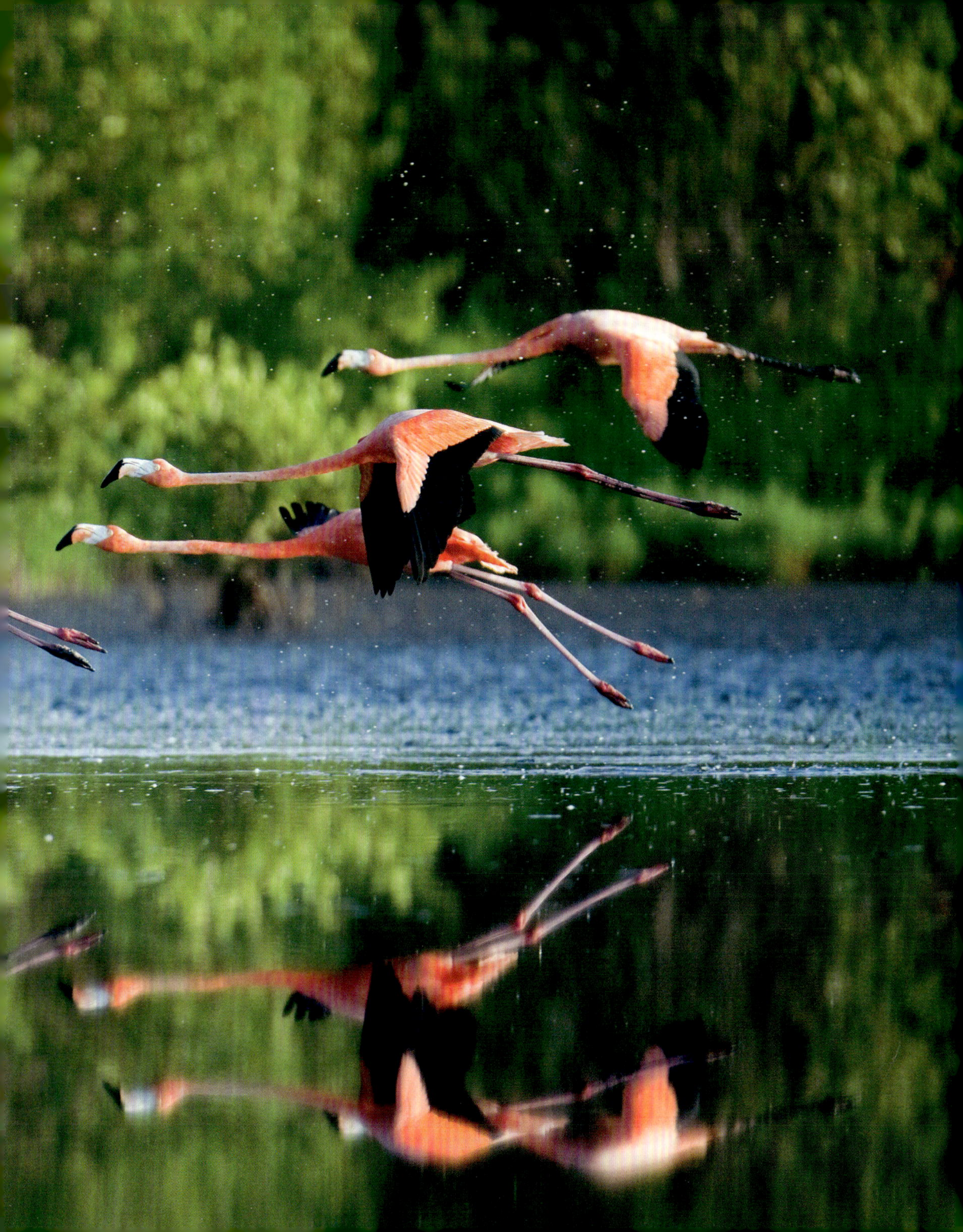

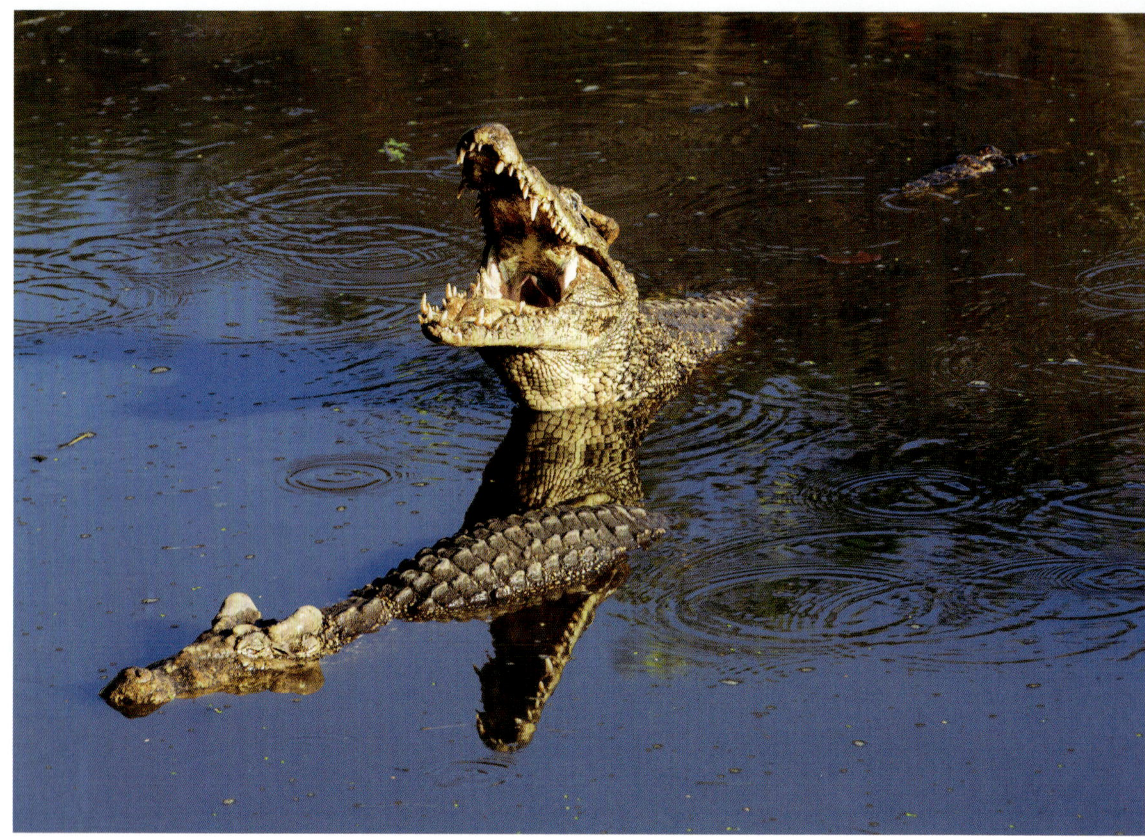

Criadero de cocodrilos, Boca de Guamá, Península de Zapata
Crocodile farm, Boca de Guamá, Zapata Peninsula

National Park Ciénaga de Zapata

The almost deserted swamp area of
the 285,650 ha (705,856 acre) Zapata
Peninsula on the south coast is part
of the Montemar Nature Park, and has
been a biosphere reserve since 2001. It
is the largest contiguous marshland in
the Caribbean and one of Cuba's richest
ecosystems, home to 20 of Cuba's 22
endemic bird species, ranging from the
bee hummingbird to Cuban flamingos
and cormorants. Boca de Guamá is a
tourist destination: in two crocodile farms
thousands of crocodiles (*Crocodylus
rhombifer)* live within walled ponds, and
are spectacularly fed and captured with a
lasso as a live show.

Parc national Ciénaga de Zapata

La région marécageuse quasiment
inhabitée de 285 650 ha de la presqu'île
de Zapata, sur la côte sud, est incluse pour
une grande part dans le parc naturel de
Montemar et est protégée depuis 2001
en tant que réserve de biosphère. Elle est
la plus vaste zone marécageuse continue
des Caraïbes et l'un des écosystèmes les
plus riches en espèces de Cuba. Elle abrite
20 des 22 espèces d'oiseaux endémiques
de l'île, du colibri-abeille aux flamants
roses et cormorans de Cuba. À la Boca de
Guamá, le tourisme bat son plein : dans 2
fermes de crocodiles vivent des milliers
d'animaux (*Crocodylus rhombifer),* nourris
théâtralement dans des mares non closes
et capturés au lasso pour le spectacle.

Nationalpark Ciénaga de Zapata

Das nahezu menschenleere Sumpfgebiet
der 285 650 ha großen Zapata-Halbinsel
an der Südküste gehört größtenteils zum
Naturpark Montemar und ist seit 2001
ein Biosphärenreservat. Es ist das größte
zusammenhängende Sumpfgebiet der
Karibik und eines der artenreichsten
Ökosysteme Kubas, in dem 20 der 22
endemischen Vogelarten Kubas leben,
von der Bienenelfe, einer Kolibri-Art, bis
hin zu Kuba-Flamingos und Kormoranen.
In Boca de Guamá geht es touristisch zu:
In zwei Krokodilfarmen leben tausende
Krokodile (*Crocodylus rhombifer)* in
ummauerten Teichen, werden spektakulär
gefüttert und als Showeinlage mit dem
Lasso eingefangen.

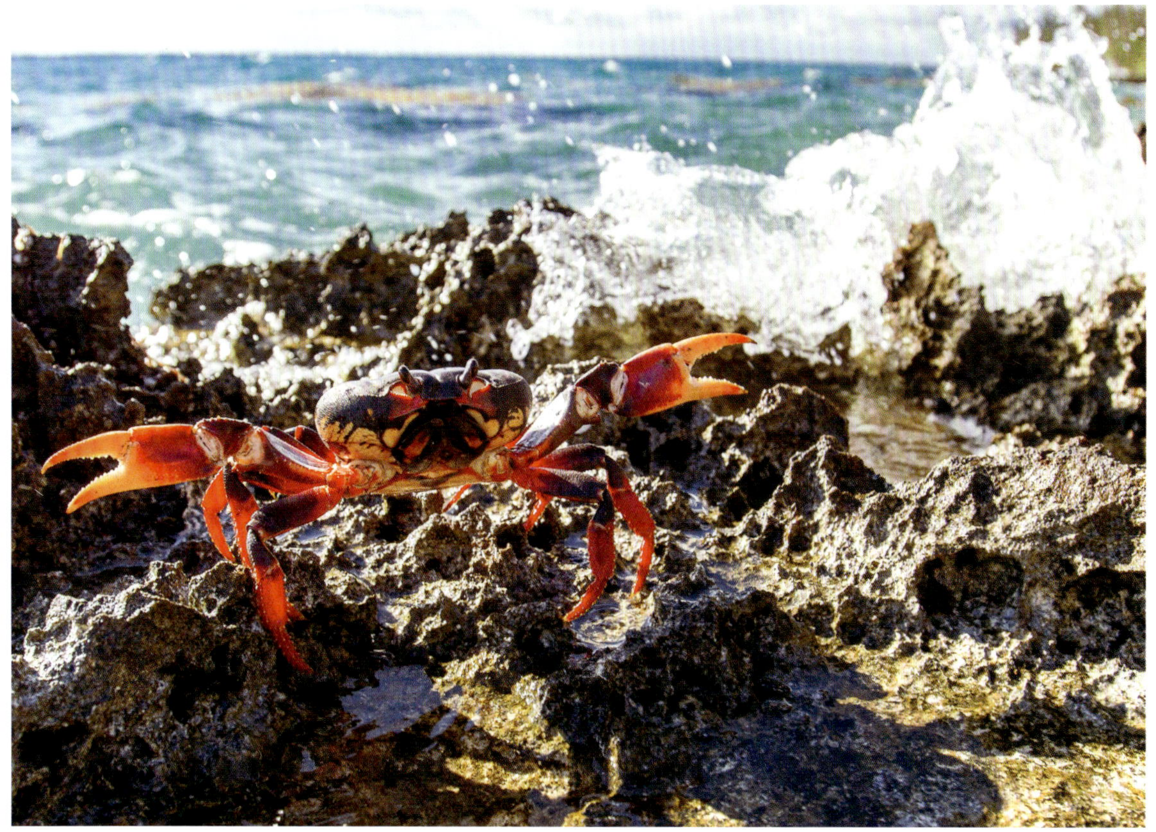

Cangrejo, Península de Zapata
Crab, Zapata Peninsula

Parque Nacional Ciénaga de Zapata

La zona pantanosa casi desierta de las
285 650 ha de la Península de Zapata, en
la costa sur, pertenece en gran medida al
Parque Natural de Montemar y ha sido una
reserva de la biosfera desde 2001. Es el
humedal contiguo más grande del Caribe y
uno de los ecosistemas más ricos de Cuba,
hogar de 20 de las 22 especies de aves
endémicas de Cuba, que van desde el elfo
de las abejas, una especie de colibrí, hasta
flamencos y cormoranes cubanos. Boca
de Guamá es un destino turístico: en dos
granjas de cocodrilos miles de cocodrilos
(*Crocodylus rhombifer*) viven en estanques
amurallados, son alimentados de manera
espectacular y capturados con un lazo
como interludio.

Parque Nacional Ciénaga de Zapata

A área de pântano quase deserta da
Península de Zapata, com 285 650 ha,
na costa sul, pertence em grande parte
ao Parque Natural de Montemar e é
uma reserva da biosfera desde 2001. É
o maior pântano contíguo do Caribe e
um dos ecossistemas mais biodiversos
de Cuba, abrigando 20 das 22 espécies
endémicas de aves de Cuba, desde o
Colibri-abelha-cubano, uma espécie de
colibri, até flamingos e corvos-marinhos
cubanos. A Boca de Guamá é um
destino turístico: em duas fazendas de
crocodilos vivem milhares de crocodilos
(*Crocodylus rhombifer*) em lagos murados,
são espetacularmente alimentados
e capturados com um laço como um
interlúdio de espetáculo.

Nationaal Park Ciénaga de Zapata

Het bijna verlaten moerasgebied van het
285 650 ha grote schiereiland Zapata aan
de zuidkust behoort grotendeels tot het
Montemar Natuurpark, en is sinds 2001
een biosfeerreservaat. Het is het grootste
aaneengesloten moerasgebied van het
Caribisch gebied en een van Cuba's rijkste
ecosystemen. Het is de thuisbasis van 20
van Cuba's 22 endemische vogelsoorten,
variërend van de bijkolibrie tot Cubaanse
flamingo's en aalscholvers. Boca de
Guamá is een toeristische bestemming:
op twee krokodillenboerderijen leven
duizenden krokodillen (*Crocodylus
rhombifer*) in ommuurde vijvers, waar ze
als showintermezzo worden ingezet. De
krokodillen worden op spectaculaire wijze
gevoed en met een lasso gevangen.

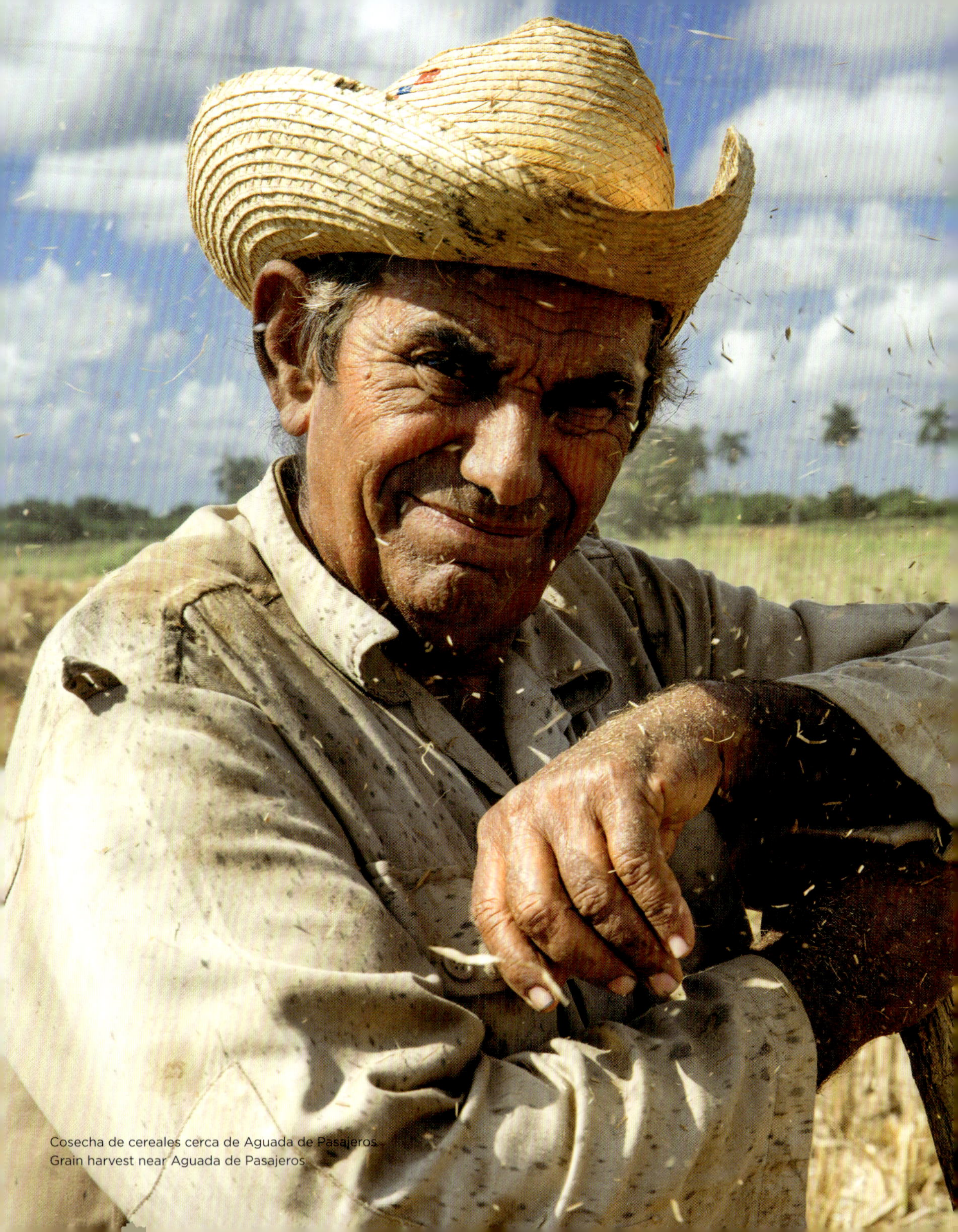

Cosecha de cereales cerca de Aguada de Pasajeros
Grain harvest near Aguada de Pasajeros

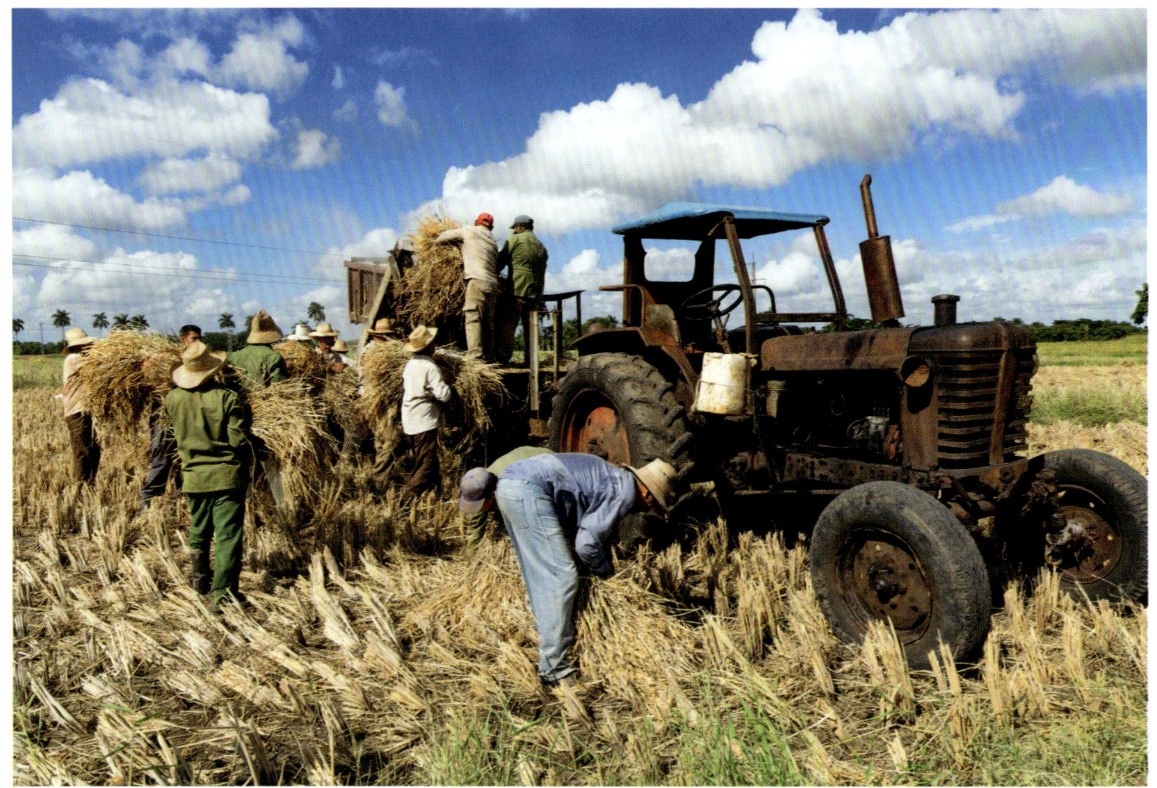

Cosecha de cereales cerca de Aguada de Pasajeros
Grain harvest near Aguada de Pasajeros

In the Country

Sugar cultivation dominated In the province of Cienfuegos until the end of the 1980s, but it has now been reduced to a minimum and all but one sugar mills have been closed. Agricultural production is focused mainly on vegetables, livestock, animal feed and rice.

En el campo

En la provincia de Cienfuegos el cultivo de azúcar dominó hasta finales de los años ochenta, pero este también se ha reducido al mínimo y se han cerrado todos los ingenios azucareros menos uno. La producción agrícola se concentra en hortalizas, ganado, piensos y arroz.

Dans les terres

Dans la province de Cienfuegos, la culture de la canne à sucre dominait l'économie jusqu'en 1980. Depuis, la pratique s'est réduite au minimum et il ne reste plus qu'un seul moulin actif. La production agricole s'est recentrée sur les légumes, l'élevage, le fourrage et la riziculture.

No país

Na província de Cienfuegos, o cultivo do açúcar dominou até o final da década de 1980, no entanto também aqui ele foi reduzido ao mínimo e quase todos os engenhos de açúcar, à excepção de um, foram fechados. A produção agrícola concentra-se sobretudo nos produtos hortícolas, na pecuária, nos alimentos para animais e no arroz.

Auf dem Land

In der Provinz Cienfuegos herrschte bis Ende der 1980er-Jahre der Zuckeranbau vor, doch mittlerweile hat er sich auch hier auf ein Minimum reduziert und es wurden bis auf eine sämtliche Zuckermühlen geschlossen. Die landwirtschaftliche Produktion konzentriert sich eher auf Gemüse, Viehwirtschaft, Viehfutter und den Reisanbau.

Op het land

In de provincie Cienfuegos domineerde tot het einde van de jaren tachtig de suikerbietenteelt, maar inmiddels is ook de suikerproductie tot een minimum beperkt, en zijn op één na alle suikerfabrieken gesloten. De landbouwproductie concentreert zich nu op groenten, vee, veevoer en rijst.

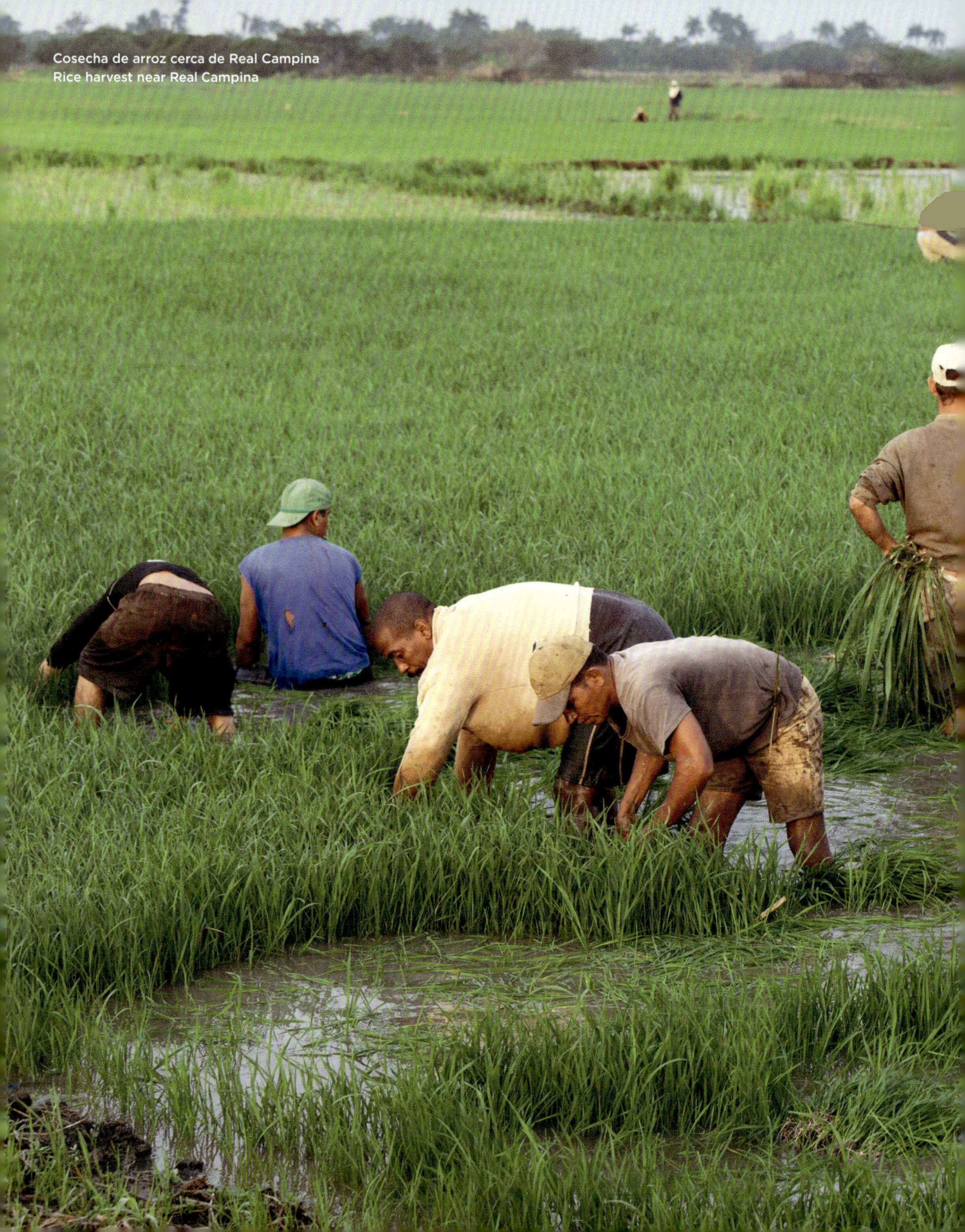

Cosecha de arroz cerca de Real Campina
Rice harvest near Real Campina

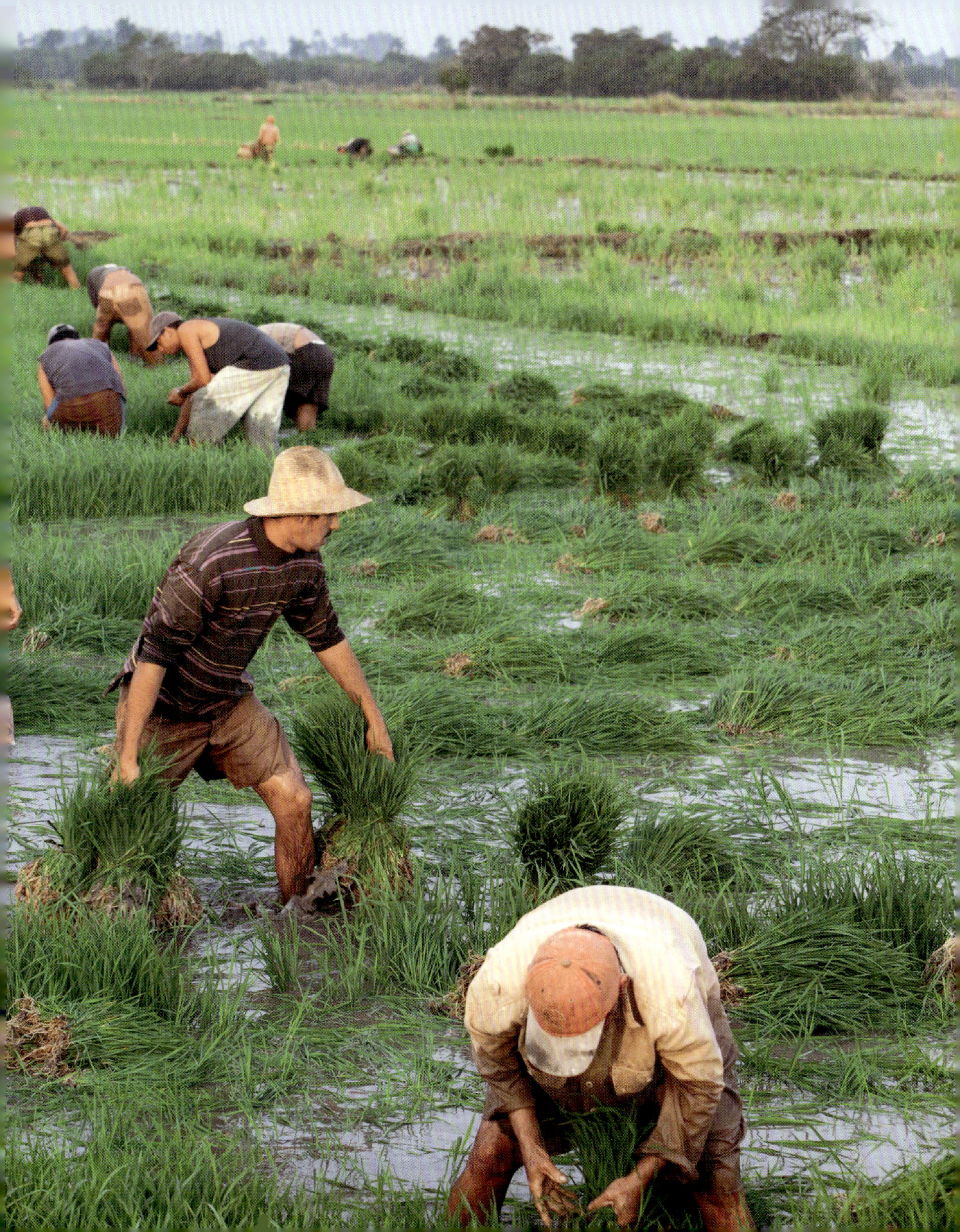

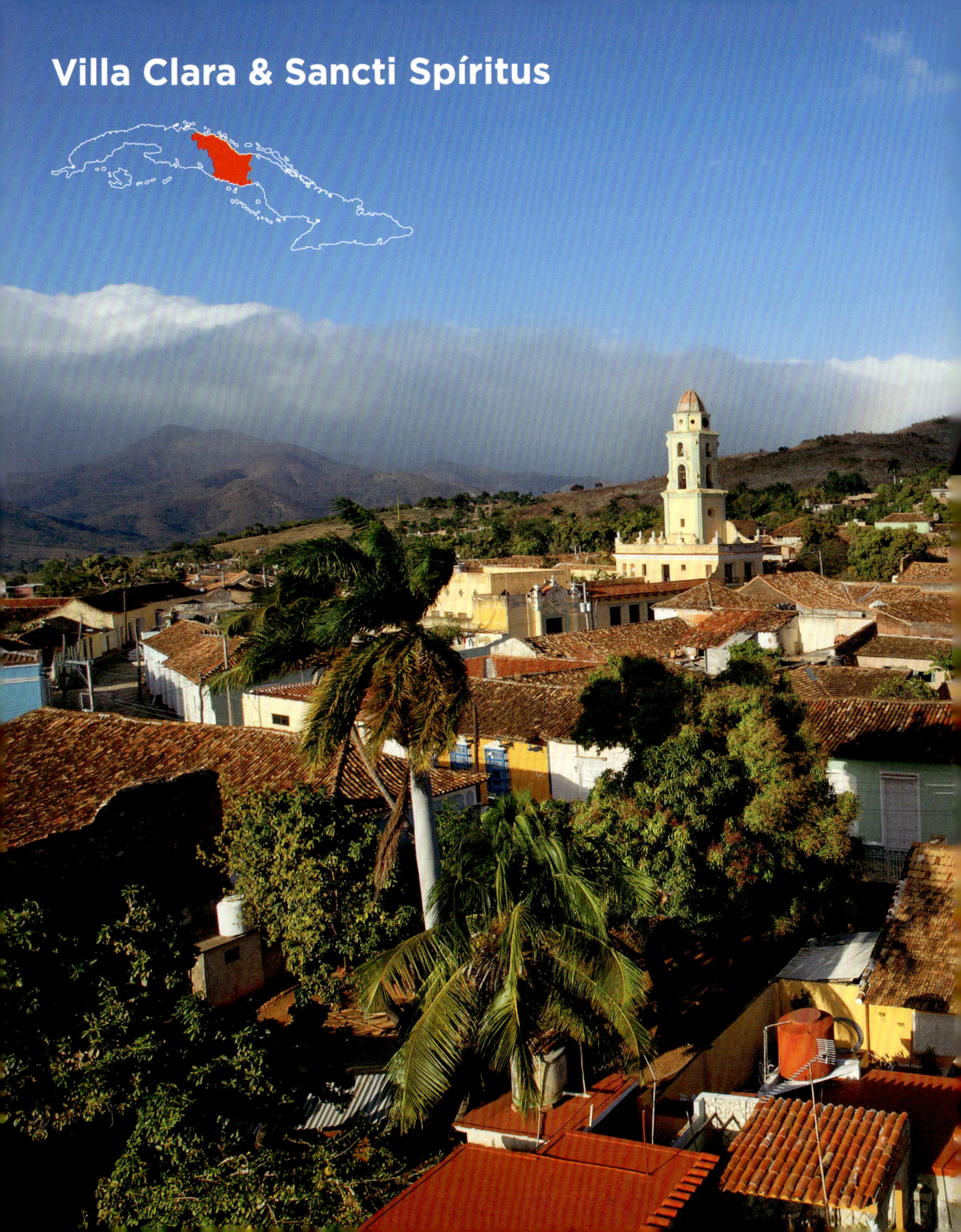

Villa Clara & Sancti Spíritus

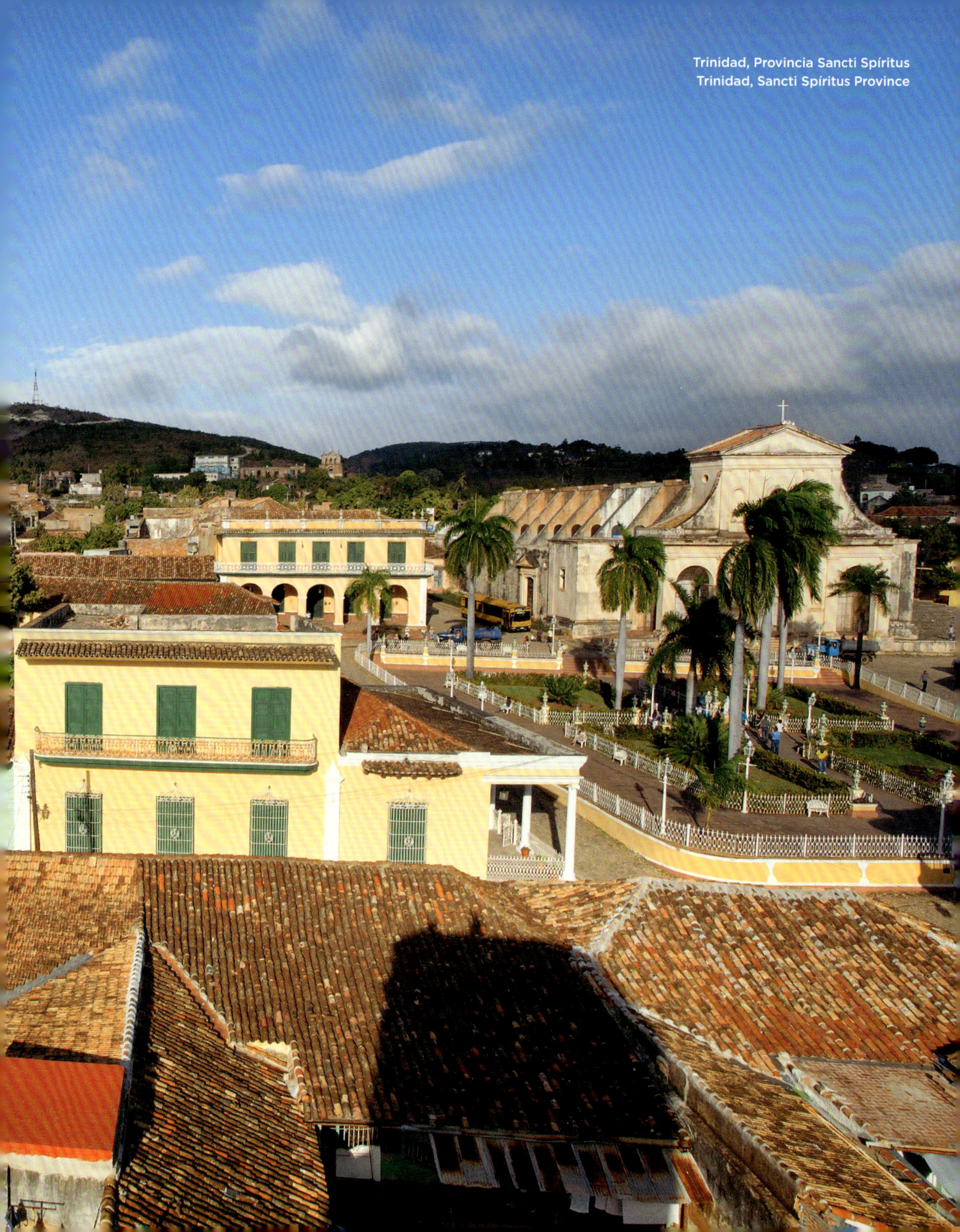

Trinidad, Provincia Sancti Spíritus
Trinidad, Sancti Spíritus Province

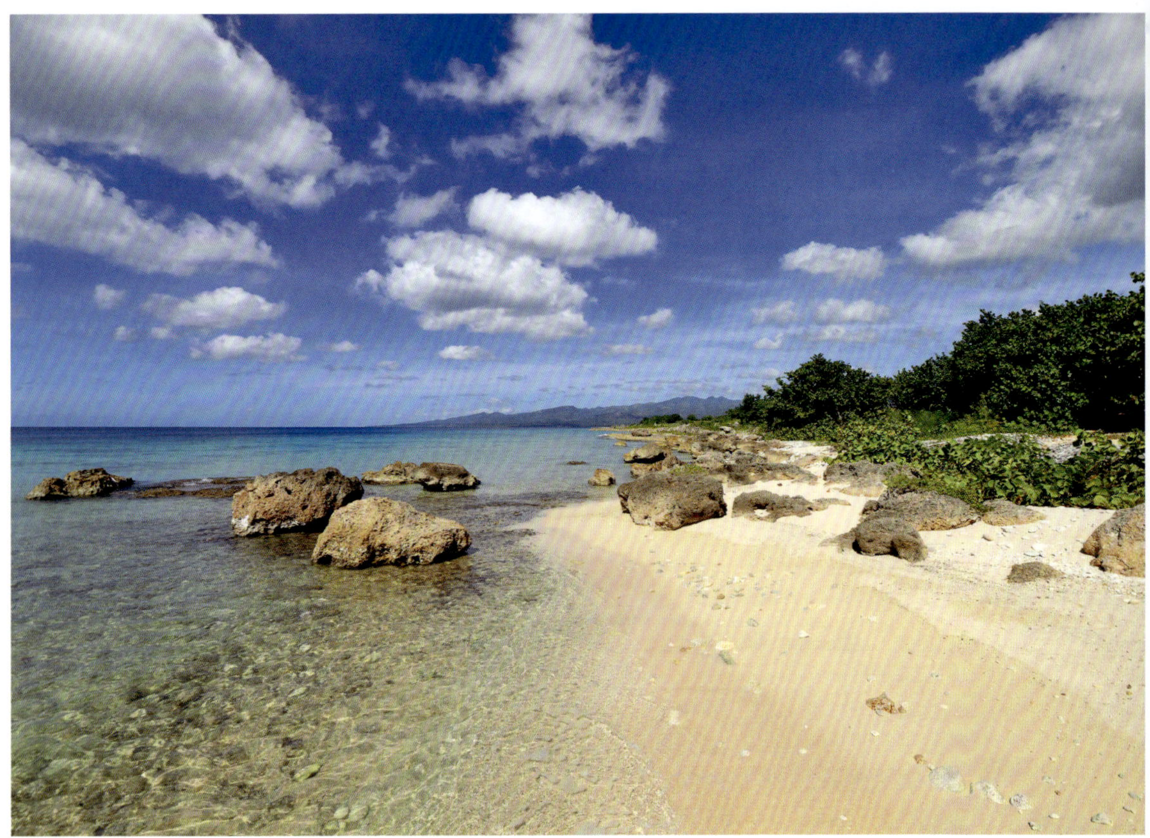

Playa Ancón, Provincia Sancti Spíritus
Ancón Beach, Sancti Spíritus Province

Villa Clara and Sancti Spíritus

In front of the north coast of the province Villa Clara in central Cuba there are some tiny idyllic islands (Cayos) with dream beaches. For centuries, the interior was strongly shaped by sugar cultivation. In the tranquil provincial capital Santa Clara, the monumental memorial with its Che Guevara mausoleum attracts many visitors, and the pretty colonial town Remedios with its musical processions (Parrandas) that take place in December is an attraction. The capital of the bordering province Sancti Spíritus is not, as one might think, the famous colonial city Trinidad, but the sleepy little city of Sancti Spíritus.

Villa Clara et Sancti Spíritus

La province de Villa Clara, au centre de Cuba, est bordée, au large de sa côte nord, par quelques îlots *(cayos)* paradisiaques dotés de plages de rêve. L'intérieur des terres est resté très imprégné par la culture de la canne à sucre. Dans sa paisible capitale, Santa Clara, le site commémoratif monumental abritant le mausolée de Che Guevara attire de nombreux visiteurs, alors que la jolie petite bourgade coloniale Remedios et ses cortèges musicaux (les Parrandas) du mois de décembre constituent une autre attraction. Dans la province voisine Sancti Spíritus, la capitale n'est pas, comme on pourrait le penser, la célèbre Trinidad coloniale, mais une petite ville endormie également dénommée « Sancti Spíritus ».

Villa Clara und Sancti Spíritus

Vor der Nordküste der Provinz Villa Clara in Zentralkuba liegen einige paradiesische Inselchen (Cayos) mit Traumstränden. Das Inland war über Jahrhunderte stark vom Zuckeranbau geprägt. In der beschaulichen Provinzhauptstadt Santa Clara zieht vor allem die monumentale Gedenkstätte mit dem Mausoleum von Che Guevara viele Besucher an, und das hübsche Kolonialstädtchen Remedios mit den im Dezember stattfindenden Musik-Umzügen (Parrandas) ist eine Attraktion. Hauptstadt der angrenzenden Provinz Sancti Spíritus ist nicht, wie man meinen könnte, die berühmte Kolonialstadt Trinidad, sondern das etwas verschlafene Städtchen Sancti Spíritus.

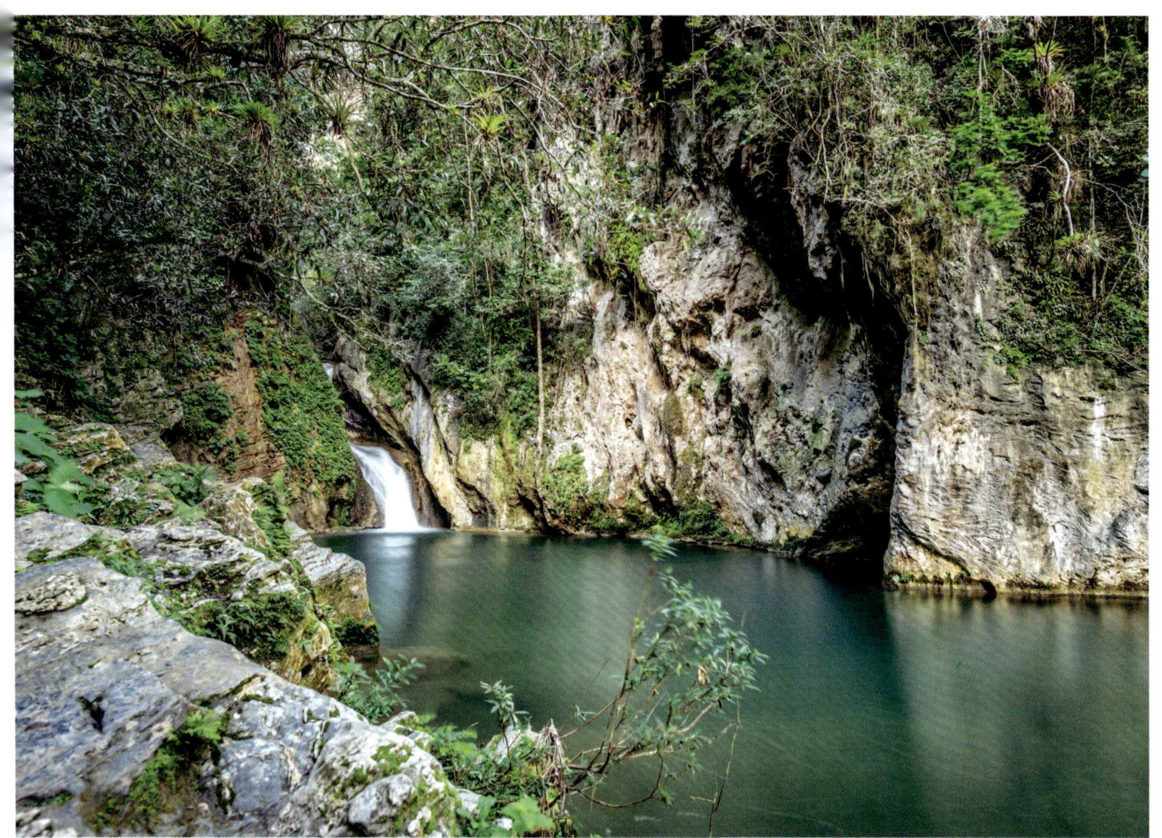

Gran Parque Natural Topes de Collantes
Topes de Collantes Natural Reserve

Villa Clara y Sancti Spíritus

Frente a la costa norte de la provincia de Villa Clara, en el centro de Cuba, hay unas paradisíacas islas (cayos) con playas de ensueño. Durante siglos, el interior del país estuvo fuertemente influenciado por el cultivo de azúcar. En la tranquila capital provincial Santa Clara, el monumental memorial con el mausoleo del Che Guevara atrae a numerosos visitantes, y la bonita ciudad colonial de Remedios con las procesiones musicales *(parrandas)* que tienen lugar en diciembre es una importante atracción. La capital de la provincia fronteriza de Sancti Spíritus no es, como se podría pensar, la famosa ciudad colonial de Trinidad, sino la tranquila y pequeña ciudad de Sancti Spíritus.

Villa Clara e Sancti Spíritus

Em frente à costa norte da província de Villa Clara, no centro de Cuba, há algumas pequenas ilhas paradisíacas (Cayos) com praias de sonho. Durante séculos, o interior foi fortemente influenciado pelo cultivo do açúcar. Na tranquila capital provincial de Santa Clara, o monumental memorial com o mausoléu de Che Guevara atrai muitos visitantes, e a bela cidade colonial Remedios com as procissões musicais (Parrandas) que acontecem em dezembro, é uma atração. A capital da província fronteiriça Sancti Spíritus não é, como se poderia pensar, a famosa cidade colonial de Trinidad, mas a pequena cidade pacata de Sancti Spíritus.

Villa Clara en Sancti Spíritus

Voor de noordkust van de provincie Villa Clara in centraal Cuba liggen enkele paradijselijke eilandjes (Cayos) met droomstranden. Het binnenland werd eeuwenlang sterk door de suikerteelt gekenmerkt. In de rustige provinciehoofdstad Santa Clara trekt het monumentale gedenkteken met het mausoleum van Che Guevara veel bezoekers, en de mooie koloniale stad Remedios met de muziekoptochten (Parrandas) die in december plaatsvinden is een attractie. De hoofdstad van de aangrenzende provincie Sancti Spíritus is niet de beroemde koloniale stad Trinidad, zoals velen denken, maar het slaperige stadje Sancti Spíritus.

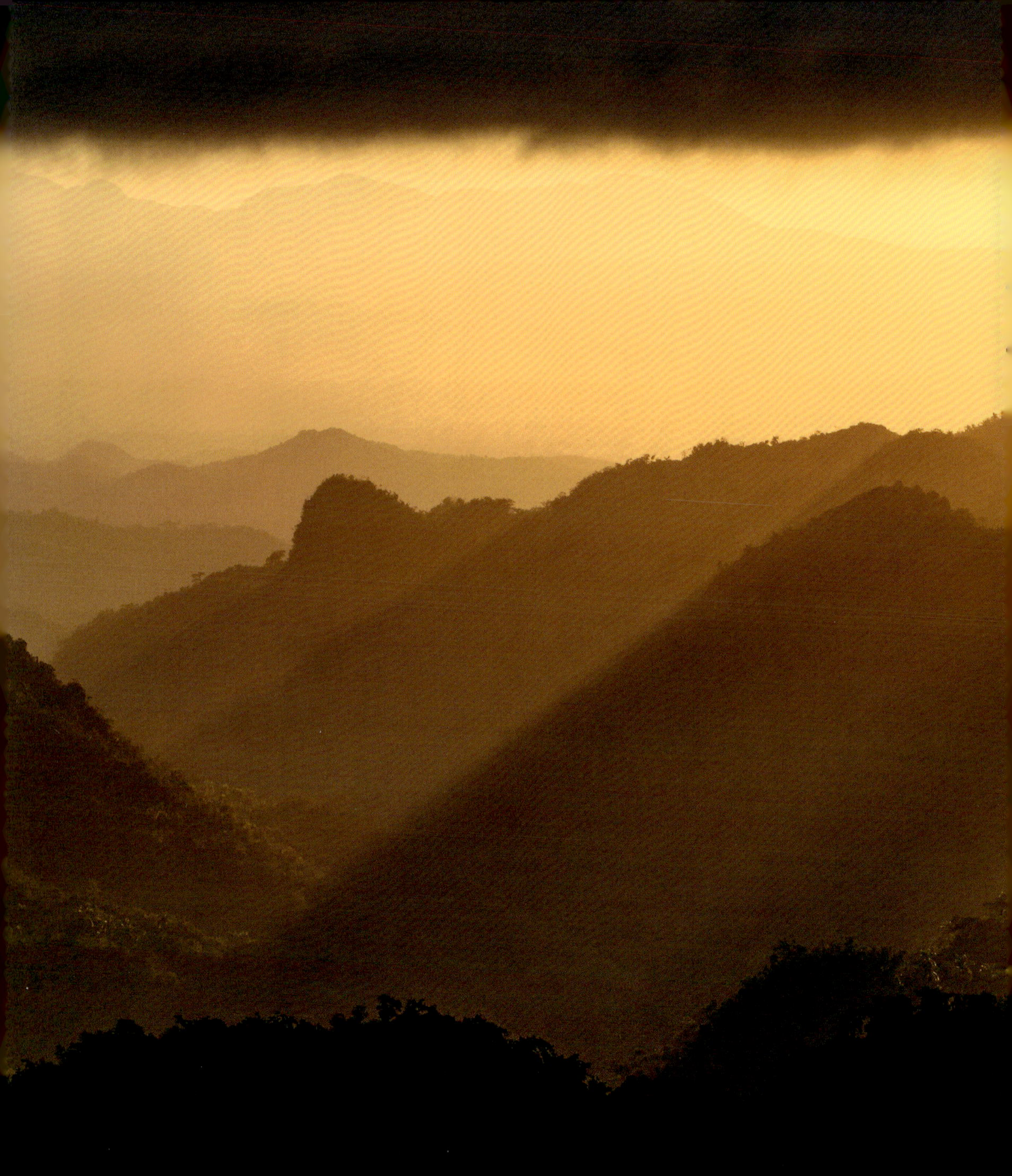

Gran Parque Natural Topes de Collantes
Topes de Collantes Natural Reserve

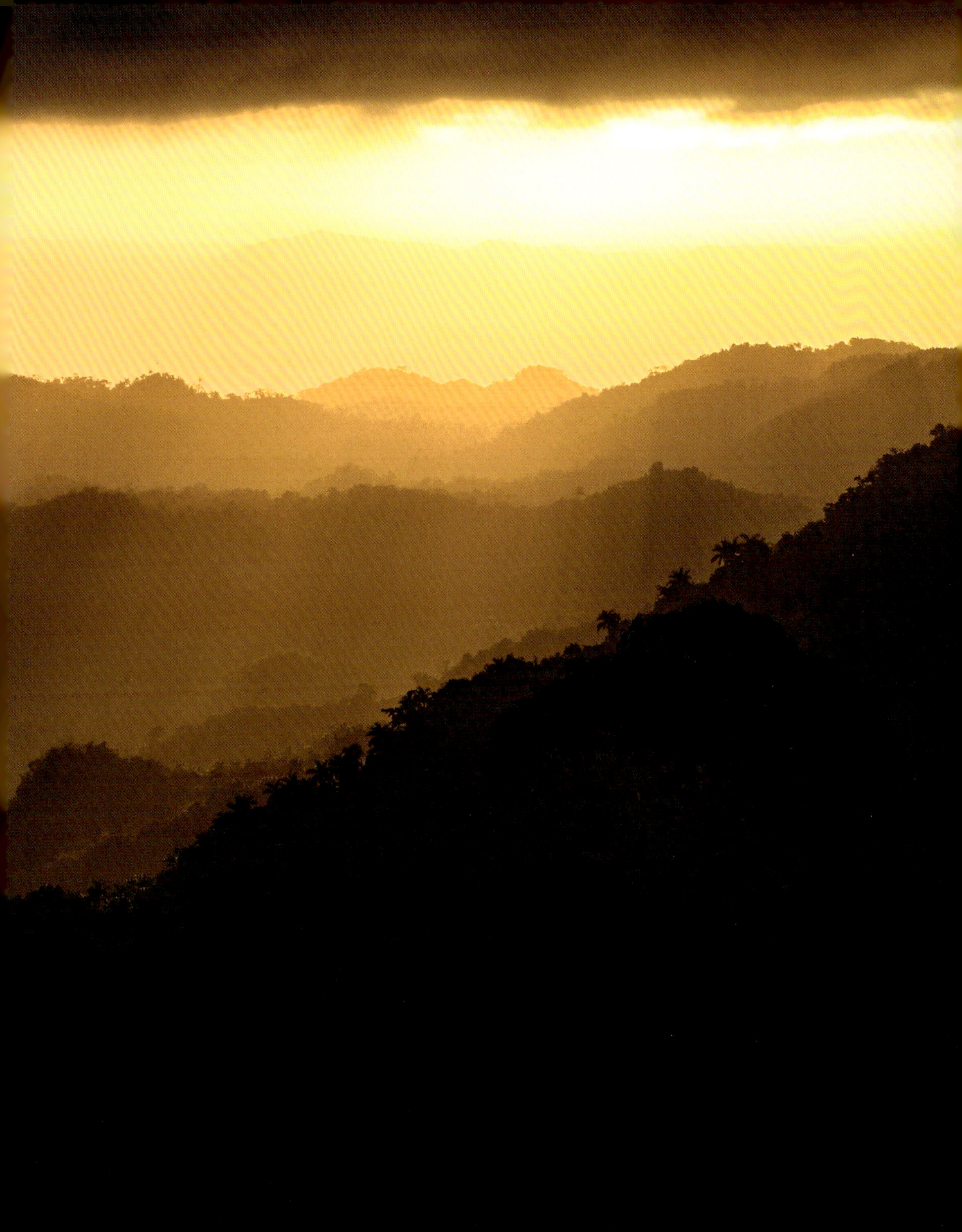

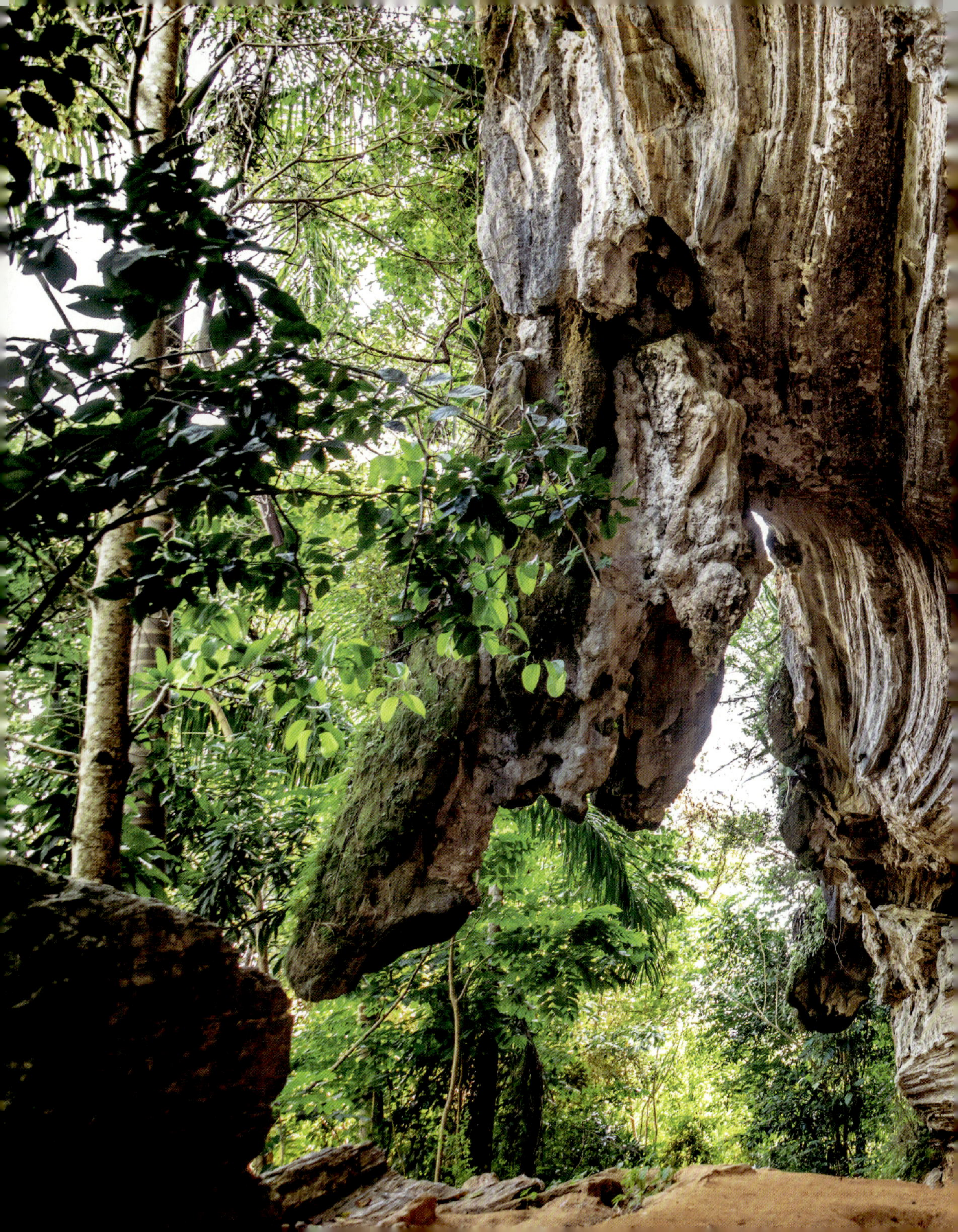

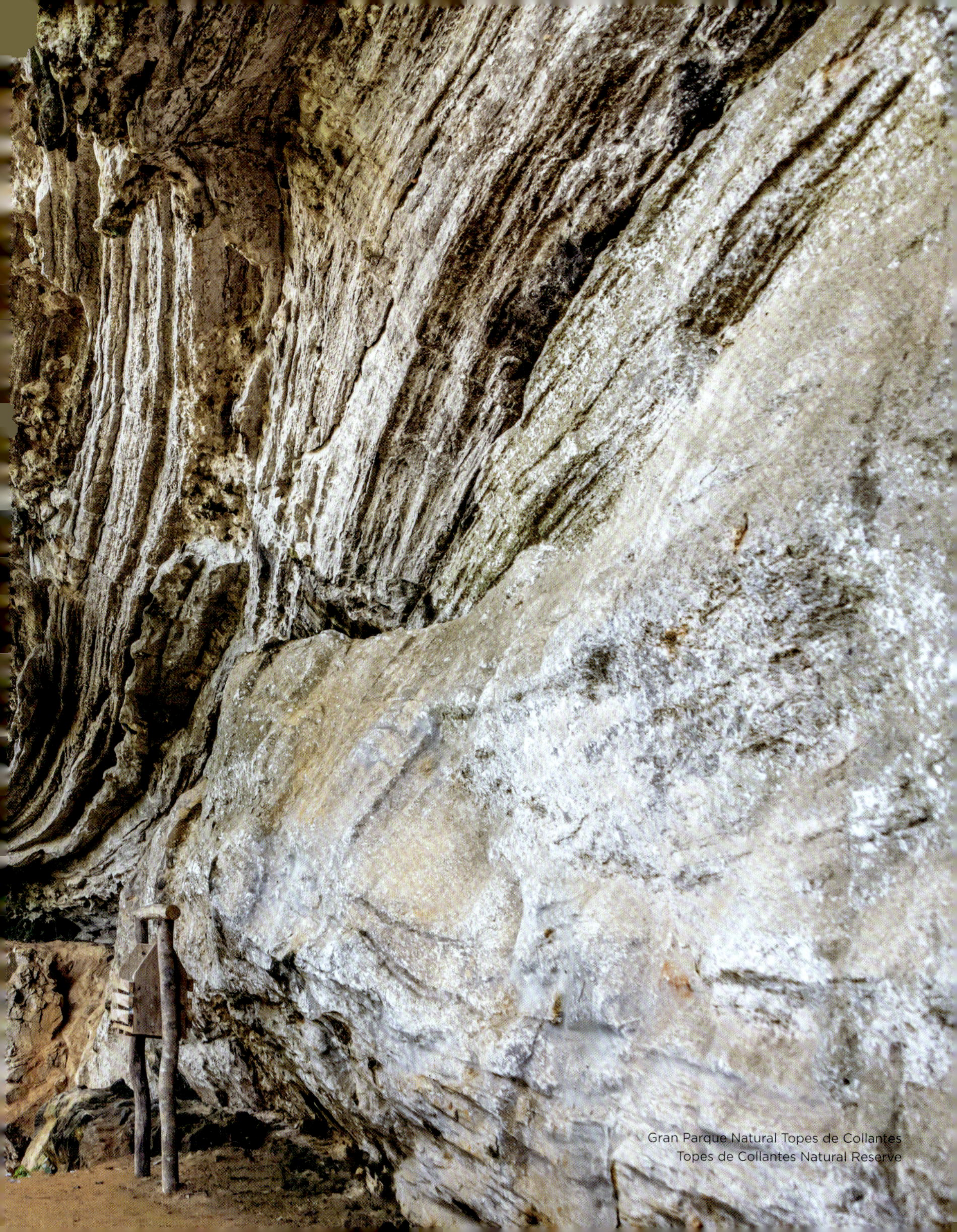

Gran Parque Natural Topes de Collantes
Topes de Collantes Natural Reserve

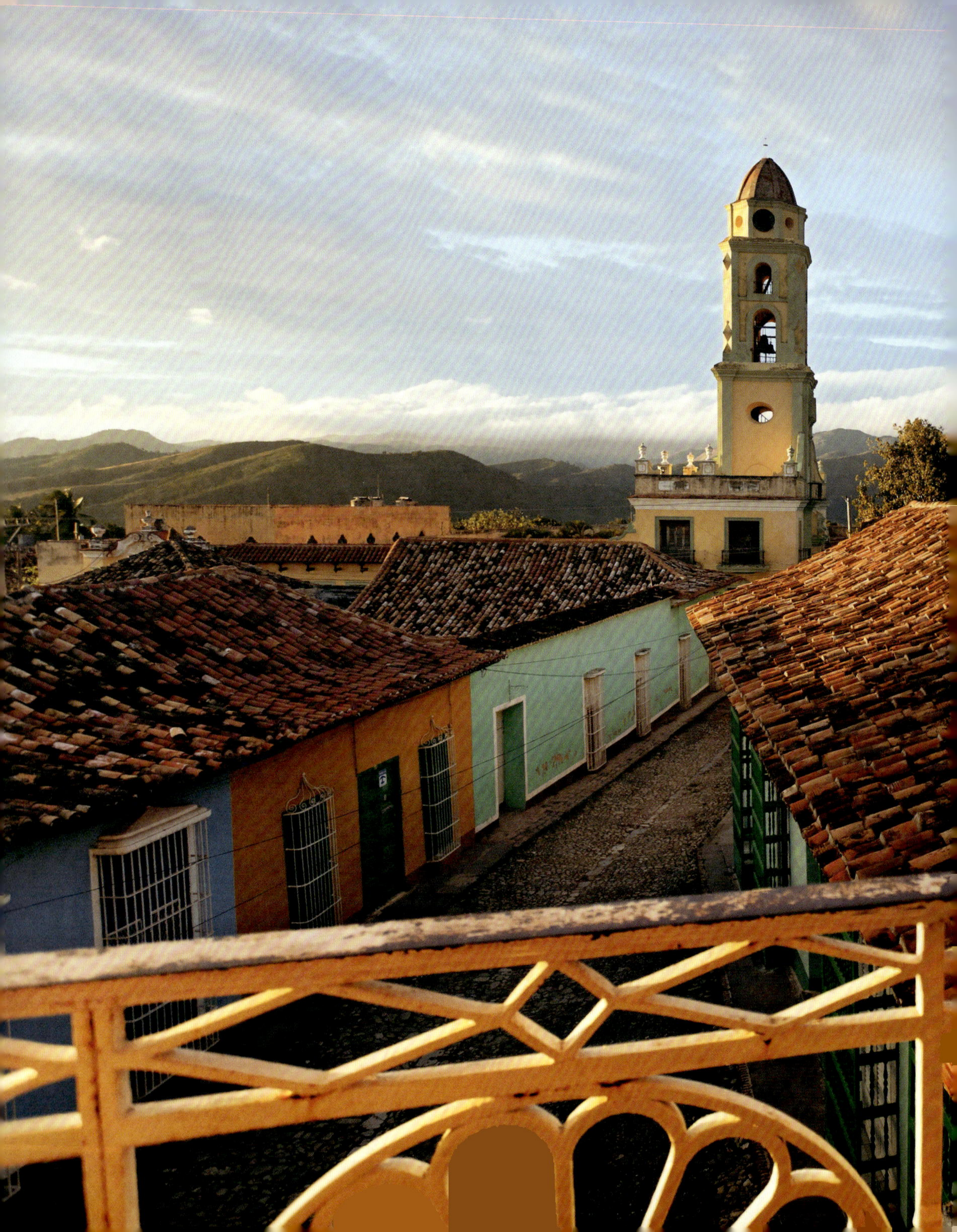

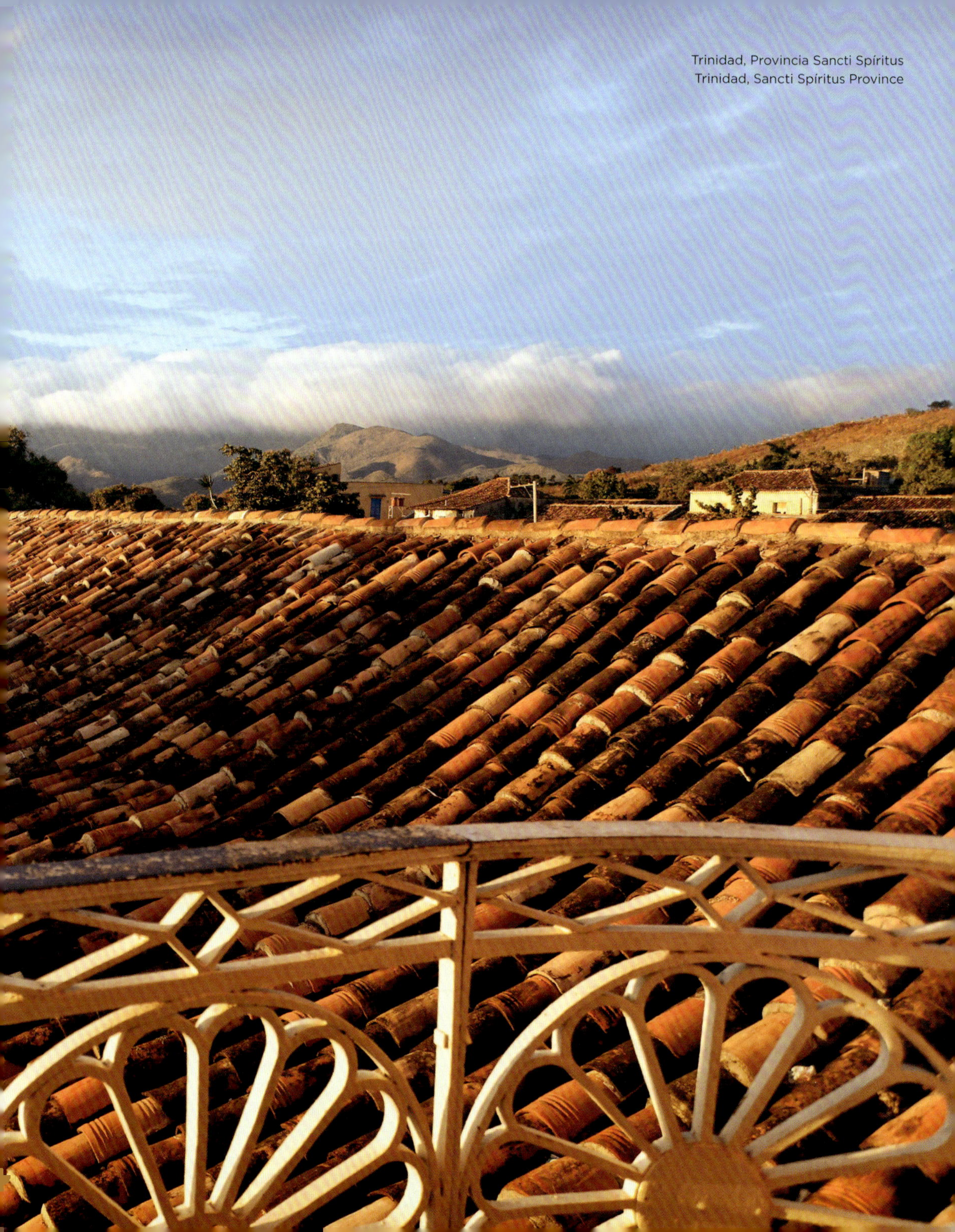

Trinidad, Provincia Sancti Spíritus
Trinidad, Sancti Spíritus Province

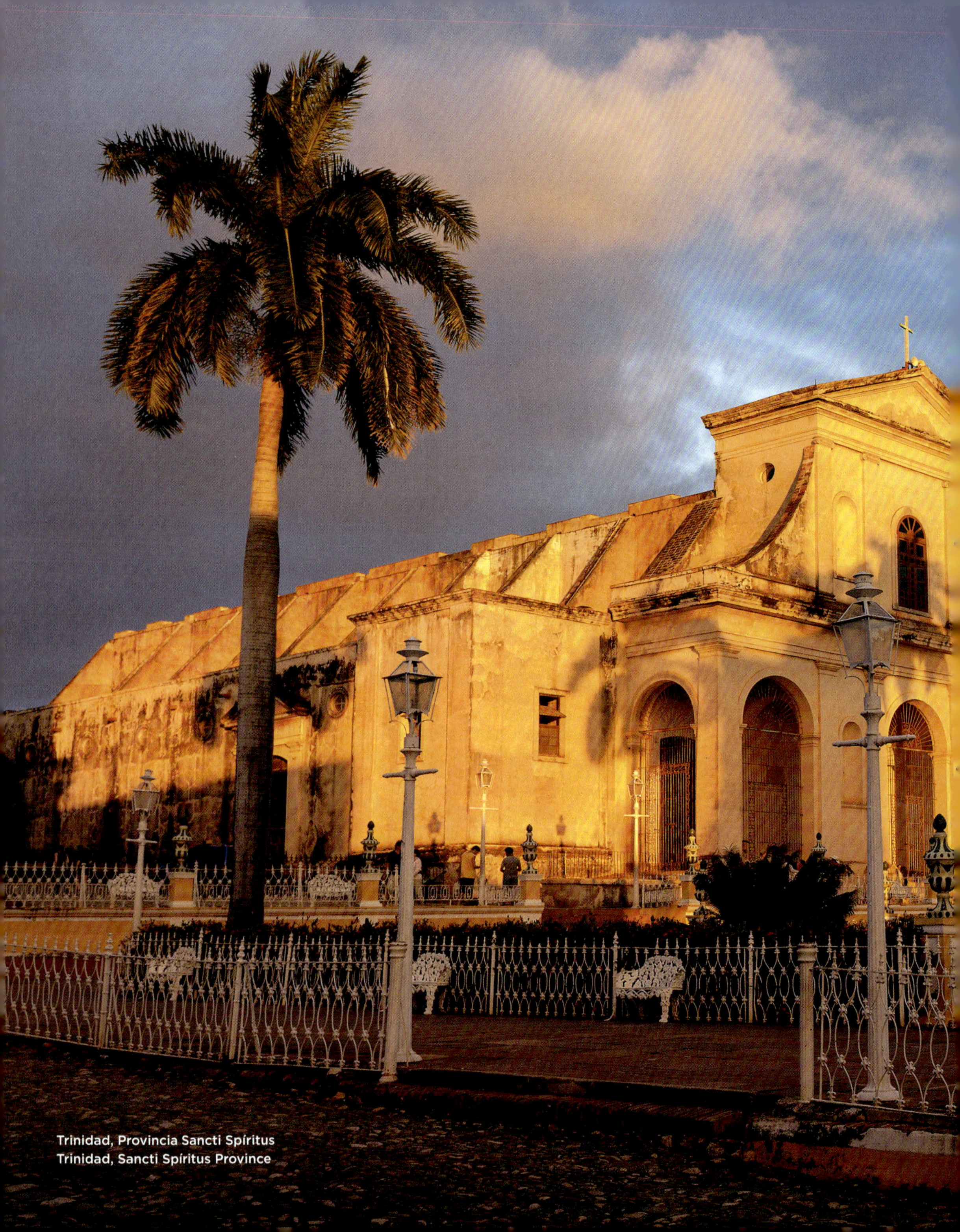

Trinidad, Provincia Sancti Spíritus
Trinidad, Sancti Spíritus Province

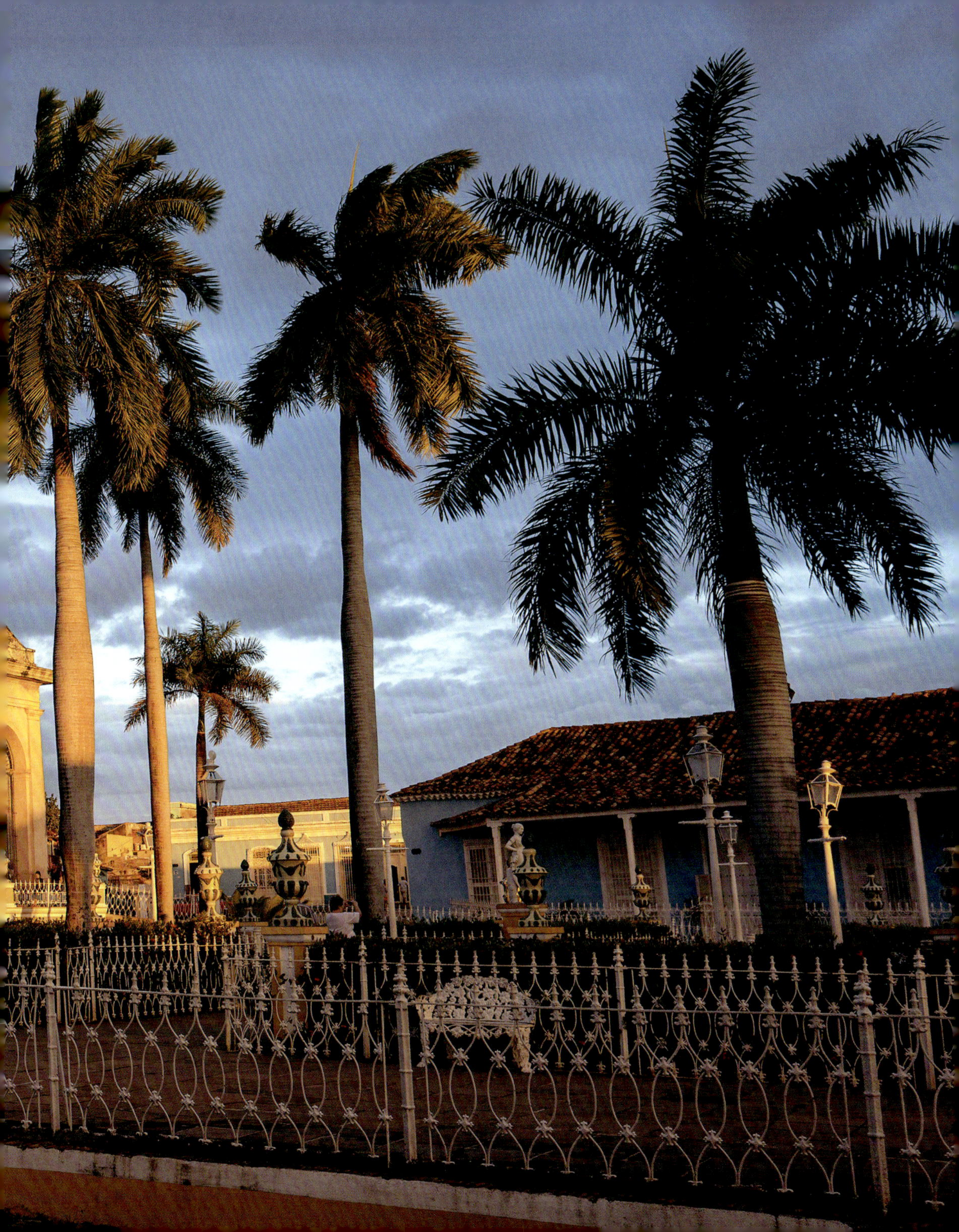

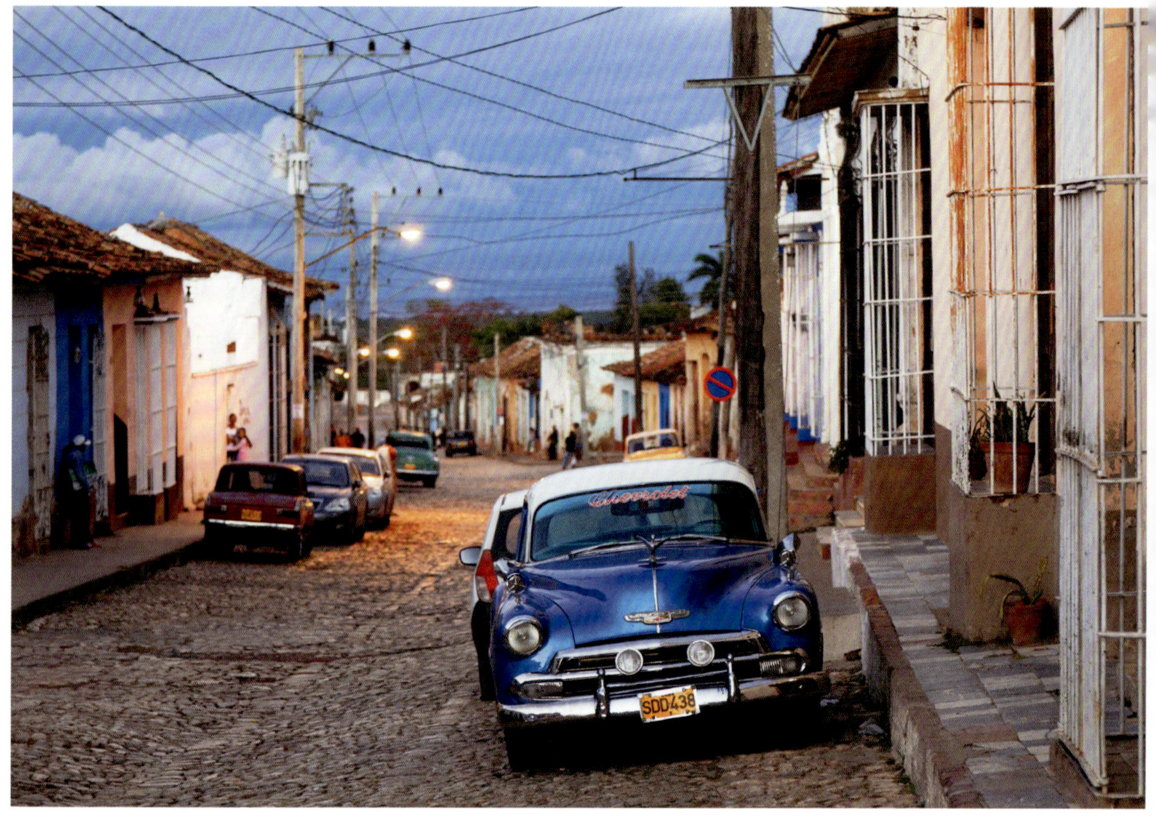

Trinidad, Provincia Sancti Spíritus
Trinidad, Sancti Spíritus Province

Trinidad

Founded in 1514 by Diego Velázquez,
for centuries Trinidad lived mainly from
smuggling (it even had its own pirate fleet)
until the sugar boom began in the middle
of the 18th century. The slave trade, sugar
cane cultivation and sugar production,
and livestock trade provided Trinidad with
an unprecedented period of prosperity,
and the city became an important trading
centre despite its remote location. The
wars of independence (1868–78, 1895–98)
brought Trinidad's economy to a standstill.
Today, everyone in Trinidad lives from
tourism: as a tourist guide, street trader,
taxi driver, cigar seller or landlord, or—last
but not least—as a musician.

Trinidad

Fondée par Diego Velázquez en 1514,
Trinidad a vécu pendant des siècles de
la contrebande (et abritait même une
flotte pirate), jusqu'à l'essor de la culture
de la canne à sucre au xviii siècle. Le
commerce des esclaves, la culture de la
canne et le négoce du sucre et du bétail
apportèrent à Trinidad une prospérité
sans pareille et la ville devint, malgré son
isolement géographique, un important
centre de négoce. L'économie de Trinidad
fut finalement mise à mal par les guerres
d'indépendance (1868–1878, 1895–1898).
Aujourd'hui, pour survivre à Trinidad, il
faut exercer une profession en lien avec
le tourisme : guide, marchand de rue,
chauffeur de taxi, vendeur de cigares,
gérant de maison d'hôtes ou musicien.

Trinidad

1514 von Diego Velázquez gegründet,
lebte Trinidad jahrhundertelang vor
allem vom Schmuggel (es gab sogar
eine eigene Piratenflotte), bis Mitte des
18. Jahrhunderts der Zuckerboom begann.
Sklavenhandel, Zuckerrohranbau, Zucker-
und Viehhandel verschafften Trinidad
eine beispiellose Blütezeit, die Stadt
wurde trotz ihrer abgeschiedenen Lage
zu einem wichtigen Handelszentrum.
Die Unabhängigkeitskriege (1868–78,
1895–98) brachten die Wirtschaft Trinidads
zum Erliegen. Wer irgend kann, lebt
heute in Trinidad vom Tourismus, als
Fremdenführer, Straßenhändler, Taxifahrer,
Zigarrenverkäufer und Zimmervermieter
sowie – nicht zuletzt – als Musiker.

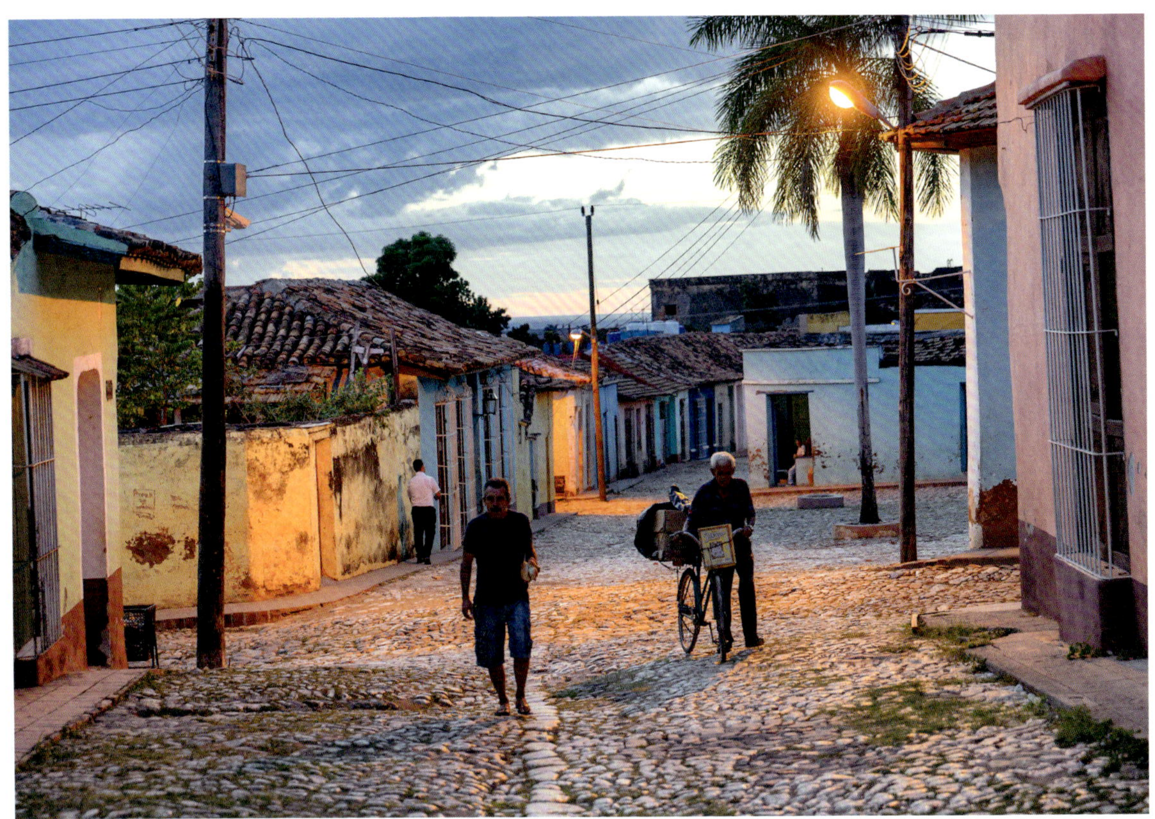

Trinidad, Provincia Sancti Spíritus
Trinidad, Sancti Spíritus Province

Trinidad

Fundada en 1514 por Diego Velázquez, Trinidad vivió durante siglos principalmente del contrabando (tenía incluso su propia flota pirata) hasta que comenzó el auge azucarero a mediados del siglo XVIII. La trata de esclavos, el cultivo de caña de azúcar, y el comercio del azúcar y de ganado proporcionaron a Trinidad un período de prosperidad sin precedentes y la ciudad se convirtió en un importante centro comercial a pesar de su remota ubicación. Las guerras de independencia (1868–78, 1895–98) paralizaron la economía de Trinidad. En la actualidad, todo el que puede vive en Trinidad del turismo, como guía turístico, comerciante ambulante, taxista, vendedor de cigarros y propietario de la habitación y por último, pero no menos importante, como músico.

Trinidad

Fundada em 1514 por Diego Velázquez, Trinidad viveu durante séculos principalmente do contrabando (havia até mesmo sua própria frota de piratas) até o começo da expansão do açúcar em meados do século XVIII. O comércio de escravos, o cultivo da cana-de-açúcar, e o comércio de açúcar e de gado proporcionaram a Trinidad um período de prosperidade sem precedentes, e a cidade tornou-se um importante centro comercial, apesar da sua localização isolada. As Guerras da Independência (1868–78, 1895–98) paralisou a economia de Trinidad. Qualquer pessoa que possa fazer qualquer coisa vive hoje em Trinidad do turismo, como guia turístico, comerciante de rua, motorista de táxi, vendedor de charutos e proprietário do quarto de aluguel e – por último, mas não menos importante – como músico.

Trinidad

Trinidad is in 1514 opgericht door Diego Velázquez en leefde eeuwenlang voornamelijk van de smokkel (er was zelfs een eigen piratenvloot) tot de suikerboom in het midden van de 18e eeuw begon. De slavenhandel, suikerrietteelt, suiker en veehandel zorgden in Trinidad voor een ongekende periode van welvaart, en de stad werd een belangrijk handelscentrum ondanks haar afgelegen ligging. De onafhankelijkheidsoorlogen (1868–78, 1895–98) brachten de economie van Trinidad tot stilstand. Tegenwoordig leven de mensen in Trinidad van het toerisme, als toeristengids, straathandelaar, taxichauffeur, sigarenverkoper en kamerexploitant en – last but not least – als muzikant.

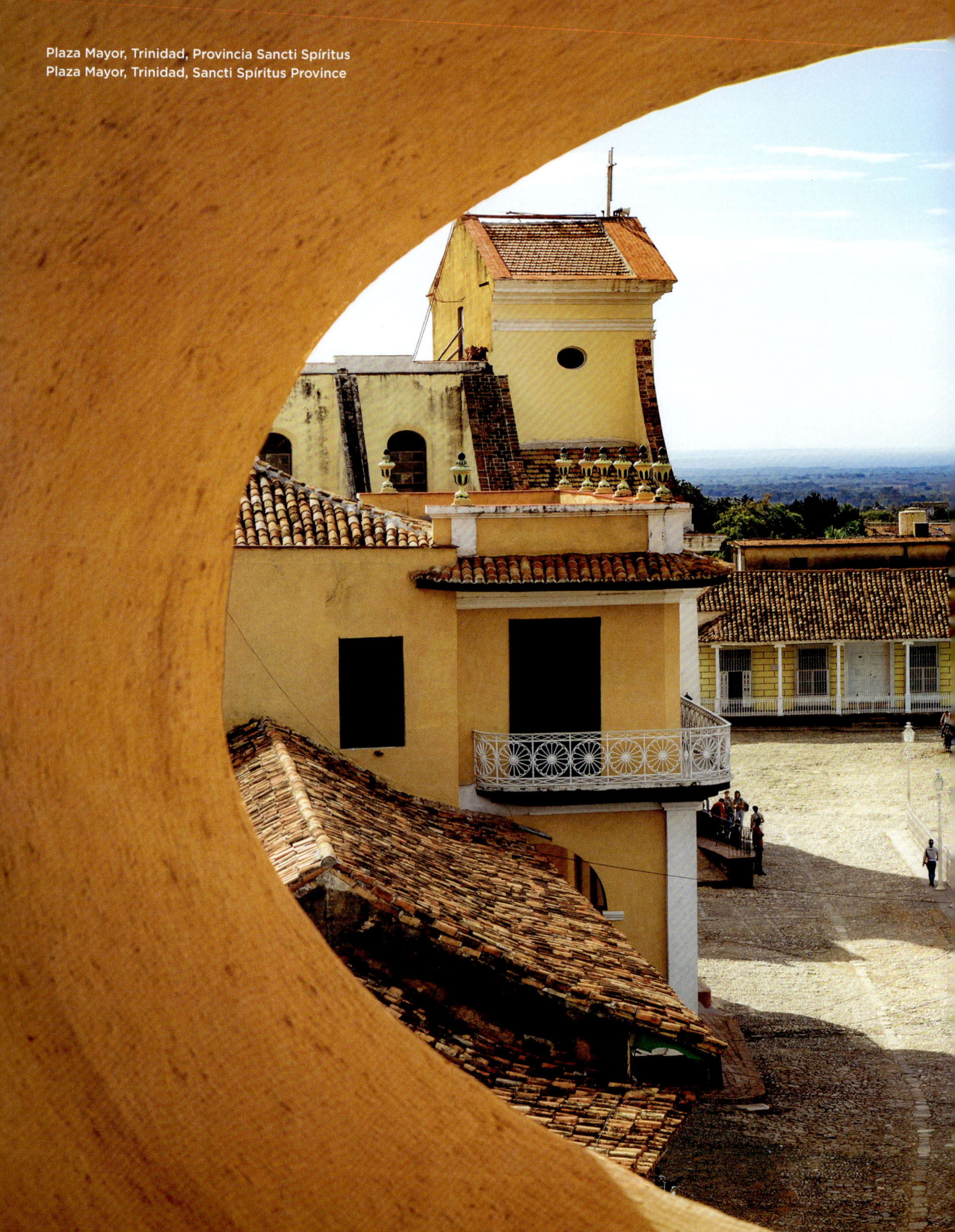
Plaza Mayor, Trinidad, Provincia Sancti Spíritus
Plaza Mayor, Trinidad, Sancti Spíritus Province

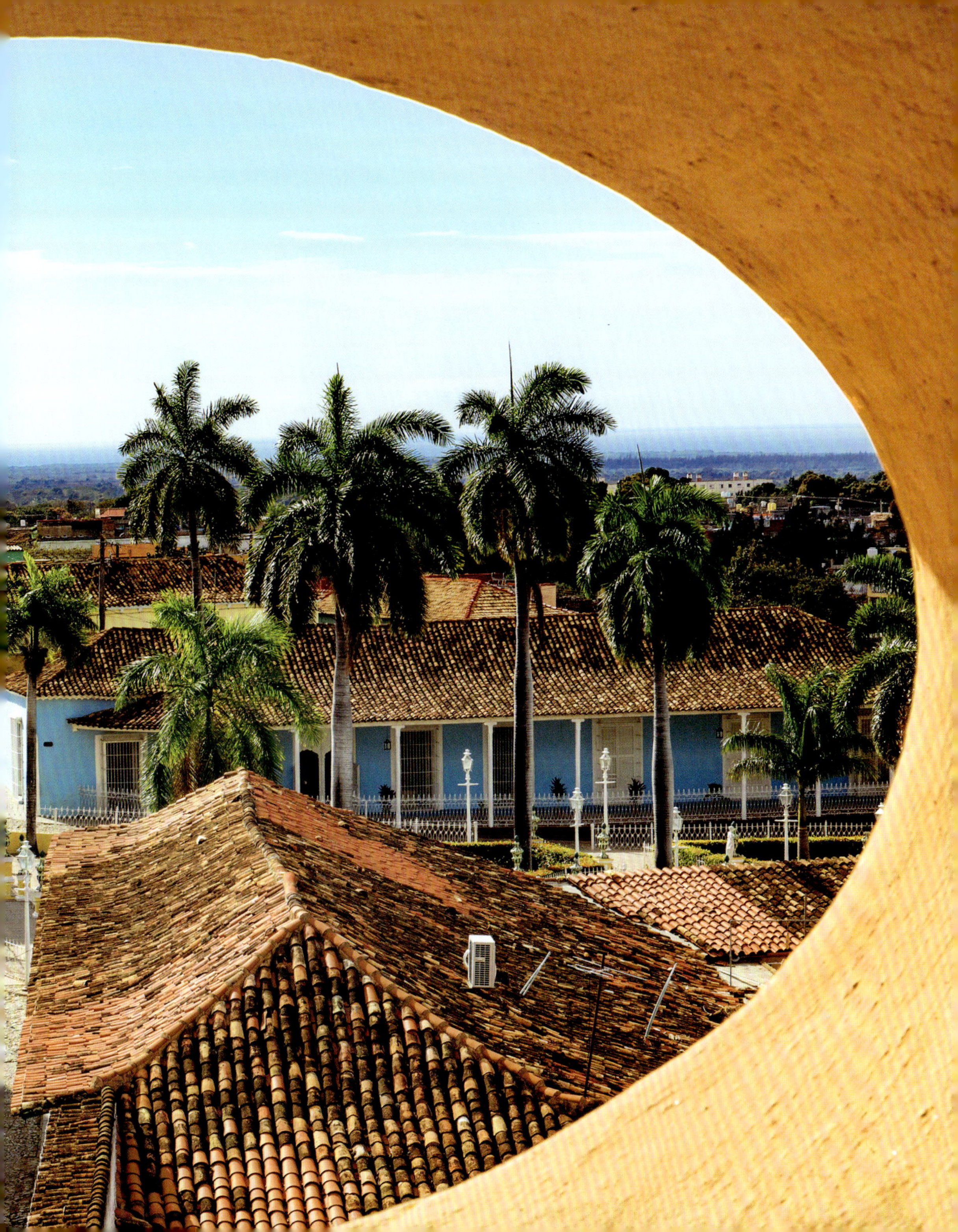

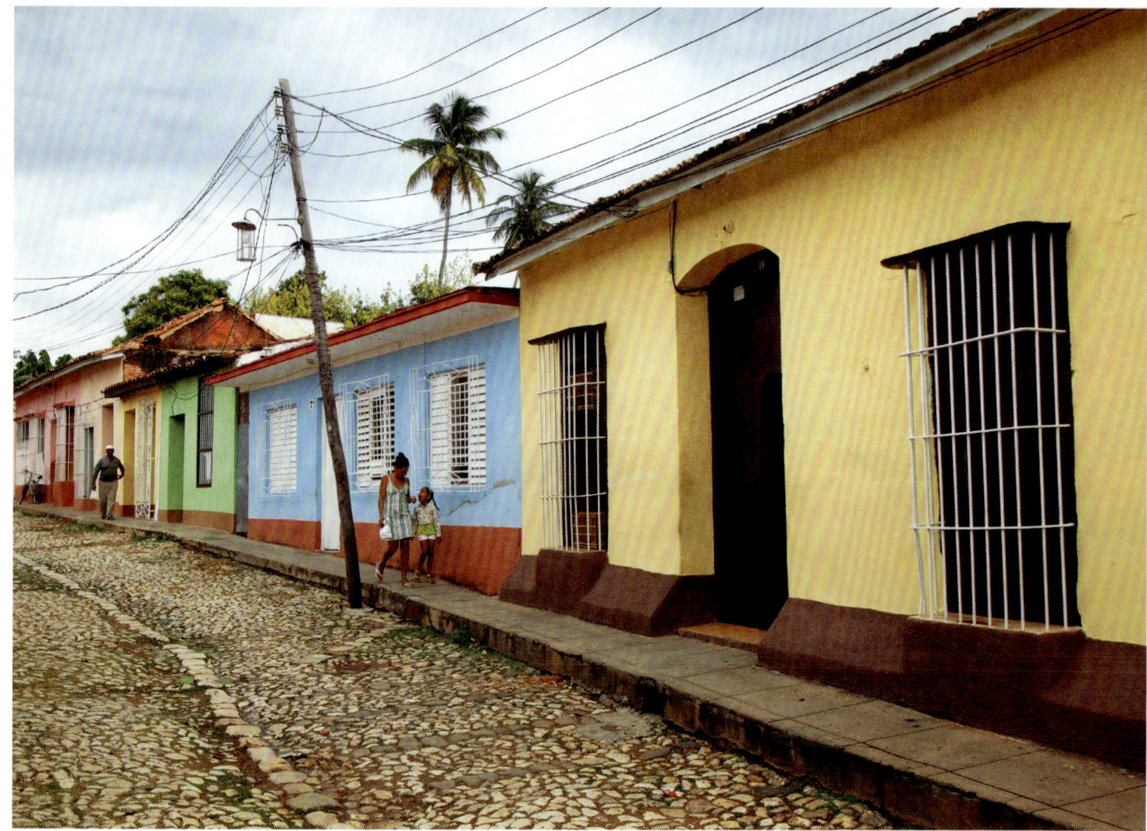

Trinidad, Provincia Sancti Spíritus
Trinidad, Sancti Spíritus Province

Plaza Mayor

The candy-coloured colonial houses with
their artistically forged window grilles,
the donkey carts rumbling over the old
cobblestone pavement and the elegant
town houses around the idyllic Plaza Mayor
are vestiges of a glorious past. Trinidad, or
at least the city centre around Plaza Mayor,
is a colonial picture-book city dominated
by the parish church of Santísima Trinidad.
Around the square are the city palaces
of the sugar barons Brunet (Romantic
Museum), Sánchez Iznaga (Museum of
Colonial Architecture), Ortíz (Art Gallery)
and Padrón (Archaeological Museum).

Plaza Mayor

Les demeures coloniales pastel parées de
grilles de fenêtres artistiquement forgées,
les vieux pavés sur lesquels cahotent les
carrioles à baudet et les élégantes maisons
de ville entourant l'idyllique Plaza Mayor
sont les témoins de pierre d'un glorieux
passé. Trinidad est la ville coloniale
typique, tout au moins son centre-ville
autour de la Plaza Mayor, dominée par
l'église paroissiale Santísima Trinidad
(Sainte-Trinité). La place est bordée de
palais municipaux érigés par les barons
du sucre Brunet (musée Romantique),
Sánchez Iznaga (musée de l'Architecture
coloniale), Ortíz (galerie d'art) et Padrón
(musée Archéologique).

Plaza Mayor

Die bonbonfarbenen Kolonialhäuser
mit ihren kunstvoll geschmiedeten
Fenstergittern, die über das alte
Kopfsteinpflaster rumpelnden Eselskarren
und die eleganten Stadthäuser rund
um die idyllische Plaza Mayor sind
steinerne Zeugen einer glorreichen
Vergangenheit. Trinidad ist eine koloniale
Bilderbuchbuchstadt, zumindest das
Stadtzentrum um die Plaza Mayor, die
von der Pfarrkirche Santísima Trinidad
(Heilige Dreifaltigkeit) dominiert wird.
Rund um den Platz liegen die Stadtpaläste
der Zuckerbarone Brunet (Romantisches
Museum), Sánchez Iznaga (Museum für
Koloniale Architektur), Ortíz (Kunstgalerie)
und Padrón (Archäologie-Museum).

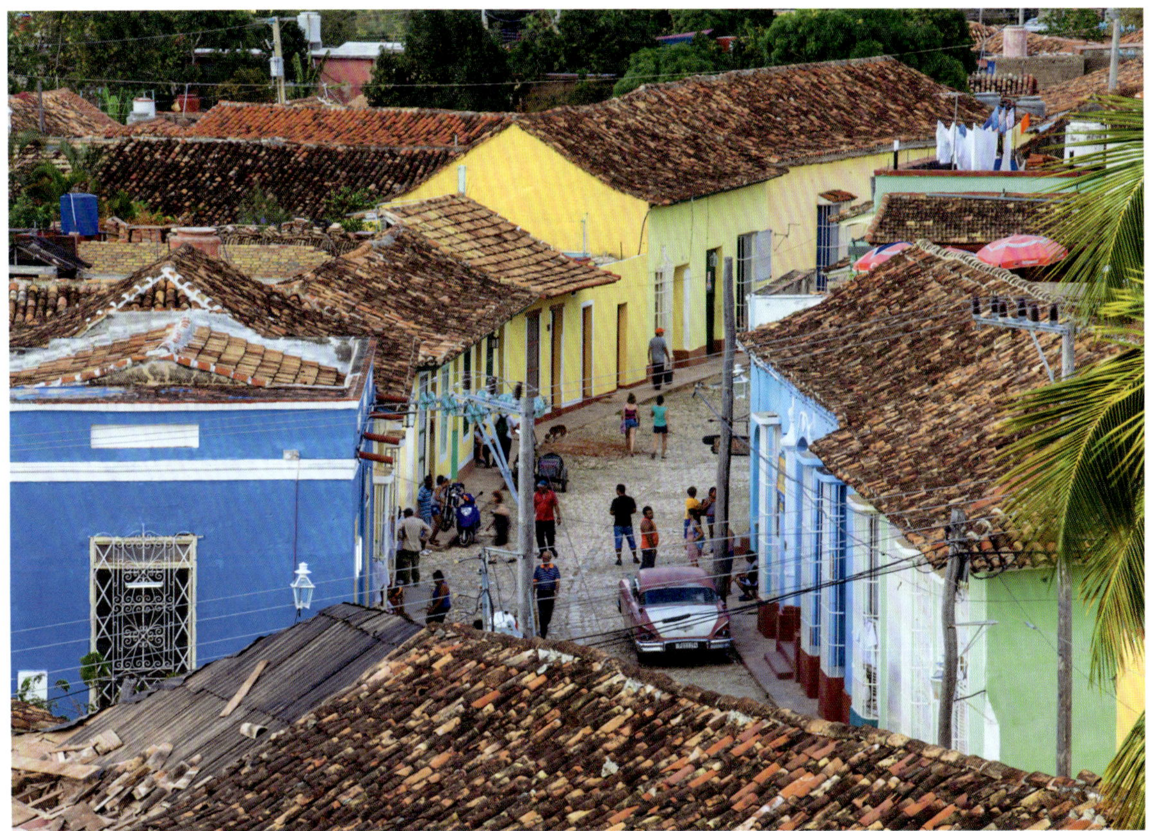

Trinidad, Provincia Sancti Spíritus
Trinidad, Sancti Spíritus Province

Plaza Mayor

Las casas coloniales de colores dulces con sus rejas de ventanas artísticamente forjadas, los carros de burro que retumban sobre el viejo pavimento de adoquines y las elegantes casas de pueblo alrededor de la idílica Plaza Mayor son testigos de un pasado glorioso. Trinidad es una ciudad colonial, al menos el centro de la ciudad alrededor de la Plaza Mayor, dominada por la iglesia parroquial de la Santísima Trinidad. Alrededor de la plaza se encuentran los palacios de los magnates del azúcar Brunet (Museo Romántico), Sánchez Iznaga (Museo de Arquitectura Colonial), Ortíz (Galería de Arte) y Padrón (Museo Arqueológico).

Plaza Mayor

As casas coloniais com cores de doces com as suas grades de janelas artisticamente ornamentadas, as carroças de burro a roncar sobre o velho pavimento de pedra e as elegantes casas da cidade à volta da idílica Plaza Mayor são testemunhas de pedra de um passado glorioso. Trinidad é uma cidade colonial de livros ilustrados, pelo menos o centro da cidade ao redor da Plaza Mayor, que é dominada pela igreja paroquial de Santísima Trinidad. Ao redor da praça estão os palácios da cidade dos barões do açúcar Brunet (Museu Romântico), Sánchez Iznaga (Museu de Arquitetura Colonial), Ortíz (Galeria de Arte) e Padrón (Museu Arqueológico).

Plaza Mayor

De snoepkleurige koloniale huizen met hun kunstzinnig gesmede raamroosters, de ezelskarren die over de oude geplaveide straatstenen rommelen en de elegante herenhuizen rond het idyllische Plaza Mayor zijn getuigen van een glorieus verleden. Trinidad is een koloniale prentenboekstad, althans het stadscentrum rond Plaza Mayor, gedomineerd door de parochiekerk van Santísima Trinidad (Drie-eenheid). Rondom het plein zijn de stadspaleizen van de suikerbaronnen Brunet (Romantisch Museum), Sánchez Iznaga (Museum voor Koloniale Architectuur), Ortíz (Kunstgalerie) en Padrón (Archeologisch Museum).

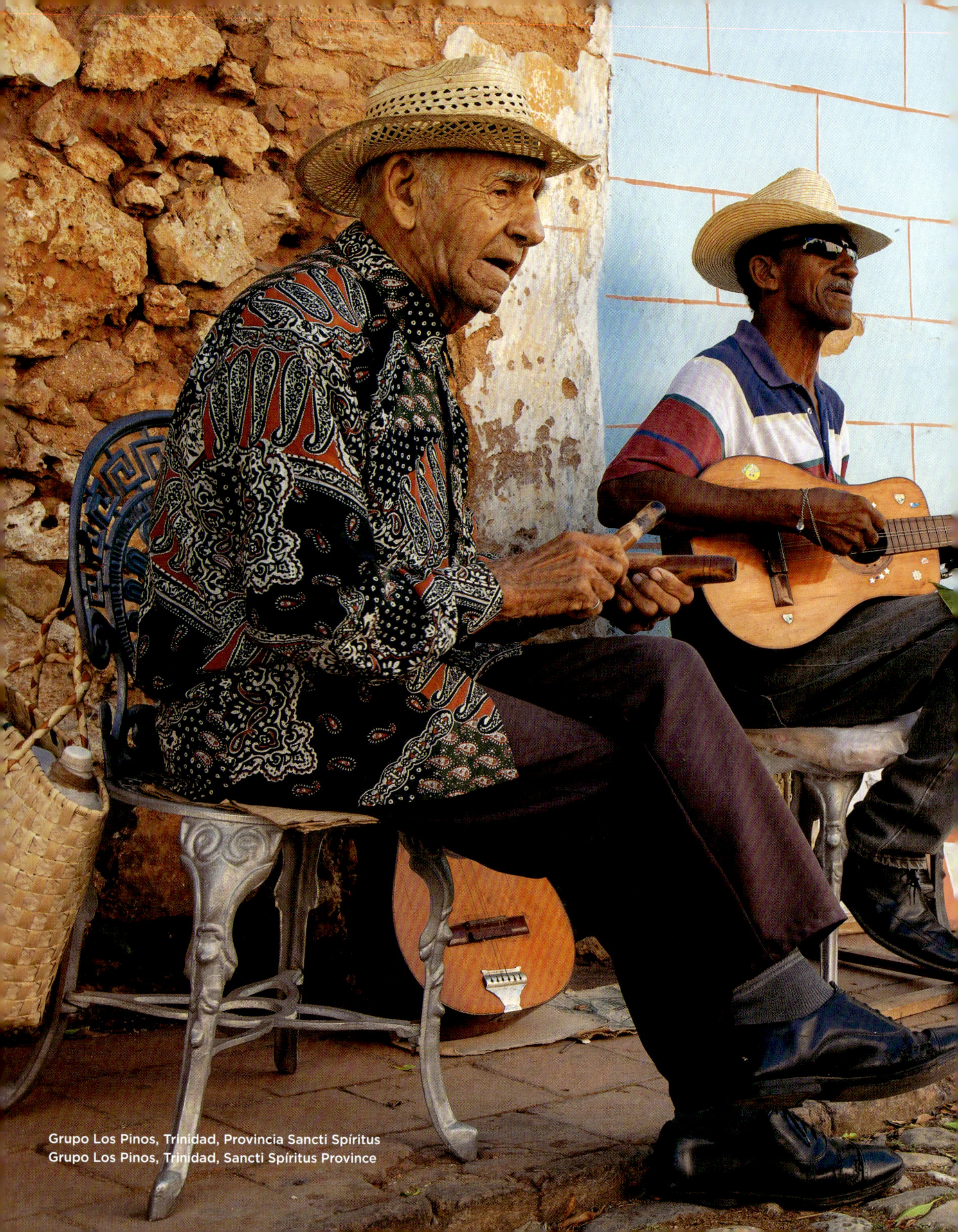

Grupo Los Pinos, Trinidad, Provincia Sancti Spíritus
Grupo Los Pinos, Trinidad, Sancti Spíritus Province

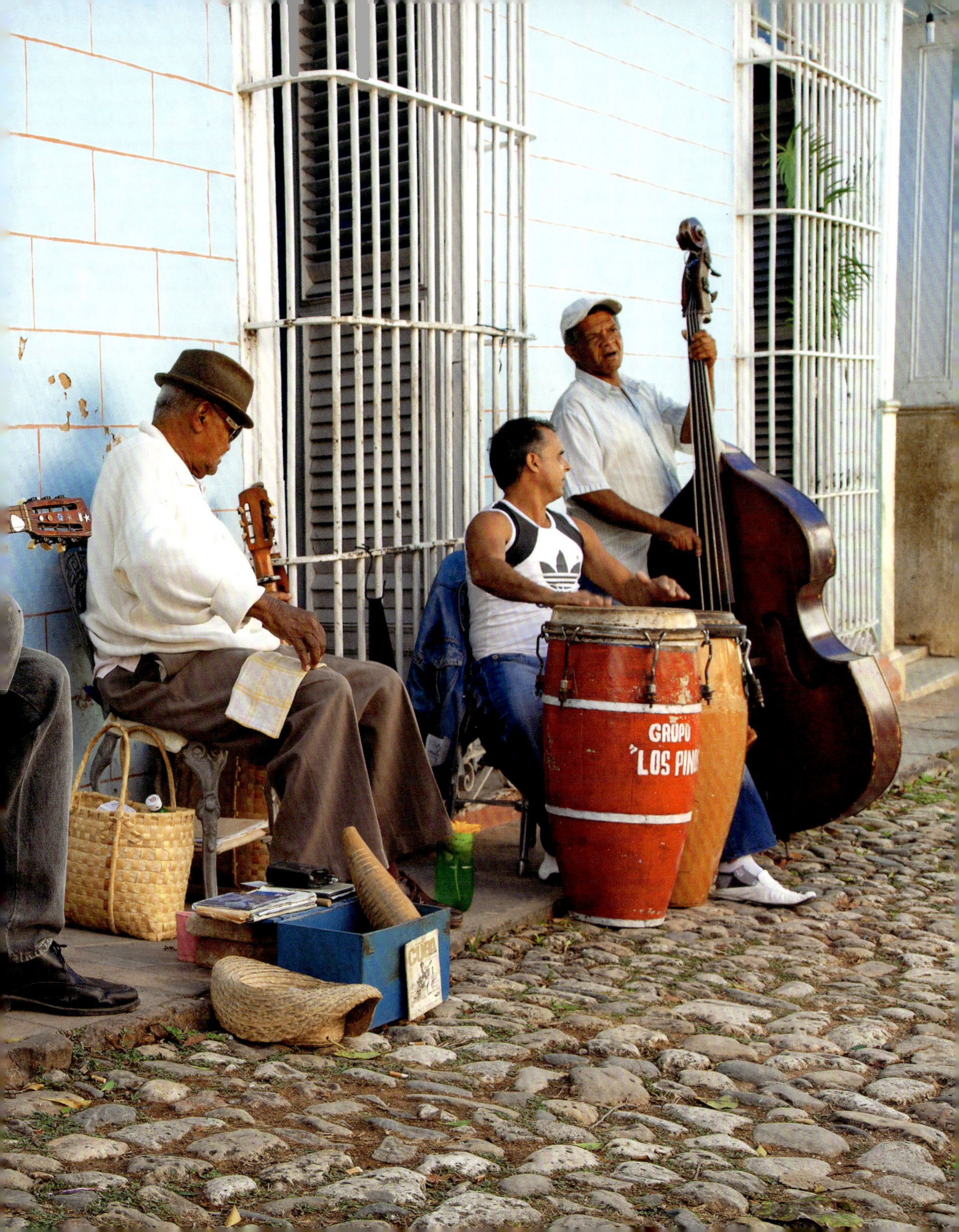
GRUPO
"LOS PINO
CUBA

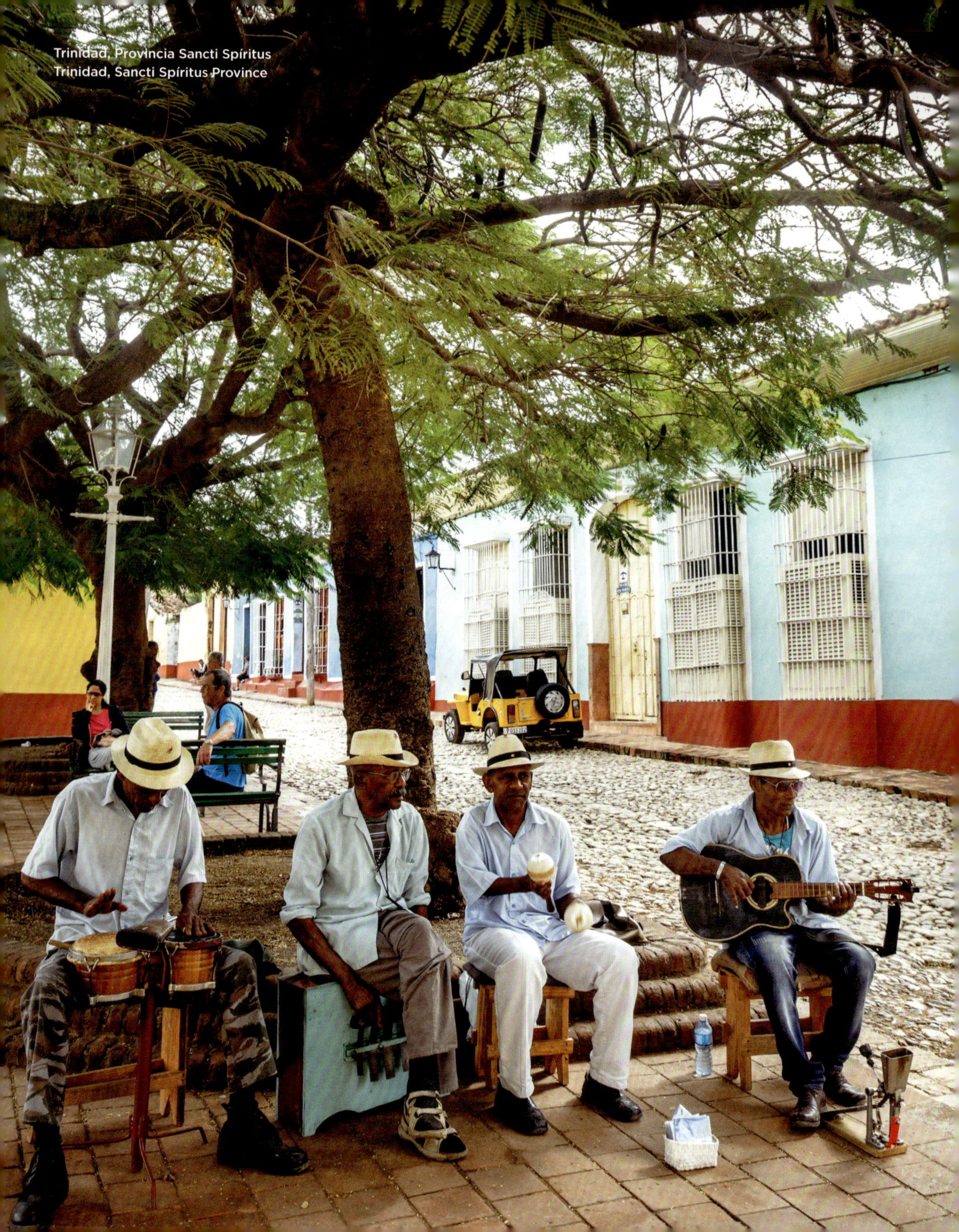

Trinidad, Provincia Sancti Spíritus
Trinidad, Sancti Spíritus Province

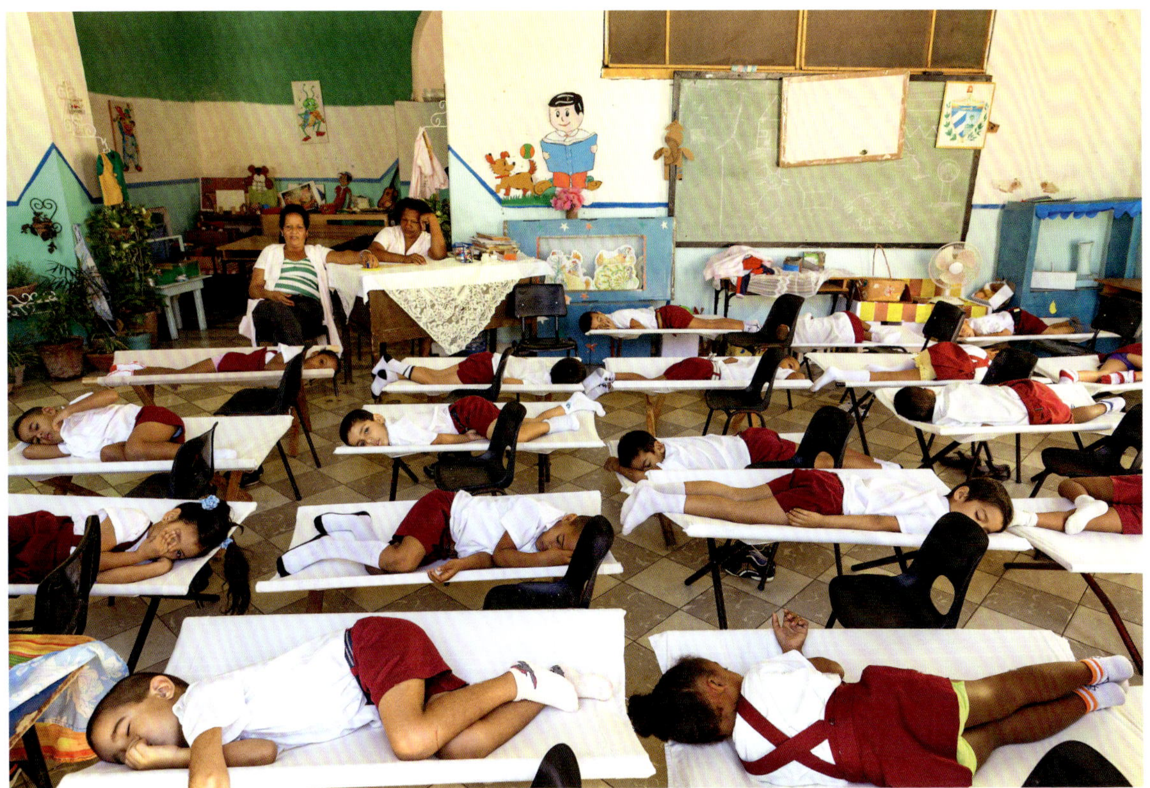

Escuela, Trinidad, Provincia Sancti Spíritus
School, Trinidad, Sancti Spíritus Province

Music Stronghold Trinidad

There is live music day and night all over Trinidad, whether in taverns and restaurants, in the Casa de la Música, in the Palenque (the seat of the Afro-Cuban folklore ensemble), in the Casa de la Trova, on the stone steps next to the parish church or simply on the street. The Son-Conjuntos traditionally play on easily carried instruments.

Fortaleza de la música Trinidad

En toda Trinidad hay música en vivo día y noche, ya sea en tabernas y restaurantes, en la Casa de la Música, en el "Palenque" (la sede del conjunto folklórico afrocubano), en la Casa de la Trova, en los escalones de piedra junto a la iglesia parroquial o simplemente en la calle. Los conjuntos de son tocan tradicionalmente en instrumentos portátiles fácil de transportar.

Trinidad, fief de la musique cubaine

À Trinidad, la musique *live* est partout, de jour comme de nuit : dans les tavernes et restaurants, dans la Casa de la Música, au Palenque (où se produisent les ensembles folkloriques afro-cubains), dans la Casa de la Trova, sur les escaliers proches de l'église paroissiale, ou simplement dans la rue. Les *son conjuntos* jouent traditionnellement sur des instruments faciles à transporter.

Fortaleza da música Trinidad

Há música ao vivo dia e noite por toda a Trindade, seja em tabernas e restaurantes, na Casa de la Música, no Palenque (a sede do grupo folclórico afro-cubano), na Casa de la Trova, nos degraus de pedra junto à igreja paroquial ou simplesmente na rua. Os conjuntos de "son" tocam tradicionalmente em instrumentos facilmente portáteis.

Musikhochburg Trinidad

Live-Musik gibt es Tag und Nacht überall in Trinidad, ob in Tavernen und Restaurants, in der Casa de la Música, im Palenque (dem Sitz des afrokubanischen Folklore-Ensembles), in der Casa de la Trova, auf der Steintreppe neben der Pfarrkirche oder einfach so auf der Straße. Die Son-Conjuntos spielen traditionell auf leicht tragbaren Instrumenten.

Muziek in Trinidad

Overal in Trinidad is dag en nacht live muziek te horen, of het nu in tavernes en restaurants is, in het Casa de la Música, in de'Palenque (de zetel van het Afro-Cubaanse folklore-ensemble), in het Casa de la Trova, op de stenen trappen naast de parochiekerk of gewoon op straat. De Son-Conjuntos spelen traditioneel op gemakkelijk draagbare instrumenten.

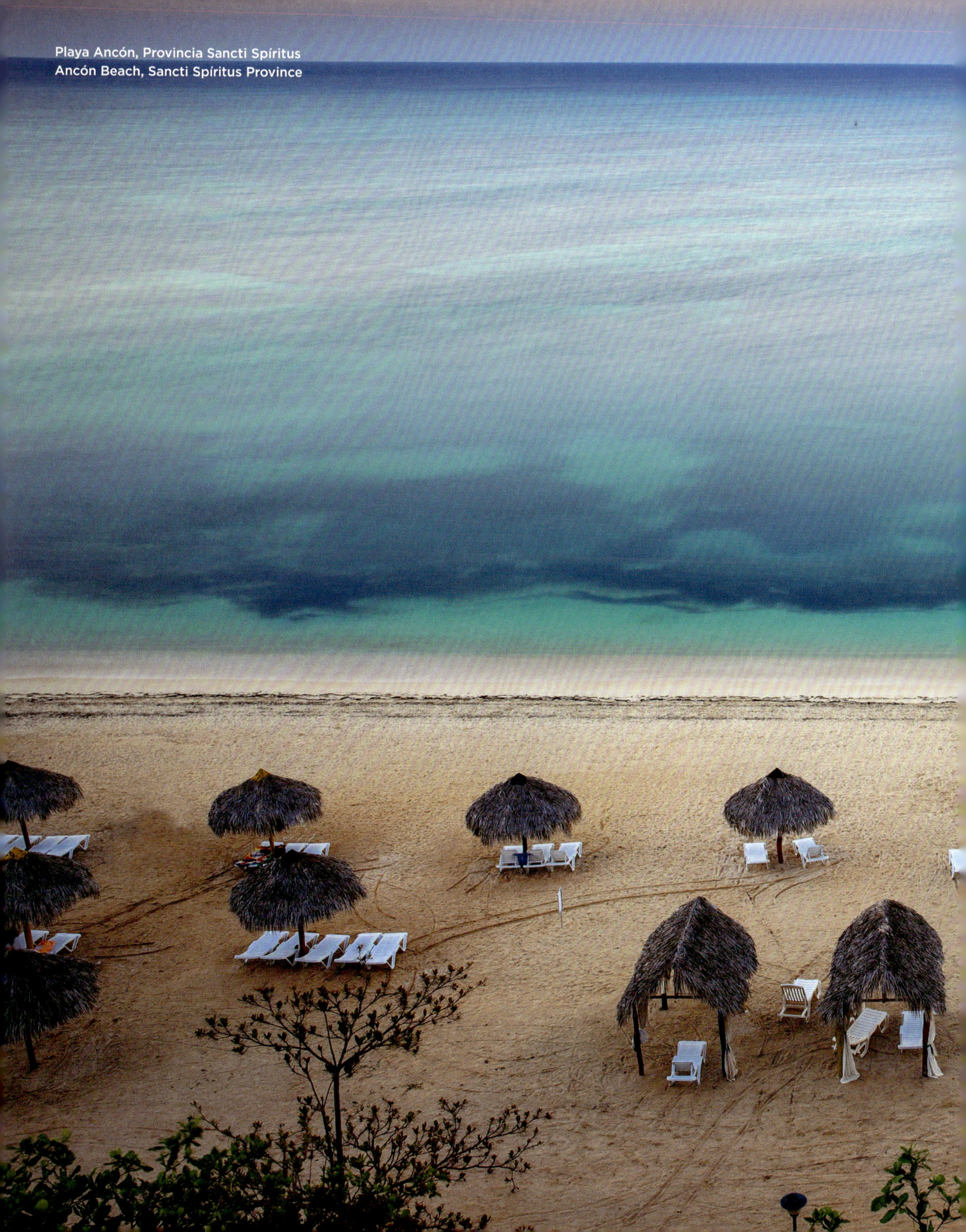

Playa Ancón, Provincia Sancti Spíritus
Ancón Beach, Sancti Spíritus Province

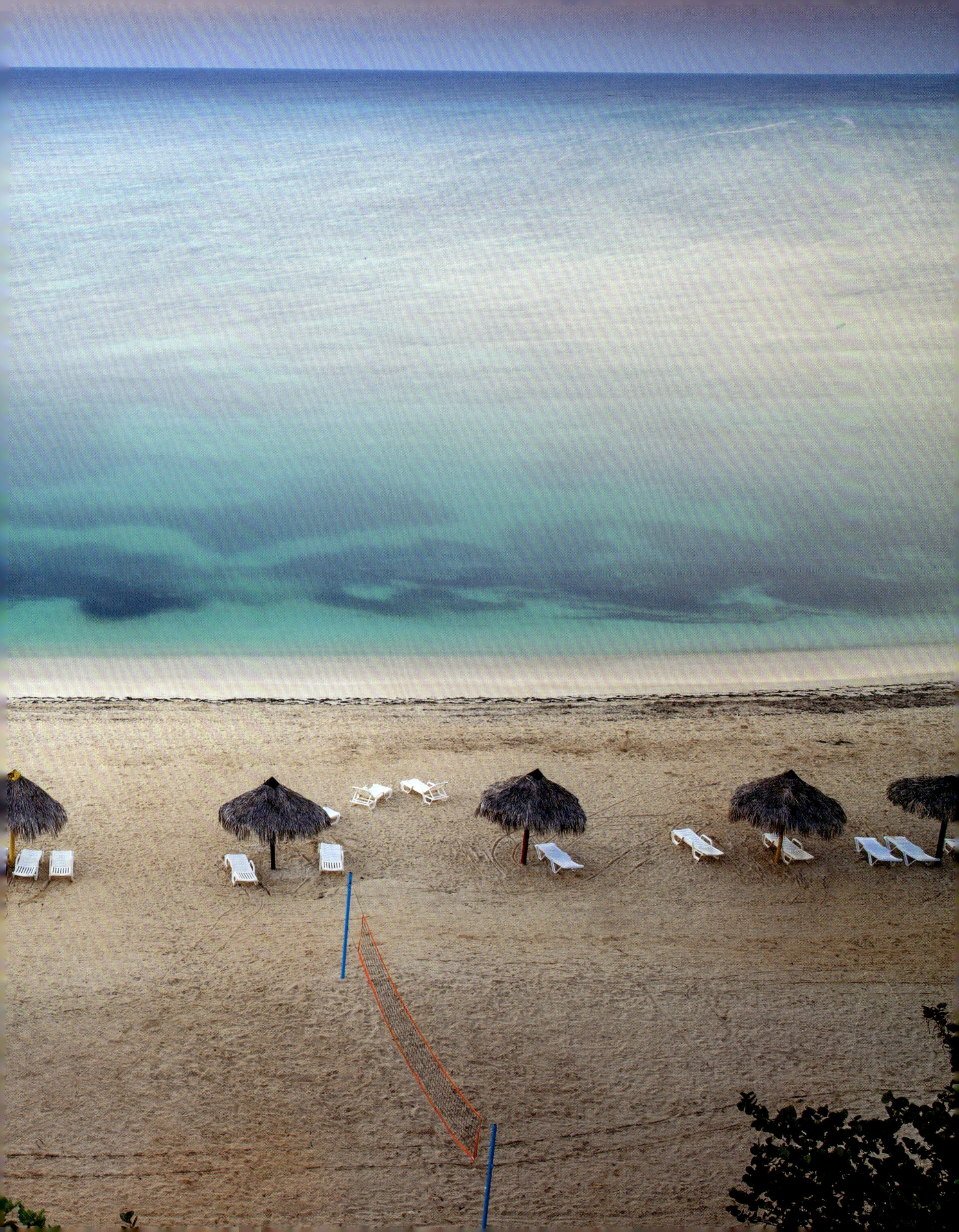

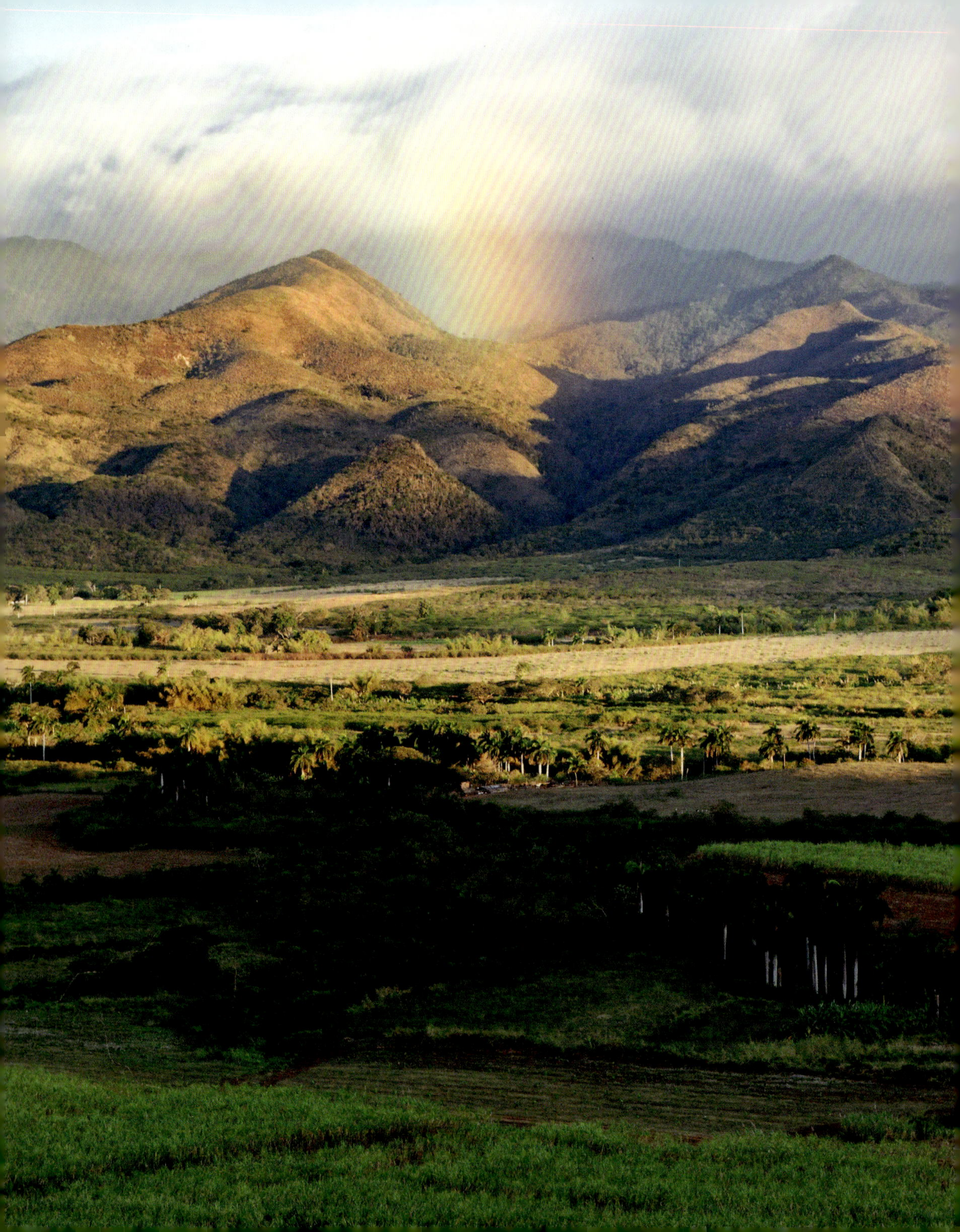

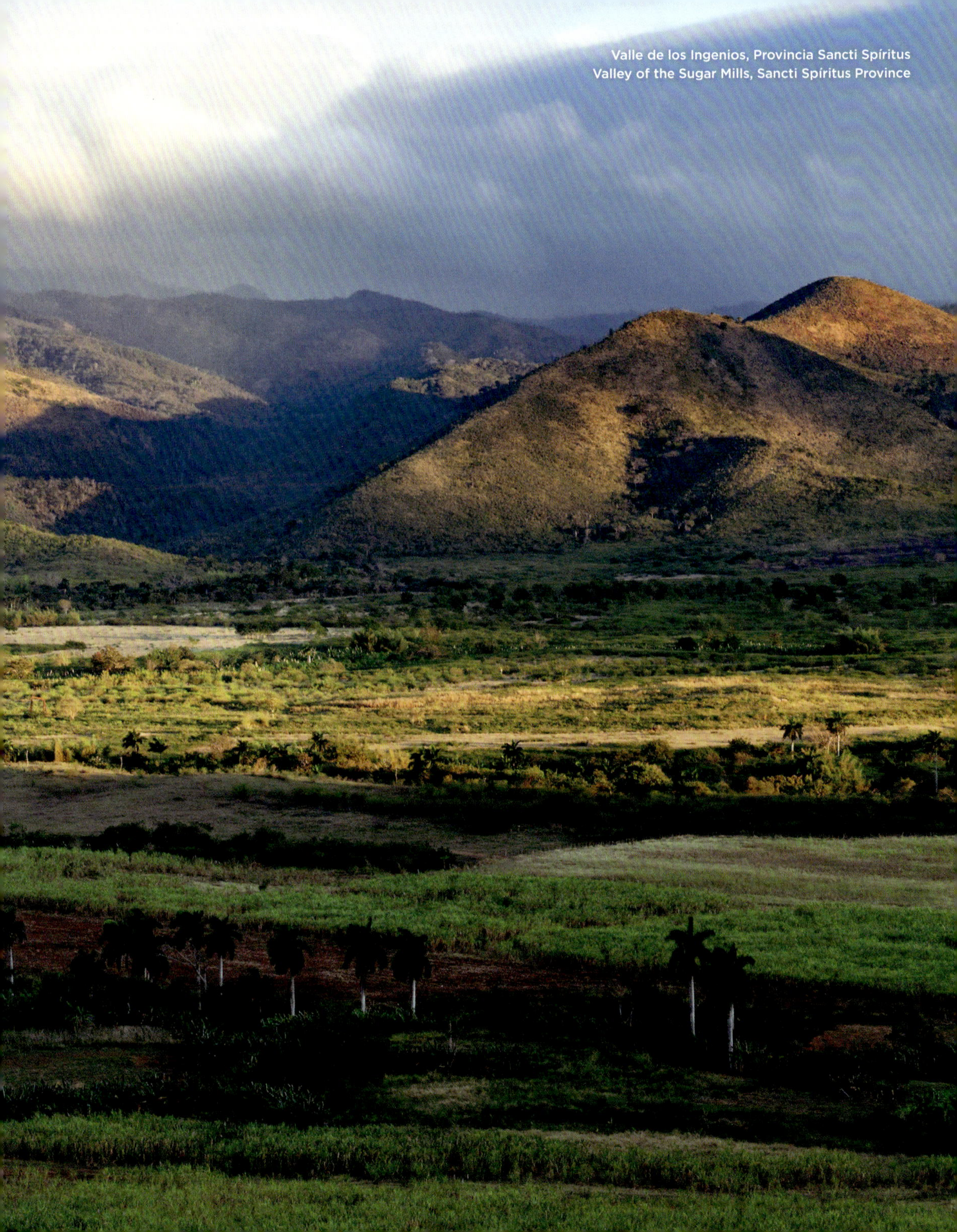
Valle de los Ingenios, Provincia Sancti Spíritus
Valley of the Sugar Mills, Sancti Spíritus Province

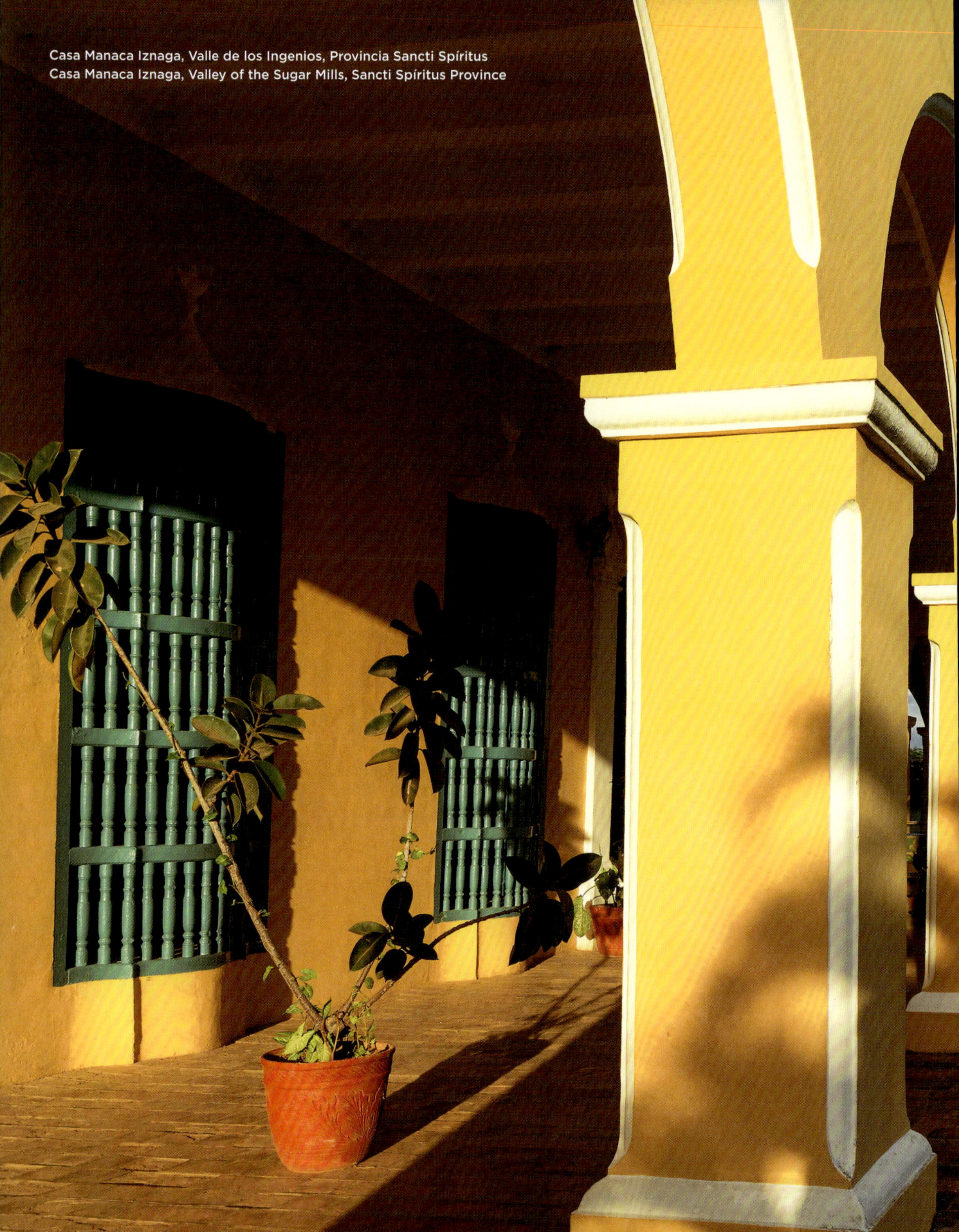

Casa Manaca Iznaga, Valle de los Ingenios, Provincia Sancti Spíritus
Casa Manaca Iznaga, Valley of the Sugar Mills, Sancti Spíritus Province

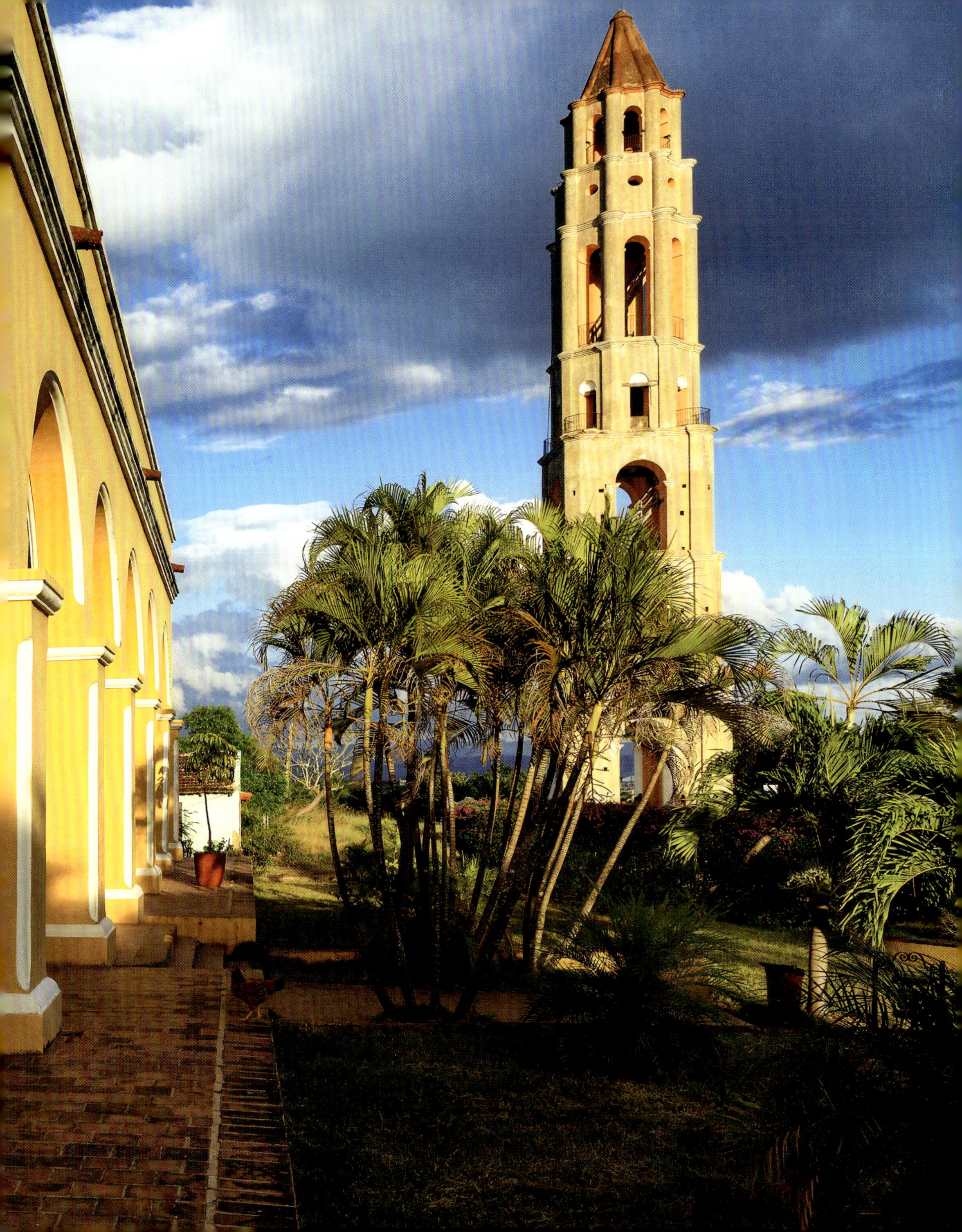

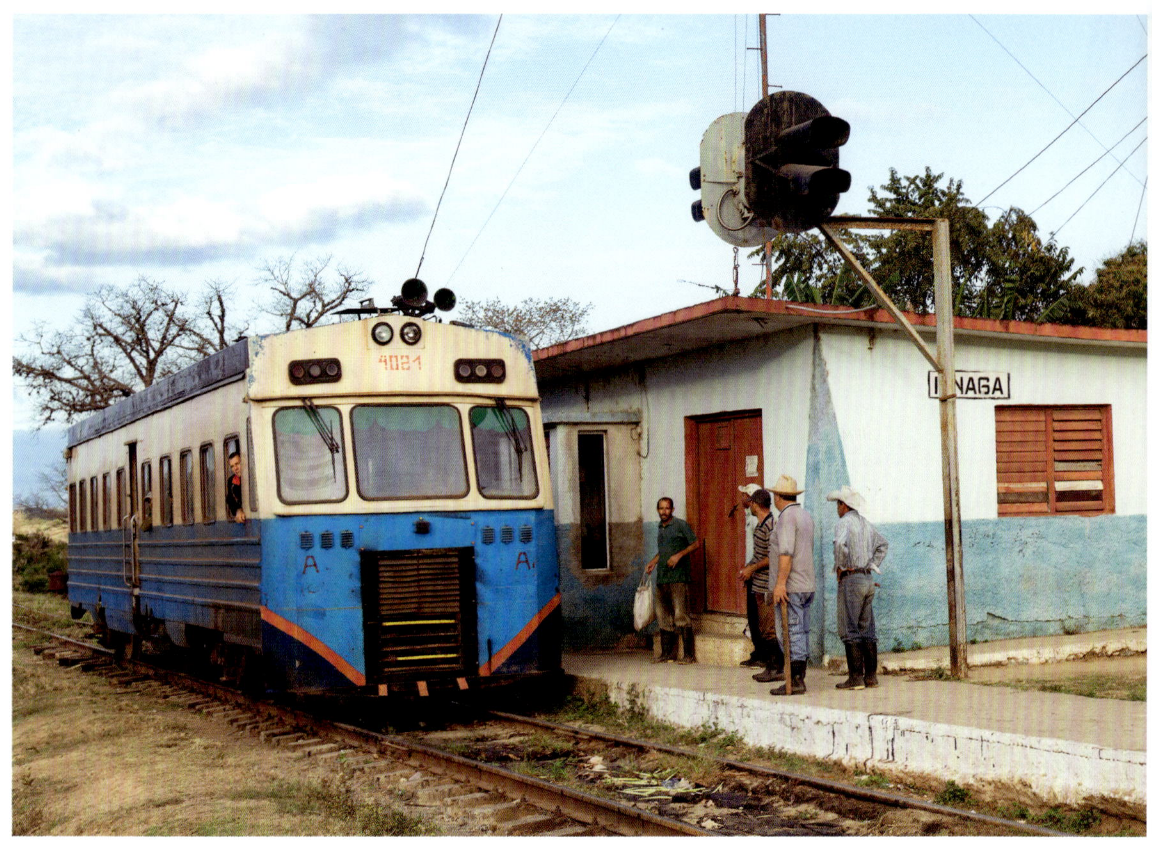

Estación Manacas, Valle de los Ingenios, Provincia Sancti Spíritus
Train Station Manacas, Valley of the Sugar Mills, Sancti Spíritus Province

Valle de los Ingenios

About 10 km (6 mi.) east of Trinidad lies the San Luís valley. In the 18th and 19th centuries, tens of thousands of slaves lived here in barracks and worked on the sugar cane fields and in the 50 sugar mills in the valley, which earned this area the name "Valley of Sugar Mills" (Valle de los Ingénios). During the wars of independence the slaves burned down all the sugar mills. Only a few ruins remain or have been rebuilt, like the former Hacienda Iznaga. From the top of the Manaca-Iznaga tower, the white lords oversaw the valley and the slaves. The sugar cane used to be transported by rail from the fields to the sugar mills.

Valle de los Ingenios

La vallée San Luís est située à environ 10 km à l'est de Trinidad. Aux XVIIIe et XIXe siècles, des dizaines de milliers d'esclaves vivaient ici dans des baraques, exploités dans les champs de canne et une cinquantaine de moulins à canne à sucre. Ces derniers valurent à la région son surnom de « Valle de los Ingénios » (vallée des sucreries). Au cours de la guerre d'indépendance, les esclaves mirent feu à la totalité des moulins et seules quelques ruines furent conservées ou reconstruites, à l'instar de l'ancienne Hacienda Iznaga. Du sommet de la tour Manaca-Iznaga, les maîtres blancs surveillaient la vallée et les esclaves. Une voie ferroviaire permettait le transport de la canne à sucre des champs jusqu'aux moulins.

Valle de los Ingenios

Etwa 10 km östlich von Trinidad liegt das Tal San Luís. Im 18. und 19. Jahrhundert lebten hier Zehntausende Sklaven in Baracken und schufteten auf den Zuckerrohrfeldern und in den 50 Zuckermühlen im Tal, was ihm den Namen „Tal der Zuckermühlen" (Valle de los Ingénios) einbrachte. Während der Unabhängigkeitskriege brannten die Sklaven sämtliche Zuckermühlen nieder, nur wenige Ruinen blieben erhalten bzw. wurden wie die ehemalige Hacienda Iznaga wiederaufgebaut. Von der Spitze des Turms Manaca-Iznaga überwachten die weißen Herren das Tal und die Sklaven. Per Eisenbahn wurde früher das Zuckerrohr von den Feldern in die Zuckermühlen transportiert.

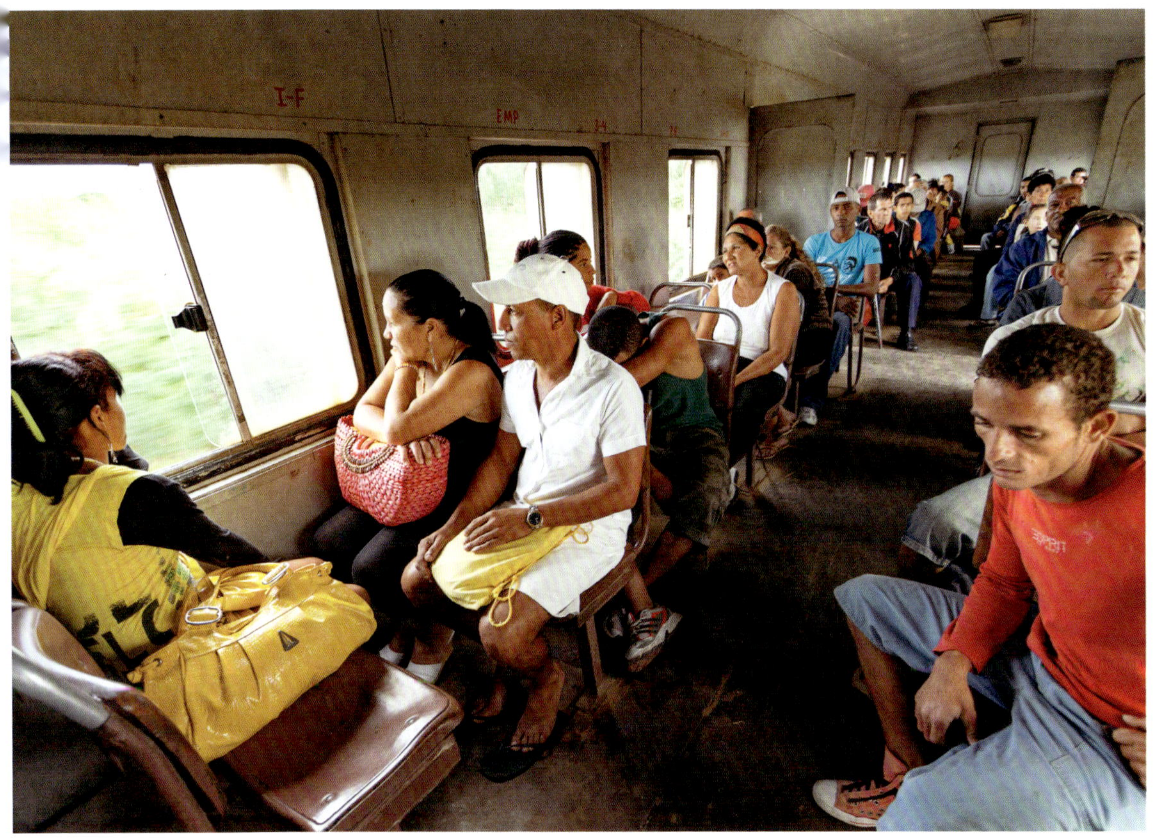

Ferrocarril, Valle de los Ingenios, Provincia Sancti Spíritus
Railway, Valley of the Sugar Mills, Sancti Spíritus Province

Valle de los Ingenios

A unos 10 km al este de Trinidad se
encuentra el valle de San Luis. En los siglos
XVIII y XIX, decenas de miles de esclavos
vivían aquí en cuarteles y trabajaban
sin descanso en los campos de caña de
azúcar y en los 50 ingenios azucareros del
valle, por lo que que se le dio el nombre
de "Valle de los Ingenios". Durante las
guerras de independencia, los esclavos
quemaron todos los ingenios azucareros;
solo quedaron unas pocas ruinas o
fueron reconstruidas como la antigua
Hacienda Iznaga. Desde lo alto de la torre
de Manaca-Iznaga, los señores blancos
supervisaban el valle y los esclavos. La
caña de azúcar era transportada por
ferrocarril desde los campos hasta los
ingenios azucareros.

Valle de los Ingenios

A cerca de 10 km a leste de Trinidad
encontra-se o vale de San Luís. Nos
séculos XVIII e XIX, dezenas de milhares
de escravos viveram aqui nas cabanas
e trabalhavam duramente nos canaviais
e nos 50 engenhos de açúcar do vale,
o que lhe valeu o nome de "Vale dos
Engenhos" (Valle de los Ingénios). Durante
as guerras de independência, os escravos
incendiaram todos os engenhos de açúcar,
restaram apenas algumas ruínas ou foram
reconstruídas como a antiga Fazenda
Iznaga. Do topo da torre Manaca-Iznaga,
os senhores brancos vigiavam o vale e os
escravos. A cana-de-açúcar costumava ser
transportada por caminho-de-ferro dos
campos para os engenhos de açúcar.

Valle de los Ingenios

Ongeveer 10 km ten oosten van Trinidad
ligt de vallei San Luís. In de 18e en 19e
eeuw leefden hier tienduizenden slaven in
kazernes en werkten op de suikerrietvelden
en in de 50 suikermolens in de vallei, wat
hem de naam 'Vallei van de Suikermolens'
(Valle de los Ingénios) opleverde. Tijdens
de onafhankelijkheidsoorlogen hebben de
slaven alle suikermolens in brand gestoken,
er zijn slechts enkele ruïnes overgebleven
of herbouwd zoals de voormalige Hacienda
Iznaga. Vanaf de top van de Manaca-
Iznaga toren, hielden de blanke heren
toezicht op de vallei en de slaven. Vroeger
werd het suikerriet per spoor van de
velden naar de suikerfabrieken vervoerd.

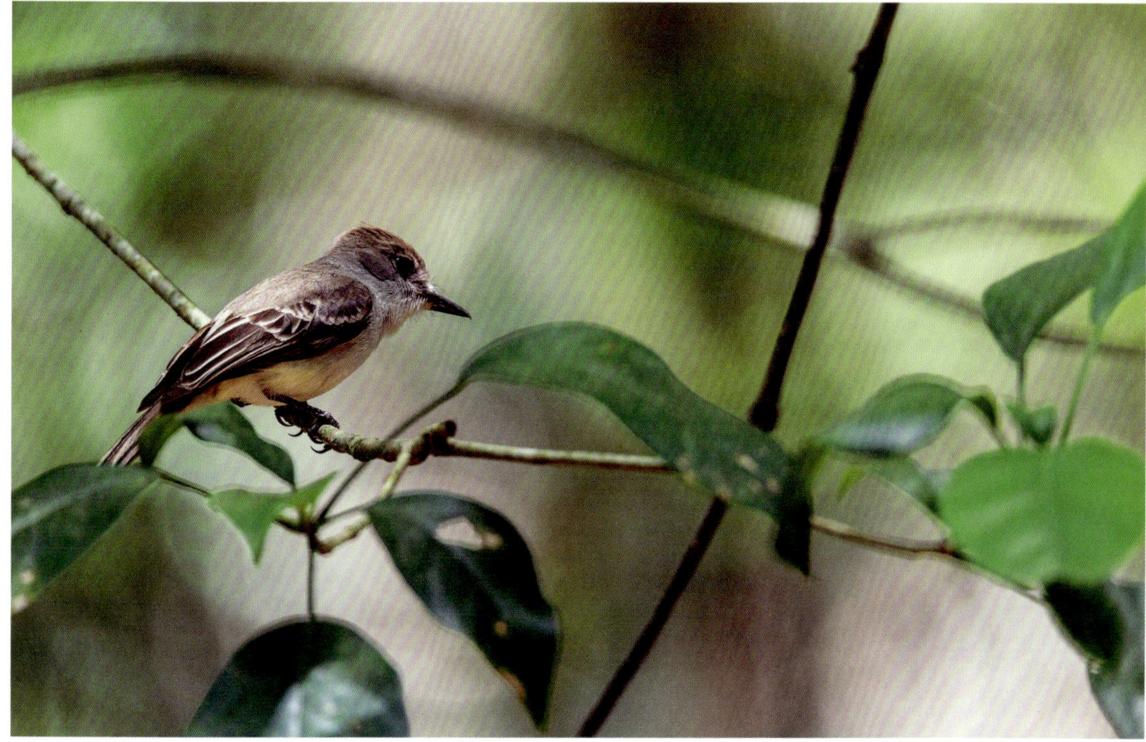

Pibí cubano, Gran Parque Natural Topes de Collantes
Cuban pewee, Topes de Collantes Natural Reserve

Parque Guanayara

A remnant of the evergreen wet forests
that covered Cuba has been preserved
in the Guanayara Nature Park. Most of
the forests were cleared for shipbuilding,
others had to give way to sugar
plantations. In the humid microclimate
of the Sierra del Escambray a lush flora
thrives, and almost half of Cuba's endemic
bird species are native.

Parque Guanayara

En el Parque Natural de Guanayara se
ha preservado un remanente de los
bosques húmedos siempre verdes que
cubrían Cuba. La mayoría de los bosques
fueron talados para la construcción naval,
mientras que otros tuvieron que ceder
el paso a las plantaciones de azúcar. En
el microclima húmedo de la Sierra del
Escambray, prospera una exuberante flora,
y casi la mitad de las especies de aves
endémicas de Cuba son autóctonas.

Parque Guanayara

Une portion de la forêt sempervirente
humide qui recouvrait autrefois l'île de
Cuba est protégée au sein du parc naturel
de Guanayara. La majorité des forêts
furent abattues pour la construction navale
ou pour laisser place aux plantations de
canne à sucre. Une végétation luxuriante
s'épanouit dans le microclimat humide
de la sierra del Escambray, où résident en
outre pratiquement la moitié des espèces
d'oiseaux endémiques de Cuba.

Parque Guanayara

No Parque Natural Guanayara foi
preservado um remanescente das florestas
úmidas sempre verdes que cobriam Cuba.
A maioria das florestas foram desmatadas
para a construção naval, outras tiveram
de ceder lugar às plantações de açúcar.
No microclima úmido da Sierra del
Escambray, floresce uma flora exuberante
e além disso, aqui estão quase metade de
todas espécies endémicas de aves nativas
de Cuba.

Parque Guanayara

Im Naturpark Guanayara ist ein Rest
der immergrünen Feuchtwälder
erhalten, von denen Kuba bedeckt war.
Die meisten Wälder wurden für den
Schiffsbau abgeholzt, andere mussten
Zuckerplantagen weichen. Im feuchten
Mikroklima der Sierra del Escambray
gedeiht eine üppige Pflanzenwelt,
außerdem sind hier fast die Hälfte aller
endemischen Vogelarten Kubas heimisch.

Parque Guanayara

In het Guanayara Natuurpark is een deel
van de altijd groene natte bossen die
Cuba bedekten bewaard gebleven. De
meeste bossen werden gekapt voor de
scheepsbouw, andere moesten wijken
voor de suikerplantages. In het vochtige
microklimaat van de Sierra del Escambray
gedijt een weelderige flora en bijna de
helft van Cuba's endemische vogelsoorten
is inheems.

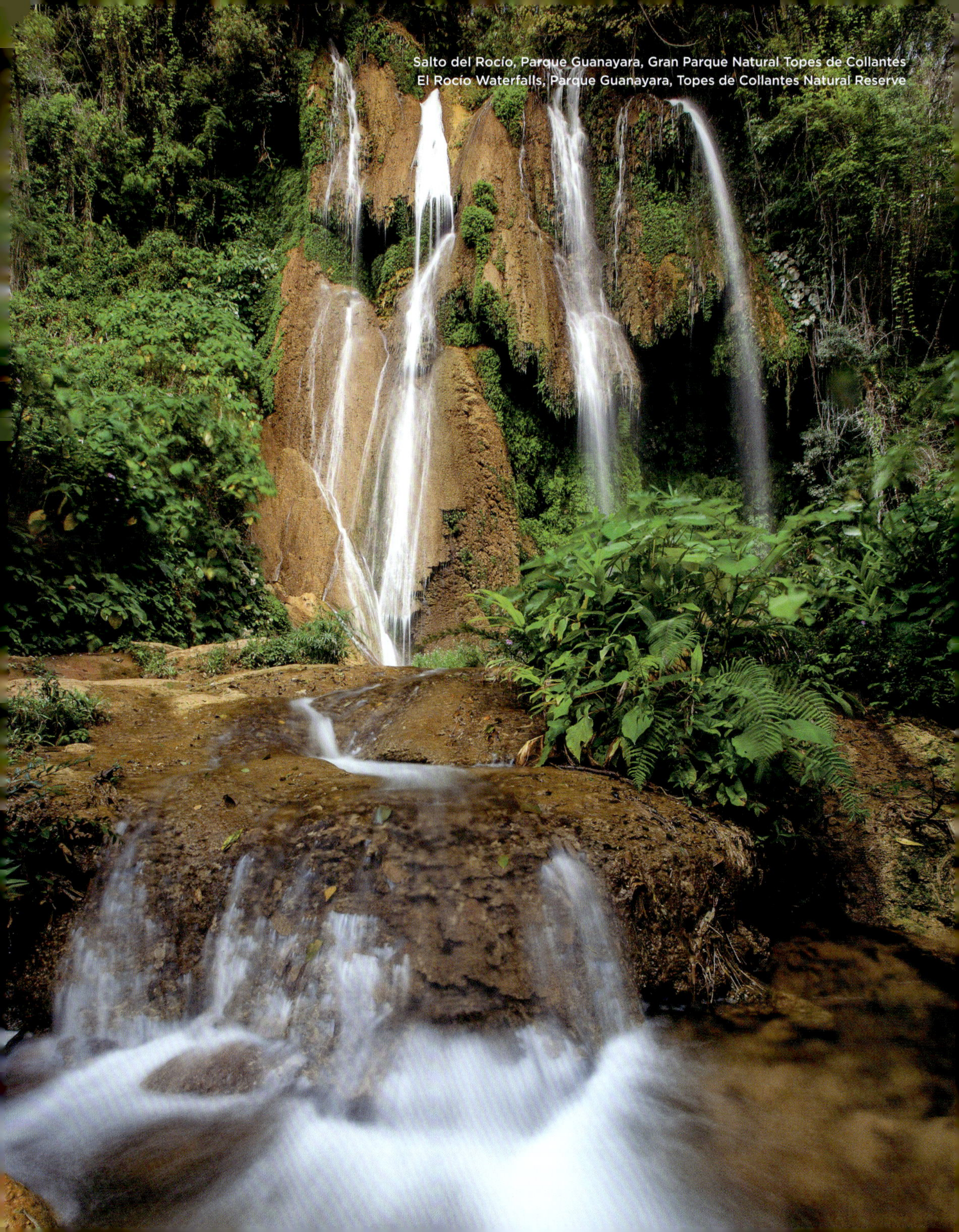

Salto del Rocío, Parque Guanayara, Gran Parque Natural Topes de Collantes
El Rocío Waterfalls, Parque Guanayara, Topes de Collantes Natural Reserve

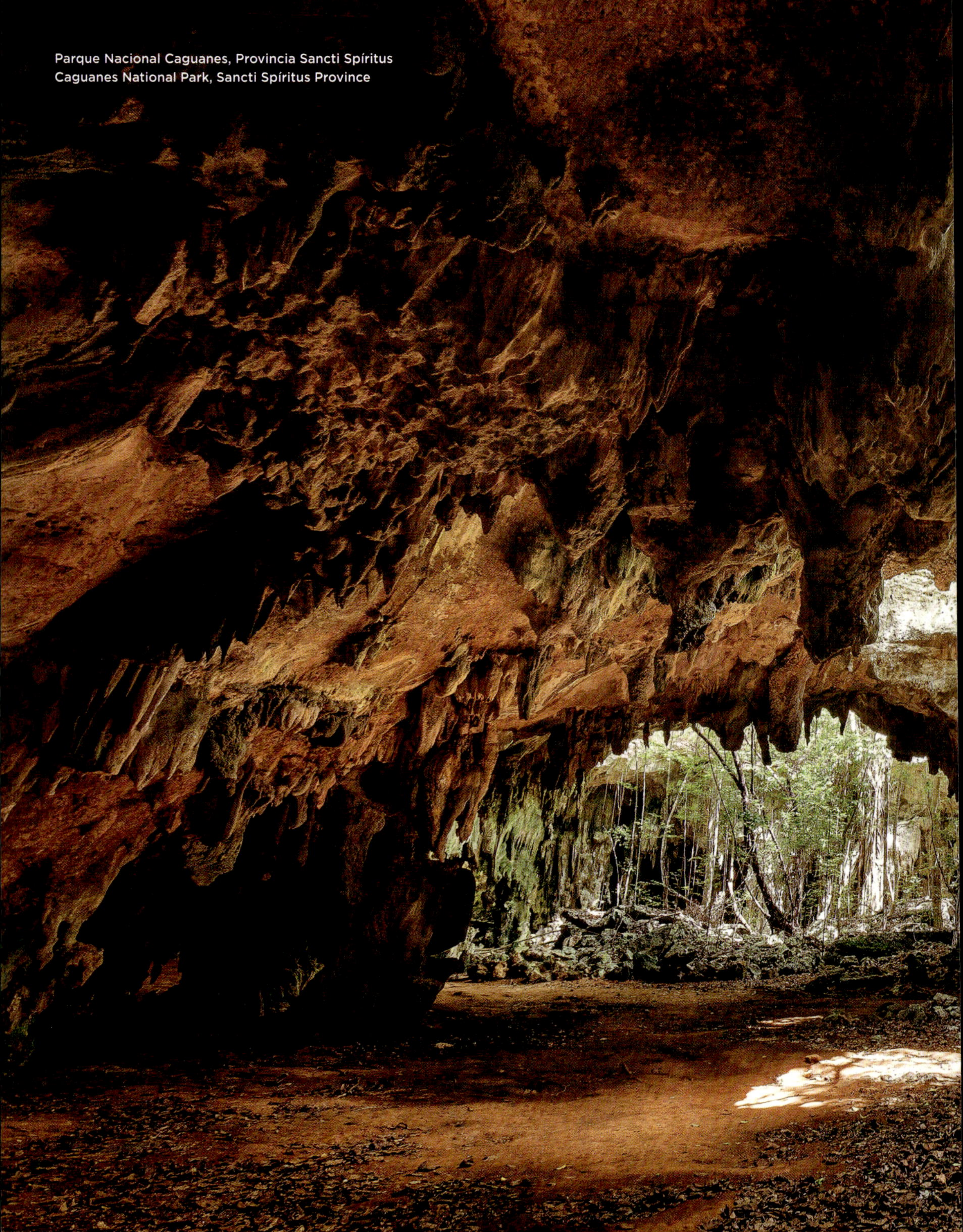

Parque Nacional Caguanes, Provincia Sancti Spíritus
Caguanes National Park, Sancti Spíritus Province

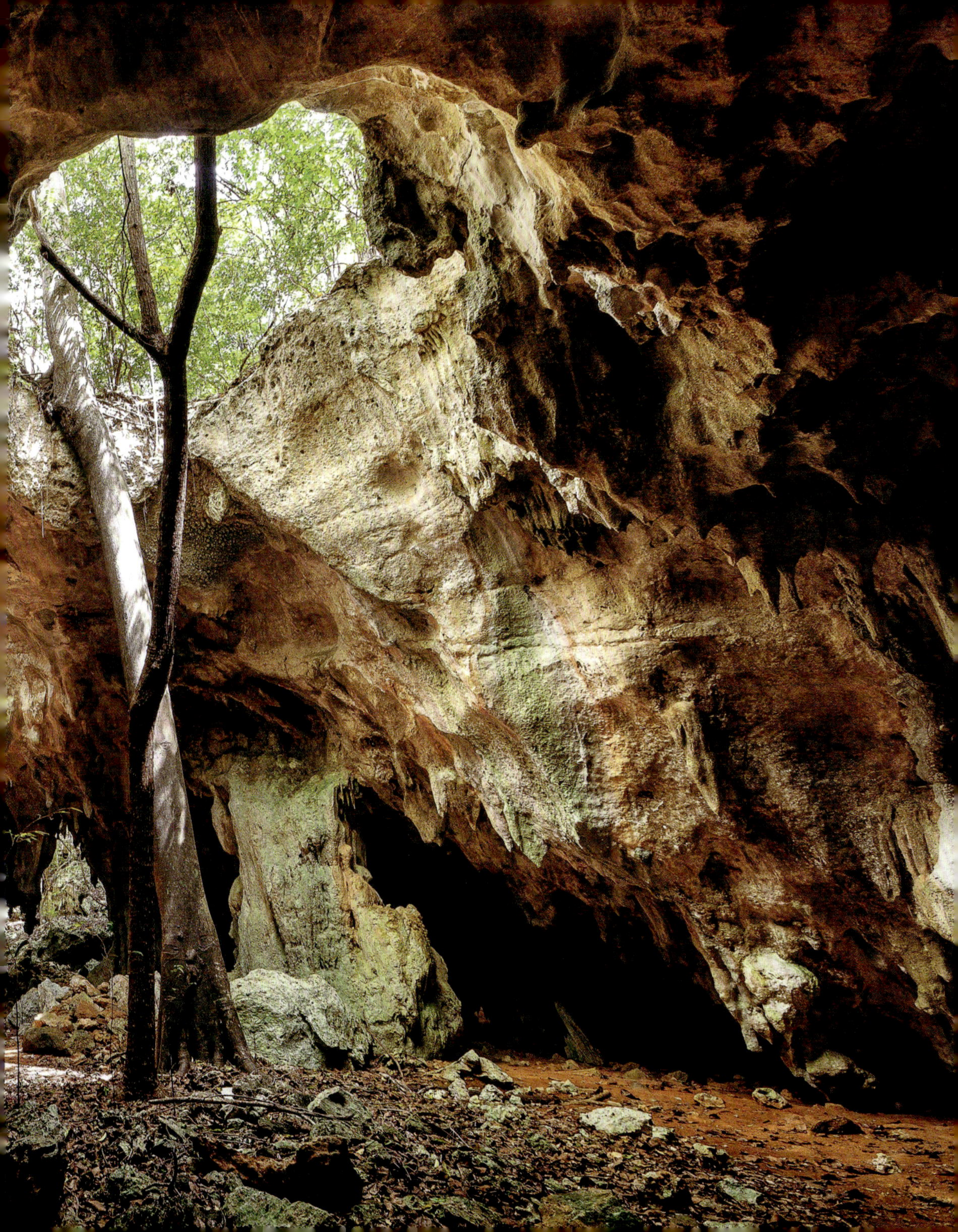

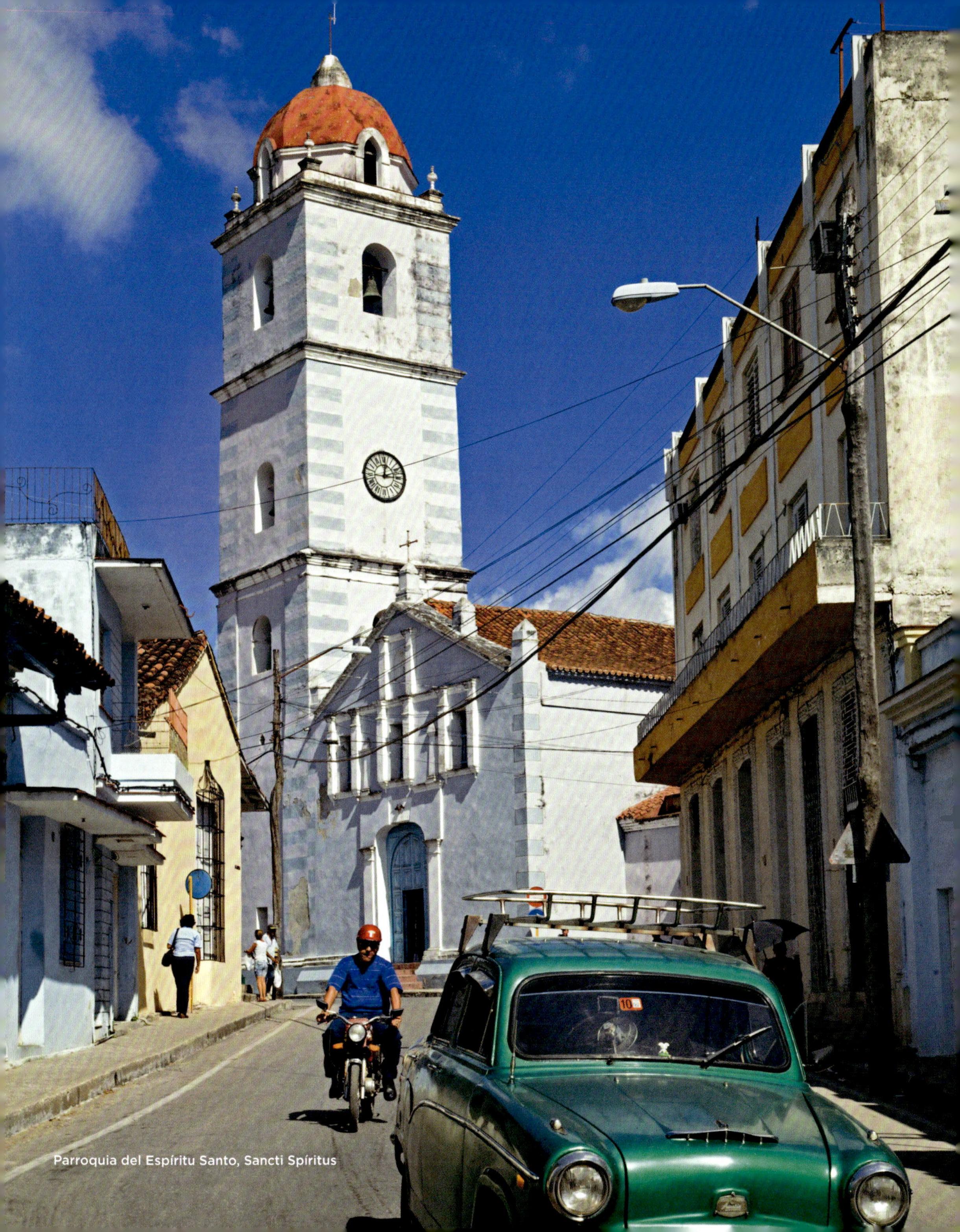

Parroquia del Espíritu Santo, Sancti Spíritus

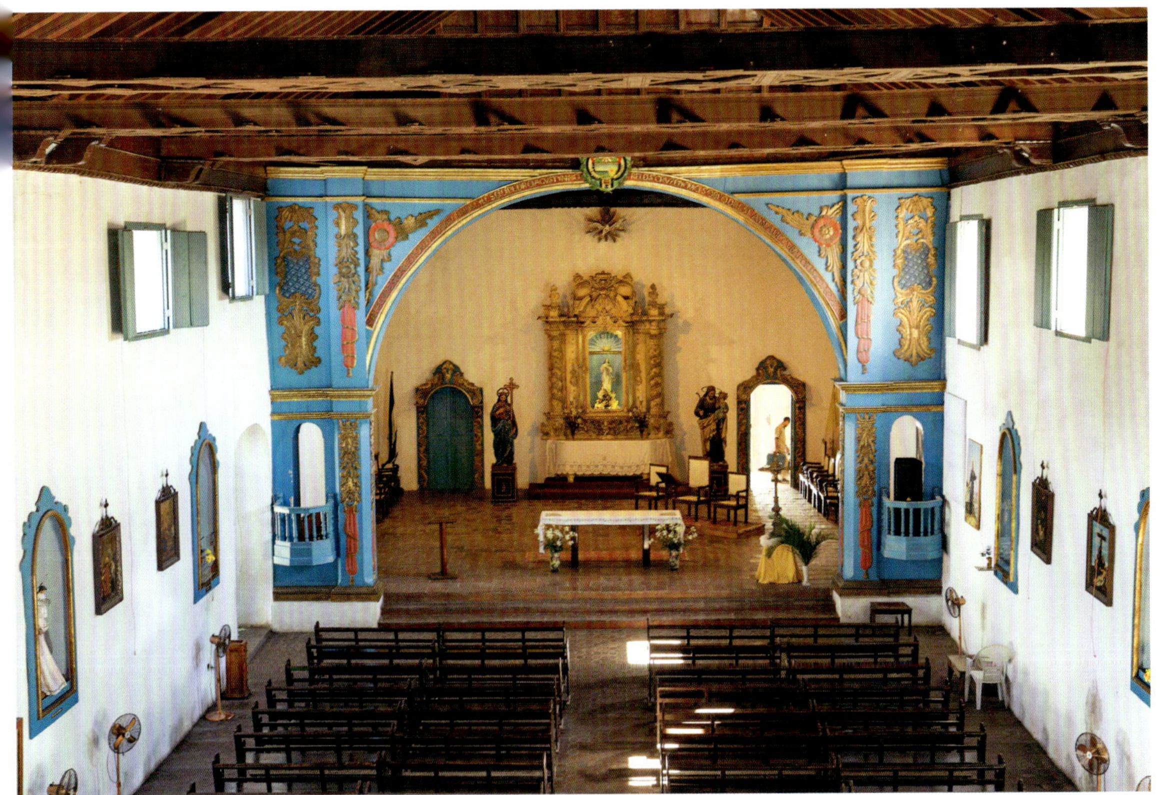

Parroquia del Espíritu Santo, Sancti Spíritus

Sancti Spíritus

The parish church of Espíritu Santo (Holy Spirit) in the provincial capital of Sancti Spíritus is considered the oldest church in Cuba. It was built of wood in 1522, and every time it was destroyed by pirate raids, hurricanes and fires it was rebuilt, most recently in 1680. Sancti Spíritus is one of the seven cities that Diego Velázquez founded in Cuba.

Sancti Spíritus

La iglesia parroquial del Espíritu Santo (en la capital provincial de Sancti Spíritus) es considerada la más antigua de Cuba. Se construyó en madera en 1522, pero cada vez que fue destruida por piratas, huracanes e incendios se volvió a reconstruir (la última reconstrucción tuvo lugar en 1680). Sancti Spíritus es una de las siete ciudades que Diego Velázquez fundó en Cuba.

Sancti Spíritus

L'église paroissiale Espíritu Santo (Saint-Esprit) de Sancti Spíritus, capitale de la province éponyme, serait la plus ancienne de l'île. Elle fut bâtie en bois en 1522 et reconstruite après chaque attaque de pirates, ouragan et incendie, jusqu'à la version actuelle datant de 1680. Sancti Spíritus est l'une des sept villes fondées par Diego Velázquez sur Cuba.

Sancti Spíritus

A igreja paroquial Espíritu Santo (Espírito Santo) na capital da província de Sancti Spíritus é considerada a igreja mais antiga de Cuba. Foi construída em madeira em 1522, mas toda vez que foi destruída por ataques de piratas, furacões e incêndios foi reconstruída, mais recentemente em 1680. Sancti Spíritus é uma das sete cidades que Diego Velázquez fundou em Cuba.

Sancti Spíritus

Die Pfarrkirche Espíritu Santo (Heiliger Geist) in der Provinzhauptstadt Sancti Spíritus gilt als älteste Kirche Kubas. 1522 wurde sie aus Holz erbaut, doch jedes Mal, wenn sie durch Piratenüberfälle, Hurrikans und Brände zerstört wurde, baute man sie wieder auf, zuletzt 1680. Sancti Spíritus gehört zu den sieben Städten, die Diego Velázquez auf Kuba gründete.

Sancti Spíritus

De parochiekerk van Espíritu Santo (Heilige Geest) in de provinciale hoofdstad van Sancti Spíritus wordt beschouwd als de oudste kerk van Cuba. Ze werd in 1522 van hout gebouwd, en elke keer dat ze door pirateninvallen, orkanen en branden werd verwoest werd het weer herbouwd, voor het laatst in 1680. Sancti Spíritus is één van de zeven steden die Diego Velázquez gesticht heeft in Cuba.

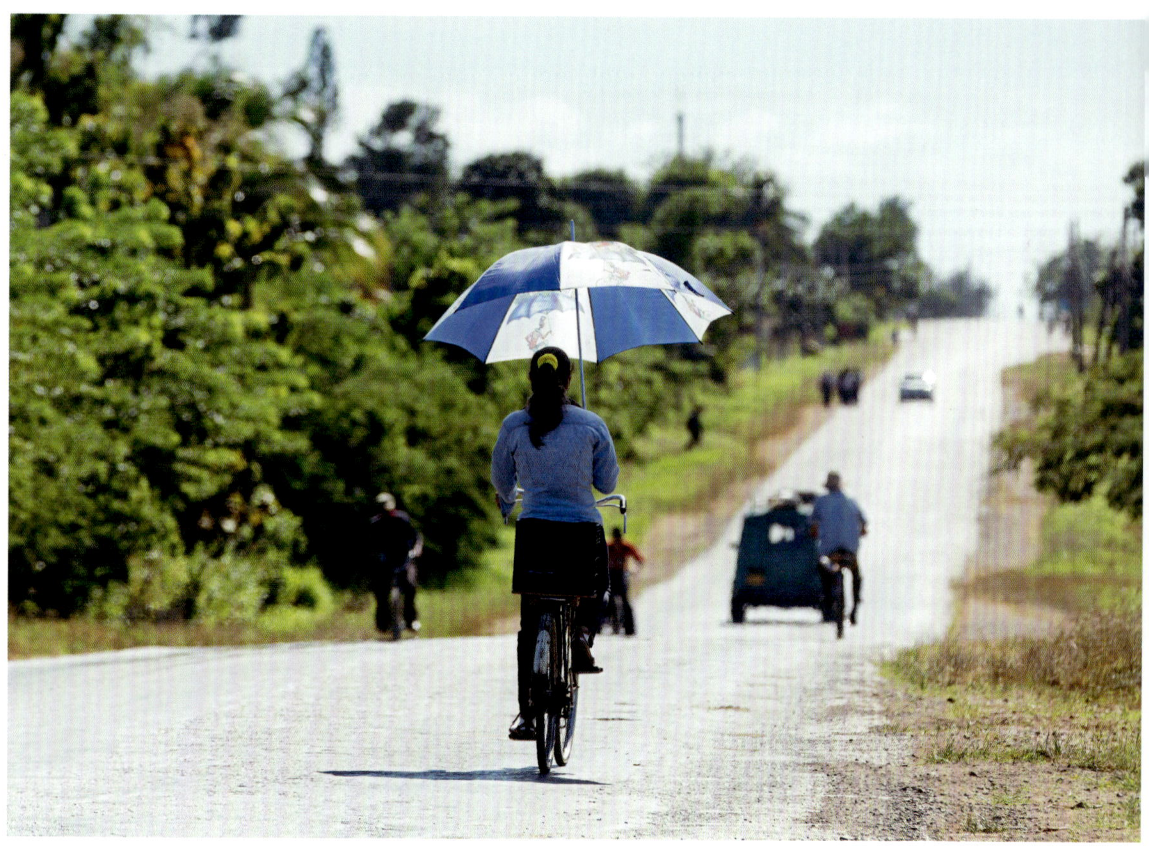

Esperanza

Revolutionary Slogan

In the early 1960s, when revolutionary icon Che Guevara was Cuba's minister of industry and head of the Cuban National Bank, the many American cars on Cuba were considered to be rolling relics of U.S. imperialism. In the meantime, they have even survived Fidel Castro, and the slogan "Always to Victory" (Hasta la victoria siempre), which has been ubiquitous since the early 1960s, is given an unintentionally ironic aftertaste in view of the supply problems that have persisted since the 1990s, the lack of transport, the failed agrarian reforms, the escalating bureaucracy and the bizarre coexistence of foreign exchange and Cuban pesos.

Slogan révolutionnaire

Au début des années 1960, alors que l'icône de la révolution, Che Guevara, était ministre de l'Industrie et directeur de la Banque nationale, les nombreuses grosses voitures américaines à Cuba étaient considérées comme des reliques mobiles de l'impérialisme américain. Elles ont pourtant survécu, même à Fidel Castro, et le slogan omniprésent des années 1960 *« Hasta la victoria siempre »* (Jusqu'à la victoire, toujours) s'est teinté d'un arrière-goût d'ironie au regard des problèmes d'approvisionnement récurrents depuis les années 1990, du manque de transports, de l'échec des réformes agraires, de l'étouffante bureaucratie et de la coexistence étrange des devises et du peso cubain.

Revolutions-Slogan

Zu Anfang der 1960er-Jahre, als die Revolutions-Ikone Che Guevara Kubas Industrieminister und Chef der kubanischen Nationalbank war, galten die vielen Ami-Schlitten auf Kuba als rollende Relikte des US-Imperialismus. Mittlerweile haben sie sogar Fidel Castro überlebt, und der seit Anfang der 1960er-Jahre allgegenwärtige Slogan „Immer bis zum Sieg" (Hasta la victoria siempre) bekommt angesichts der seit den 1990er-Jahren anhaltenden Versorgungsprobleme, des fehlenden Transports, der gescheiterten Agrarreformen, der ausufernden Bürokratie und der bizarren Koexistenz von Devisen und kubanischen Peso einen ungewollt ironischen Beigeschmack.

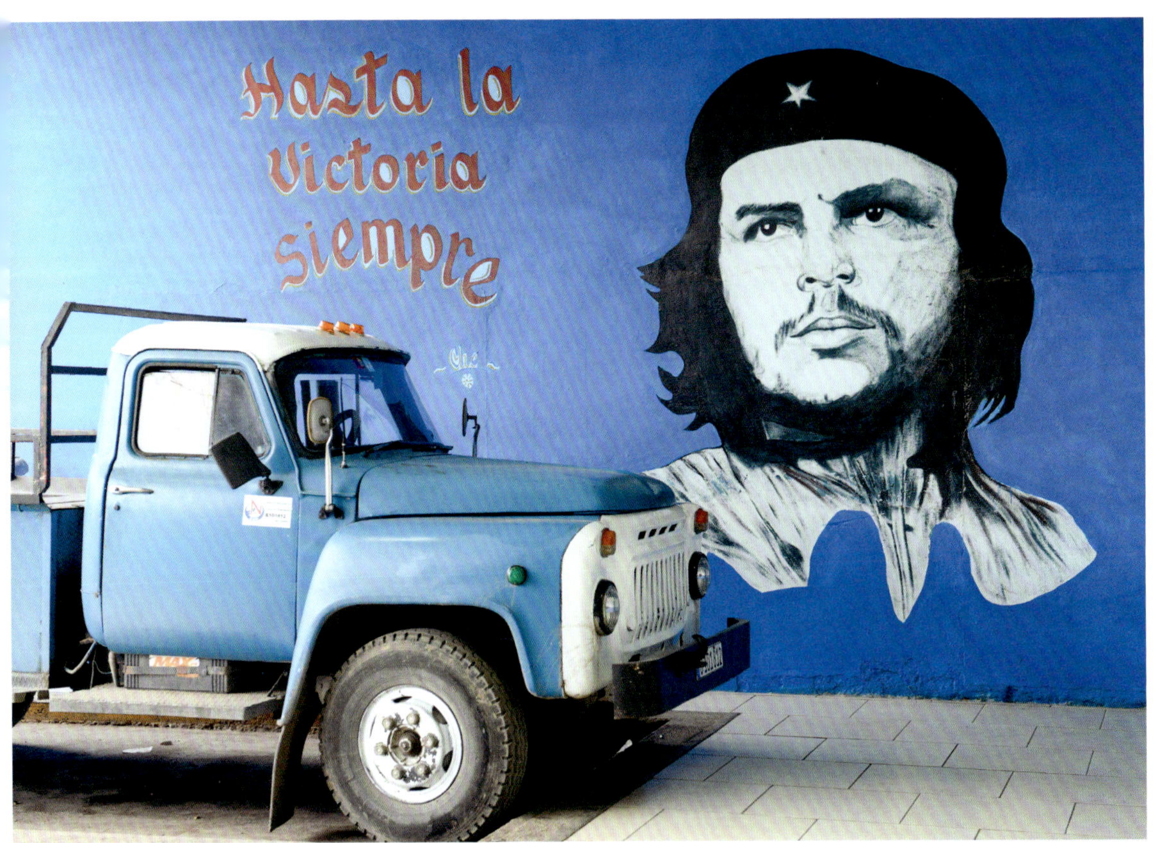

Santa Clara, Provincia Villa Clara
Santa Clara, Villa Clara Province

Lema revolucionario

A principios de la década de 1960, cuando el icono revolucionario Che Guevara era ministro de industria de Cuba y jefe del Banco Nacional de Cuba, los numerosos coches estadounidenses de Cuba se consideraban reliquias rodantes del imperialismo estadounidense. Mientras tanto, incluso han sobrevivido a Fidel Castro, y el eslogan "Hasta la victoria siempre", que ha sido omnipresente desde principios de los años sesenta, tiene un sabor irónico involuntario en vista de los problemas de suministro que han persistido desde los años noventa, la falta de transporte, las fallidas reformas agrarias, la escalada de la burocracia y la extraña coexistencia de divisas y pesos cubanos.

Slogan revolucionário

No início da década de 1960, quando o ícone revolucionário Che Guevara era Ministro da Indústria de Cuba e Chefe do Banco Nacional Cubano, os muitos carros antigos coloridos americanos em Cuba eram considerados relíquias circulantes do imperialismo dos EUA. De lá para cá, eles até sobreviveram a Fidel Castro, e o slogan "Sempre à vitória" (Hasta la victoria siempre), que tem sido onipresente desde o início dos anos 60, recebe um sabor irônico e não intencional diante dos problemas de abastecimento que persistem desde os anos 90, da falta de transporte, das reformas agrárias fracassadas, da burocracia crescente e da bizarra coexistência de divisas e pesos cubanos.

Revolutionaire slogan

In het begin van de jaren zestig, toen het revolutionaire icoon Che Guevara Cuba's minister van Industrie en hoofd van de Cubaanse Nationale Bank was, werden de vele Amerikaanse sleeën op Cuba beschouwd als rollende overblijfselen van het Amerikaanse imperialisme. Ondertussen hebben ze zelfs Fidel Castro overleefd, en de slogan 'Always to Victory' (Hasta la victoria siempre), die alomtegenwoordig is sinds het begin van de jaren zestig, krijgt een onbedoeld ironische nasmaak, gezien de bevoorradingsproblemen die sinds de jaren negentig zijn blijven bestaan, het gebrek aan vervoer, de mislukte landbouwhervormingen, de escalerende bureaucratie en de bizarre coëxistentie van deviezen en Cubaanse pesos.

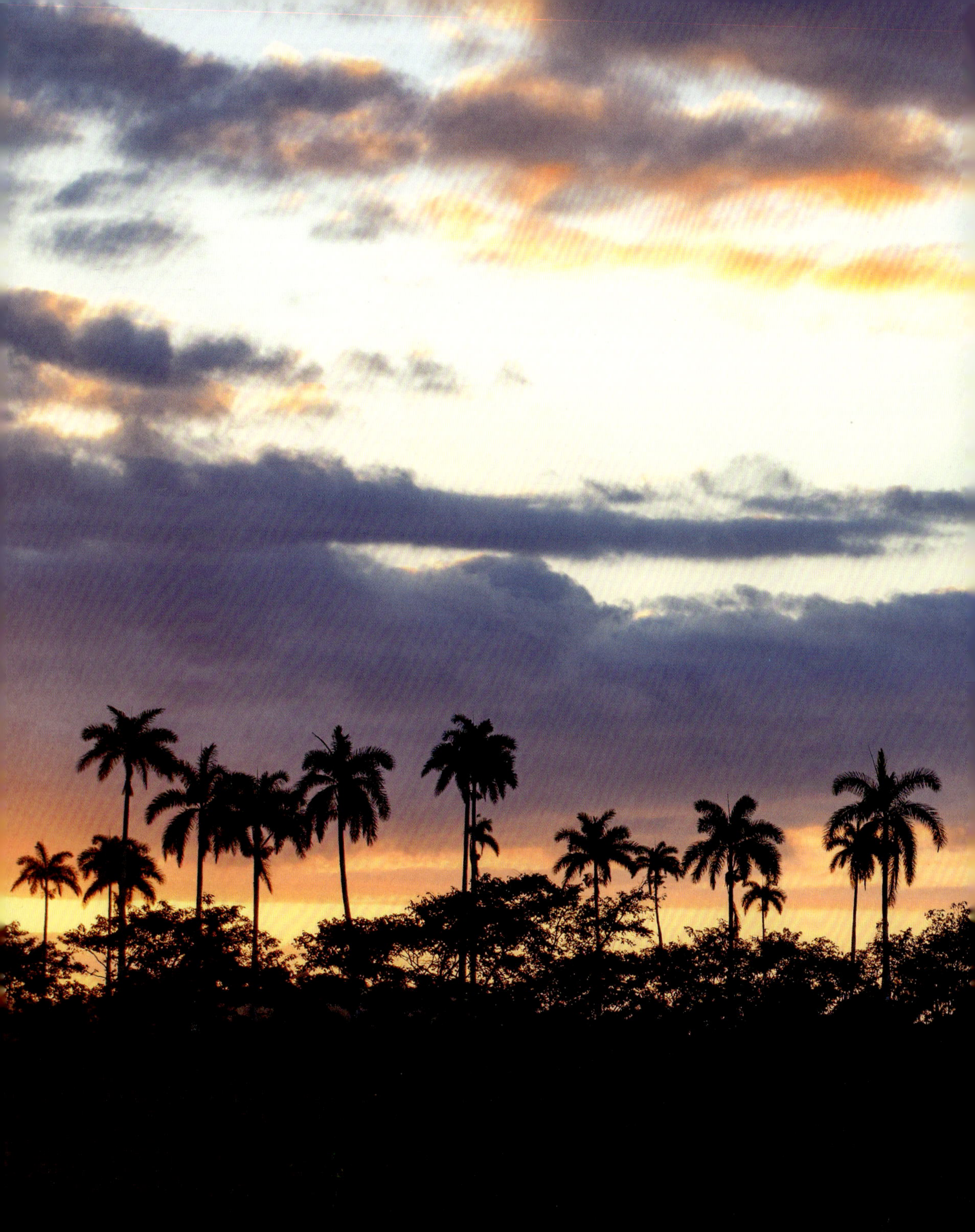

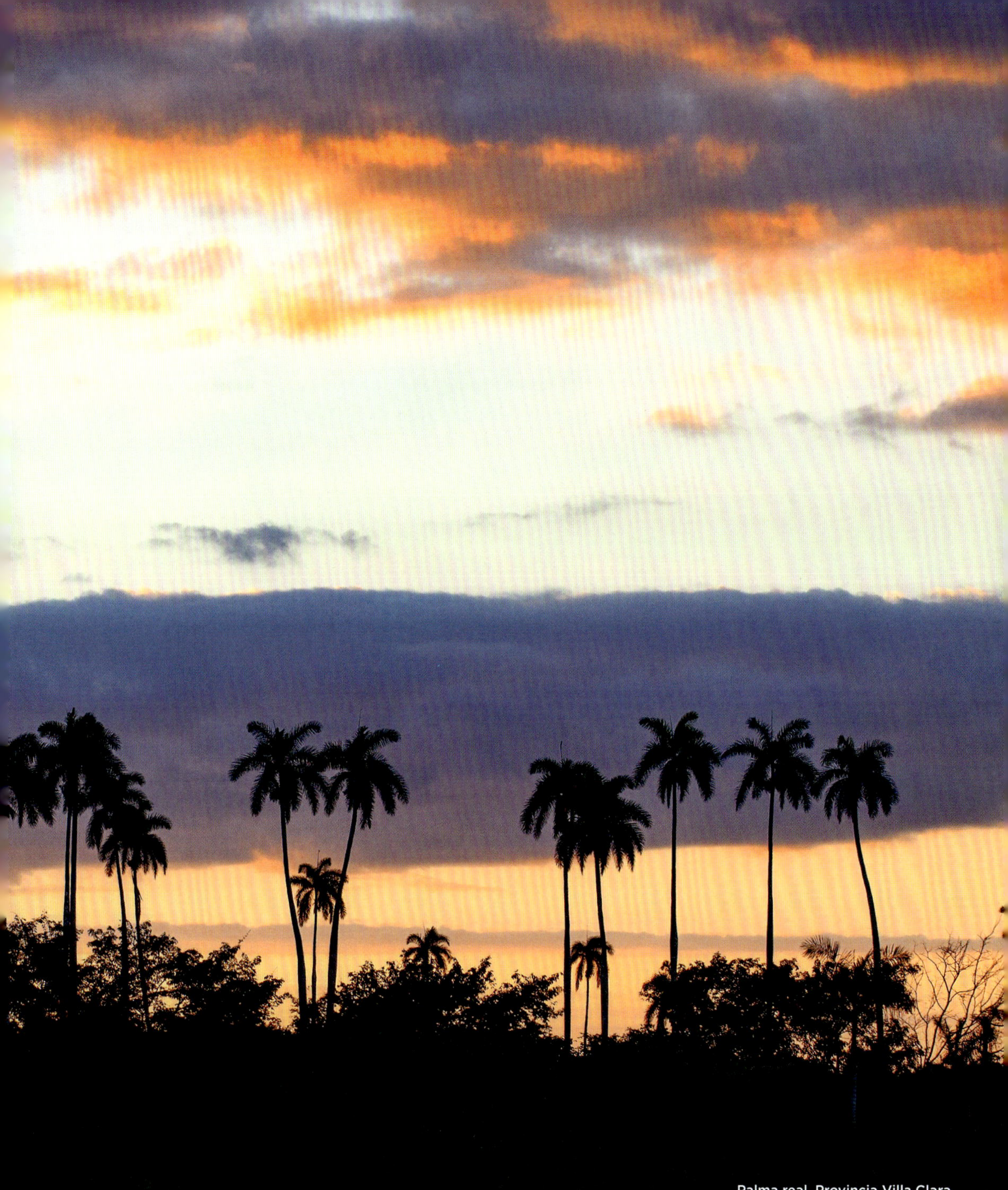

Palma real, Provincia Villa Clara
Cuban royal palm, Villa Clara Province

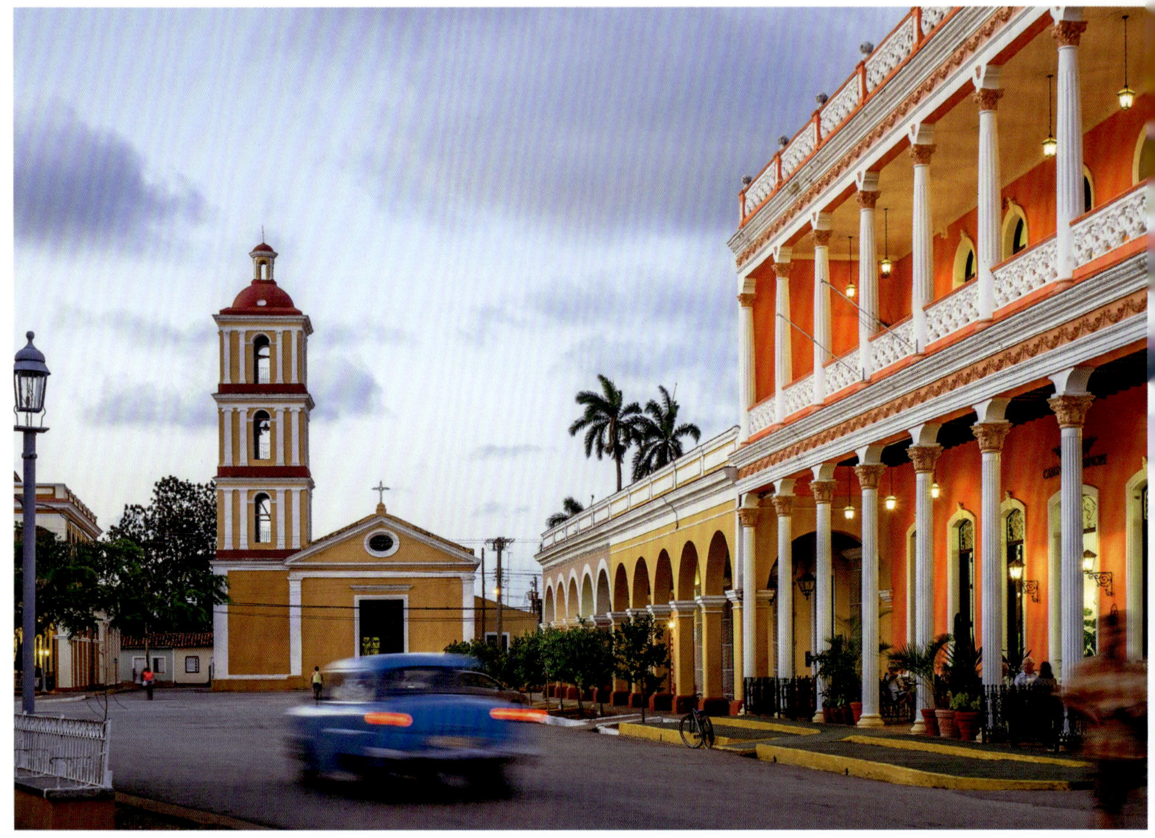

Remedios, Provincia Villa Clara
Remedios, Villa Clara Province

Remedios

Remedios is by no means as famous as Trinidad, and perhaps that's why the little town has been able to preserve much of its dreamy charm. Like almost all cities in central Cuba, Remedios, founded in 1514 by Diego Velázquez, benefited from slaves and sugar cultivation, which is clearly reflected in the cityscape. A special feature: The central Plaza Martí is flanked by two Catholic churches, one from the 18th century and one from 1692 (Parish Church of St. John the Baptist). The square is named after Cuba's national hero José Martí (1853–95), spiritual leader of the independence movement, journalist, intellectual and poet.

Remedios

Remedios est nettement moins célèbre que Trinidad et a, peut-être pour cette raison, conservé nombre de ses charmes idylliques. Comme pratiquement toutes les villes au centre de Cuba, Remedios, fondée par Diego Velázquez en 1514, a tiré profit des esclaves et de la culture de la canne à sucre, ce dont témoigne clairement la physionomie de la ville. Elle compte une particularité : la place centrale, Plaza Martí, est flanquée de deux églises catholiques, l'une datant du XVIIIᵉ siècle et l'autre de 1692 (église paroissiale San Juan Bautista). La place porte le nom du héros national cubain José Martí (1853–1895), guide spirituel du mouvement de l'indépendance, journaliste, intellectuel et poète.

Remedios

Remedios ist längst nicht so berühmt wie Trinidad, vielleicht konnte das Städtchen deshalb viel von seinem verträumten Charme bewahren. Wie nahezu alle Städte in Zentralkuba profitierte auch das 1514 von Diego Velázquez gegründete Remedios von Sklaven und vom Zuckeranbau, was sich deutlich im Stadtbild widerspiegelt. Eine Besonderheit: Die zentrale Plaza Martí wird gleich von zwei katholischen Kirchen flankiert, eine aus dem 18. Jahrhundert, eine von 1692 (Pfarrkirche Johannes der Täufer). Benannt ist der Platz nach Kubas Nationalheld José Martí (1853–95), geistiger Führer der Unabhängigkeitsbewegung, Journalist, Intellektueller und Dichter.

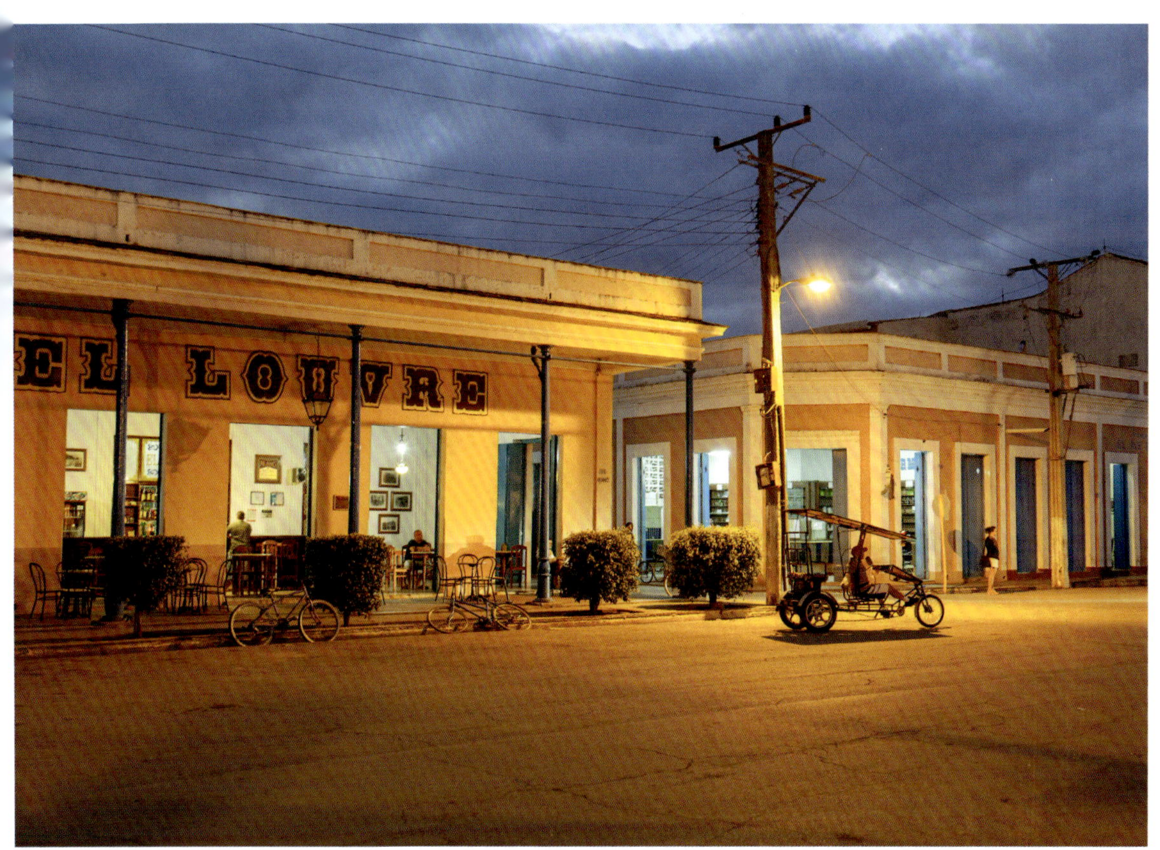

Plaza Mayor, Remedios, Provincia Villa Clara
Plaza Mayor, Remedios, Villa Clara Province

Remedios

Remedios no es tan famoso como Trinidad, y tal vez por eso el pequeño pueblo pudo conservar gran parte de su encanto de ensueño. Como casi todas las ciudades del centro de Cuba, Remedios (fundada en 1514 por Diego Velázquez) se benefició de los esclavos y del cultivo de azúcar, lo que se refleja claramente en el paisaje urbano. Una particularidad: la céntrica Plaza Martí está flanqueada por dos iglesias católicas, una del siglo XVIII y otra de 1692 (iglesia parroquial de San Juan Bautista). La plaza lleva el nombre del héroe nacional cubano José Martí (1853–95), líder espiritual del movimiento independentista, periodista, intelectual y poeta.

Remedios

Remedios está longe de ser tão famoso como Trinidad, talvez por isso a pequena cidade tenha sido capaz de preservar muito do seu charme sonhador. Como quase todas as outras cidades do centro de Cuba, Remedios, fundada em 1514 por Diego Velázquez, se beneficiava dos escravos e do cultivo de açúcar, que se reflete claramente na paisagem urbana. Uma característica especial: a Plaza Martí central é cercada por duas igrejas católicas, uma do século XVIII e outra de 1692 (igreja paroquial de São João Batista). A praça recebeu o nome do herói nacional de Cuba, José Martí (1853–95), líder espiritual do movimento independentista, jornalista, intelectual e poeta.

Remedios

Remedios is lang niet zo beroemd als Trinidad, misschien is dat wel de reden waarom het stadje veel van zijn dromerige charme heeft weten te behouden. Zoals bijna alle steden in Centraal Cuba, profiteerde Remedios, gesticht in 1514 door Diego Velázquez, van de slaven- en suikerteelt, wat duidelijk terug te vinden is in het stadsbeeld. Een bijzonderheid: Het centrale Plaza Martí wordt geflankeerd door twee katholieke kerken, een uit de 18e eeuw en een uit 1692 (parochiekerk van Johannes de Doper). Het plein is vernoemd naar Cuba's nationale held José Martí (1853–95), de geestelijke leider van de onafhankelijkheidsbeweging, journalist, intellectueel en dichter.

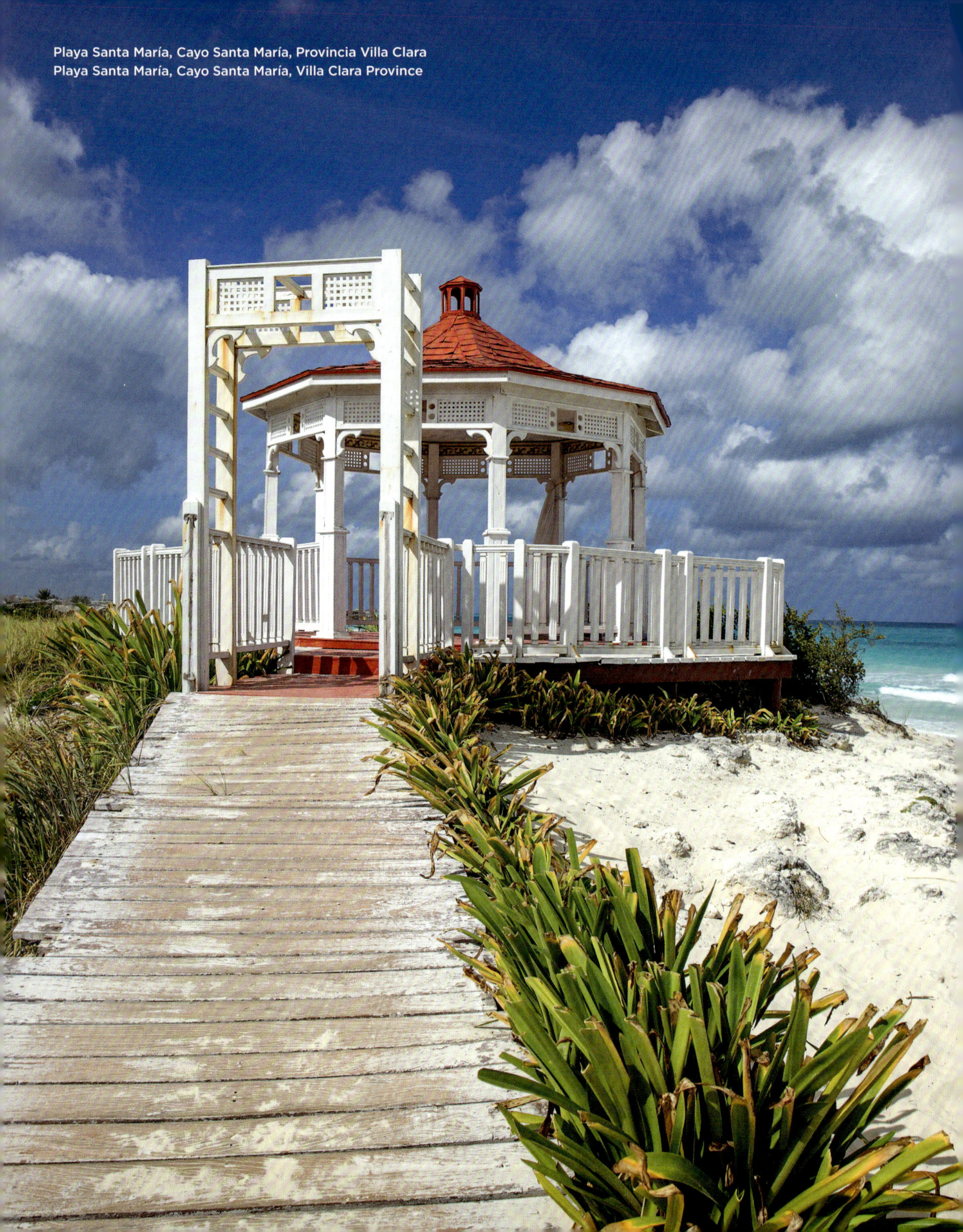

Playa Santa María, Cayo Santa María, Provincia Villa Clara
Playa Santa María, Cayo Santa María, Villa Clara Province

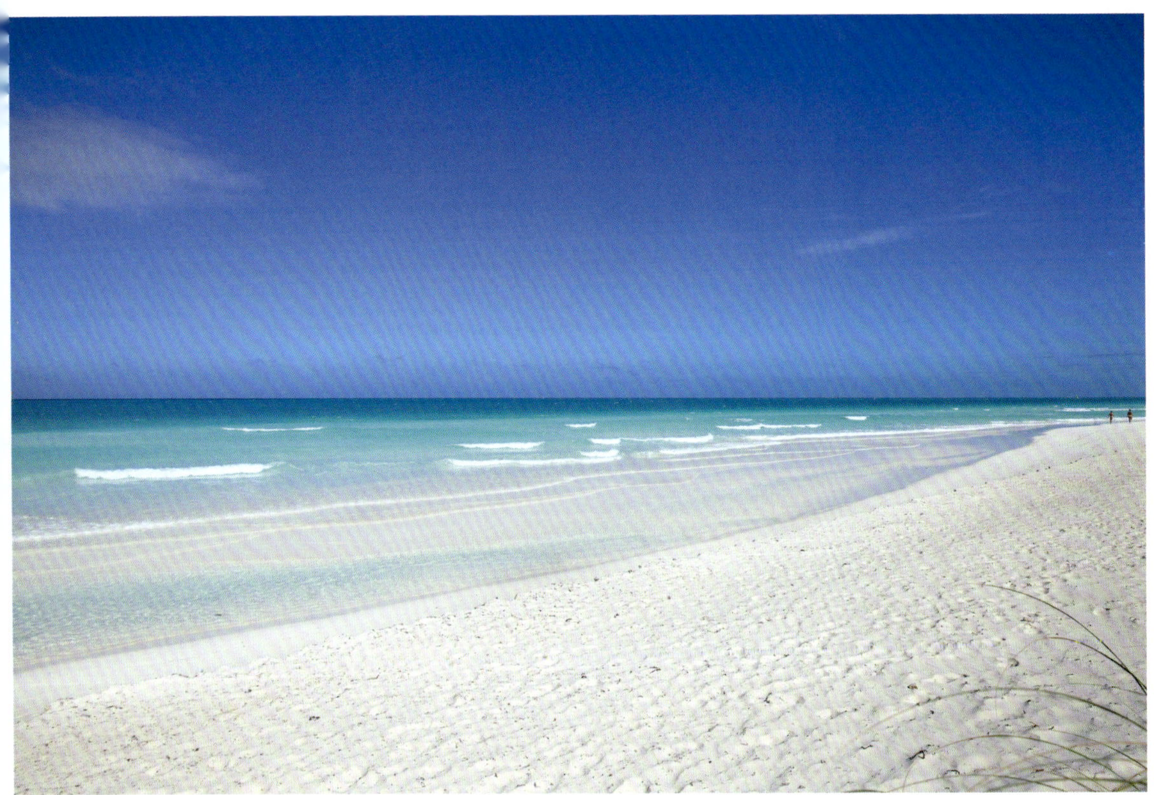

Playa Santa María, Cayo Santa María, Provincia Villa Clara
Playa Santa María, Cayo Santa María, Villa Clara, Province

Cayo Santa María

From Caibarién on the north coast, a 50 km (30 mi.) long stone dam leads through the turquoise sea to the idyllic islets of the Cayería del Norte. Only after 38 km (23 mi.) will you reach the first Cayo (Las Brujas). The Cayo Santa María is the largest island of the archipelago, and is the best developed for tourism. Nevertheless, you can find secluded dream beaches here.

Cayo Santa María

Desde Caibarién, en la costa norte, una presa de piedra de 50 km de longitud conduce a través del mar turquesa hasta los paradisíacos islotes de la Cayería del Norte. Solo después de 38 km se llega al primer Cayo (Las Brujas). El Cayo Santa María es la isla más grande del archipiélago y la mejor desarrollada para el turismo. Y aun así aquí se encuentran playas de ensueño.

Cayo Santa María

Sur la côte nord, une digue de pierres de 50 km de long s'avance dans les eaux turquoise et relie Caibarién aux îlots de la Cayería del Norte. Le premier *cayo* (Las Brujas) que rejoint la digue est à 38 km. Cayo Santa María est la plus grande île de l'archipel et la plus développée d'un point de vue touristique. On y trouve tout de même des plages idylliques isolées.

Cayo Santa Maria

De Caibarién, na costa norte, uma barragem de pedra de 50 km de comprimento leva através do mar azul-turquesa até os ilhéus paradisíacos da Cayería del Norte. Só depois de 38 km se chega ao primeiro Cayo (Las Brujas). O Cayo Santa María é a maior ilha do arquipélago e melhor desenvolvida para o turismo. Mesmo assim, aqui se encontram praias desertas de sonho.

Cayo Santa María

Von Caibarién an der Nordküste führt ein 50 km langer Steindamm durch die türkisfarbene See auf die paradiesischen Inselchen der Cayería del Norte. Erst nach 38 km hat man den ersten Cayo (Las Brujas) erreicht. Der Cayo Santa María ist die größte Insel des Archipels und am besten touristisch erschlossen. Trotzdem findet man hier einsame Traumstrände.

Cayo Santa Maria

Vanaf Caibarién aan de noordkust leidt een 50 km lange stenen dam door de turquoise zee naar de paradijselijke eilandjes van de Cayería del Norte. Pas na 38 km bereik je de eerste Cayo (Las Brujas). De Cayo Santa Maria is het grootste eiland van de archipel en het best ontwikkeld voor het toerisme. Toch vindt men hier eenzame droomstranden.

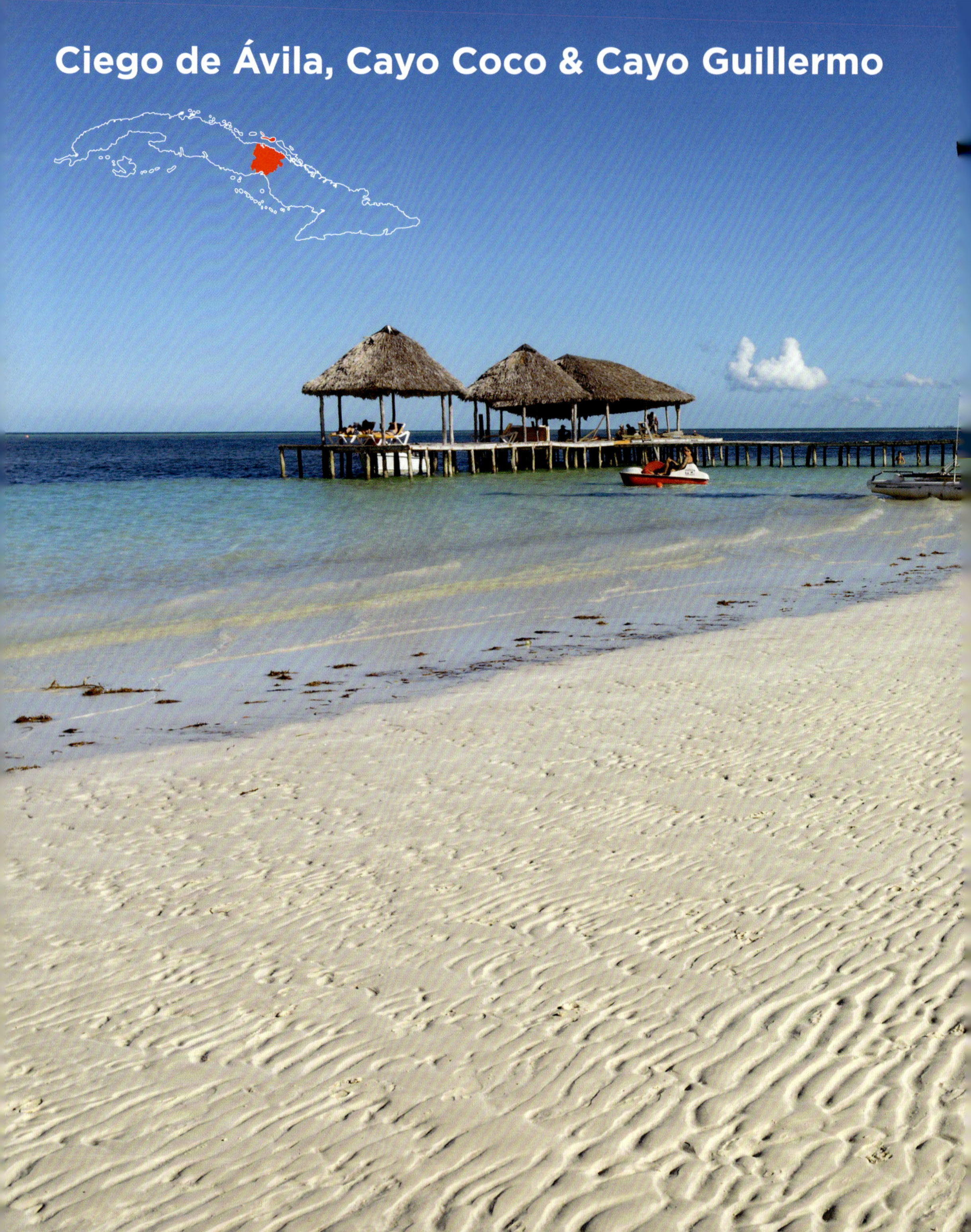
Ciego de Ávila, Cayo Coco & Cayo Guillermo

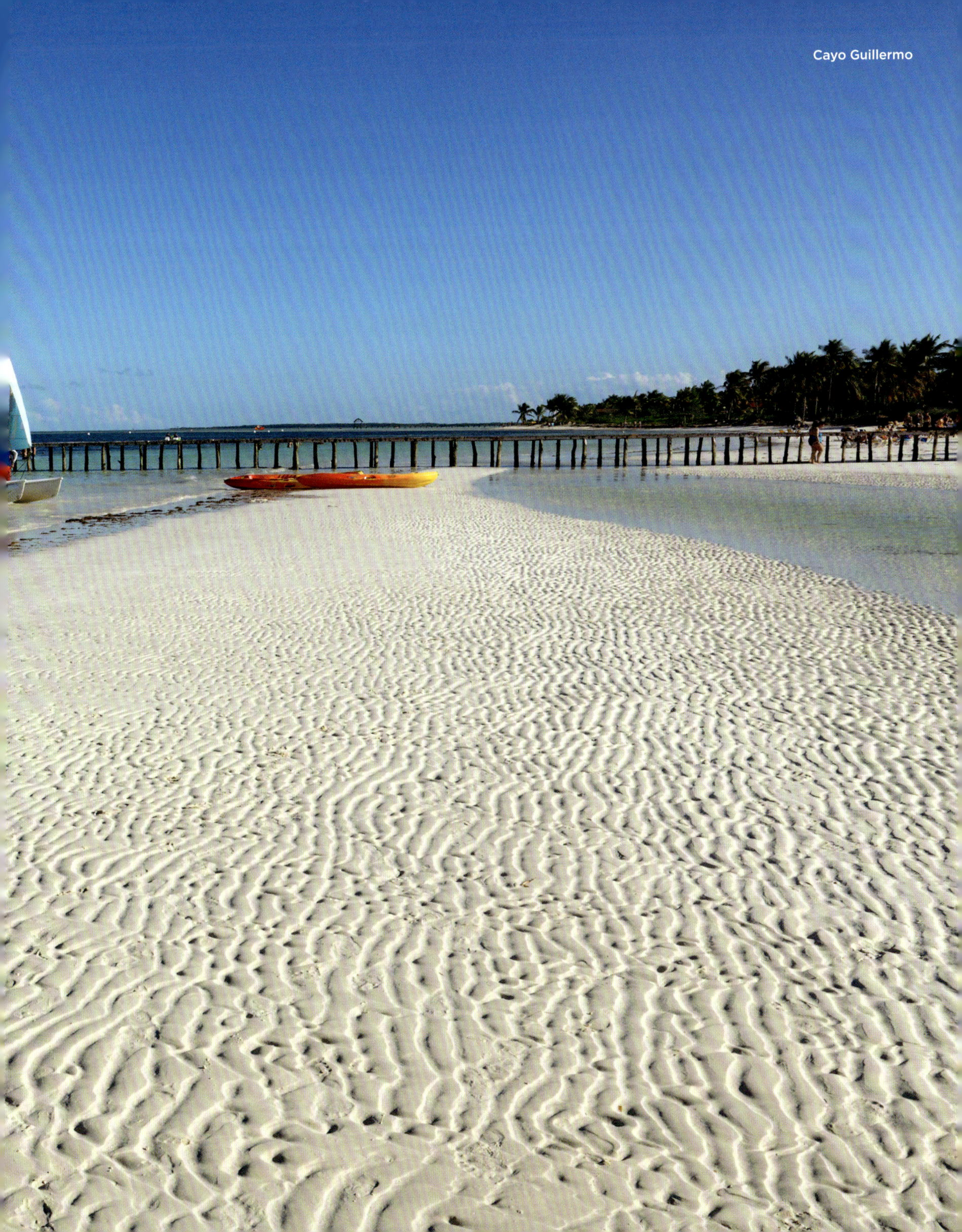
Cayo Guillermo

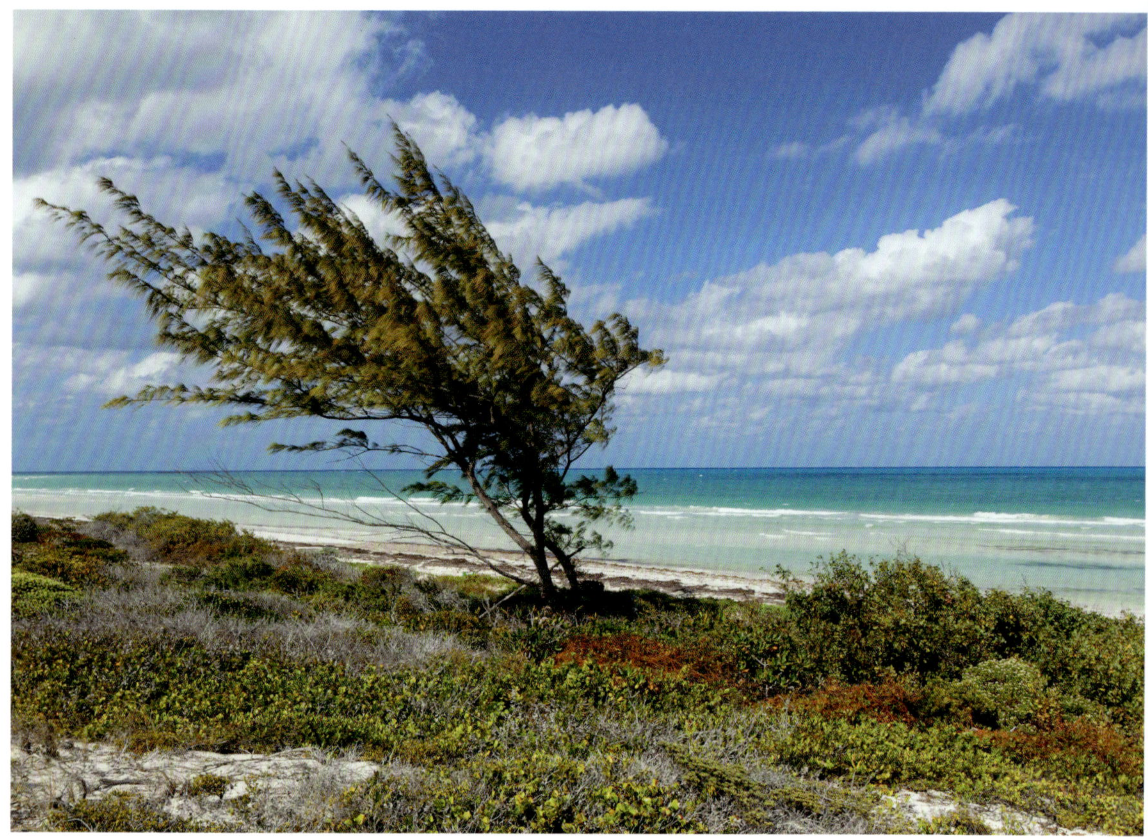

Playa del Norte, Cayo Coco

Ciego de Ávila, Cayo Coco and Cayo Guillermo

The flat province of Ciego de Ávila lies on a vast plain where sugar plantations used to stretch to the horizon. Today it is mainly used for cattle breeding, citrus fruit and pineapples. Most tourists ignore the provincial capital of the same name because the absolute jewel of the province is located off the north coast: the countless tiny islands of the "Garden of the King" (Jardines del Rey) archipelago, among them Cayo Coco and Cayo Guillermo, with their kilometers of white sandy beaches. The Cayos are protected by a 400 km (250 mi.) long coral reef, the second largest in the world, and mangrove forests.

Ciego de Ávila, Cayo Coco et Cayo Guillermo

La plate province de Ciego de Ávila se situe sur un vaste plateau autrefois recouvert à perte de vue de plantations de canne. Aujourd'hui, la région pratique essentiellement l'élevage et la culture des agrumes et des ananas. La majorité des touristes délaisse la capitale locale homonyme pour le grand atout de la province, au large de la côte nord : les innombrables îlots de l'archipel Jardines del Rey (jardins du roi), dont Cayo Coco et Cayo Guillermo, arborent des kilomètres de plages de sable blanc. Les *cayos* sont protégés par un récif de corail de 400 km de long, le plus vaste du monde, et par des forêts de mangrove.

Ciego de Ávila, Cayo Coco und Cayo Guillermo

Die tischflache Provinz Ciego de Ávila liegt in einer weiten Ebene, in der sich früher die Zuckerplantagen bis zum Horizont dehnten. Heute wird hier vor allem Viehzucht betrieben, Zitrusfrüchte und Ananas angebaut. Die meisten Touristen lassen die gleichnamige Provinzhauptstadt links liegen, denn vor der Nordküste befindet sich der absolute Joker der Provinz: die unzähligen winzigen Inseln des Archipels „Gärten des Königs" (Jardines del Rey), darunter Cayo Coco und Cayo Guillermo, mit ihren kilometerlangen blütenweißen Sandstränden. Geschützt werden die Cayos von einem 400 km langen Korallenriff, das zweitgrößte der Welt, sowie Mangrovenwäldern.

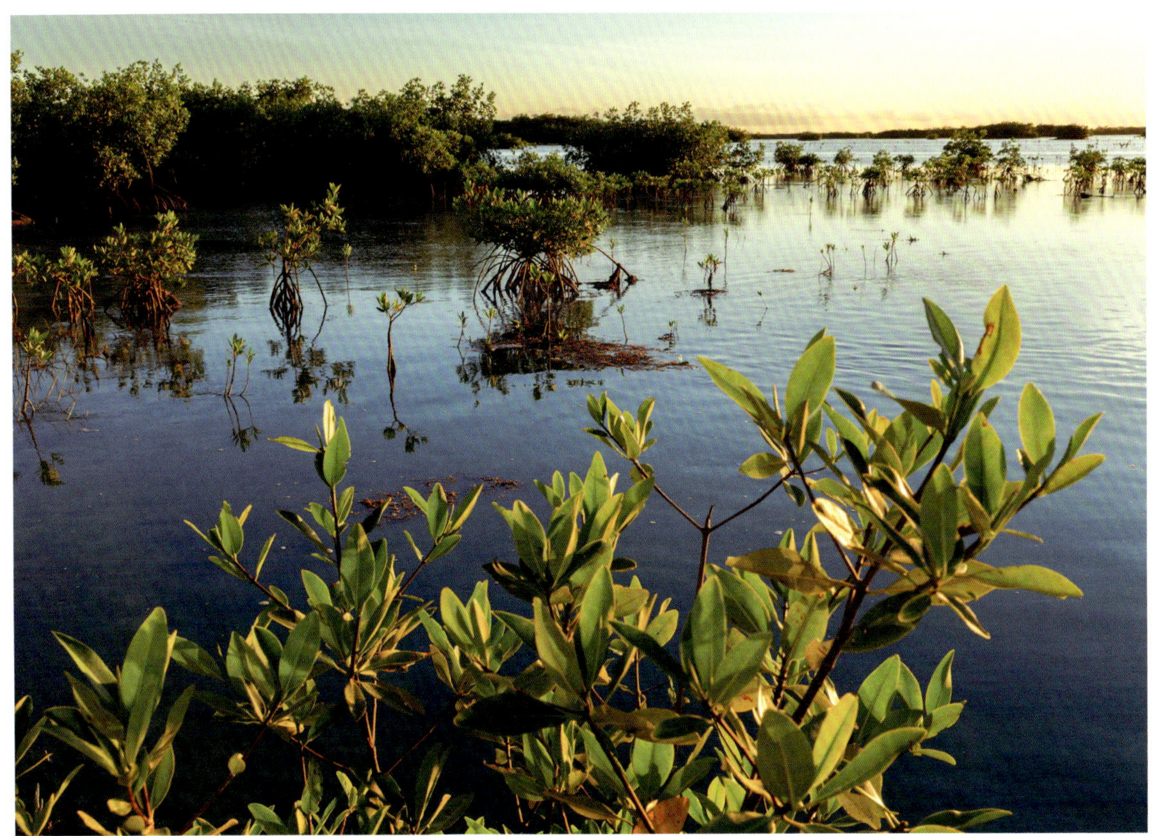

Parque Natural El Bagá, Cayo Coco
El Bagá Natural Park, Cayo Coco

Ciego de Ávila, Cayo Coco
y Cayo Guillermo

La llana provincia de Ciego de Ávila se
encuentra en una vasta llanura donde antes
se extendían las plantaciones de azúcar
hasta el horizonte. Hoy en día se utiliza
principalmente para la cría de ganado,
cítricos y piñas. La mayoría de los turistas
dejan la capital de la provincia del mismo
nombre a la izquierda porque el comodín
absoluto de la provincia se encuentra
frente a la costa norte: las innumerables
islas diminutas del archipiélago "Jardines
del Rey", entre ellas Cayo Coco y Cayo
Guillermo, con sus kilométricas playas de
arena blanca. Los cayos están protegidos
por un arrecife de coral de 400 km de
largo, el segundo más grande del mundo, y
por bosques de manglares.

Ciego de Ávila, Cayo Coco
e Cayo Guillermo

A província de Ciego de Ávila situa-se
numa vasta planície onde as plantações de
açúcar se estendem até ao horizonte. Hoje
em dia,encontram-se aqui principalmente
a criação de gado, e o cultivo de frutas
cítricas e ananases. A maioria dos turistas
deixa de lado a capital provincial de
mesmo nome, porque o coringa absoluto
da província está localizado em frente à
costa norte: as inúmeras e pequenas ilhas
do arquipélago "Jardim do Rei" (Jardines
del Rey), entre elas Cayo Coco e Cayo
Guillermo, com seus quilômetros de praias
de areia branca. Os Cayos são protegidos
por um recife de corais de 400 km de
comprimento, o segundo maior do mundo,
e por florestas de mangue.

Ciego de Ávila, Cayo Coco Coco
en Cayo Guillermo

De vlakke provincie Ciego de Ávila ligt
op een uitgestrekte vlakte waar vroeger
suikerplantages tot aan de horizon reikten.
Tegenwoordig wordt het voornamelijk
gebruikt voor de veeteelt, en de aanbouw
van citrusvruchten en ananas. De
meeste toeristen laten de gelijknamige
provinciehoofdstad links liggen omdat voor
de noordkust de absolute joker bevindt: de
ontelbare kleine eilandjes van de archipel
'Garden of the King' (Jardines del Rey),
waaronder Cayo Coco en Cayo Guillermo,
met hun kilometers witte zandstranden.
De Cayos worden beschermd door een
400 km lang koraalrif, het op een na
grootste koraalrif ter wereld, zoals ook
mangrovebossen.

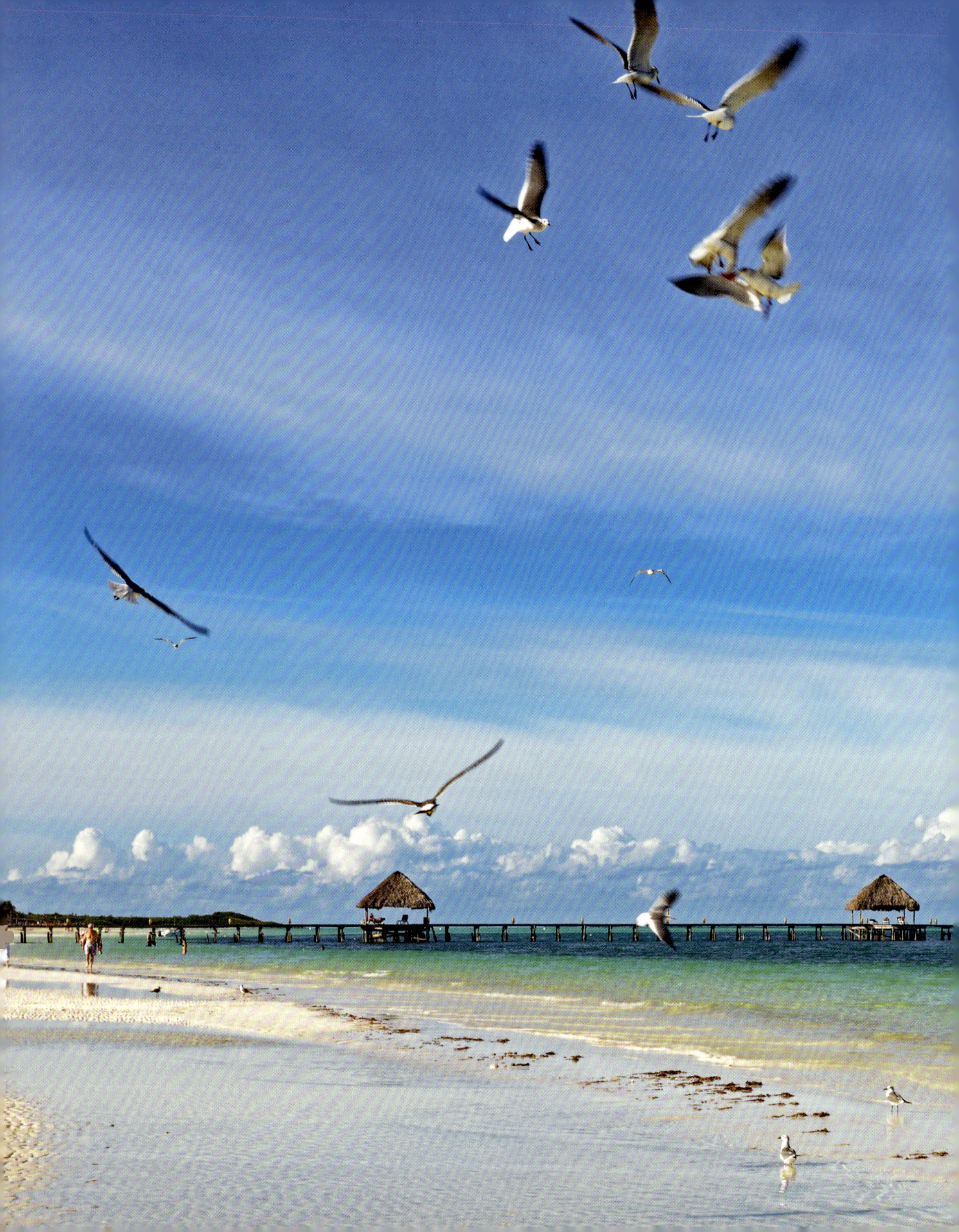

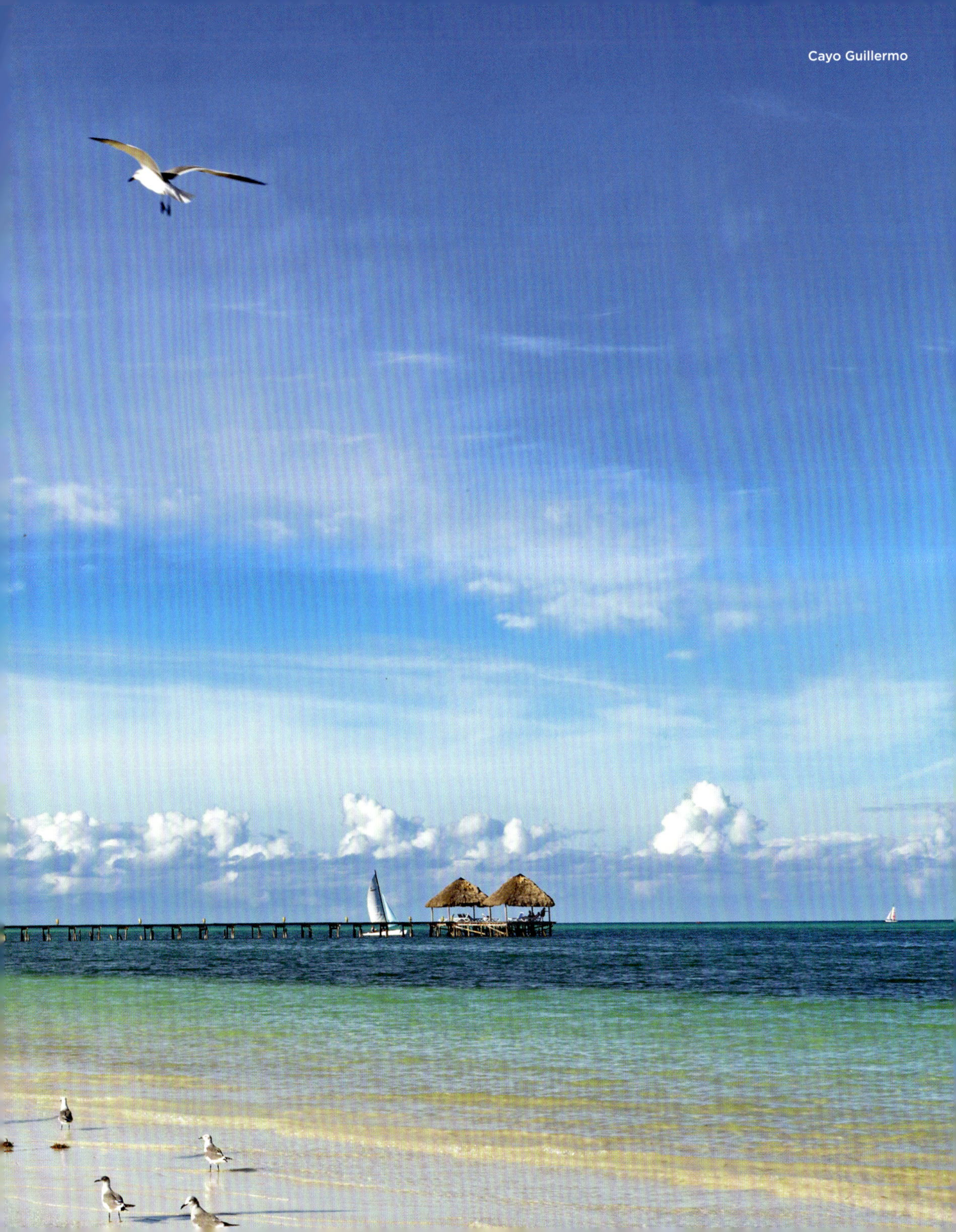

Cayo Guillermo

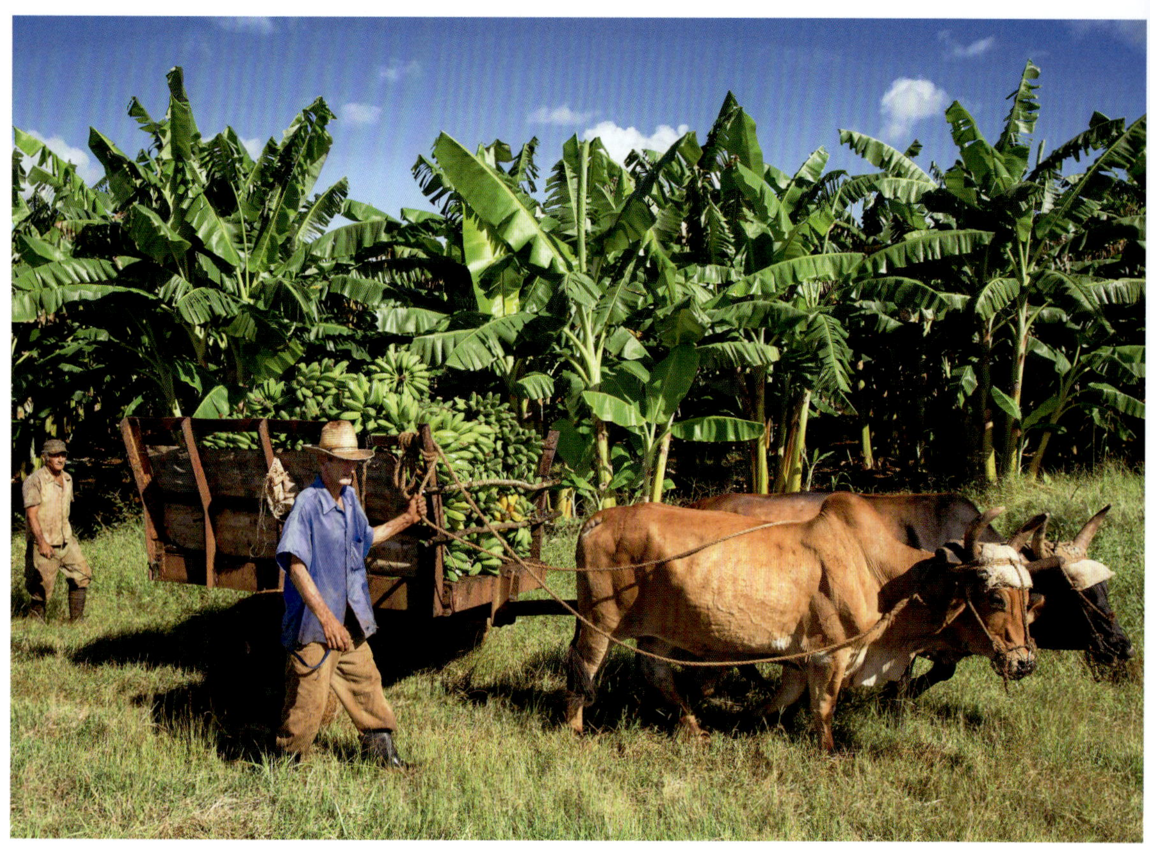

Plantación de bananas, Morón
Banana plantation near Morón

Pineapple

The province of Ciego de Ávila is the leader in Cuban pineapple production. The particularly sweet and juicy hybrid variety MD-2, which has also been exported to Europe since 2015, is cultivated here. In the eastern provinces of Cuba, pineapples are also popular in the kitchen, and chicken braised in pineapple is a popular dish. But above all, pineapple is needed for the Piña Colada cocktail, prepared in a blender with white rum, sugar, lime juice, coconut cream, ice cream and pineapple juice. The green harvested plantains (*plátano*) are as popular in Cuba as potatoes elsewhere, and are on the daily menu.

Ananas

La province Ciego de Ávila est la grande productrice d'ananas de l'île. La variété principale cultivée est l'hybride MD-2, exportée vers l'Europe depuis 2015. Dans les provinces est de Cuba, l'ananas est également très présent dans la cuisine, avec notamment le très apprécié poulet à l'ananas à l'étuvée. Toutefois, le fruit entre surtout dans la composition du cocktail piña colada, qui marie rhum blanc, sucre, jus de limette, crème de noix de coco, glaçons et jus d'ananas. Les bananes plantains (*plátano*) récoltées vertes sont aussi courantes à Cuba que les pommes de terre ailleurs et sont consommées quotidiennement.

Ananas

Die Provinz Ciego de Ávila ist Spitzenreiter der kubanischen Ananas-Produktion. Hier wird vor allem die besonders süße und saftige Hybrid-Sorte MD-2 angebaut, die seit 2015 auch nach Europa exportiert wird. In den östlichen Provinzen Kubas verwendet man die Ananas auch gern in der Küche, mit Ananas geschmortes Hühnchen ist ein beliebtes Gericht. Doch vor allem braucht man die Ananas für den Cocktail Piña Colada, im Mixer zubereitet mit weißem Rum, Zucker, Limettensaft, Kokosnusscreme, Eis und Ananassaft. Die grün geernteten Kochbananen (*plátano*) sind in Kuba so populär wie andernorts die Kartoffeln und stehen täglich auf dem Speiseplan.

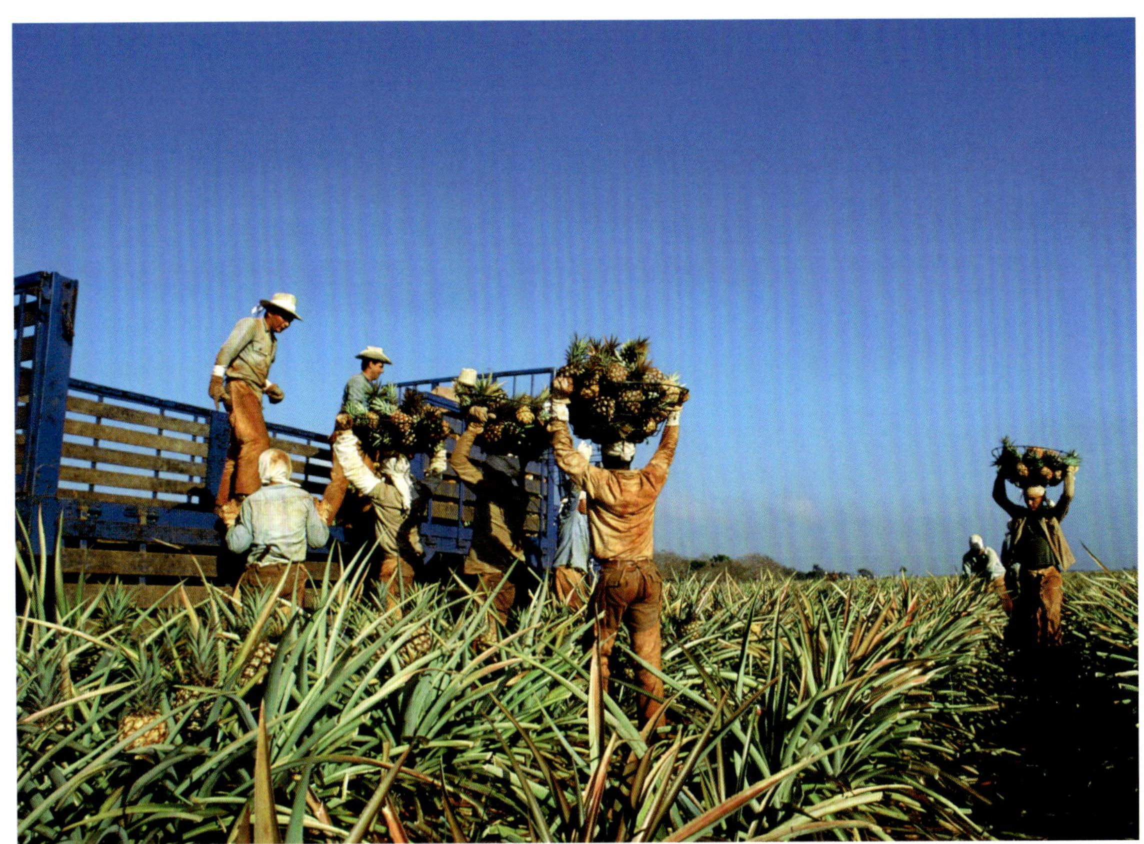

Cosecha de piña cerca de Ciego de Ávila
Pineapple harvest near Ciego de Ávila

Piña

La provincia de Ciego de Ávila es líder en la producción de piña cubana. Aquí se cultiva la variedad híbrida MD-2, especialmente dulce y jugosa, que también se exporta a Europa desde 2015. En las provincias orientales de Cuba, las piñas también son populares en la cocina, y el pollo cocido con piña es un plato popular. Pero sobre todo, la piña es necesaria para elaborar el cóctel de Piña Colada, que se prepara en una licuadora con ron blanco, azúcar, jugo de limón, crema de coco, helado y jugo de piña. Los plátanos verdes cosechados son tan populares en Cuba como las patatas en otros lugares, y forman parte del menú diario.

Ananás

A província de Ciego de Ávila é líder na produção de ananás cubanos. Aqui, especialmente, é cultivada a variedade híbrida particularmente doce e suculenta MD-2, que também é exportada para a Europa desde 2015. Nas províncias do leste de Cuba, os ananasess também são populares na cozinha, e o frango assado com ananás é um prato popular. Mas, acima de tudo, o ananás é necessário para o coquetel Piña Colada, preparado em um liquidificador com rum branco, açúcar, suco de limão, creme de coco, gelo e suco de abacaxi. As bananas-da-terra (plátano) são tão populares em Cuba, como as batatas em outros lugares, e fazem parte do cardápio diário.

Ananas

De provincie Ciego de Ávila is de koploper betreffende de Cubaanse ananasproductie. Het bijzonder zoete en sappige hybride ras MD-2, dat sinds 2015 ook naar Europa wordt geëxporteerd, wordt hier geteeld. In de oostelijke provincies van Cuba is ananas ook populair in de keuken, en kip gestoofd met ananas is een populair gerecht. Maar ananas is vooral nodig voor de Piña Colada cocktail, bereid in een blender met witte rum, suiker, limoensap, kokosroom, ijs en ananassap. De groen geoogste bakbananen (*plátano*) zijn in Cuba net zo populair als de aardappelen elders en staan dagelijks op het menu.

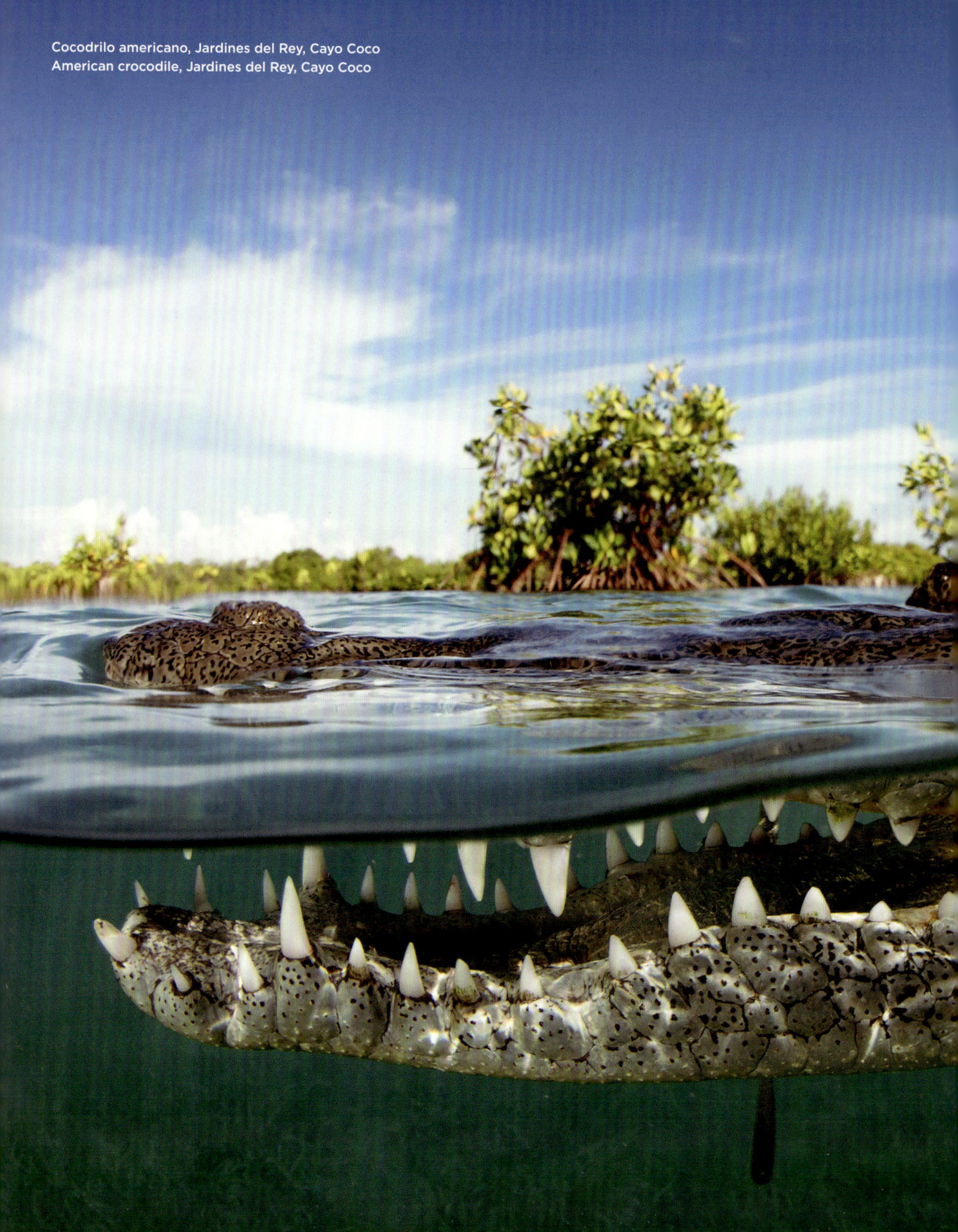

Cocodrilo americano, Jardines del Rey, Cayo Coco
American crocodile, Jardines del Rey, Cayo Coco

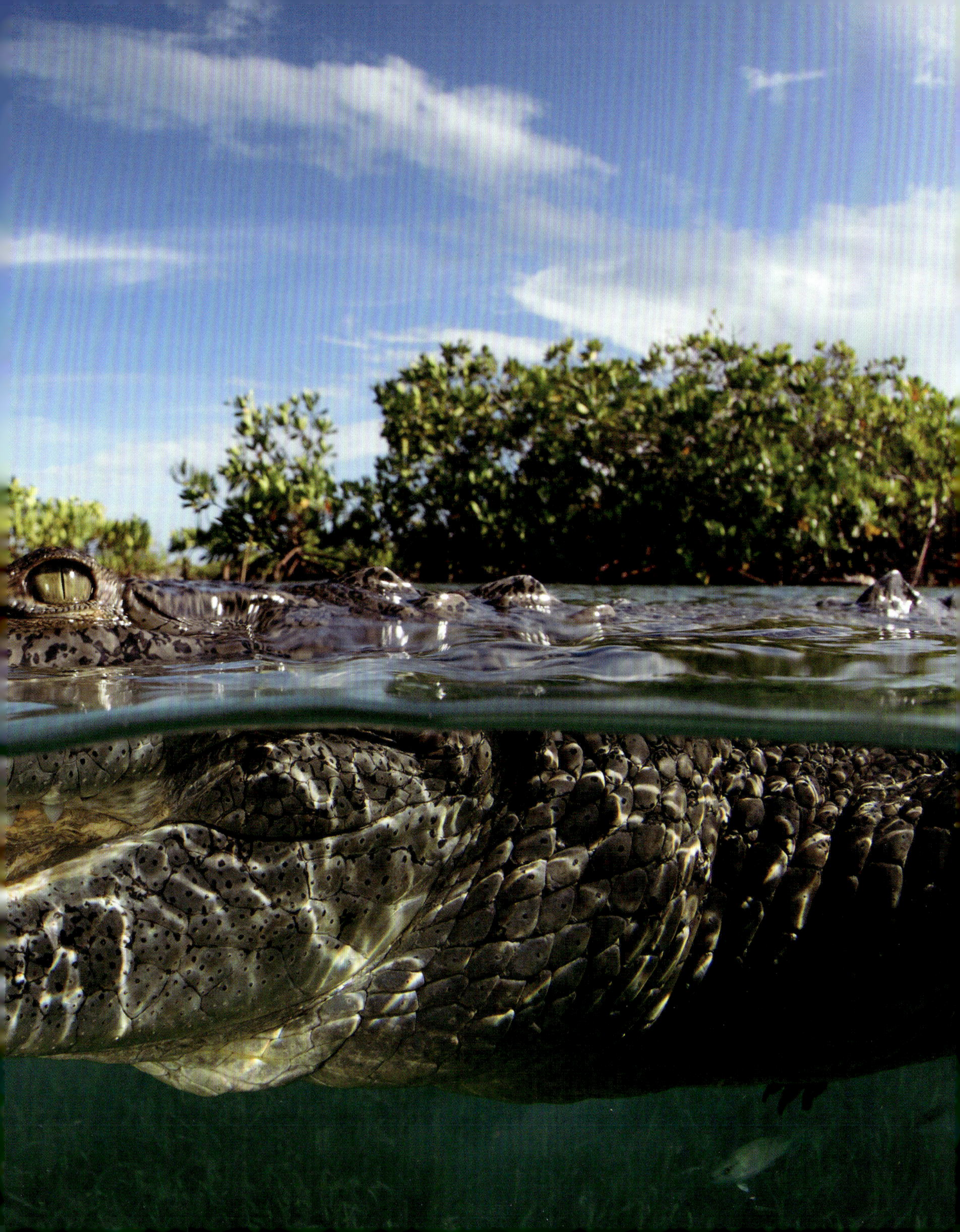

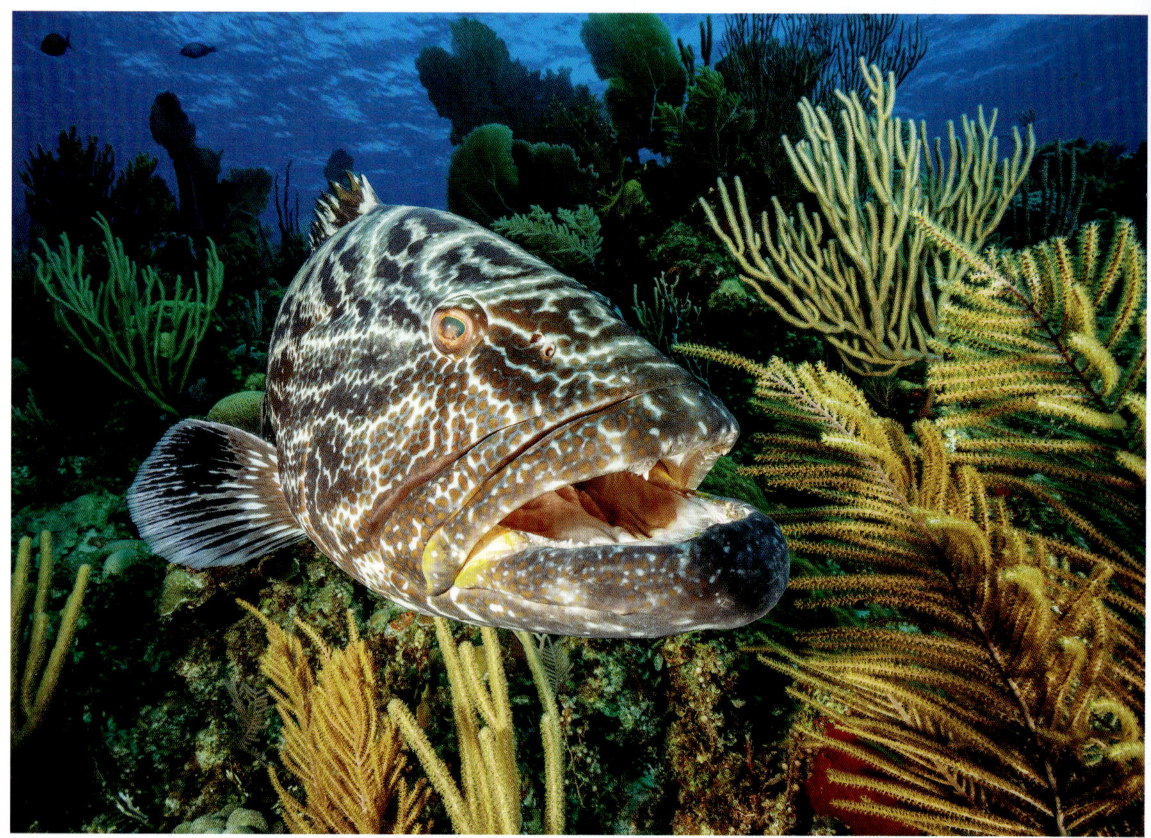

Mero negro, Jardines del Rey
Black grouper, Jardines del Rey

Underwater World of Jardines del Rey

The underwater world of the coral reef off
the Cayos offers an overwhelming variety
of species. Divers will encounter sea
turtles, hake, mackerel, flounders, marlins,
macabis, sea breams, groupers, rays and
spotted eagle rays, to name but a few.
Sponges of various sizes and colors as
well as various types of coral, from stony
coral to octocoral and even black coral find
ideal conditions here. Crocodiles are not
encountered while diving, but can be seen
on a small farm in the Bagá nature park on
Cayo Coco.

Le royaume sous-marin de Jardines del Rey

Au large des *cayos*, les fonds marins du
récif corallien présentent une faune et
une flore d'une richesse exceptionnelle.
Les plongeurs y croisent notamment
des tortues marines, des gadiformes,
des maquereaux, des flets, des marlins,
des Albulidae, des pageots communs,
des Epinephelinae, des raies Dasyatis
et des raies léopards. Ces eaux offrent
également des conditions de vie idéales à
des éponges de toutes tailles et couleurs,
ainsi qu'à diverses variétés de coraux,
scléractiniaires, octocoralliaires ou coraux
noirs, entre autres. Une petite ferme du
parc naturel de Bagá, sur Cayo Coco, élève
des crocodiles.

Unterwasserwelt Jardines del Rey

Die Unterwasserwelt am Korallenriff vor
den Cayos bietet einen überwältigenden
Artenreichtum. Taucher begegnen hier
Meeresschildkröten, Seehechten, Makrelen,
Flundern, Marlinen, Macabí (Grätenfisch),
Rotbrassen, Zackenbarschen, Rochen
und Gefleckten Adlerrochen, um nur
einige wenige zu nennen. Schwämme in
den verschiedensten Größen und Farben
ebenso wie diverse Korallenarten von
Steinkorallen über Oktokorallen und sogar
Schwarze Korallen finden hier ideale
Bedingungen vor. Krokodilen begegnet
man allerdings nicht beim Tauchen,
sondern auf einer kleinen Farm im
Naturpark Bagá auf Cayo Coco.

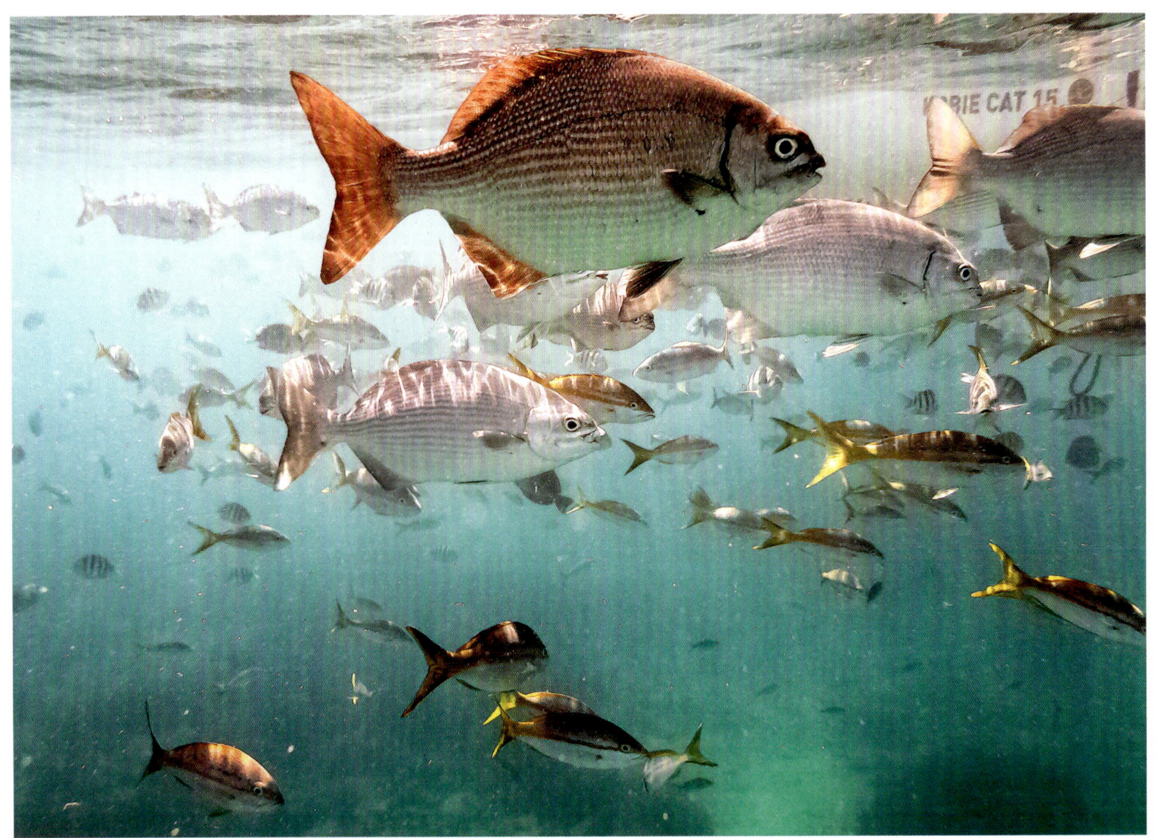

Jardines del Rey

Mundo submarino Jardines del Rey

El mundo submarino en el arrecife de coral frente a los cayos alberga una gran variedad de especies. Los buzos encontrarán tortugas marinas, gadiformes, platijas europeas, lenguados, marlines, macabís, pagros, meros mediterráneos, rayas y rayas jaspeadas, por nombrar solo algunos. Esponjas de diferentes tamaños y colores, así como diversos tipos de corales, desde corales pétreos hasta octocorales e incluso corales negros, encuentran aquí las condiciones ideales. Los cocodrilos no se encuentran mientras se bucea, sino en una pequeña granja en el parque natural Bagá en Cayo Coco.

Mundo subaquático Jardines del Rey

O mundo subaquático no recife de corais em frente ao Cayos oferece uma variedade impressionante de espécies. Os mergulhadores encontrarão tartarugas marinhas, pescadas, cavalas (ou sardas), solha-das-pedras, marlins-negro, flechas (peixes ósseos), vermelhos-cioba, garoupas, arraias e raia-pintada, só para citar algumas. Esponjas em vários tamanhos e cores, bem como vários tipos de corais, desde corais-pétreos a octocorais e até mesmo corais negros encontram aqui as condições ideais de vida. Os crocodilos, todavia, não são encontrados durante o mergulho, mas em uma pequena fazenda no parque natural Bagá, no Cayo Coco.

Onderwaterwereld Jardines del Rey

De onderwaterwereld bij het koraalrif voor de Cayos biedt een overweldigende soortenrijkdom. Duikers komen onder andere zeeschildpadden, heken, makrelen, botvissen, zeilvissen, gratenvisachtigen, gewone zeebrasems, tandbaarzen, roggen en gevlekte adelaarsroggen tegen. Sponsdieren in verschillende maten en kleuren, verschillende soorten koralen, van rifkoralen tot octocorallia en zelfs zwarte koralen zijn hier te vinden. Krokodillen zijn niet te vinden tijdens het duiken, maar op een kleine boerderij in het natuurpark Bagá op Cayo Coco Coco.

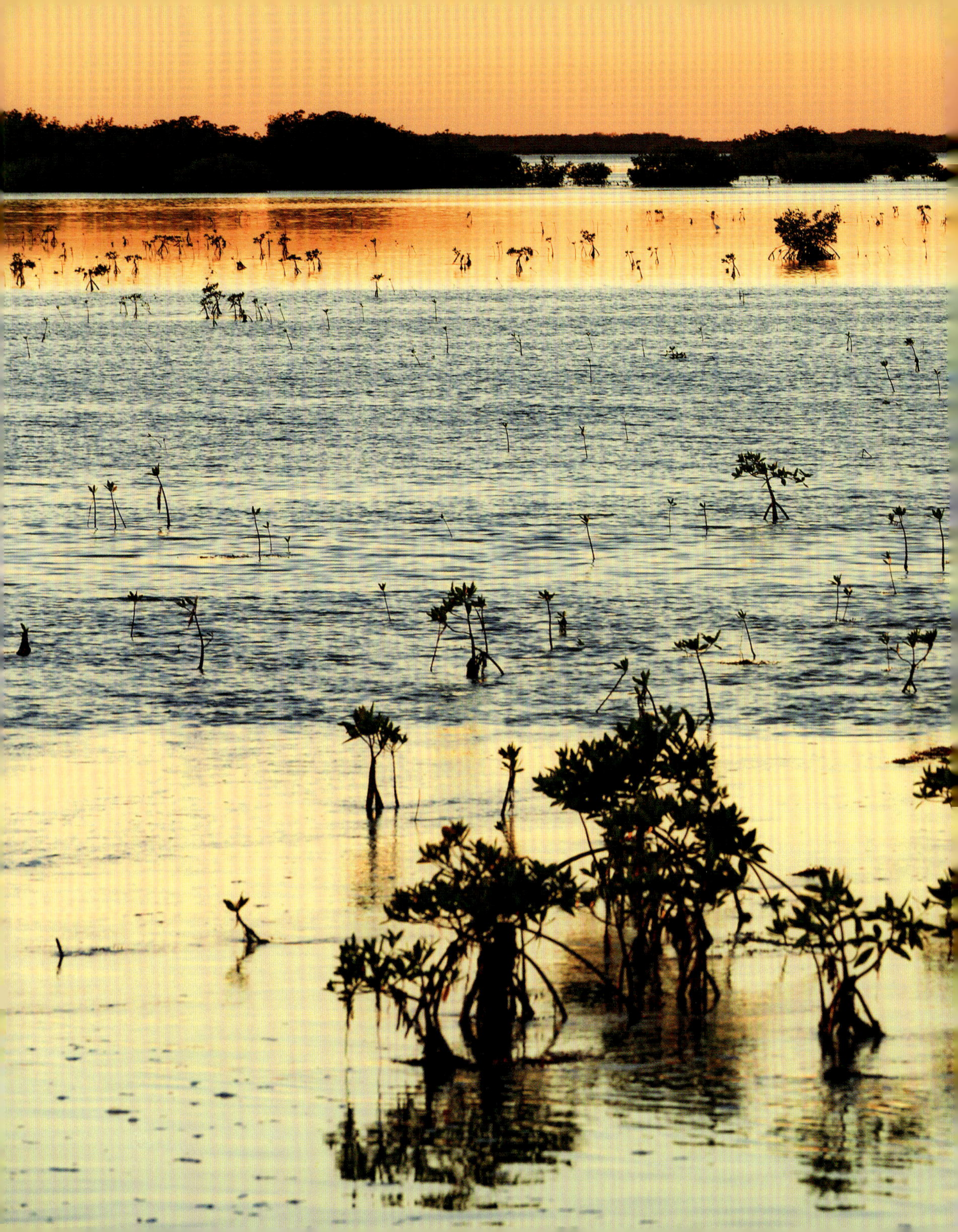

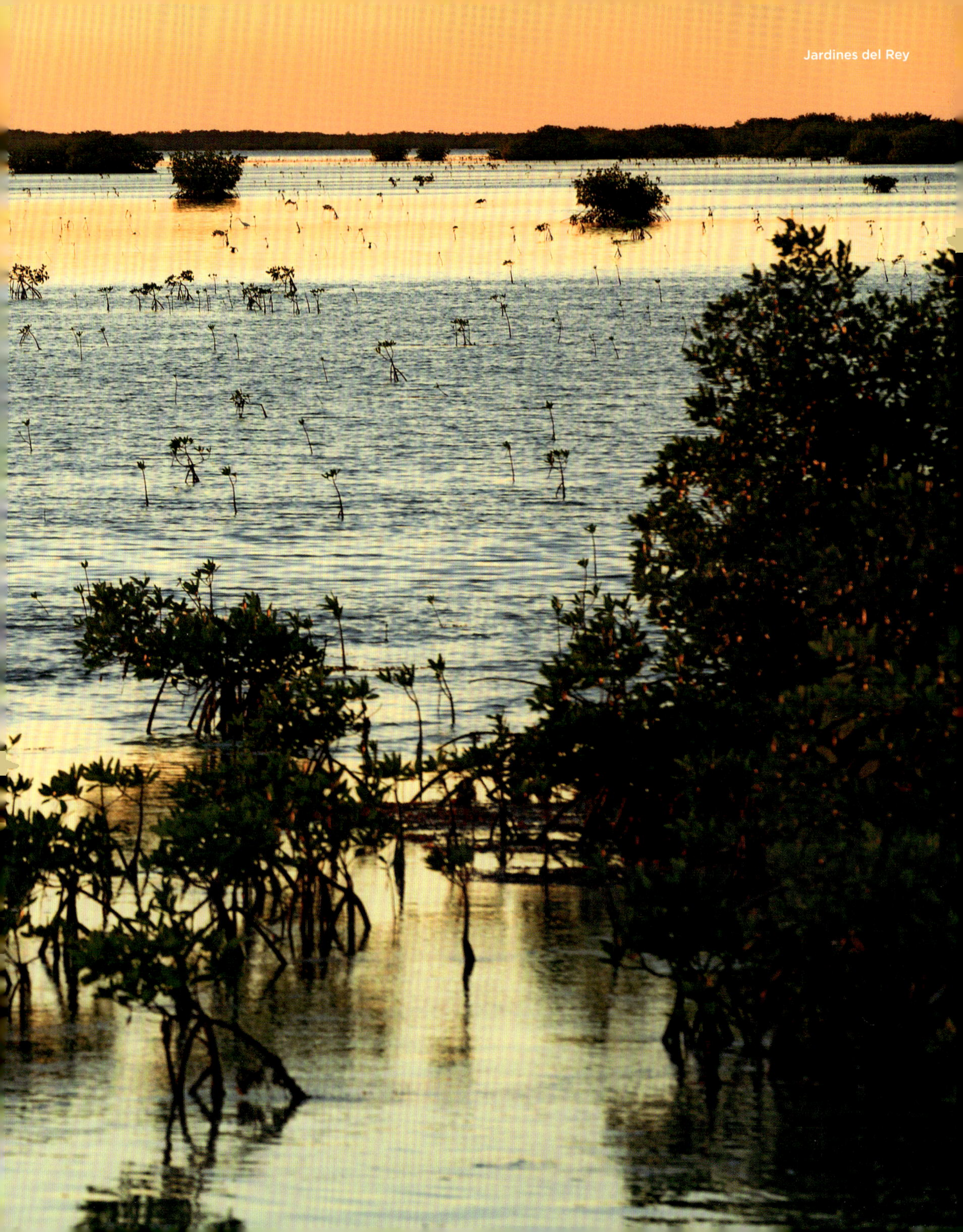
Jardines del Rey

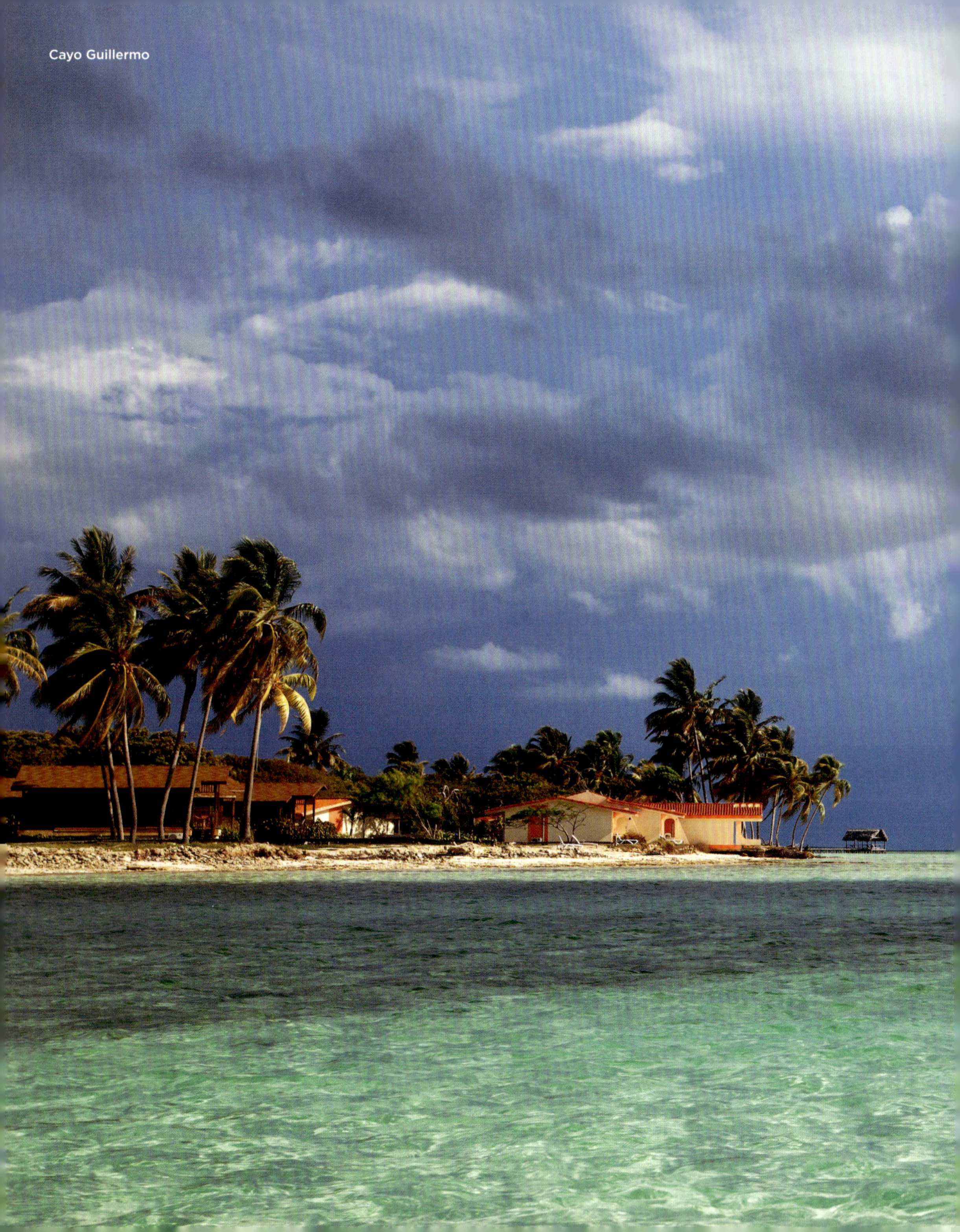

Cayo Guillermo

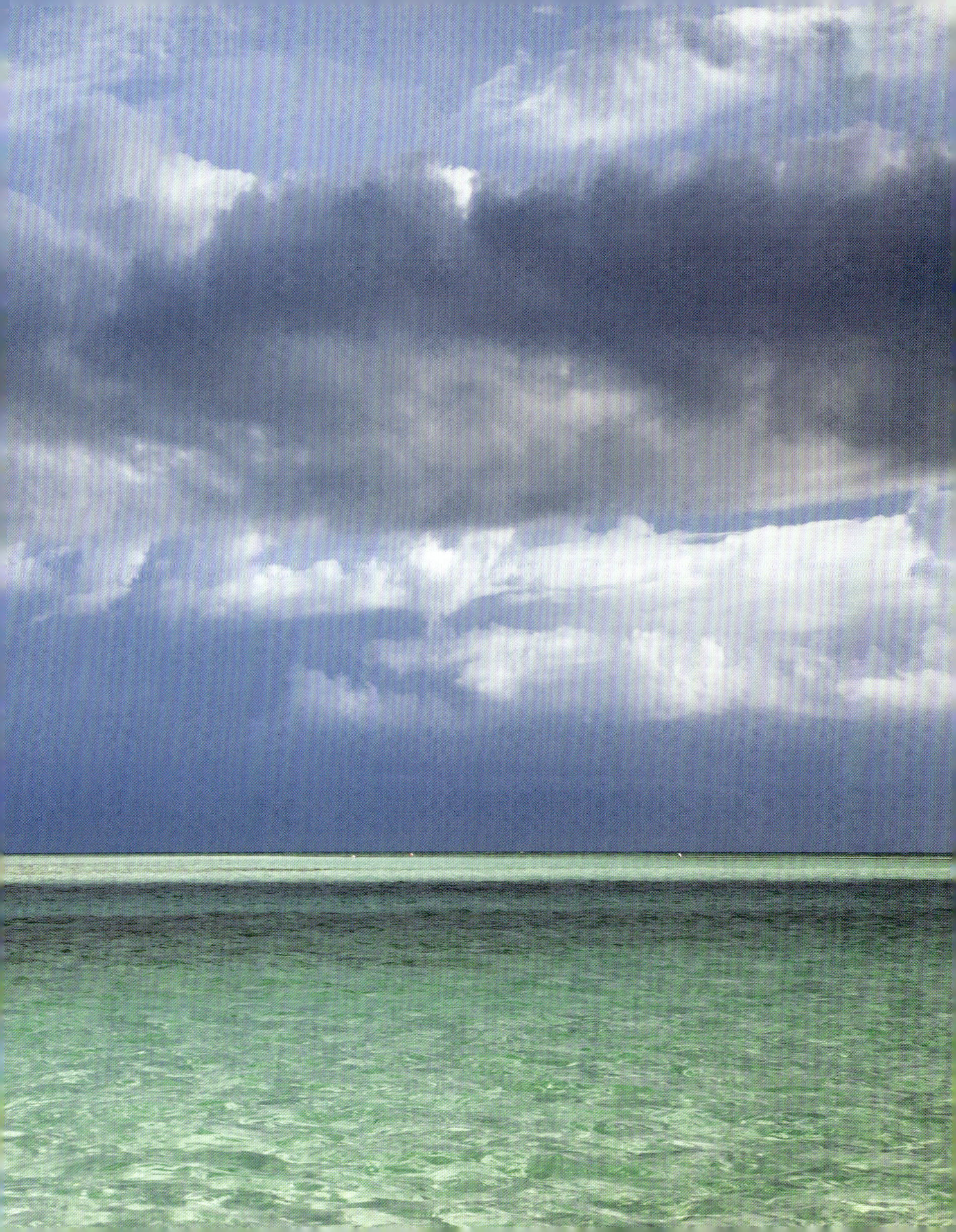

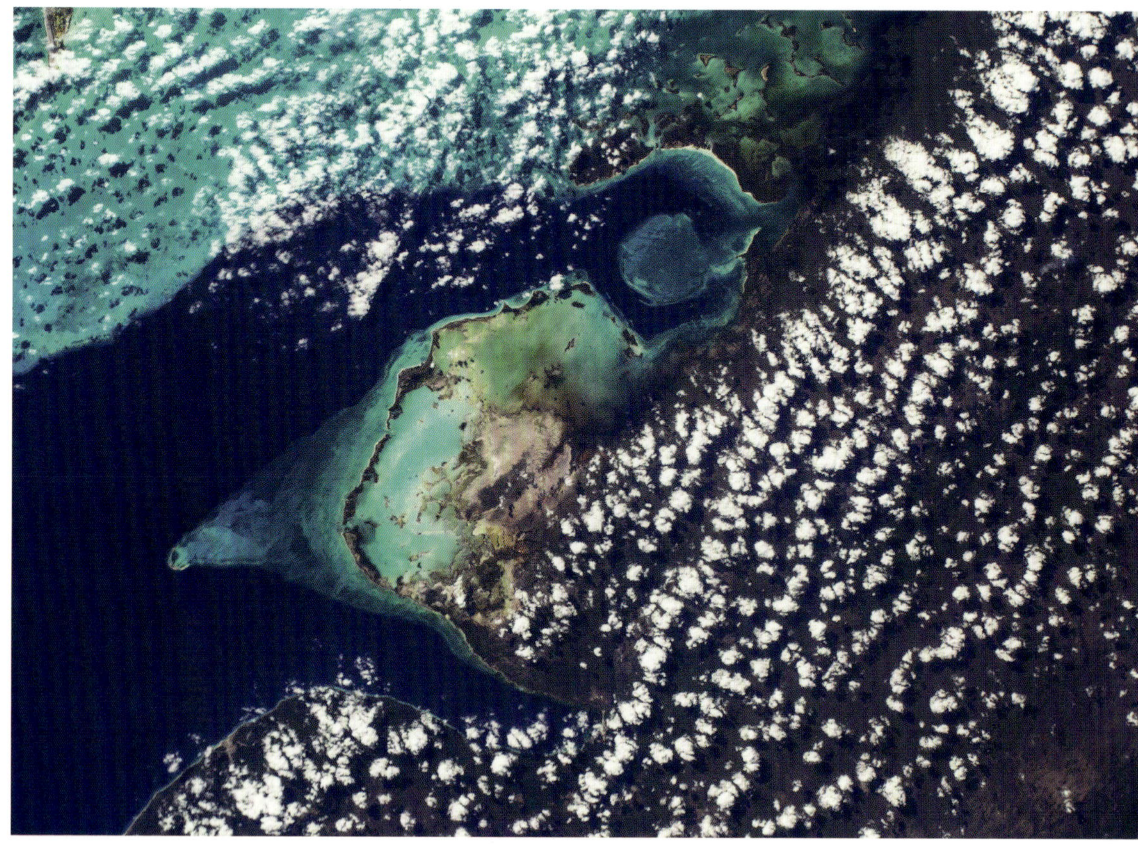

Cayo Coco

Cayo Coco and Cayo Guillermo

The entire archipelago is protected. Cayo Coco is the largest of the islets that have been developed for tourism, and if gets its name not from coconut palms, but from the small white heron Ibis Blanco, colloquially known as "Coco". The fine sandy beaches are located on the north coasts of the Cayos; on the south coasts there are mangrove forests that stretch to the "mainland" of the main island, inhabited by large colonies of pink flamingos. Many migratory birds stop at the archipelago on their way north. Ernest Hemingway created a literary monument to this paradisiacal island world in his novel *Islands in the Stream.*

Cayo Coco et Cayo Guillermo

L'ensemble de l'archipel est constitué en réserve naturelle. Cayo Coco est la plus grande des îles aménagées pour le tourisme ; elle ne doit pas son nom aux palmiers, mais à un petit héron, *Ibis blanco,* communément appelé « coco ». Les plages de fin sable blanc bordent la côte nord des *cayos,* alors que les forêts de mangrove s'étendent sur leur côte sud, jusqu'aux terres de l'île centrale. Elles abritent de vastes colonies de flamants roses. De nombreux oiseaux migrateurs font également escale sur l'archipel au cours de leur périple vers le nord. Ernest Hemingway érigea un monument littéraire à ce monde insulaire paradisiaque dans son roman *Îles à la dérive.*

Cayo Coco und Cayo Guillermo

Der gesamte Archipel steht unter Naturschutz. Cayo Coco ist die größte der touristisch erschlossenen Inselchen und hat seinen Namen nicht von Kokospalmen, sondern von dem kleinen weißen Reiher Ibis Blanco, umgangssprachlich „Coco" genannt. Die feinsandigen Strände liegen jeweils an den Nordküsten der Cayos, an den Südküsten erstrecken sich Mangrovenwälder, die sich bis zum „Festland" der Hauptinsel ziehen, bewohnt von großen Kolonien rosafarbener Flamingos. Viele Zugvögel machen auf dem Weg nach Norden auf dem Archipel Station. Ernest Hemingway setzte der paradiesischen Inselwelt in seinem Roman *Inseln im Strom* ein literarisches Denkmal.

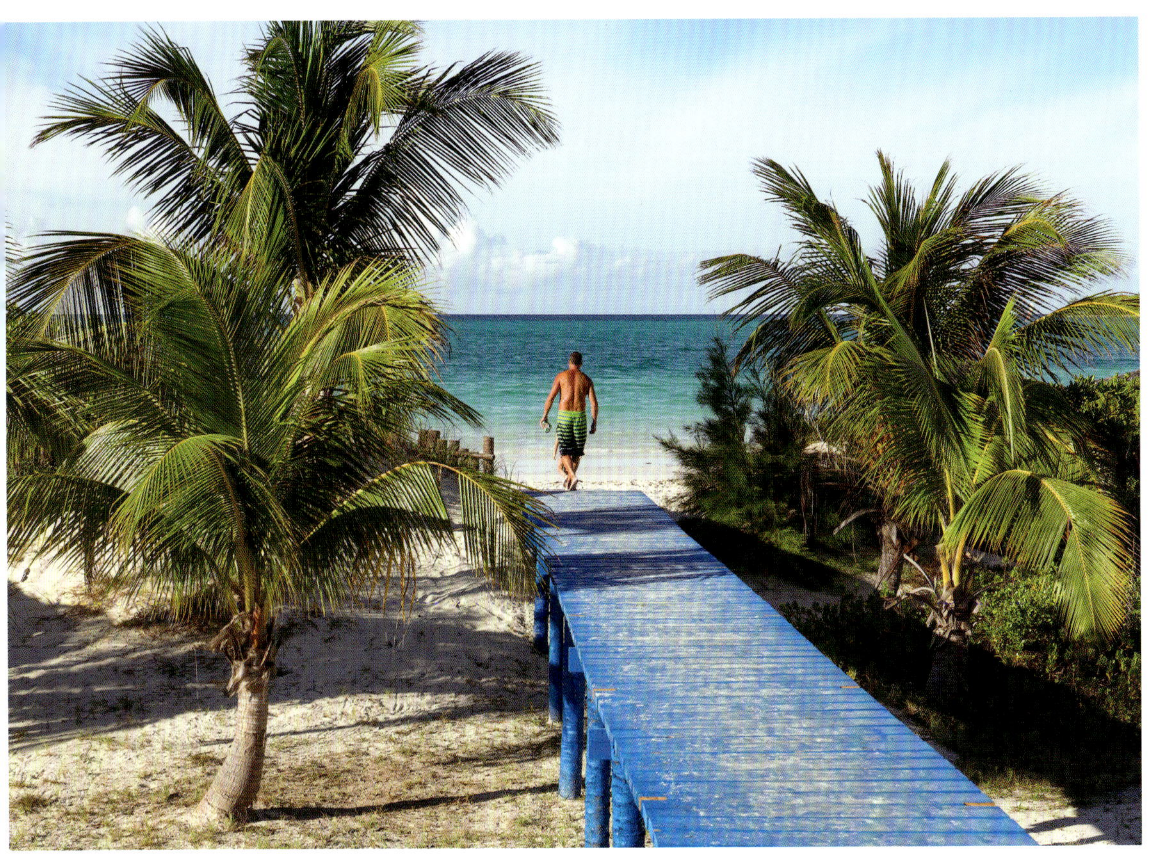

Cayo Guillermo

Cayo Coco y Cayo Guillermo

Todo el archipiélago está protegido. Cayo Coco es el más grande de los islotes turísticos y su nombre no proviene del cocotero, sino de la pequeña garza blanca Ibis Blanco, coloquialmente llamada "coco". Las playas de arena fina se encuentran en la costa norte de los Cayos; en la costa sur hay manglares que se extienden hasta el "continente" de la isla principal, habitada por grandes colonias de flamencos rosados. Muchas aves migratorias se detienen en el archipiélago en su camino hacia el norte. Ernest Hemingway ha creado un monumento literario al paradisíaco mundo insular en su novela *Islands in the Stream*.

Cayo Coco e Cayo Guillermo

Todo o arquipélago está sob proteção ambiental. Cayo Coco é o maior dos ilhéus turísticos desenvolvidos e seu nome não vem de coqueiros, mas da pequena garça branca Ibis Blanco, coloquialmente chamada de "Coco". As praias de areia fina estão localizadas na costa norte dos Cayos, na costa sul há florestas de mangues, que se estendem até o "continente" da ilha principal, habitadas por grandes colônias de flamingos rosados. Muitas aves migratórias fazem uma parada no arquipélago a caminho do norte. Ernest Hemingway estabeleceu um monumento literário ao mundo paradisíaco das ilhas em seu romance *Ilhas na Corrente (Islands in the Stream)*.

Cayo Coco en Cayo Guillermo

De hele archipel is beschermd. Cayo Coco Coco is het grootste van de toeristisch ontwikkelde eilandjes en heeft zijn naam niet van kokospalmen, maar van de kleine witte reiger Ibis Blanco, in de volksmond 'Coco' genoemd. De fijne zandstranden liggen aan de noordkust van de Cayos, aan de zuidkust zijn er mangrovebossen die zich uitstrekken tot het 'vasteland' van het hoofdeiland, en wordt bewoond door grote kolonies roze flamingo's. Veel trekvogels stoppen bij de archipel op weg naar het noorden. Ernest Hemingway heeft in zijn roman *Islands in the Stream* een literair monument voor de paradijselijke eilandwereld opgericht.

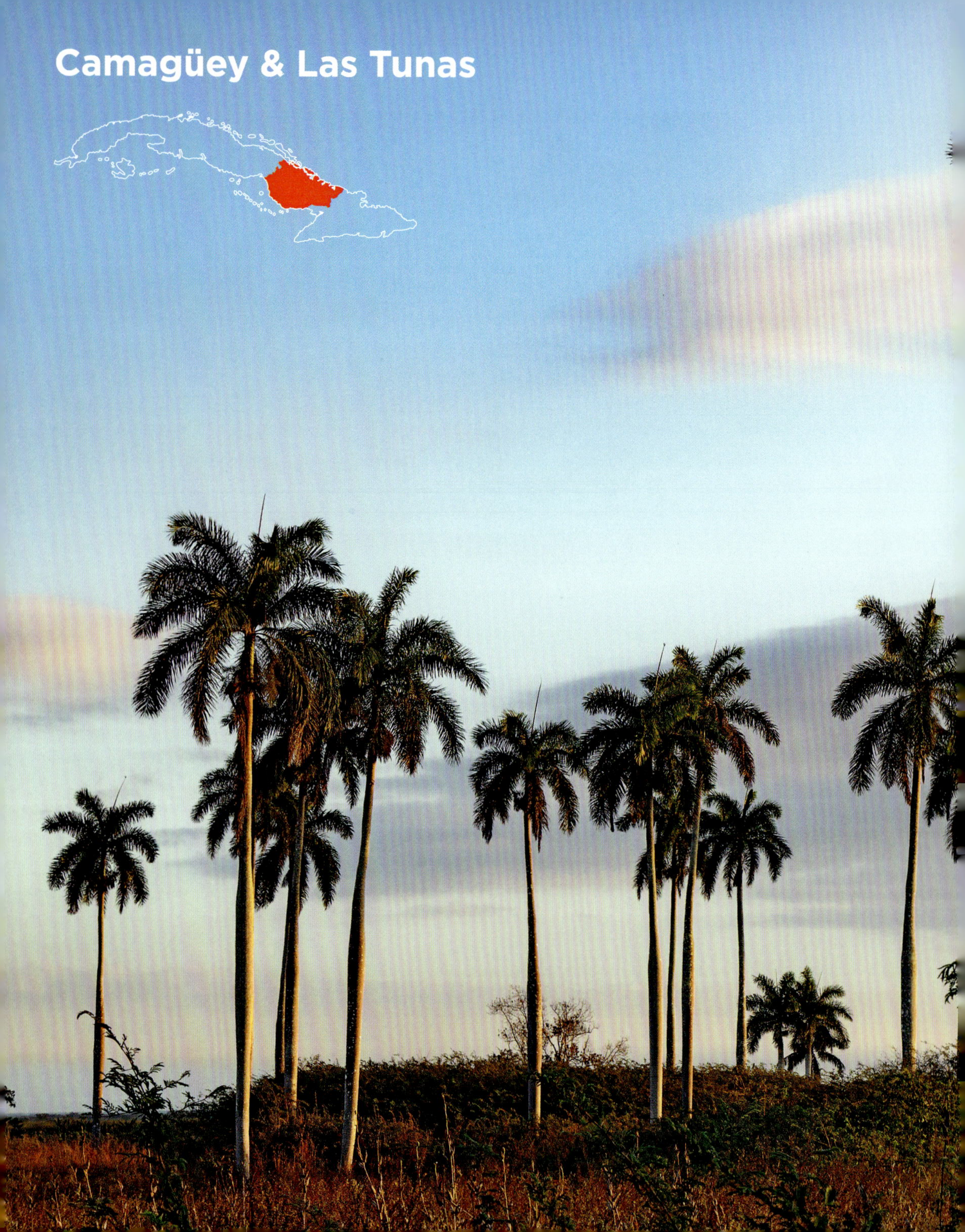

Camagüey & Las Tunas

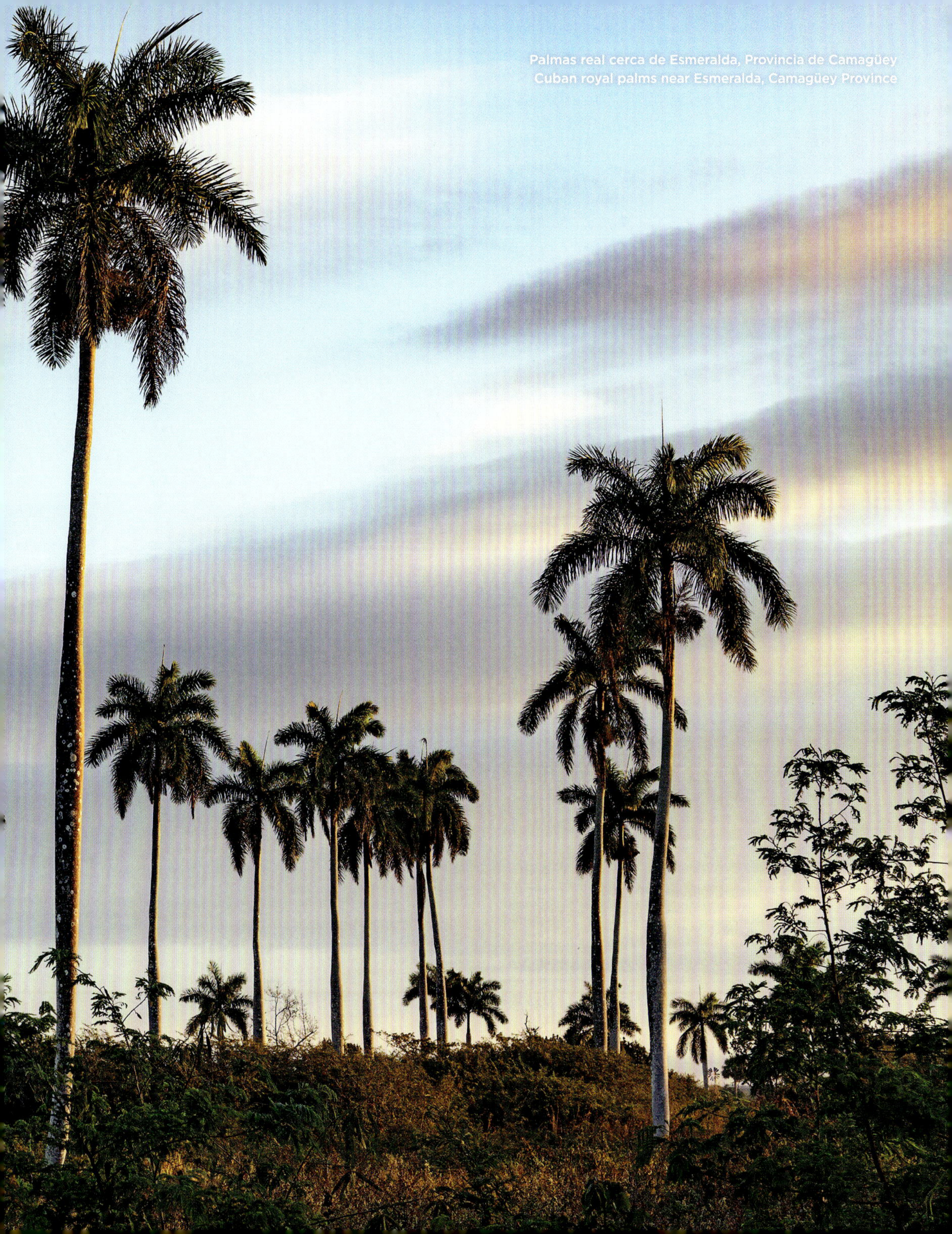
Palmas real cerca de Esmeralda, Provincia de Camagüey
Cuban royal palms near Esmeralda, Camagüey Province

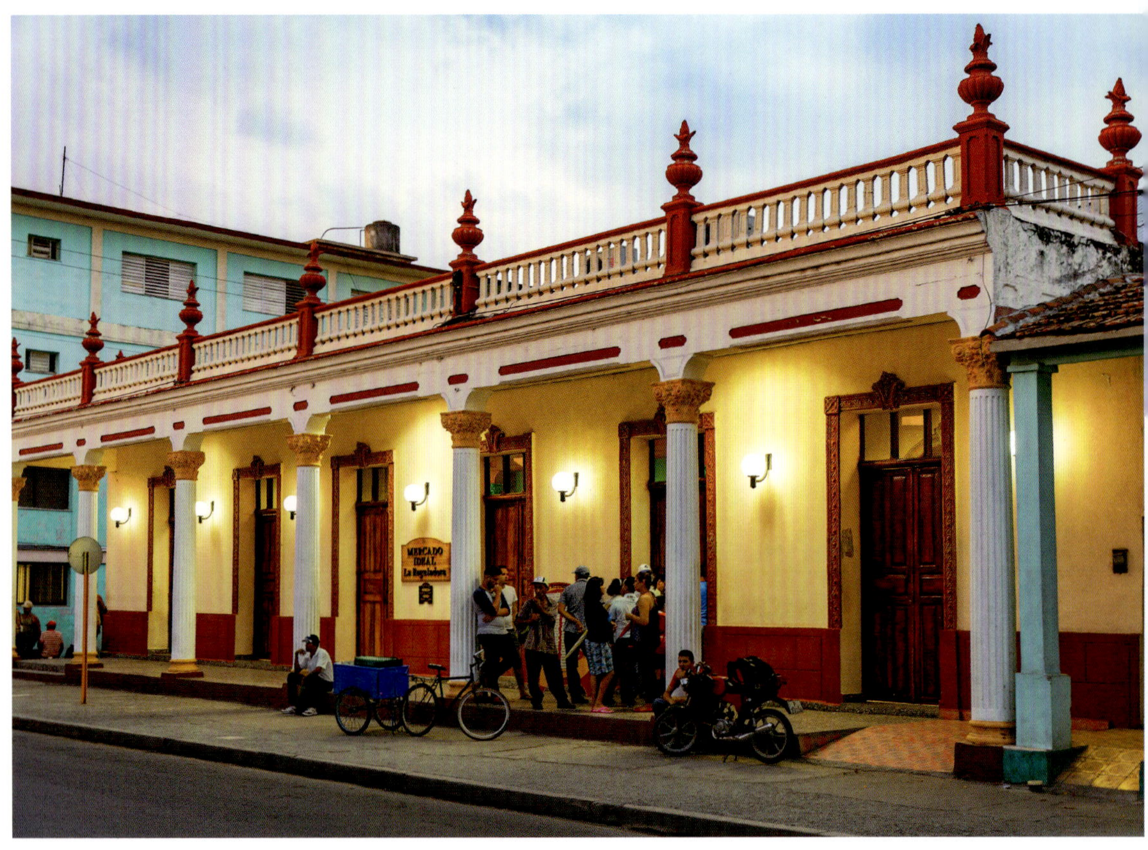

Las Tunas

Camagüey and Las Tunas

These two provinces in central Cuba are characterized by gently rolling pastures and sugar plantations. Camagüey in particular is known for its extensive cattle breeding, and the provincial capital of the same name has a lively creative scene. On the north coast the fine sandy beach of Playa Santa Lucía attracts with its crystal clear water and coral reefs, and the island world off Camagüey is largely untouched. On the north coast of Las Tunas there are also very beautiful beaches, of which only the Playa Covarrubias is developed for tourism. The provincial capital Las Tunas is a sleepy provincial town that exists far from tourist crowds.

Camagüey et Las Tunas

Le paysage de ces deux provinces centrales de l'île se compose essentiellement d'herbages ondoyants et de plantations de canne à sucre. Camagüey est particulièrement célèbre pour son élevage bovin extensif. Sa capitale, homonyme, connaît une scène créative dynamique. Sur la côte nord, le sable fin de la plage Playa Santa Lucía, ses eaux cristallines et ses récifs coralliens dépeignent un splendide paysage insulaire encore vierge. La côte nord de Las Tunas est occupée par de belles plages, dont la Playa Covarrubias, aménagée pour le tourisme. La capitale de la province Las Tunas est une petite ville calme, où la vie suit son cours loin du tourisme.

Camagüey und Las Tunas

Die beiden Provinzen in Zentralkuba sind von sanft gewelltem Weideland und Zuckerplantagen geprägt. Vor allem Camagüey ist bekannt für die extensiv betriebene Rinderzucht. Die gleichnamige Provinzhauptstadt hat eine lebendige Kreativ-Szene. An der Nordküste lockt der feinsandige Strand Playa Santa Lucía mit kristallklarem Wasser und Korallenriffen, die Inselwelt vor Camagüey ist weitgehend unberührt. Auch an der Nordküste von Las Tunas liegen sehr schöne Strände, von denen nur die Playa Covarrubias touristisch erschlossen ist. Die Provinzhauptstadt Las Tunas ist ein verschlafenes Provinzstädtchen, das fernab vom Tourismus lebt.

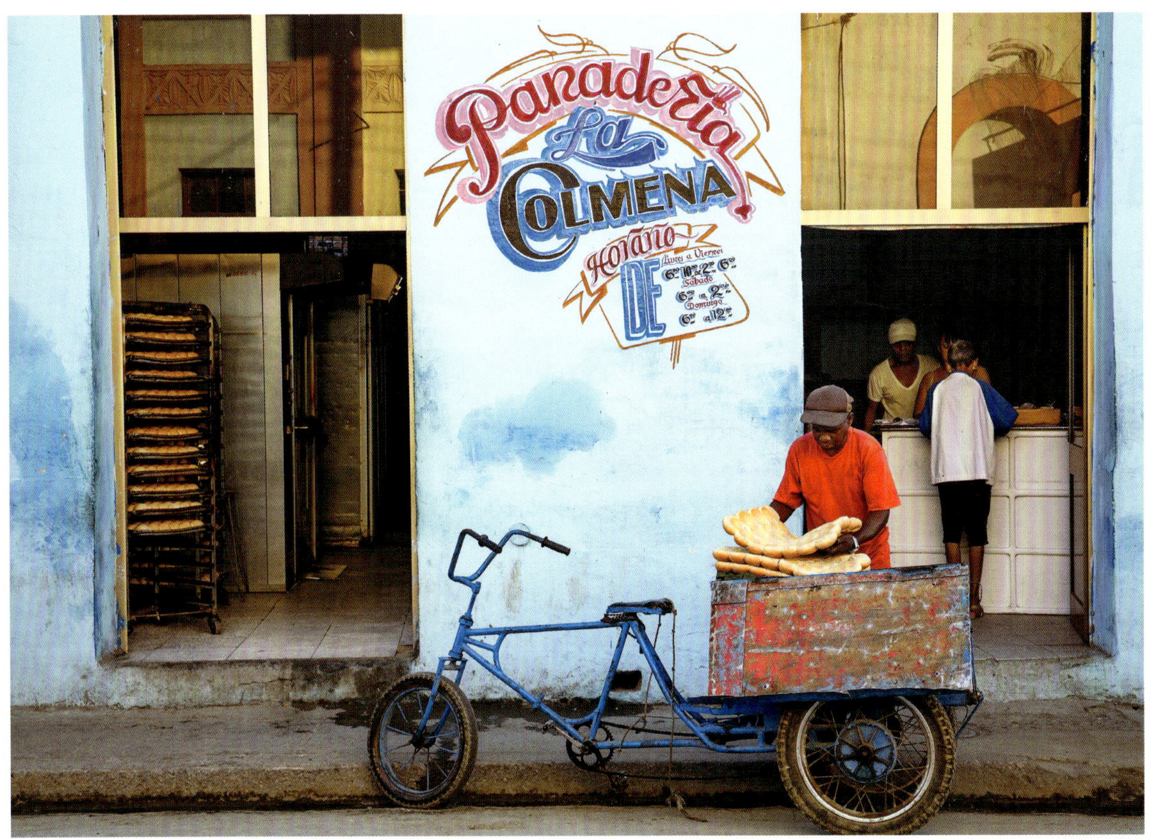

Las Tunas

Camagüey y Las Tunas

Las dos provincias del centro de Cuba se caracterizan por sus pastizales suavemente ondulados y sus plantaciones de azúcar. Camagüey, en particular, es conocida por su ganadería extensiva. La capital de la provincia del mismo nombre tiene una animada escena creativa. En la costa norte la playa de arena fina Playa Santa Lucía es muy atractiva, con aguas cristalinas y arrecifes de coral. El mundo de la isla antes de Camagüey permanece en gran medida intacto. También en la costa norte de Las Tunas hay playas muy bonitas, de las cuales solo la Playa Covarrubias está desarrollada para el turismo. La capital de la provincia, Las Tunas, es una tranquila ciudad de provincia que vive ajena al turismo.

Camagüey e Las Tunas

As duas províncias do centro de Cuba são caracterizadas por pastagens suaves e plantações de açúcar. Camagüey, em particular, é conhecida pela sua criação extensiva de gado. A capital provincial com o mesmo nome tem um cenário animado e criativo. Na costa norte, a praia de areia fina Playa Santa Lucía encanta com águas cristalinas e recifes de corais, o mundo da ilha em frente a Camagüey é praticamente intocada. Também na costa norte de Las Tunas há praias muito bonitas, das quais apenas a Playa Covarrubias é desenvolvida turisticamente. A capital provincial Las Tunas é uma pacata cidade provincial que vive longe do turismo.

Camagüey en Las Tunas

De twee provincies in centraal Cuba worden door weideland en suikerplantages gekenmerkt. Vooral Camagüey staat bekend om zijn extensieve veeteelt. De gelijknamige provinciehoofdstad heeft een levendige creatieve scene. Aan de noordkust trekt het fijne zandstrand Playa Santa Lucía met kristalhelder water en koraalriffen, de eilandwereld voor Camagüey is grotendeels onaangetast. Ook aan de noordkust van Las Tunas zijn zeer mooie stranden, waarvan alleen het Playa Covarrubias toeristisch ontwikkeld is. De ver van het toerisme gelegen provinciale hoofdstad Las Tunas is een slaperige stad.

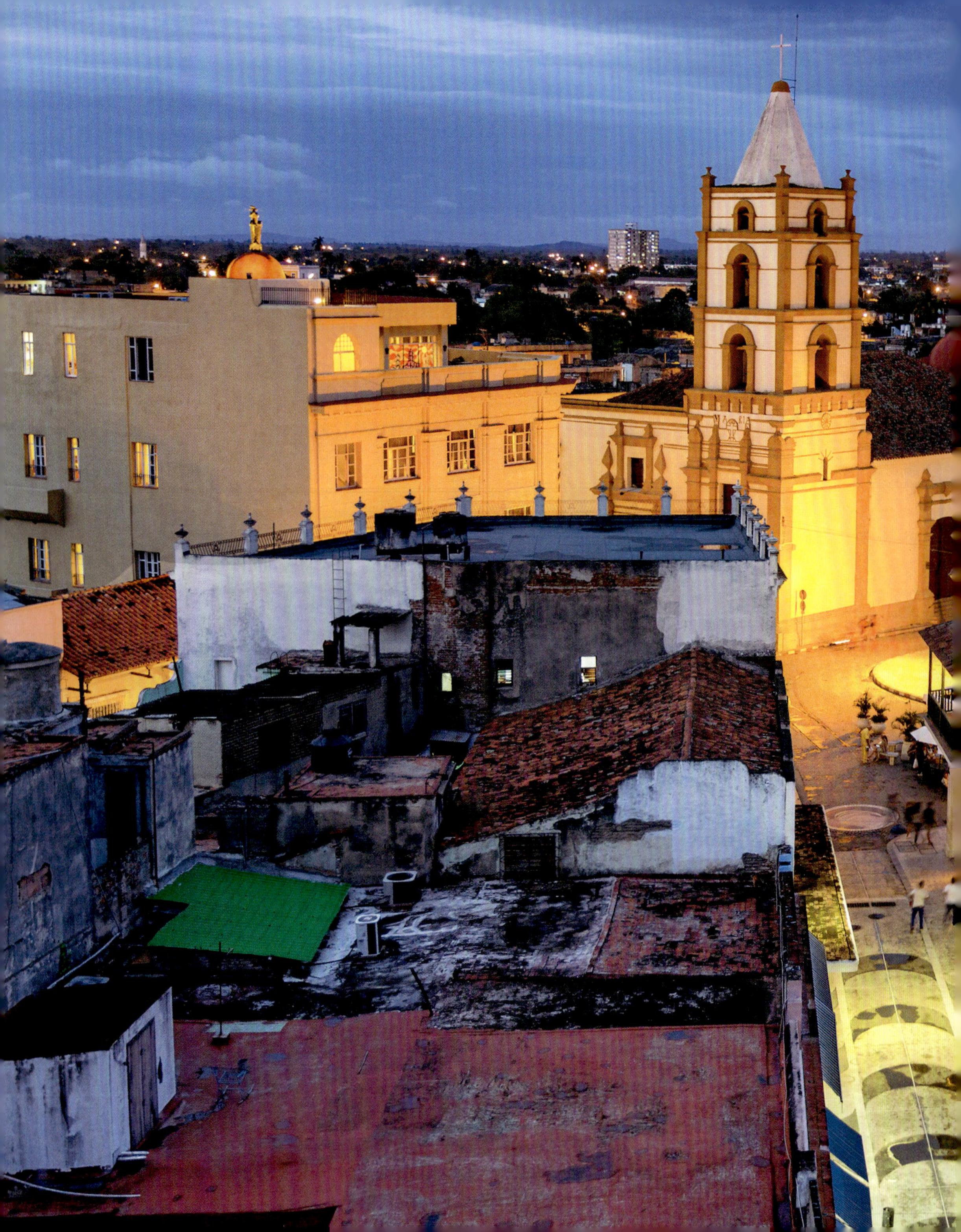

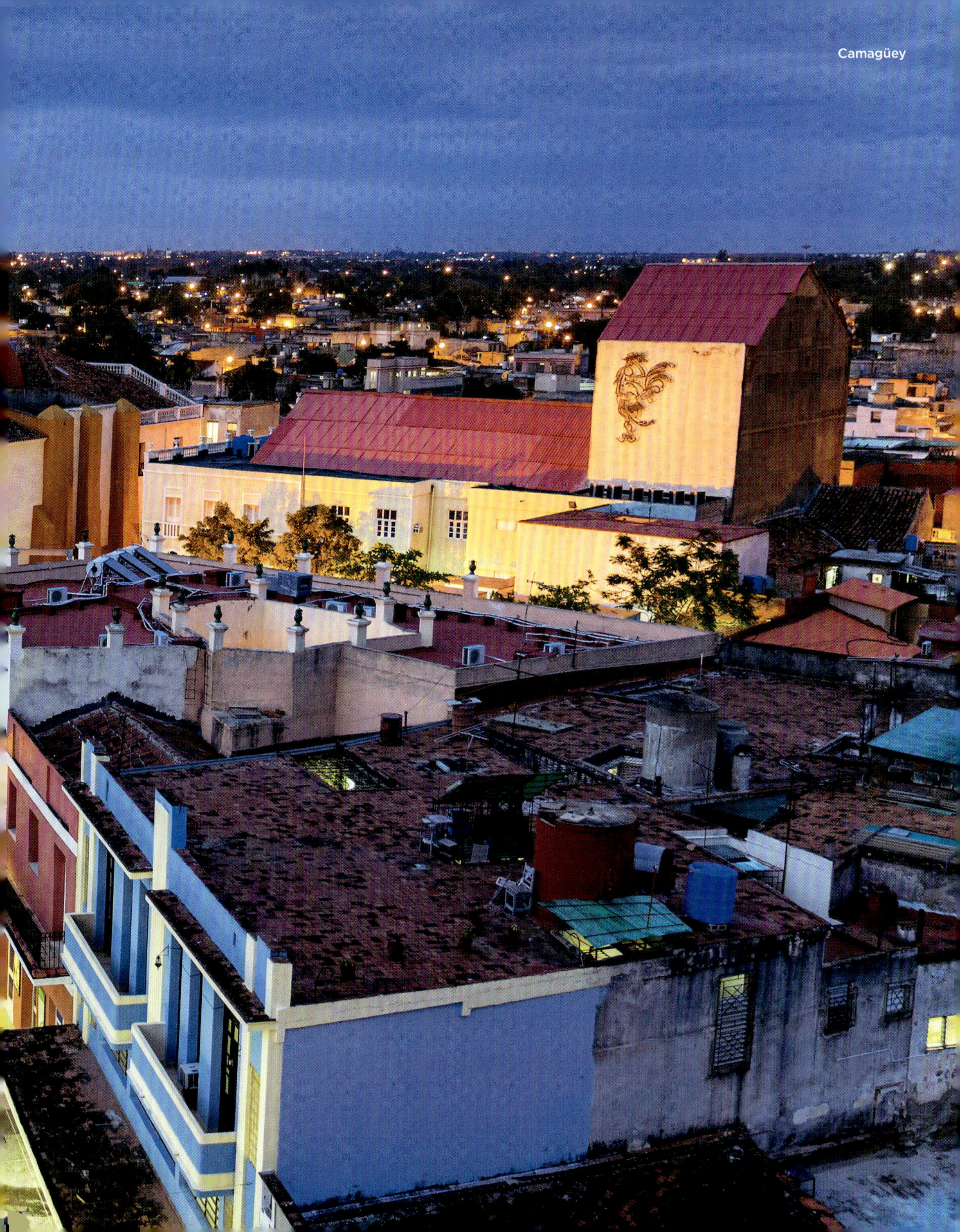

Camagüey

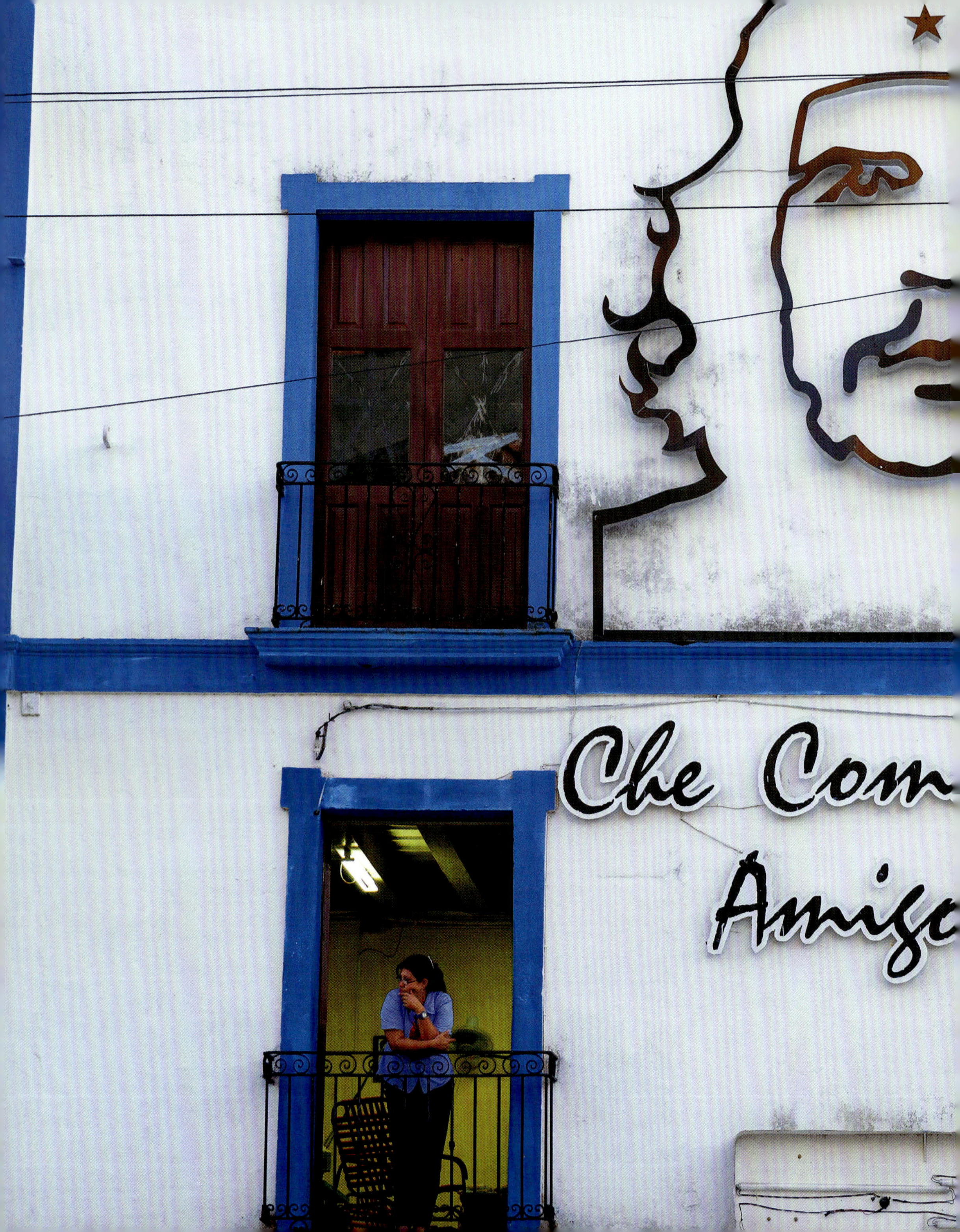
Che Com
Amigo

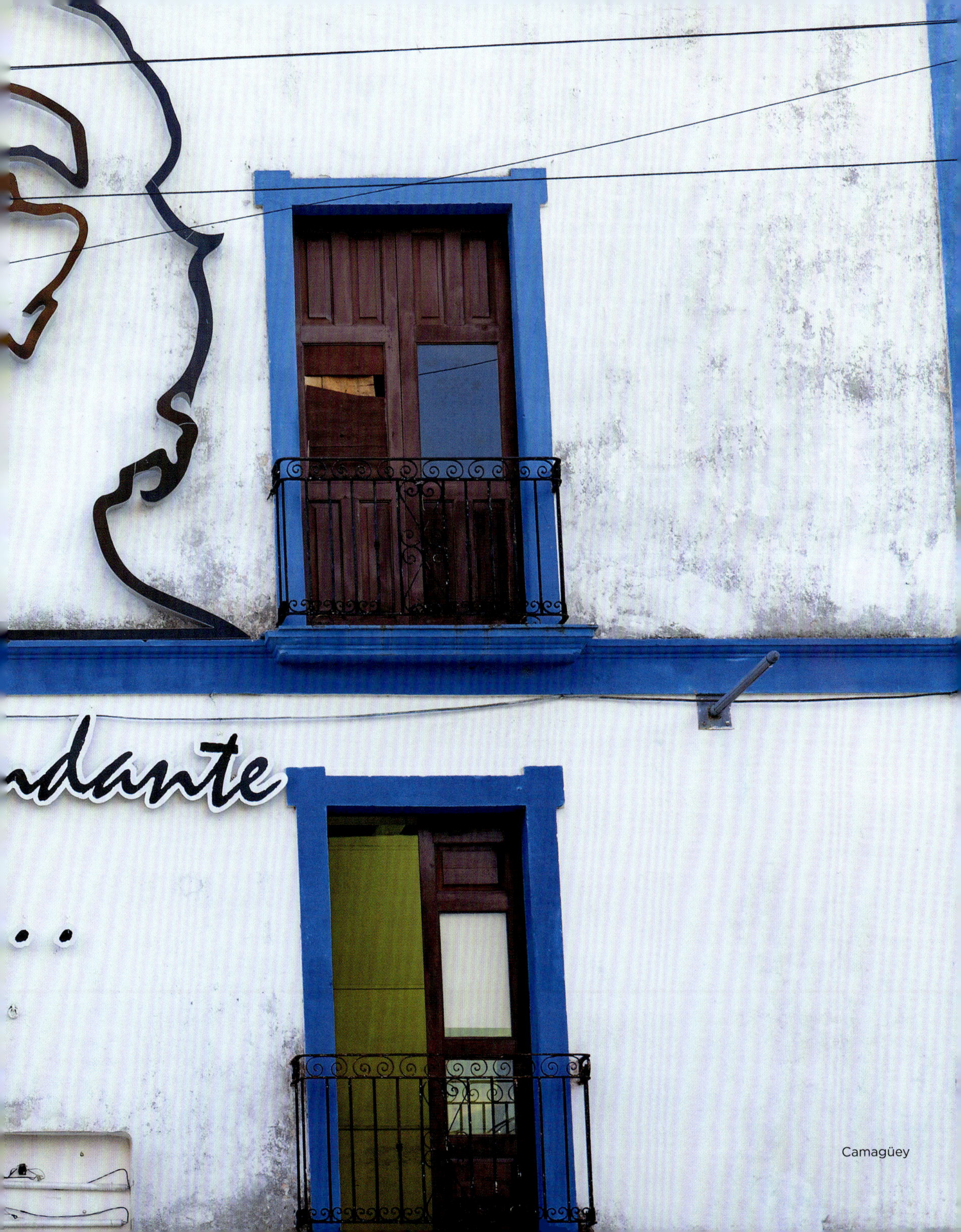

Camagüey

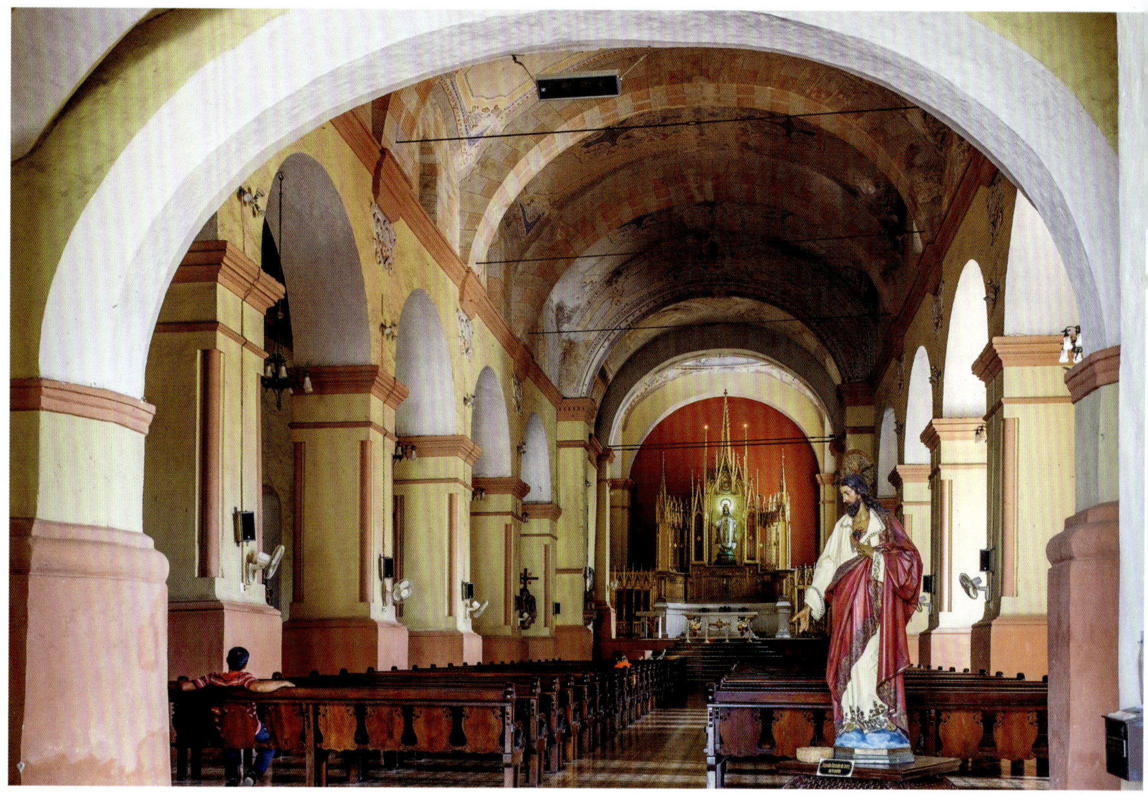

Iglesia de Nuestra Señora de la Merced, Camagüey

Provincial Capital Camagüey

Also founded by Velázquez, Camagüey is the third largest city in Cuba. In contrast to other cities, the streets do not have a chessboard pattern but form a labyrinth with many small squares to protect them from pirate attacks. The church Nuestra Señora del Carmen is located at the Plaza del Carmen, the most beautiful place in Camagüey.

Camagüey, capital de provincia

Fundada también por Velázquez, Camagüey es la tercera ciudad más grande de Cuba. A diferencia de otras ciudades, las calles de la ciudad no tienen un patrón de ajedrez, sino que forman un laberinto de calles con muchas plazas pequeñas para protegerla de los ataques de los piratas. La iglesia Nuestra Señora del Carmen está ubicada en la Plaza del Carmen, el lugar más hermoso de Camagüey.

Camagüey, capitale provinciale

Également fondée par Velázquez, Camagüey est la troisième ville de Cuba. Contrairement à l'habituel plan urbain cubain, le quadrillage des rues est remplacé par un labyrinthe tortueux composé de ruelles et de nombreuses petites places, destiné à protéger la population des attaques de pirates. L'église Nuestra Señora del Carmen trône sur la Plaza del Carmen, plus belle place de Camagüey.

Camagüey, a capital da província

Também fundada por Velázquez, Camagüey é a terceira maior cidade de Cuba. Ao contrário de outras cidades, as ruas da cidade não têm um padrão quadriculado, mas formam um labirinto de ruas com muitas praças pequenas para serem protegidas de ataques de piratas. A igreja Nuestra Señora del Carmen está localizada na Plaza del Carmen, o lugar mais bonito de Camagüey.

Provinzhauptstadt Camagüey

Ebenfalls von Velázquez gegründet, ist Camagüey die drittgrößte Stadt Kubas. Anders als sonst verlaufen die Straßen der Stadt nicht im Schachbrettmuster, sondern bilden zum Schutz vor Piratenüberfällen ein verwinkeltes Gassenlabyrinth mit vielen kleinen Plätzen. Die Kirche Nuestra Señora del Carmen liegt an der Plaza del Carmen, dem schönsten Platz Camagüeys.

Provinciale hoofdstad Camagüey

Camagüey, wat ook door Velázquez is gesticht, is de derde grootste stad van Cuba. In tegenstelling tot andere steden hebben de straten van de stad geen schaakbordpatroon, maar vormen ze een labyrint van straten met veel kleine pleintjes om ze te beschermen tegen piratenaanvallen. De kerk Nuestra Señora del Carmen is gelegen aan de Plaza del Carmen, de mooiste plek van Camagüey.

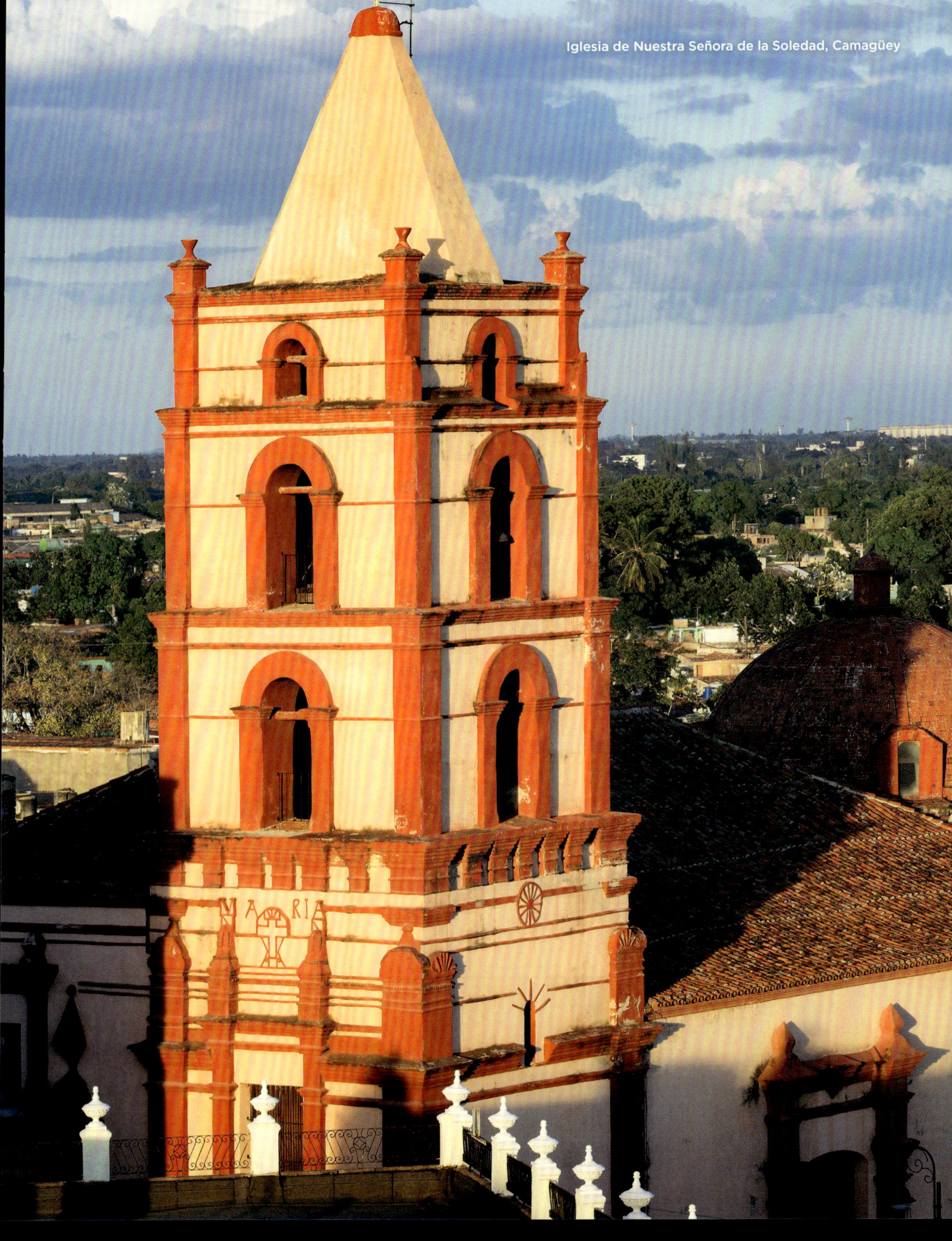

Iglesia de Nuestra Señora de la Soledad, Camagüey

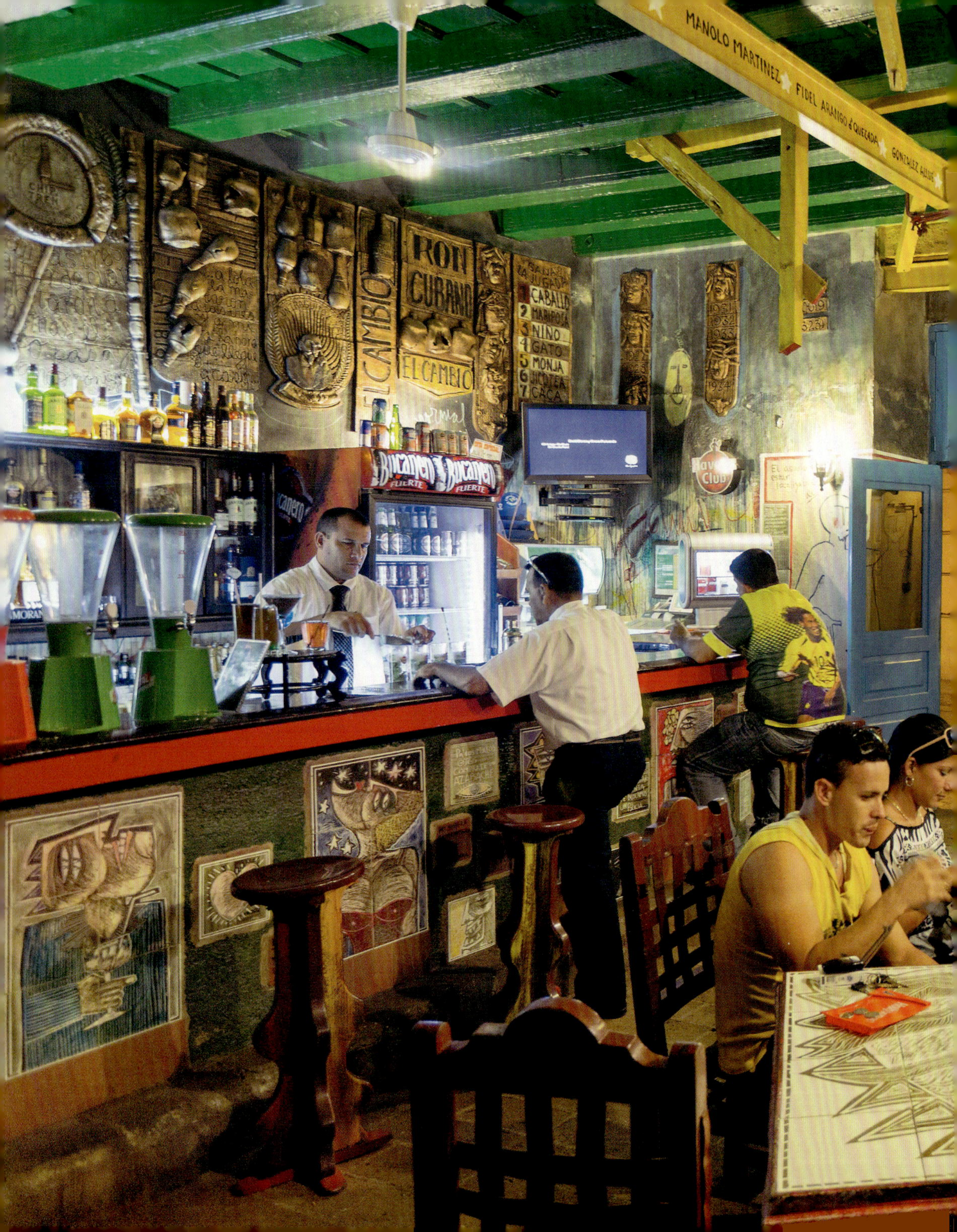

MANOLO MARTINEZ
FIDEL ARANGO y QUEZADA
GONZÁLEZ
RON
CUBANO
EL CAMBIO
EL CAMBIO
CABALLO
MARIPOSA
NIÑO
GATO
MONJA
JICOTEA
CACA
Bucanero
FUERTE
Bucanero
FUERTE
Havana
Club

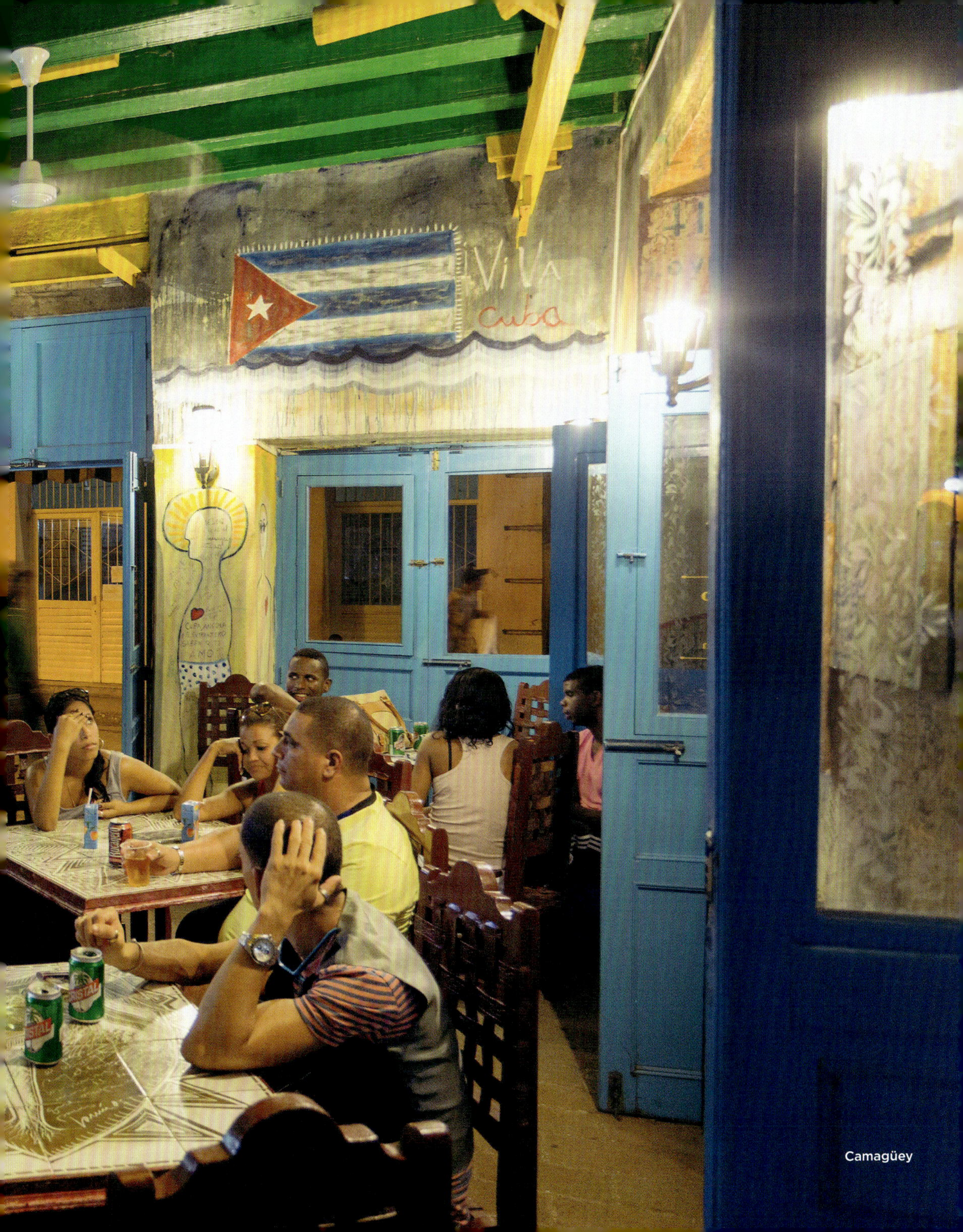

Camagüey

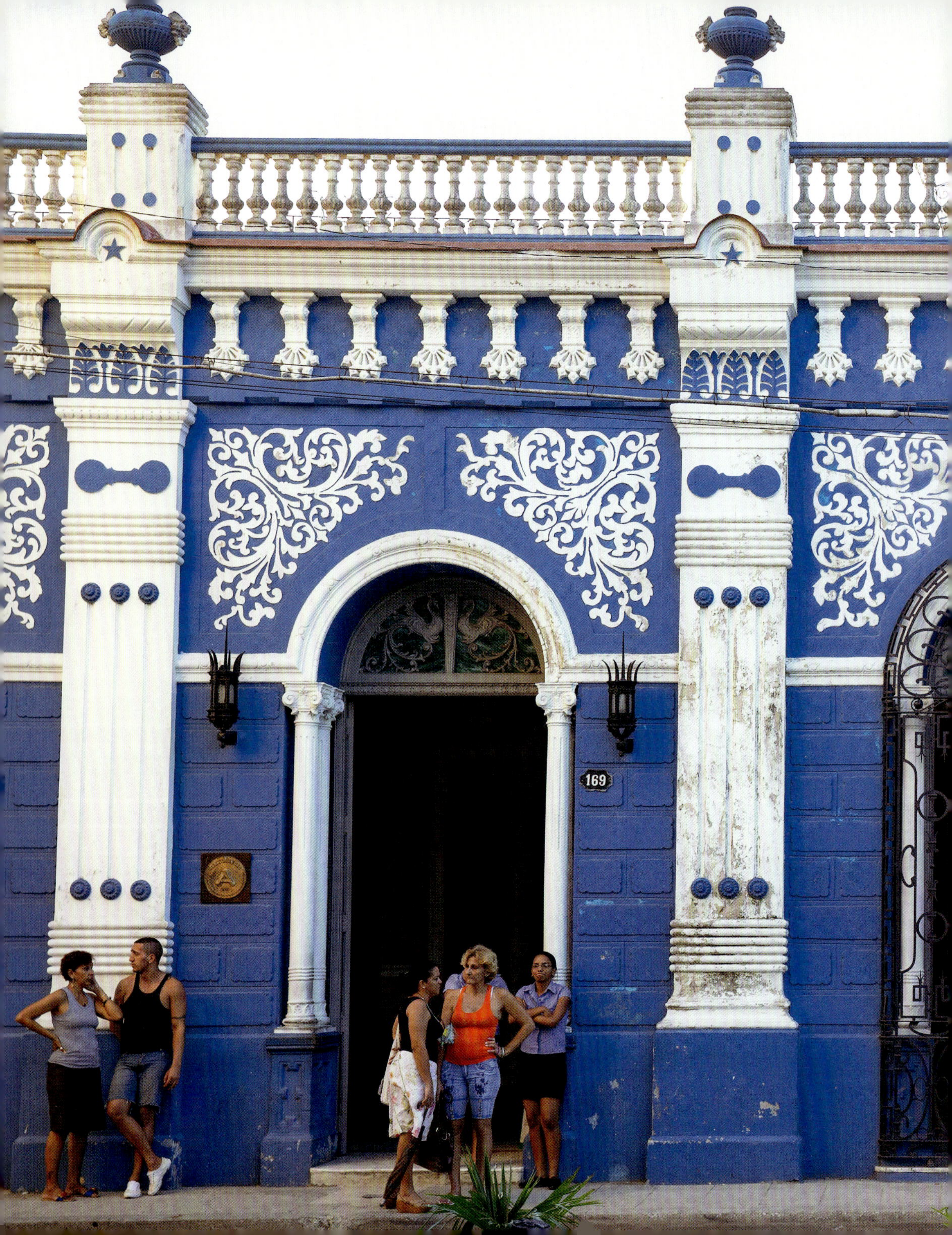
169

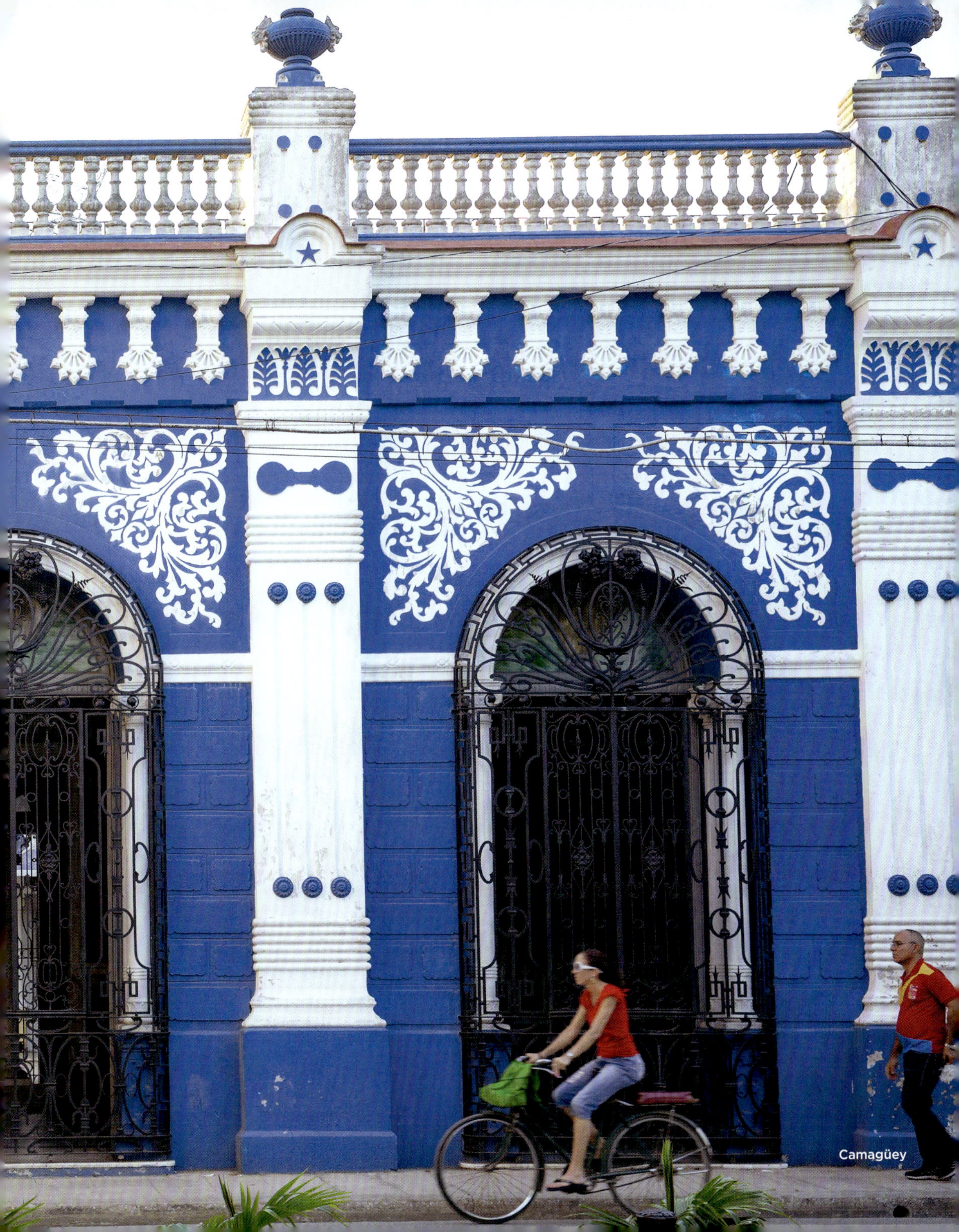
Camagüey

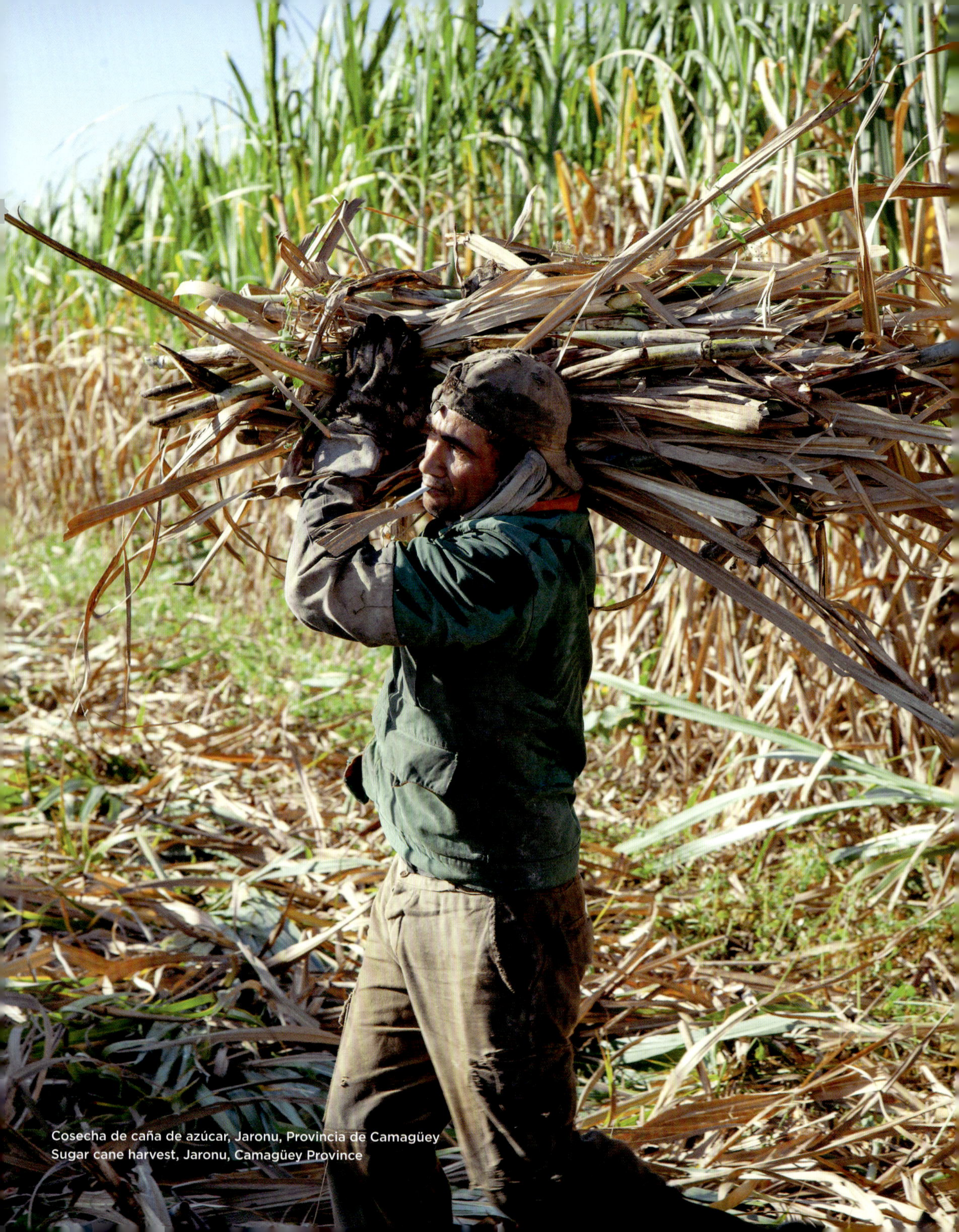

Cosecha de caña de azúcar, Jaronu, Provincia de Camagüey
Sugar cane harvest, Jaronu, Camagüey Province

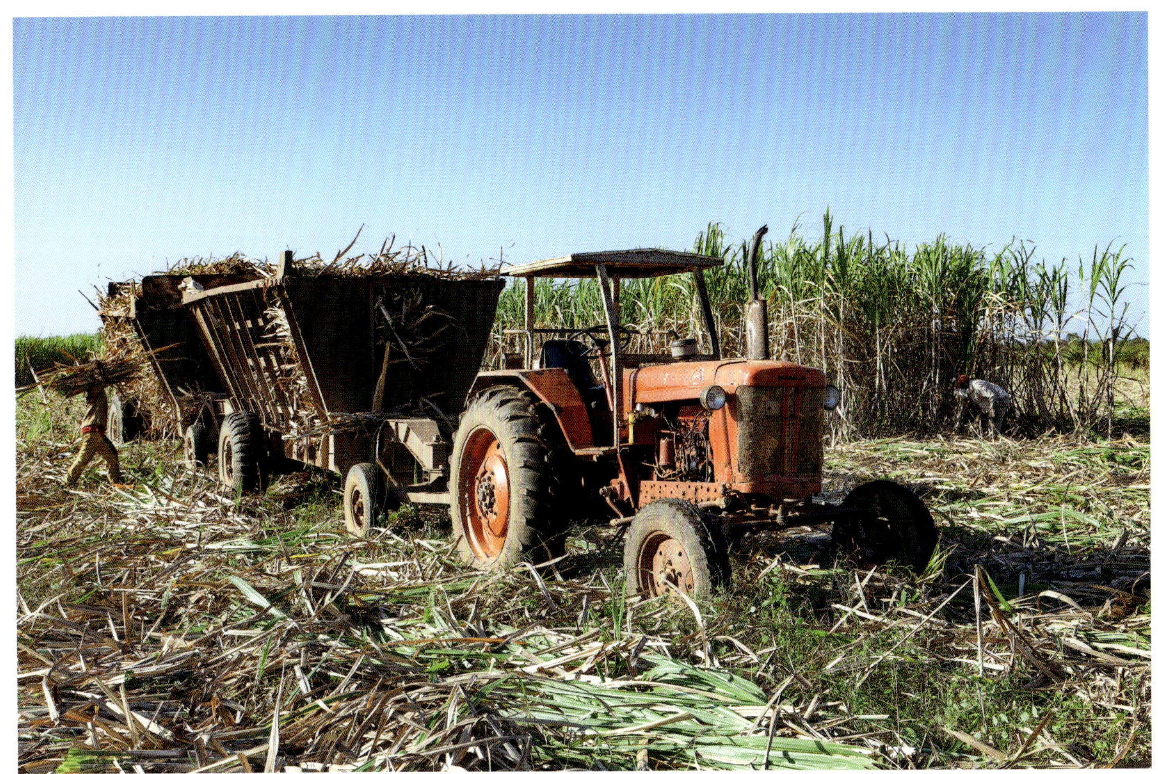

Cosecha de caña de azúcar, Jaronu, Provincia de Camagüey
Sugar cane harvest, Jaronu, Camagüey Province

Sugar

Sugar is in short supply in Cuba because the sugar monoculture that produced Cuba's wealth until the 20th century has been reduced to a minimum. Sugar production fell from around 8 million tonnes (9 million tons) at the end of the 1980s to 1.1 million tonnes (1.2 million tons) in 2018. More than half of the sugar production goes to China in exchange for cheap credit, trains, buses and trucks.

Azúcar

El azúcar escasea en Cuba porque el monocultivo azucarero que produjo la riqueza de Cuba hasta el siglo XX se redujo al mínimo. La producción de azúcar cayó de unos 8 millones de toneladas a finales de los años 80 a 1,1 millones de toneladas en 2018, y más de la mitad de la producción de azúcar va a China a cambio de créditos baratos, trenes, autobuses y camiones.

Sucre

À Cuba, le sucre se fait rare, car la monoculture de la canne à sucre, qui fit la richesse de Cuba pratiquement jusqu'à la fin du xxᵉ siècle, a été réduite au minimum. La production de sucre a chuté drastiquement, d'environ 8 millions de tonnes à la fin des années 1980 à 1,1 million de tonnes en 2018. Plus de la moitié de la production est exportée vers la Chine, en échange de crédits avantageux, trains, bus et camions.

Açucar

O açúcar é escasso em Cuba porque a monocultura de açúcar, que produziu a riqueza de Cuba até o século XX, foi reduzida ao mínimo. A produção de açúcar caiu de cerca de 8 milhões de toneladas no final dos anos 80 para 1,1 milhões de toneladas em 2018. Mais da metade da produção de açúcar vai para a China em troca de crédito barato, trens, ônibus e caminhões.

Zucker

Zucker wird in Kuba knapp, denn die Zucker-Monokultur, die bis ins 20. Jahrhundert den Reichtum Kubas hervorbrachte, wurde auf ein Minimum reduziert. Die Zuckerproduktion fiel von rund 8 Millionen Tonnen Ende der 1980er-Jahre auf 1,1 Millionen. Tonnen 2018. Über die Hälfte der Zuckerproduktion geht nach China, im Tausch gegen günstige Kredite, Züge, Busse und Lastwagen.

Suiker

Er is een tekort aan suiker in Cuba omdat de suikermonocultuur die tot de 20e eeuw de rijkdom van Cuba produceerde, tot een minimum werd beperkt. De suikerproductie daalde van ongeveer 8 miljoen ton eind jaren tachtig tot 1,1 miljoen ton in 2018. Meer dan de helft van de suikerproductie gaat naar China in ruil voor goedkope kredieten, treinen, bussen en vrachtwagens.

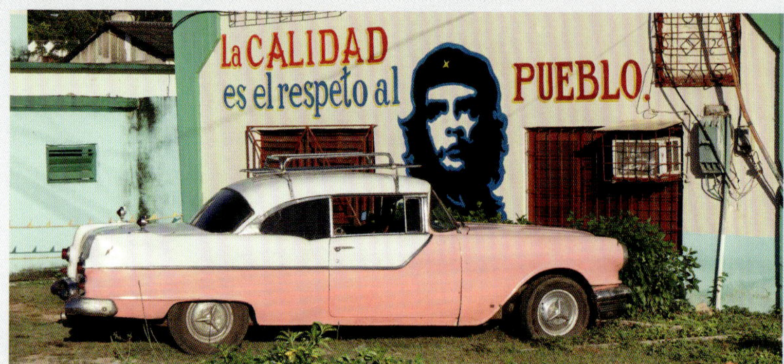

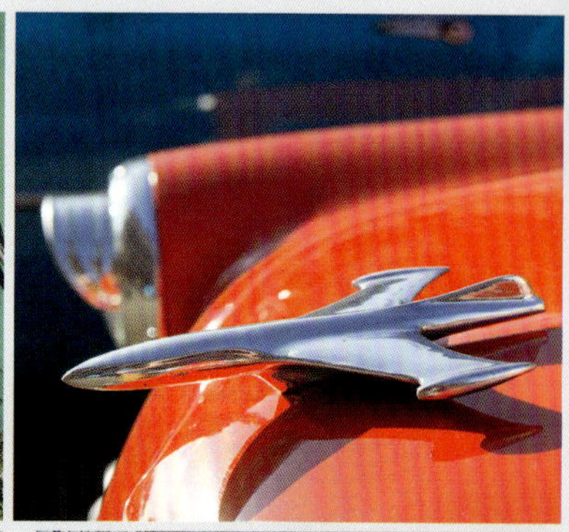

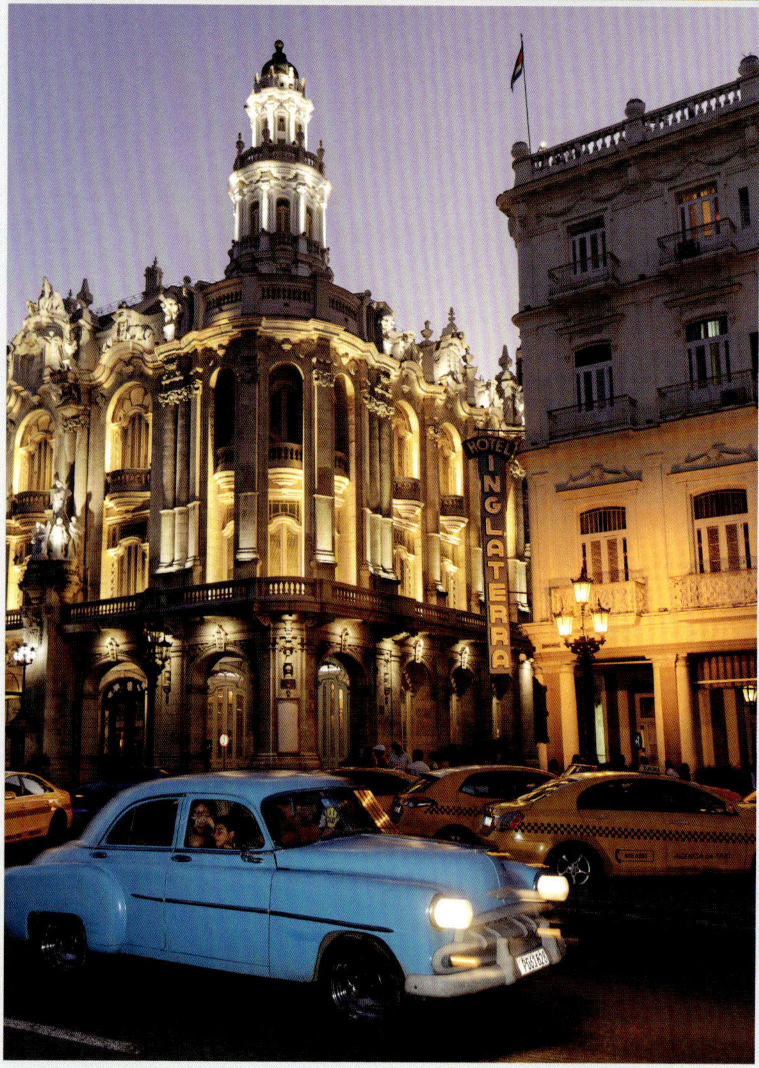

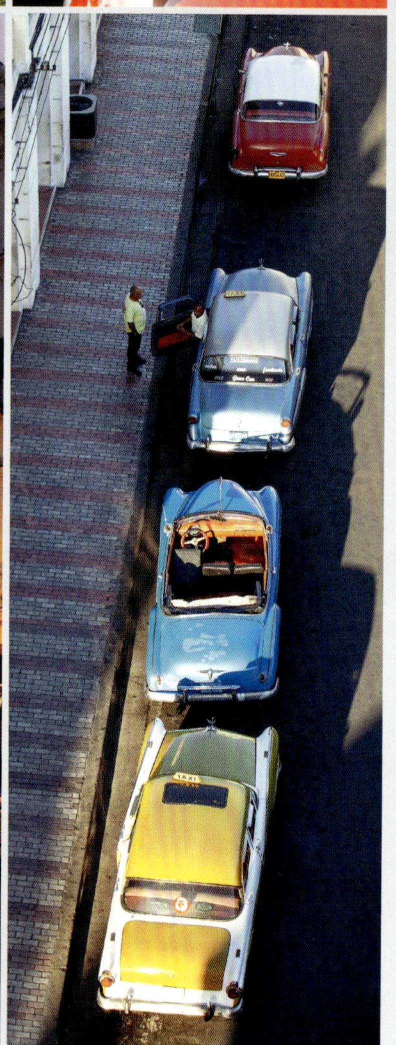

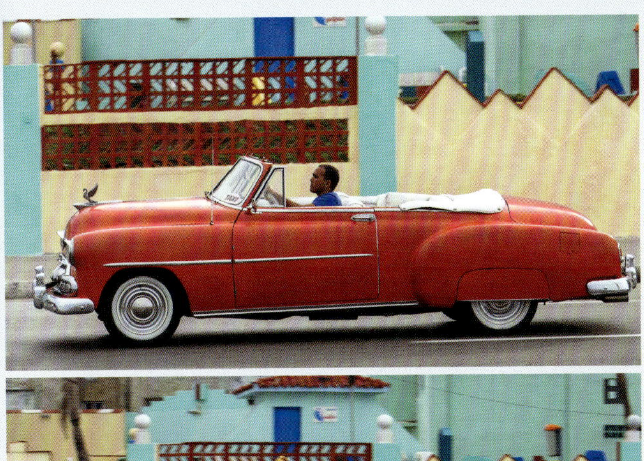

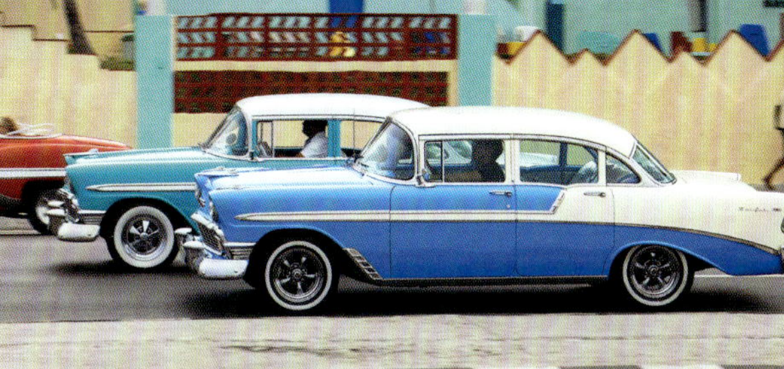

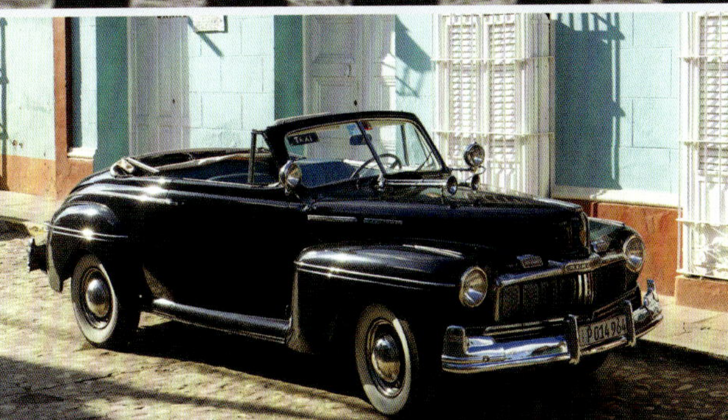

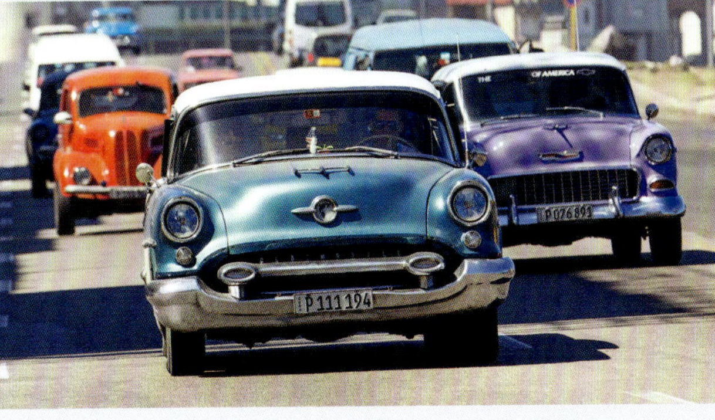

Vintage Cars

There are about 75,000 classic American cars on Cuba, but hardly any of them are still in their original condition, because after 1959 spare parts were not available. Converting an old car into a pastel-colored jewel is very expensive and labor-intensive. Since private people can acquire a taxi license and are allowed to use these oldtimers as shared taxis or for tourists, the business flourishes.

Vieilles américaines

Environ 75 000 vieilles voitures américaines sont toujours en usage à Cuba, mais pratiquement toutes ont subi des modifications, car les pièces de rechange sont indisponibles depuis 1959. Transformer un vieux tacot en bijou pastel revient très cher et requiert beaucoup de travail. Depuis que les personnes privées sont autorisées à acheter une licence de taxi et que les vieilles américaines sont converties en taxis collectifs ou en voitures de location pour touristes, leur commerce est florissant.

Oldtimer

Rund 75 000 amerikanische Oldtimer gibt es auf Kuba, doch kaum einer ist noch im Originalzustand, denn nach 1959 fehlten Ersatzteile. Einen alten Schlitten in ein pastellfarbenes Juwel zu verwandeln, ist sehr teuer und arbeitsaufwändig. Seit Privatleute eine Taxilizenz erwerben und die Oldtimer als Sammeltaxis oder für Touristen einsetzen dürfen, floriert das Geschäft.

Coches de época

En Cuba hay alrededor de 75 000 coches clásicos americanos, pero casi ninguno de ellos se encuentra en su estado original, porque después de 1959 faltaban piezas de repuesto. Convertir un coche antiguo en una joya de color pastel es muy caro y requiere mucha mano de obra. Dado que los particulares adquieren una licencia de taxi y se les permite utilizar los coches de época como taxis compartidos o para turistas, el negocio florece.

Carro antigo

Há cerca de 75 000 carros clássicos americanos em Cuba, mas quase nenhum deles ainda está no seu estado original, porque desde 1959 faltam peças de reposição. Transformar um carro antigo em uma jóia de cor pastel é muito caro e requer trabalho intensivo. A partir do momento que as pessoas privadas puderam adquirem uma licença de táxi e foram autorizados a usar os carros antigos como táxis compartilhados ou para turistas, o negócio floresce.

Klassieke auto

Er zijn ongeveer 75 000 Amerikaanse klassieke auto's op Cuba, maar bijna geen enkele is nog in originele staat, want na 1959 ontbraken er onderdelen. Een oude slee ombouwen tot een pastelkleurig juweel is erg duur en arbeidsintensief. Omdat particulieren een taxivergunning kunnen krijgen en de oldtimers mogen gebruiken als gedeelde taxi's of voor toeristen, bloeit het bedrijf.

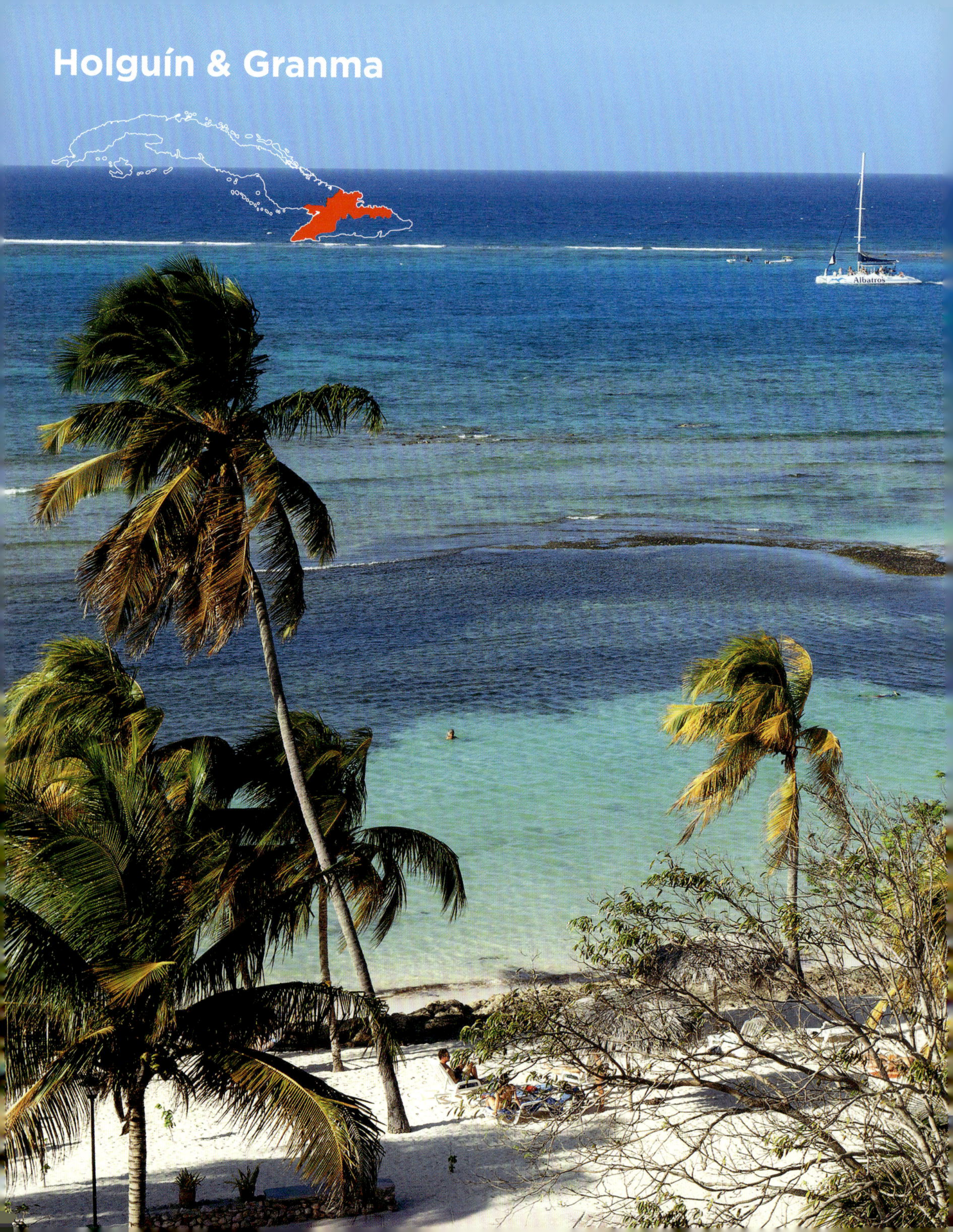

Holguín & Granma
Albatros

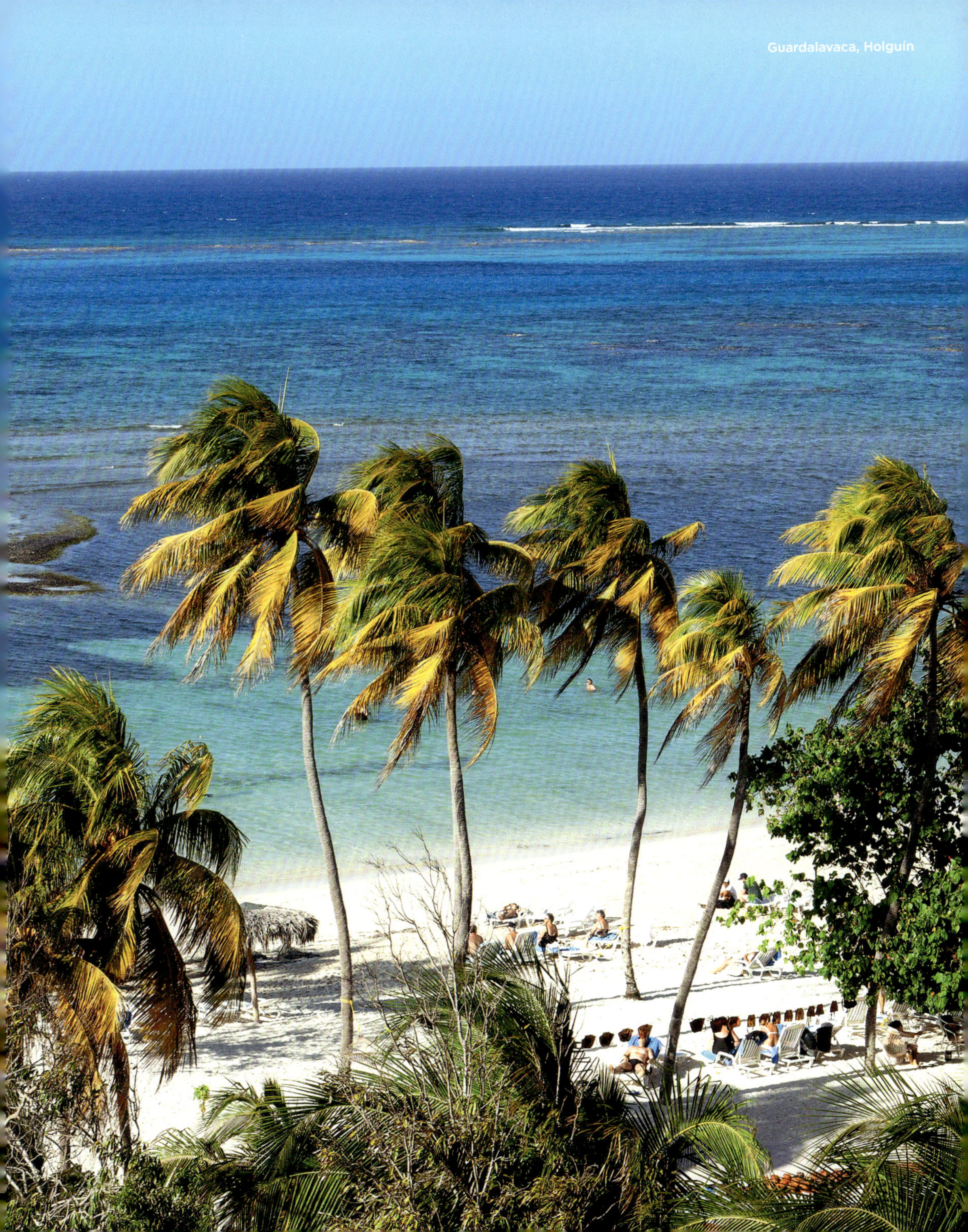
Guardalavaca, Holguín

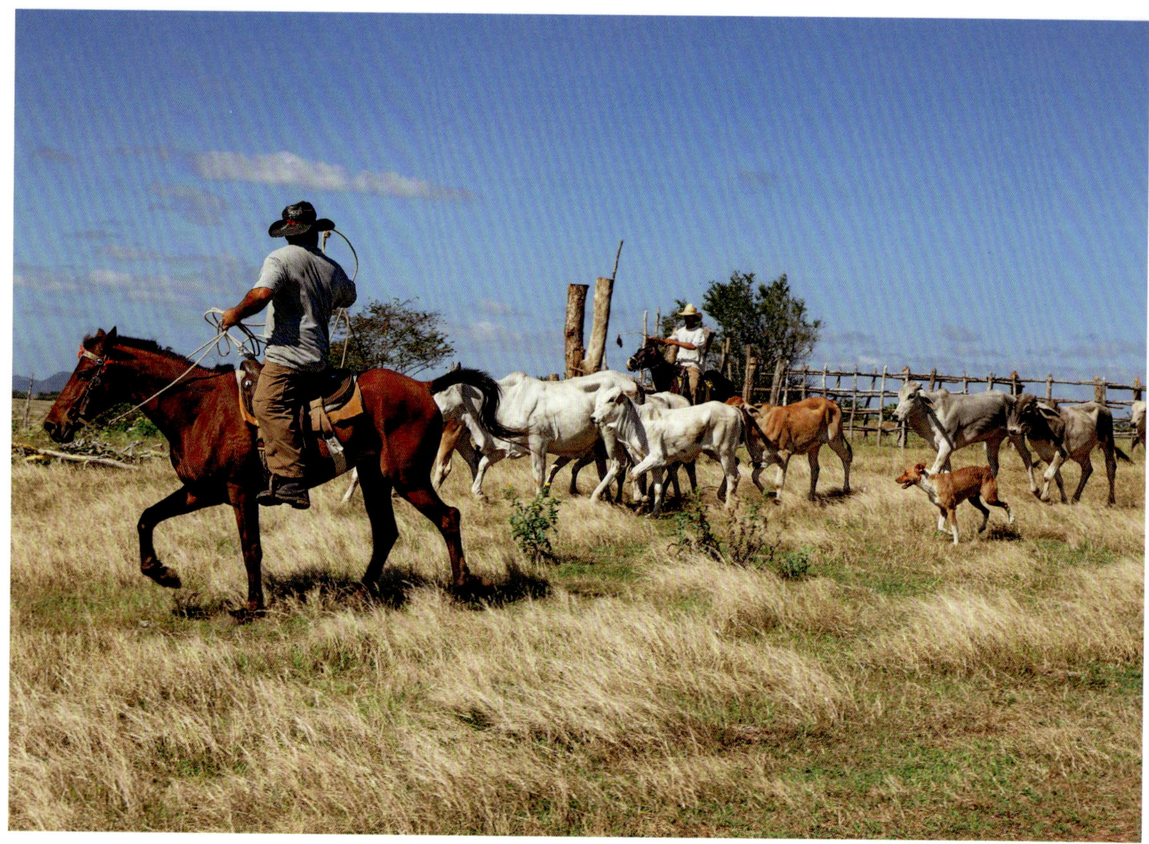

Fray Benito, Holguín

Holguín and Granma

On 28 October 1492, Columbus landed in Bariay Bay on the north coast of Holguín province, where up to 300,000 Taíno and Siboney Indians lived. The monument in the bay is a reminder of this historical turning point: sixteen Indian statues of gods are almost pushed aside by columns arranged in the shape of a ship's hull. The entire coastal region with the town of Gibara, the white beaches of Guardalavaca and the excavation sites of Banes, where the largest Indian cemetery in the Caribbean was found, is part of the Bariay National Park. To the south is the province of Granma with the mountains of the Sierra Maestra and the cities of Bayamo and Manzanillo.

Holguín et Granma

Le 28 octobre 1492, Christophe Colomb accosta dans la baie de Bariay, sur la côte nord de la province d'Holguín, où vivaient 300 000 Indiens des peuples Taïno et Siboney. Le monument érigé dans la baie immortalise cet événement décisif : 17 statues de dieux indiens sont disposées en une forme de coque de bateau. L'ensemble de la région côtière fait partie du parc national de Bariay, y compris le site de Gibara, les plages blanches de Guardalavaca et le site archéologique de Banes, où fut découvert le plus vaste cimetière indien des Caraïbes. Au sud, la province de Granma est bordée par la chaîne montagneuse de la sierra Maestra et les petites villes de Bayamo et Manzanillo.

Holguín und Granma

Am 28. Oktober 1492 landete Kolumbus in der Bariay-Bucht an der Nordküste der Provinz Holguín, wo bis zu 300 000 Taíno- und Siboney-Indianer lebten. Das Denkmal in der Bucht erinnert an diese historische Zäsur: Sechzehn indianische Götterstatuen werden von in Form eines Schiffsrumpfes angeordneten Säulen geradezu abgedrängt. Die gesamte Küstenregion mit dem Ort Gibara, den weißen Stränden Guardalavacas bis zu den Ausgrabungsstätten von Banes, wo der größte indianische Friedhof der Karibik gefunden wurde, gehört zum Nationalpark Bariay. Im Süden schließt sich die Provinz Granma mit der Sierra Maestra und den Städten Bayamo und Manzanillo an.

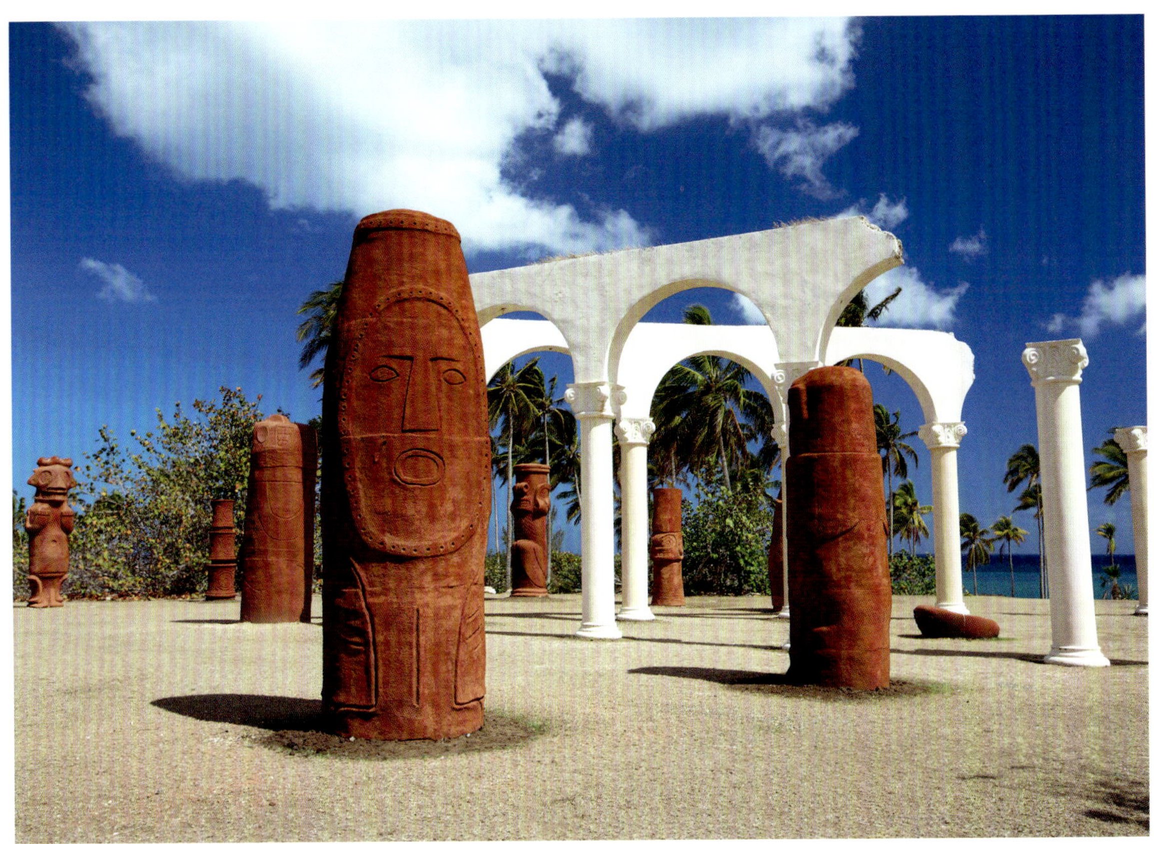

Parque Nacional Monumento Bariay, Holguín

Holguín y Granma

El 28 de octubre de 1492, Colón desembarcó en la bahía de Bariay, en la costa norte de la provincia de Holguín, donde vivían hasta 300 000 indios Taíno y Siboney. El monumento de la bahía recuerda esta histórica cesura: dieciséis estatuas indias de dioses son casi empujadas hacia un lado por columnas dispuestas en forma de casco de barco. Toda la región costera con la ciudad de Gibara, las playas blancas de Guardalavaca y los sitios de excavación de Banes, donde se encontró el cementerio indígena más grande del Caribe, pertenece al Parque Nacional Bariay. Al sur se encuentra la provincia de Granma con la Sierra Maestra y las ciudades de Bayamo y Manzanillo.

Holguín e Granma

Em 28 de outubro de 1492, Colombo desembarcou na Baía de Bariay, na costa norte da província de Holguín, onde viviam até 300 000 índios Taíno e Siboney. O monumento na baía comemora este momento histórico: dezesseis estátuas de deuses indianos que são quase empurradas para o lado por colunas dispostas sob a forma de casco de navio. Toda a região costeira, incluindo a cidade de Gibara, as praias brancas de Guardalavaca e os sítios de escavação arqueológica de Banes, onde foi encontrado o maior cemitério indígena do Caribe, pertencem ao Parque Nacional Bariay. Ao sul está a província de Granma com a Serra Mestra e as cidades de Bayamo e Manzanillo.

Holguín en Oma

Op 28 oktober 1492 landde Columbus in de baai van Bariay aan de noordkust van de provincie Holguín, waar tot 300 000 Taíno en Siboney Indianen woonden. Het monument in de baai herinnert aan deze historische cesuur: zestien Indiase godenbeelden worden bijna terzijde geschoven door zuilen in de vorm van een scheepsromp. Het hele kustgebied met de stad Gibara, de witte stranden van Guardalavaca en de opgravingsplaatsen van Banes, waar de grootste indiaanse begraafplaats van het Caribisch gebied is gevonden, behoort tot het Bariay National Park. In het zuiden ligt de provincie Granma met de Sierra Maestra en de steden Bayamo en Manzanillo.

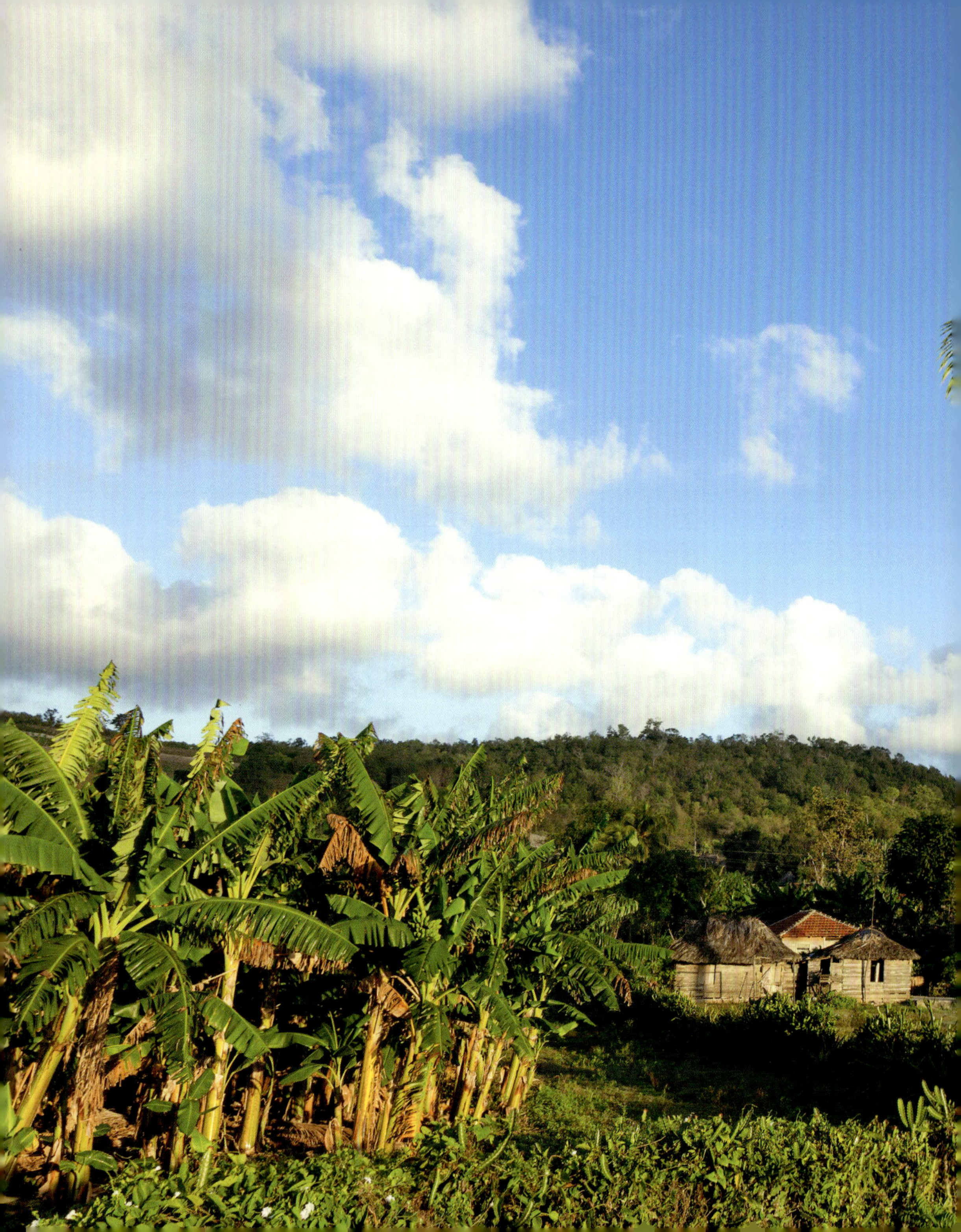

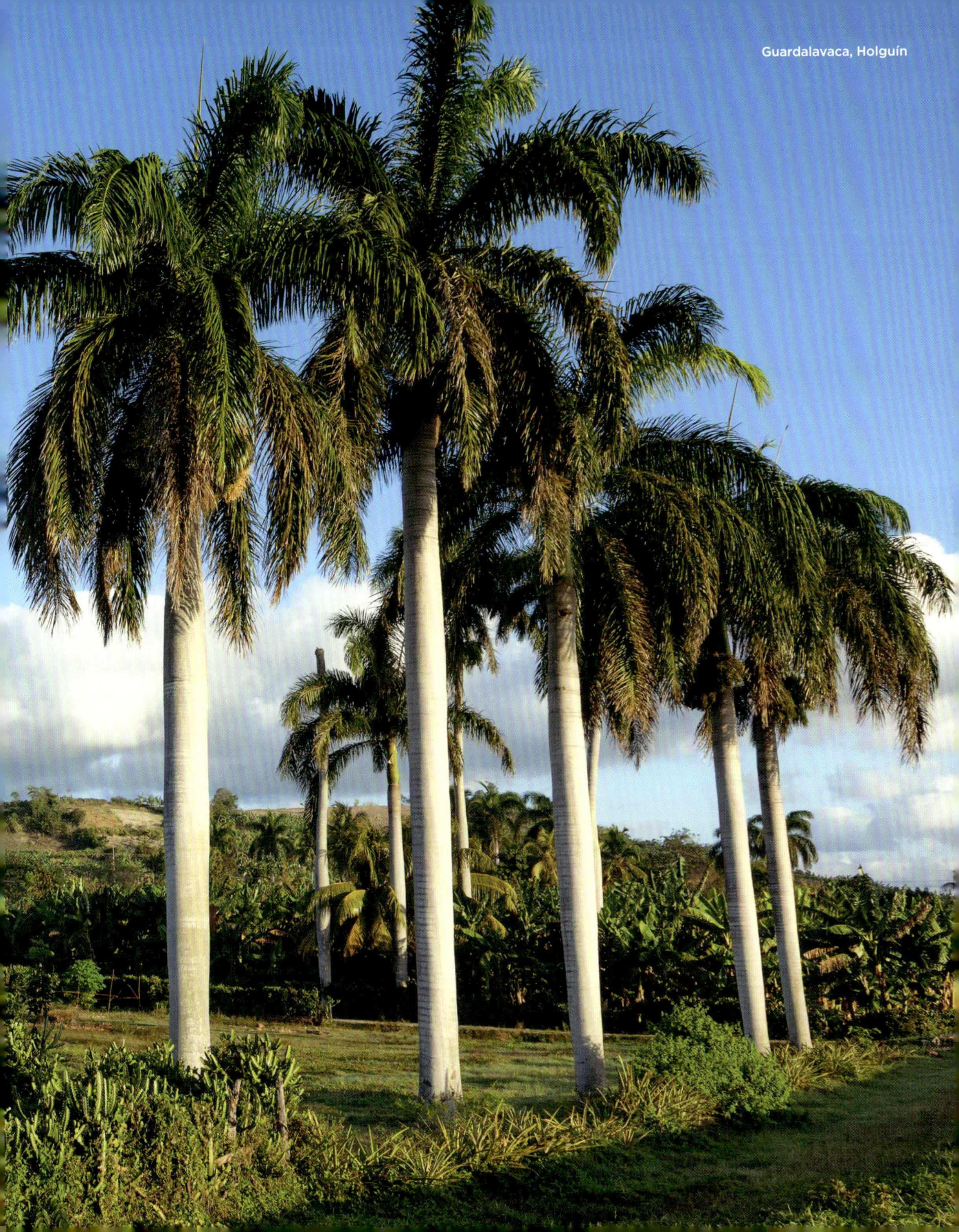
Guardalavaca, Holguín

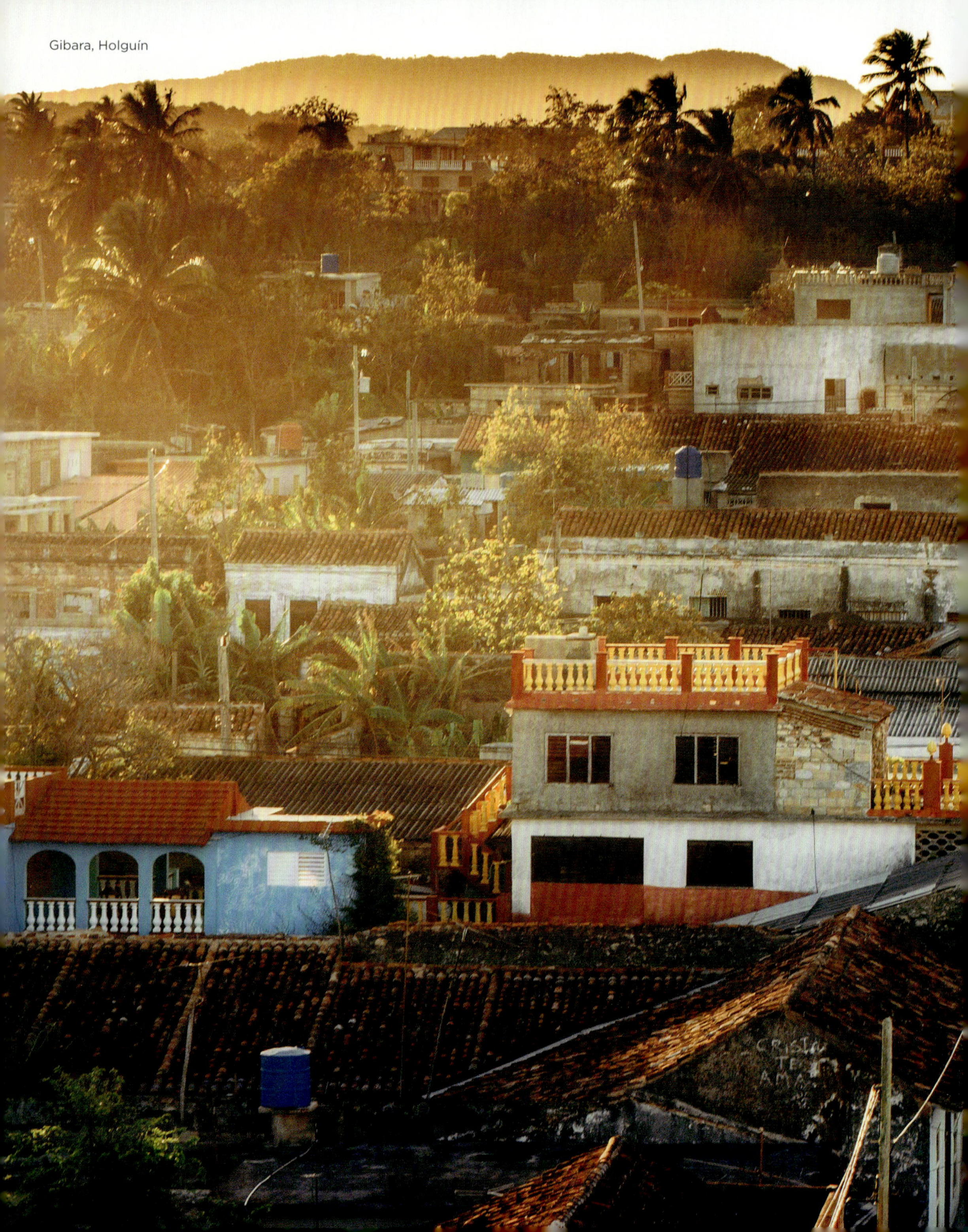
Gibara, Holguín

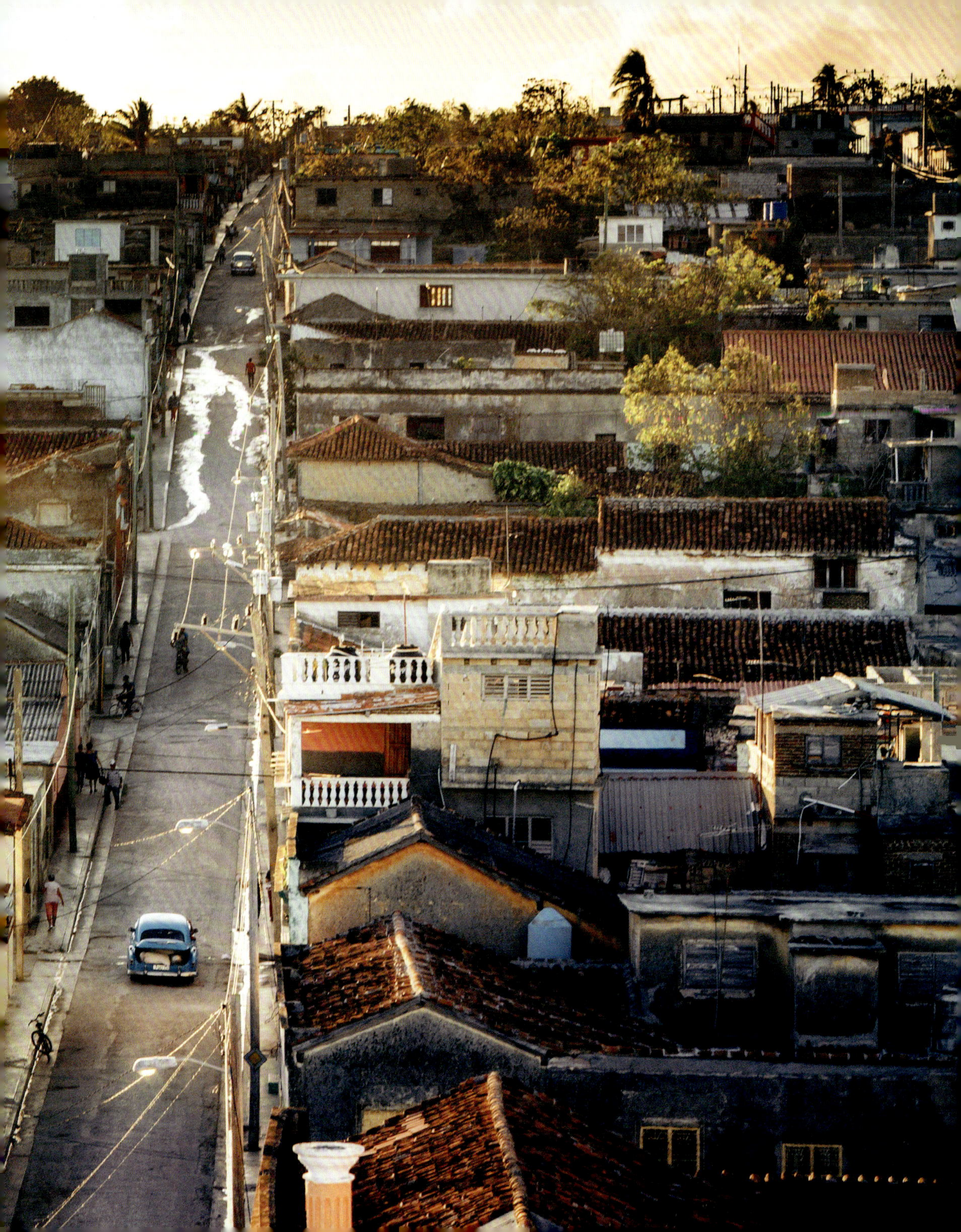

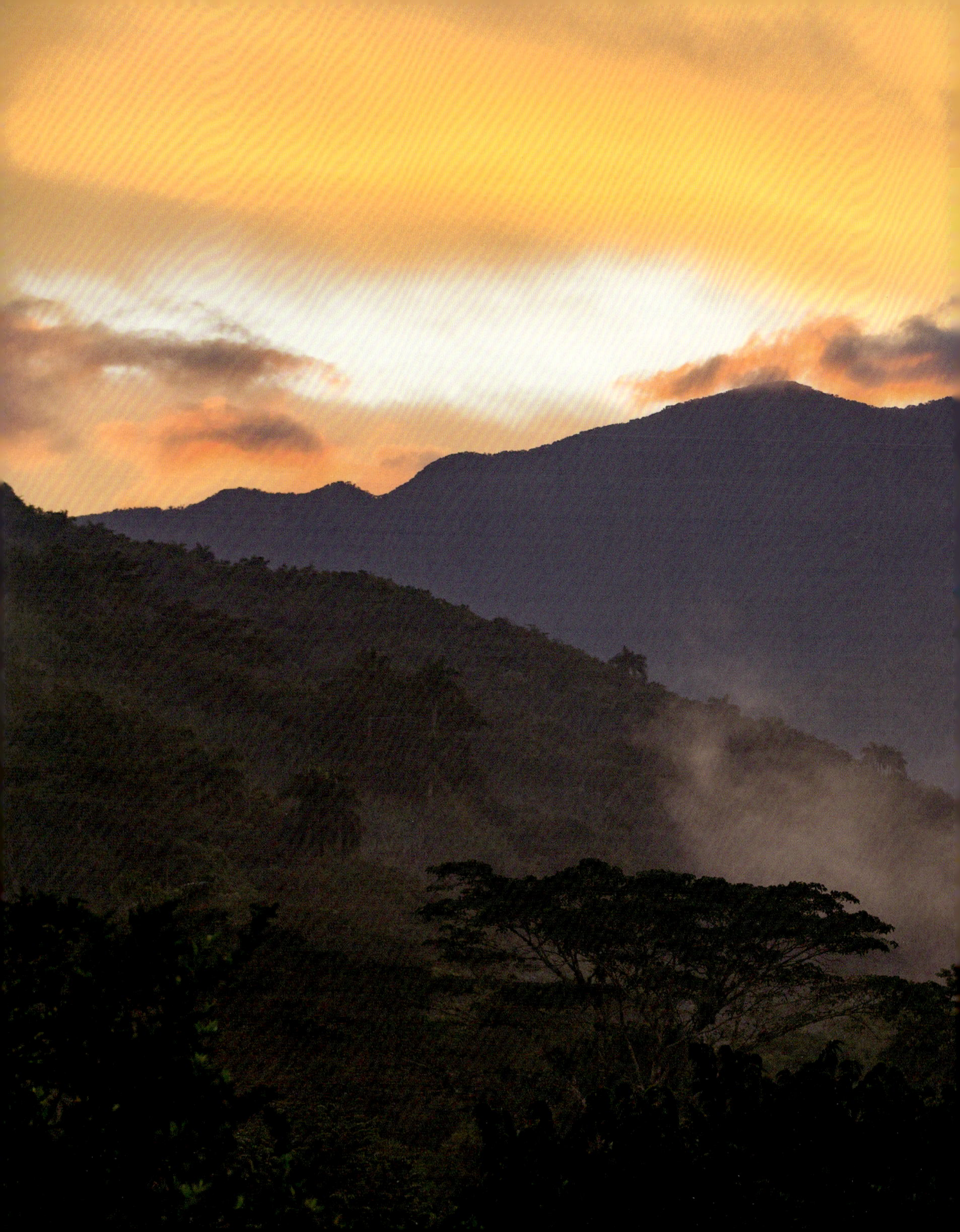

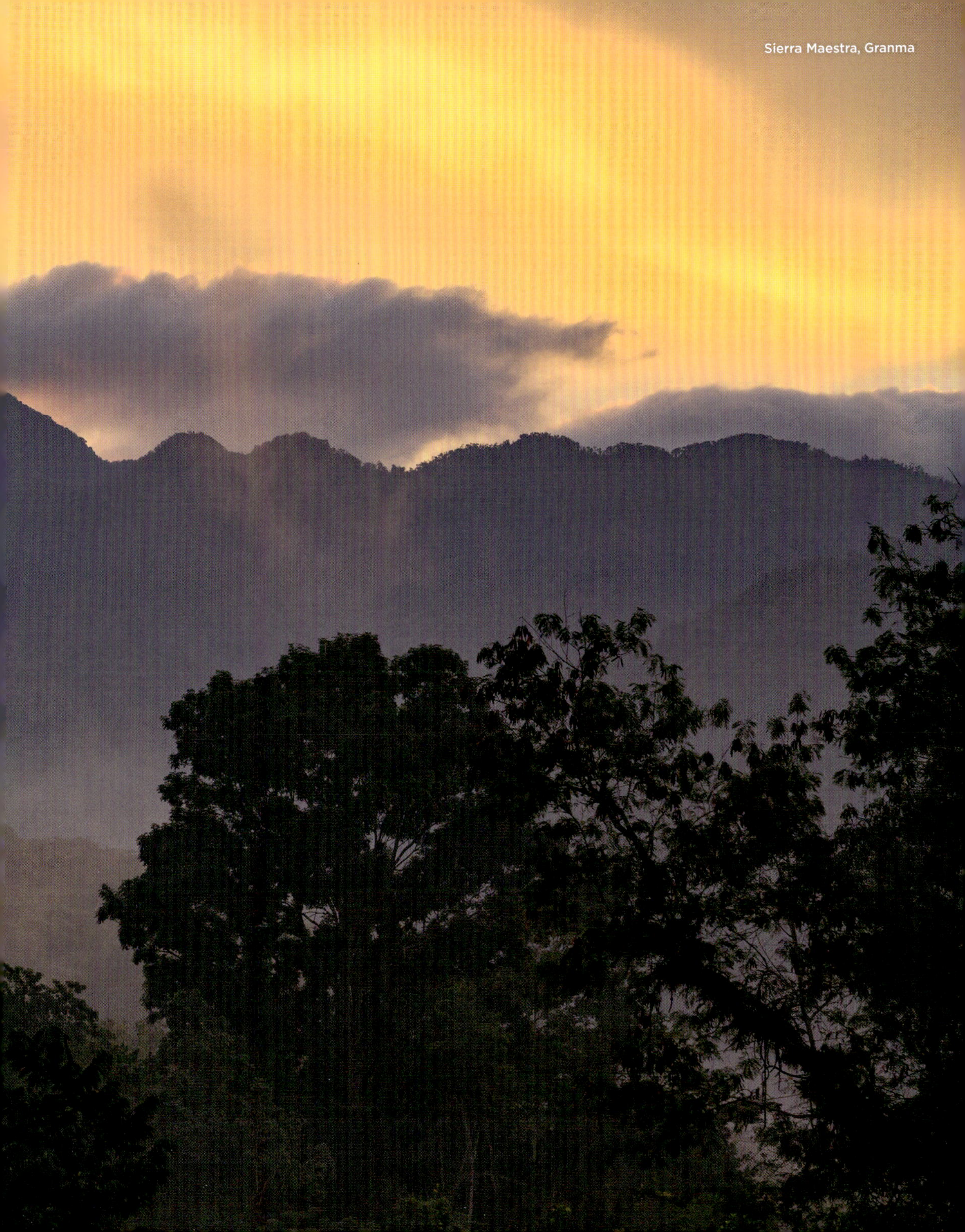
Sierra Maestra, Granma

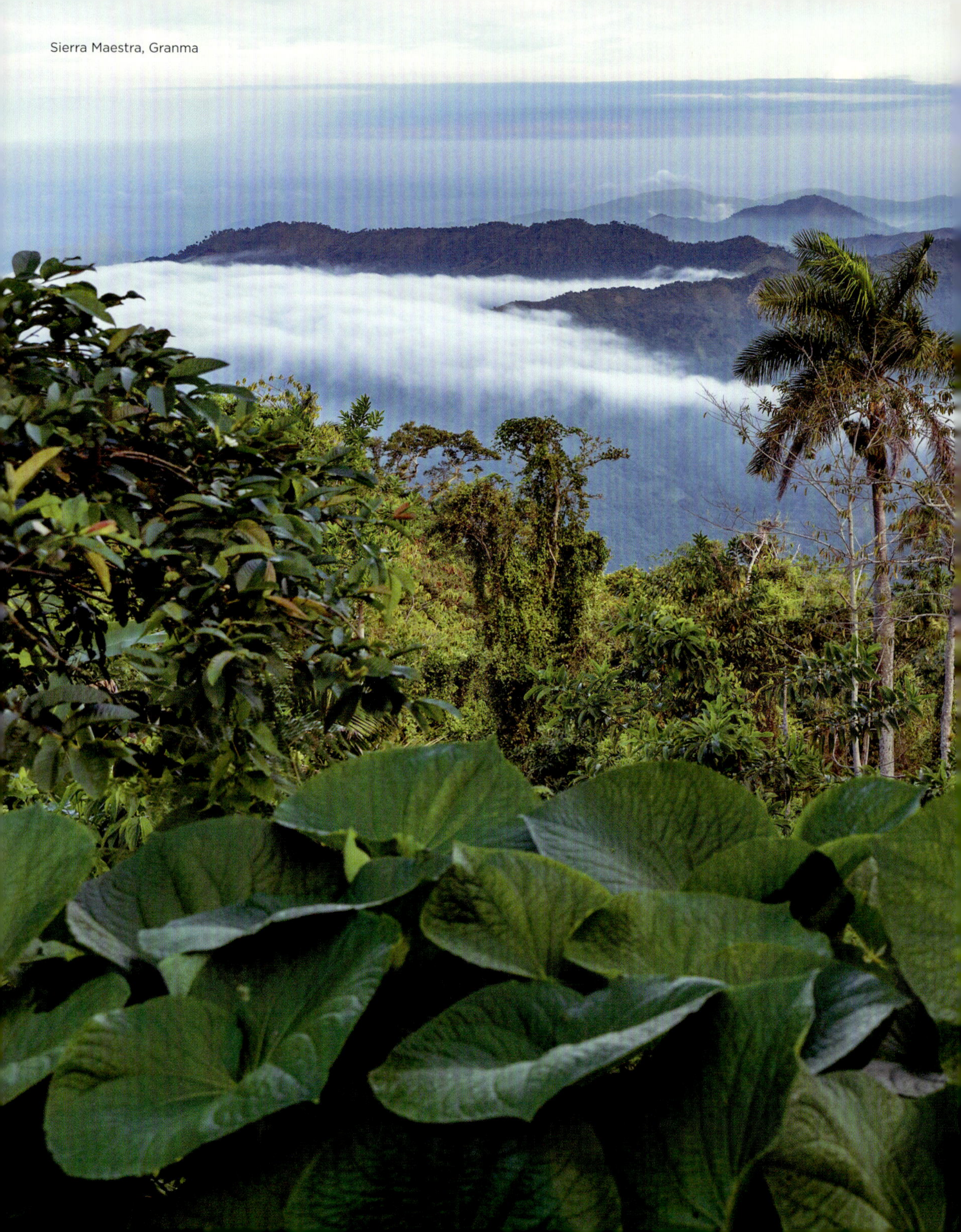
Sierra Maestra, Granma

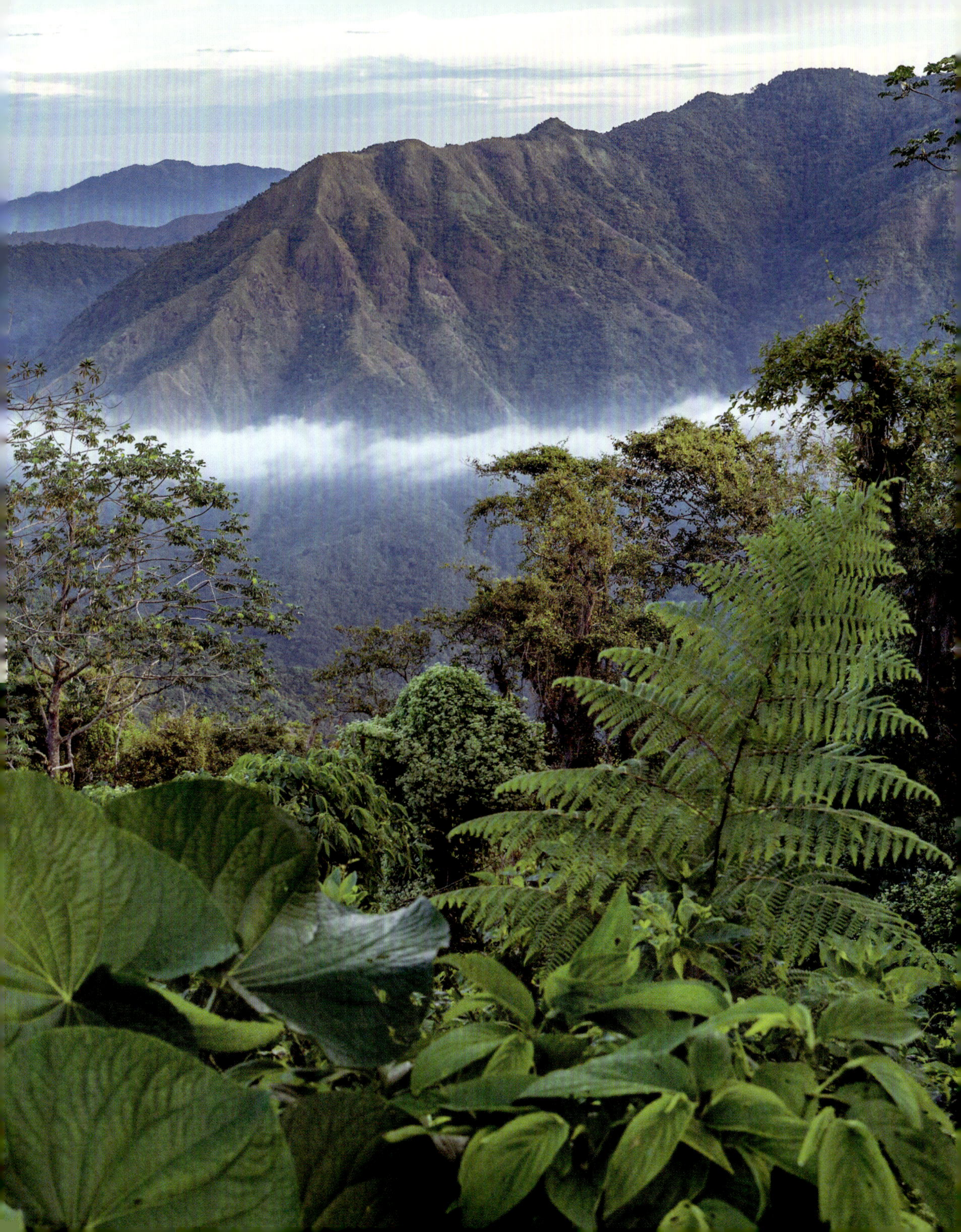

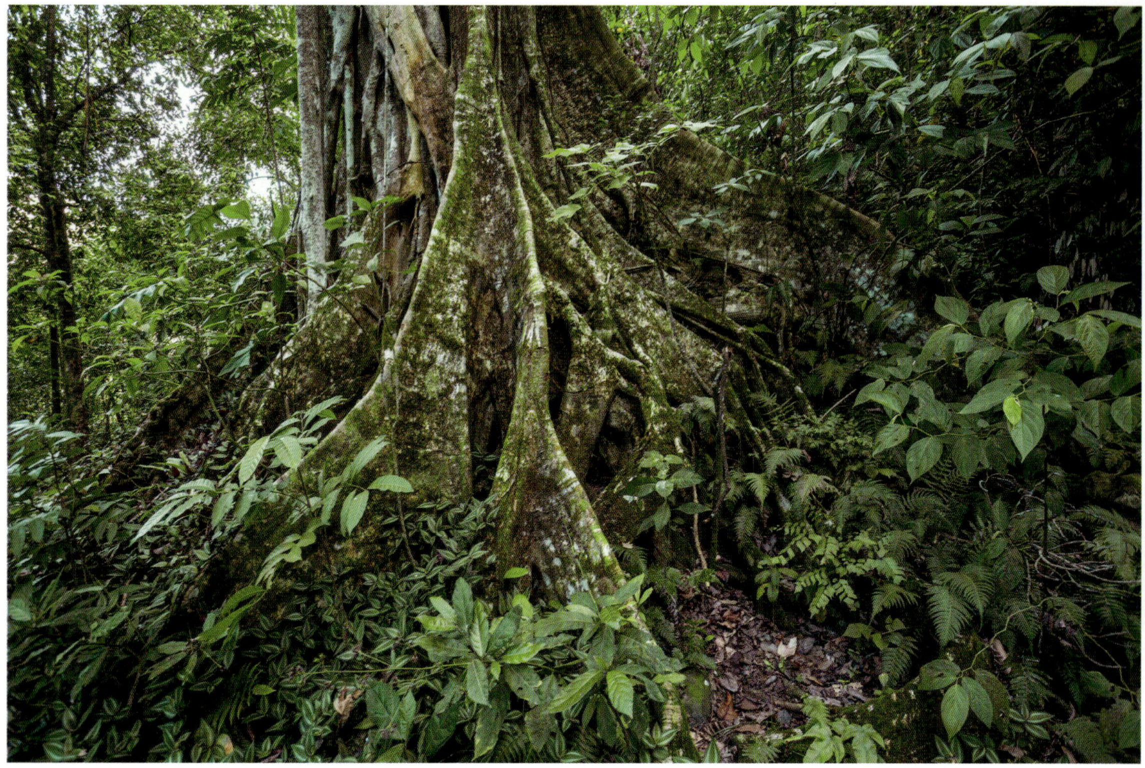

Sierra Maestra, Granma

Sierra Maestra National Park

In the mountains of the Sierra Maestra, the largest mountain range in Cuba and overgrown with rain and cloud forests, a very species-rich flora and fauna survives, some of which can only be found here. At the foot of Pico Turquino, at 1974 m (6476 ft) the highest mountain of Cuba, the rebel army under Fidel Castro had its headquarters (Comandancia de la Plata). Today it is a museum.

Parc national de la sierra Maestra

Dans les montagnes de la sierra Maestra, plus haute chaîne de Cuba, recouverte de forêts pluvieuses et de forêts de nuages, prospèrent une faune et une flore diverses, dont certaines espèces ont disparu du reste du globe. L'armée rebelle de Fidel Castro avait installé son quartier général (Comandancia de la Plata) au pied du pico Turquino, plus haut sommet de l'île culminant à 1974 m. Le site est aujourd'hui un musée.

Nationalpark Sierra Maestra

In den mit Regen- und Nebelwäldern bewachsenen Bergen der Sierra Maestra, dem größten Gebirge Kubas, überlebt eine sehr artenreiche Flora und Fauna, die es teilweise nur noch hier gibt. Zu Füßen des Pico Turquino, mit 1974 m der höchste Berg Kubas, hatte die Rebellenarmee unter Fidel Castro ihr Hauptquartier (Comandancia de la Plata), heute ein Museum.

Parque Nacional Sierra Maestra

En las montañas de la Sierra Maestra, la cordillera más grande de Cuba y que se encuentra cubierta de bosques lluviosos y nublados, sobrevive una flora y una fauna muy ricas en especies, algunas de las cuales solo se pueden encontrar aquí. Al pie del Pico Turquino que, con sus 1974 m, es la montaña más alta de Cuba, el ejército rebelde de Fidel Castro tenía su cuartel general (Comandancia de la Plata), que hoy es un museo.

Parque Nacional Sierra Maestra

Nas montanhas da Sierra Maestra, a maior cadeia montanhosa de Cuba, coberta de florestas tropicais e de nevoeiros, sobrevive uma variedade muito rica de flora e fauna, algumas das quais só podem ser encontradas aqui. Ao pé do Pico Turquino, a montanha mais alta de Cuba com 1974 m, o exército rebelde de Fidel Castro tinha sua sede (Comandancia de la Plata), hoje um museu.

Sierra Maestra Nationaal Park

In de met regen en nevelwouden begroeide bergen van Sierra Maestra (de grootste gebergte van Cuba), overleefde een zeer diverse flora en fauna, waarvan sommige alleen hier te vinden zijn. Aan de voet van Pico Turquino, met 1974 m de hoogste berg van Cuba, had het rebellenleger onder Fidel Castro zijn hoofdkwartier (Comandancia de la Plata), tegenwoordig een museum.

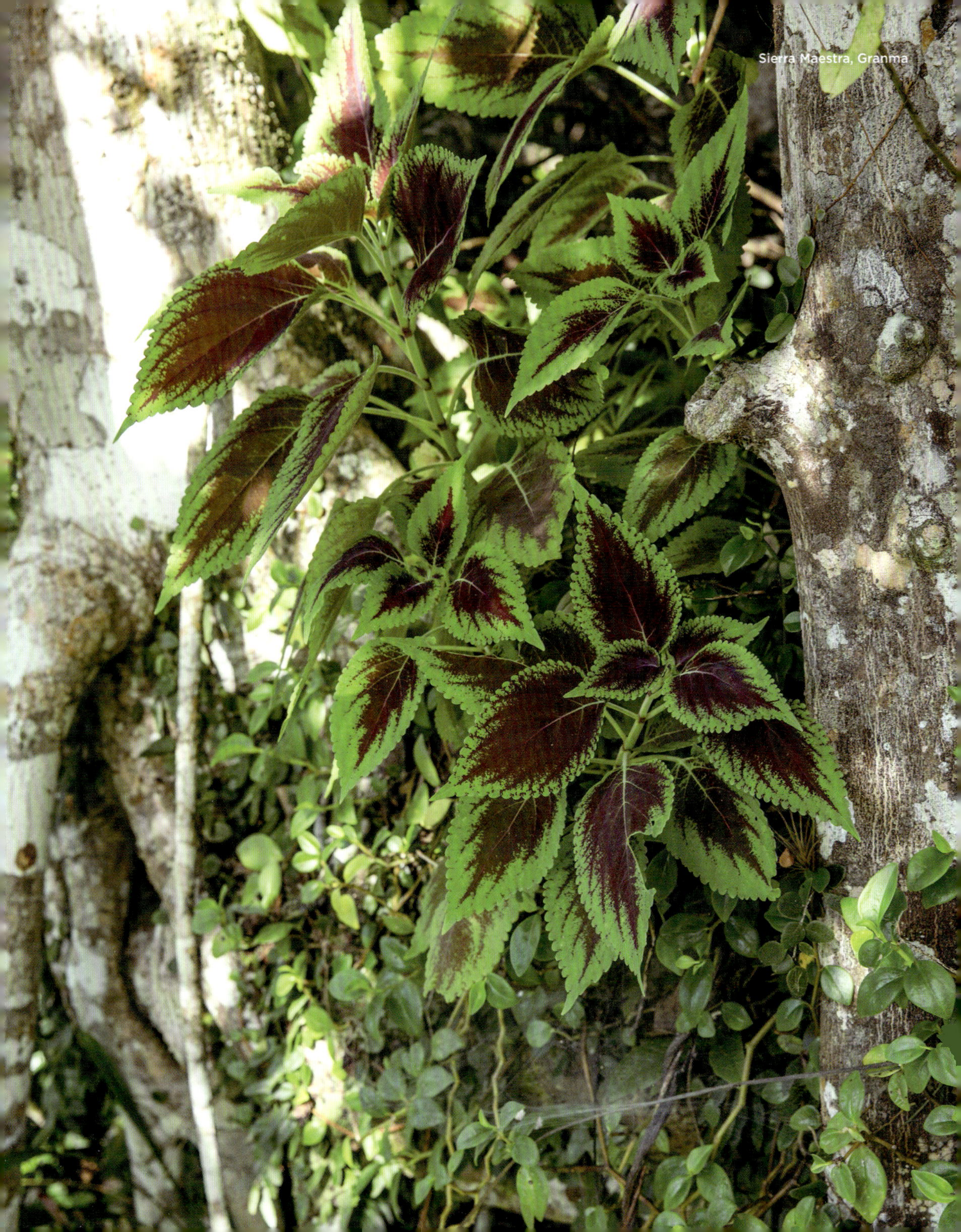
Sierra Maestra, Granma

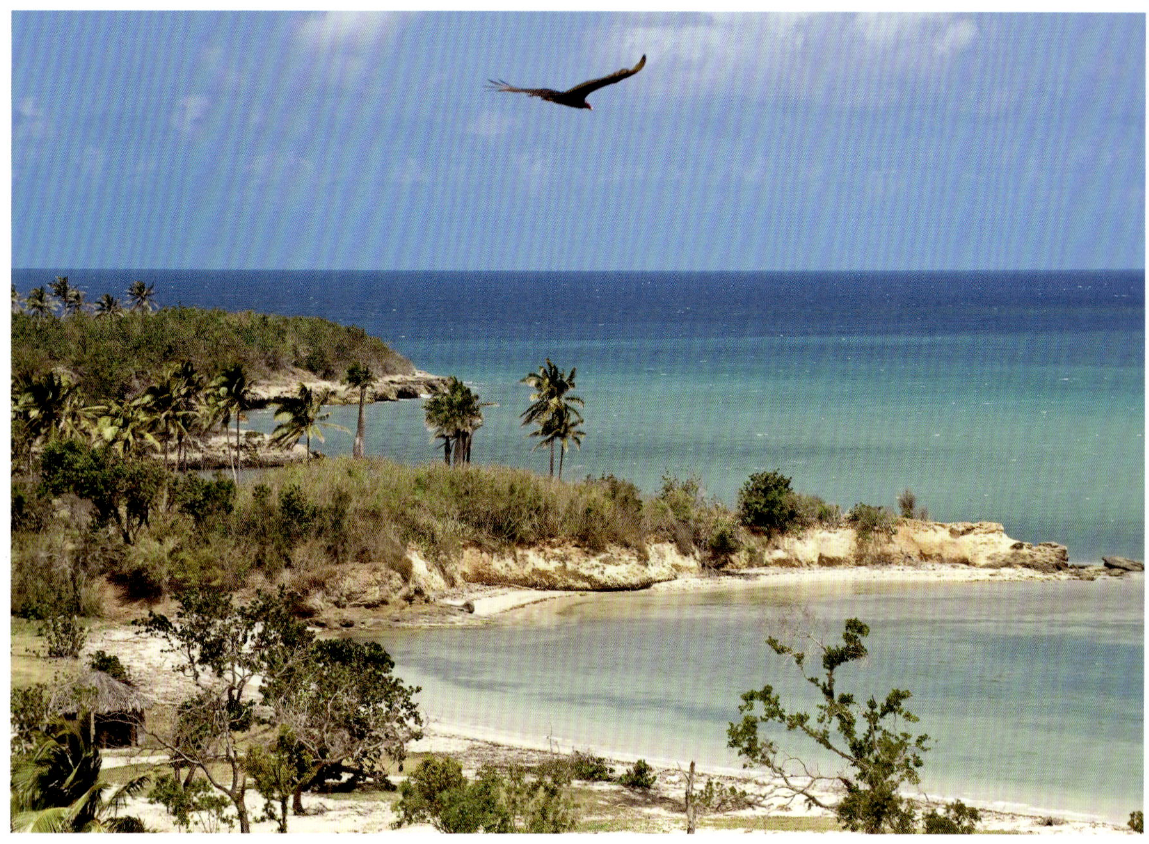

Parque Nacional de Bariay, Holguín

Bariay National Park

Even today it is easy to understand why Columbus wrote in his logbook that this island was "the most beautiful country that human eyes have ever seen". The region from Gibara to Banes is extremely scenic. The idyll of the coast continues inland, with lush green hills and gentle valleys, palm forests, flowering trees and here and there a palm straw-covered Bohío. The Taínos and Siboneyes living here believed that the foreign arrivals were emissaries of their gods, who had come to protect them from the attacks of the warring Aruak Indians; they received them with great respect.

Parc national de Bariay

Aujourd'hui encore, on comprend parfaitement pourquoi Christophe Colomb décrivit dans son journal cette île comme étant « la plus belle terre sur laquelle l'homme ait jamais posé les yeux ». La région entre Gibara et Banes offre un paysage au charme extraordinaire. Le tableau idyllique de la côte se prolonge à l'intérieur des terres par des collines vert intense et des vallons délicats parsemés de palmeraies, d'arbres fleuris et de quelques *bohíos* à toit de chaume de palmier. Les Taïnos et Siboneyes habitant la région pensaient que les arrivants étrangers étaient des descendants de leurs dieux, venus pour les défendre contre les attaques du peuple guerrier Aruak, et les accueillirent avec beaucoup de respect.

Nationalpark Bariay

Noch heute lässt sich gut nachvollziehen, warum Kolumbus in sein Bordbuch notierte, diese Insel sei „das schönste Land, das Menschenaugen je gesehen haben." Die Region von Gibara bis Banes ist landschaftlich außerordentlich reizvoll. Die Idylle an der Küste setzt sich im Inland fort, mit sattgrünen Hügeln und sanften Tälern, Palmwäldern, blühenden Bäumen und hier und da einem palmstrohgedeckten Bohío. Die hier lebenden Taínos und Siboneyes glaubten, die fremden Ankömmlinge seien Abgesandte ihrer Götter, die gekommen waren, um sie vor den Angriffen der kriegerischen Aruak-Indianer zu schützen, und nahmen sie mit großem Respekt auf.

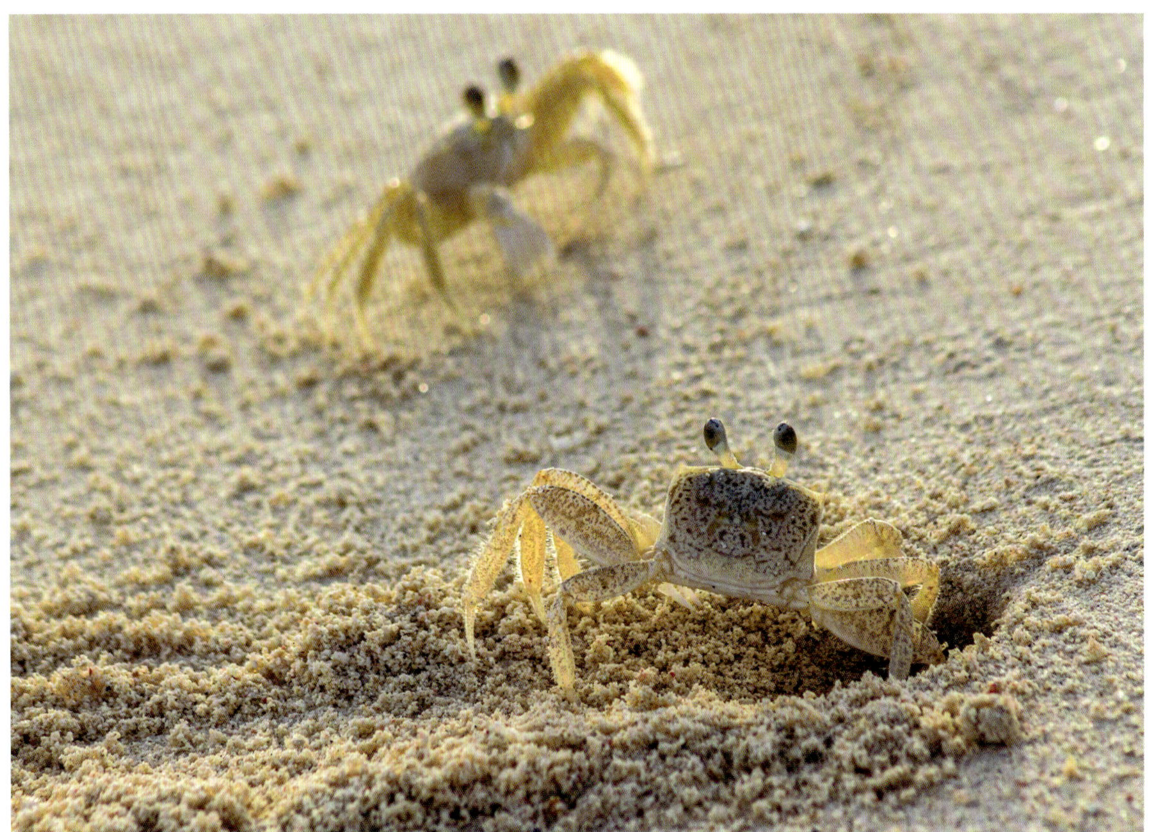

Cangrejos
Crabs

Parque Nacional de Bariay

Aún hoy es fácil entender por qué Colón escribió en su diario de a bordo que esta isla era "la tierra más hermosa que ojos humanos hubieran visto". La región de Gibara a Banes es extremadamente pintoresca. El idilio de la costa continúa hacia el interior, con exuberantes colinas verdes y valles suaves, bosques de palmeras, árboles florecientes y aquí y allá un bohío cubierto de paja de palma. Los Taínos y Siboneyes que vivían aquí creían que los extranjeros que llegaban eran emisarios de sus dioses, que habían venido a protegerlos de los ataques de los guerreros indios Aruak, y los recibieron con gran respeto.

Parque Nacional de Bariay

Ainda hoje, é fácil de entender porque Colombo escreveu em seu diário de bordo que esta ilha era "a terra mais bela que os olhos humanos jamais viram". A região de Gibara até Banes é uma paisagem extraordinariamente atraente. O idílio na costa continua no interior, com colinas verdejantes e vales suaves, florestas de palmeiras, árvores floridas e aqui e ali uma choupana coberta de palha de palmeira. Os Taínos e Siboneyes, que aqui viviam, acreditavam que os estrangeiros chegados eram emissários de seus deuses, que vieram para protegê-los dos ataques dos índios guerreiros Aruak, e os receberam com grande respeito.

Bariay Nationaal Park

Zelfs vandaag de dag is het goed te begrijpen waarom Columbus in zijn logboek schreef dat dit eiland 'het mooiste land was dat de mensenogen ooit hebben gezien'. De regio van Gibara tot Banes is zeer schilderachtig. De idylle aan de kust gaat verder landinwaarts, met weelderige groene heuvels en zachte valleien, palmbomen, bloeiende bomen en hier en daar een met palmenstro bedekte Bohío. De hier wonende Taíno's en Siboneyes geloofden dat de buitenlanders afgezanten van hun goden waren, die waren gekomen om hen te beschermen tegen de aanvallen van de strijdende Aruak-indianen, en ontvingen hen met groot respect.

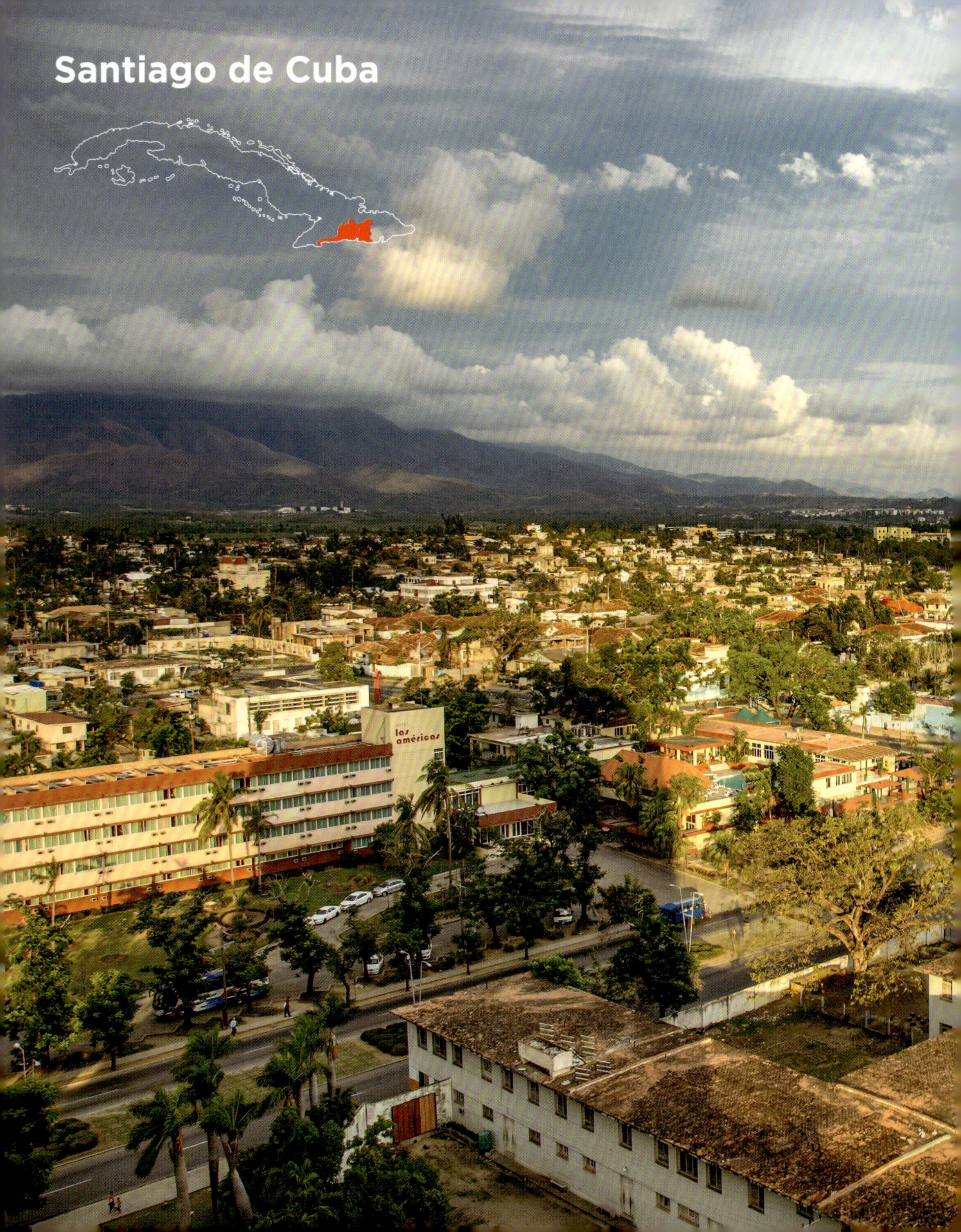
Santiago de Cuba
las américas

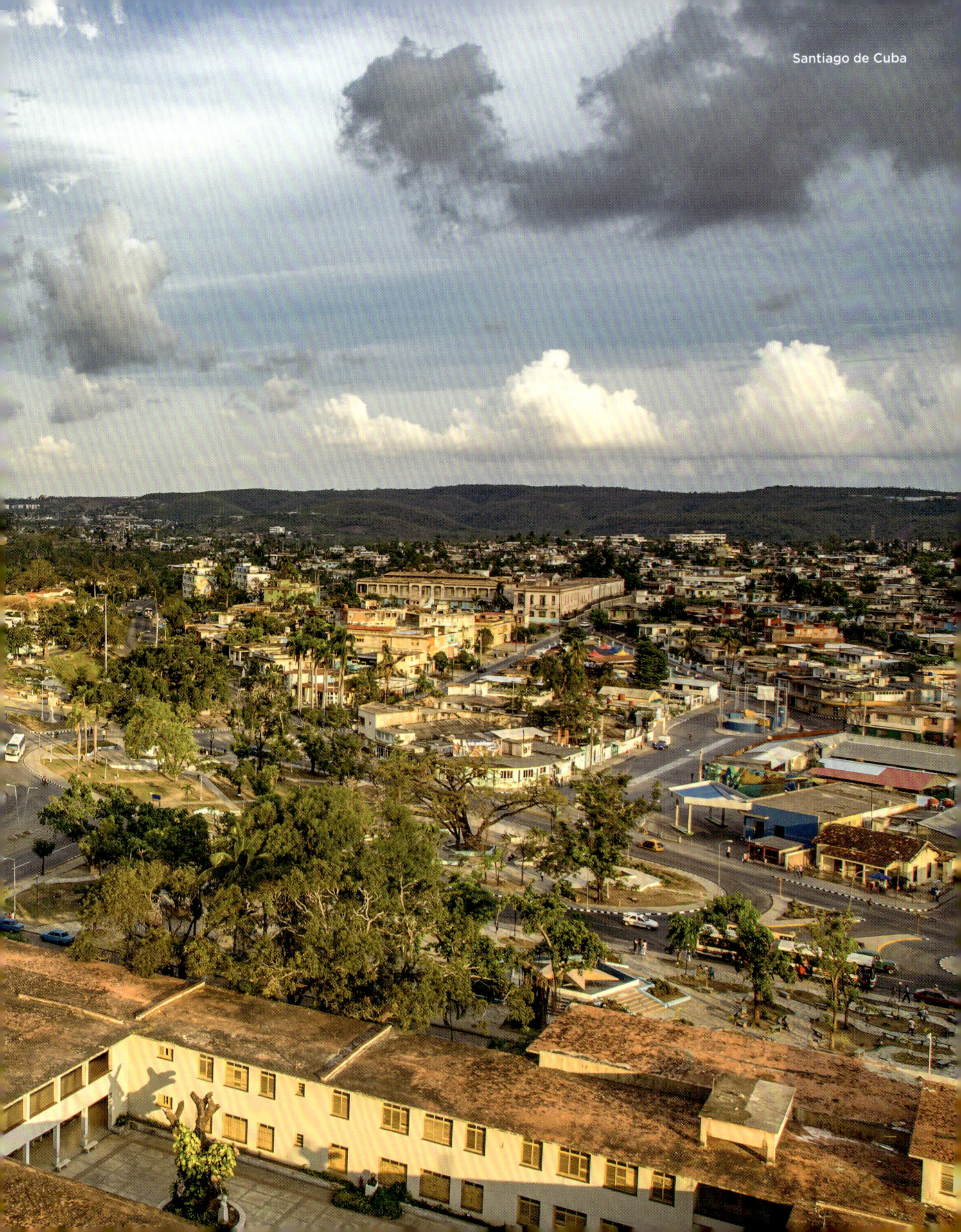
Santiago de Cuba

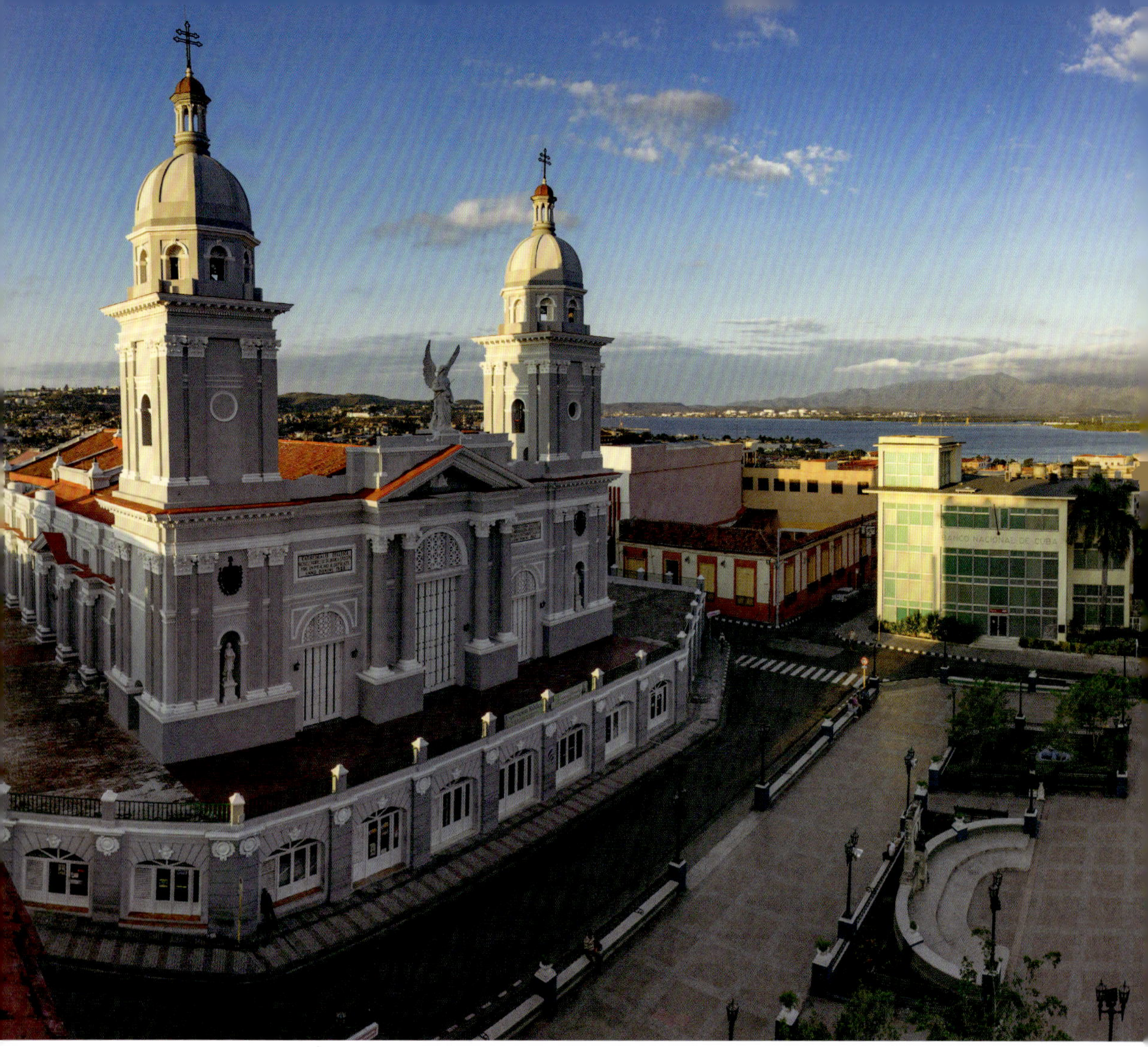

Santiago de Cuba

Santiago de Cuba is the "secret capital" of Cuba, picturesquely situated between the green foothills of the Sierra Maestra and the cobalt blue sea. A city full of charm and music, with steep narrow streets and shady squares, colonial treasures, legendary musicians and the colorful street carnival that turns the whole of Santiago into a drumming and dancing witch's cauldron. The city, like the province, is also known as the "cradle of the revolution", which began here in the 1950s.

Santiago de Cuba

Santiago de Cuba est la « capitale sacrée » de Cuba, idéalement installée entre les contreforts verts de la sierra Maestra et la mer bleu de cobalt. C'est une ville débordant de charme et de musique, appréciée pour ses ruelles étroites escarpées et placettes ombragées, ses trésors coloniaux, ses musiciens légendaires et son carnaval de rue coloré qui la transforme en un chaudron bouillonnant de rythmes et de danses. La ville, tout comme la province, sont considérées comme le berceau de la révolution qui débuta dans les années 1950.

Santiago de Cuba

Santiago de Cuba ist die „heimliche Hauptstadt" Kubas, malerisch gelegen zwischen den grünen Ausläufern der Sierra Maestra und dem kobaltblauen Meer. Eine Stadt voller Charme und Musik, mit steilen engen Straßen und schattigen Plätzen, kolonialen Kostbarkeiten, legendären Musikern und dem bunten Straßenkarneval, der ganz Santiago in einen trommelnden und tanzenden Hexenkessel verwandelt. Die Stadt, wie die Provinz, gilt auch als die „Wiege der Revolution", die hier in den 1950er-Jahren begann.

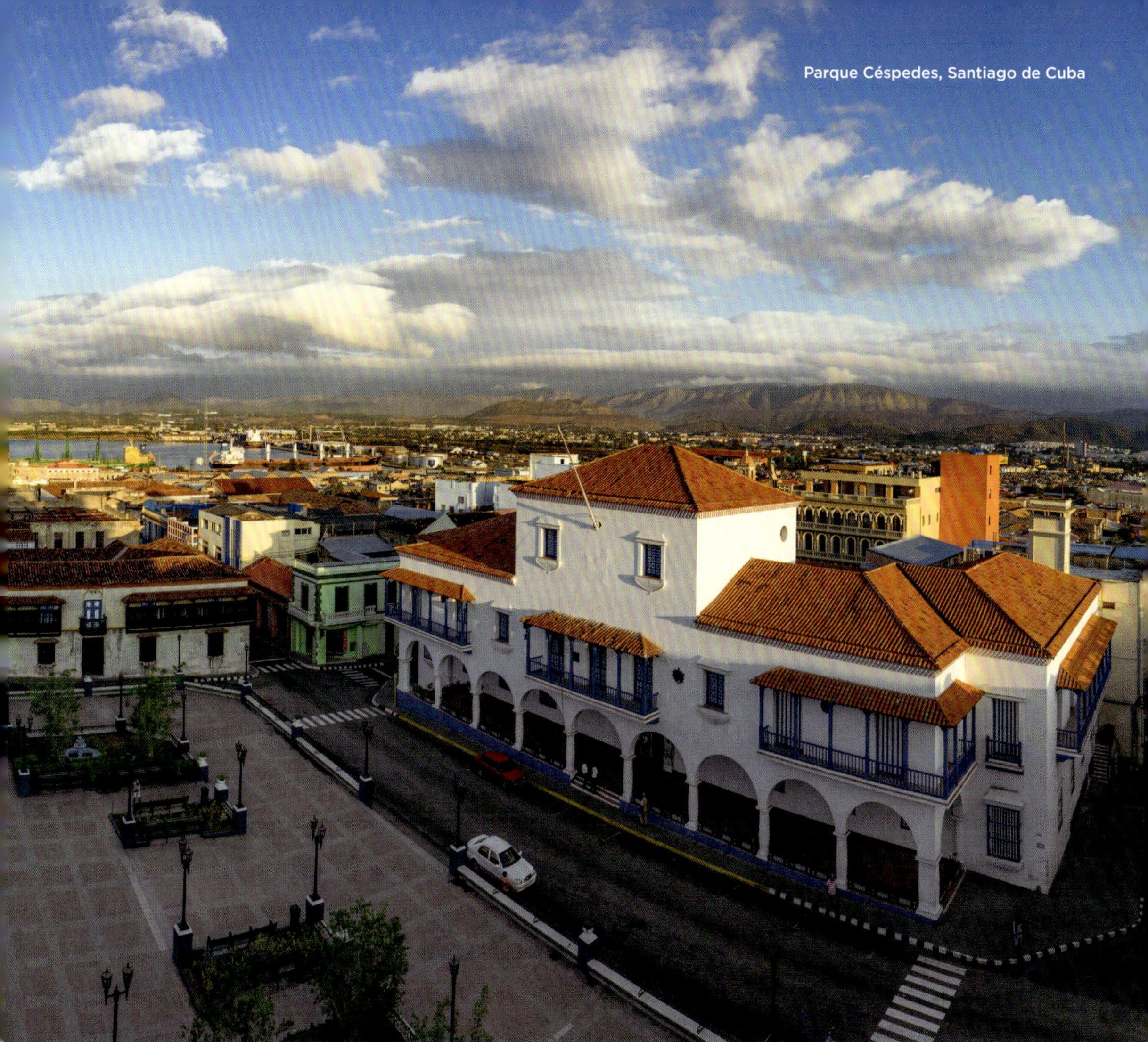

Santiago de Cuba

Santiago de Cuba es la "capital secreta" de Cuba, pintorescamente situada entre las verdes estribaciones de la Sierra Maestra y el mar azul cobalto. Una ciudad llena de encanto y música, con calles estrechas y empinadas y plazas sombreadas, tesoros coloniales, músicos legendarios y el colorido carnaval callejero que convierte a todo Santiago en una caldera de tambores y bailes de brujas. La ciudad, al igual que la provincia, también es conocida como la "cuna de la revolución", que comenzó aquí en la década de 1950.

Santiago de Cuba

Santiago de Cuba é a "capital secreta" de Cuba, pitorescamente situada entre as colinas verdes da Sierra Maestra e o mar azul-cobalto. Uma cidade cheia de charme e música, com ruas estreitas e íngremes e praças sombrias, tesouros coloniais, músicos lendários e o colorido carnaval de rua que transforma toda a cidade de Santiago em um caldeirão de bruxas de danças e tambores. A cidade, como a província, também é conhecida como o "berço da revolução", que começou aqui na década de 1950.

Santiago de Cuba

Santiago de Cuba is de 'geheime hoofdstad' van Cuba, schilderachtig gelegen tussen de groene uitlopers van de Sierra Maestra en de kobaltblauwe zee. Een stad vol charme en muziek, met steile smalle straatjes en schaduwrijke pleinen, koloniale schatten, legendarische muzikanten en het kleurrijke straatcarnaval dat het hele Santiago verandert in een drummende en dansende heksenketel. De stad staat net als de provincie ook bekend als de 'wieg van de revolutie', die hier in de jaren vijftig begon.

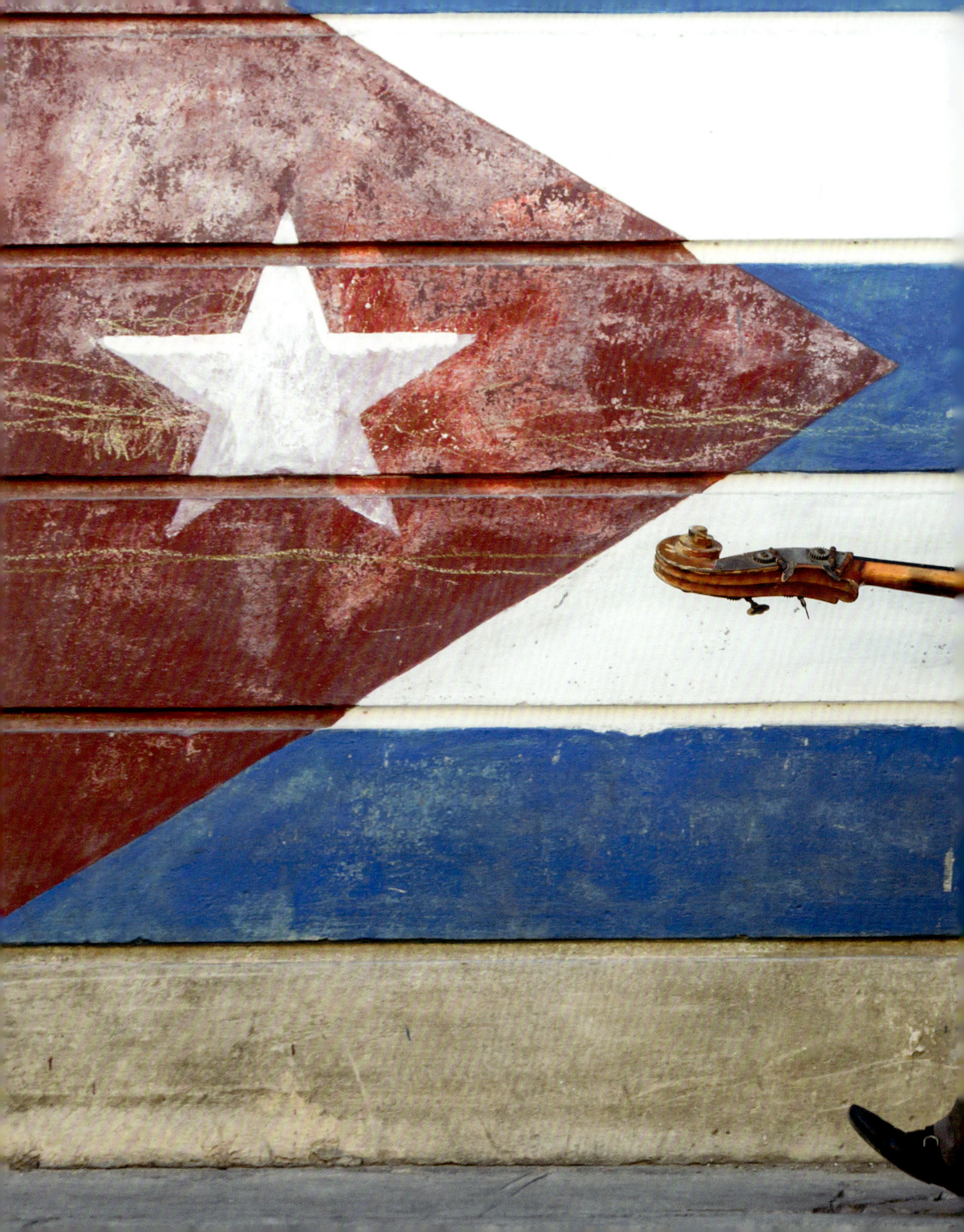

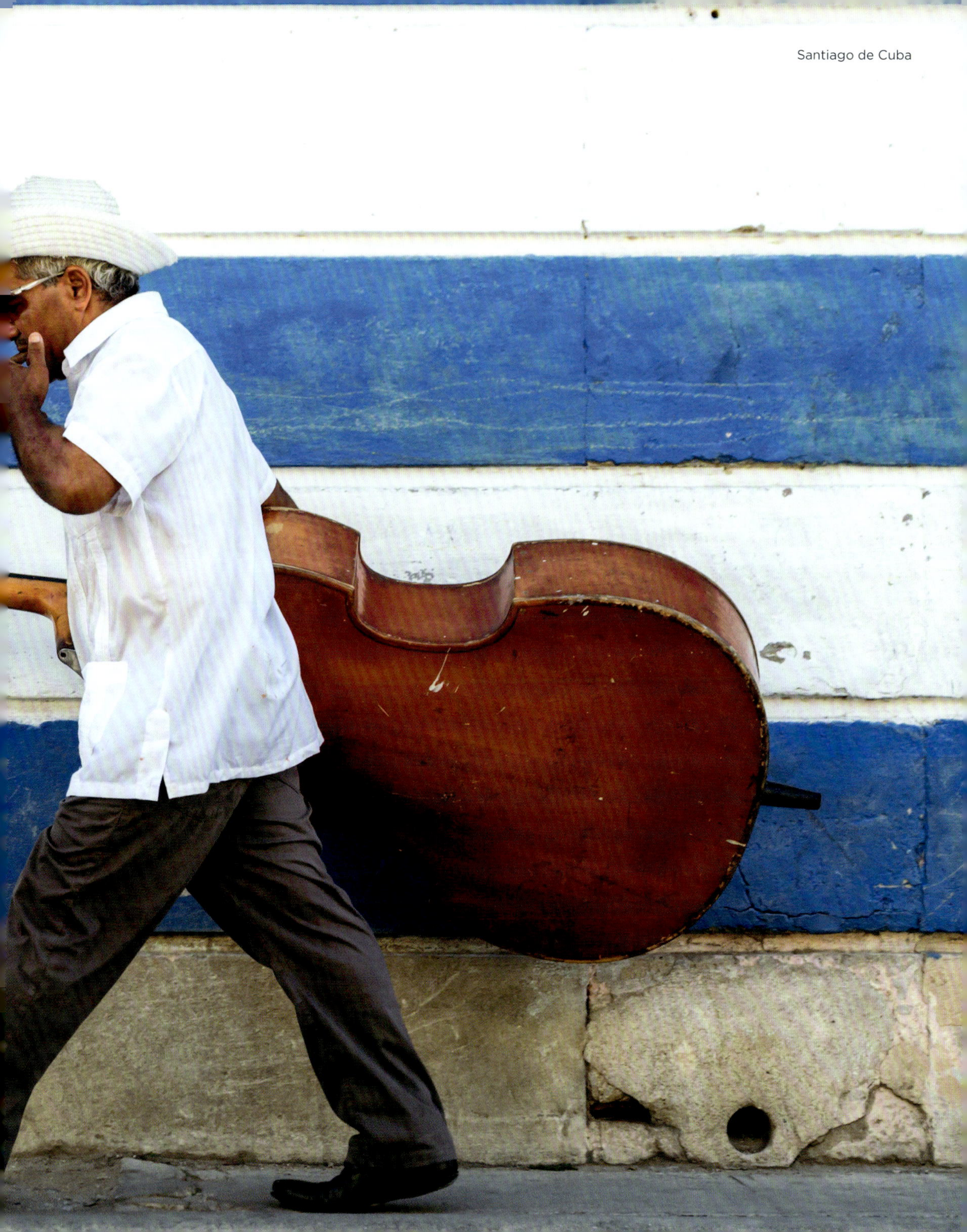
Santiago de Cuba

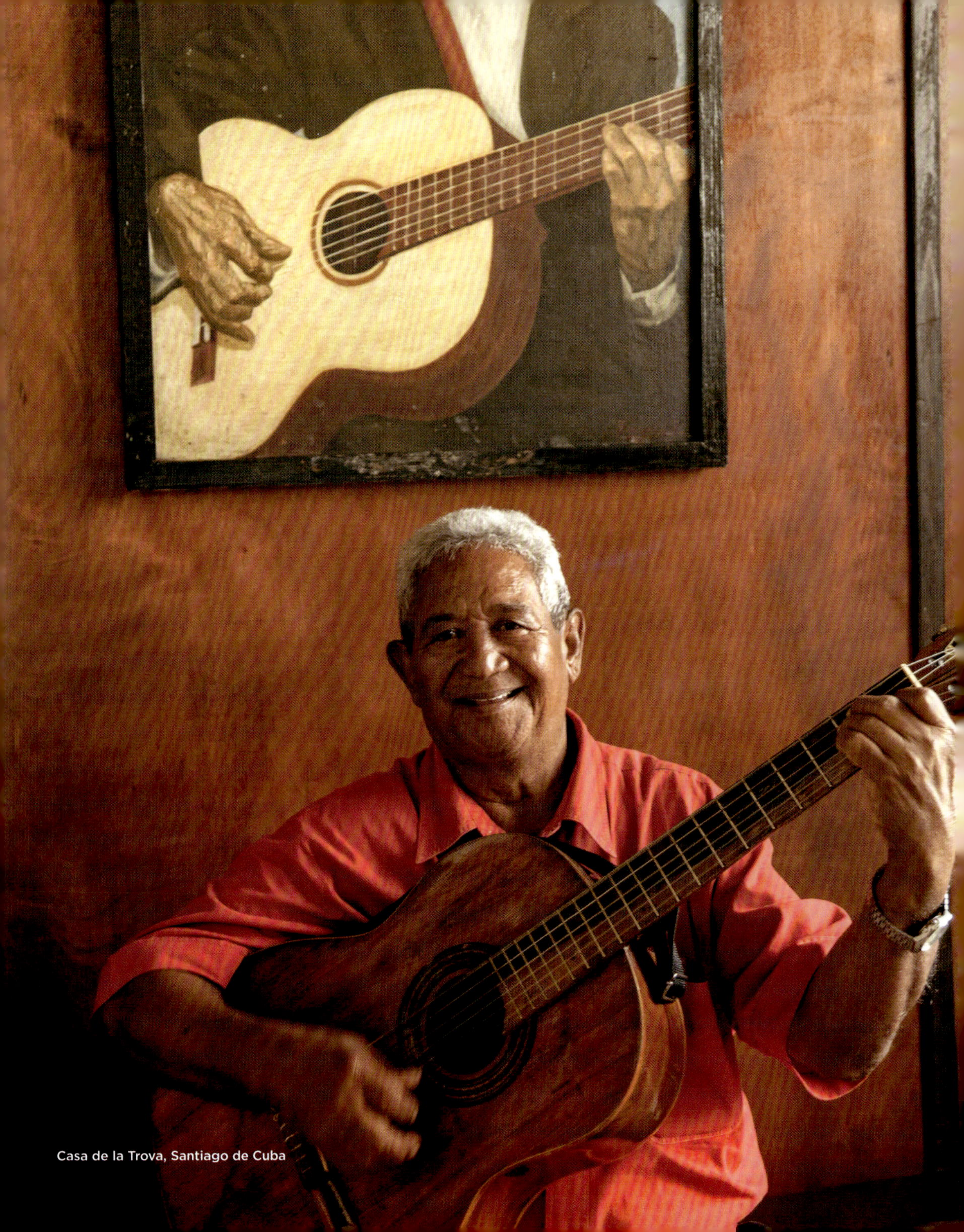

Casa de la Trova, Santiago de Cuba

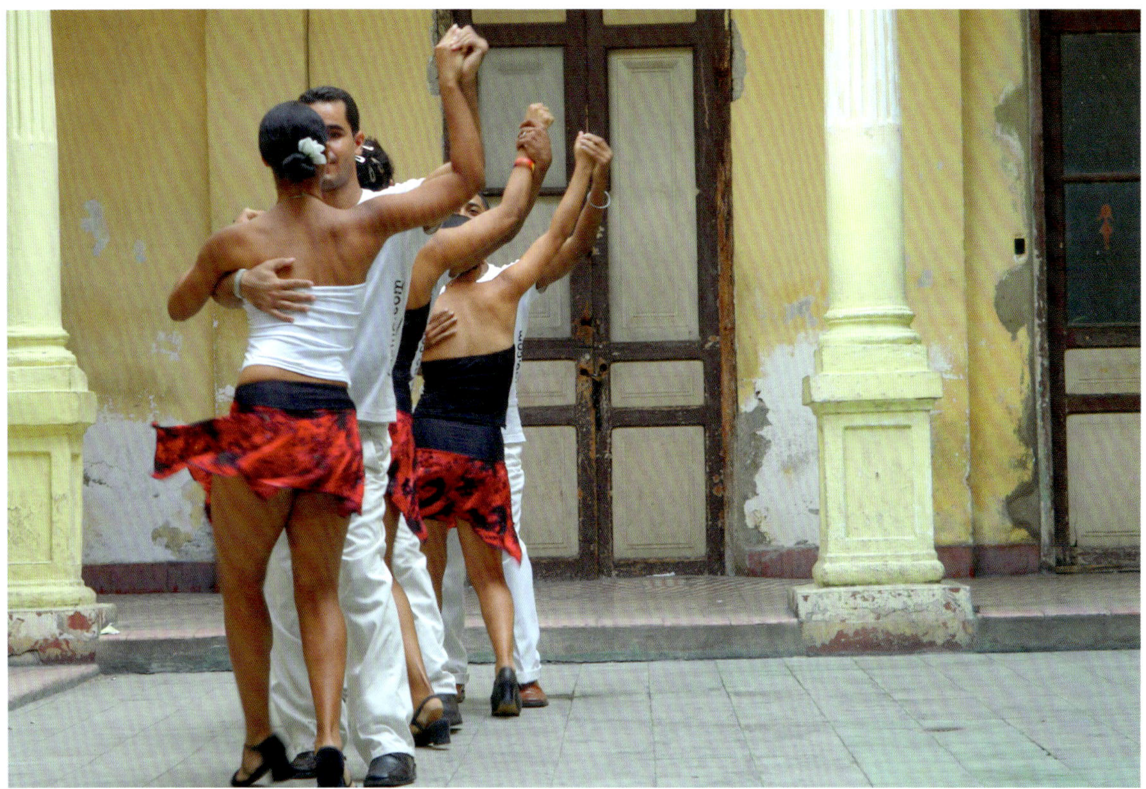

Santiago de Cuba

Casa de la Trova

The "Casa de la Trova" in Santiago is the most famous of all "Casas de la Trova" in Cuba. Originally a tobacconist's shop where people sang, it quickly became the meeting place for the best musicians and Soneros Santiago. The portraits of the legendary Soneros Sindo Garay and Miguel Matamoros, whose sones can still be heard everywhere, still hang here today.

Casa de la Trova

La Casa de la Trova de Santiago es la más famosa de todas las Casas de la Trova de Cuba. Originalmente era una tienda de tabaco donde la gente cantaba, y rápidamente se convirtió en el lugar de encuentro de los mejores músicos y soneros santiaguinos. Todavía se conservan aquí los retratos de los legendarios Soneros Sindo Garay y Miguel Matamoros, cuyos sones todavía se pueden escuchar en todas partes.

Casa de la Trova·

La *Casa de la Trova* de Santiago est la plus célèbre de toutes les Casa de la Trova de Cuba. Cette ancienne boutique de tabac, dans laquelle on venait chanter, est rapidement devenue le lieu de rencontre des meilleurs musiciens et *soneros* de Santiago. Aujourd'hui encore, y sont exposés les portraits des légendaires Sindo Garay et Miguel Matamoros, dont les célèbres *son* sont encore joués partout.

Casa de la Trova

A "Casa de la Trova" em Santiago é a mais famosa de todas as "Casas de la Trova" em Cuba. Originalmente uma loja de tabacaria onde as pessoas cantavam, tornou-se rapidamente o ponto de encontro dos melhores músicos e "soneros" de Santiago. Ainda hoje encontram-se aqui os retratos dos lendários Soneros Sindo Garay e Miguel Matamoros, cujas músicas na cadência do "son" ainda podem ser ouvidas em toda a parte.

Casa de la Trova

Die „Casa de la Trova" in Santiago ist von allen „Casas de la Trova" die berühmteste Kubas. Ursprünglich ein Tabakladen, in dem gesungen wurde, wurde sie schnell zum Treffpunkt der besten Musiker und Soneros Santiagos. Noch heute hängen hier die Portraits der legendären Soneros Sindo Garay und Miguel Matamoros, deren Sones man noch heute überall hört.

Casa de la Trova

Het 'Casa de la Trova' in Santiago is het bekendste van alle 'Casas de la Trova' in Cuba. Oorspronkelijk een tabakswinkel waar men zong, werd het al snel de ontmoetingsplaats voor de beste muzikanten en Soneros Santiago. De portretten van de legendarische Soneros Sindo Garay en Miguel Matamoros, wier zonen nog steeds overal te horen zijn, hangen hier nog steeds.

Son

They say in Cuba that those who are born in Santiago de Cuba run, speak and dance to the rhythm of Son. The Son, a song form and dance, originated at the beginning of the 20th century in Santiago and spread rapidly across the island. It blends Spanish verses and guitars with Afro-Cuban rhythms and drums, a typical Creole mixture.

Son

Les natifs de Santiago de Cuba marchent, parlent et dansent au rythme du *son,* dit-on à Cuba. Le *son* est un type de chant et de danse apparu au début du xxᵉ siècle à Santiago et qui s'est rapidement répandu dans toute l'île. Il marie paroles et guitares espagnoles à des rythmes et percussions afro-cubains, composant une authentique fusion créole.

Son

Wer in Santiago de Cuba geborenen wird, läuft, spricht und tanzt im Rhythmus des Son, sagt man in Kuba. Der Son, Liedform und Tanz, entstand Anfang des 20. Jahrhunderts in Santiago und verbreitete sich rasch über die Insel. Er verschmilzt spanische Verse und Gitarren mit afrokubanischen Rhythmen und Trommeln, ein typisch kreolisches Mischprodukt.

Son

Los nacidos en Santiago de Cuba corren, hablan y bailan al ritmo del son, dicen en Cuba. El son, forma de canción y danza, se originó a principios del siglo XX en Santiago y se extendió rápidamente por toda la isla. Mezcla versos y guitarras españolas con ritmos y tambores afrocubanos, una típica mezcla criolla.

Son

Aqueles que nascem em Santiago de Cuba correm, falam e dançam ao ritmo do "son", dizem em Cuba. O son, forma de canção e dança, surgiu no início do século XX em Santiago e espalhou-se rapidamente por toda a ilha. Ele mistura versos e violões espanhóis com ritmos e tambores afro-cubanos, uma mistura típica crioula.

Son

Wie in Santiago de Cuba geboren is, rent, spreekt en danst op het ritme van Son, zeggen ze in Cuba. De Son, zangvorm en dans, ontstond in het begin van de 20e eeuw in Santiago en verspreidde zich snel over het eiland. Hij mengt Spaanse verzen en gitaren met Afro-Cubaanse ritmes en drums, een typisch Creoolse mix.

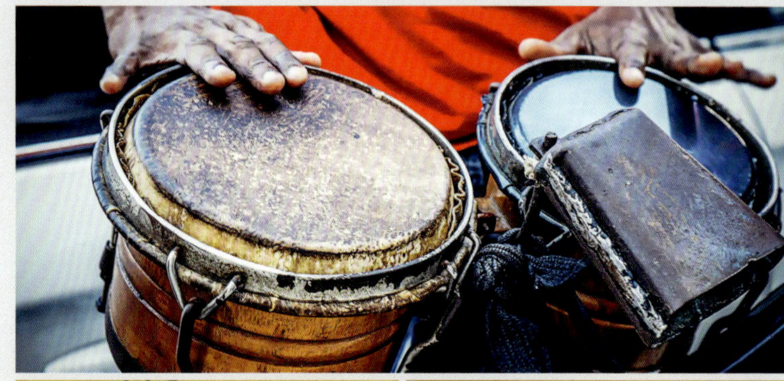

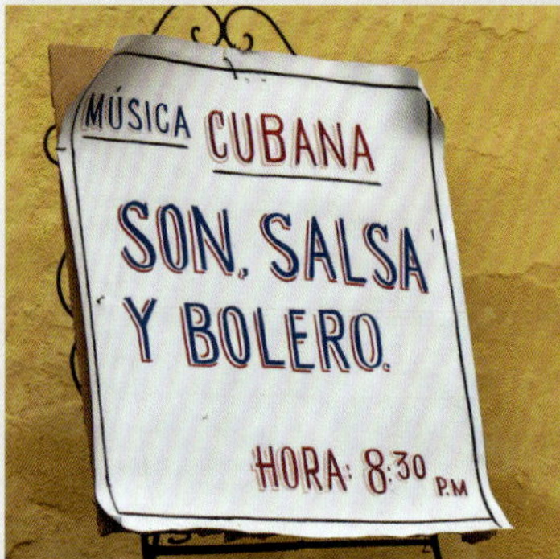

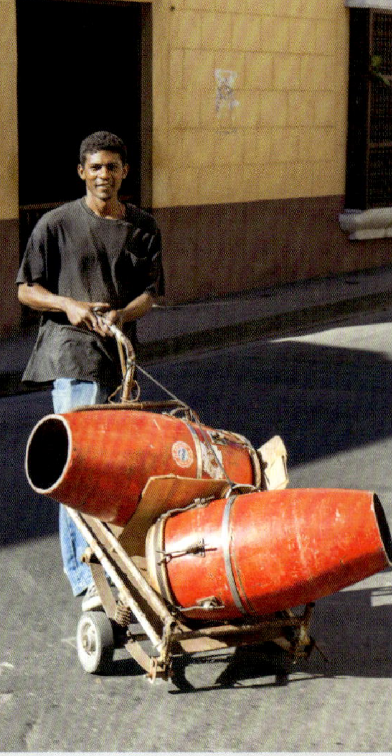

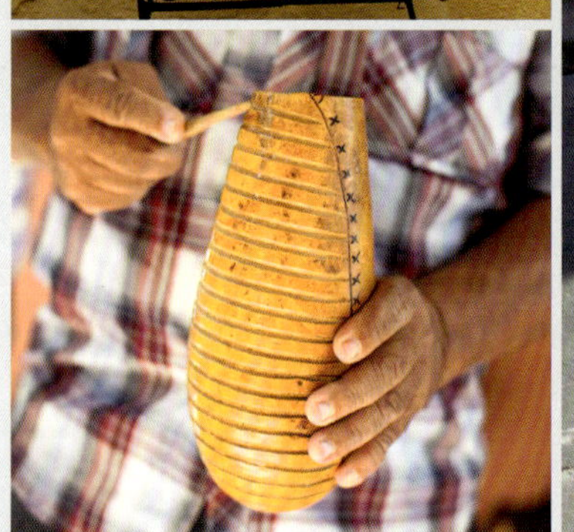

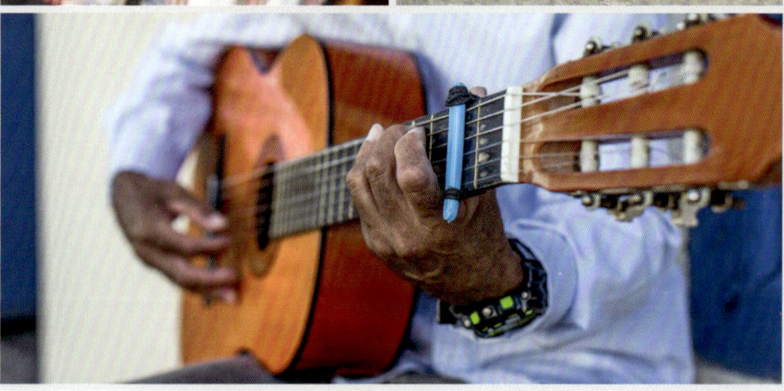

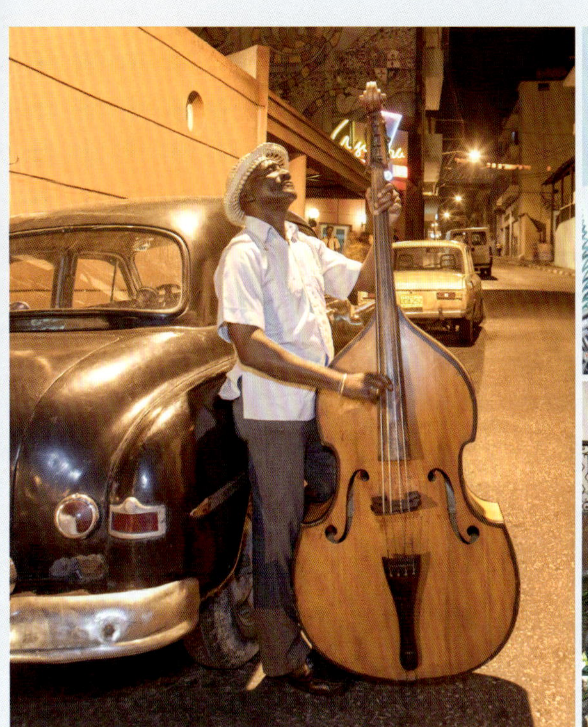

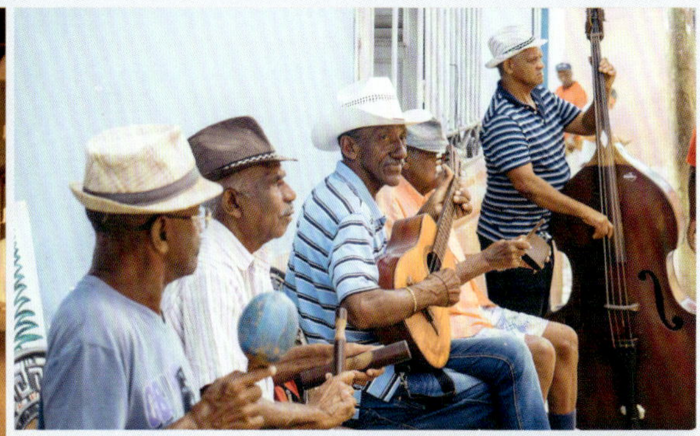

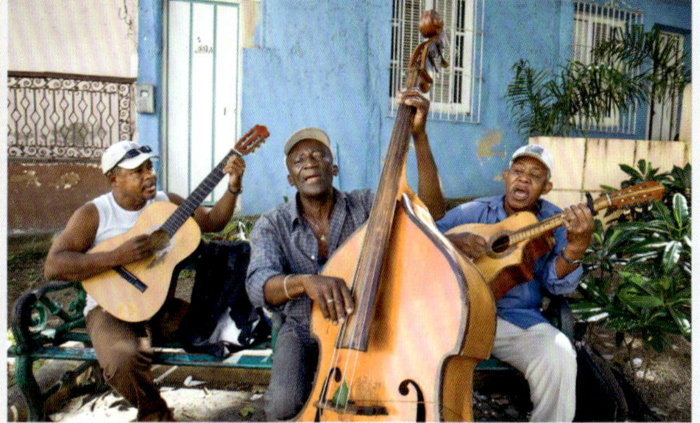

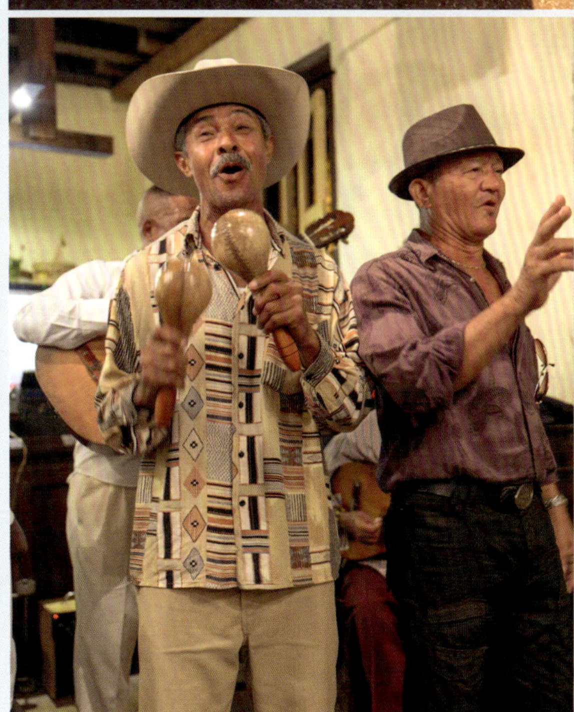

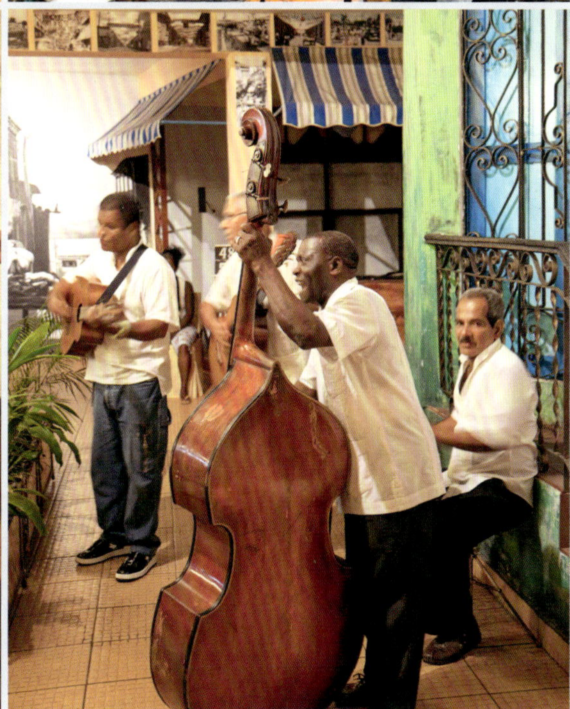

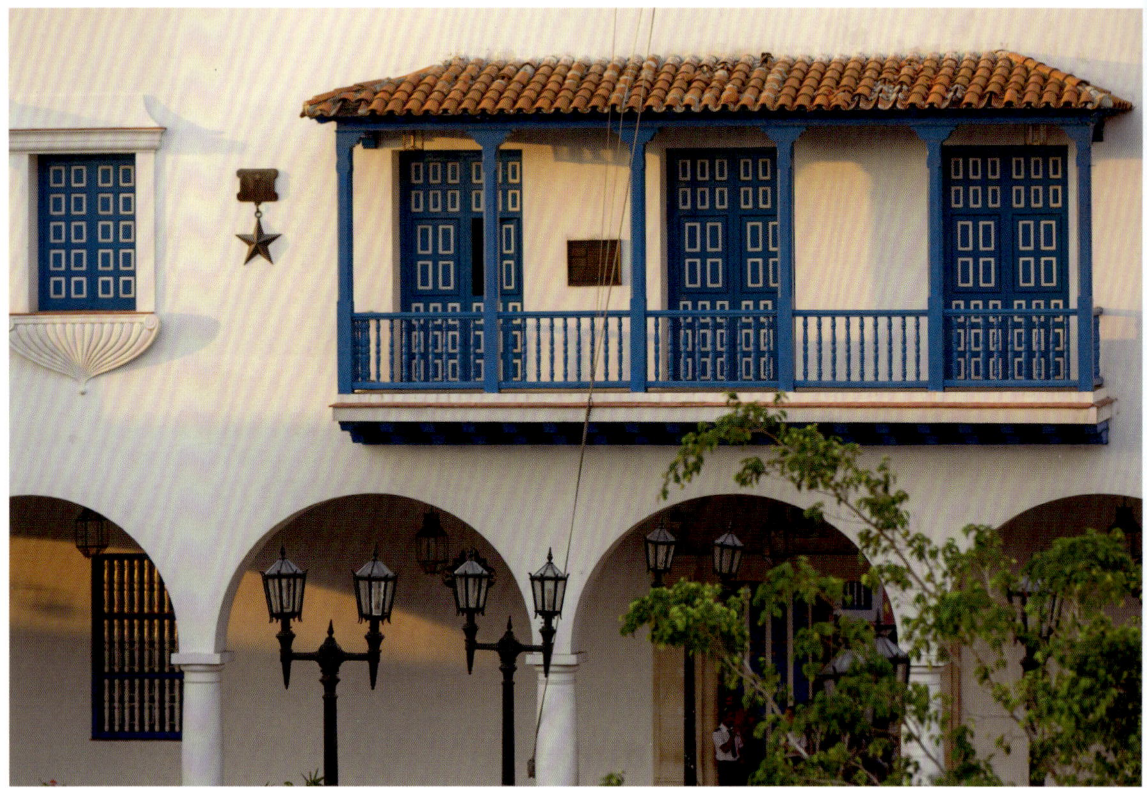

Santiago de Cuba

Parque Céspedes

This is a square steeped in history: from the balcony of the Town Hall at the central Parque Céspedes, Fidel Castro announced the victory of the revolution on 1 January 1959. Next to the oldest building in Cuba stands Diego Velázquez's 1516 residence. Here the Aztec gold stolen in Mexico was melted down before it was brought to Spain.

Parque Céspedes

Una plaza cargada de historia: desde el balcón del Ayuntamiento en el céntrico Parque Céspedes, Fidel Castro anunció la victoria de la revolución el 1 de enero de 1959, junto al edificio más antiguo de Cuba, la residencia de Diego Velázquez de 1516, que es la más antigua. Aquí el oro azteca robado en México fue fundido antes de ser traído a España.

Parque Céspedes

Parque Céspedes est une place chargée d'histoire : du haut du balcon de son hôtel de ville central, Fidel Castro annonça le 1er janvier 1959 la victoire de la révolution, à quelques pas du plus vieux bâtiment de Cuba, la demeure de Diego Velázquez bâtie en 1516. C'est dans cette bâtisse que fut fondu l'or des Aztèques dérobé au Mexique, avant d'être transporté jusqu'en Espagne.

Parque Céspedes

Um lugar cheio de história: da varanda da Câmara Municipal no Parque Céspedes central, Fidel Castro anunciou a vitória da revolução em 1º de janeiro de 1959, ao lado do edifício mais antigo de Cuba, a residência de Diego Velázquez, construída em 1516. Aqui, o ouro dos astecas roubado do México foi derretido, antes de ser levado para Espanha.

Parque Céspedes

Ein geschichtsträchtiger Platz: Vom Balkon des Rathauses am zentralen Parque Céspedes verkündete Fidel Castro am 1. Januar 1959 den Sieg der Revolution, gleich daneben steht das älteste Gebäude Kubas, das 1516 erbaute Wohnhaus von Diego Velázquez. Hier wurde das in Mexiko geraubte Gold der Azteken eingeschmolzen, bevor man es nach Spanien brachte.

Parque Céspedes

Een plein vol geschiedenis: vanaf het balkon van het stadhuis in het centrale Parque Céspedes kondigde Fidel Castro op 1 januari 1959 de overwinning van de revolutie aan, gelijk daarnaast staat het oudste gebouw van Cuba, het in 1516 gebouwde woonhuis van Diego Velázquez. Hier werd het in Mexico gestolen Azteekse goud gesmolten voordat het naar Spanje werd gebracht.

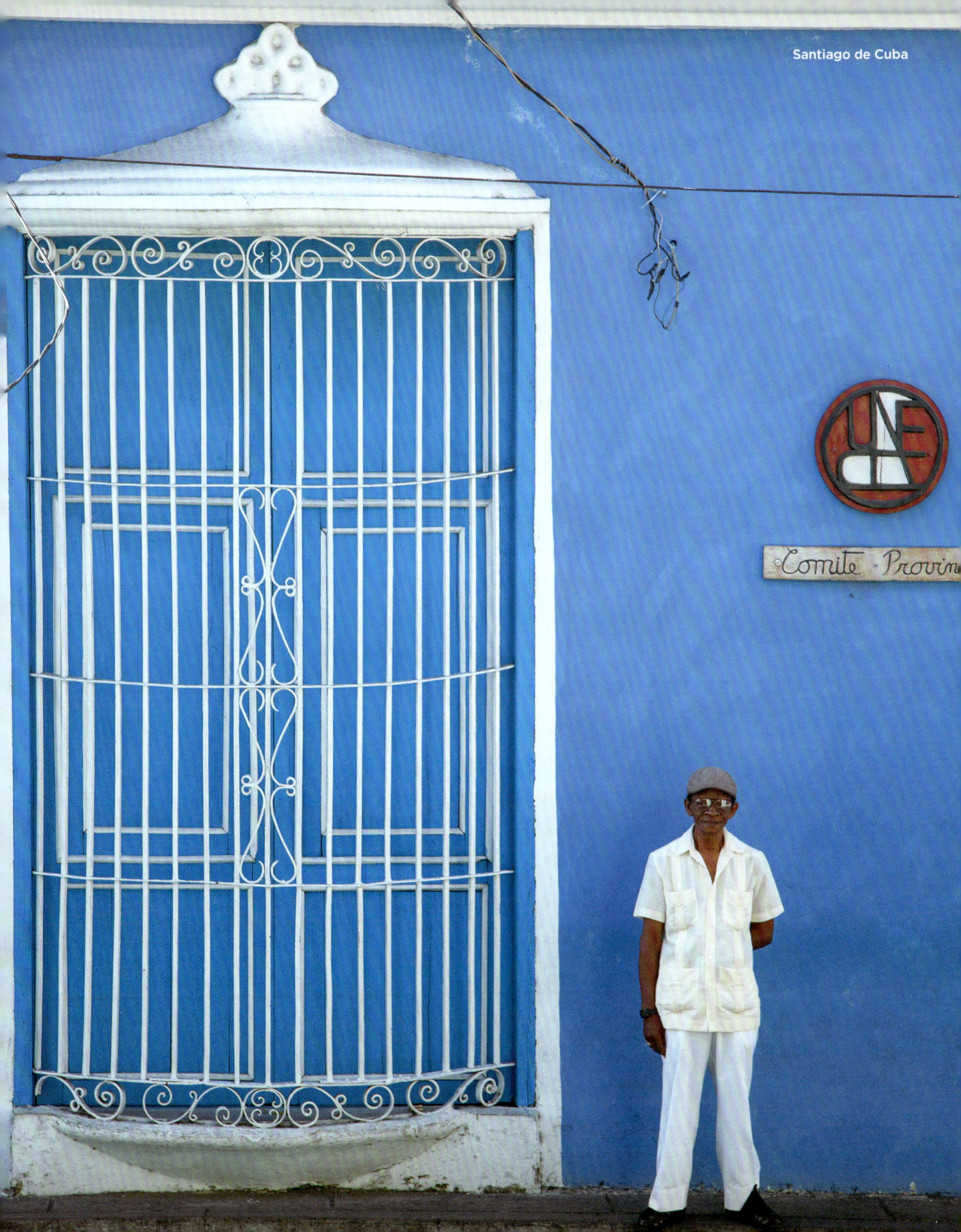

Santiago de Cuba
Comité Provin

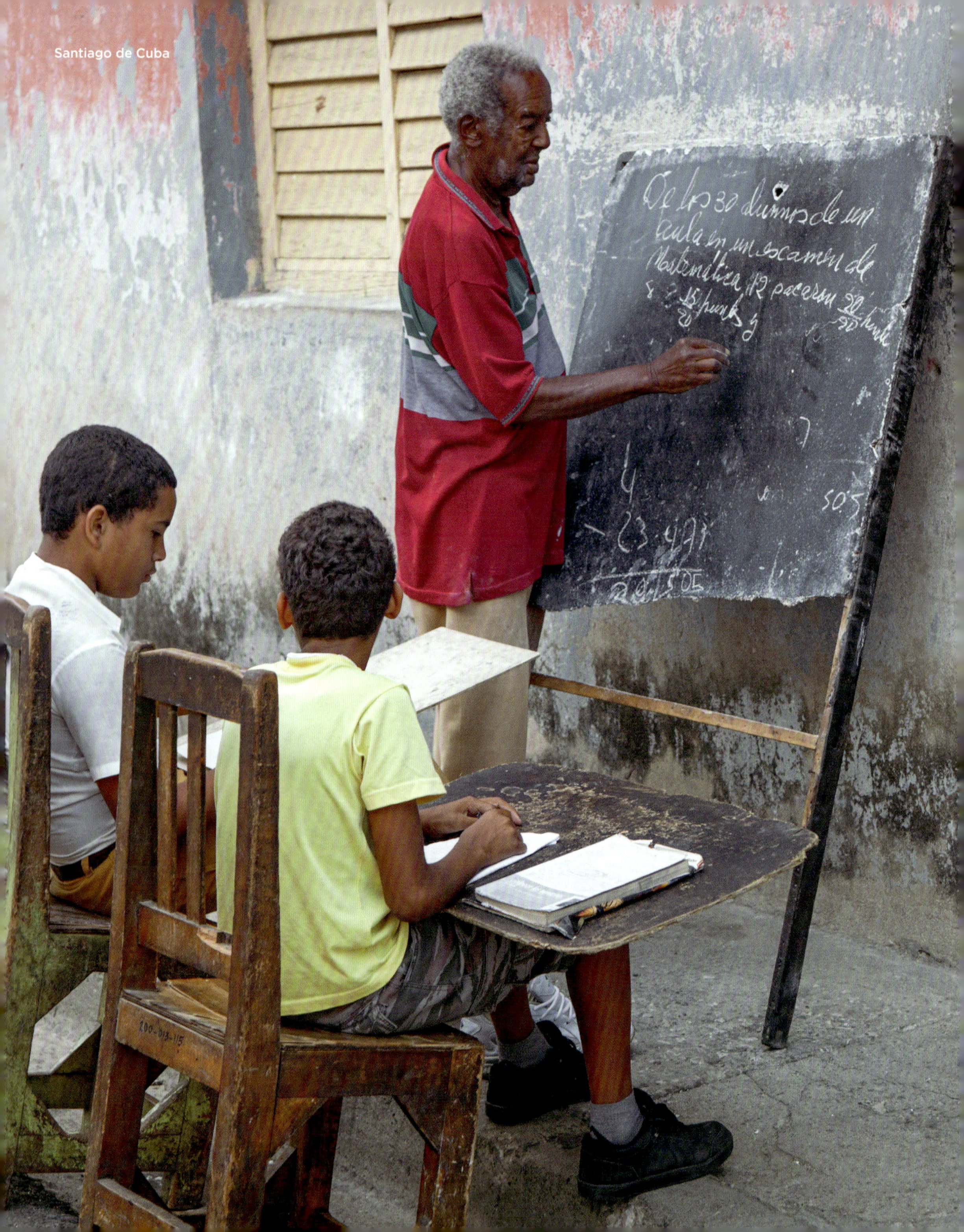

Santiago de Cuba

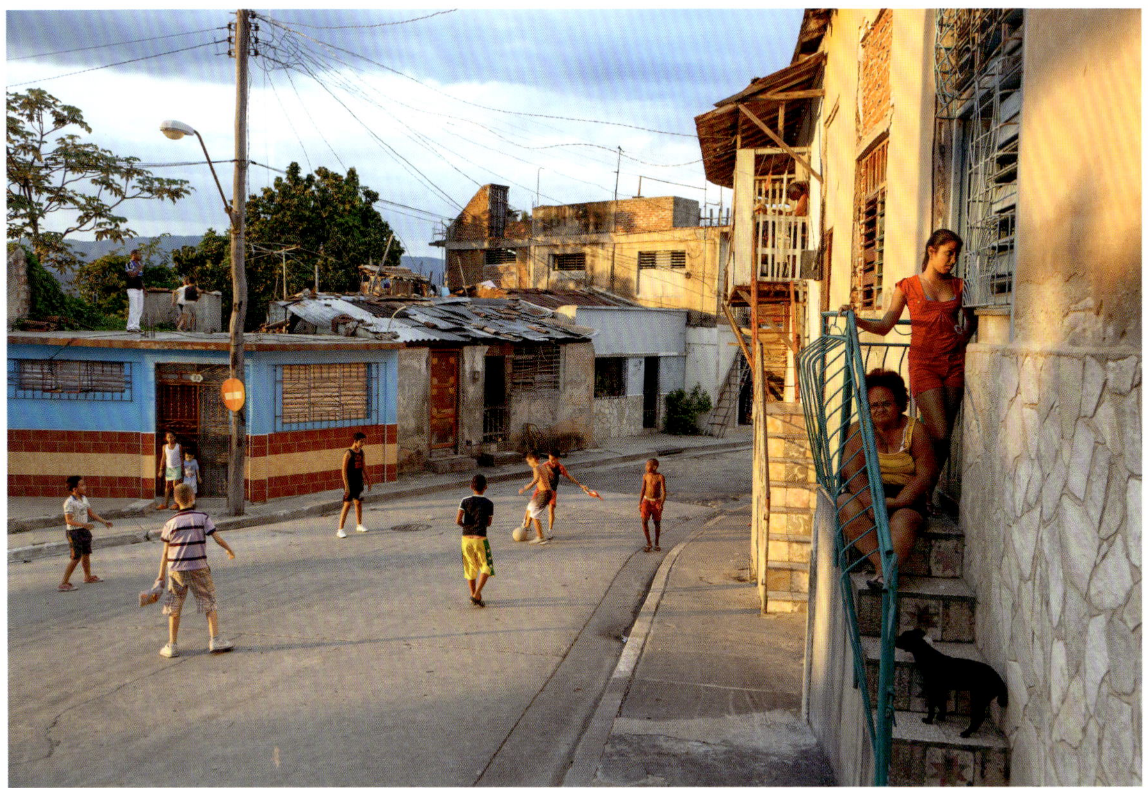

Santiago de Cuba

Cuban Everyday Life

Life in Santiago de Cuba also takes place on the streets. The Santiagueros are music and dance enthusiasts, but their everyday life has little to do with a Caribbean idyll, but is rather a roller coaster ride due to the continual shortages. You need a lot of patience, inventiveness and humor to survive in Cuba.

La vida cotidiana cubana

La vida en Santiago de Cuba también se desarrolla en las calles. Los santiagueros son entusiastas de la música y la danza, pero su vida cotidiana tiene poco que ver con un idilio caribeño, sino más bien con un paseo en montaña rusa debido a su situación de escasez. Se necesita mucha paciencia, inventiva y humor para sobrevivir en Cuba.

Vie quotidienne à Cuba

À Santiago de Cuba également, la vie se joue dans la rue. Les *santiagueros* sont certes passionnés de musique et de danse, mais les conditions de pénurie ont transformé leur quotidien en une expérience chaotique bien éloignée du tableau idyllique des Caraïbes. (Sur)vivre à Cuba nécessite beaucoup de patience, d'ingéniosité et d'humour.

A vida cotidiana cubana

A vida em Santiago de Cuba também acontece nas ruas. Os Santiagueros são entusiastas da música e da dança, mas sua vida cotidiana tem pouco a ver com um idílio caribenho, mas sim com um passeio de montanha-russa devido à situação de excassez. É preciso muita paciência, inventividade e humor para (sobre)viver em Cuba.

Kubanischer Alltag

Das Leben spielt sich auch in Santiago de Cuba auf der Straße ab. Die Santiagueros sind zwar musik- und tanzbegeistert, doch ihr Alltag hat wenig mit karibischer Idylle, sondern aufgrund der Mangelsituation eher mit einer Achterbahnfahrt zu tun. Man braucht viel Geduld, Erfindungsreichtum und Humor, um in Kuba zu (über)leben.

Cubaans dagelijks leven

Het leven in Santiago de Cuba vindt ook op straat plaats. De Santiagueros zijn muziek- en dansliefhebbers, maar hun dagelijks leven heeft weinig te maken met een Caribische idylle, maar eerder met een achtbaanritje vanwege het ontbreken van een structuur. Je hebt veel geduld, inventiviteit en humor nodig om in Cuba te overleven.

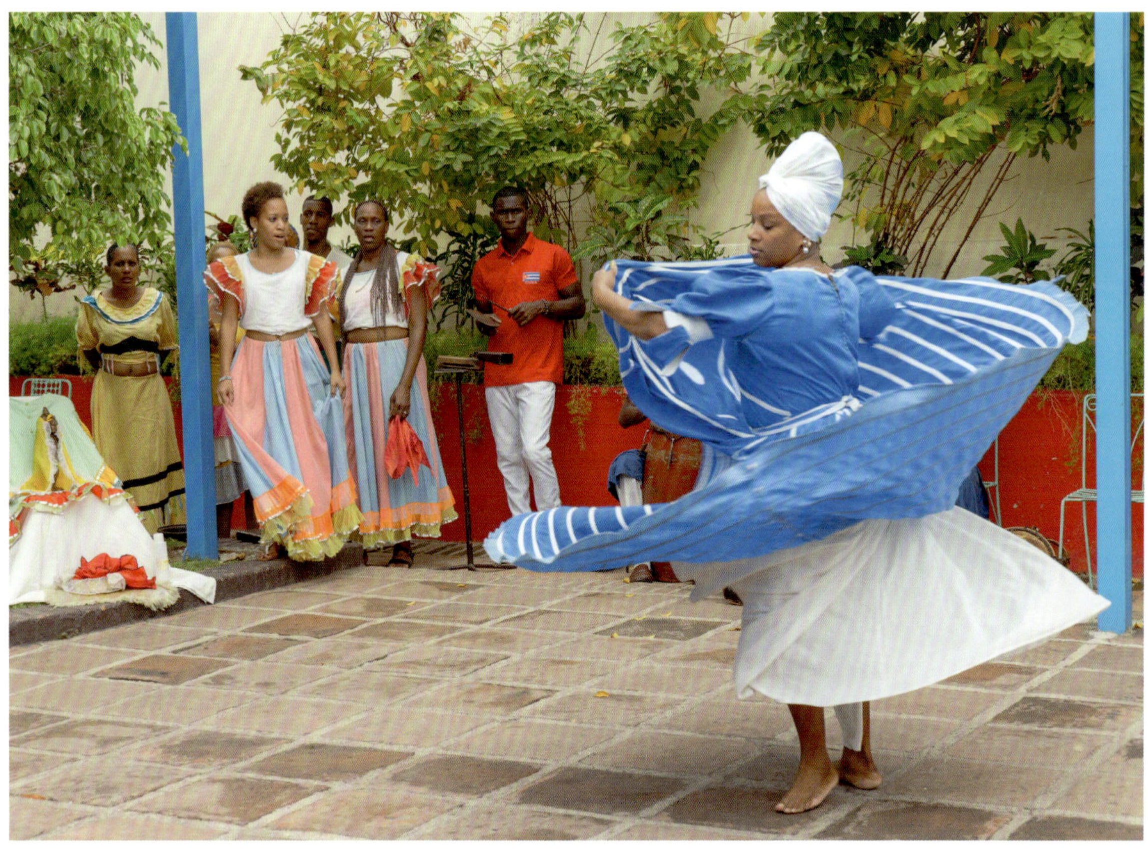

Museo el Carnaval, Santiago de Cuba

Tumba francesa and Carnival

After the bloody revolution in Haiti in 1791, many plantation owners and freed slaves fled to Santiago. These "French" people brought coffee plants and their drums, known as *tumba francesa* in Santiago, and the Cocoyé dance, a Caribbean variant of French minuets. "Tumba francesa" in Santiago means the music of the immigrants, as well as the cultural associations of their descendants. Typical of the carnival are the *congas*, groups of hundreds of drummers dancing through the streets—in short fast steps, because the slaves danced in leg irons.

Tumba francesa et carnaval

À la fin de la révolution haïtienne de 1791, de nombreux propriétaires de plantations et leurs esclaves affranchis ont émigré à Santiago. Ces « Français » ont importé à Santiago leurs plants de café, leurs tambours, surnommés *tumba francesa*, et leur danse, *cocoyé*, version caribéenne du menuet français. À Santiago, la *tumba francesa* est la danse des immigrés, tout comme les associations culturelles de leurs descendants. Les *congas* sont une spécificité du carnaval ; ce sont des groupes d'une centaine de tambours, accompagnés de danseurs qui déambulent dans les rues à petits pas, puisque les esclaves dansaient enchaînés.

Tumba francesa und Karneval

Nach der blutigen Revolution auf Haiti 1791 flohen viele Plantagenbesitzer und freigelassene Sklaven nach Santiago. Die „Franzosen" brachten Kaffeepflanzen und ihre paukenartigen Trommeln mit, die in Santiago *tumba francesa* genannt werden, und den Tanz Cocoyé, eine karibische Variante französischer Menuette. „Tumba francesa" heißt in Santiago die Musik der Einwanderer, ebenso wie die Kulturvereine ihrer Nachfahren. Typisch für den Karneval sind die Congas, hundertköpfige Trommlergruppen, die tanzend durch die Straßen ziehen – in kurzen schnellen Schritten, denn die Sklaven tanzten in Fußketten.

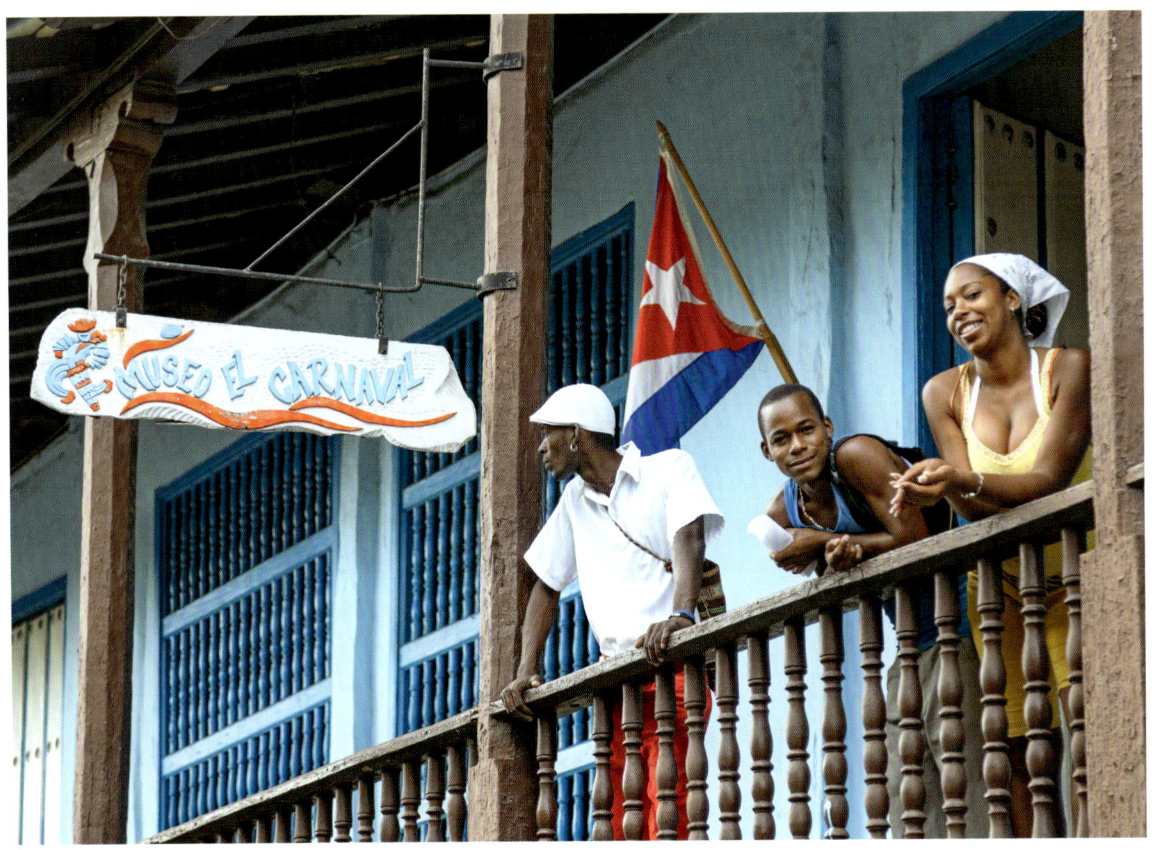

Museo el Carnaval, Santiago de Cuba

Tumba francesa y Carnaval

Después de la sangrienta revolución en Haití en 1791, muchos dueños de plantaciones y esclavos liberados huyeron a Santiago. Los "franceses" trajeron a Santiago los cafetos y sus tambores, llamados "tumba francesa", y el baile Cocoyé, una variante caribeña de los minuetos franceses. "Tumba francesa" en Santiago significa la música de los inmigrantes, así como las asociaciones culturales de sus descendientes. Típico del carnaval son las "congas", grupos de cien tamborileros que bailan por las calles, en cortos pasos rápidos, porque los esclavos bailaban en cadenas de pies.

Tumba francesa e Carnaval

Após a sangrenta revolução no Haiti em 1791, muitos proprietários de plantações e escravos libertados fugiram para Santiago. Os "franceses" trouxeram plantas de café e seus tambores do tipo timbales, chamados *tumba francesa* em Santiago, e a dança Cocoyé, uma variante caribenha dos minuetos franceses. "Tumba francesa" em Santiago significa a música dos imigrantes, bem como as associações culturais dos seus descendentes. Típico para o carnaval são as "congas", grupos de cem bateristas dançando pelas ruas – em passos curtos e rápidos, porque os escravos dançavam com correntes presas no tornozelo.

Tumba francesa en Carnaval

Na de bloedige revolutie in Haïti in 1791 vluchtten veel plantage-eigenaren en bevrijde slaven naar Santiago. De 'Fransen' brachten koffieplanten en hun trommels, die in Santiago *tumba francesa* wordt genoemd, en de dans Cocoyé, een Caribische variant van Franse menuetten. 'Tumba francesa' in Santiago betekent de muziek van de immigranten en de culturele verenigingen van hun nakomelingen. Kenmerkend voor het carnaval zijn de 'conga's', groepen van honderd trommelaars die door de straten dansen – korte snelle stappen maken omdat de slaven met voetkettingen om dansten.

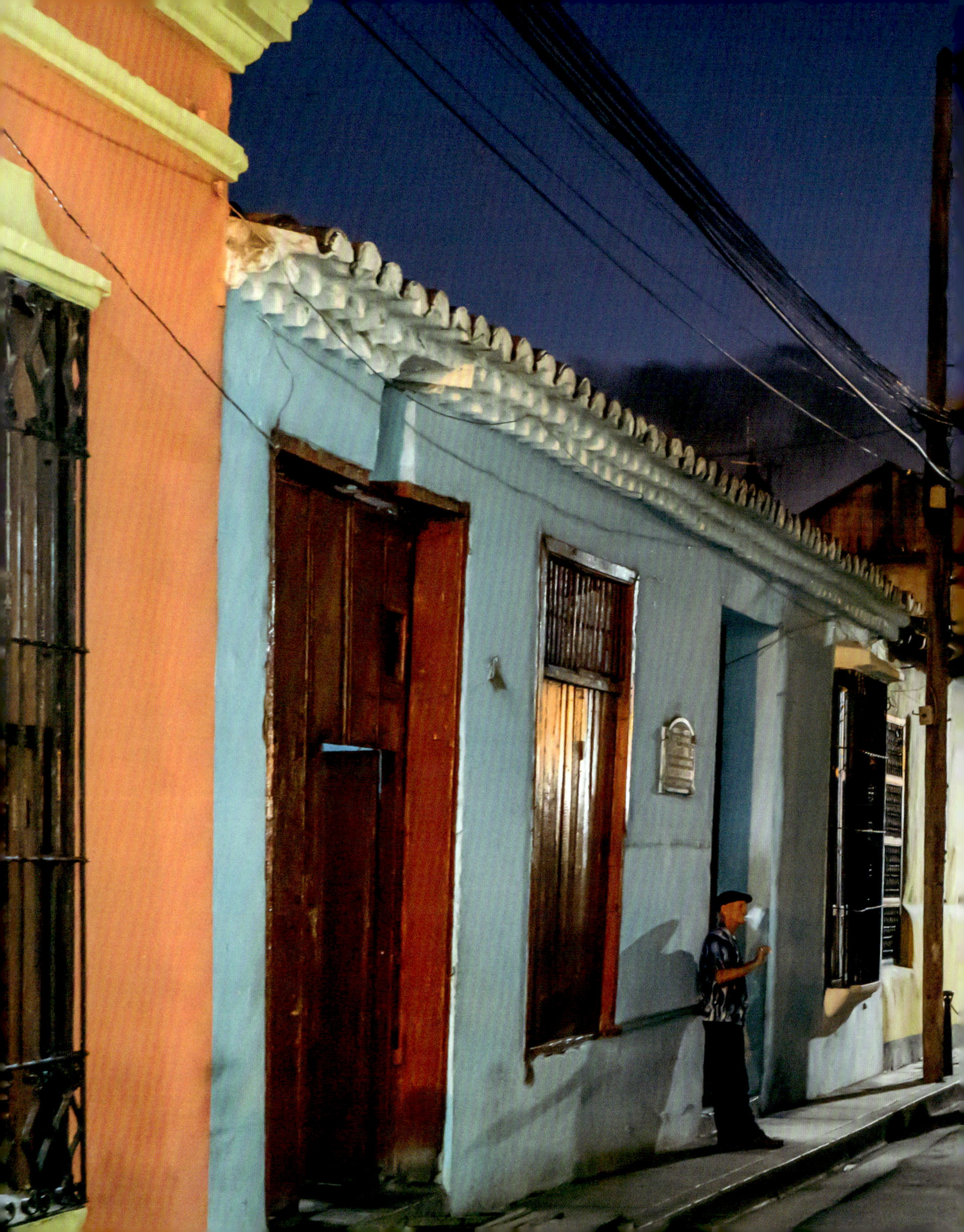

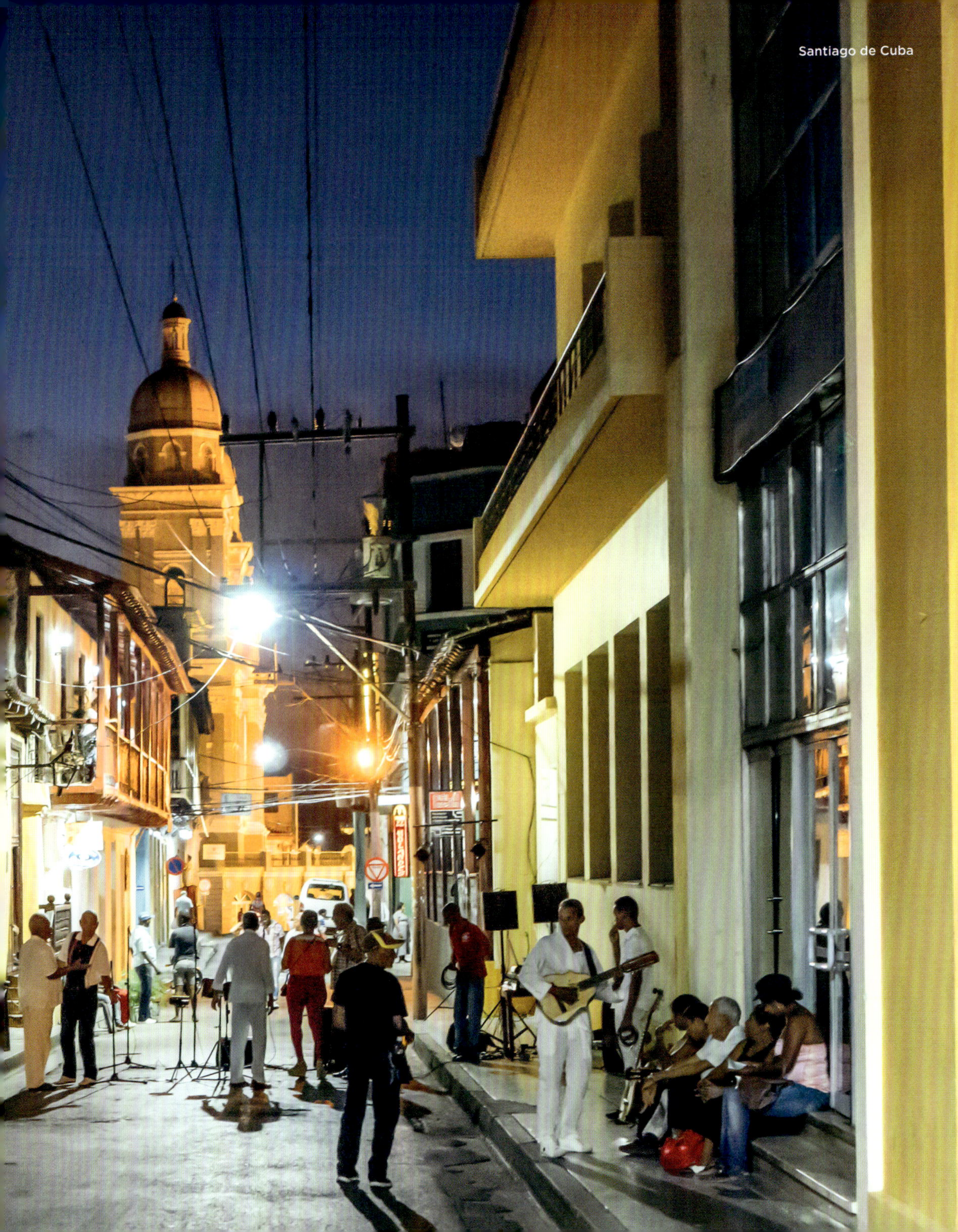
Santiago de Cuba

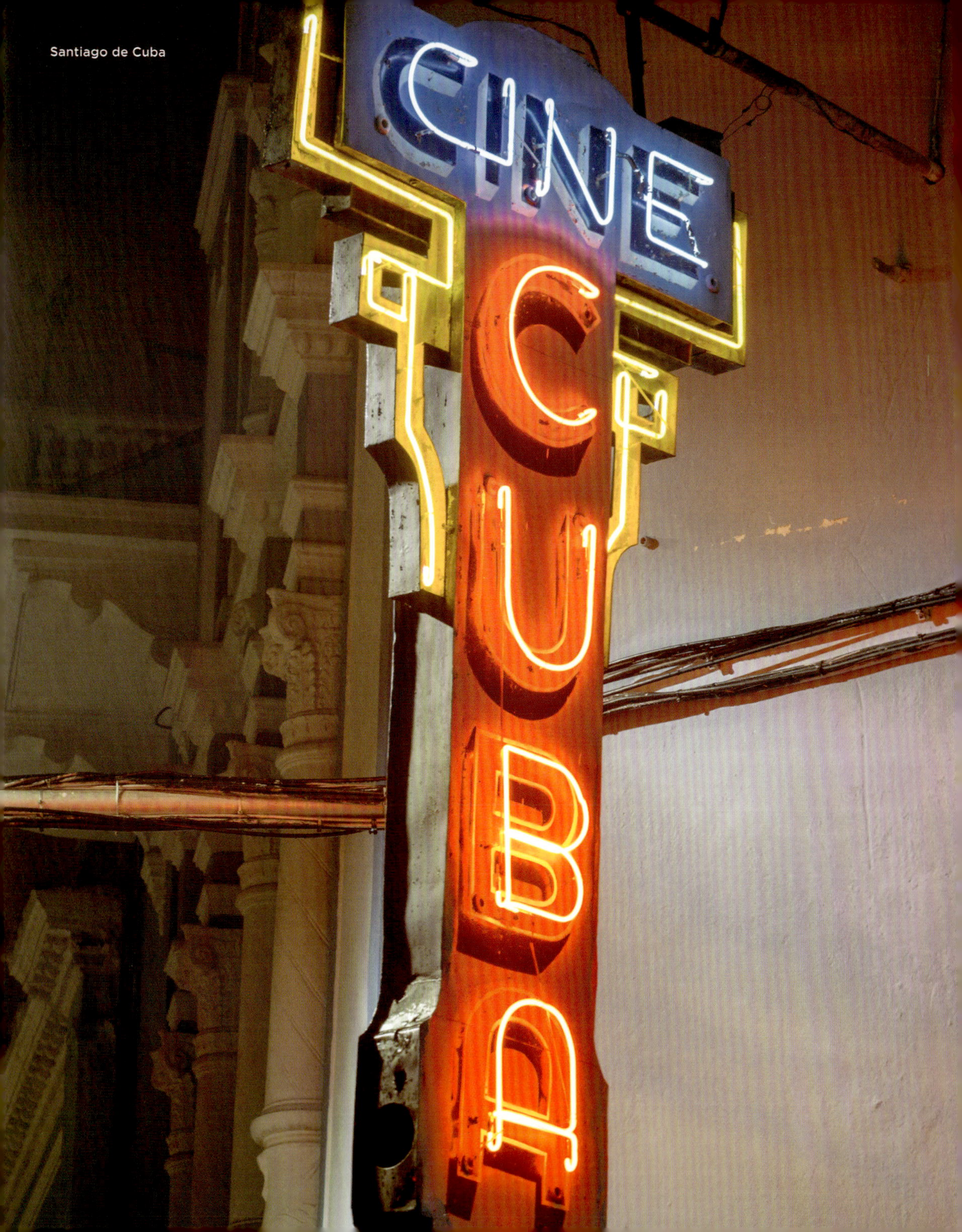

Santiago de Cuba

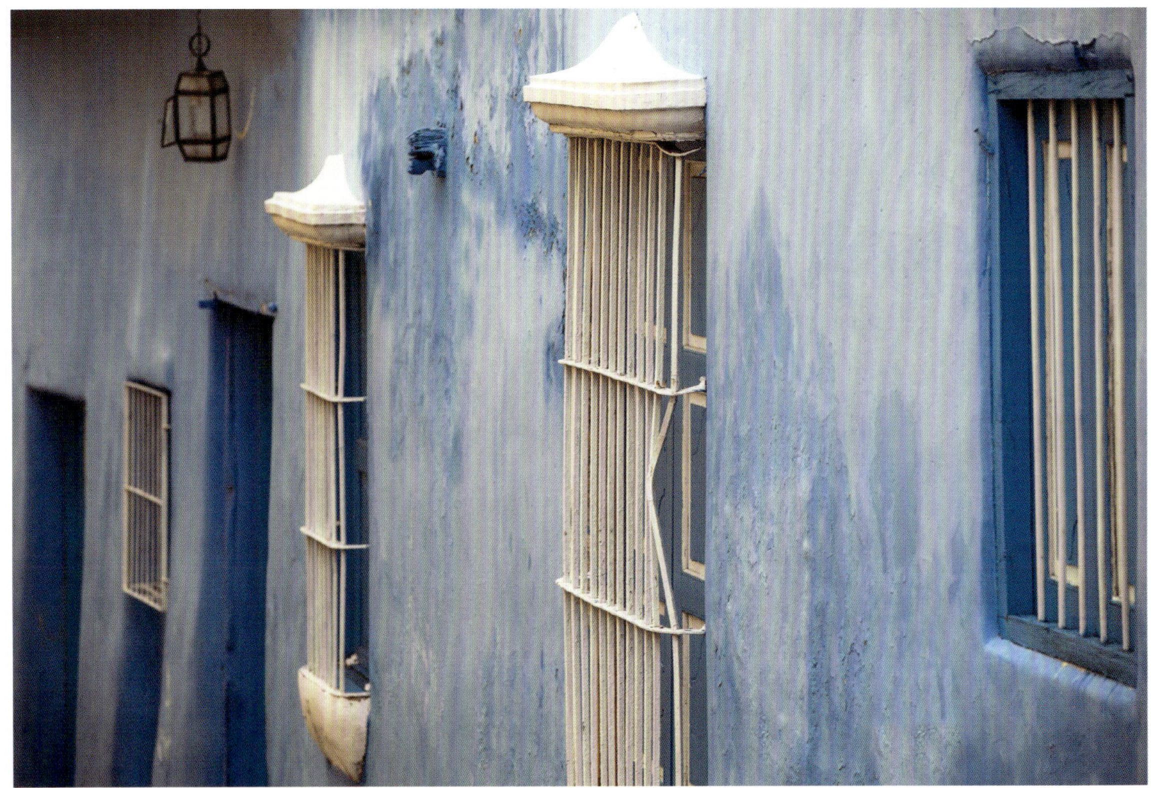

Santiago de Cuba

Calle Heredia

Calle Heredia is Santiago's lively "Cultural Street", with art galleries, bookshops, the Casa de la Trova and small museums. Especially popular is the Carnival Museum, with its most beautiful costumes and props of the three big carnival associations Carabalí Izuama, Carabalí Ozugo and Tumba Francesa. There are live performances everywhere.

Calle Heredia

La calle Heredia est la rue culturelle animée de Santiago où sont installées les galeries d'art, les librairies, la Casa de la Trova et de petits musées. Celui consacré au carnaval est particulièrement apprécié ; il présente les costumes et accessoires de trois grandes associations de carnaval : Carabalí Izuama, Carabalí Ozugo et Tumba Francesa. Des présentations en public sont organisées partout.

Calle Heredia

Die Calle Heredia ist Santiagos lebendige „Kulturstraße", mit Kunstgalerien, Buchhandlungen, der Casa de la Trova und kleinen Museen. Besonders beliebt ist das Karnevalsmuseum mit den schönsten Kostümen und Requisiten der drei großen Karnevalsvereine Carabalí Izuama, Carabalí Ozugo und der Tumba Francesa. Überall gibt es Live-Vorführungen.

Calle Heredia

La calle Heredia es el animado "Camino Cultural" de Santiago, con galerías de arte, librerías, la Casa de la Trova y pequeños museos. Especialmente popular es el Museo del Carnaval con los más bellos trajes y accesorios de las tres grandes asociaciones carnavalescas Carabalí Izuama, Carabalí Ozugo y Tumba Francesa. Hay actuaciones en vivo en todas partes.

A Calle Heredia

A Calle Heredia é a animada "Rua Cultural" de Santiago, com galerias de arte, livrarias, a Casa de la Trova e pequenos museus. Especialmente popular é o Museu do Carnaval com os mais belos trajes e adereços das três grandes associações carnavalescas Carabalí Izuama, Carabalí Ozugo e Tumba Francesa. Há espectáculos ao vivo por todo o lado.

Calle Heredia

Calle Heredia is de levendige 'Culturele Weg' van Santiago, met kunstgalerijen, boekhandels, het Casa de la Trova en kleine musea. Vooral het Carnavalsmuseum met de mooiste kostuums en rekwisieten van de drie grote carnavalsverenigingen Carabalí Izuama, Carabalí Ozugo en Tumba Francesa is populair. Overal zijn er live optredens.

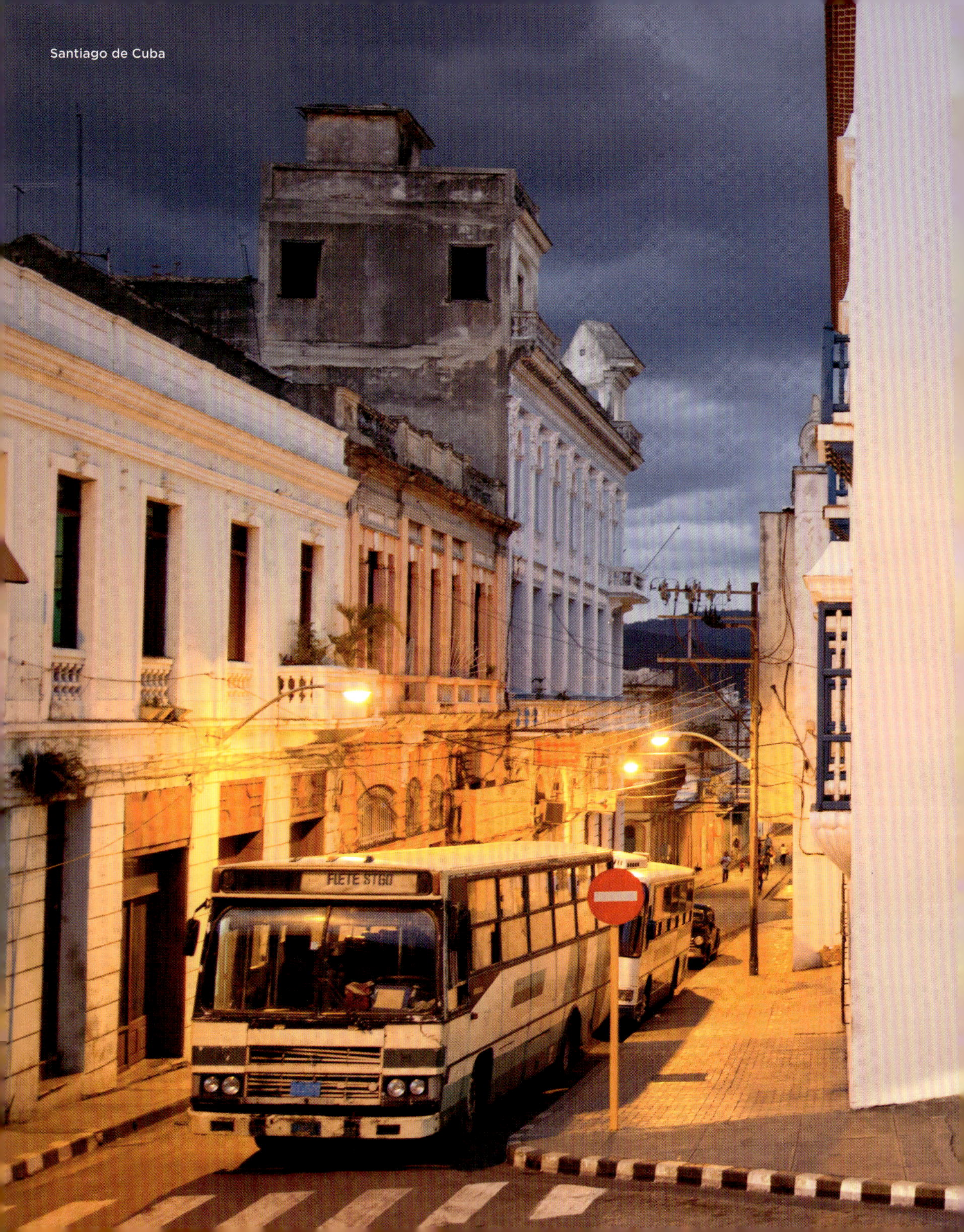

Santiago de Cuba
FLETE STGO

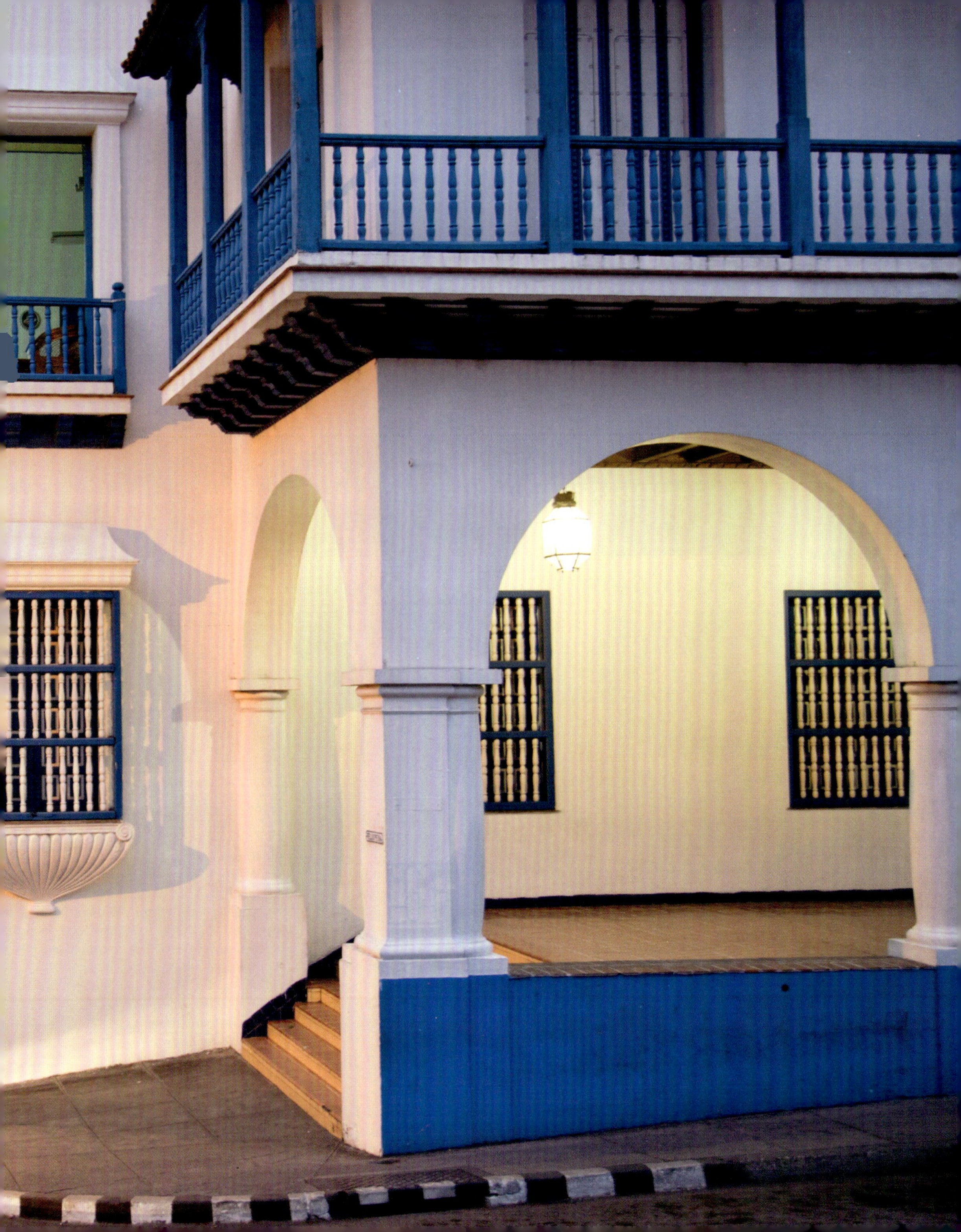

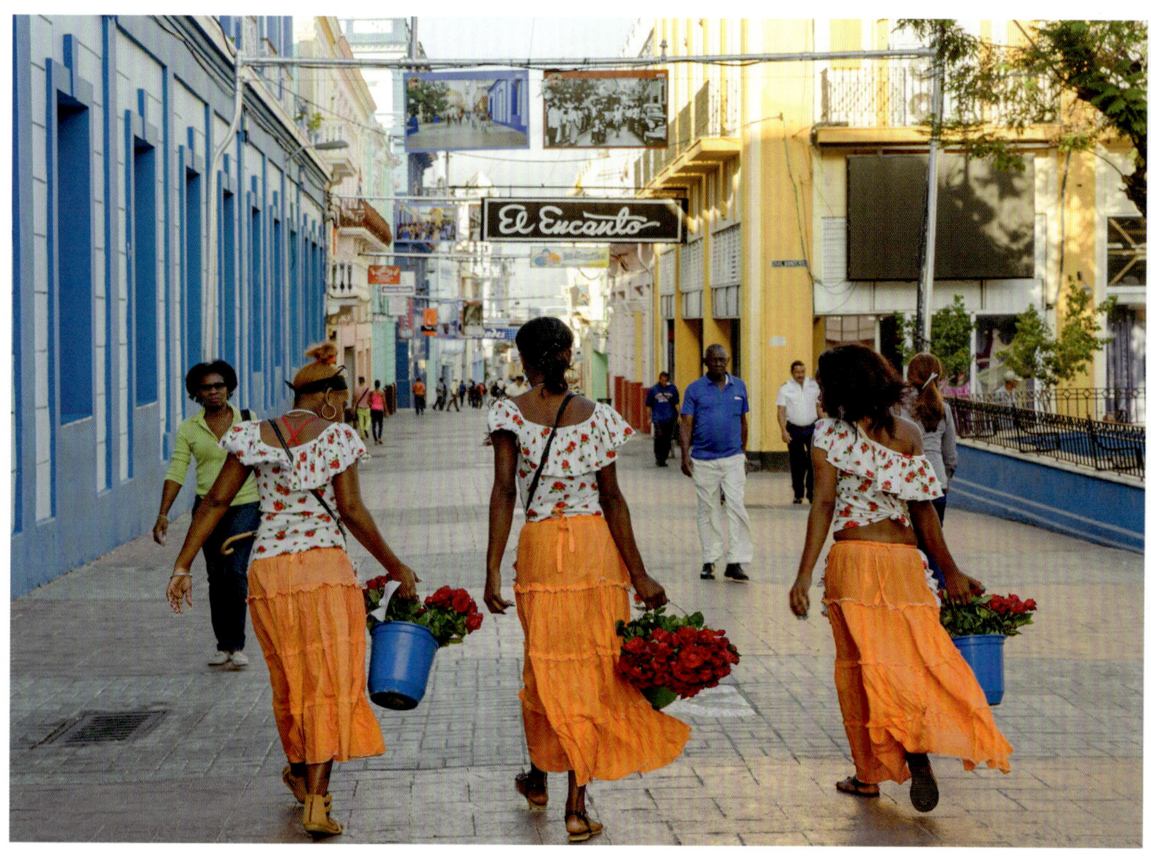

Santiago de Cuba

Calle Enramadas

North of the Parque Céspedes is José António Saco Avenue, a pedestrian zone better known as Calle Enramadas. In colonial times there was a pillory here where criminals and escaped slaves were punished. In the 20th century the "Enramadas" with its two theatres, newspaper editorial offices, and numerous shops, department stores, restaurants and cafés became a cultural centre. Although there hasn't been much to buy on the traditional promenade for a long time, the extinct neon signs from the 1950s create a nostalgic charm.

Calle Enramadas

Au nord de Parque Céspedes s'étend la rue piétonne Avenida José Antonio Saco, plus connue sous le nom de « calle Enramadas ». À l'époque coloniale, c'est là qu'était installé le pilori, auquel les délinquants et les esclaves enfuis étaient condamnés. Les Enramadas, comprenant deux théâtres, les rédactions des journaux locaux et de nombreuses entreprises, boutiques, restaurants et cafés, sont devenus un centre culturel. Le long de la traditionnelle promenade, les boutiques n'ont certes depuis longtemps plus grand-chose à vendre, mais les enseignes en néon des années 1950 distillent un charme nostalgique.

Calle Enramadas

Nördlich vom Parque Céspedes verläuft die fußläufige Avenida José Antonio Saco, besser bekannt unter dem Namen Calle Enramadas. Zu Kolonialzeiten stand hier der Schandpfahl bzw. Pranger, an dem Delinquenten und entlaufende Sklaven bestraft wurden. Im 20. Jahrhundert wurde die „Enramadas" mit ihren beiden Theatern, den Zeitungsredaktionen, den vielen Geschäften, Kaufhäusern, Restaurants und Cafés zu einem kulturellen Zentrum. Auf der traditionellen Flaniermeile gibt es zwar schon lange nicht mehr viel zu kaufen, doch die erloschenen Neonreklamen aus den 1950er Jahren verbreiten einen nostalgischen Charme.

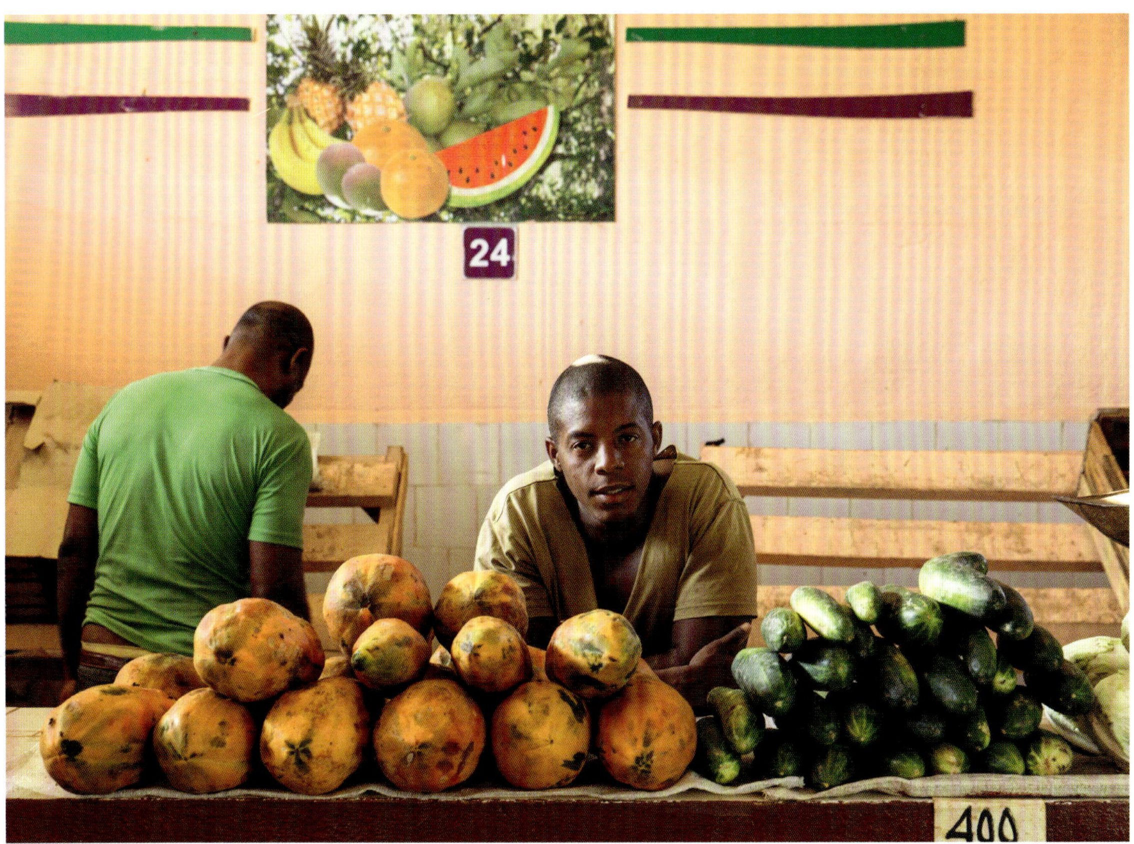

Santiago de Cuba

Calle Enramadas

Al norte del Parque Céspedes se encuentra la Avenida José Antonio Saco, más conocida como Calle Enramadas, que se recorre a pie. En la época colonial existía la picota donde se castigaba a los delincuentes y a los esclavos que escapaban. En el siglo XX, las "Enramadas" con sus dos teatros, la redacción de los periódicos, las numerosas tiendas, los grandes almacenes, los restaurantes y los cafés, se convirtieron en un centro cultural. Aunque no ha habido mucho que comprar en el paseo tradicional durante mucho tiempo, los extintos letreros de neón de la década de 1950 propagan un encanto nostálgico.

Calle Enramadas

A norte do Parque Céspedes fica a Avenida José Antonio Saco, mais conhecida por Calle Enramadas, uma avenida de pedestre. Nos tempos coloniais havia o "pilar da vergonha" ou pelourinho onde delinquentes e escravos fugitivos eram punidos. No século XX as "Enramadas", com os seus dois teatros, as redações dos jornais, as muitas lojas, lojas de departamento, restaurantes e cafés tornaram-se um centro cultural. Embora, durante muito tempo, não tenha havido muito o que comprar no calçadão tradicional, os letreiros de néon extintos dos anos 50 espalharam um encanto nostálgico.

Calle Enramada's

Ten noorden van het Parque Céspedes ligt op loopafstand de Avenida José Antonio Saco, beter bekend als de Calle Enramadas. In de koloniale tijd was er de schandpaal waar misdadigers en ontsnapte slaven werden gestraft. In de 20e eeuw werden de 'Enramadas' een cultureel centrum met twee theaters, krantenredacties, winkels, warenhuizen, restaurants en cafés. Hoewel er op de traditionele promenade al lang niet meer veel te koop is, verspreiden de uitgestorven neonlichten uit de jaren vijftig een nostalgische charme.

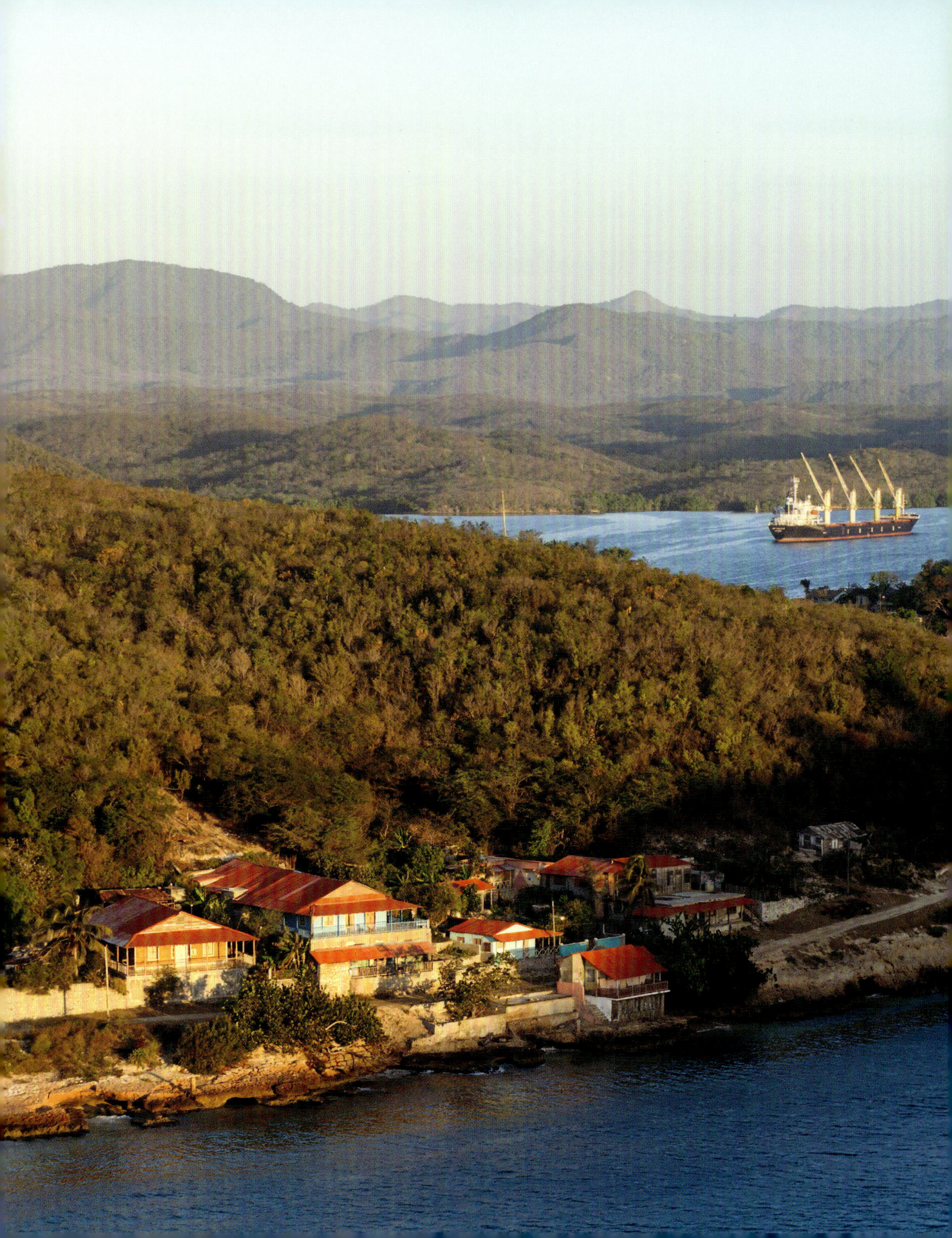

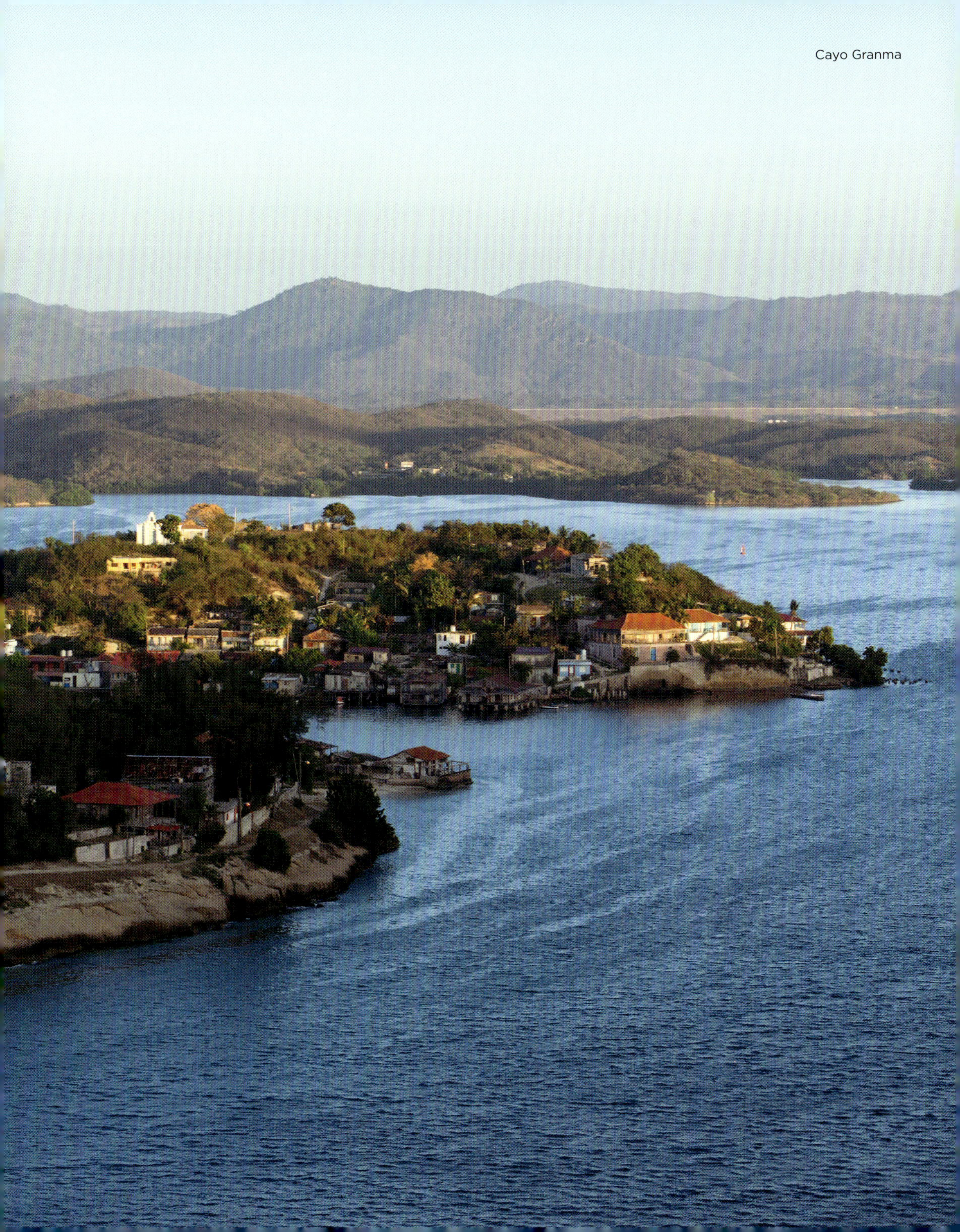

Cayo Granma

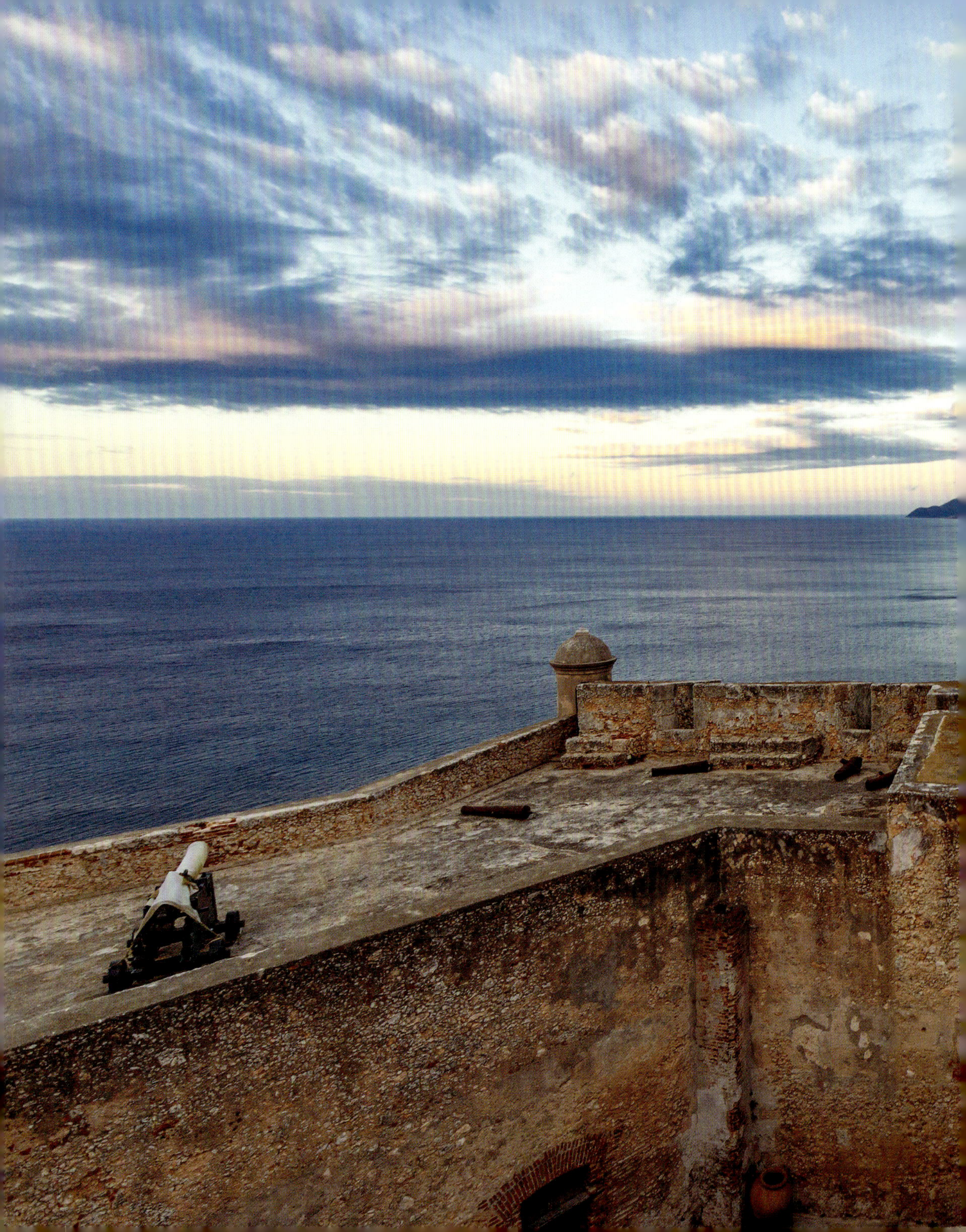

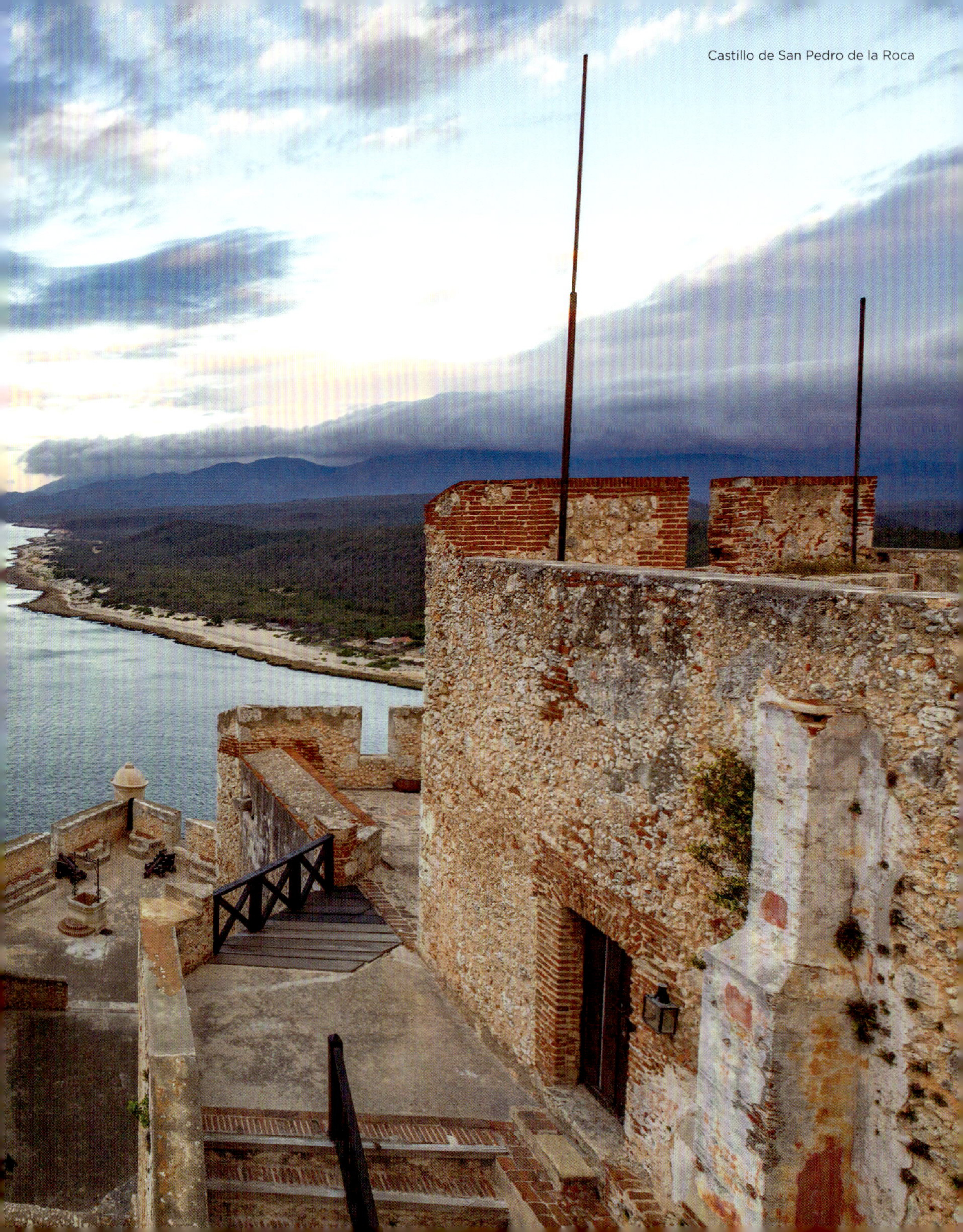

Castillo de San Pedro de la Roca

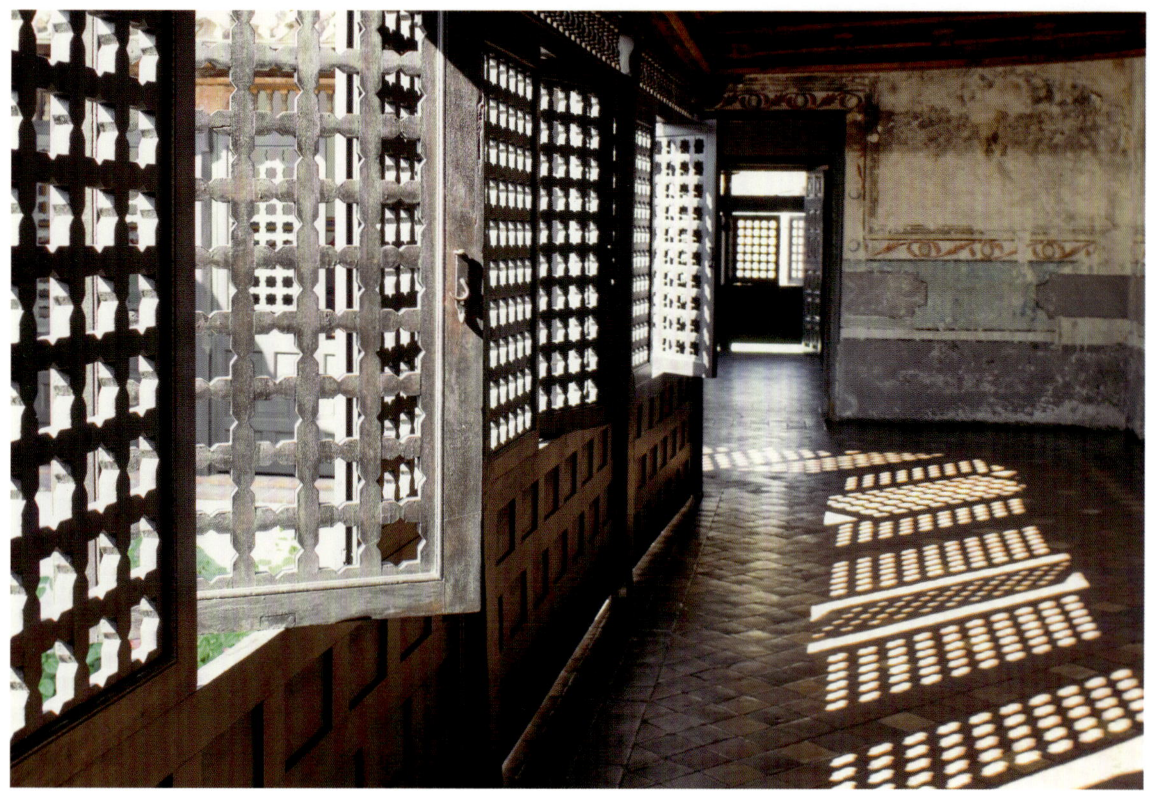

Castillo de San Pedro de la Roca

Fortress El Morro

El Morro (Castillo de San Pedro de la Roca), built in 1640 to protect against pirates, is a fortress 10 km (6 mi.) outside Santiago built on a high coastal rock. It overlooks the bay of Santiago, the mountains of the Sierra Maestra and the Caribbean Sea. El Morro has been a UNESCO World Heritage Site since 1997, and inside is the Piracy Museum.

Fortaleza El Morro

El Morro (Castillo de San Pedro de la Roca), construido en 1640 para protegerse de los piratas, es una fortaleza a 10 km de Santiago situada sobre una alta roca costera. Tiene vistas a la bahía de Santiago, las montañas de la Sierra Maestra y el Mar Caribe. El Morro es Patrimonio de la Humanidad de la UNESCO desde 1997, y en su interior se encuentra el Museo de la Piratería.

Le fort El Morro

La forteresse El Morro (Castillo de San Pedro de la Roca), bâtie en 1640 pour se défendre des pirates, trône au sommet du littoral rocheux à 10 km à l'extérieur de Santiago. De là s'étend la vue sur la baie de Santiago, les montagnes de la sierra Maestra et la mer des Caraïbes. El Morro est inscrite depuis 1997 au patrimoine mondial de l'UNESCO et abrite dans ses locaux le musée de la Piraterie.

Fortaleza El Morro

El Morro (Castillo de San Pedro de la Roca), construído em 1640 para proteger contra os piratas, é uma fortaleza que fica a 10 km de Santiago sobre uma alta rocha costeira. A partir daqui tem-se a vista para a baía de Santiago, as montanhas da Sierra Maestra e o Mar do Caribe. El Morro é Patrimônio Mundial da UNESCO desde 1997, e no seu interior encontra-se o Museu da Pirataria.

Festung El Morro

Die 1640 zum Schutz gegen Piraten erbaute Festung El Morro (Castillo de San Pedro de la Roca) thront 10 km außerhalb Santiagos auf einem hohen Küstenfelsen. Von hier aus überblickt man die Bucht von Santiago, die Berge der Sierra Maestra und die karibische See. El Morro gehört seit 1997 zum UNESCO-Weltkulturerbe, im Inneren befindet sich das Piraterie-Museum.

Fort El Morro

El Morro (Castillo de San Pedro de la Roca), gebouwd in 1640 ter bescherming tegen piraten, is een fort 10 km buiten Santiago op een hoge kustrots. Het kijkt uit over de baai van Santiago, de bergen van de Sierra Maestra en de Caribische Zee. El Morro staat sinds 1997 op de Werelderfgoedlijst van de UNESCO en binnenin bevindt zich het Piraterijmuseum.

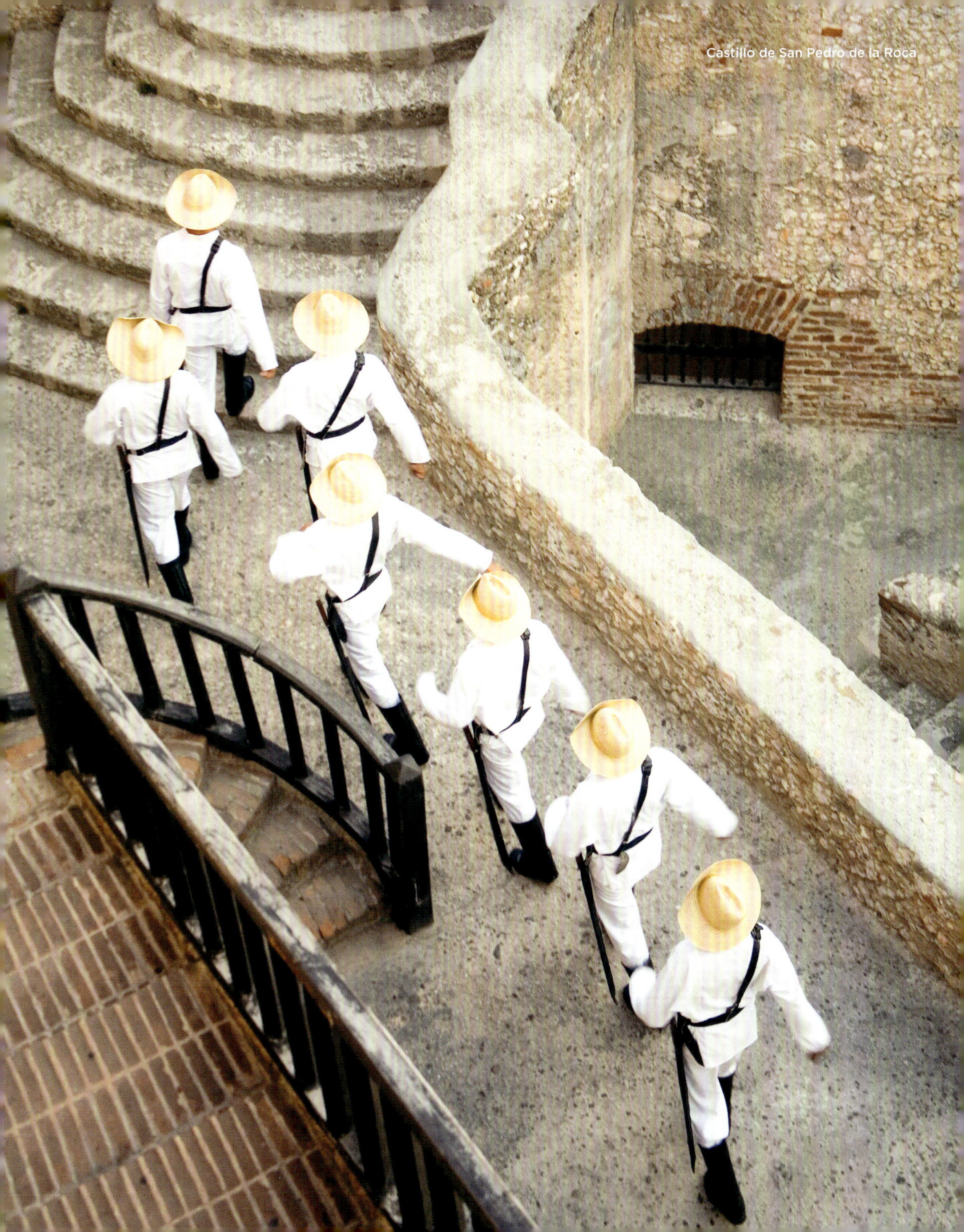

Castillo de San Pedro de la Roca

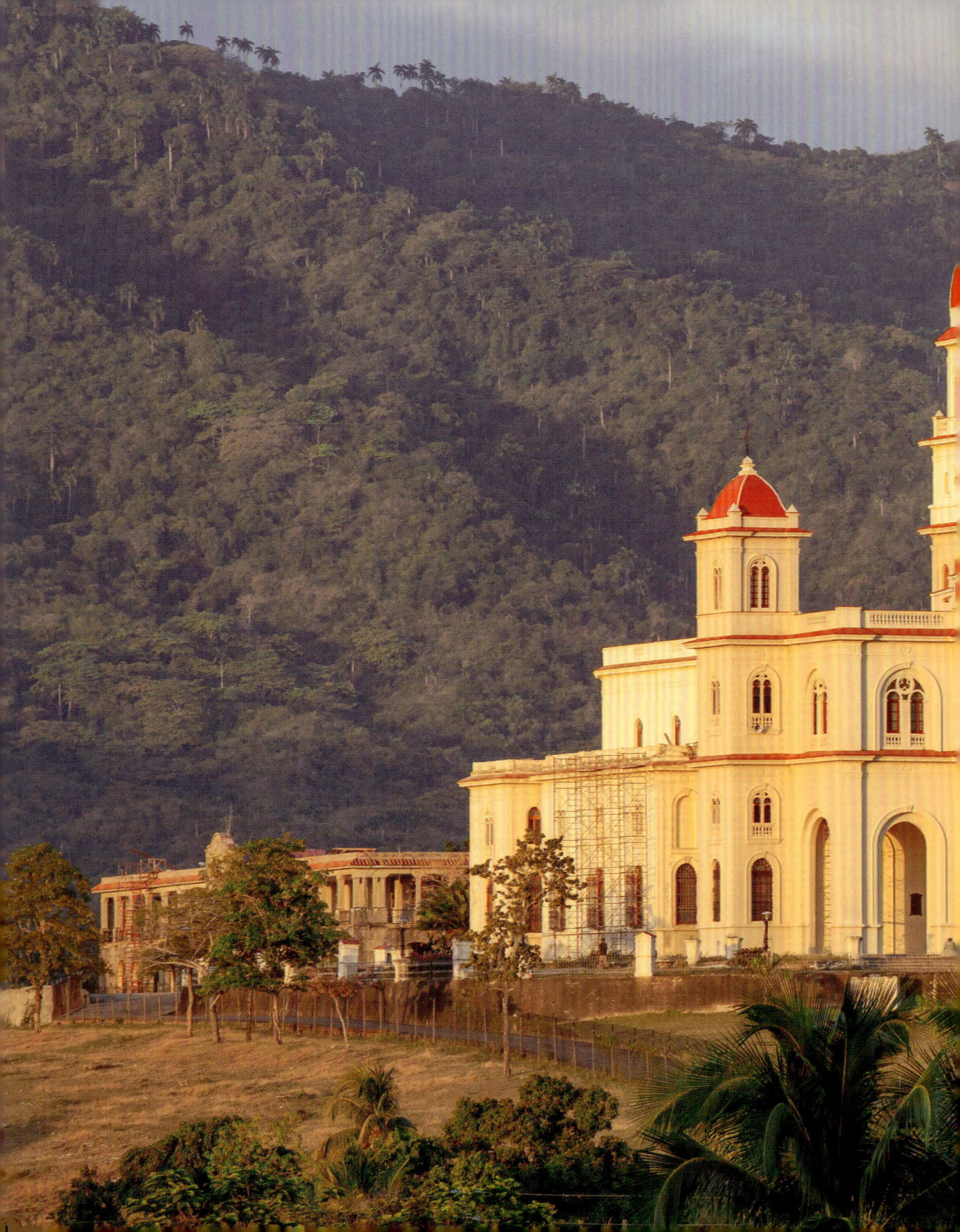

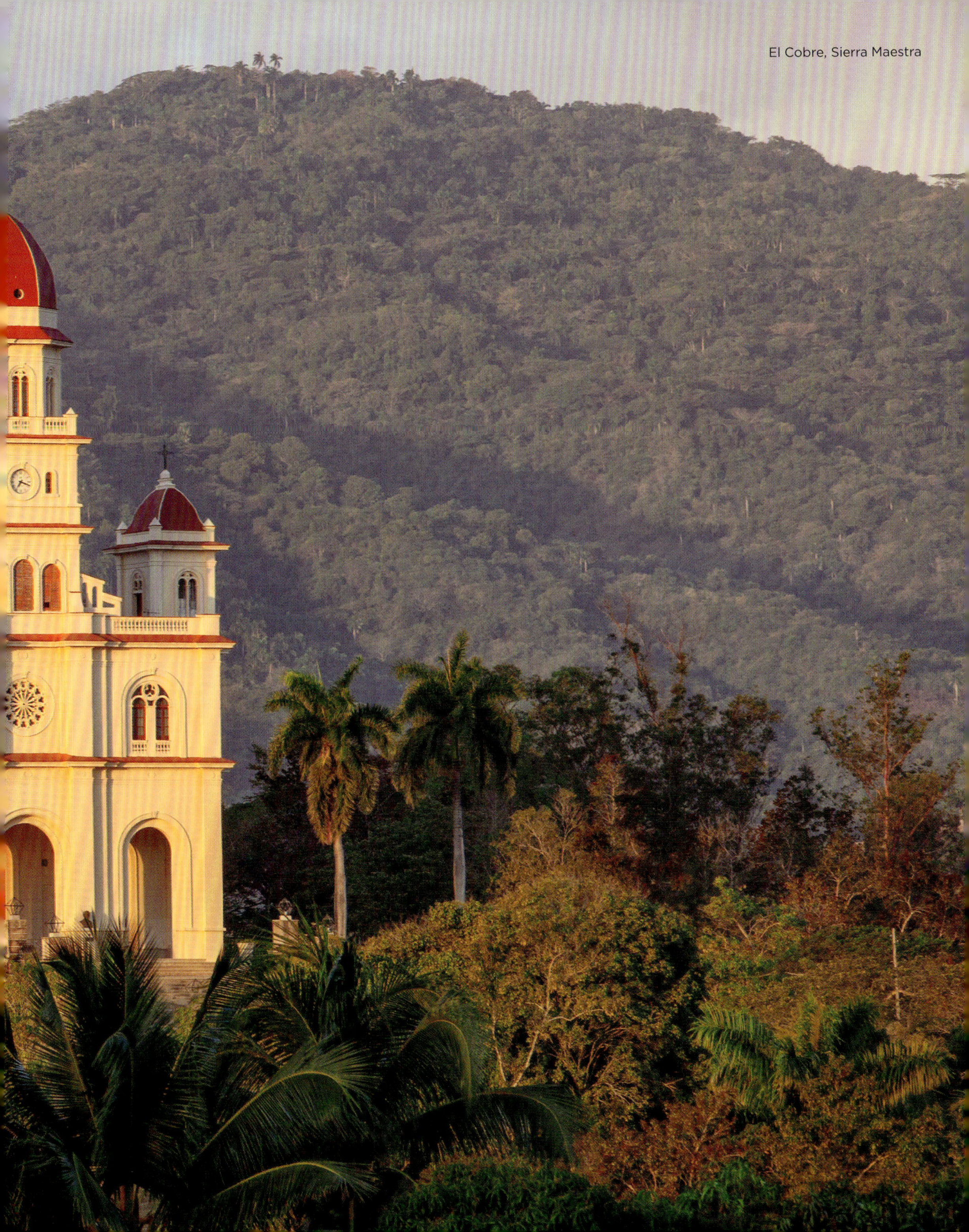

El Cobre, Sierra Maestra

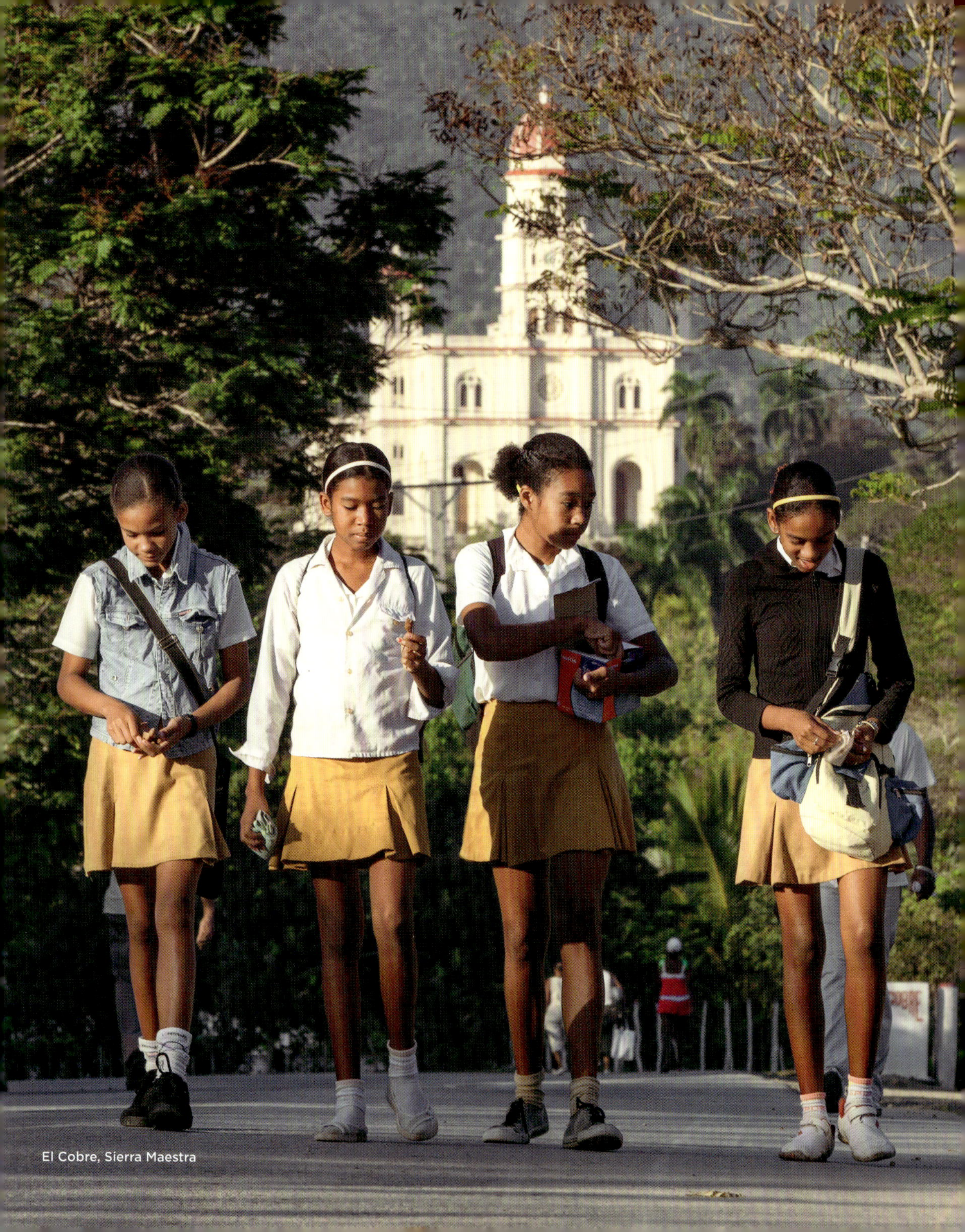

El Cobre, Sierra Maestra

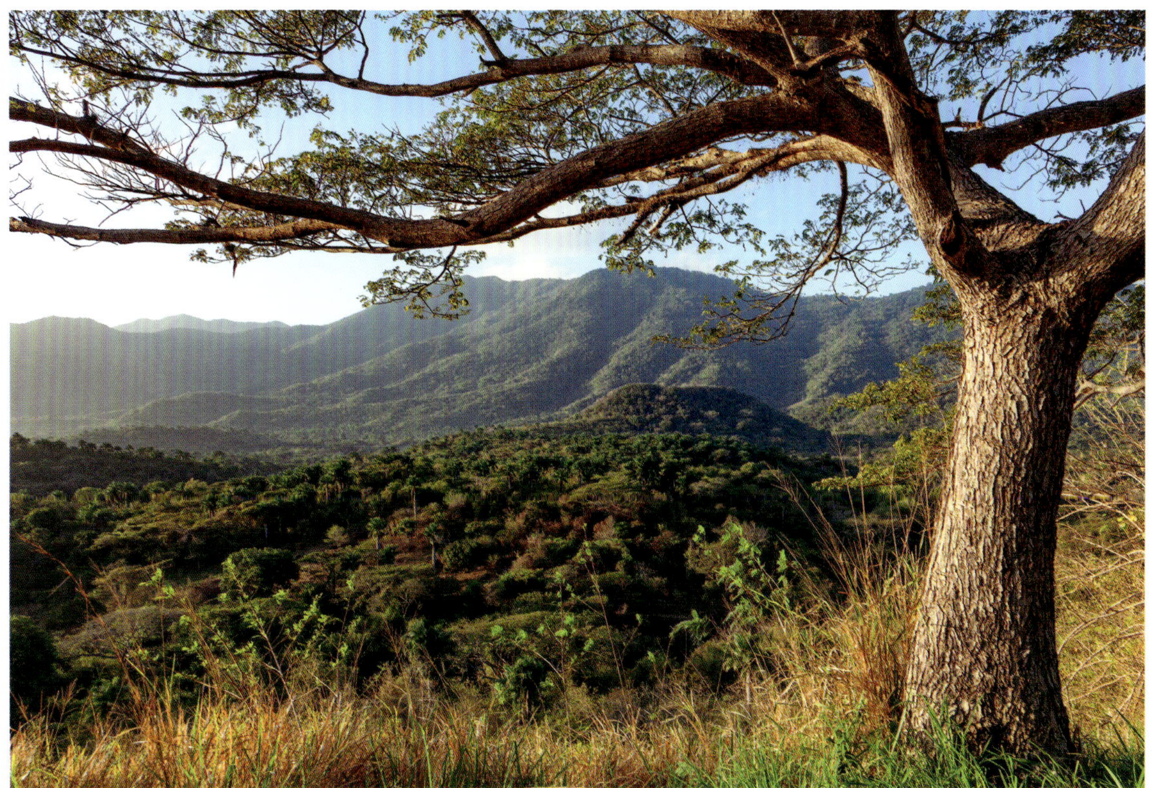

Sierra Maestra

El Cobre

The copper mine in Valle El Cobre made Santiago rich by the 19th century. Today, the valley is dominated by the Basilica of El Cobre, dedicated to the Merciful Virgin of Copper, patron saint of Cuba. In popular belief, however, the Virgin is none other than Ochún, the Afro-Cuban goddess of love. Hemingway donated his Nobel Prize medal to her.

El Cobre

La mina de cobre en Valle El Cobre enriqueció a Santiago hasta el siglo XIX. Hoy en día, el valle está dominado por la Basílica del Cobre, dedicada a la Virgen Misericordiosa del Cobre, patrona de Cuba. En la creencia popular, sin embargo, la Virgen no es otra cosa que la diosa afrocubana del amor Ochún. Hemigway le donó su medalla del Premio Nobel.

El Cobre

La mine de cuivre de la Valle El Cobre a assuré la richesse de Santiago jusqu'au milieu du xixe siècle. Aujourd'hui, la vallée est dominée par la basilique El Cobre, dédiée à la Vierge de la Charité d'El Cobre, sainte patronne de Cuba. Selon la croyance populaire, cette vierge n'est autre que la déesse de l'amour afro-cubaine Ochún. Hemingway lui offrit sa médaille du prix Nobel.

El Cobre

A mina de cobre do Valle El Cobre enriqueceu Santiago até o século XIX. Hoje, o vale é dominado pela Basílica de El Cobre, dedicada à Virgem Misericordiosa do Cobre, padroeira de Cuba. Na crença popular, porém, a Virgem não é outra senão a deusa afro-cubana do amor de Oxum. Hemigway doou-lhe a sua medalha de Prémio Nobel.

El Cobre

Das Kupferbergwerk im Valle El Cobre machte Santiago bis ins 19. Jahrhundert reich. Beherrscht wird das Tal heute von der Basilika El Cobre, die der Barmherzigen Jungfrau des Kupfers gewidmet ist, der Patronin Kubas. Im Volksglauben ist die Jungfrau jedoch niemand anderes als die afrokubanische Liebesgöttin Ochún. Hemigway stiftete ihr seine Nobelpreis-Medaille.

El Cobre

De kopermijn in Valle El Cobre heeft Santiago tot de 19e eeuw rijk gemaakt. Tegenwoordig wordt de vallei gedomineerd door de Basiliek van El Cobre, gewijd aan de Barmhartige Maagd van Koper, beschermheilige van Cuba. In het volksgeloof is de Maagd echter niemand minder dan de Afro-Cubaanse godin van de liefde Ochún. Hemigway schonk haar zijn Nobelprijs medaille.

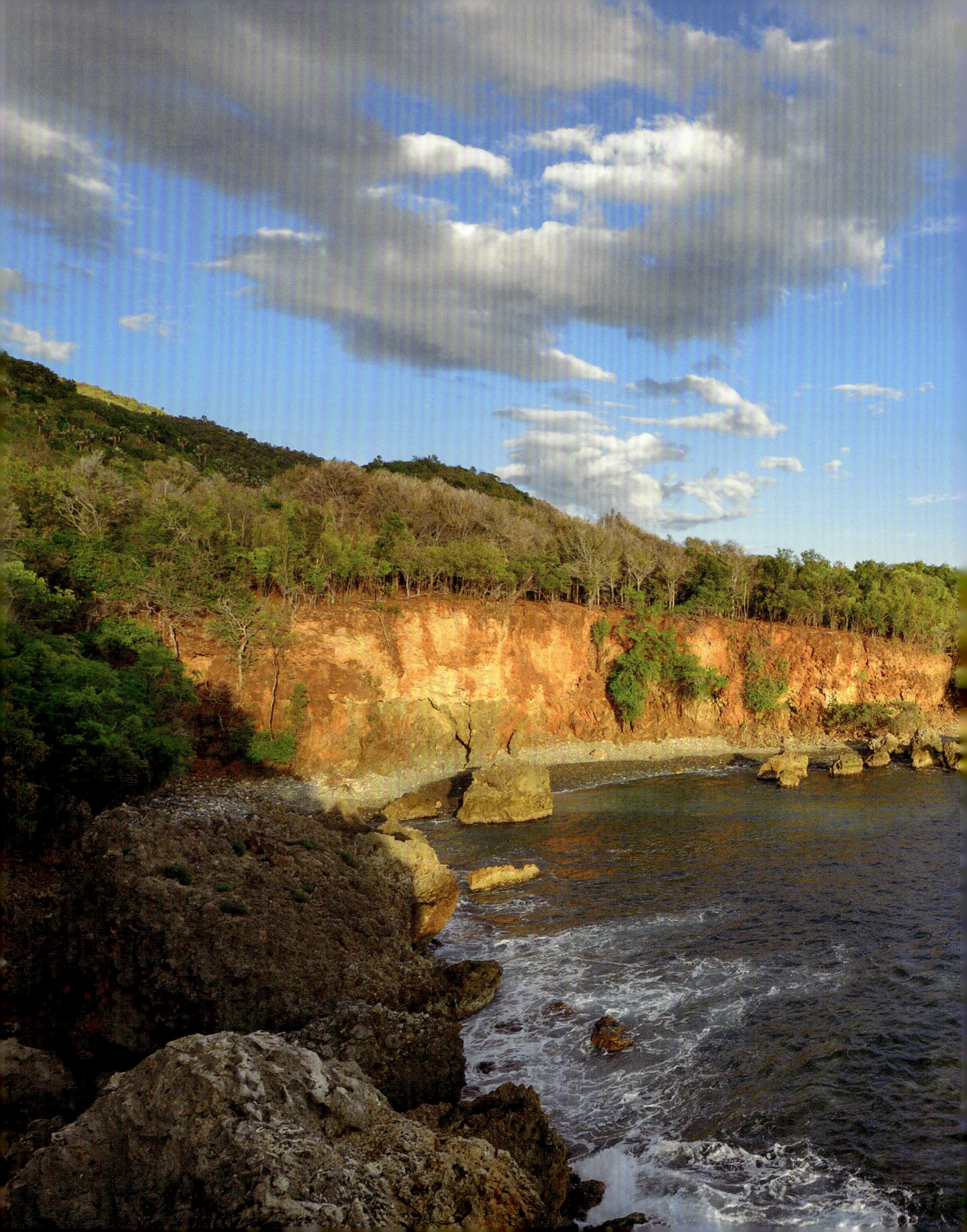

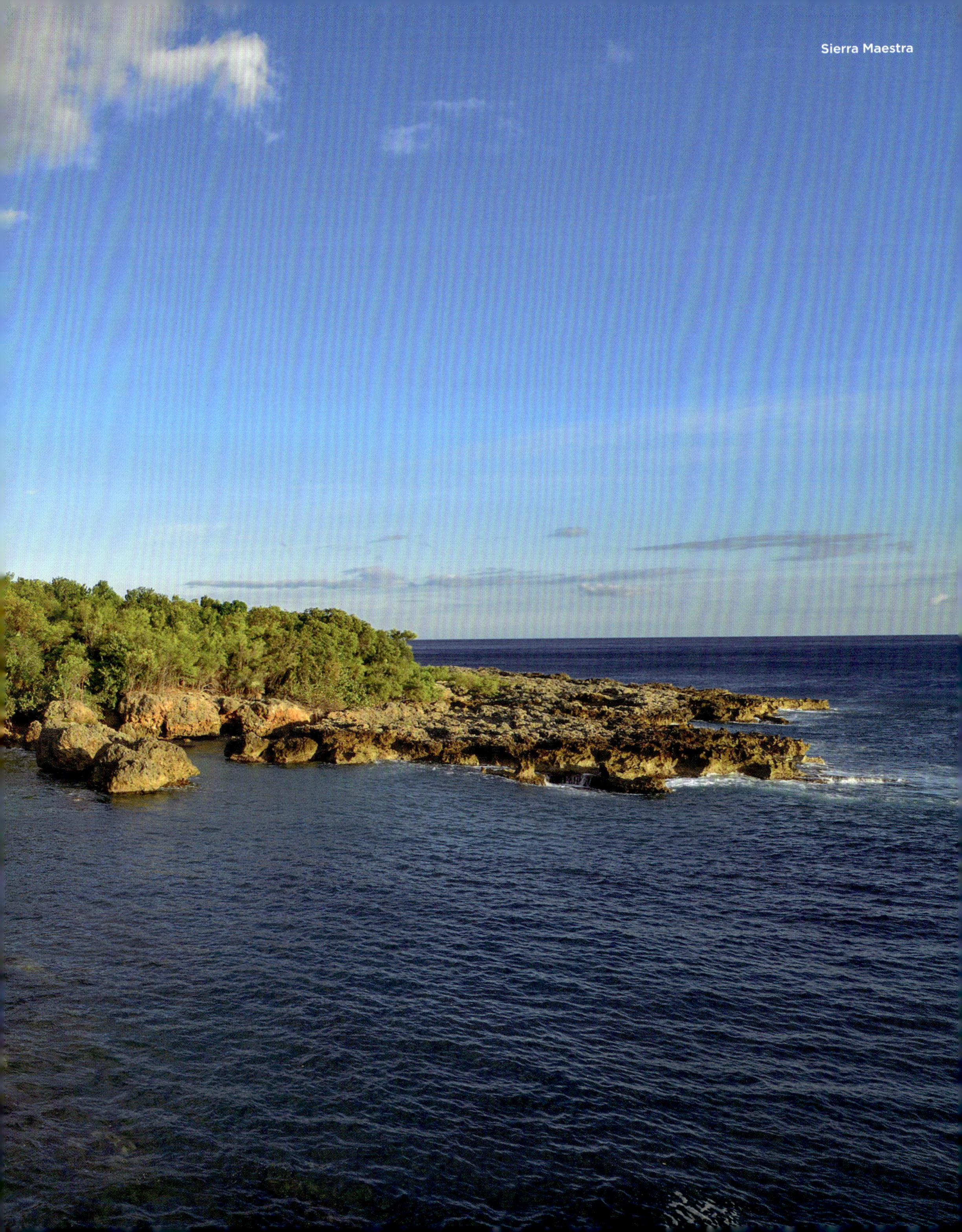
Sierra Maestra

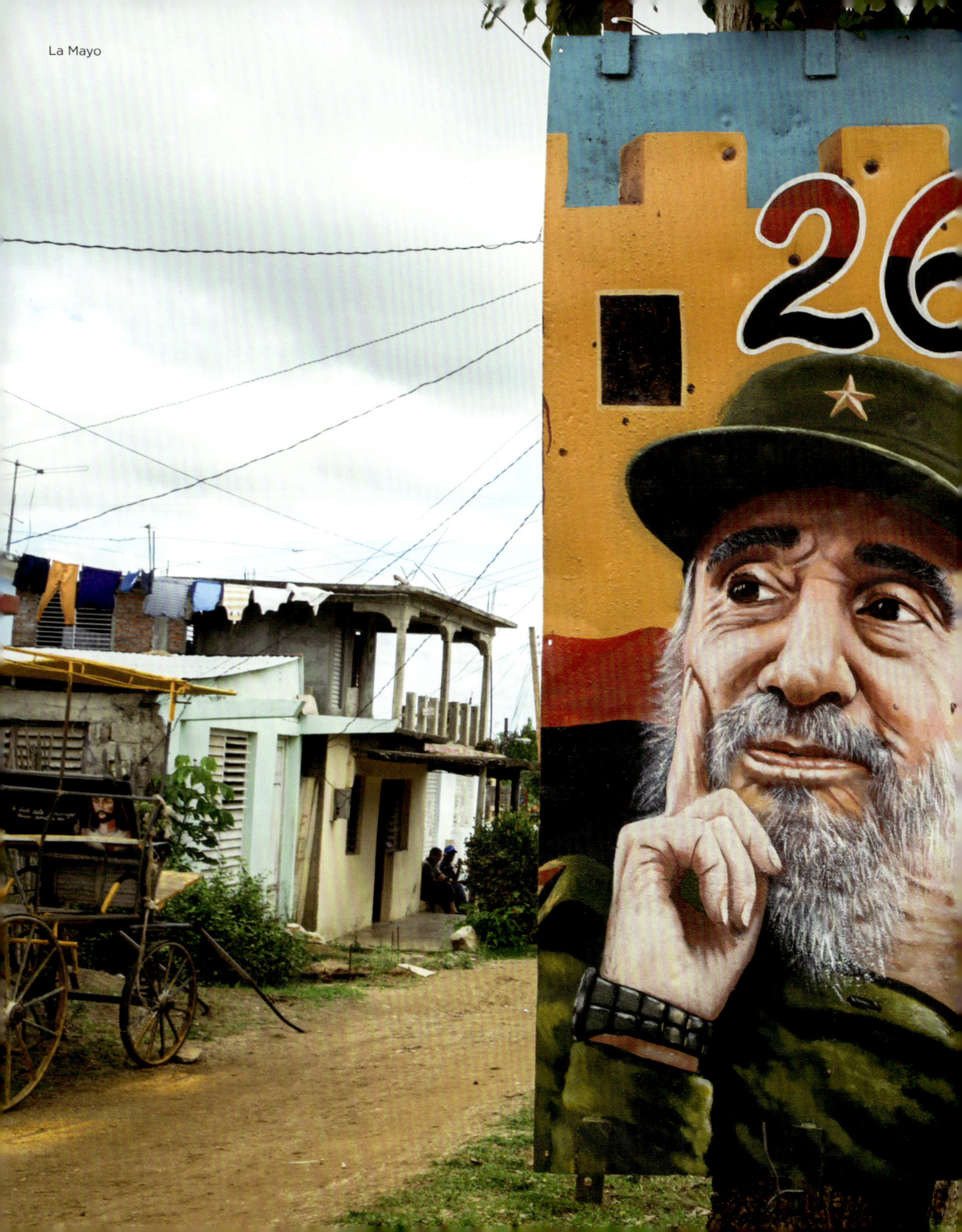

La Mayo

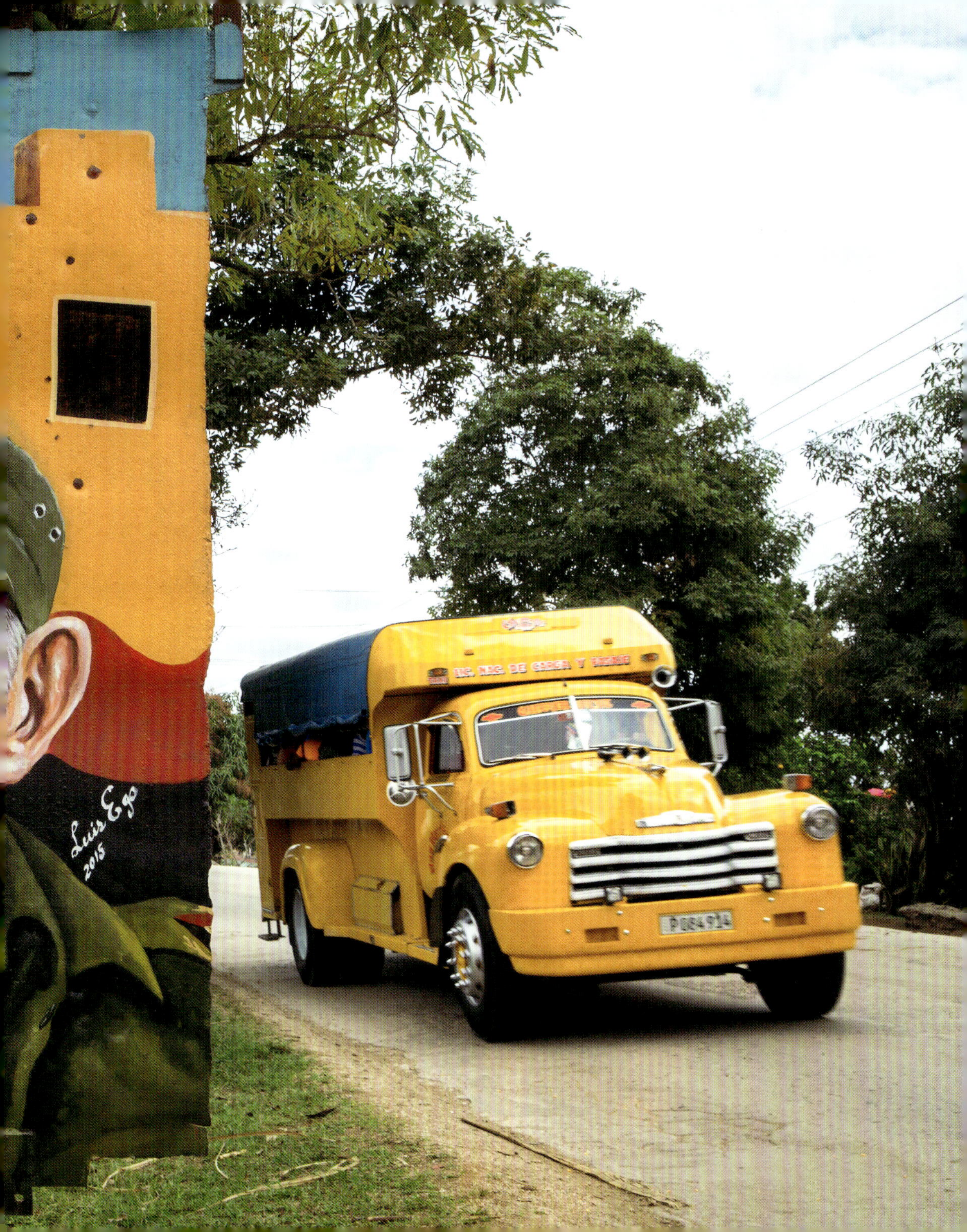

Luis Ego
2015

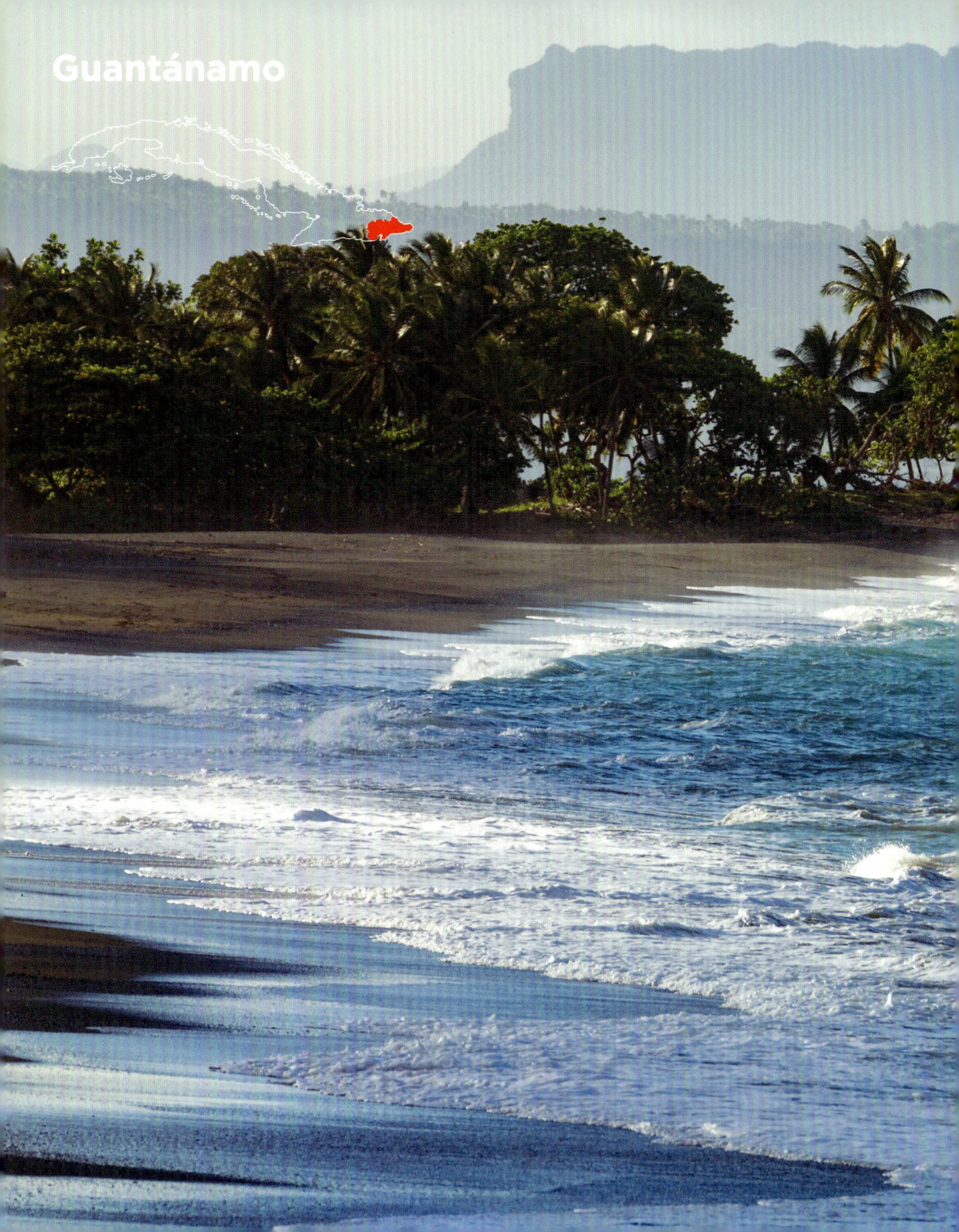

Guantánamo

Playa Barigua

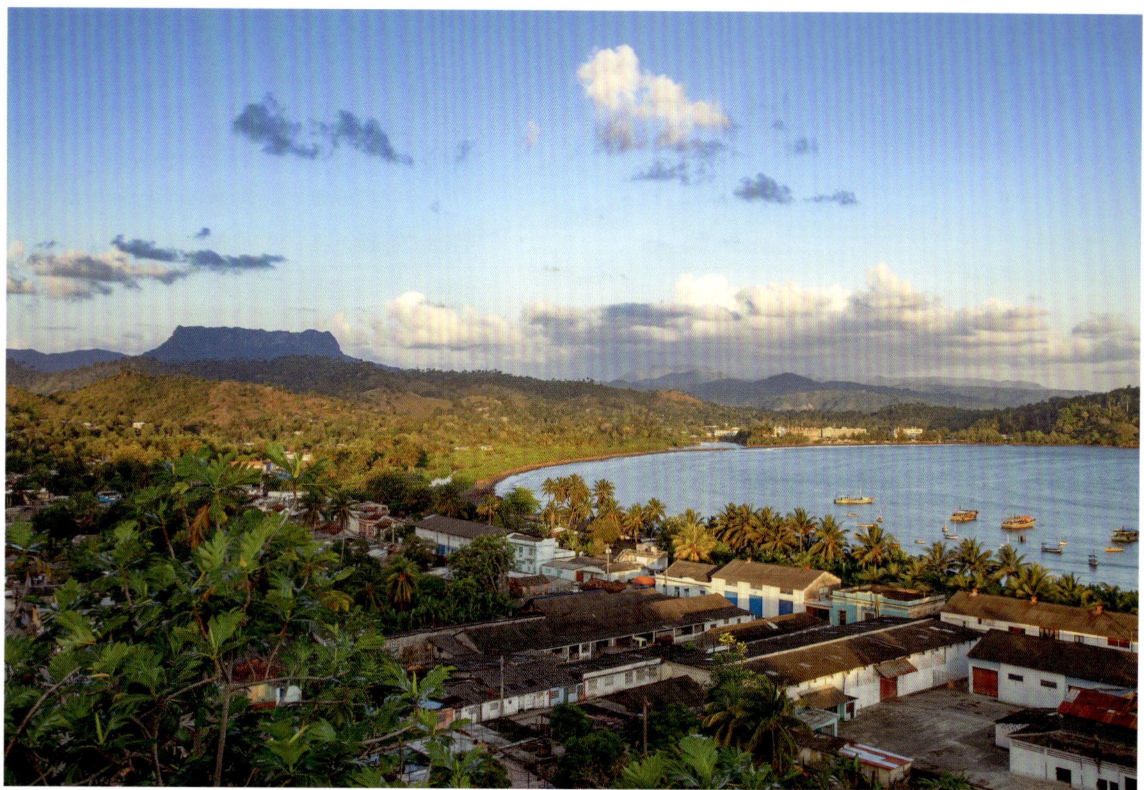

Baracoa

Guantánamo

The most mountainous eastern province of Cuba is by name the most famous—because of the song *Guajira Guantanamera* and because of the US military base built in 1903. The provincial capital of the same name, Guantánamo, in the shadow of the naval base, plays a minor role in Cuba, unlike the colonial town of Baracoa in the easternmost corner of the island.

Guantánamo

La province montagneuse la plus à l'est de Cuba est la plus connue de nom, d'une part grâce à la célèbre chanson *Guajira Guantanamera* et, d'autre part, pour la présence de la base militaire américaine installée en 1903. La capitale homonyme de la province, Guantánamo, dans l'ombre de la base militaire, joue un rôle secondaire à Cuba, contrairement à la petite ville coloniale de Baracoa, située à la pointe la plus orientale de l'île.

Guantánamo

Die gebirgige östlichste Provinz Kubas ist vom Namen her die bekannteste – wegen des Liedes *Guajira Guantanamera* und wegen des 1903 errichteten US-Militärstützpunktes. Die gleichnamige Provinzhauptstadt Guantánamo im Schatten der Marine-Basis spielt in Kuba eine Nebenrolle, ganz anders als das Kolonialstädtchen Baracoa im äußersten Ostzipfel der Insel.

Guantánamo

La provincia más montañosa del este de Cuba es la más famosa por la canción *Guajira Guantanamera* y por la base militar estadounidense construida en 1903. La capital de la provincia del mismo nombre, Guantánamo, a la sombra de la base naval, desempeña un papel menor en Cuba, a diferencia de la ciudad colonial de Baracoa, que se encuentra en el extremo oriental de la isla.

Guantánamo

A província mais montanhosa do leste de Cuba é por nome a mais famosa – por causa da canção *Guajira Guantanamera* e por causa da base militar americana construída em 1903. A capital provincial do mesmo nome, Guantánamo, à sombra da base naval, desempenha um papel menor em Cuba, ao contrário da cidade colonial de Baracoa, no extremo leste da ilha.

Guantánamo

De meest bergachtige oostelijke provincie van Cuba is met naam de bekendste – vanwege het lied *Guajira Guantanamera* en vanwege de Amerikaanse militaire basis gebouwd in 1903. De gelijknamige provinciehoofdstad Guantánamo, in de schaduw van de marinebasis, speelt in Cuba een ondergeschikte rol, in tegenstelling tot de koloniale stad Baracoa in de meest oostelijke hoek van het eiland.

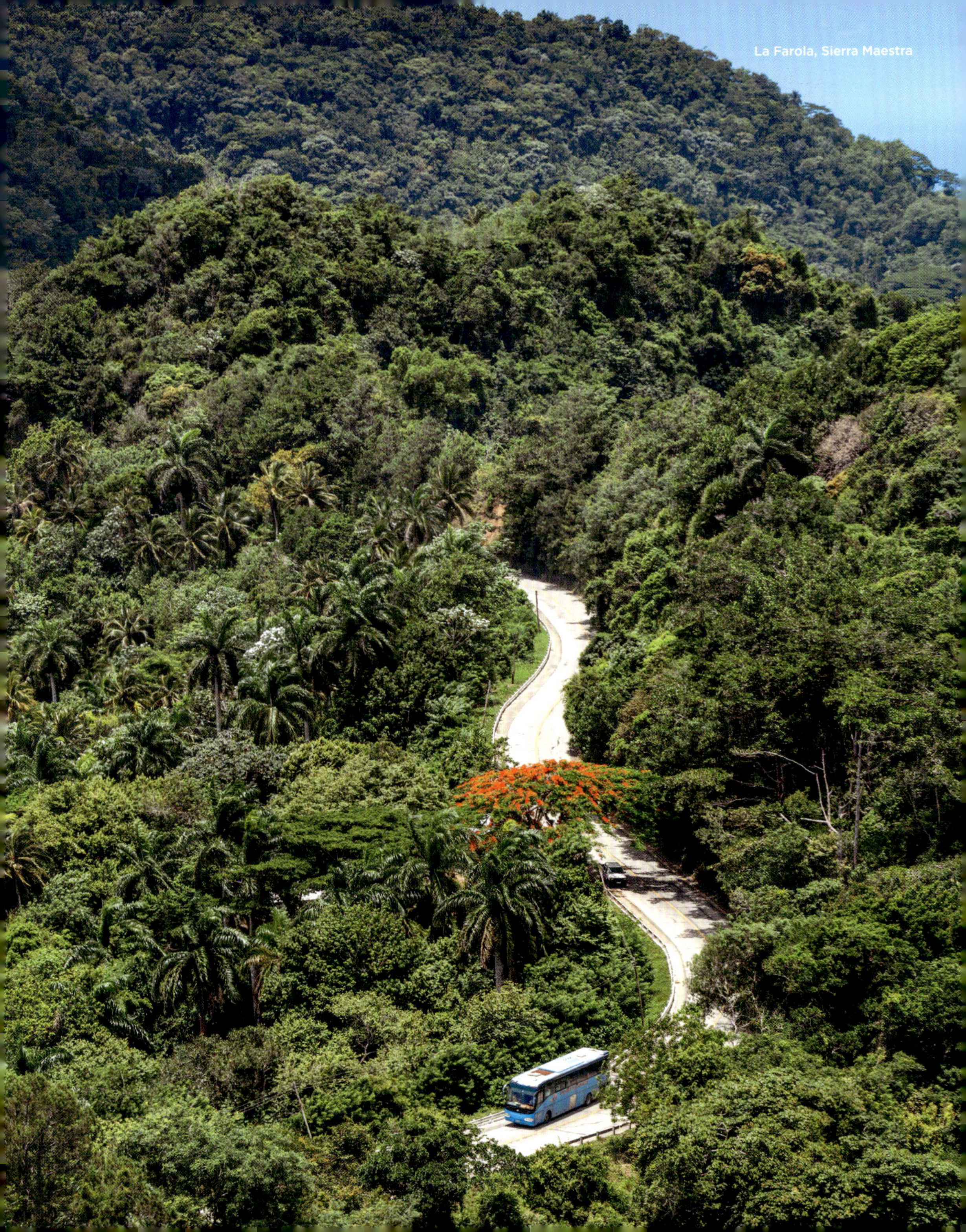
La Farola, Sierra Maestra

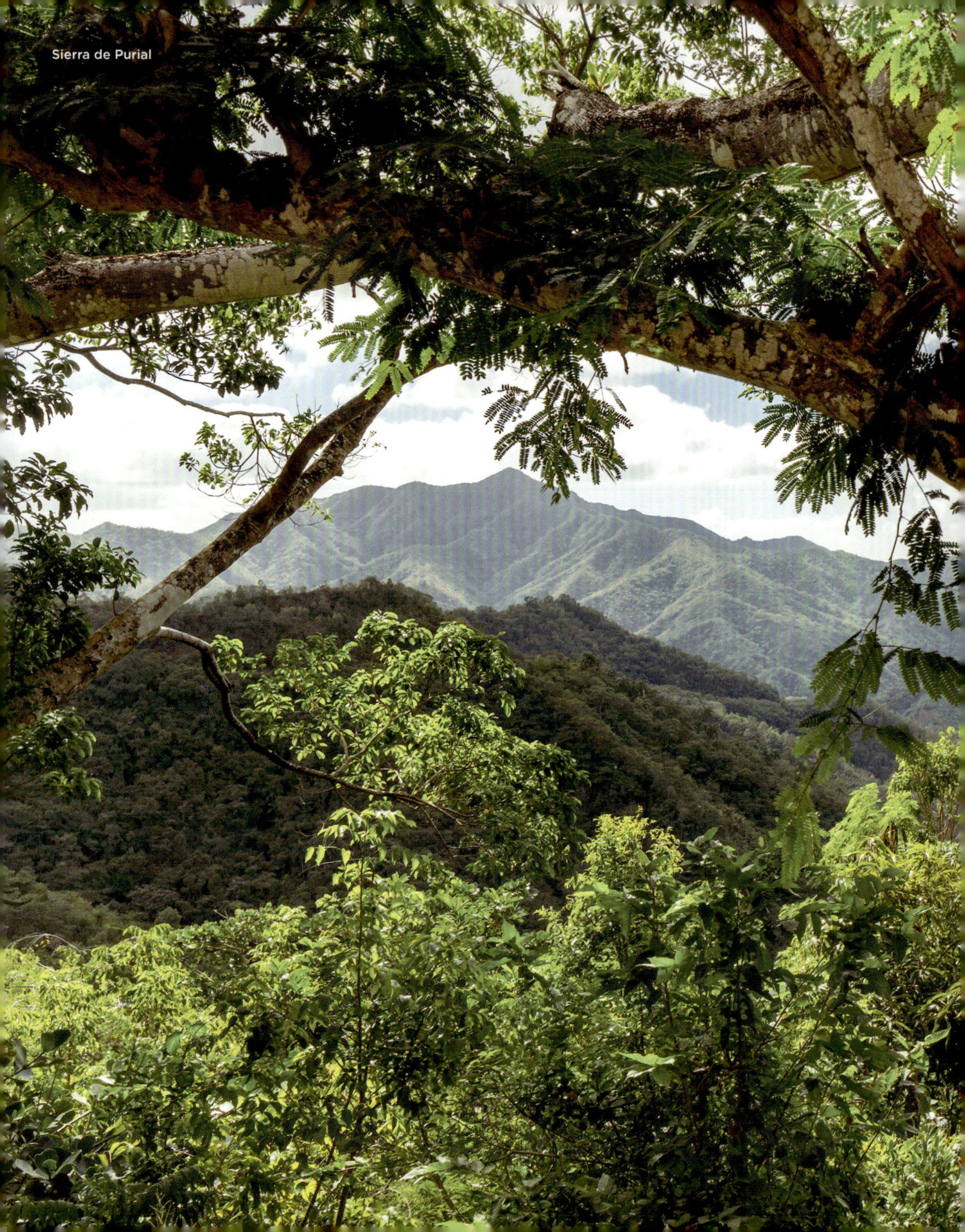
Sierra de Purial

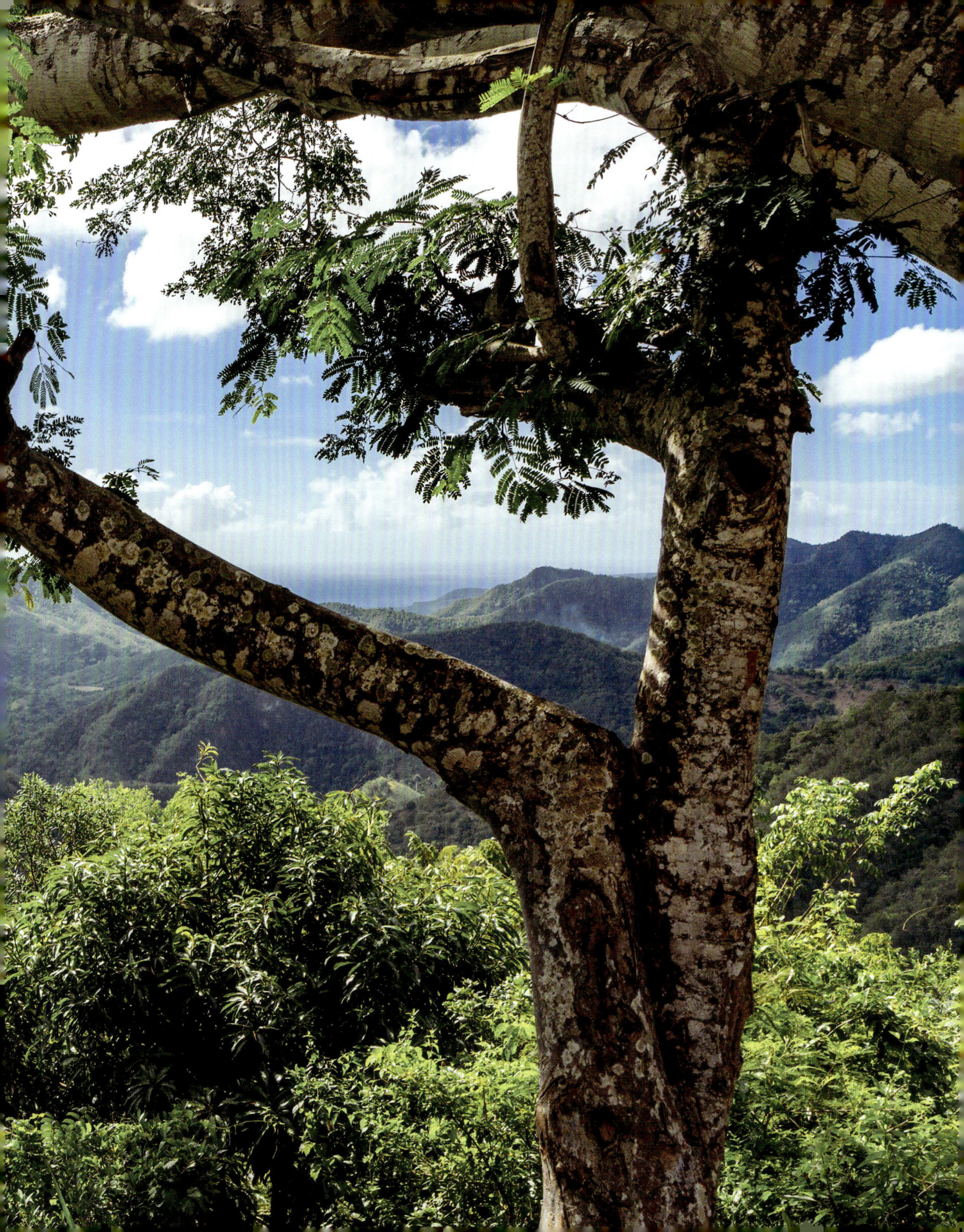

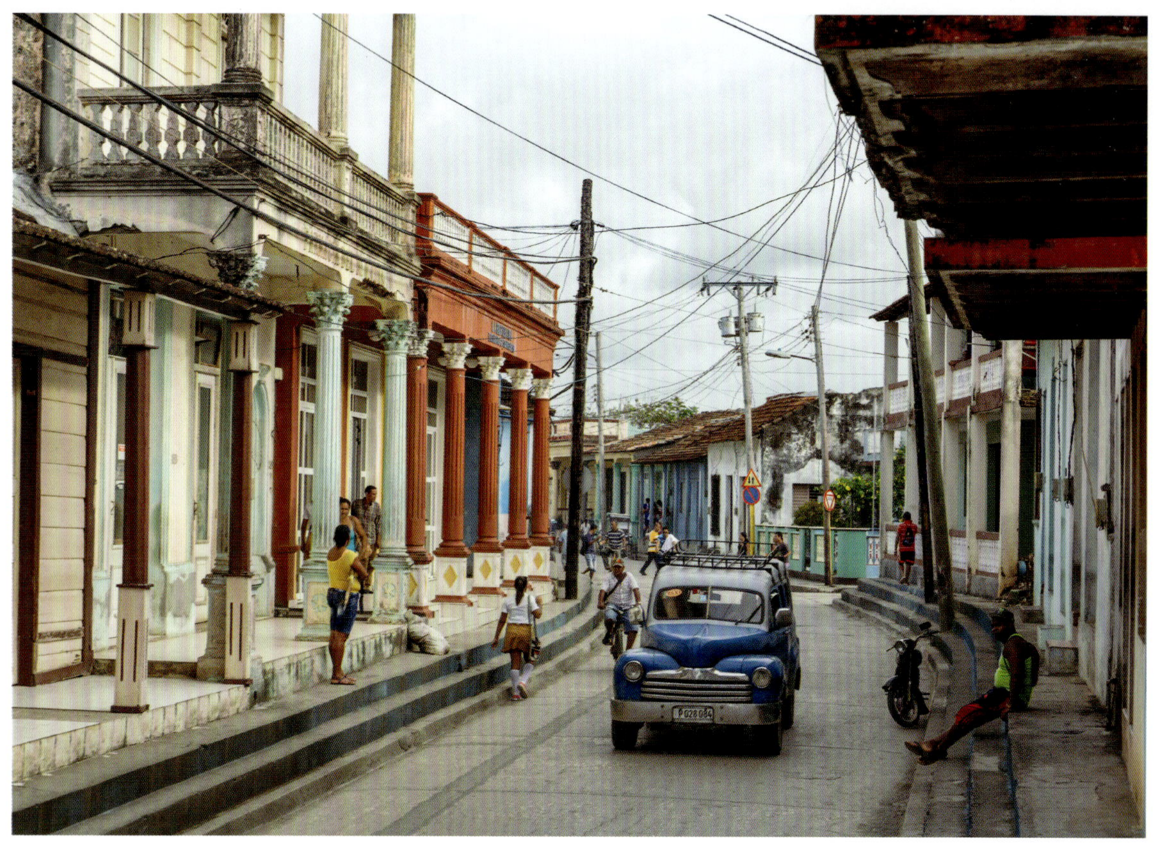

Baracoa

Baracoa

In 1492 Columbus landed briefly in the bay of Baracoa, and Diego Velázquez founded a settlement here in 1511; this was the capital of Cuba for several years. Baracoa is therefore the oldest city of Cuba and Latin America. The name Baracoa is Indian and means "high country". This small town located between the mountains (landmark: the table mountain El Yunque), four river estuaries and the green-blue "honey bay" (Boca de Miel) lives with its back to the country and its face to the sea. Smuggling and bartering with the neighboring islands and constant pirate attacks shaped the city. Until 1964 when a road was finally built, Baracoa could only be reached by sea.

Baracoa

En 1492, Christophe Colomb fit une halte rapide dans la baie de Baracoa, mais ce n'est qu'en 1511 que Diego Velázquez y fonda une première colonie, qui fut pendant quelques années la capitale de Cuba. Baracoa est ainsi la plus vieille ville de Cuba et d'Amérique latine, dont le nom indien signifie «haute terre». La petite ville, nichée entre les montagnes (dont la remarquable montagne à plateau El Yunque), quatre embouchures de fleuve et les eaux turquoise de la Boca de Miel (bouche de miel), vit dos à la terre et face à la mer. Elle porte les vestiges de la contrebande et du négoce avec les îles voisines, ainsi que des attaques incessantes des pirates. Jusqu'en 1964, Baracoa n'était accessible que par la mer.

Baracoa

1492 landete Kolumbus kurz in der Bucht von Baracoa, doch erst Diego Velázquez gründete hier 1511 eine Siedlung, die einige Jahre lang Hauptstadt Kubas war. Somit ist Baracoa die älteste Stadt Kubas und Lateinamerikas. Der Name Baracoa ist indianisch und bedeutet „hohes Land". Das Städtchen zwischen Bergen (Landmarke: der Tafelberg El Yunque), vier Flussmündungen und der grünblauen „Honigbucht" (Boca de Miel) lebt mit dem Rücken zum Land und dem Gesicht zum Meer. Schmuggel und Tauschhandel mit den Nachbarinseln und ständige Piratenüberfälle prägten die Stadt. Bis 1964 war Baracoa nur übers Meer zu erreichen, der Landweg wurde erst 1964 gebaut.

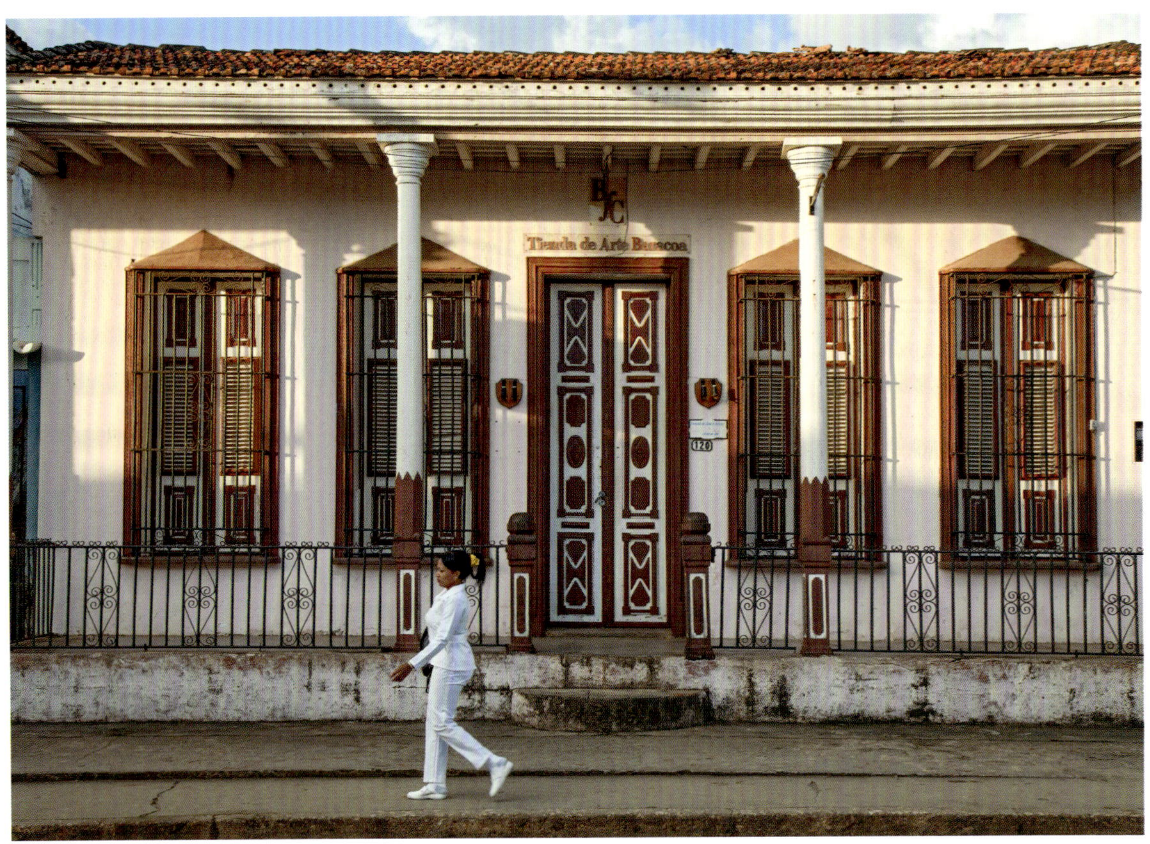

Baracoa

Baracoa

En 1492 Colón desembarcó brevemente en la bahía de Baracoa, pero fue Diego Velázquez quien fundó un asentamiento aquí en 1511, que fue la capital de Cuba durante varios años. Así, Baracoa es la ciudad más antigua de Cuba y de América Latina. El nombre Baracoa es indio y significa "país alto". El pequeño pueblo situado entre montañas (punto de referencia: la montaña de mesa El Yunque), cuatro estuarios fluviales y la bahía de miel (Boca de Miel), de color verde azulado, vive de espaldas al campo y de cara al mar. El contrabando y el trueque con las islas vecinas y los constantes ataques de piratas dieron forma a la ciudad. Hasta 1964 solo se podía llegar a Baracoa por mar; la carretera terrestre se construyó en 1964.

Baracoa

Em 1492, Colombo desembarcou brevemente na Baía de Baracoa, mas apenas Diego Velázquez fundou aqui um povoado em 1511, que por vários anos foi a capital de Cuba. Assim, Baracoa é a cidade mais antiga de Cuba e da América Latina. O nome Baracoa é indiano e significa "terras altas". A pequena cidade entre montanhas (marco: o planalto El Yunque), quatro estuários fluviais e a "Baía de Mel" (Boca de Miel) verde-azulada, vive de costas para a terra e de frente para o mar. O contrabando e as trocas comerciais com as ilhas vizinhas e os constantes ataques de piratas moldaram a cidade. Até 1964 Baracoa só podia ser alcançada por via marítima, a rota terrestre foi construída em 1964.

Baracoa

In 1492 landde Columbus kortstondig in de baai van Baracoa, Diego Velázquez stichtte hier in 1511 een nederzetting, die enkele jaren de hoofdstad van Cuba was. Baracoa is daarmee de oudste stad van Cuba en Latijns-Amerika. De naam Baracoa is Indiaas en betekent 'hoogland'. Het stadje tussen de bergen (kenmerkend: de tafelberg El Yunque). Vier riviermondingen en de groen-blauwe 'honingbaai' (Boca de Miel) leeft met de rug naar het land en het gezicht naar de zee. Smokkel en ruilhandel met de naburige eilanden en voortdurende piratenaanvallen vormden de stad. Tot 1964 kon Baracoa alleen over zee worden bereikt, de landweg werd in 1964 aangelegd.

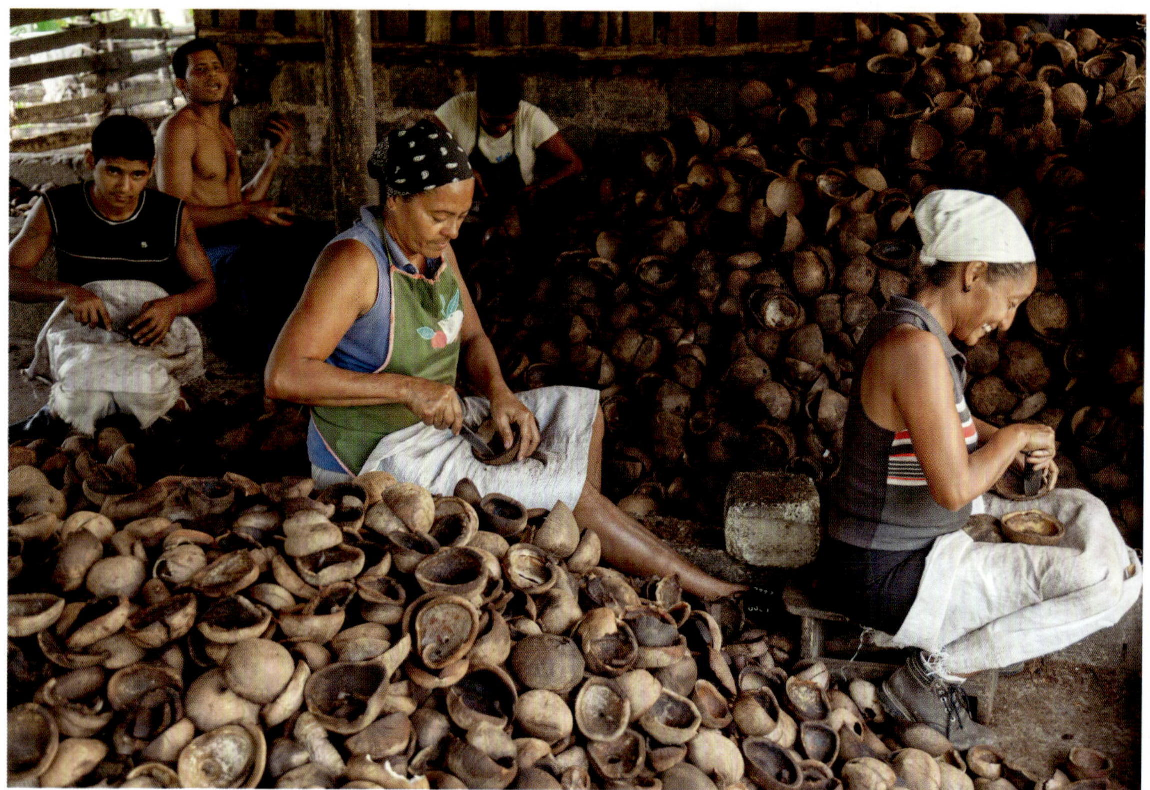

Procesado de coco, Baracoa
Coconut processing, Baracoa

Cocoa and Coconuts

In the areas around Baracoas there are
many plantations run by cooperatives
where cocoa, coffee, bananas and
coconuts are grown. The cocoa beans are
processed directly in the local chocolate
factory (popular brand: Hatuey), and
coconut oil and coconut flour are obtained
from the coconuts. Baracoa has the only
coconut oil factory in Cuba.

Cacao y cocos

En los alrededores de Baracoa hay muchas
plantaciones gestionadas por cooperativas
en las que se cultiva cacao, café, bananas
y cocos. Los granos de cacao se procesan
directamente en la fábrica local de
chocolate (marca popular: Hatuey), el
aceite de coco y la harina de coco se
obtienen de los cocos. Baracoa tiene la
única fábrica de aceite de coco en Cuba.

Cacao et noix de coco

La région autour de Baracoa compte de
nombreuses plantations coopératives
où sont cultivés cacao, café, bananes et
noix de coco. Les fèves de cacao sont
directement transformées dans l'immense
usine de chocolat (produisant la célèbre
marque Hatuey), alors que les noix de coco
servent à produire de l'huile et de la farine.
L'unique usine d'huile de coco de Cuba est
installée à Baracoa.

Cacau e cocos

Nos arredores de Baracoa há muitas
plantações operadas por cooperativas,
que cultivam cacau, café, banana e cocos.
Os grãos de cacau são processados
diretamente na fábrica local de chocolate
(marca popular: Hatuey), óleo de coco e
farinha de coco são obtidos a partir dos
cocos. Baracoa tem a única fábrica de óleo
de coco em Cuba.

Kakao und Kokosnüsse

In der Umgebung Baracoas liegen viele von
Genossenschaften betriebene Plantagen,
auf denen Kakao, Kaffee, Bananen und
Kokosnüsse angebaut werden. Die
Kakaobohnen werden in der hiesigen
Schokoladenfabrik direkt weiterverarbeitet
(populäre Marke: Hatuey), aus den
Kokosnüssen gewinnt man Kokosöl
und -mehl. In Baracoa steht die einzige
Kokosölfabrik Kubas.

Cacao en kokosnoten

In de omgeving van Baracoas zijn veel
plantages van coöperaties waar cacao,
koffie, bananen en kokosnoten worden
verbouwd. De cacaobonen worden
rechtstreeks verwerkt in de plaatselijke
chocoladefabriek (populair merk: Hatuey),
kokosolie en kokosmeel worden uit de
kokosnoten verkregen. Baracoa heeft de
enige kokosnootolie fabriek in Cuba.

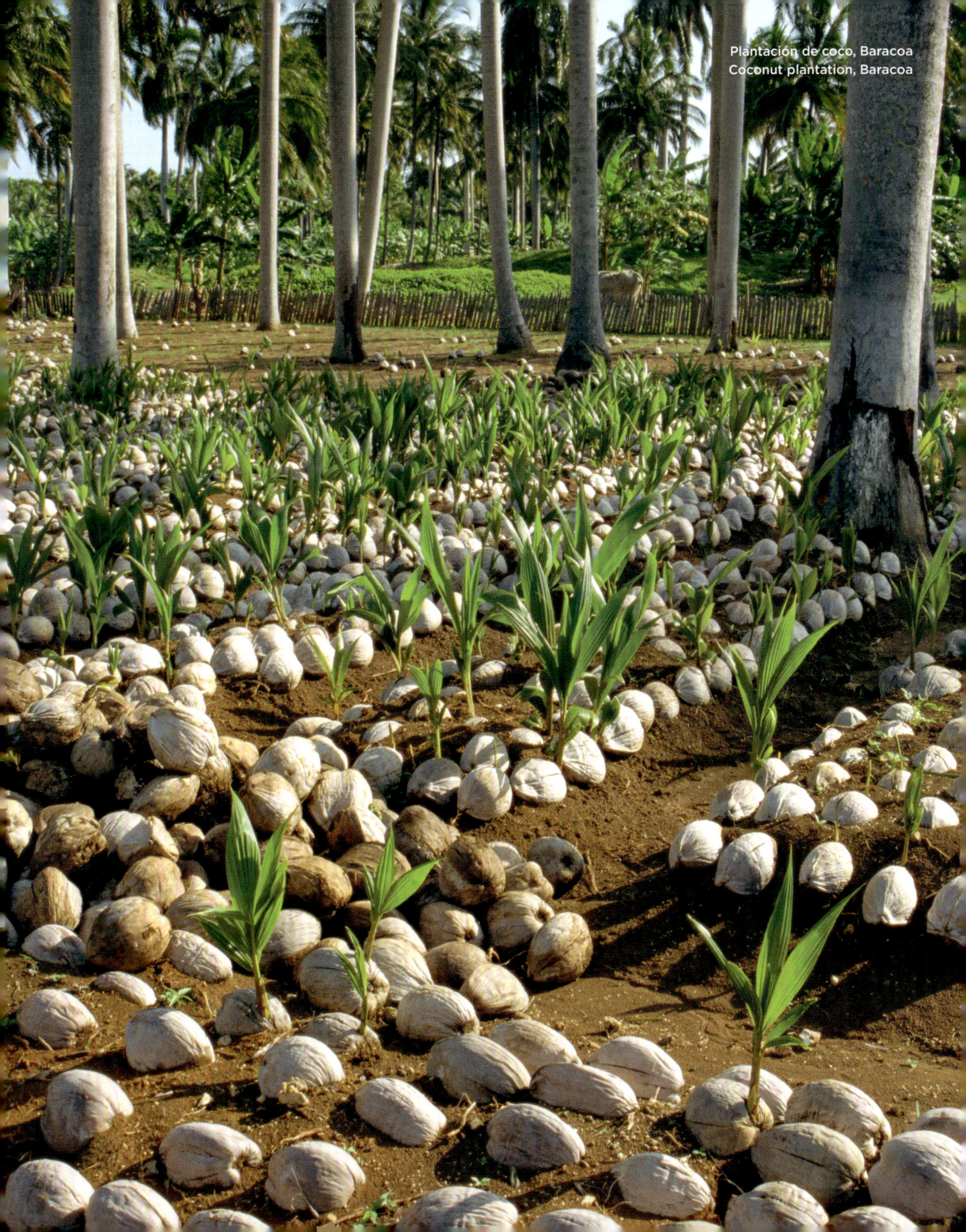

Plantación de coco, Baracoa
Coconut plantation, Baracoa

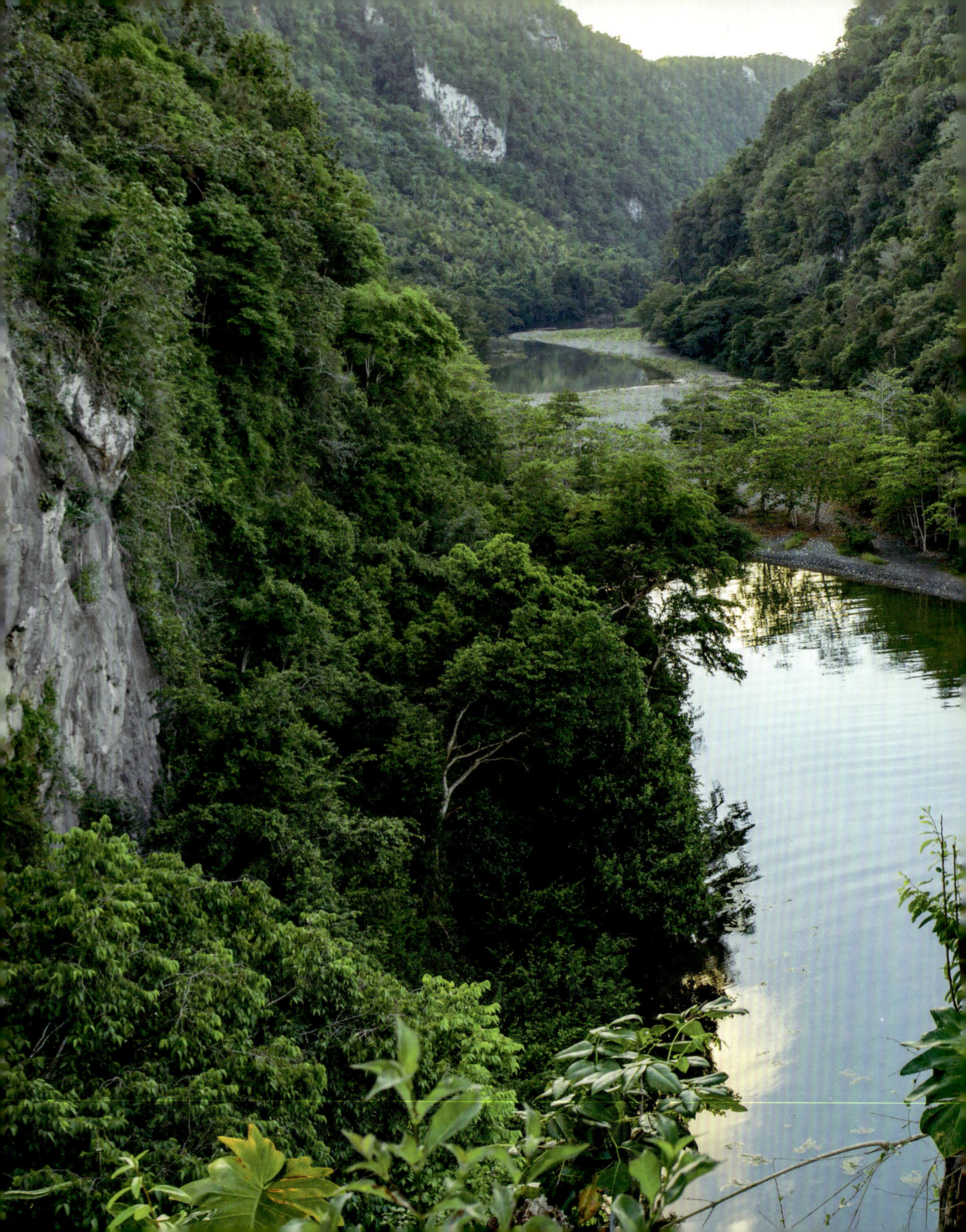

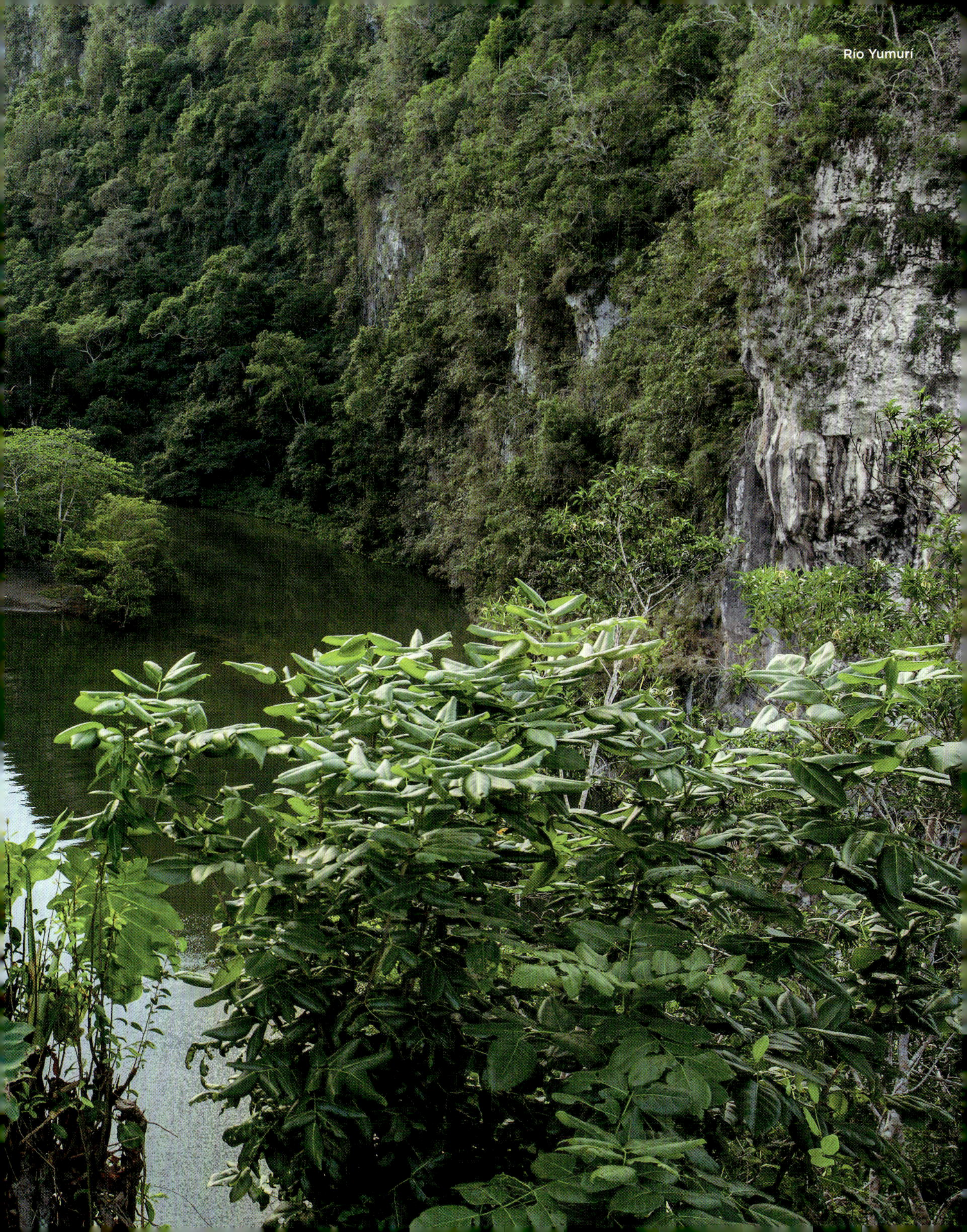
Río Yumurí

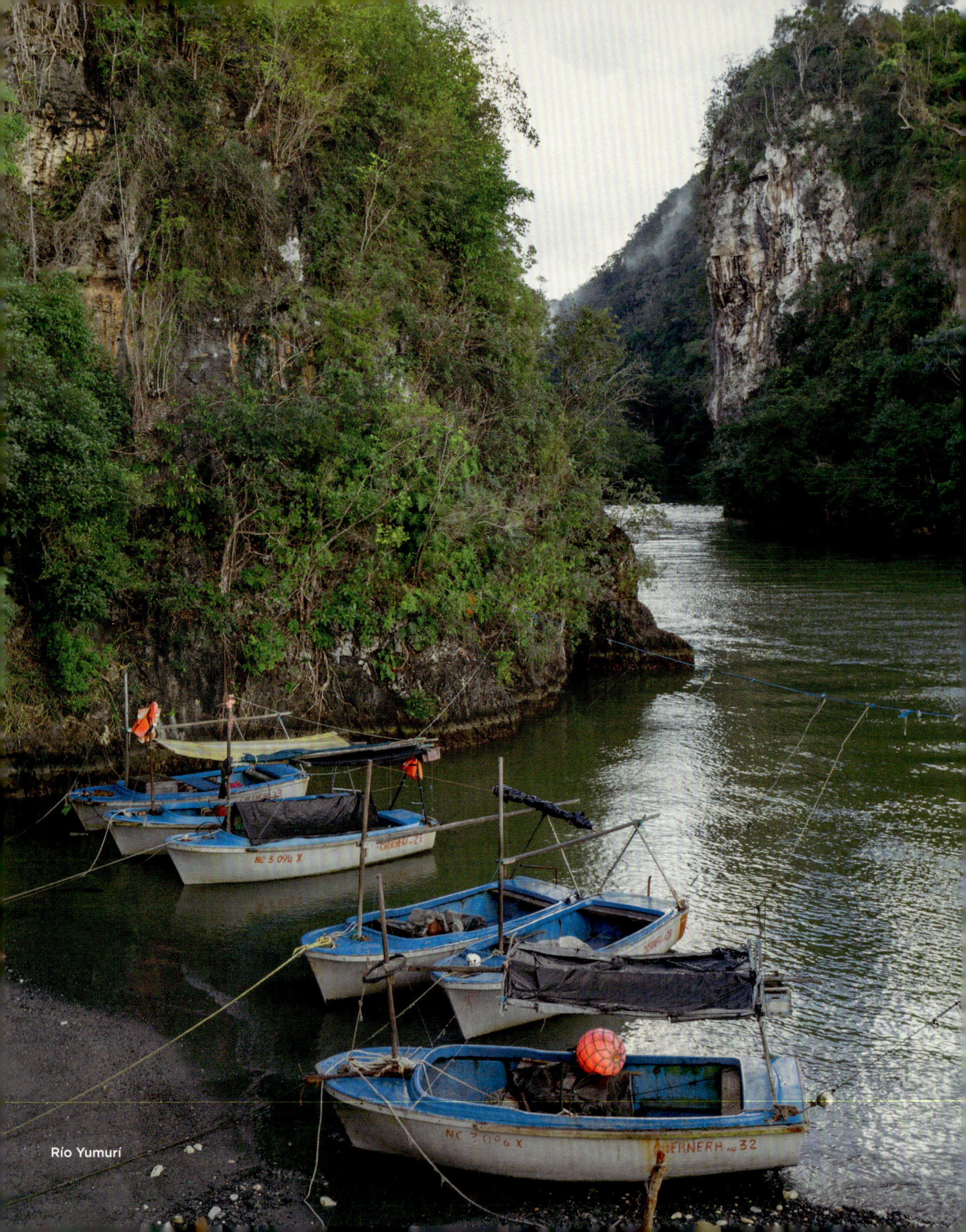

Río Yumurí

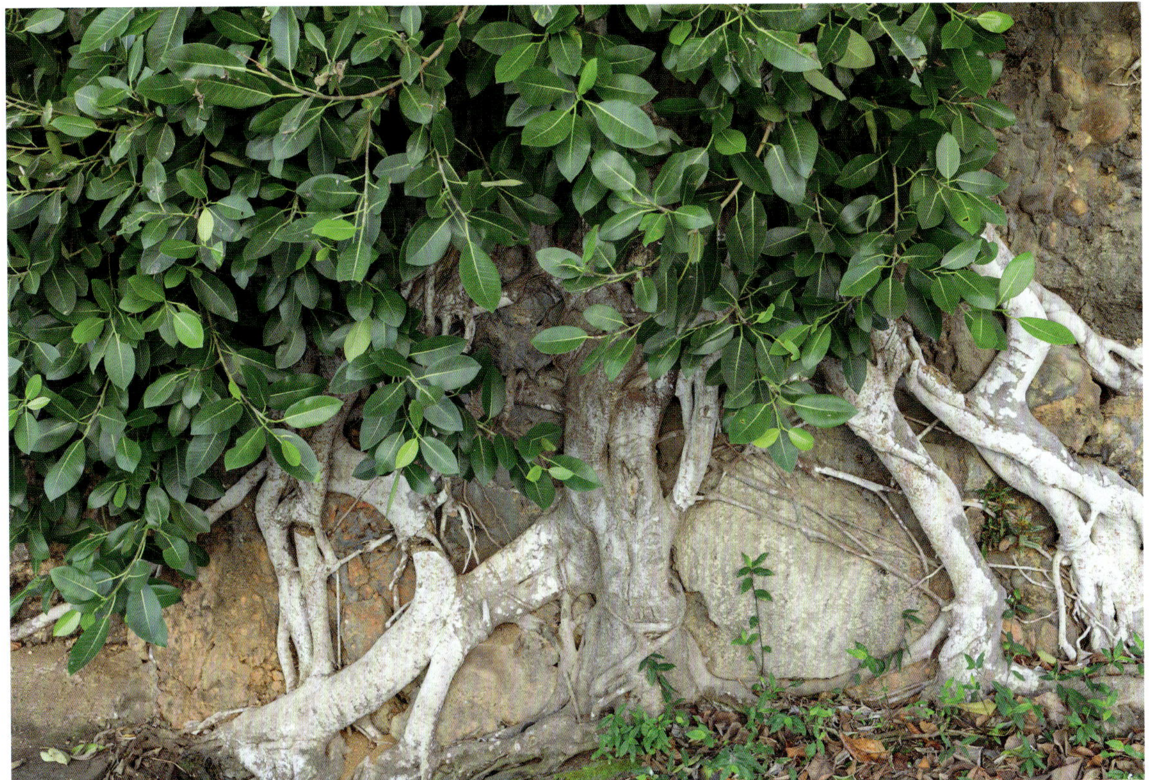

Boca de Yumurí

Yumurí River

The Yumurí flows through two canyons and the spectacular mountain world of the Sierra del Purial with its dense subtropical rainforests. Baracoas, the greenest city in Cuba, is a well-preserved ecosystem, due in part to the geographical remoteness of the region, and is now a centre of ecotourism.

Río Yumurí

El Yumurí fluye a través de dos cañones y el espectacular mundo montañoso de la Sierra del Purial con densos bosques subtropicales. Los alrededores de Baracoa, la ciudad más verde de Cuba, son un ecosistema bien conservado debido, en parte, a la lejanía geográfica de la región, que ahora es un centro de ecoturismo.

Fleuve Yumurí

Le fleuve Yumurí s'écoule le long de deux canyons et traverse le spectaculaire paysage montagnard de la sierra del Purial, couverte de forêts denses subtropicales. La périphérie de Baracoa, ville la plus verdoyante de Cuba, est l'un des écosystèmes les mieux préservés, grâce notamment à sa situation géographique isolée. Elle est aujourd'hui un centre d'écotourisme.

Rio Yumurí

O Yumurí atravessa dois cânions e o espetacular mundo montanhoso da Sierra del Purial com densas florestas subtropicais. Toda a área circundante de Baracoa, a cidade mais verde de Cuba, é um ecossistema bem preservado, devido em parte ao isolamento geográfico da região, que é agora um centro de ecoturismo.

Yumurí-Fluss

Der Yumurí fließt durch zwei Canyons und die spektakuläre Bergwelt der Sierra del Purial mit dichten subtropischen Regenwäldern. Das gesamte Umland Baracoas, der grünsten Stadt Kubas, ist ein bestens erhaltenes Ökosystem, wozu auch die geographische Abgeschiedenheit der Region beigetragen hat, die heute ein Zentrum des Ökotourismus ist.

Yumurí rivier

De Yumurí stroomt door twee canyons en de spectaculaire bergwereld van de Sierra del Purial met zijn dichte subtropische regenwouden. Baracoas, de groenste stad van Cuba, is een goed bewaard gebleven ecosysteem, mede door de geografische afstand van de regio, die nu een centrum van ecotoerisme is.

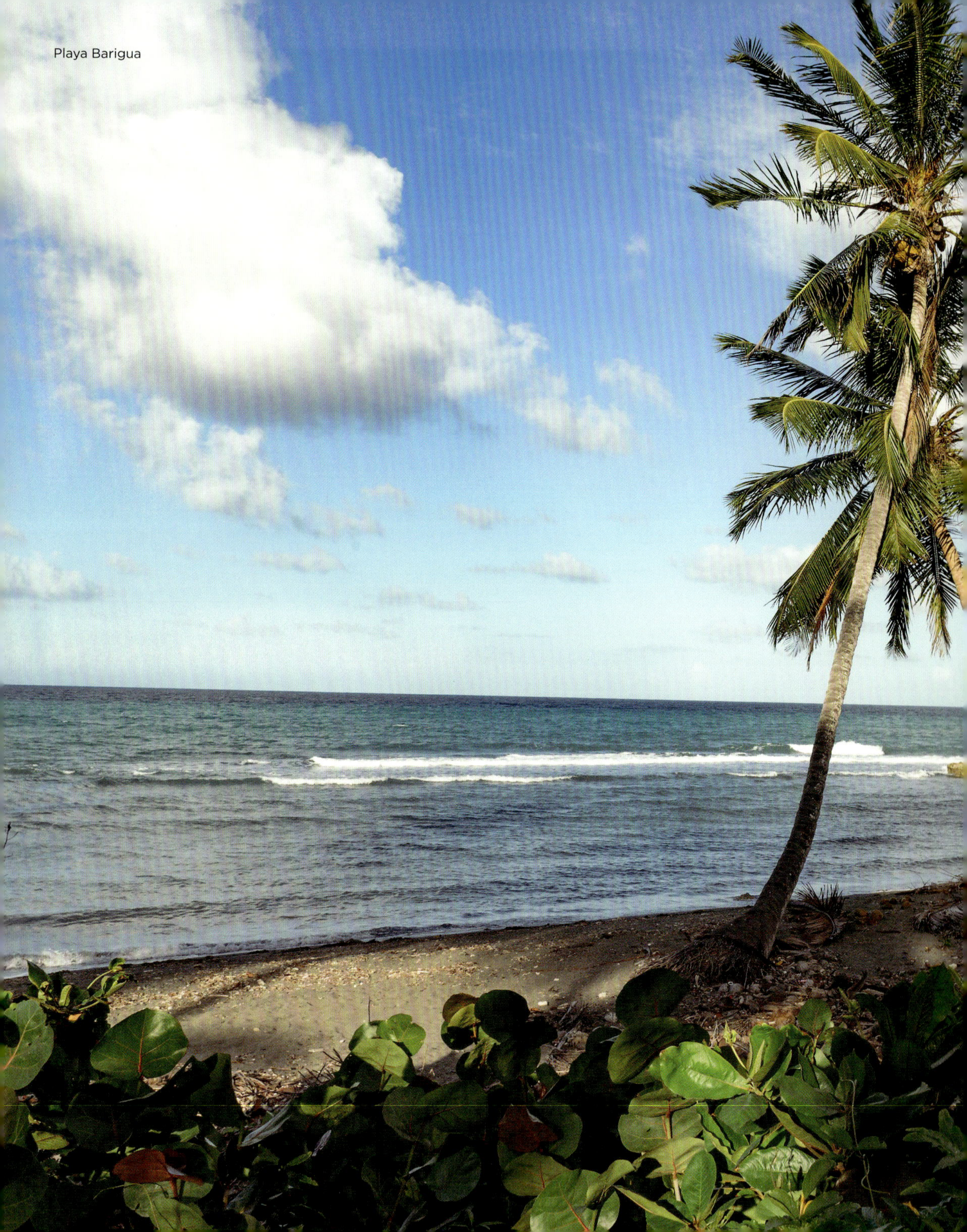

Playa Barigua

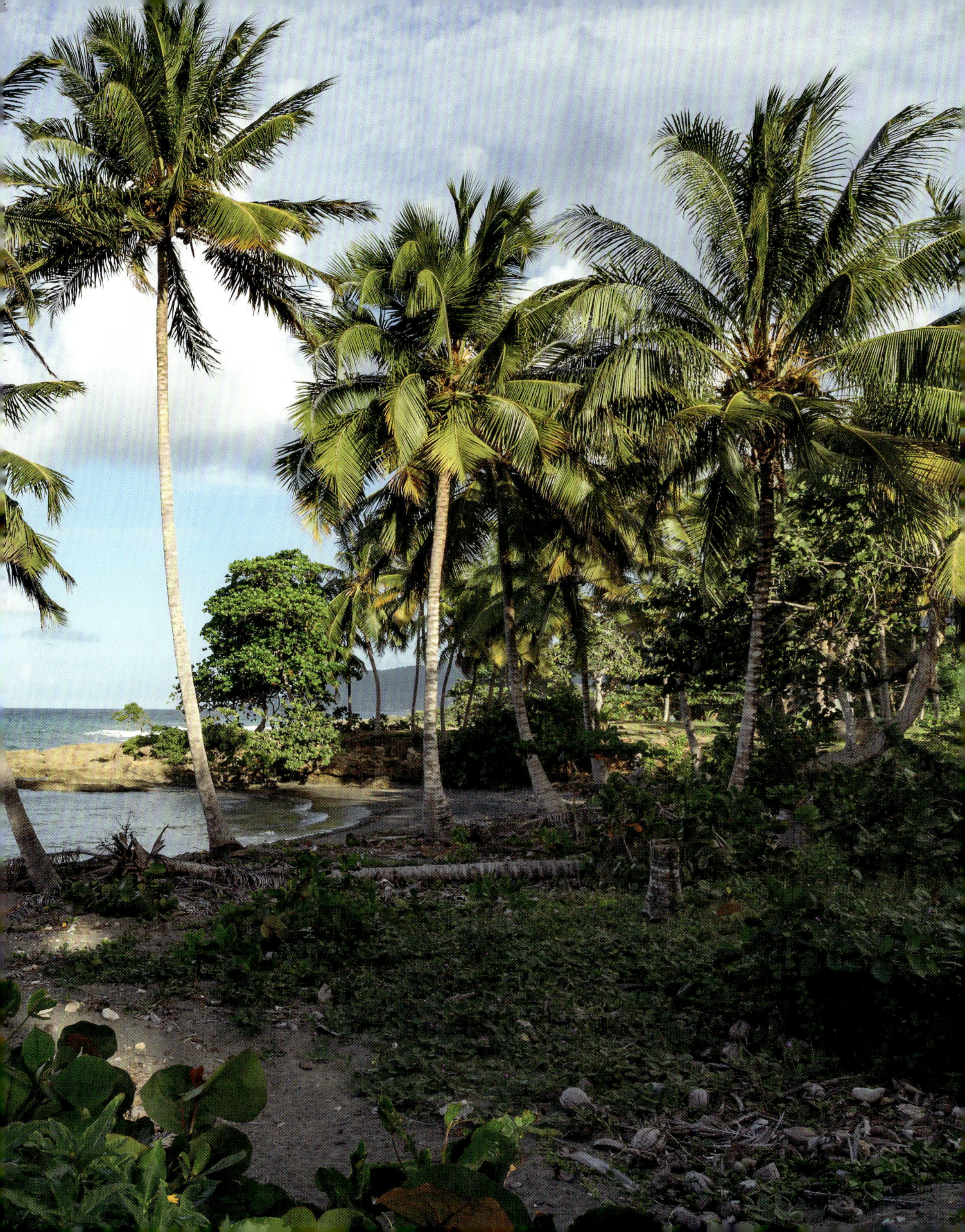

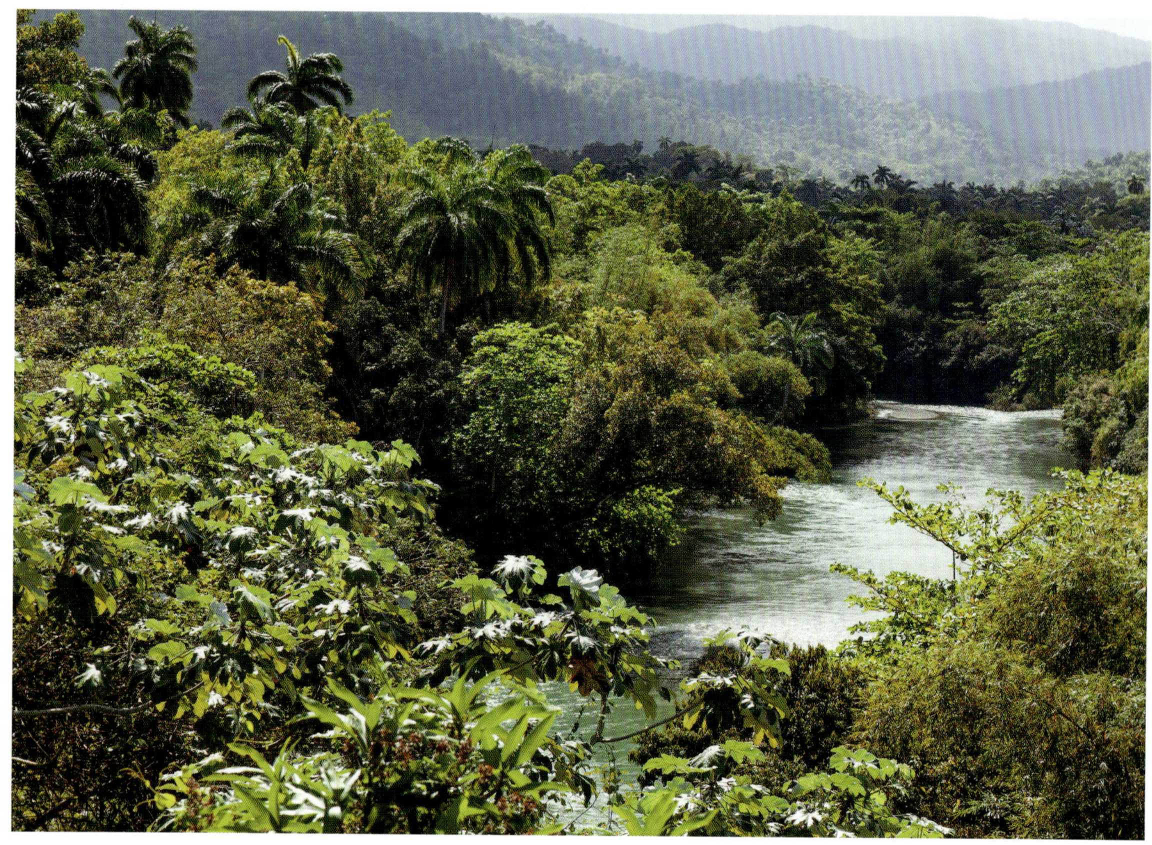

Río Duaba

Humboldt National Park

The three rivers Duaba, Tóa and Yumurí rise in the Alexander von Humboldt National Park (the naturalist visited Cuba twice). At 700 km² (270 sq.mi.), the park is Cuba's largest protected area and covers large parts of the provinces of Holguín and Guantánamo, including the coastal regions. In the rainforests, which are difficult to access, the largest number of all plant and animal species in Cuba have been preserved, including dragon trees, coral trees and rain trees, the endemic and endangered Cuban solenodon, Cuban land snails with their colorful shells and the Monte Iberia eleuth, a frog that is only one centimeter (0.5 inch) long.

Parc national d'Humboldt

Les trois fleuves Duaba, Tóa et Yumurí prennent leur source dans le parc national Alexander von Humboldt (naturaliste qui visita deux fois Cuba). Avec ses 700 km², le parc est le plus grand territoire protégé de Cuba ; il englobe une grande partie des provinces d'Holguín et Guantánamo, dont les régions côtières. Les forêts pluvieuses difficilement accessibles hébergent la majorité des variétés de plantes et d'animaux de Cuba, et notamment des dragonniers, des espèces du genre *Erythrina* et des arbres de pluie, le solénodon de Cuba endémique et menacé d'extinction, les gastéropodes à coquille colorée du genre *Polymita* et l'*Eleutherodactylus iberia,* amphibien d'un cm.

Humboldt-Nationalpark

Die drei Flüsse Duaba, Tóa und Yumurí entspringen im Nationalpark „Alexander von Humboldt" (der Naturforscher besuchte Kuba zwei Mal). Mit 700 km² ist der Park das größte Schutzgebiet Kubas und umfasst große Teile der Provinzen Holguín und Guantánamo, inklusive der Küstenregionen. In den schwer zugänglichen Regenwäldern hat sich die größte Anzahl aller in Kuba vorhandenen Pflanzen- und Tierarten erhalten, darunter Drachen-, Korallen- und Regenbäume, der auf der Insel endemische und vom Aussterben bedrohte Kubanische Schlitzrüssler, die Polymita-Landschnecken mit ihren bunten Gehäusen und der nur ein Zentimeter kleine Monte-Iberia-Frosch.

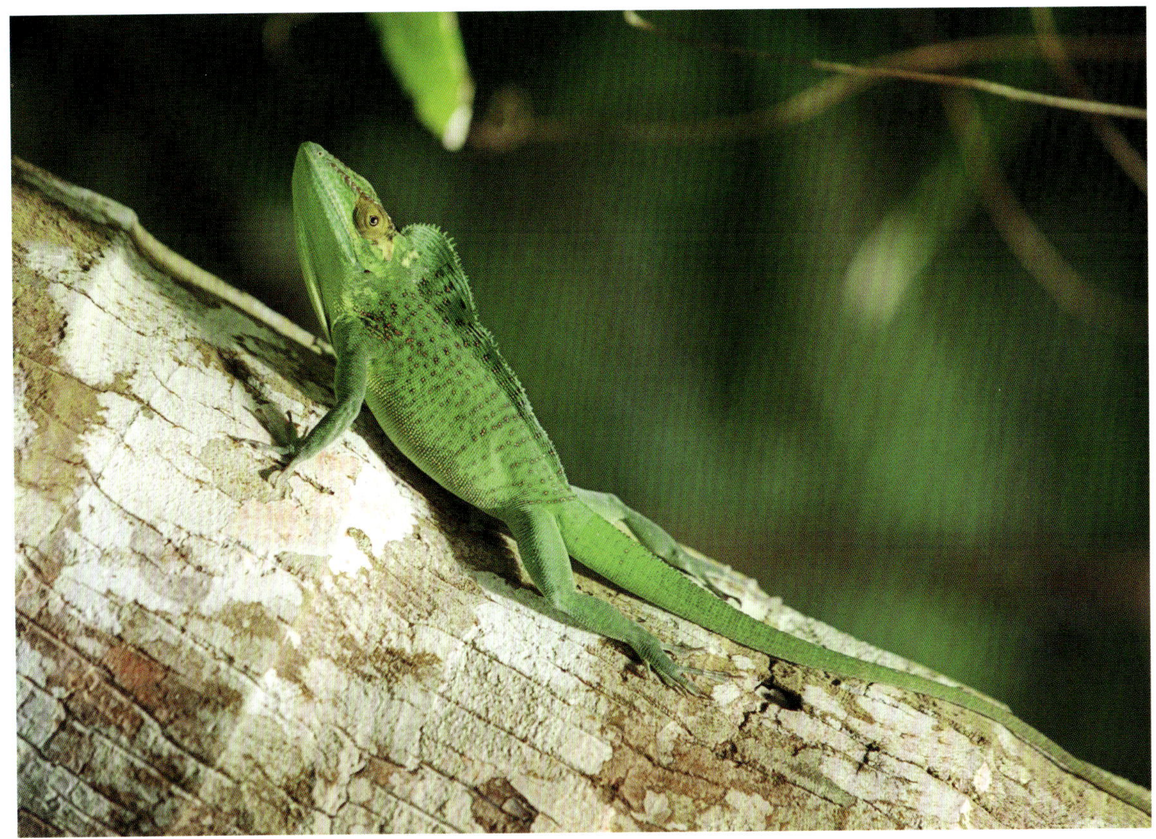

Anolis baracoae, Parque Nacional Alejandro de Humboldt
Anolis baracoae, Alejandro de Humboldt National Park

Parque Nacional Humboldt

Los tres ríos Duaba, Tóa y Yumurí nacen en el parque nacional "Alexander von Humboldt" (el naturalista visitó Cuba dos veces). Con 700 km², el parque es el área protegida más grande de Cuba y cubre gran parte de las provincias de Holguín y Guantánamo, incluyendo las regiones costeras. En las selvas tropicales, a las que es difícil acceder, se ha conservado el mayor número de especies de plantas y animales de Cuba, incluyendo dracaenas, erythrinas y árboles de lluvia, el endémico y amenazado almiquí de Cuba, los caracoles Polymita con sus coloridas conchas y la ranita monte Iberia, de solo un centímetro de tamaño.

Parque Nacional de Humboldt

Os três rios Duaba, Tóa e Yumurí nascem no Parque Nacional "Alexander von Humboldt" (o naturalista visitou Cuba duas vezes). Com 700 km², o parque é a maior área protegida de Cuba e cobre grande parte das províncias de Holguín e Guantánamo, incluindo as regiões costeiras. Nas florestas tropicais, de difícil acesso, foi preservado o maior número de todas as espécies vegetais e animais em Cuba, incluindo dragoeiros, arvores-de-coral e árvores da chuva, o solenodonte cubano endémico e ameaçado de extinção, os caracóis da Polymita com as suas casas coloridas e o sapo Monte-Iberia, de apenas um centímetro de tamanho.

Humboldt Nationaal Park

De drie rivieren Duaba, Tóa en Yumurí ontspringen in het nationale park 'Alexander von Humboldt' (de naturalist bezocht Cuba twee keer). Met 700 km² is het park het grootste beschermde gebied van Cuba en omvat grote delen van de provincies Holguín en Guantánamo, inclusief de kustgebieden. In de moeilijk toegankelijke regenwouden is het grootste aantal planten- en diersoorten in Cuba bewaard gebleven, waaronder draak-, koraal- en regenbomen, de endemische en bedreigde Cubaanse solenodon, de Polymita-landslakken met hun kleurrijke behuizingen en de Monte-Iberia kikker, die slechts een centimeter groot is.

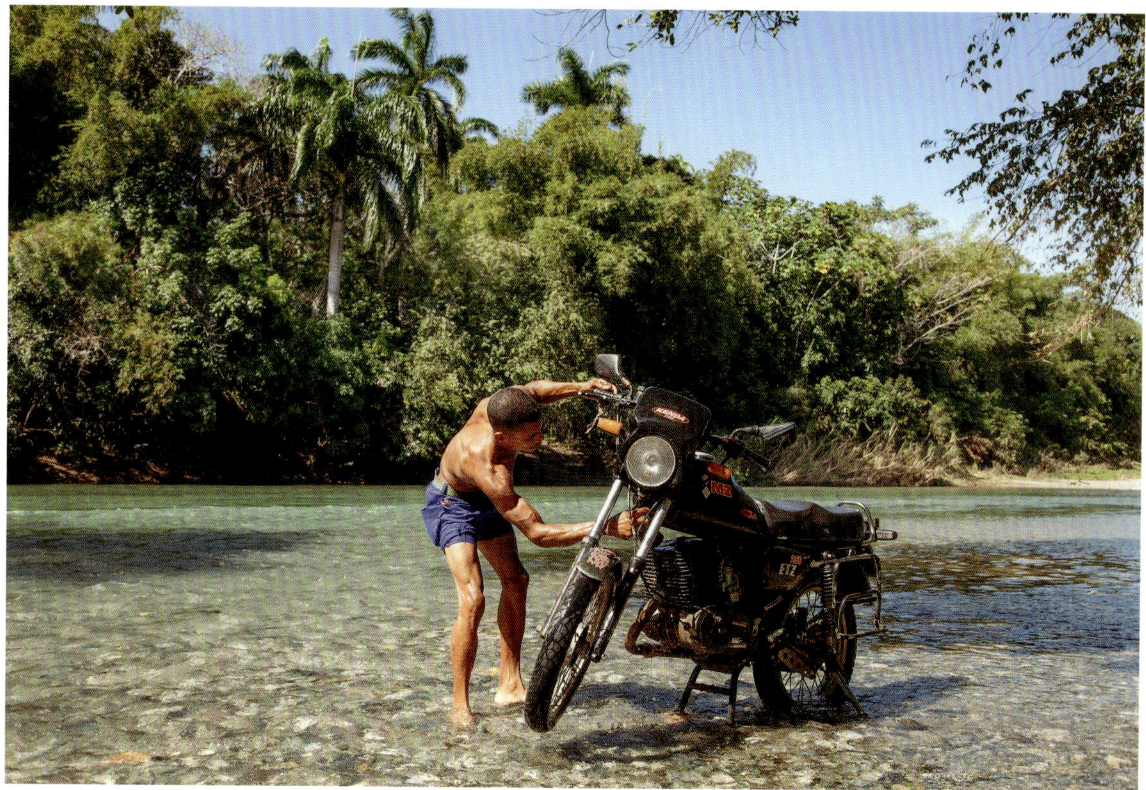

Rio Duaba

Duaba and Yumurí

Of the approximately 20 rivers in the region, the Toa, Duaba, Miel (= honey) and Yumurí are the largest. On the crystal clear Duaba there are many idyllic bathing places, and at the mouth lies the only black sand beach of Cuba. It is said that many Indians would have preferred to throw themselves off the cliffs into the Yumurí rather than become subjects of Spain.

Duaba y Yumurí

De los aproximadamente 20 ríos de la región, el Toa, Duaba, Miel y Yumurí son los más grandes. En la cristalina Duaba hay muchos lugares idílicos para bañarse, en la desembocadura se encuentra la única playa de arena negra de Cuba. Se dice que muchos indios habrían preferido lanzarse de los acantilados al Yumurí antes que convertirse en súbditos de España.

Duaba et Yumurí

De la vingtaine de fleuves parcourant la région, le Tóa, la Duaba, le Miel et le Yumurí sont les plus grands. Les rives de la Duaba cristalline recèlent de nombreux sites de baignades paradisiaques, et son embouchure côtoie les uniques plages noires de Cuba. On raconte que de nombreux Indiens ont préféré se jeter du haut des parois à pic bordant le Yumurí plutôt que de se soumettre aux Espagnols.

Duaba e Yumurí

Dos aproximadamente 20 rios da região, o Toa, o Duaba, o Miel (= mel) e Yumurí são os maiores. No cristalino Duaba há muitos locais de banho idílicos, na foz encontra-se a única praia de areia preta de Cuba. Diz-se que muitos índios teriam preferido atirar-se dos penhascos para o Yumurí em vez de se tornarem súditos da Espanha.

Duaba und Yumurí

Von den rund 20 Flüssen der Region sind der Toa, der Duaba, der Miel (= Honig) und der Yumurí die größten. Am kristallklaren Duaba locken viele idyllische Badestellen, an der Mündung liegt der einzige schwarzsandige Strand Kubas. Man erzählt, viele Indianer hätten sich lieber von den Steilwänden in den Yumurí gestürzt, als Untertanen Spaniens zu werden.

Duaba en Yumurí

Van de ongeveer 20 rivieren in de regio zijn de Toa, Duaba, Miel (= honing) en Yumurí de grootste. Bij de kristalheldere Duaba zijn er veel idyllische badplaatsen, bij de monding ligt het enige zwarte zandstrand van Cuba. Men zegt dat veel indianen zich liever van de kliffen in de Yumurí wierpen dan dat ze onderdanen van Spanje waren geworden.

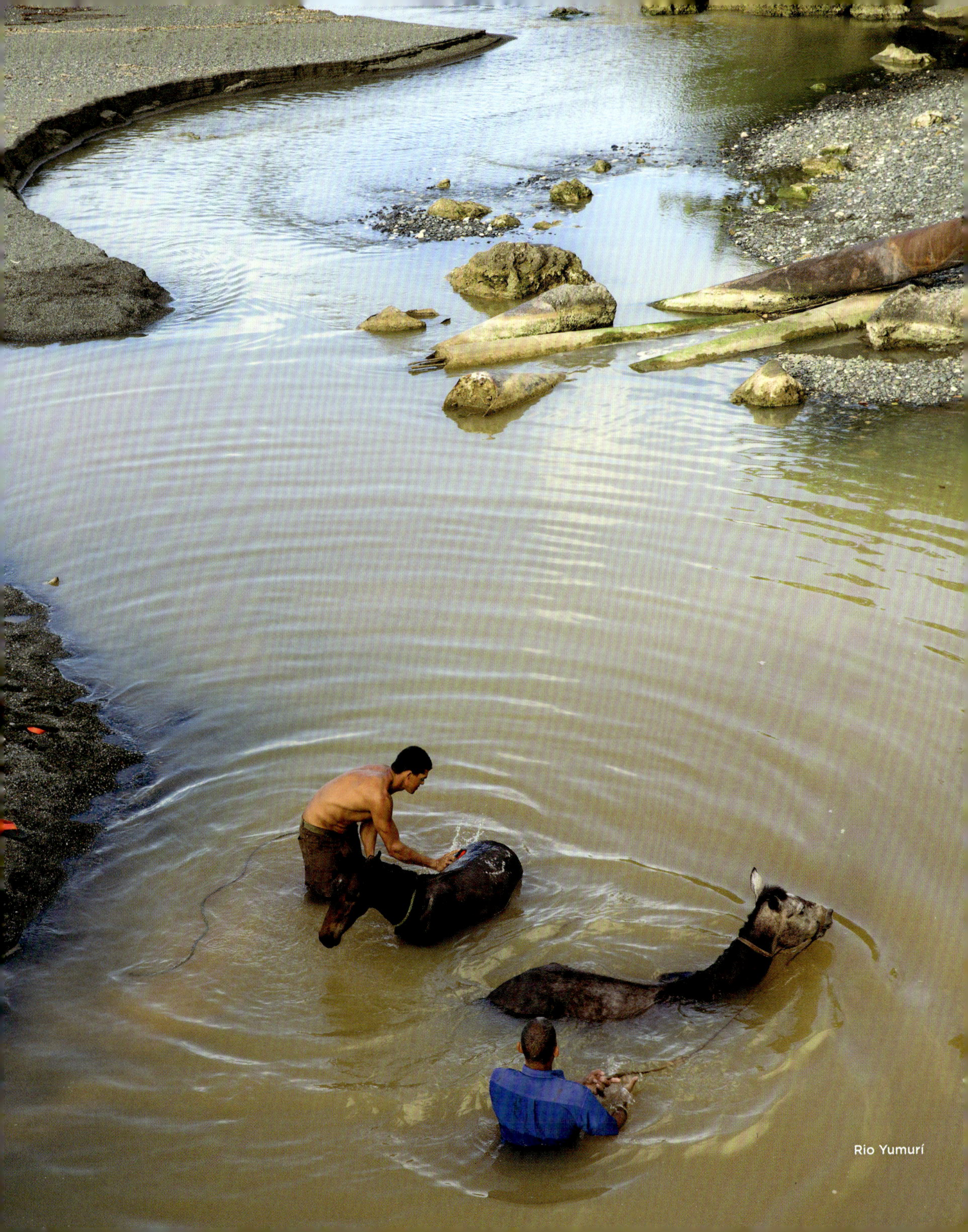

Rio Yumurí

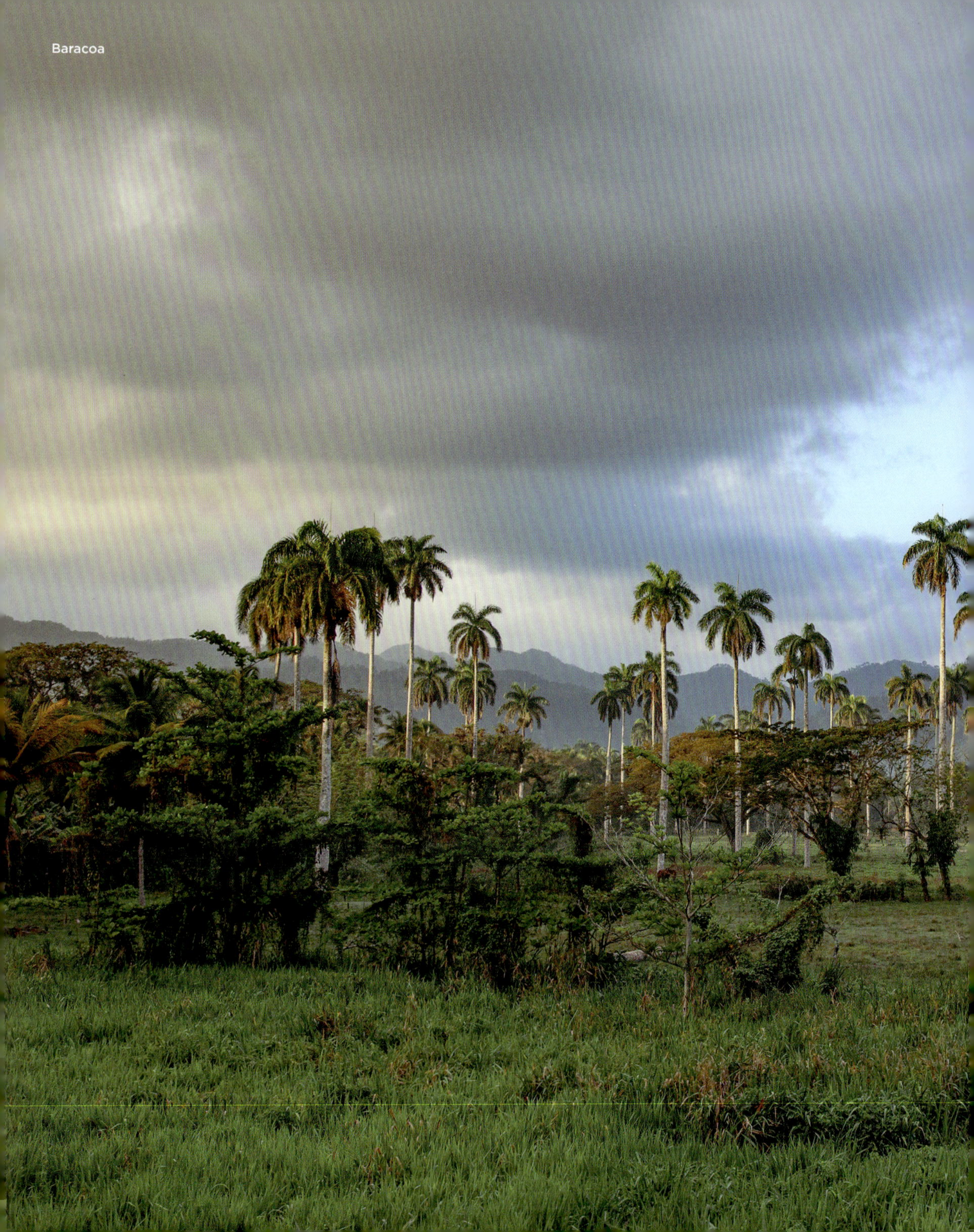
Baracoa

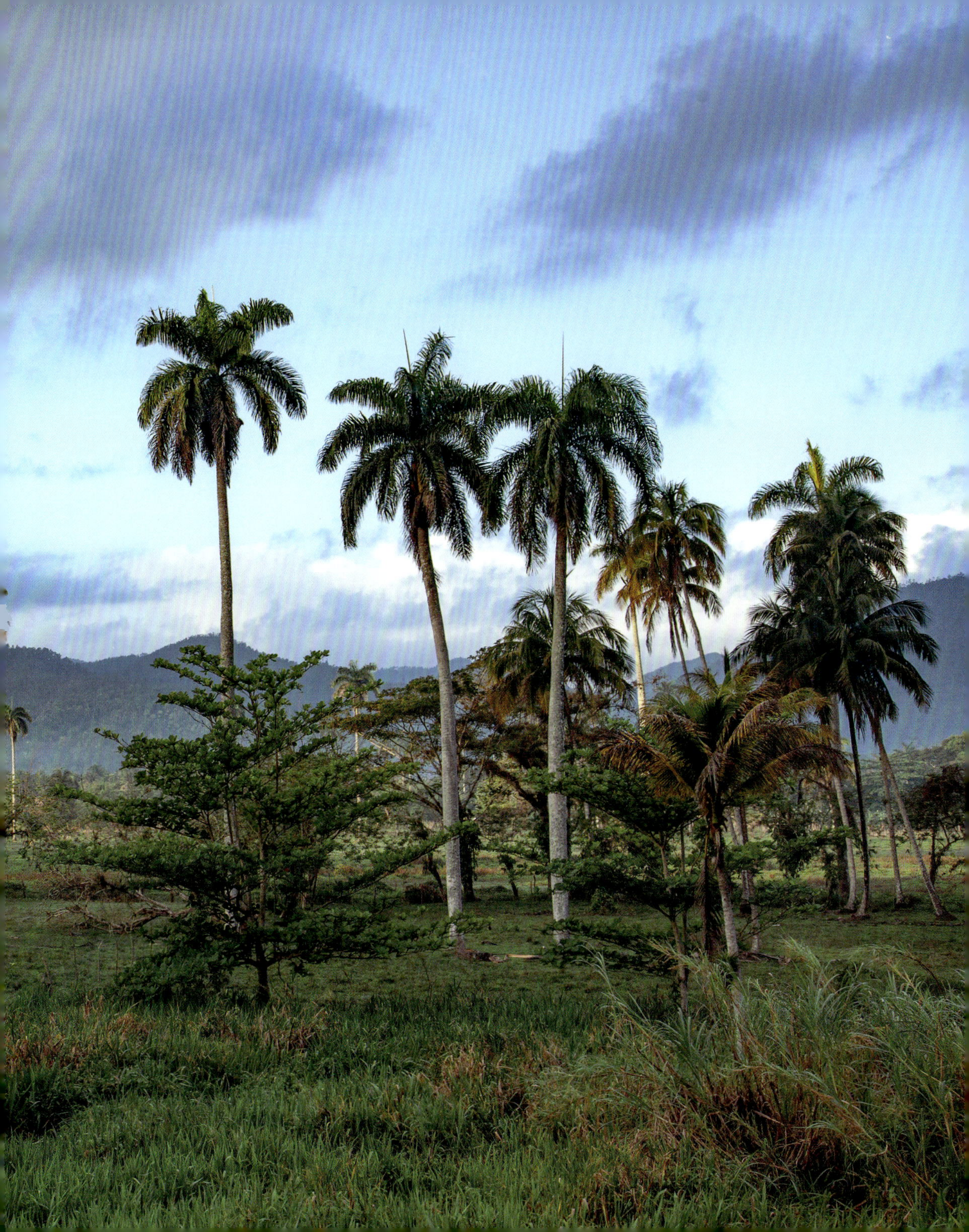

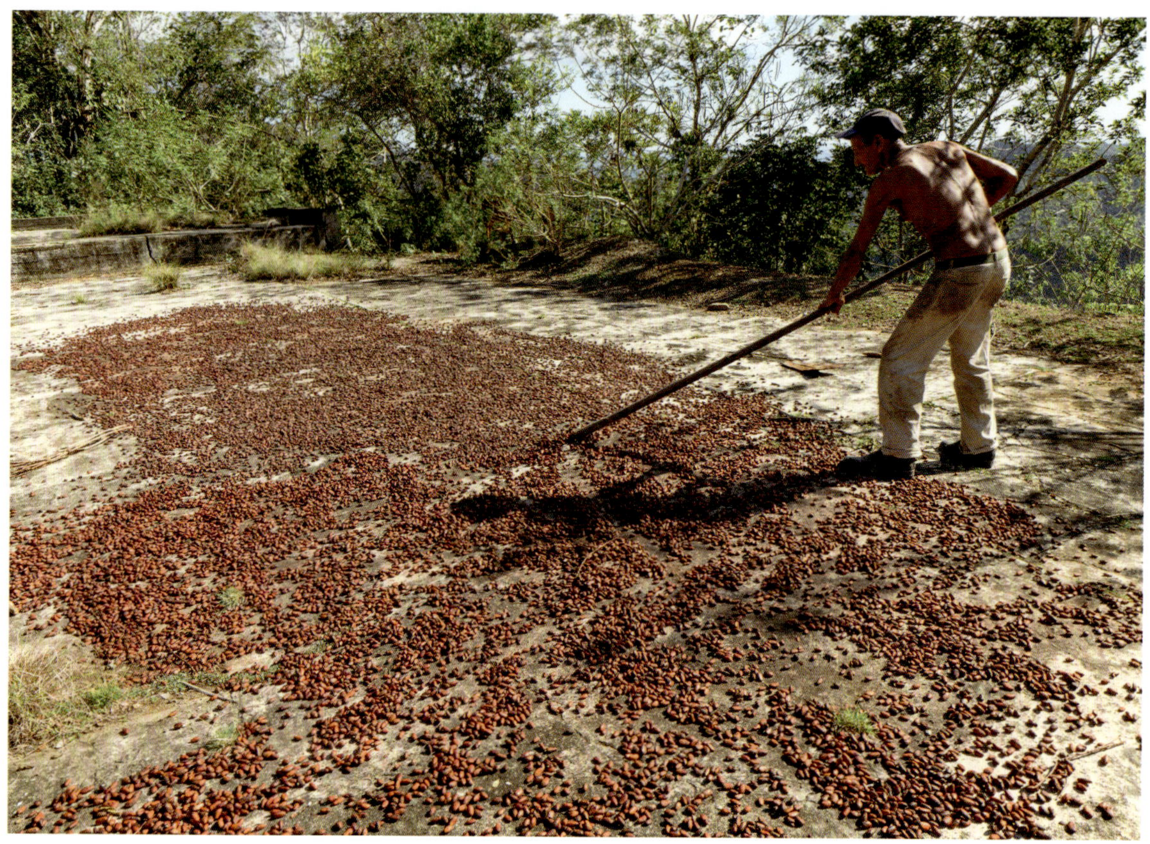

Granos de café, Cuchillas de Baracoa
Coffee beans, Cuchillas de Baracoa

Coffee

French settlers brought coffee plants from Haiti in the 18th century, and since then coffee has also been cultivated in Baracoa by small farmers, but not in large quantities. A special feature of their cultivation here is that the coffee is planted in the shade of naturally grown forest trees or under ornamental trees, so that the coffee plants are integrated into the natural flora. This method of production is rare, so the cultivation areas are considered to be a UNESCO World Cultural Heritage Site. Similarly to the tobacco farmers, coffee growers must sell their harvest to the state at fixed prices. Because production does not meet demand, Cuba imports a lot of coffee.

Café

Depuis que les colons français de Haïti importèrent au xviiie siècle leurs plants de café, les précieux grains sont également cultivés en quantité restreinte dans la région de Baracoa par de petits producteurs. Particularité locale, le café pousse dans l'ombre d'arbres forestiers ou ornementaux sauvages et les plants sont donc intégrés à la flore locale. Ce type de production est devenu très rare, ce pourquoi ces cultures sont inscrites au patrimoine de l'Unesco. Tout comme les cultivateurs de tabac, les propriétaires de plantations de café doivent vendre leur récolte à l'État, à prix fixe. La production étant insuffisante pour couvrir les besoins, Cuba importe beaucoup de café.

Kaffee

Seit im 18. Jahrhundert französische Siedler aus Haiti Kaffeepflanzen mitbrachten, wird auch in Baracoa von Kleinbauern Kaffee angebaut, allerdings nicht in großen Mengen. Die Besonderheit: Der Kaffee wird im Schatten natürlich gewachsener Waldbäume bzw. unter Zierbäumen angepflanzt, wodurch die Kaffeepflanzen in die natürliche Flora integriert werden. Diese Produktionsweise existiert ansonsten nur noch selten, daher gelten die Anbaugebiete als UNESCO-Weltkulturerbe. Ähnlich wie die Tabakbauern müssen auch die Kaffeepflanzer ihre Ernte zu Fixpreisen an den Staat verkaufen. Weil die Produktion den Bedarf nicht deckt, importiert Kuba viel Kaffee.

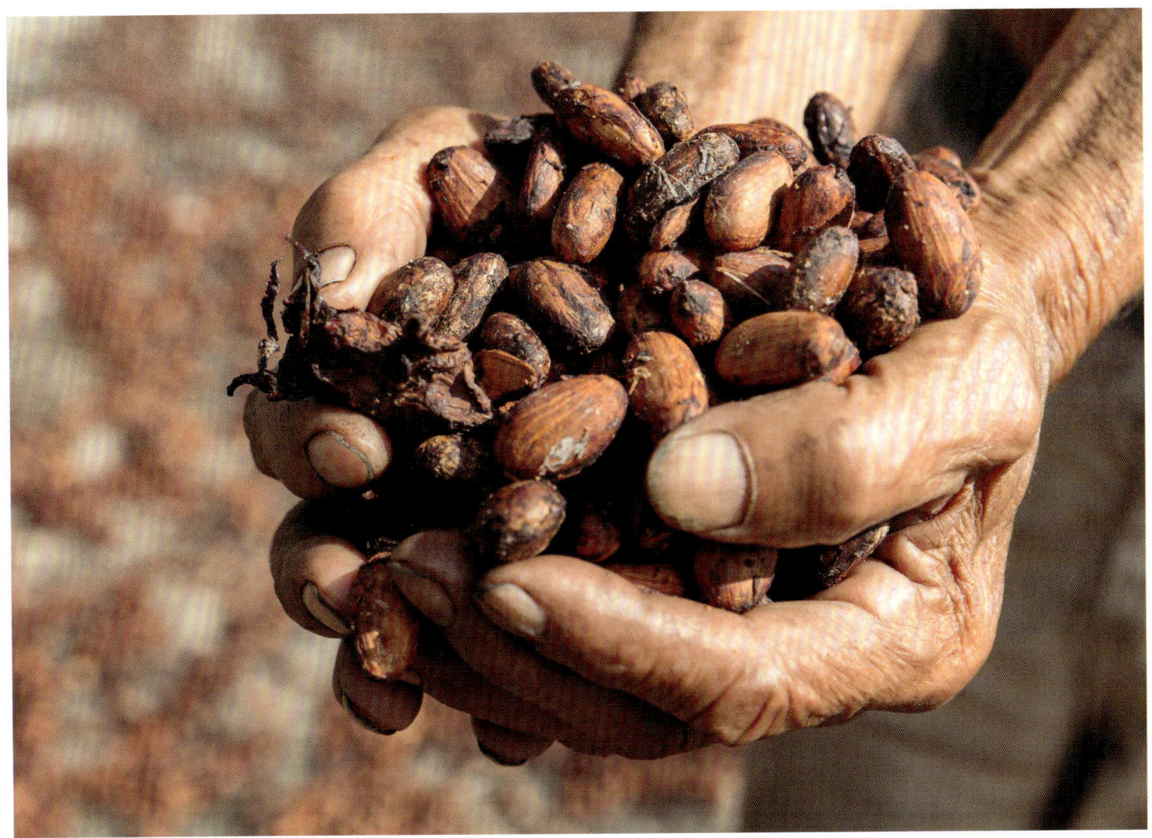

Granos de café, Cuchillas de Baracoa
Coffee beans, Cuchillas de Baracoa

Café

Desde que los colonos franceses trajeron plantas de café de Haití en el siglo XVIII, el café también ha sido cultivado en Baracoa por pequeños agricultores, pero no en grandes cantidades. La particularidad es que el café se planta a la sombra de árboles forestales naturales o bajo árboles ornamentales, por lo que los cafetos se integran en la flora natural. Este método de producción es poco frecuente, por lo que las zonas de cultivo son Patrimonio Cultural de la Humanidad por la UNESCO. Al igual que los cultivadores de tabaco, los caficultores tienen que vender sus cosechas al Estado a precios fijos. Debido a que la producción no satisface la demanda, Cuba importa mucho café.

Café

Desde que os colonos franceses trouxeram plantas de café do Haiti no século XVIII, o café também tem sido cultivado em Baracoa por pequenos agricultores, mas não em grandes quantidades. A característica especial: o café é plantado à sombra de árvores florestais cultivadas naturalmente ou sob árvores ornamentais, onde os cafeeiros são integrados à flora natural. Este método de produção é raro, motivo pelo qual as áreas de cultivo são consideradas Património Cultural da Humanidade pela UNESCO. À semelhança dos produtores de tabaco, os produtores de café têm de vender as suas colheitas ao Estado a preços fixos. Como a produção não atende à demanda, Cuba importa muito café.

Koffie

Sinds de Franse kolonisten in de 18e eeuw koffieplanten uit Haïti meebrachten, wordt er in Baracoa door kleine boeren ook koffie verbouwd, maar niet in grote hoeveelheden. Het bijzondere: de koffie wordt geplant in de schaduw van natuurlijk groeiende bosbomen of onder sierbomen, waarbij de koffieplanten in de natuurlijke flora worden geïntegreerd. Deze productiemethode zie je zo goed als niet meer, zodat de teeltgebieden als UNESCO-wereldcultuurerfgoed worden beschouwd. Net als de tabakstelers moeten de koffieboeren hun oogsten tegen vaste prijzen aan de staat verkopen. Omdat de productie niet aan de vraag voldoet, importeert Cuba veel koffie.

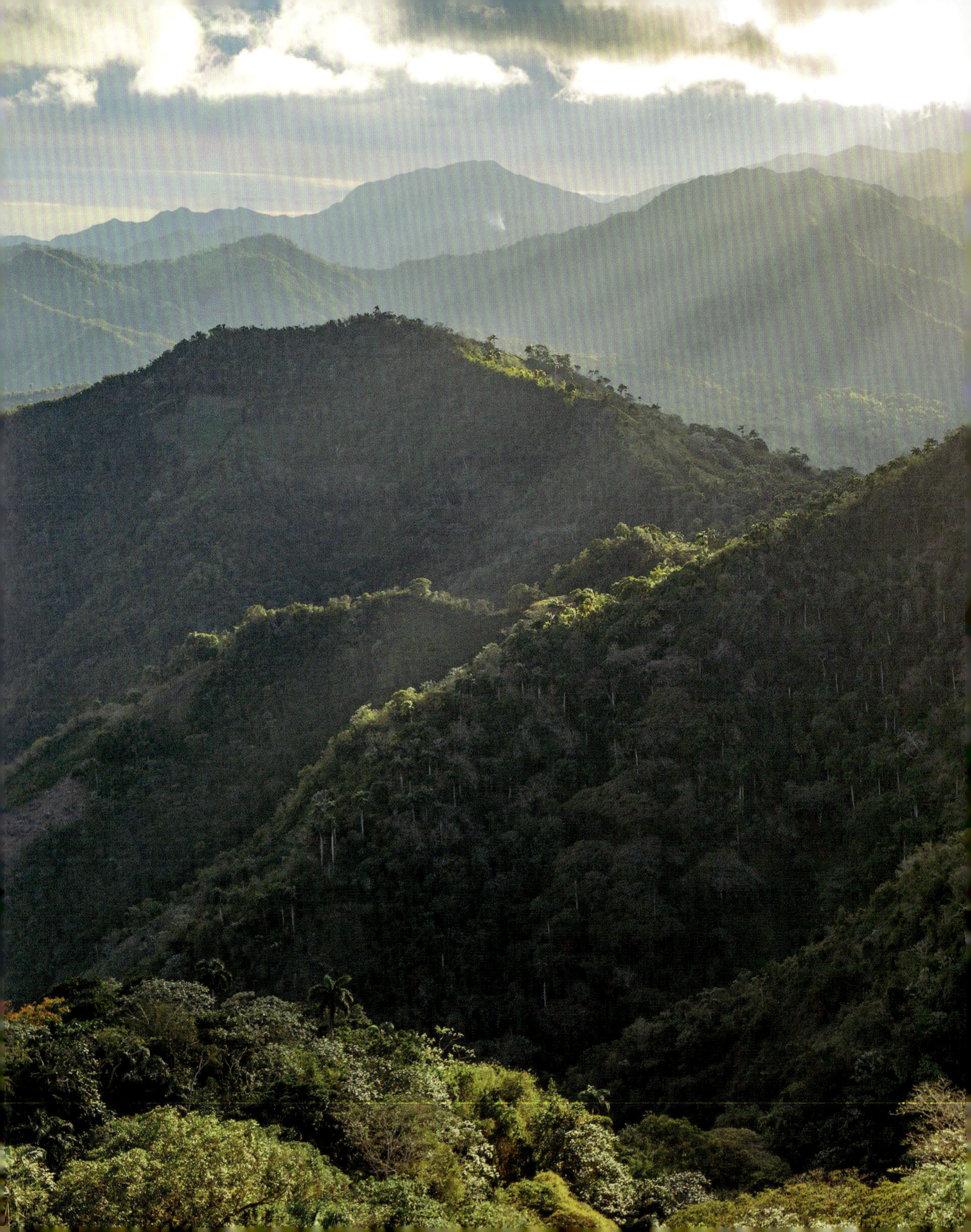

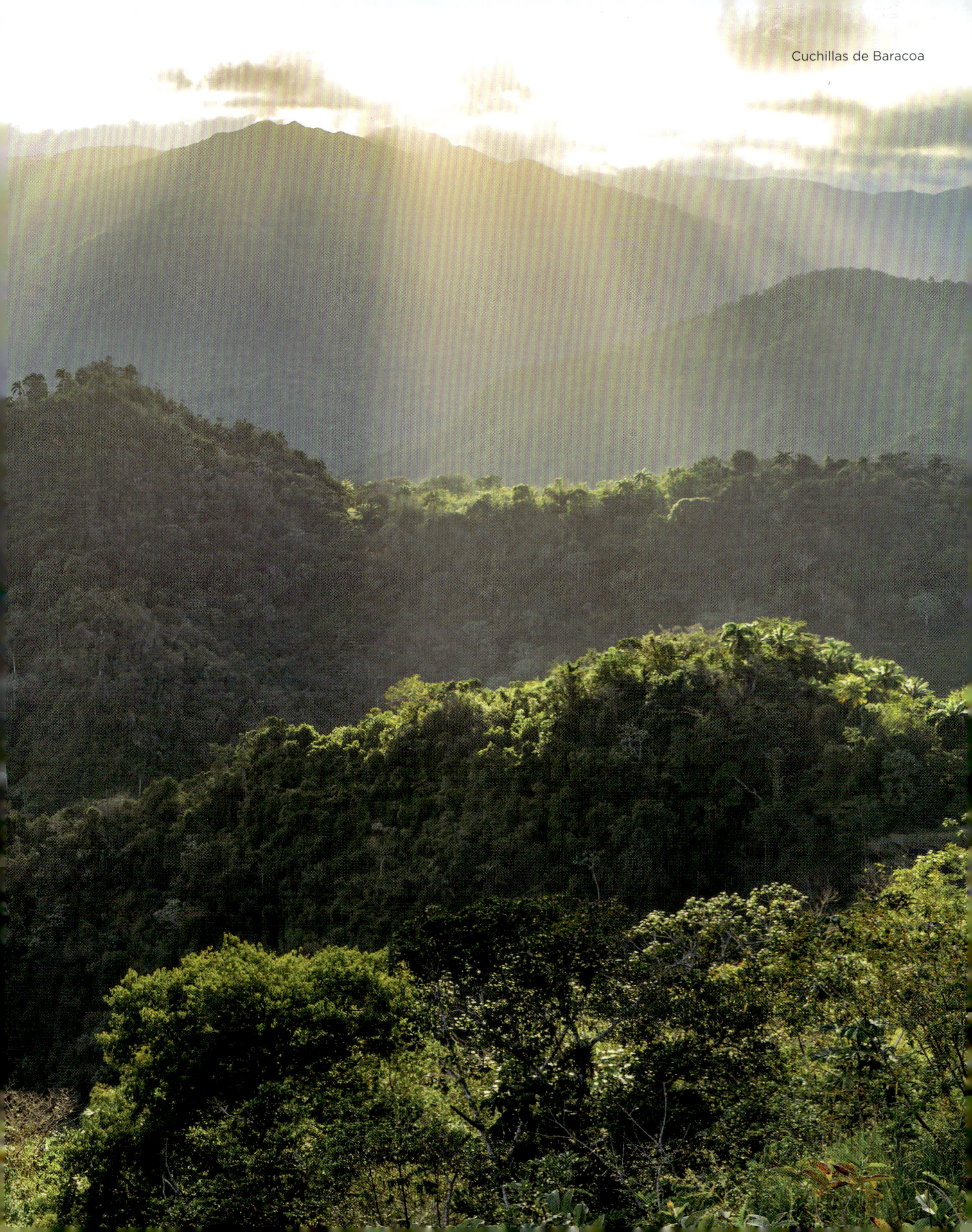
Cuchillas de Baracoa

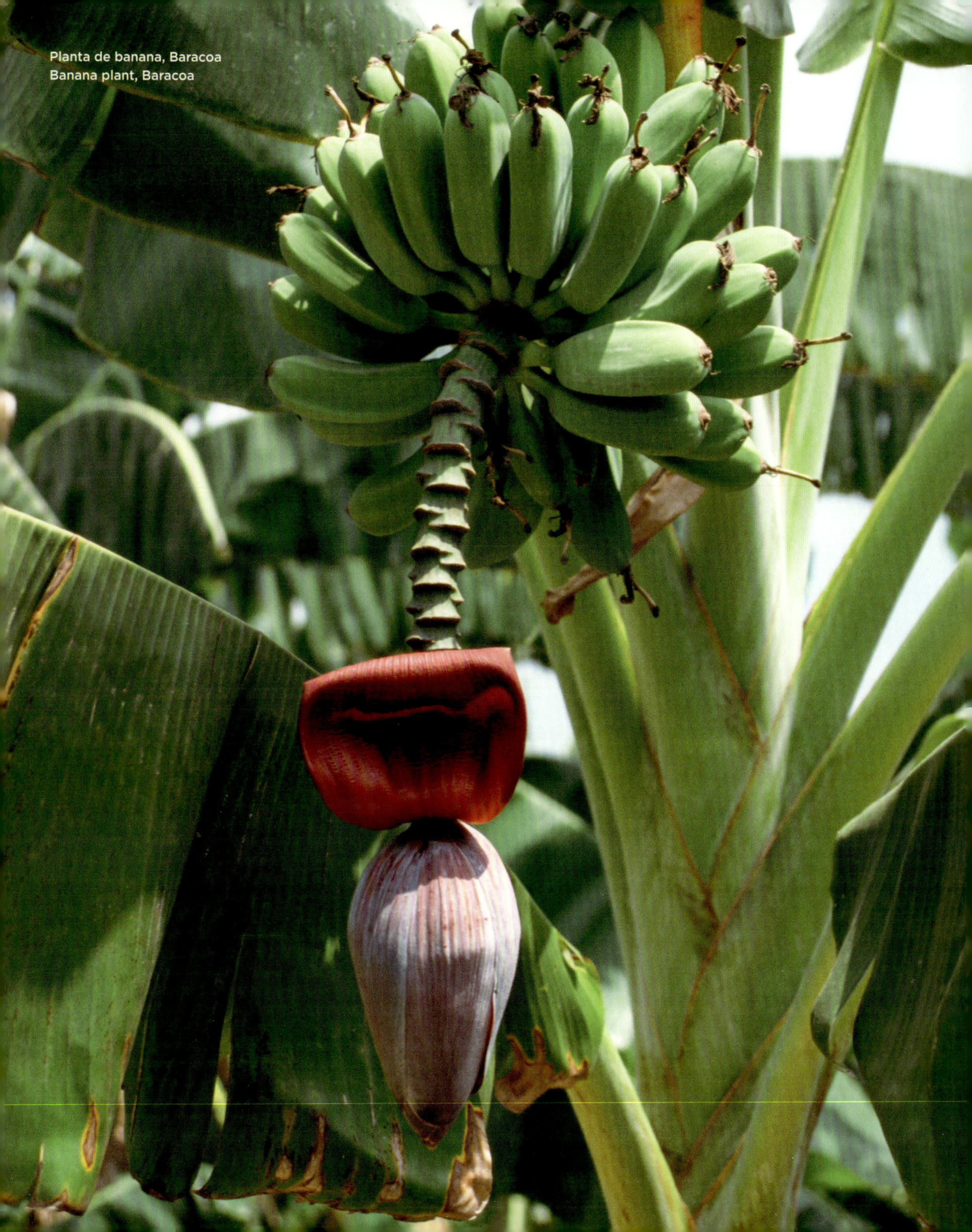
Planta de banana, Baracoa
Banana plant, Baracoa

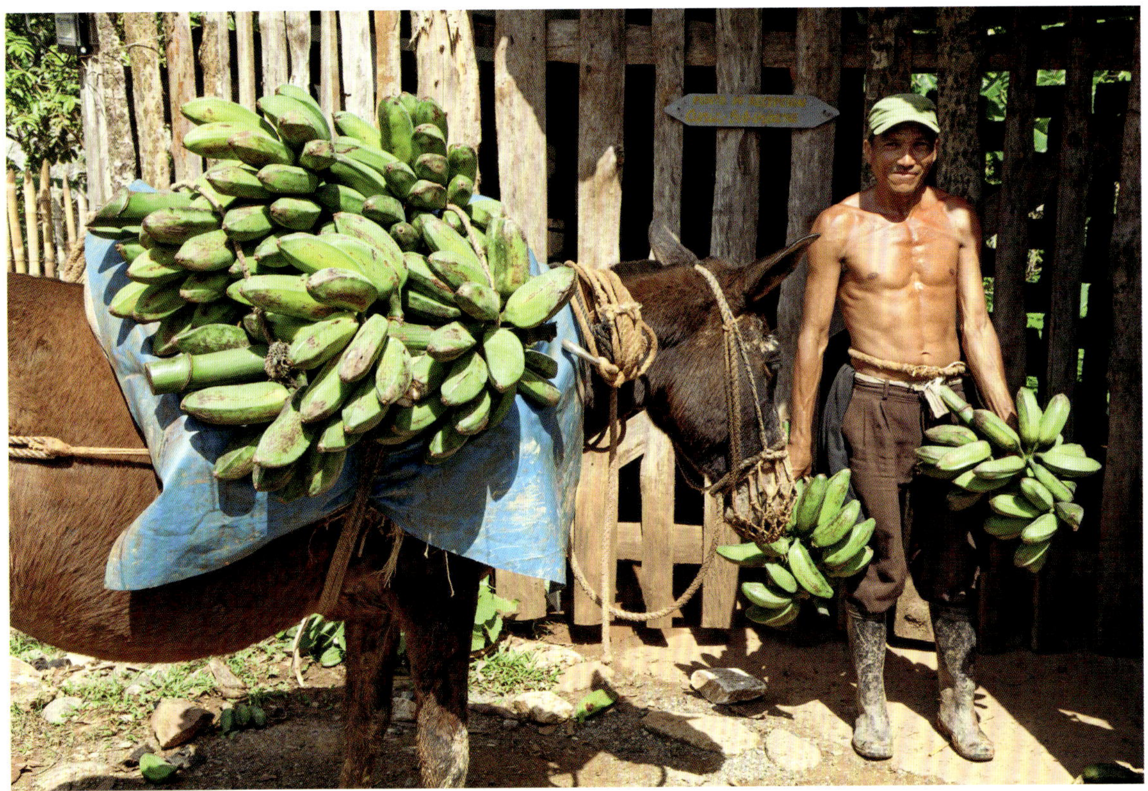

Baracoa

Plantains

You can't do anything in Baracoa without plantains. For example *plátanos* are used here to create "cannon balls". The production of these is quite complex, and the result is mini baskets made of fried banana strips and filled with tuna. Also popular is a hearty *fufú,* for which the plantains are boiled rather than fried.

Plátanos

No se puede hacer nada en Baracoa sin plátanos. Aquí se sacan de los *plátanos* por ejemplo las "balas de cañón". La producción es bastante compleja, el resultado son minicestas llenas de atún y hechas de tiras de plátano frito. También es popular un fuerte fufú, para el cual los plátanos se cocinan en lugar de freírse.

Bananes plantains

Baracoa ne serait pas ce qu'elle est sans la banane plantain. Ici les *plátanos* sont par exemple cuisinés en «boulets de canon». Ce mets, très long à préparer, se présente sous la forme de mini-paniers de tranches de bananes frites, farcies de thon. Autre spécialité fort appréciée, le *fufú,* pour lequel les bananes ne sont exceptionnellement pas frites mais bouillies.

Bananas-da-terra

Sem bananas-da-terra não se pode fazer nada em Baracoa. Aqui cria-se por exemplo "bolas de canhão" feitas de banana-da-terra. A produção é bastante complexa, o resultado são mini cestos cheios de atum e feitos de tiras de banana frita. Também popular é um *fufú* forte, para o qual as bananas-da-terra não são fritas, e sim cozidas.

Kochbananen

Ohne Kochbananen geht auch in Baracoa nichts. Hier zaubert man aus den *plátanos* zum Beispiel „Kanonenkugeln". Die Herstellung ist recht aufwändig, das Ergebnis sind mit Thunfisch gefüllte Mini-Körbchen aus frittierten Kochbananenstreifen. Beliebt ist auch ein kräftiges *fufú,* für das die Kochbananen ausnahmsweise nicht frittiert, sondern gekocht werden.

Bakbananen

Zonder bakbananen gaat niets in Baracoa. Hier tovert men uit de *plátanos* bijvoorbeeld 'kanonskogels'. De productie is vrij complex, het resultaat zijn kleine manden gevuld met tonijn en gemaakt van gefrituurde bananenreepjes. Een sterke *fufú* is ook populair, waarvoor de bakbananen eerder gekookt dan gebakken worden.

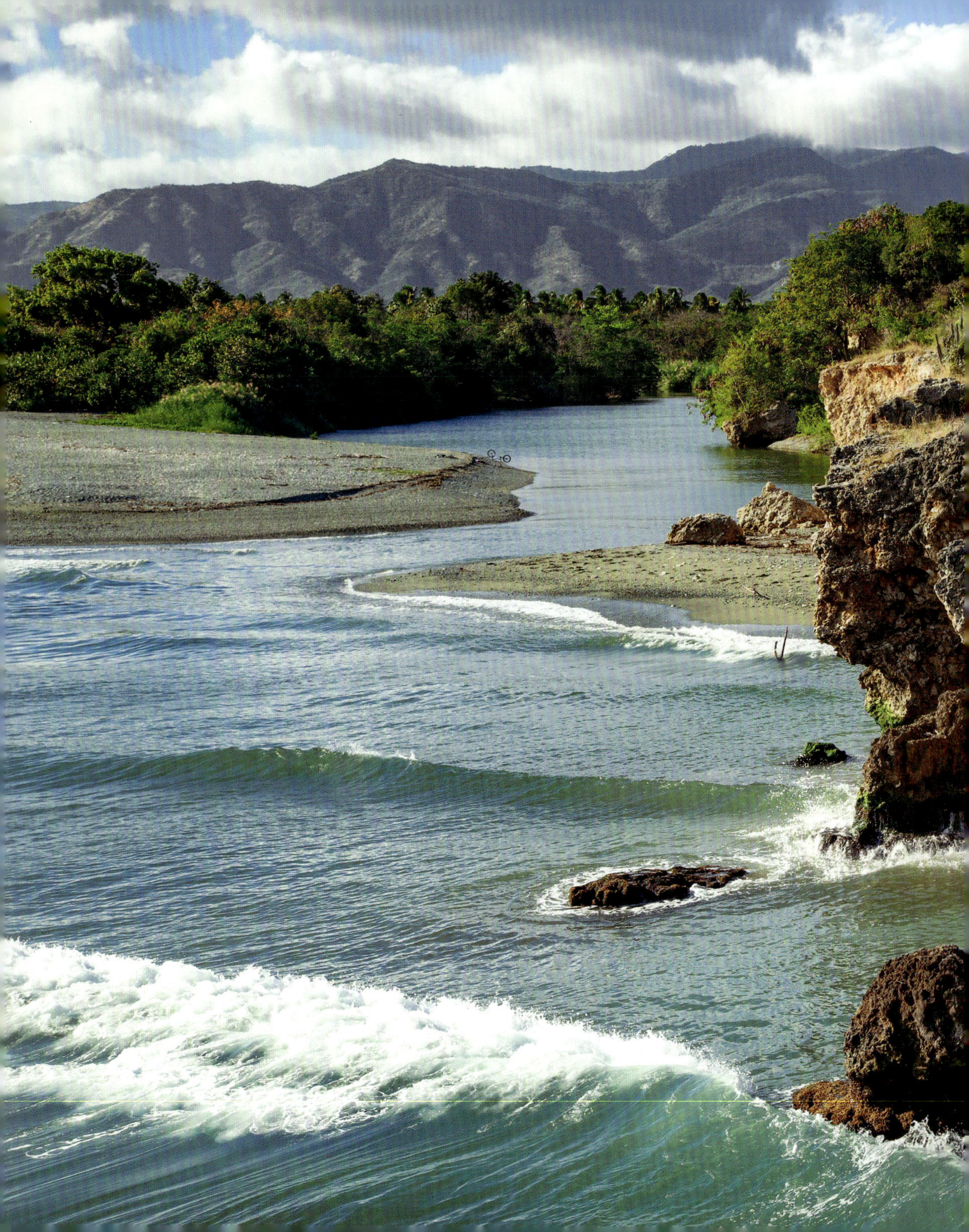

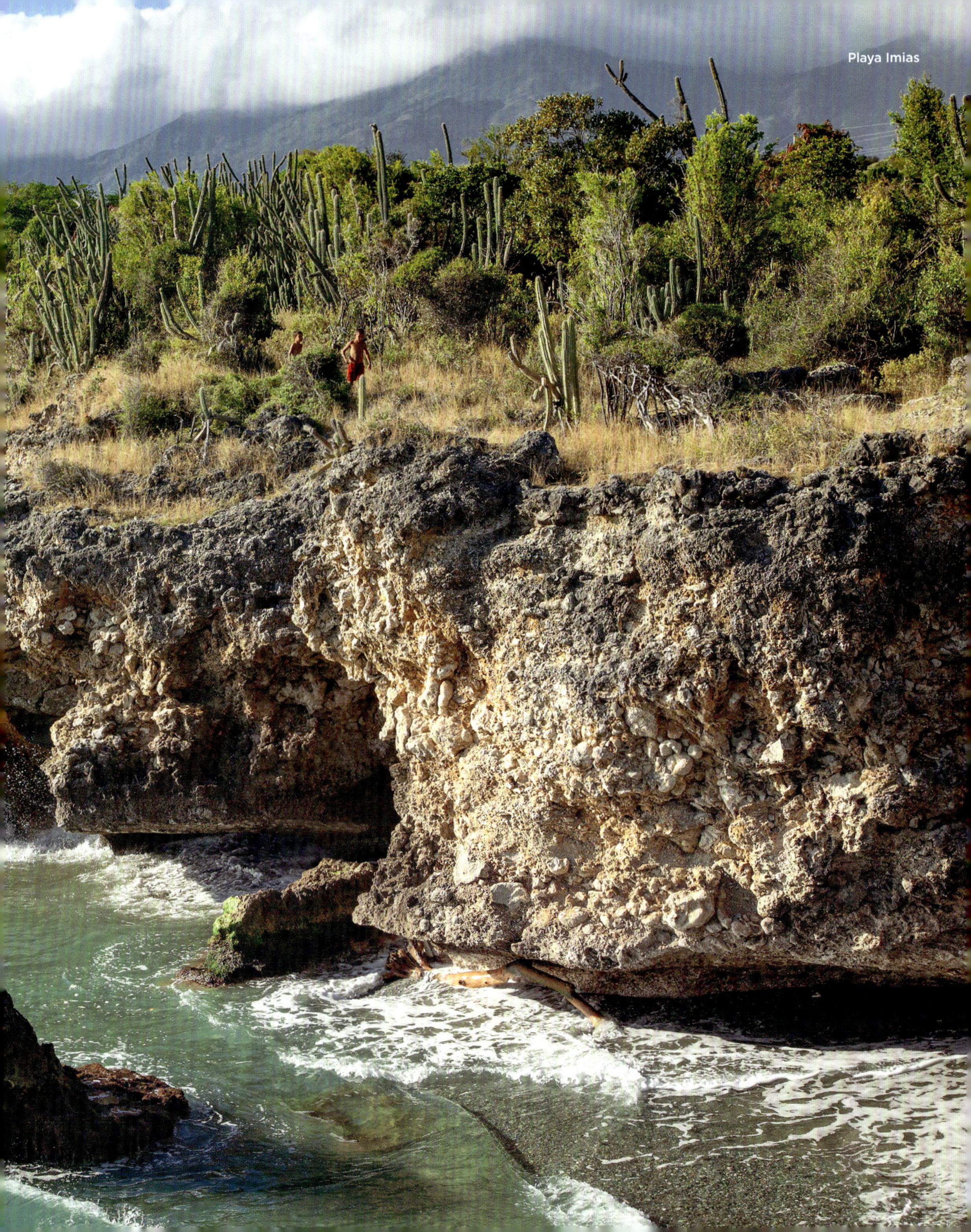
Playa Imias

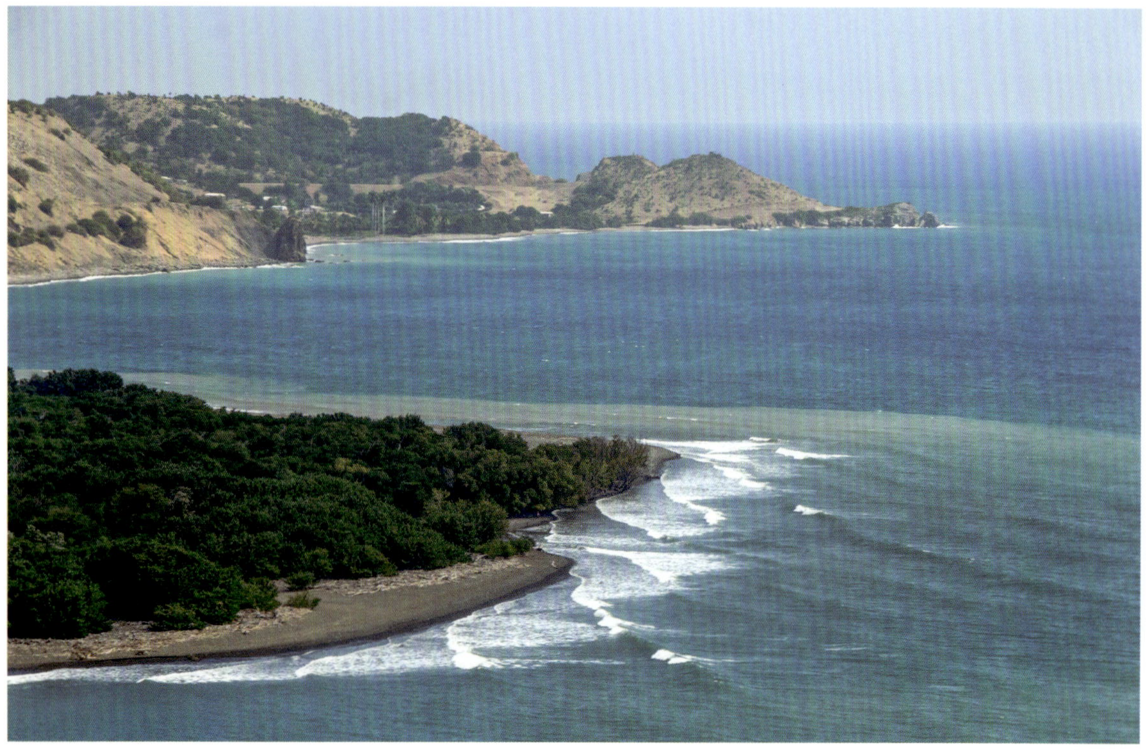

Punta Negra

Punta Negra

Punta Negra is located at the northern end of Guantánamo Bay, which extends 20 km (12 mi.) inland. The US naval base is further south on the Caribbean Sea. For decades, Cuba has been unsuccessfully demanding the return of the 117 km² (45 sq.mi.) area from the USA. The coastal forests, mangroves and coral reefs are habitats for endangered plants, land and sea animals that are worth protecting.

Punta Negra

Punta Negra est située à l'extrême nord de la baie de Guantánamo, qui remonte sur 20 km à l'intérieur des terres. La base militaire américaine est installée plus au sud, au bord de la mer des Caraïbes, sur un territoire de 117 km² que Cuba réclame aux États-Unis depuis des dizaines d'années. Les forêts côtières, mangroves et récifs coralliens sont les espaces de vie sensibles d'une flore et d'une faune marines et terrestres menacées.

Punta Negra

Punta Negra liegt am nördlichen Ende der Guantánamo-Bucht, die 20 km weit ins Land reicht. Die US-Marinebasis liegt weiter südlich am Karibischen Meer. Seit Jahrzehnten fordert Kuba das 117 km² große Areal vergeblich von den USA zurück. Die Küstenwälder, Mangroven und Korallenriffe sind schützenswerte Lebensräume für bedrohte Pflanzen, Land- und Meerestiere.

Punta Negra

Punta Negra se encuentra en el extremo norte de la Bahía de Guantánamo, que se extiende 20 km en el interior del país. La base naval de EE.UU. está más al sur, en el Mar Caribe. Durante décadas, Cuba ha exigido en vano la devolución de la superficie de 117 km² de Estados Unidos. Los bosques costeros, los manglares y los arrecifes de coral son hábitats que vale la pena proteger para las plantas, la tierra y los animales marinos que se encuentran en peligro de extinción.

Punta Negra

Punta Negra está localizada no extremo norte da Baía de Guantánamo, que chega a 20 km terra adentro. A base naval dos EUA fica mais ao sul, no Mar das Caraíbas. Durante décadas, Cuba exigiu em vão que a área de 117 km² fosse devolvida pelo os EUA. As florestas costeiras, manguezais e recifes de coral são habitats dignos de proteção para plantas, animais terrestres e marinhos ameaçados de extinção.

Punta Negra

Punta Negra ligt aan het noordelijke uiteinde van Guantánamo Bay, dat zich 20 km in het land uitstrekt. De Amerikaanse marinebasis ligt verder naar het zuiden aan de Caribische Zee. Cuba eist al tientallen jaren tevergeefs het 117 km² grote gebied terug van de VS. De kustbossen, mangroven en koraalriffen zijn habitats die het beschermen waard zijn voor bedreigde planten, land- en zeedieren.

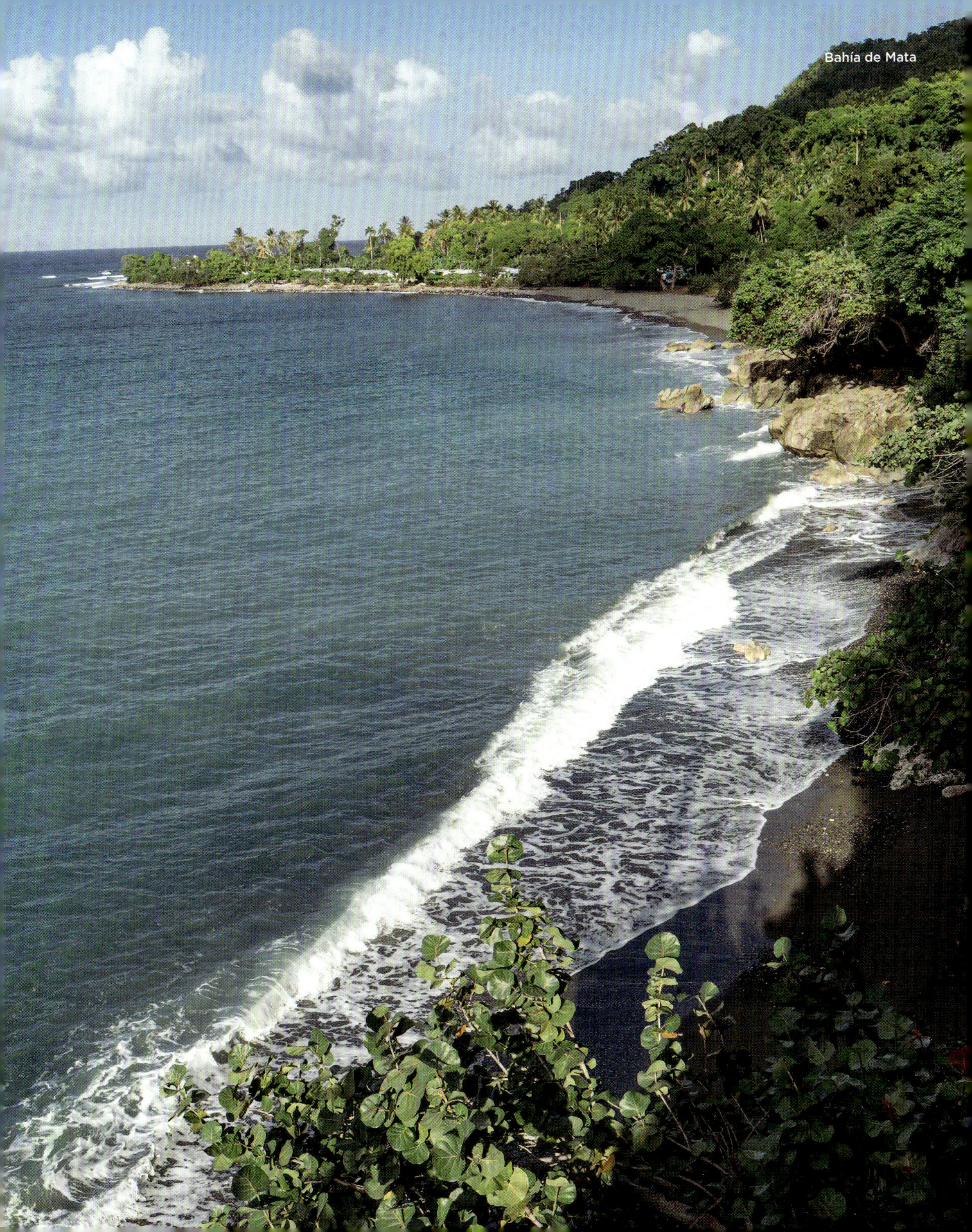
Bahía de Mata

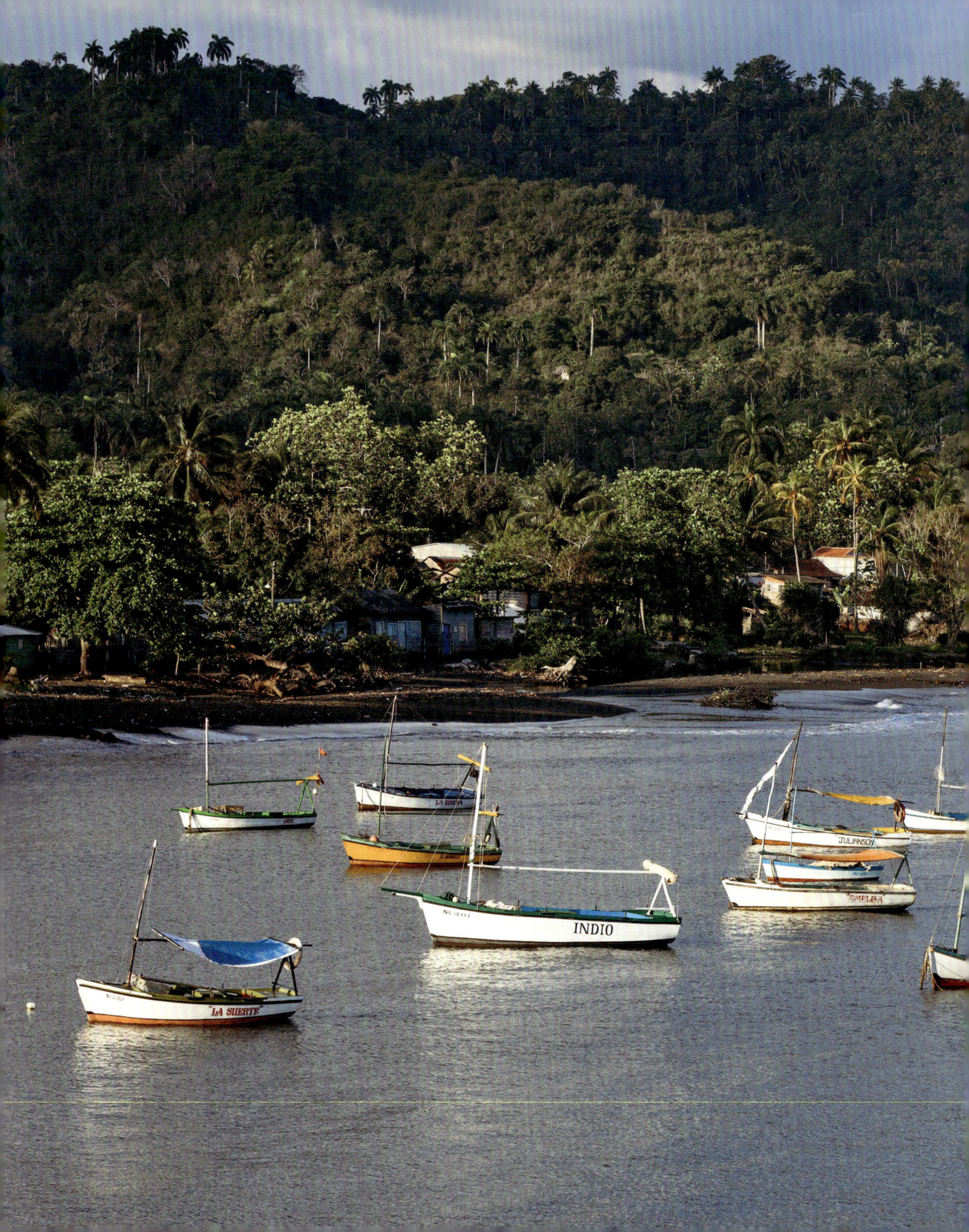

"LA SIRENA"
"INDIO"
"JULIANSON"
"EMELINA"
"LA SUERTE"

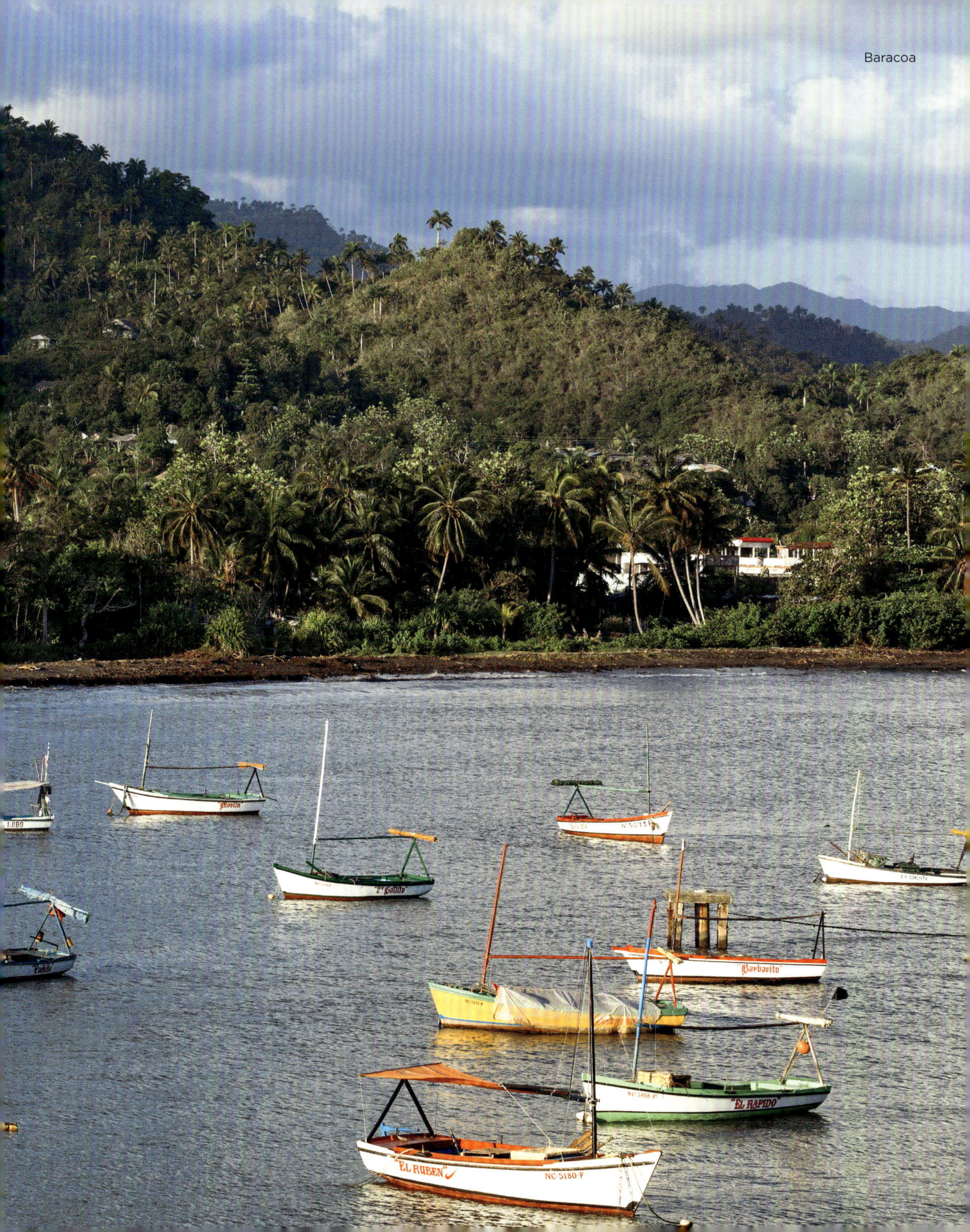

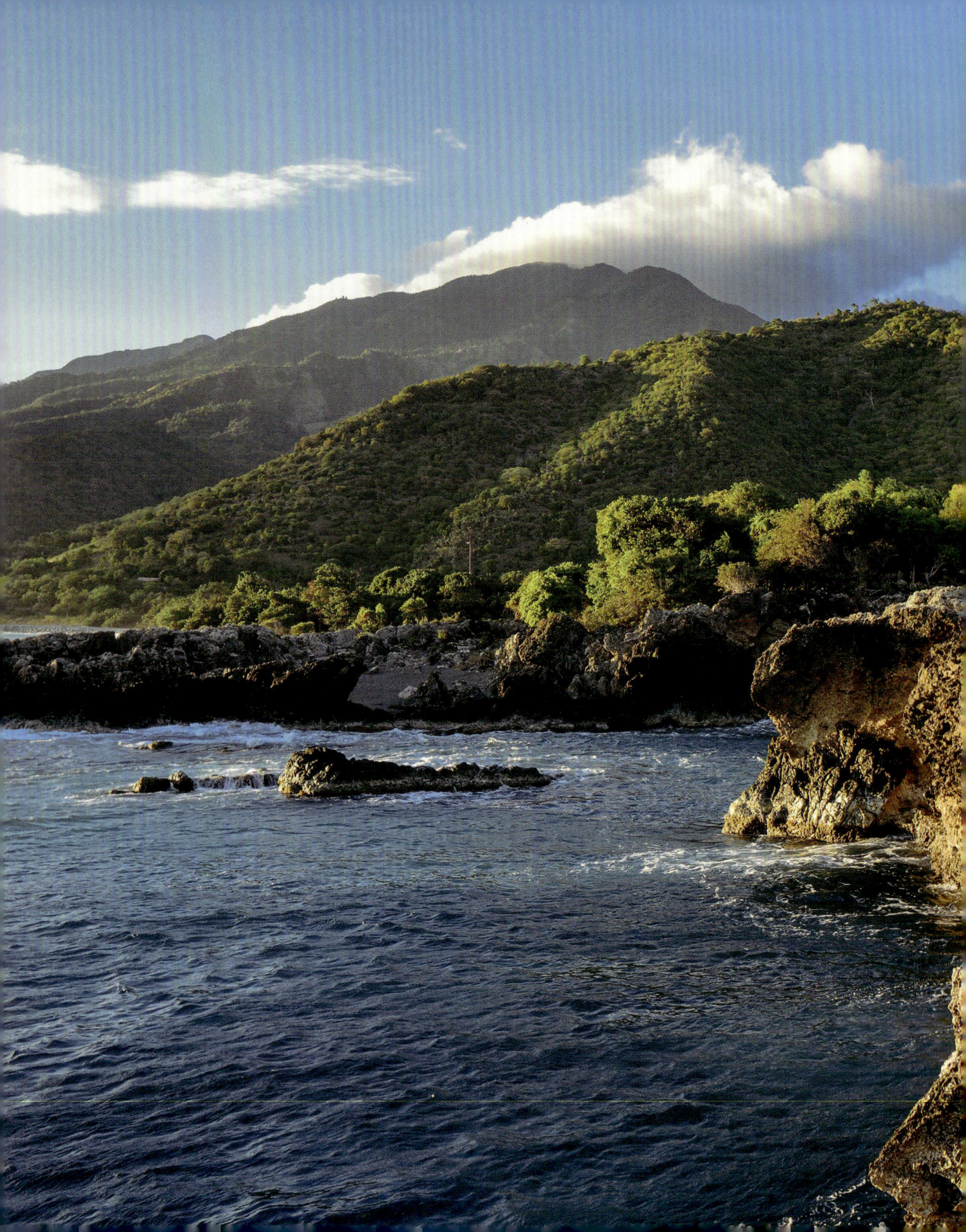

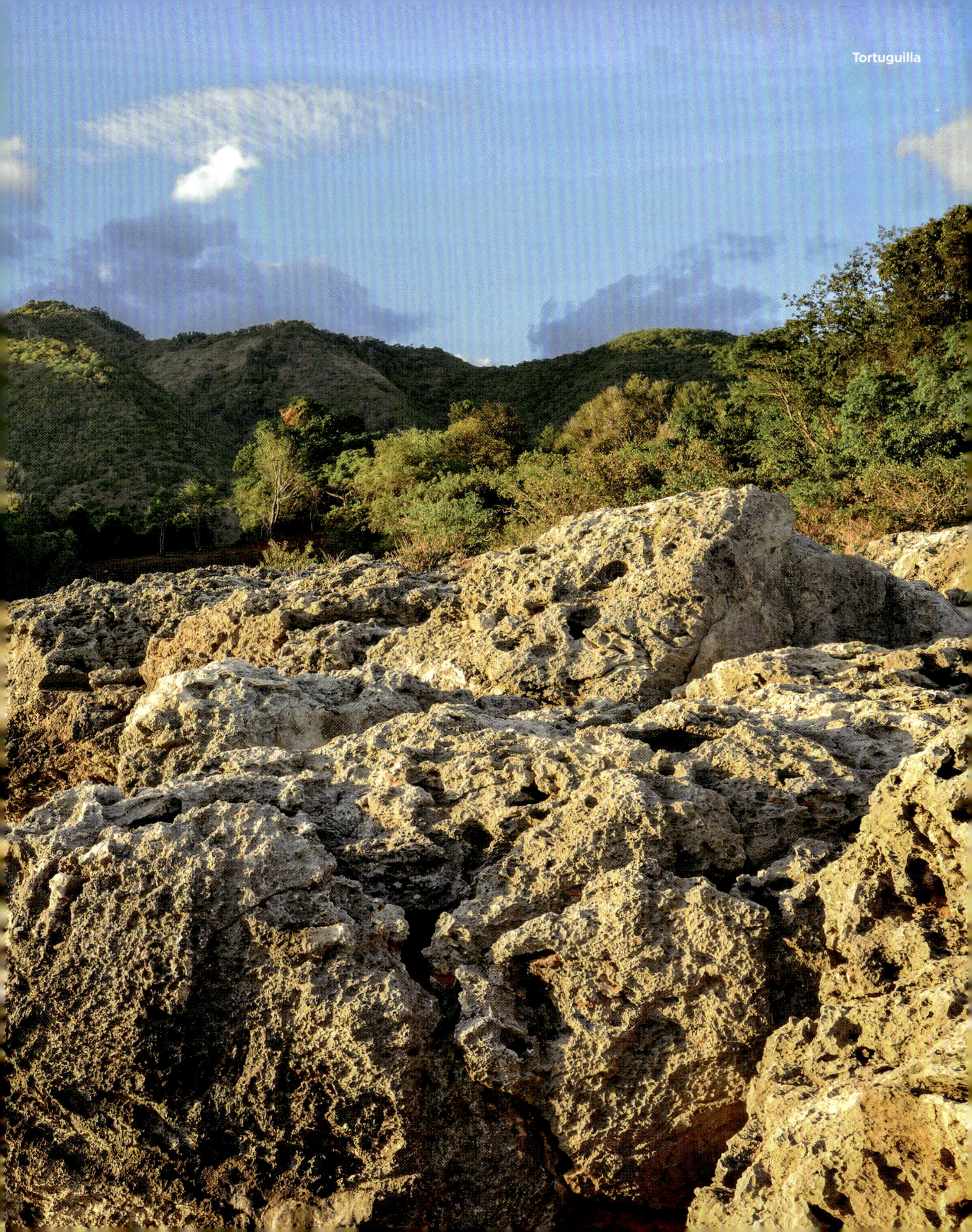
Tortuguilla

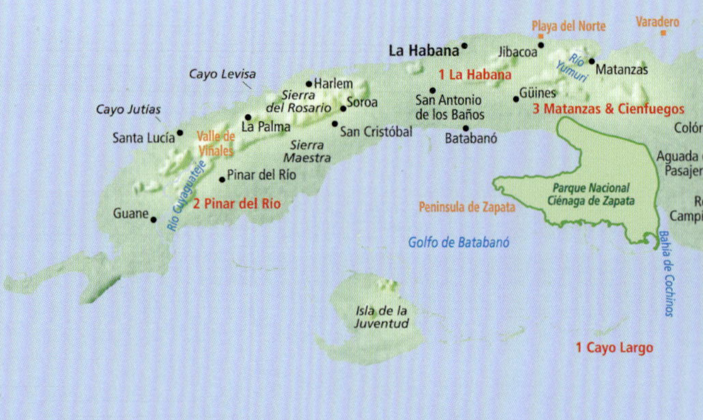

USA
Golfo de México
Playa del Norte
Varadero
La Habana
Jibacoa
Río Yumurí
Matanzas
1 La Habana
Cayo Levisa
Harlem
Güines
Cayo Jutías
Sierra del Rosario
Soroa
San Antonio de los Baños
3 Matanzas & Cienfuegos
Colón
Santa Lucía
La Palma
San Cristóbal
Batabanó
Aguada de Pasajeros
Valle de Viñales
Sierra Maestra
Río Guaniguanico
Pinar del Río
Peninsula de Zapata
Parque Nacional Ciénaga de Zapata
Real Campina
Guane
2 Pinar del Río
Golfo de Batabanó
Bahía de Cochinos
Isla de la Juventud
1 Cayo Largo
A n t
Mar Caribe
La Habana
Artemisa
Maya beque
Matanzas
Villa Clara
Pinar del Río
Cienfuegos
Sancti Spíritus
Ciego de Ávila
Isla de la Juventud
Camagüey
Las Tunas
Holguín
Granma
Santiago de Cuba
Guantánamo

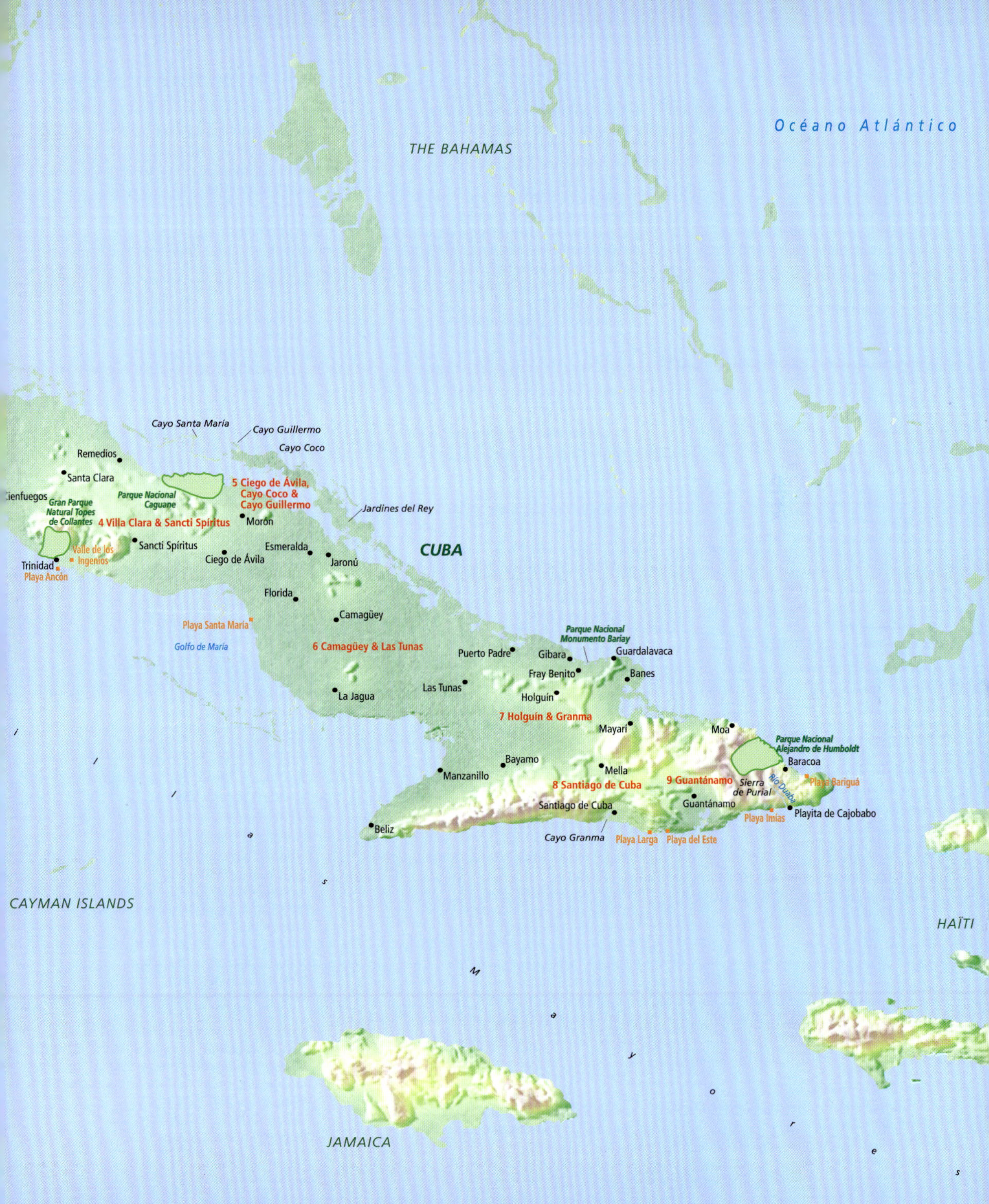

Océano Atlántico
THE BAHAMAS
CUBA
CAYMAN ISLANDS
JAMAICA
HAÏTI
Cayo Santa María
Cayo Guillermo
Cayo Coco
Remedios
Santa Clara
Cienfuegos
Gran Parque
Natural Topes
de Collantes
Parque Nacional
Caguane
5 Ciego de Ávila,
Cayo Coco &
Cayo Guillermo
4 Villa Clara & Sancti Spíritus
Morón
Jardines del Rey
Valle de los
Ingenios
Sancti Spíritus
Trinidad
Playa Ancón
Ciego de Ávila
Esmeralda
Jaronú
Florida
Playa Santa María
Golfo de María
Camagüey
6 Camagüey & Las Tunas
Puerto Padre
Gibara
Guardalavaca
Parque Nacional
Monumento Bariay
Fray Benito
Banes
La Jagua
Las Tunas
Holguín
7 Holguín & Granma
Mayarí
Moa
Parque Nacional
Alejandro de Humboldt
Baracoa
Bayamo
Mella
9 Guantánamo
Sierra
de Purial
Playa Bariguá
Manzanillo
8 Santiago de Cuba
Santiago de Cuba
Guantánamo
Río Duaba
Playita de Cajobabo
Playa Imías
Beliz
Cayo Granma
Playa Larga
Playa del Este

Photo credits

Getty Images

Huber Images

laif

Mauritius Images

Karl-Heinz Raach

Shutterstock

KÖNEMANN
© 2020 koenemann.com GmbH
www.koenemann.com

© Éditions Place des Victoires
6, rue du Mail – 75002 Paris
www.victoires.com
Dépôt légal : 1er trimestre 2020
ISBN 978-2-8099-1796-3

Series Concept: koenemann.com GmbH

Responsible Editor: Jennifer Wintgens
Picture Editing: Karl-Heinz Raach
Layout: Regine Ermert
Colour Separation: Prepress GmbH, Cologne
Text: Karl-Heinz Raach
Translation into French: Véronique Valentin
Translation into English, Spanish, Portuguese and Dutch: koenemann.com GmbH
Maps: Angelika Solibieda
Front cover: janesweeney/robertharding/laif

Printed in China by Shyft Publishing / Hunan Tianwen Xinhua Printing Co., Ltd.

ISBN 978-3-7419-2513-9